CANADIAN FOREST POLICY:
ADAPTING TO CHANGE

Edited by Michael Howlett

The forest sector, historically Canada's largest industry and largest employer, remains today the source of most of Canada's positive balance of trade on goods and commodities. Why, then, is there a dearth of policy literature devoted to exploring the industry within Canada?

Arguing that the complexity of policy-making in the forest sector has led many analysts to focus exclusively on specific activities or jurisdictions, this collection of essays offers a framework of analysis, based on comparative public policy studies, to address the current status of Canadian forest policy. Using case studies of historical and contemporary federal and provincial forest policies, the essays examine the manner in which changes in resource management ideas, subsystem membership, industrial organization, policy processes, international affairs, and intergovernmental initiatives have affected the sector.

Insightful and authoritative, this volume will be an indispensable resource for scholars in the fields of political science, forestry, public administration, history, and geography, and in Canadian, environmental, and labour studies. It will also be of value to policy-makers who must grapple with complex issues of forest policy on a day-to-day basis.

(Studies in Comparative Political Economy and Public Policy)

MICHAEL HOWLETT is a professor in the Department of Political Science, Simon Fraser University.

Studies in Comparative Political Economy and Public Policy

Editors: Michael Howlett, David Laycock, and Stephen McBride, Simon Fraser University. *Studies in Comparative Political Economy and Public Policy* is designed to showcase innovative approaches to political economy and public policy from a comparative perspective. While originating in Canada, the series will provide attractive offerings to a wide international audience, featuring studies with local, subnational, cross-national, and international empirical bases and theoretical frameworks.

For a list of books published in the series, see page 449.

Canadian Forest Policy

Adapting to Change

EDITED BY
MICHAEL HOWLETT

Donated to
Augustana
University College
by
Augustana's
Students' Union
Capital Development Fund
2001-2004

UNIVERSITY OF TORONTO PRESS
Toronto Buffalo London

© University of Toronto Press Incorporated 2001
Toronto Buffalo London
Printed in Canada

ISBN: 0-8020-4351-8 (cloth)
ISBN: 0-8020-8175-4 (paper)

Printed on acid-free paper

National Library of Canada Cataloguing in Publication Data

Main entry under title:
Canadian forest policy : adapting to change

(Studies in comparative political economy and public policy)
Includes bibliographical references.
ISBN 0-8020-4351-8 (bound)   ISBN 0-8020-8175-4 (pbk.)

1. Forest policy – Canada – History.   2. Forest policy –
Canada.   I. Howlett, Michael, 1955–   II. Series.

SD567.C39 2001   333.75′0971   C2001-901400-7

This book has been published with the help of a grant from the Humanities
and Social Sciences Federation of Canada, using funds provided by the Social
Sciences and Humanities Research Council of Canada.

The University of Toronto Press acknowledges the financial assistance to its
publishing program of the Canada Council for the Arts and the Ontario Arts
Council.

The University of Toronto Press acknowledges the financial support for its
publishing activites of the Government of Canada through the Book Publishing Industry Development Program (BPIDP).

Contents

PART 5 CONCLUSION

Figures and Tables

Acknowledgments

This book owes its origins to work done by a group of political scientists concerned with environmental and forestry issues in Canada and elsewhere. Elements of this work have appeared in various forums and publications over the past several years. Special thanks go to Monique Ross of the Canadian Institute for Resources Law for having begun the process of bringing these works and authors together. Collaborations undertaken by the British Columbia T4 Group and the British Columbia Forest Policy Network (FPN) helped shape the context and identify the complex of problems addressed in this book. Discussions at various forums including the British Columbia Political Studies Association Annual Meeting and the Annual General Meeting of the Canadian Political Science Association helped to hone the arguments. At Simon Fraser University thanks go to Alex Netherton for his translation of the chapter on Quebec and the vice-president research Bruce Clayman for extending funding towards the costs of manuscript preparation. Thanks also go to the Institute for Governance Studies – and especially Paddy Smith, Laurent Dobuzinskis, Steve McBride, and David Laycock – for continual support and encouragement.

PART 1
INTRODUCTION

Chapter One

Introduction: Policy Regimes and Policy Change in the Canadian Forest Sector

Michael Howlett

The forest sector, historically, has been Canada's largest industry and largest employer and remains today the source of most of Canada's positive balance of trade on goods and commodities.[1] Forestry continues to play a major role in every region of the country and, in this sense, is one of a very few truly national Canadian industries.[2] Despite its significance, however, the sector has received relatively little treatment in the policy literature. This is because of a number of reasons related to the decentralized nature of the forest industry with regard to both production and jurisdiction. Divided into several major industrial subsectors (softwood lumber, pulp, and newsprint) and fragmented into eleven major jurisdictions, the forest sector displays many different forms of institutionalization and organizational or associative behaviour; this makes it a complex subject for policy analysis.

The complexity of policy-making in the forest sector has challenged many analysts. Often they have reacted by choosing to focus their attention on specific sectoral activities or specific jurisdictions. Important volumes such as *Green Gold*,[3] by Patricia Marchak for example, focused exclusively on British Columbia; other books such as *The Temagami Experience* by Bruce Hodgins and Jaime Benidickson and *The Last Great Forest* by Larry Pratt and Ian Urquhart discuss only Northern Ontario or Alberta, respectively.[4] Donald MacKay's essay *Heritage Lost* and Peter Gillis and Thomas Roach's book *Lost Initiatives*[5] direct their focus to specific historical epochs, while MacKay, Moore, Swift, and Drushka[6] examined aspects of the forest industry, but not government policy-making per se. McGonigle, Kimmins, and Marchak investigated contemporary issues surrounding environmentalism and internationalization of the forest industry but, once again, without systematically spelling out the implications for overall forest policy and policy-making in Canada.[7]

Nevertheless, some effort has to be made to deal with the vast array of issues that currently face this critical sector of the Canadian economy.[8] Understanding which issues are significant and why requires a nuanced, multidimensional framework for policy analysis. In addition, Canadian forest policy has to be analysed in such a way as to take full recognition of the decentralized, provincially led nature of the Canadian forest policy process.[9]

The present volume uses the notion of a *policy regime* to deal with the complexity of policy-making in the forest sector.[10] It examines the current status of the Canadian forest policy regime, the nature of various factors driving change in this sector, and the impact that such factors have had and continue to have in actually effecting change in different Canadian jurisdictions. First, we consider the principal ideas, institutions, interests, and instruments that comprise the Canadian forest policy regime. Then we address the regime dynamics. We examine the manner in which changes in ideas about resource management, subsystem membership, industrial organization, policy processes, international affairs, and intergovernmental initiatives have affected forestry, both the sector as a whole and in terms of specific jurisdictions singled out for case study or comparative analysis.

In this way the book accomplishes two goals. First, it provides an up-to-date overview of forest policy and policy-making in Canada, including an empirical examination of many aspects of the existing relationships between state and societal actors in this sector. Second, it contributes more generally to discussions about the process of policy-making and change in a policy regime – a subject of some current interest to political scientists, administrators, and others.

The Concept of a Policy Regime

The term 'policy regime' helps to capture the overall nature of Canadian forest policy and policy-making in a way that makes sense both to cross-national and subnational comparativists.[11] Although it is sometimes confused with the related terms 'political regime'[12] or an 'international regime,'[13] it is actually quite distinct. Like a political regime or an international regime, a policy regime attempts to describe the domestic and/or international institutions, norms, conventions, rules, and behaviour that influence state actions. Unlike the two other terms, however, a 'policy regime' focused specifically on policy outcomes and the process of policy-making, is usually at the meso or sectoral level.

Policy regime analysis attempts to capture the more-or-less long-term, quasi-permanent, social, political, economic, and cultural arrangements that underlie government actions. However, a policy regime is concerned less with understanding a specific political or economic arrangement, such as a particular administrative agency or policy relationship, than with the identification, description, and analysis of the overall tenor and types of interactions existing among institutions, actors, and ideas that tend to congeal into relatively long-term, institutionalized, patterns of policy and policy-making.[14]

Origins

U.S. students of regulation have long argued that regulatory arrangements tend to ossify into widespread institutionalized patterns of interactions between the state and society.[15] Marc Eisner, for example, argues that regulatory arrangements can usefully be viewed as quasi-permanent arrangements, or 'regulatory regimes,' in which: 'A regulatory regime is a historically specific configuration of policies and institutions which establishes certain broad goals that transcend the problems specific to particular industries.'[16]

A similar perspective informs the work of European observers of contemporary governments and political–economic arrangements. Alain Lipietz and Michel Aglietta, for example, argue that there are particular and specific sets of political–economic relationships for each different stage in the development of productive technology; each set of relationships constituting a 'regime of regulation' or a 'regime of production' designed to facilitate capital accumulation and avoid the economic and political crises associated with tensions specific to particular historical epochs. In their work, each regime involves the application of the coercive powers of the state to control labour and aid in the reproduction and expansion of capital. In the modern era, they argue, the regime must also maintain a certain consumption norm to ensure that the mass production of commodities does not result in oversupply and a decline in prices and profits. Hence, government adherence to Keynesianism demand management techniques, in the post–Second World War era, for example, is seen as an outgrowth of the development of a modern, 'Fordist' regime of mass production.[17]

Gosta Esping-Anderson suggests that a similar concept could describe long-term patterns of sectoral policy-making. In his work on social policy-making in western European democracies, he defines such social policy regimes as 'specific institutional arrangements adopted by societies in the pursuit of work and welfare.'[18] Such policy regimes, argues Esping-Anderson, have been linked to larger national patterns of organizing relations between the state and the market-based institutions: 'A given organization of state-economy relations associated with a particular social policy logic.'[19] His initial focus was on national concerns and institutions, but in later works he became more selective, arguing that there are various policy-specific regimes, and these can be identified in a host of sectors, including the labour market, pension arrangements, the distribution of goods and services, and employment policy.[20]

Elements

The concept of a policy regime, as developed by Esping-Anderson and others, combines aspects of two other concepts previously used in the policy sciences to describe long-term patterns of public policy-making, namely, *policy paradigm*[21] and *policy style*.[22] A policy paradigm, as used by Peter Hall and other authors, captures the notion that relatively long-lived patterns of policy-relevant 'ideas,' 'discourses,' or 'epistemes' can be observed in many policy sectors, such as fiscal and monetary policy-making.[23] The concept of a policy style, as developed by David Vogel, refers to the long-term configurations of specific processes of interaction among actors in a variety of national and sectoral policy areas.[24] A policy regime is a larger concept than either a paradigm or style, encompassing both elements to describe and explain long-term, persistent patterns in both the substance and process of policy-making.[25]

Ideas and procedural routines, however, are not the only components of a policy regime. In their work on regulatory regimes, Richard Harris and Sidney Milkis identified a third, institutional, element. In their observations of a variety of U.S. cases, they noted that regimes to regulate economic activities comprise 'a constellation of (1) new ideas justifying governmental control over business activity, (2) new institutions that structure regulatory politics, and (3) a new set of policies impinging on business.'[26] These three elements describe the basic contents of a policy regime, that is, a policy regime can be defined as a persistent and regular political arrangement composed of (1) a set of state–societal relations affecting the style or process of sectoral policy-making; (2) a set of ideas related to governing these interactions and effecting policy contents and instrument choices; and (3) a set of institutions designed to regularize and routinize the content and style of policy-making in the sector concerned.

This notion of a policy regime is a significant conceptual tool in the analysis of policy dynamics, particularly because it helps show how sectoral policy-making tends to develop so that the same actors, institutions, instruments, and governing ideas tend to dominate policy-making for extended periods of time and in so doing generate similar policies. Understanding how regimes form, how they are maintained, and how they change are the principal components of policy regime analysis.

Dynamics

The principal assumptions made by a regime approach to the study of sectoral policies and policy-making are: (1) The substance of sectoral policies as well as sectoral policy-making processes both tend to congeal into recognizable long-term patterns; (2) These patterns can be disaggregated into their component parts – actors, ideas, institutions, and instruments – but they can also usefully be studied together as a policy regime; and (3) Studying sectoral policy-making as a policy regime not only helps to identify the component parts of a regime, but also helps to illuminate the reasons for shifts or changes in regimes.

Although little direct work has been done on the phenomenon of policy regime change, current work on the subject of policy styles and policy paradigms suggests a variety of factors that may lead to regime change. In their work on policy styles, for example, Howlett and Ramesh argue that the two most significant variables affecting the development of a sectoral policy style are (1) the range of ideas and actors found within the sector, and (2) the ad-ministrative capacity and the nature of the resource constraints under which state actors operate.[27] Similar factors were advanced by others in their explanations of the development of a policy paradigm.

This raises the questions of how these variables can change and what would be the effect of such changes on long-term policy patterns. In his discussion of the evaluation of a policy paradigm, Peter A. Hall suggested that the process of long-term paradigm change is largely endogenous in nature, as internal debates among policy-makers lead to a search for new solutions (policy-learning) which can inject new ideas into policy processes.[28] Others emphasize the manner in which exogenous events can also alter the range or number of actors involved in policy processes and perhaps thus introduce new ideas into the policy process.[29] Frank R. Baumgartner and Bryan D. Jones, for example, place great store in shifts policy paradigms occasioned by interest group behaviour, for example, shifting policy venues or expanding, or otherwise altering, predominant policy frames and images.[30] Howlett has shown how different issue areas can converge or intersect, again potentially injecting new dimensions to existing policy debates and discourses;[31] and Coleman and others have noted that phenomena such as globalization and the increasing internationalization of decision-making have also destabilized the membership composition and idea sets present in many subsystems.[32]

The key questions involved in the contemporary analysis of the dynamics of policy regimes hence relate to the role played by the exogenous and endogenous sources of changes in policy actors and policy ideas and, subsequently, the relationship between changes in these variables and changes in the regime.[33] In what follows in this volume, Canadian forest policies are systematically evaluated using a policy regime framework. Individual chapters analyze the components of the present-day regime (including the range of actors in the subsystem and their configuration); the impact on the existing regime of changes in the key variables such as technology, internationalization of the industry; and the entry into policy processes of environmentalists and environmental ideas. The chapters trace the process through which these dynamics have affected subsystem membership and the capacities of the state and resulted in significant alterations in forest administration. These essays provide both a description of the overall elements and composition of the Canadian forest policy regime, as well as an analysis of its evolution and its propensity for change in the future.

The Contemporary Canadian Forest Policy Regime

The contemporary Canadian forest policy regime is usually described as one of 'public forest management for private timber harvesting.' It dates back to the middle years of the twentieth century, when governments began regulating company harvesting practices in order to ensure that timber supplies were not wasted or damaged by harvesting activities, and encompasses a gradual shift from a reliance on natural regeneration to artificial regeneration of the resource base.[34]

Key policy issues which continue to face this regime involve the creation of cutting plans and management units on existing tenures, the establishment of area-based and volume-based timber supply agree-ments with harvesting companies, and the imposition of de jure or de facto quota regimes restricting entry of new firms into the forest sector. In most jurisdictions, forest regimes have been created which have involved the reorganization or 'rationalization' of leases into large-scale, contiguous areas of land, under different forms of forest management agreements or licences, and the extension of government regulations to privately held forest lands.[35]

The transition from an earlier regime of conservation to one of timber management occurred in most Canadian jurisdictions after inventories taken in the 1930s revealed the extent to which forest resources had been depleted under earlier licensing systems, threatening the long-term via-bility of the resource and the industries and communities that depended on it. The interventionist atmosphere of the Second World War years, in which governments assumed extensive powers to direct the economy, and the ensuing era of 'province-building,' were both conducive to more activist federal and provincial forest policies. At hearings before a series of royal commissions in many jurisdictions, the fledgling Canadian for-estry profession successfully argued that there was a fundamental conflict between the industry's demand for timber, at whatever levels the market would bear, and the interests of the governments in creating and main-taining long-term prospects for revenue and employment.[36] Most argued that a new system of licences to cut Crown timber could be made to work as long as their terms could be manipulated so as to provide sufficient incentives for industry to provide a stable or increasing supply of wood fibre, while still ensuring that governments received an economic rent for the land being licensed.[37] Postwar forest policy in Canada has been dominated by the attempt to balance these two aims.

Regime Dynamics in the Canadian Forest Sector

A number of significant conflicts and controversies currently affect the operation of the contemporary Canadian forest management regime and threaten to undermine many of its central elements.[38] Conflicts between different resource users, for example, have grown significantly in recent years and have become a major source of tension in the devel-opment of forest policy. This is especially true of conflicts involving new actors such as environmentalists and Native groups that have challenged the right of landowners to continue to dispose of timber and forest lands for industrial purposes.[39] These disputes have been heightened as the limits of existing timber supplies are reached and forest companies have begun to log previously marginal wilderness areas and to demand concessions in parks and timber reserves.[40]

Although the most highly publicized, these are not the only disputes that characterize the current regime. New disputes have emerged in other areas, including those between capital and labour over productivity concerns that have grown as industry profits can no longer be increased by simply increasing production.[41] Increasing profitability now involves enhancing the productivity of existing mills to produce more output with essentially the same inputs of labour and capital, or, to put it another way, by intensifying work. Efforts in this direction have centred either on developing new production technologies that promise greater yields[42] or on decreasing production costs while retaining essentially the same production techniques.[43] This last effort has resulted in the industry focusing its attention on reducing both labour costs and the costs of government regulation and taxation.[44]

Efforts at reorganizing the labour process have provoked a major response from affected unions in the form of strikes, work stoppages, and industrial unrest. They have also prompted environmentalists to draw attention to the seemingly inexorable trend of declining employment per unit of wood processed in an effort to recruit unions to the cause of tenure reform, with mixed results. Efforts by the industry to transfer the costs of modernization and reforestation to governments have also provoked conflicts between industry and governments over shares of profits and rents collected in the industry.[45]

Finally, governments themselves have changed and altered administrative arrangements in recent years in order to deal with these and other concerns. The primary organization utilized to implement forest policies in Canada has been the administrative department, and the process of development of these agencies in each jurisdiction has closely followed the gradual extension of government regulation in the sector. Although forest departments have usually been combined with the administration of lands in long-lasting departments of lands and forests, in recent years there have been two opposing tendencies apparent in terms of administrative reorganizations. One has been the emergence of larger, omnibus departments of natural resources, encompassing regulatory authority for a variety of natural resource sectors including forests, mines, and energy. The other has seen the development of single-purpose forest ministries.

This is only a very general pattern, however, as there have also been efforts to combine forest administration with such areas as tourism, water resources, or parks, and in some jrisdictions to combine forestry with environmental protection. At the federal level, reflecting the ambiguous nature of the federal role in the fomation of forest policy, a variety of idiosyncratic organizational forms have been used – from a Department of the Interior at the time of Confederation to the more recent Ministry of State for Forests and Mines. The need for governments at both levels greater administrative capacity in order to better coordinate increasingly sophisticated policy regimes has been evident in efforts made at the intergovernmental level to develop more effective forest policy structures. At this level, forest issues have been addressed, since 1960, both in the context of other natural resources issues in forums such as the Canadian Council of Resource and Environment Ministers (CCREM) and in the creation of a specific Canadian Council of Forest Ministers in 1985.[46]

Chapter-by-Chapter Outline

As has been pointed out, the observations that new members have entered into existing regimes and that existing state capacities have been altered leads to the expectation that change in the overall forest sector regime might not be far away. The chapters in this volume investigate and evaluate this hypothesis.

First we establish the elements of the current Canadian forest policy regime by describing the institutions, actors, ideas, and interests which comprise it. Then we discuss several specific elements that are effecing changes in this mix, such as new production technology, the rise of environmentalism, new managerial ethos, shifts in international 'forces,' and new government administrative reforms. The book then presents a number of case studies that illustrate how general regime elements and dynamics vary by jurisdiction.

This first part contains introductory material setting out the origins of the regime framework, its elements, and a review of the literature on regime dynamics. Part 2 then presents the basic elements of the present-day Canadian forest policy regime. In their contribution to this section, Howlett and Rayner describe the historic pillars of the contemporary regime, including the organization of business interests, labour, and the forestry profession. Their chapter discusses the evolution of forest management paradigms, the usual instruments used in the regulatory regime, the key actors in the forest policy subsystem, the key interests involved in the accumulation regime, and the general policy style found in the forest sector.

Part 3 looks at several of the exogenous and endogenous avenues and forces that are leading towards regime change. These include the impact of internationalization on policy-making in the forest sector, the diffusion and dissemination of new ideas about forest management, the impact of technological change and industrial restructuring, the emergence of new actors (like environmentalists) in policy networks and communities, and the creation of new institutions and processes for the administration of land and natural resources. Each chapter in this part describes the current situation and shows how policy outcomes and processes have been influenced by these factors and developments.

In Chapter 3 Cashore and Bernstein examine the linkages between international and domestic forest policies. They argue that internationalization is a complex process involving different types of actors and effects on domestic policy-making, but that in the Canadian forest sector, the introduction of new international actors and ideas into existing processes has had a substantial impact on numerous aspects of the domestic regime. In Chapter 4, Wilson examines new methods for the management of ecosystems and how they affect forest policy outcomes. Although these new ideas have received a great deal of publicity, only recently have they begun to be implemented. In many cases, Wilson finds, the new methods pose little threat to the general pattern of the 'liquidation–conversion' paradigm that characterized the past century of Canadian forest policy-making. Hayter and Holmes, in Chapter 5, examine the impact of globalization and technical change on the forest industry and government policy in this sector. They describe recent changes in labour processes and technology, and discuss how their impact on the restructuring of forest sector employment, community structure, and royalty and tax rates has affected policy-making. In Chapter 6, Stefanick looks at the role lay environmental actors and ideas have played in altering many aspects of forest management and forest policy-making; while in Chapter 7, Beyers shows how efforts at policy process reform, such as alternative decision-making and model forest programs, have also influenced forest policy outcomes.

Part 4 provides case studies of Canadian jurisdictions that assess how the factors and linkages described in Part 3 have actually determined the evolution of the policy practices of different provincial and federal governments. The case studies show how the general forces at work in forestry have been filtered through existing institutional arrangements, resulting in a common model of regime development and change, albeit one with significant jurisdictional differences and/or nuances.

In Chapter 8, Clancy examines the evolution of forest policy regimes in the Atlantic provinces. These developed very slowly – from their colonial foundations in the seventeenth century to the current era of timber management. He finds the federal government and the industry to have been at the forefront of change in the region but also shows how existing property relations and forest resource endowments significantly affect innovation in the sector. Bouthillier, in Chapter 9, argues that Quebec, too, has made only a slow transition towards sustainable forestry, indeed, at a rate that threatens the overall project. Lawson, Levy, and Sandberg analyse Ontario in Chapter 10. Like Clancy and Bouthillier, they find the pattern of forest policy in that province to have evolved through several distinct stages, very slowly and over a long period of time. Each regime has had a distinctive pattern of industry–government relations, with the more recent transitions greatly influenced by the rise of the forestry profession and the development of environmental groups. In Chapter 11, Urquhart examines the Western provinces, focusing on Alberta, the largest forest-producing province in the region. His analysis highlights the provincial government's role in bolstering, supporting, or otherwise subsidizing the forest industry as an economic or regional development project – a project that actively engages various globalized forest resource companies in a process of significant regime change. In Chapter 12, Hoberg looks at British Columbia's recent development of formal, legal forest codes as a mode of resource regulation. His analysis addresses the difficulties encountered in forcing change on the sector and points to the continued informality of many policy processes and practices within the contemporary regime. In Chapter 13, Howlett examines the history of federal government forest regulation, painting a slightly different picture of policy-making in lands and territories under federal jurisdiction. Here policy-making proceeded along provincial lines only until 1930, when the best federal forest lands were transferred to the provincial governments of the three prairie provinces. Since then, the federal government has consistently attempted, and failed, to play a major leading role in coordinating provincial policies and the overall Canadian regime.

In Part 5, Wellstead and Lindquist review the literature on, and approaches to, forest policy analysis in Canada and then reflect on the contents of this entire volume and its contribution to the field. Their chapter concludes with a proposed agenda for future research on the subject.

NOTES

1 On the history of the forests and the forest industry of Canada, see Arthur Lower, *The North American Assault on the Canadian Forest* (Toronto: Ryerson Press, 1938); Arthur Lower, *Great Britain's Woodyard* (Montreal: McGill-Queen's University Press, 1973); Robert G. Albion, *Forests and Sea-Power: The Timber Problems of the Royal Navy, 1652–1862* (Hamden, Conn.: Archon Books, 1926); Esdras Minville, ed., *La Forêt* (Montreal: Editions Fides, 1944).

2 See J. Britton, ed., *Canada and the Global Economy* (Montreal: McGill-Queen's University Press, 1996); M. Hessing and M. Howlett, *Canadian Natural Resource and Environmental Policy: Political Economy and Public Policy* (Vancouver: UBC Press, 1997).

3 Patricia Marchak, *Green Gold* (Vancouver: University of British Columbia Press, 1983).

4 Bruce Hodgins and Jaime Benidickson, *The Temagami Experience* (Toronto: University of Toronto Press, 1989); L. Pratt and I. Urquhart, *The Last Great Forest: Japanese Multinationals and Alberta's Northern Forests* (Edmonton: NeWest Press, 1994).

5 Donald MacKay, *Heritage Lost: The Crisis in Canada's Forests* (Toronto: Macmillan, 1985); R. Peter Gillis and Thomas R. Roach, *Lost Initiatives: Canada's Forest Industries, Forest Policy, and Forest Conservation* (New York: Greenwood, 1986).

6 See Donald MacKay, *Empire of Wood: The Macmillan Bloedel Story* (Vancouver: Douglas and McIntyre, 1982); Jamie Swift, *Cut and Run: The Assault on Canada's Forests* (Toronto: Between the Lines, 1983); A. Milton Moore, *Forestry Tenures and Taxes in Canada: The Economic Effects of Taxation and the Regulating of the Crown Forests by the Provinces* (Toronto: Canadian Tax Foundation, 1957); Ken Drushka, *Stumped: The Forest Industry in Transition* (Vancouver: Douglas and McIntyre, 1985).

7 See R. Michael McGonigle, and Ben Parfitt, *Forestopia: A Practical Guide to the New Forest Economy* (Madeira Park, BC: Harbour Publishers, 1994); J.P. Kimmins, *Balancing Act: Environmental Issues in Forestry* (Vancouver: UBC Press, 1992); Patricia Marchak, *Logging the Globe* (Montreal: McGill-Queen's University Press, 1995).

8 See Peter N. Nemetz, ed., *Emerging Issues in Forest Policy* (Vancouver: UBC Press, 1992); M.K. Luckert and F.J. Salkie, 'Forestry in Canada: Transitions

and Emerging Policy Issues,' *Canadian Public Policy* 24, Supplement – Special issue no. 2, 1998, S1–S10; Bill Wilson, G.C. Van Kootew, Ilan Vertinsky, and Louise Arthur, eds., *Forest Policy: International Case Studies* (New York: CABI Publishing, 1999).

9 See Michael Howlett, 'The 1987 National Forest Sector Strategy and the Search for a Federal Role in Canadian Forest Policy,' *Canadian Public Administration* 32(4), 1989, 545–63; M. Howlett, 'The Politics of Constitutional Change in a Federal System: Institutional Arrangements and Political Interests in the Negotiation of Section 92A of the Canadian Constitution Act (1982),' *Publius* 21(1), 1991, 121–42; Elizabeth May, *At the Cutting Edge: The Crisis in Canada's Forests* (Toronto: Key Porter Books, 1998). For a comparison with the situation in other countries, see Peter Gluck, 'European Forest Politics in Progress,' paper presented at the Forest Policy Research Forum, Joensuu, Finland, 1997.

10 Although there is some dispute over the definition, dimensions, and elements of such regimes, a growing literature has employed the concept of a policy regime with great success in illuminating the nature of policy-relevant institutions, ideas, actors, and instruments in different countries and sectors. See, e.g., Gosta Esping-Andersen, 'Power and Distributional Regimes,' in *Politics and Society* 14(2), 1985, 223–56; Martin Rein, Gosta Esping-Andersen, and Lee Rainwater, eds., *Stagnation and Renewal in Social Policy: The Rise and Fall of Policy Regimes* (Armonk, NY: M.E. Sharpe, 1987); Marc Allen Eisner, *Regulatory Politics in Transition* (Baltimore: Johns Hopkins University Press, 1993); George Hoberg, *Pluralism by Design: Environmental Policy and the American Regulatory State* (New York: Praeger, 1992).

11 See Bruce Doern, 'The Interplay among Regimes: Mapping Regulatory Institutions in the U.K., U.S., and Canada,' in G. Bruce Doern and Stephen Wilks, eds., *Changing Regulatory Institutions in Britain and North America* (Toronto: University of Toronto Press, 1998), 29–50.

12 Even this term has been used in two senses. The first refers to the general arrangement of political institutions found in a country. See, e.g., Richard Gunther, 'The Impact of Regime Change on Public Policy: The Case of Spain,' *Journal of Public Policy* 16(2), 1996, 157–202; Valerie Summers, *Regime Change in a Resource Economy: The Politics of Underdevelopment in Newfoundland since 1825* (St John's: Breakwater, 1994). The second refers to the values and general ideological orientation of a country. See, e.g., Stephen L. Elkin, 'Regulation and Regime: A Comparative Analysis,' *Journal of Public Policy* 6(1), 1986, 49–72.

13 On the development of this concept, see Stephen D. Krasner, ed., *International Regimes* (Ithaca: Cornell University Press, 1983); Oran R. Young,

'International Regimes: Problems of Concept Formation,' *World Politics,* 32(2), 1980, 331–56; A. Claire Cutler and Mark W. Zacher, eds., *Canadian Foreign Policy and International Economic Regimes* (Vancouver: UBC Press, 1992).

14 George Hoberg, 'Distinguishing Learning from Other Sources of Policy Change: The Case of Forestry in the Pacific Northwest,' paper presented to the Annual Meeting of the American Political Science Association, Boston, 1998. See also, Christoph Knill, 'European Policies: The Impact of National Administrative Traditions,' *Journal of Public Policy* 18(1), 1998, 1–28; Carter A. Wilson, 'Policy Regimes and Policy Change,' *Journal of Public Policy* 20(3), 2000, 247–71.

15 Theodore J. Lowi, 'Four Systems of Policy, Politics and Choice,' in *Public Administration Review* 32 , 1972, 298–310; Richard Harris and Sidney Milkis, *The Politics of Regulatory Change* (New York: Oxford University Press, 1989).

16 Eisner, *Regulatory Politics* xv.

17 See Robert Brenner and Mark Glick, 'The Regulation Approach: Theory and Practice,' *New Left Review* (188), 1991, 45–120; R. Boyer, ed., *Capitalismes fin de siècle* (Paris: PUF, 1986). See also, Alain Lipietz, 'Towards Global Fordism?' *New Left Review* (132), 1982, 33–48; Michel Aglietta, *A Theory of Capitalist Regulation* (London: Verso, 1979).

18 Rein et al., *Stagnation.*

19 Ibid.

20 See Gosta Esping-Anderson, *The Three Worlds of Welfare Capitalism* (London: Polity Press, 1990). See also Jon Eivind Kolberg and Gosta Esping-Anderson, 'Welfare States and Employment Regimes,' in J.E. Kolberg, ed., *The Study of Welfare State Regimes* (New York: M.E. Sharpe, 1992). The term has also been used by economists and others in recent years in a similar vein. See George Alogoskoufis, 'Greece: The Two Faces of Janus – Institutions, Policy Regimes and Macroeconomic Performance' in *Economic Policy*, no. 20, 1995, 147–92.

21 See Peter A. Hall, 'Policy Paradigms, Social Learning and the State: The Case of Economic Policy-Making in Britain,' *Comparative Politics* 25(3), 1993, 275–96.

22 See Jeremy Richardson, Gunnel Gustafsson, and Grant Jordan, 'The Concept of Policy Style' J.J. Richardson, ed., *Policy Styles in Western Europe,* (London: George Allen and Unwin, 1982) 1–16.

23 Hall, 'Policy Paradigms.'

24 David Vogel, *National Styles of Regulation: Environmental Policy in Great Britain and the United States* (Ithaca: Cornell University Press, 1986).

25 Doern, G. Bruce. 'Interplay among Regimes.' G. Bruce Doern, Margaret M. Hill, Michael J. Prince and Richard J. Schultz., eds., *Changing the Rules: Cana-*

dian Regulatory Regimes and Institutions (Toronto: University of Toronto Press, 1999).

26 Harris and Milkis, *Politics of Regulatory Change* 25.

27 M. Howlett and M. Ramesh, *Studying Public Policy: Policy Cycles and Policy Subsystems* (Toronto: Oxford University Press, 1995) 187. On state autonomy generally, see Eric Nordlinger, *On the Autonomy of the Democratic State* (Cambridge, Mass.: Harvard University Press, 1981).

28 Hall, 'Policy Paradigms.' See also William D. Coleman, Grace D. Skogstad, and Michael Atkinson, 'Paradigm Shifts and Policy Networks: Cumulative Change in Agriculture,' *Journal of Public Policy* 16(3), 1996, 273–302

29 See Paul A. Sabatier and Hank C. Jenkins-Smith, eds., *Policy Change and Learning: An Advocacy Coalition Approach* (Boulder: Westview, 1993). See also Gregory F. Intoccia, 'Governing Telecommunications: A New Regime in Public Law and Public Policy,' *Glendale Law Review* 10(1/2), 1991, 1–32. Hall, of course, also noted the manner in which changes in the electoral fortunes of government could raise new actors and ideas to the forefront. Hall, 'Policy Paradigms.'

30 Frank R. Baumgartner, and Bryan D. Jones, 'Agenda Dynamics and Policy Subsystems,' *Journal of Politics* 53(4), 1991, 1044–74; Paul A. Sabatier, 'An Advocacy Coalition Framework of Policy Change and the Role of Policy-Oriented Learning Therein,' *Policy Sciences* 21(2/3), 1988, 129–68.

31 Michael Howlett, 'Policy Paradigms and Policy Change: Lessons from the Old and New Canadian Policies towards Aboriginal Peoples,' *Policy Studies Journal* 22(4), 1994, 631–51. See also Jeremy J. Richardson, William A. Maloney, and Wolfgang Rudig, 'The Dynamics of Policy Change: Lobbying and Water Privatization,' *Public Administration* 70, 1992, 157–75.

32 William D. Coleman and Grace Skogstad, 'Neo-Liberalism, Policy Networks and Policy Change: Agricultural Policy Reform in Australia and Canada,' *Australian Journal of Political Science* 30, 1995, 242–63. See also Judith Goldstein and Robert O. Keohane, eds., *Ideas and Foreign Policy: Beliefs, Institutions and Political Change* (Ithaca: Cornell University Press, 1993); Wolfgang Streeck, 'Neo-Voluntarism: A New European Social Policy Regime?' *European Law Journal* 1(1), 1995, 31–59, and Peter M. Haas, 'Introduction: Epistemic Communities and International Policy Coordination,' *International Organization* 46(1), 1992, 1–36.

33 In the area of citizenship policy, e.g., Jenson and Phillips have attributed a regime shift to 'institutional changes that have removed advocates for certain categories of citizens ... from within the state; the diminished capacity and credibility of public interest groups in gaining access to the state; and the definition of government through service delivery partnerships.' See

Jane Jenson and Susan D. Phillips, 'Regime Shift: New Citizenship in Canada,' *International Journal of Canadian Studies* 14, 1996, 111–36. See also Thomas H. Hammond and Jack H. Knott, 'The Deregulatory Snowball: Explaining Deregulation in the Financial Industry,' *Journal of Politics* 50(1), 1988, 3–30; M. Howlett and M. Ramesh, 'Patterns of Policy Instrument Choice Policy Styles, Policy Learning and the Privatization Experience,' *Policy Studies Review* (U.S.), 12(1), 1993, 3–24.

34 See Michael Howlett and Jeremy Rayner, 'The Framework of Forest Management in Canada,' in Monique Ross, ed., *Forest Management in Canada* (Calgary: Canadian Institute for Resources Law, 1995), 43–118. See also M. Howlett and J. Rayner, 'Opening Up the Woods?: The Origins and Future of Contemporary Canadian Forest Policy Conflicts,' *National History* 1(1), 1997; and Jeremy Wilson, *Talk and Log: Wilderness Politics in British Columbia* (Vancouver: UBC Press, 1998).

35 See Carlos Galindo-Leal and Fred L. Bennell, 'Eco-System Management: Implications and Opportunities of a New Paradigm,' *Forestry Chronicle* 71(5), 1995, 601–6.

36 Christopher K. Leman, 'A Forest of Institutions: Patterns of Choice on North American Timberlands,' in Elliot Feldman and Michael Goldberg, eds., *Land Rites and Wrongs: The Management, Regulation, and Use of Land in Canada and the United States* (Lincoln Institute of Land Policy, 1987), 116–34. See also I.C.M. Place, 'Forestry in Canada,' *Journal of Forestry* 76(9), 1978, 557–62; Frances Wetton, 'Evolution of Forest Policies in Canada,' *Journal of Forestry* 76(9), 1978, 563–5, A.J. Herridge, 'The Development of Forestry Policy,' *Forestry Chronicle* 40(4), 1964, 425–8.

37 C.M. Johnson, 'Legislative Mechanisms to Balance Public and Private Interests in Forest Management,' paper presented to the International Forest Congress, Quebec City, Quebec, 1984. On the basic elements of tenure agreements as they developed in this period, see David H. Jackson, 'Some Structural Components of Contracts as They Relate to Canadian Forest Tenures,' *Forestry Chronicle* 53(1), 1977, 33–6; Jagdish Kumar Rawat, 'Forest Tenure Systems in Canada and Their Role in the Investment Behaviour of Integrated Forestry Firms, doctoral dissertation, University of Toronto, 1985.

38 Peter Duinker and David L. Euler, 'Forest Issues in Canada: Towards a Productive Discussion on Directions for Canada's Forests Into the 21st Century,' paper prepared for the National Forest Congress, Ottawa, 1998.

39 Although the current form of such disputes is new, it is not the first time that such conflicts have surfaced in Canadian forestry policy formation. In the early period of agricultural settlement of the country, such disputes were common and involved competing land-use claims of farmers and loggers.

See A.R.M. Lower, 'Settlement and the Forest Frontier,' in *Settlement and the Frontier in Eastern North America*, A.R.M. Lower and H.A. Innis. eds. (Toronto: Macmillan, 1936) 1–123.

40 See Claudia Notzke, *Aboriginal Peoples and Natural Resources in Canada* (Toronto: Captus University Publications, 1994); Phillip Dearden and Rick Rollins, eds., *Parks and Protected Areas in Canada: Planning and Management* (Toronto: Oxford University Press, 1993). Because of the role of most provincial governments as major forest landlords, these governments have on the whole been unsympathetic to the demands and concerns of Native and environmental groups that have challenged government authority in the disposition and management of national resources. As a result, the direct impact of these actors on existing policies has been muted. See Michael Howlett and Jeremy Rayner, 'Do Ideas Matter? Policy Subsystem Configurations and the Continuing Conflict over Canadian Forest Policy,' *Canadian Public Administration* 38(3), 1995, 382–410.

41 Given the limitations of established markets and the dangers posed to the industry by overproduction, forestry companies cannot increase production in an absolute or extensive sense unless new markets can be found. Markets for Canadian forestry products are well known and virtually fully exploited in terms of sales of existing products. Opportunities for growth in a mature industry through expansion of output itself are limited and such an industry must look inward if it is to achieve any significant growth. See Roger Hayter, 'Innovation Policy and Mature Industries: The Forest Products Sector of British Columbia,' in K. Chapman and G. Humphrys, eds., *Technical Change and Industrial Policy* (Oxford: Basil Blackwell, 1987) 215–32. More generally, see Richard P. Rumelt, *Strategy, Structure and Economic Performance* (Boston: Harvard University School of Business Administration, 1974) 130–1.

42 On pulping processes developed in the 1980s and implemented in the 1990s, see Marchak, *Logging the Globe*; P. Marchak, 'For Whom the Tree Falls: Restructuring of the Global Forest Industry,' *BC Studies* 90, 1991, 3–24. In the wood products industry, see Brian J. Greber and David E. White, 'Technical Change and Productivity Growth in the Lumber and Wood Products Industry,' in *Forest Science* 28(1), 1982, 135–47.

43 See Luis Constantino and David Haley, *Concepts and Measurement of Productivity in the Forest Industries* (Vancouver: UBC Forest Economics and Policy Analysis Project, 1986) 85–9; M. Sandoe and M. Wayman, 'Productivity of Capital and Labour in the Canadian Forest Products Industry, 1965–1972,' *Canadian Journal of Forest Research* 7, 1977, 85–93; H.F. Kaiser, 'Productivity Gains in Forest Products Industries,' *Forest Products Journal* 21(5), 1971, 14–16.

44 See Ian Urquhart and Larry Pratt, *The Last Great Forest: Japanese Multinationals and Alberta's Northern Forests* (Edmonton: NeWest Press, 1994); L. Anders Sandberg, ed., *Trouble in the Woods: Forest Policy and Social Conflict in Nova Scotia and New Brunswick* (Halifax: Gorsebrook Research Institute for Atlantic Canada Studies, 1993).
45 See T.J. Barnes, and R. Hayter, 'Economic Restructuring, Local Development and Resource Towns: Forest Communities in Coastal British Columbia,' *Regional Studies* 26, 1992, 647–63; Thomas A. Hutton, *Visions of a 'Post-Staples' economy: Structural Change and Adjustment Issues in British Columbia* (Vancouver: UBC Centre for Human Settlements, 1994).
46 See Michael Howlett, 'Forest Policies in Canada: Resource Constraints and Political Conflicts in the Canadian Forest Sector,' doctoral dissertation, Queen's University, 1988.

PART 2
THE CANADIAN FOREST POLICY REGIME

Chapter Two

The Business and Government Nexus: Principal Elements and Dynamics of the Canadian Forest Policy Regime

Michael Howlett and Jeremy Rayner

Introduction: The Historical Pattern of Canadian Forest Policy

For over 300 years, the competing interests of governments in rents, industry in profits, and labour in wages have led to a succession of forestry policy regimes in Canada. Both before and after Confederation these regimes have been heavily influenced by the differing political strengths of capital, labour, and landowners, as well as by how the major actors have exercised their power within the prevailing context and organization of the Canadian state. The defining contextual feature since 1867 has been the authority of the provincial governments over forests and forest land as granted to them by Canada's constitution.[1] The result is a decentralized pattern of forest policy-making, reinforced by significant jurisdictional variations in the political–economic importance of forests as a resource base. In sum, the type of forest industry found in each Canadian jurisdiction and the capacity and willingness of the different jurisdictions to regulate the forest industry varies significantly, as does the record of policy development within each jurisdiction.

Nevertheless, a number of signficant factors in the evolution of policy transcend provincial boundaries, making it possible to discern the outlines of a general pattern of forest policy development in Canada. Markets for Canadian forest products, for example, have been and remain primarily international. The technology of production is quite similar across regions and provinces. Companies and trade unions, as well, operate across provinces, and provincial governments meet regularly to learn from each other's experiences. A national forest policy regime, albeit with distinct regional and provincial variations in terms of local actors, ideas, and institutions, emerges from this complex interplay of local, national, and international forces. Like all policy regimes, the Canadian forest policy regime contains a generally accepted set of ideas, called a policy paradigm, and a relatively distinct policy-making process, called a policy style, within which local variations unfold.

This chapter identifies the basic sets of ideas, actors, and institutions that comprise the current forest policy regime by examining the characteristics of policy-making within it. After establishing the general nature of the historical evolution of regimes in this sector, the elements and dynamics of the contemporary timber management regime are explored in some detail. The current policy paradigm of liquidating the natural forest and converting it to managed timber plantations is described, followed by a discussion of the quasi-corporatist policy style in this sector, as well as the stresses and strains both have encountered in recent years.

Forest Policy Regimes in Canadian History

Before discussing in detail the elements and dynamics of the contemporary forest regime, it should be noted that the contemporary regime is only the most recent of four regimes that have characterized Canadian forest policy. The first regime was established by European powers in the early settlement period of the country. It was a regime of essentially unregulated small-scale exploitation of the existing forest by settlers who needed wood for domestic fuel and construction purposes. In the early nineteenth century this regime was transformed by the creation of the first licensing schemes for the removal of timber. Such schemes were designed, for the most part, to capture resource rents from the nascent export trade in square timber for governments, who were the owners of the forest lands. This second regime was followed, in the last two decades of the nineteenth century and the first decades of the twentieth century, by one comprising early efforts to ensure the long-term conservation of forest resources; usually this was through the issuance of regulations designed to avoid waste and promote natural regeneration. The fourth, and current, regime emerged in the years surrounding the Second World War. Increasing demands on the resource base associated with the rise of the newsprint and pulp and paper industries led to efforts to promote and guarantee long-term resource supplies; these were augmented by campaigns to promote artificial regeneration of the forests, and cemented by the establishment of long-term timber management agreements with producing firms.[2]

The current regime is, at the very least, contested, and there is much evidence to suggest that it is in the process of being replaced by a new regime of an as yet undetermined character. Ideas, actors, and institutions are all in a state of flux, creating considerable uncertainty, and some discomfort, for many elements of the forest policy community. In the concluding section, we speculate a little about the form that this fifth regime may take. However, much of what we say concerns the surprising ability of the current policy regime to resist demands for change or to deflect those demands towards piecemeal and incremental adjustments. It should also be noted that, although the accounts of foresters often tend to represent the successive regimes as 'stages,' we do not mean to imply a progressive development in the rational or scientific character of policy from one stage to the next. On the contrary, no such implication is intended here at all.

The Regime of Unregulated Exploitation

In the first regime of unregulated exploitation, tenure arrangements did not usually exist, and where they did they merely amounted to reservations of specific tree species for use by the French and British navies in jurisdictions where these species occurred in abundance.[3] During this era, small-scale exploitation of Canadian forests began for settlement purposes. Napoleon's imposition of the Continental Blockade in 1806 cut England off from its traditional supplies of timber in the Baltic regions, leading to a rapid growth in exports from Canada, as British markets suddenly opened.[4]

The system of largely unregulated exploitation of forest resources by a plethora of small logging outfits associated with the square timber trade was inordinately wasteful of timber resources. Limited technology and poor communications raised the spectre of scarcity, as easily accessible forests were denuded through excessive cutting or cleared to allow agricultural settlement. The ensuing competition for accessible resources led to the first government regulation of the industry – both to enforce exclusive cutting privileges and to prevent the monopolization of forest lands.

The Regime of Revenue Enhancement

After 1806 governments began to realize that substantial revenues could be generated from the industry for the privilege of removing timber from Crown lands. This led to the creation and enforcement of specific forest tenure and licensing policies and to the introduction of stumpage and ground rents.

The implementation of licensing policies signalled the transition from a regime of unregulated exploitation to one of regulation for revenue enhancement. Throughout this second period, governments strove to extract high rents or returns from Crown-owned timber, instituting stumpage and export duties, and prohibiting the sale or granting of Crown timber lands. Exceptions were made in order to subsidize railway development; however, in most cases the ban on Crown land alienations remained in effect. By the mid-nineteenth century, New Brunswick had led the way for governments in both Upper and Lower Canada to develop various types of leases or 'tenures,' providing long-term timber supplies to established sawmill operations and to the newly developing pulp and paper industry.[5] Later in the century, similar leases were adopted in other provinces extending the system to the rest of the country.

The Conservation Regime

By the mid-nineteenth century the first legislation controlling access to the forest had begun to appear; this legislation was supplemented, around the turn of the century, by increased regulation of harvesting to eliminate wasteful practices.[6] The development of the pulp and paper industry changed forest policies. Its capital-intensive nature, large scale of production, and need for an extensive transportation and service sector infrastructure required considerably different government policies than those needed for the small-scale, labour-intensive, and transitory lumber industry.[7] The most important change brought on by the pulp and paper industry, however, was its impact on the forest resource base. Although it exploited species like spruce and fir, which had not been favoured by the lumber industry, the large appetite of the pulp and paper industry for fibre led to ever-increasing problems in matching the supply and demand of timber over both the short and the long term. This, in turn, led to increased efforts by Canadian governments to augment the Crown's timber supply by artificial means and to implement closer regulation of harvesting to ensure maximum use of present and future resources.

Under this conservation regime, governments began to regulate the industry to minimize the accidental or careless destruction of remaining forests.[8] Relatively unfettered small-scale competition had by this time given way to large-scale forest operations which dominated existing markets and resource supplies and cut increasingly larger volumes of timber. Around the turn of the century, the provinces created provincial forest services to design and implement conservation and to establish the professional forestry schools that would staff them. Efforts were made to institute fire protection legislation and to ensure that the forest was left in a condition that would allow natural regeneration to take place.[9]

The conservation regime was designed to provide the industry with supplies that would justify the capital requirements of large-scale forest-products processing plants. Long-term leases were extended to companies that agreed to establish production facilities in the jurisdiction concerned and to abide by existing forest-legislation and conservation regulations.[10] Provincial and national associations were formed to help promote conservation principles,[11] along with a federal commission of conservation that published numerous reports on forest issues over the first two decades of the twentieth century.[12]

The Current Timber Management Regime

Inventories carried out in the 1930s revealed the extent to which forest resources continued to be depleted under the system of licensing associated with earlier regimes, threatening the long-term viability of the resource and the industries and communities that depended on it.[13] Both the interventionist atmosphere of the Second World War years, in which governments assumed extensive powers to direct the economy, and the ensuing era of 'province-building,' were factors conducive to more activist provincial forest policies.

The current regime, that of timber management, was created as the limits of naturally occurring forests were approached. It poses somewhat different problems in different regions of Canada. In the Maritimes and parts of southern Ontario and Quebec, the old forests were already gone, and the primary objective was to reconstitute viable managed Crown forests from the patchwork of abandoned cutovers and failed settlements found around substantial private forest holdings. In the newly opened boreal forest, which stretched from northern Quebec to the Yukon and, above all, into the productive temperate forests of coastal British Columbia, the problem was how to manage an orderly transition from the old forest to the new. This new regime was intended to facilitate and speed the process of converting natural forests to tree farms, or plantations, which could sustain the long-term fibre needs of industry.

The transition to this regime was marked by government attempts to regulate company harvesting practices to ensure that timber supplies were not wasted or damaged by harvesting activities. There was a gradual shift from a reliance on natural regeneration to artificial regeneration; with the creation of cutting plans and management units on existing tenures, there was a shift from area-based timber supply agreements without management responsibilities to volume-based timber supply agreements (then back to area-based ones with licensees responsible for basic silvicultural activities); an imposition of quota regimes restricted entry into the forest sector; and a general increase in government regulation of all aspects of the industry.[14]

In most jurisdictions, the timber management regime involved the reorganization or 'rationalization' of scattered and relatively small-scale leases into large-scale, contiguous areas of land under different forms of forest management agreements or licenses, and the extension of government regulations to privately held forest lands. In most jurisdictions, the timber management regime was adopted after royal commissions of inquiry, or other investigative bodies, immediately following the Second World War reported on the poor prospects for continued industrial use of the forests over the medium to long term.[15]

The Overall Pattern of Regime Evolution

In the development of their forest policies, all Canadian governments, with the exceptions of Prince Edward Island, the federal government, and the Northwest and Yukon territories, passed sequentially through the four different regimes. P.E.I. was exceptional since all land in that province had been sold to absentee landlords early in its history, leaving the provincial government with very little forest to administer. Without rents to collect and with only a small forest base to begin with, P.E.I. never passed through a stage of regulation for revenue enhancement. Nevertheless, after 1938 it began to reacquire abandoned agricultural lands, and gradually started to regulate the cut of timber from private lands – adopting most of the tenets of a general conservation strategy. After 1969, with the aid of federal funding, P.E.I. began promoting a regime of intensive forest management on private lands and moved into the era of timber management.[16]

In the case of the federal and territorial governments the pattern is also quite different, and this is addressed in Chapter 13 below.[17] In short, however, having inherited a regime of regulation for revenue

Table 2.1 Chronological pattern of the development of Canadian forest policy

	Unregulated before	Regulation for		
		Revenue	Conservation	Management
New Brunswick	1837	1837	1883	1937
Ontario	1849	1849	1898	1947
Quebec	1849	1849	1909	1974
Saskatchewan	1872	1872	1906	1947
Alberta	1872	1872	1906	1949
Manitoba	1872	1872	1906	1952
Fed/NWT/Yukon	1872	1872	1906	–
Newfoundland	1875	1875	1955	1970
Nova Scotia	1882	1882	1921	1977
British Columbia	1888	1888	1910	1947
PEI	1938	–	1938	1969

Source: Michael Howlett and Jeremy Rayner, 'The Framework of Forest Policy in Canada,' in Monique M. Ross, ed., *Forest Management in Canada* (Calgary: Canadian Institute of Resources Law, 1995).

enhancement from the United Provinces of Canada and the Maritime Provinces in 1867, the federal government never encountered a situation of unregulated forest exploitation. Revenue enhancement was generalized to federal lands in the Dominion Lands Act of 1872, and after 1906 it was replaced by a regime of conservation policies. The extent of federally controlled forest lands was substantially reduced in 1930, when the three Prairie provinces were granted control over their own natural resources. The federal government retained ownership only of poor quality and inaccessible timberlands in the Northwest Territories and the Yukon, as well as of very limited forest areas contained in national parks, Indian reserves, or armed forces bases; on its remaining lands it continued to practise conservation policies.[18]

The pattern of policy development in the various jurisdictions can be seen in Table 2.1. As befits a national policy regime characterized by provincial jurisdiction and variations in regional and local forest resources, there are differences between jurisdictions in terms of both the length of time each policy regime was left in place and the specific point in time at which a new regime was instituted. Different governments in the various jurisdictions adopted similar forestry policies, usually in the same order or sequence, but not at the same times.

Similar regimes developed in disparate jurisdictions for the reasons alluded to above. Despite the independence formally granted to provincial governments by Canada's constitution, similar sets of problems – largely associated with the increasingly intensive industrial use of a restricted range of tree species – led to similar legislative and regulatory responses across the country. Significant actors in the forest sector, such as the forest industry and forestry professionals, have been active throughout Canada, and while they have operated in different jurisdictions, they brought with them similar approaches to and ideas about appropriate solutions to common forest policy problems. Moreover, in all jurisdictions, Canadian governments are constrained by the moves and actions of their predecessors' policy regimes. Early decisions to establish lease-based systems of exploitation, rather than simply selling off public forest land or creating publicly owned forest companies, for example, set the basic framework within which each successive regime was established. More recent decisions, such as those made to link expanded forest tenures to industrial processing plants, also 'lock-in' certain policy options while restricting the ability of governments to adopt alternatives.[19]

The same problem appearing in different jurisdictions and the common problem of having predecessors' policies in place before them has resulted in the tendency towards enacting similar policies in different jurisdictions. Where differences occur most is in the timing. However, the intensity of the impact and nature of the problems related to the industrial use of provincial, federal, and territorial forests vary directly by jurisdiction in terms of the basic endowments of commercial tree species that each enjoys, as well as the level of development of the forest industry in exploiting that resource in that jurisdiction. The different intensities of commercial forest exploitation affect the timing at which regulatory problems emerged historically, resulting in the pattern of lagged policy innovation and adoptions, as shown in Table 2.1.

Constituent Elements of the Contemporary Timber Management Regime

The current Canadian forest policy regime encompasses the idea that forests can be 'cropped' for industrial timber production on a continuous or 'managed' basis. The adoption of the sustained yield objective, and the characteristic instruments of licensing and regulation designed to achieve it, proceeded at different paces in the different jurisdictions. It is now adopted across the country, having been in place in most jurisdictions for nearly half a century. Over the past fifty years or so, Canada has witnessed a gradual convergence of a very similar set of forest policies involving a preference for large, area-based tenures carrying extensive management responsibilities for private forest operators; an emphasis on artificial regeneration of cutovers, with penalties for failure to achieve adequate cover within a specified time; and increasingly intensive government regulation of company harvesting practices, both in order to ensure timber supplies are not wasted or permanently damaged by harvesting activities and to protect other forest values from the externalities of industrial forestry.

Both the advantages and disadvantages of this regime are now becoming apparent, stimulating intense debate at the level of ideas and some considerable experimentation in the use of policy instruments. It is striking that, despite the decentralization of policy-making in Canada, the appearance of new provincial forest-related groups and actors, and the considerable controversy generated by their attempts to promote policy change, the fundamental features of the Canadian forest policy regime have remained remarkably stable. In all Canadian jurisdictions forests continue to be managed primarily for commercial timber production by incentive-based tenure arrangements between the provincial Crown as landowner and large forest products corporations as harvesters.

The Founding Idea: Liquidation–Conversion or 'Maximum Sustained Yield'

At the heart of the current timber management regime is a particular concept of sustainability known as 'maximum sustained yield.' This means that the forests that survived earlier regimes will be managed to provide a steady stream of fibre for industrial production. Under exceptional circumstances, forests may be left uncut because they are too inaccessible or contain the wrong kinds of trees. Often it is possible to provide benefits such as recreation access or improved hunting as a by-product of managing for fibre. However, over the long term, the idea is to sustain fibre production for industrial production by gradually liquidating the original forest and converting it to a managed plantation.[20]

Even before the rise of modern environmentalism, with its ambitious goal of preserving indigenous ecosystems, serious tensions emerged in the timber management regime around exactly what it was that was being sustained: jobs, capital, resource rents, or trees. Historical patterns of forest land use by both indigenous and non-indigenous populations were swept aside with little consultation or means of redress for these groups. At the same time, the forest industry itself was subject to a series of 'rationalizations,' fundamentally altering the nature of work in the woods and driving down employment in mills, with destabilizing consequences for timber-dependent communities. Nevertheless, the 'liquidation–conversion' paradigm has remained a central pillar of the existing timber management regime.

The overall policy style associated with the liquidation–conversion paradigm in the Canadian timber management regime has several specific features. Often referred to as a 'closed, bilateral, negotiative' style, the policy process in this sector is typically one in which governments and industry work out policies through private negotiations. In this quasi-corporatist style, agenda-setting is largely a matter of inside initiation; policy formulation is dominated by a small, closed, subsystem; and decision-making is largely incremental in nature. In addition, implementation is largely a matter of 'command and control' regulation, and any evaluations are usually formal ones undertaken by government agencies.[21]

Just as the liquidation–conversion paradigm has evolved over the past several decades, some minor changes in this policy style have also occurred. The increasing visibility of environmental organizations in Canada, and reference to 'multiple stakeholders,' supports the idea that the style is moving towards an increased public involvement in policy processes. However, the nature and impact of public involvement is often exaggerated.

New actors, for example, face numerous constraints that impede their ability to affect forestry policy agendas. The informal and discretionary basis of issue identification continues to ensure that all serious issues are not placed on the agenda, although media attention may help the most provocative ones to be addressed. This means that interests supported by money, power, political connections, or other backing come to be addressed by governments, while other, often chronic, and perhaps as yet unidentified issues, serving no visible economic interest, tend to remain less visible. Procedurally, there are no means to ensure that such items will move onto the agenda, let alone that they will remain there.

The Traditional Actors: Bilateral Industry–Government Networks

Since forest land in Canada is predominantly owned by the Crown, in the policy network of most timber-producing provinces, the state, and its agencies, in the forest policy sector, have a special place over and above the usual roles available to a legitimate government. As landlords, provincial governments can set the terms for access to Crown forest resources, impose more onerous restrictions on harvesting activities, and use more intrusive policy instruments for regulation than would be tolerated if private forest lands were involved. However, the widespread use of forest-generated income for general revenue purposes and the unwillingness of cash-strapped provincial governments to invest in timber management has created a strong bargaining position for private firms. Under the timber management regime, the business sector has become the critical partner of the state, providing not only the large-scale processing facilities and international marketing skills needed to turn trees into revenue, but increasingly, the technical and professional knowledge essential to timber management itself. This symbiotic, though by no means always friendly, relationship between capital and the state constitutes the core of the forest policy network in every Canadian province, with only minor variations for local conditions.

While other actors have had commensurate difficulty breaking into these closed and unwelcoming policy networks, they have not been without resources of their own. Labour, although a significant actor in some provinces, suffers from fragmented organization. Where organized labour has achieved significant gains in wages and working conditions, companies have been able to respond by substituting capital for labour. The seemingly inexorable trend for employment per unit of wood cut to decline shows no signs of abating, with the result that organized labour has tended to resist efforts to reduce cut levels.[22] In this, labour has been joined by organizations representing rural, timber-dependent communities and their bureaucratic allies.

Business

Forest products companies in Canada have a long history, with the roots of many currently viable firms stretching back to the earliest days of timber exploitation. Forest companies are among Canada's largest firms, although, by international standards they are middle-sized, well behind such giants as Fletcher Challenge of New Zealand, Daiwa of Japan, or Georgia-Pacific of the United States.[23] Although divided, both sectorally and by jurisdiction, the forest industry, and especially the pulp and paper industry, has long had a strong position on appropriate government policy towards the forest sector, and it has clearly articulated its interests in maintaining and enhancing profits through its business associations.

Table 2.2 Top ten forest products companies, Canada 1984 and 1997 (by revenue in hundreds of thousands of dollars)

Company	1984 Revenue	Company	1997 Revenue
MacMillan Bloedel	2,044	MacMillan Bloedel	4,584
Domtar	1,820	Abitibi-Consolidated	3,747
Abitibi Price	1,660	Noranda Forest (Nexfor)	2,279
Consolidated Bathurst	1,393	Cascades	2,254
CIP	1,213	Avenor	2,186
Canadian Forest Products	995	Domtar	1,964
B.C. Forest Products	899	West Fraser Timber	1,872
Crown Forest	727	Canfor	1,862
Weldwood	586	Donohue	1,747
Great Lakes Paper	495	Kruger	1,661

Sources: Richard Schwindt, *An Analysis of Vertical Integration and Diversification Strategies in the Canadian Forest Sector* (Vancouver: UBC Forest Economics and Policy Analysis Project, 1985) 57; Jim Rowland, 'The Great Paper Chase,' in *Pulp and Paper Journal* 40(7), 1987, 30–1; 'The Top 1000,' in *Globe and Mail, Report on Business Magazine*, July 1998, 160.

The organizational structure of individual businesses and the structure of the sector as a whole is constantly changing. This can be seen in the comparison of the top ten forest products companies in Canada in the mid-1980s and the late 1990s, as set out in Table 2.2 above.

The overall tendency in the forest industry has been for ever greater consolidation and concentration. Many of the Canadian top ten companies have been involved in a spate of takeovers and mergers in the post-1997 period, with ownership or control of these companies moving outside of Canada. Avenor, for example, was sold to Bowater in 1999, Mac-Millan Bloedel was taken over by Weyerhaeuser, and the Canadian assets of New Zealand's Fletcher Challenge Corporation were sold to the Norwegian firm Norske Skogindustrier ASA in 2000, as were those of Weldwood of Canada to International Paper Co. via that company's U.S. $7.3 billion acquisition of rival Champion International Corporation. The best example of consolidation involved Abitibi Price, which merged with Stone Consolidated in 1997 to become Abitibi-Consolidated, which then merged with Donohue to become Abitibi-Donohue in 2000. This movement has been accompanied by a proliferation of spin-off firms established by leading companies to rid themselves of obsolete or high-cost mills. Names of some firms – such as CIP and Avenor – have also changed, as parent conglomerates have spun-off entire divisions to concentrate on holdings in other sectors. Many companies have aggressively moved offshore and count international operations as a significant share of their total investments.[24]

Historically, forest sector capital has, above all else, desired a private sector solution to any problems that arise in the industry.[25] However, it has also sought government largesse on many occasions in aid of its activities, from road construction to mill modernization and employment training. In practice, this has meant bilateral bargaining between industry and provincial governments, with the outcome largely dependent on the ability of the forest industry operators in particular provinces to organize for maximum leverage. To this end, for policy purposes, the pulp and paper industry has been represented since 1913 by a national organization, the Montreal-based Canadian Pulp and Paper Association (CPPA), which was itself renamed, becoming the Forest Products Association of Canada (FPAC).[26] The lumber industry, on the other hand, has not had an authoritative national organization until relatively recently.[27] Previously, the lumber industry relied heavily on provincial associations, and, especially in the modern era, on the large association in British Columbia, to carry out its lobbying and other activities.[28] Both industries have resisted any effort to expand subsystem membership; contesting the right of environmental groups, for example, to participate in allocating forest lands and organizing residents of timber-dependent communities to counter grass-roots environmentalism.[29]

Governments

The expansion of forest policy objectives with each successive forest policy regime has resulted in several major administrative challenges for provincial governments. The primary organization utilized to implement forest policies in Canada has been the administrative department, although there have been occasional uses of Crown corporations to rescue unprofitable mills, and in some provinces marketing boards were established for small-scale timber producers. Forest ministries have often been combined with the administration of lands in several long-lasting provincial departments of lands and forests, yet in recent years there have been two opposing tendencies apparent in terms of administrative reorganizations. One has been the emergence of larger, omnibus

Table 2.3 Pattern of development of forest administrative agencies

	Type 1: Lands	Type 2: Forests	Type 3: Natural resources	Type 4: Environment
Newfoundland	1930	1970	1992	–
Nova Scotia	1848	1926	–	–
New Brunswick	1824	1913	1966	–
P.E.I.	–	–	1897	–
Quebec	1841	1905–93	1979	–
Ontario	1841	1906	1972	–
Manitoba	–	–	1930	–
Saskatchewan	–	–	1930	1991
Alberta	1930	1949–86	1975	1993
British Columbia	18741	1945	–	–
Federal	1867	1960–90	1966–93	1970

Source: Michael Howlett and Jeremy Rayner, 'The Framework of Forest Policy in Canada,' in Monique M. Ross, ed., *Forest Management in Canada* (Calgary: Canadian Institute of Resources Law, 1995).

ministries of natural resources, encompassing regulatory authority for a variety of natural resource sectors including forests, mines, and energy. The other has been the entrenchment of powerful forest ministries. This is only a very general pattern, however, as there have also been efforts to combine forest administration with such areas as tourism, water resources, or parks.

In general, government administrative agencies of all stripes have become more sophisticated as their direct involvement in forest operations has declined. The development of single or dual-purpose administrative agencies displays a much greater effort to monitor and control forest administration, while in the recent past organizational changes have represented increased efforts to integrate forest planning activities with natural resource and environmental planning in general (see Table 2.3).

At the federal level, reflecting the ambiguous nature of the federal role in forest policy formation, a variety of idiosyncratic organizational forms have been used – from the original Department of the Interior to the more recent Ministry of State for Forests and Mines. While the federal government has been aggressively signing on to various international conventions with a potential forest impact, notably, the Conventions on Biodiversity Conservation and Global Climate Change, implementation remains the responsibility of the provinces. However, the need for greater coordination of these increasingly sophisticated policy regimes has been recognized in efforts made at the intergovernmental level, and the federal government has assumed the leading role in developing effective forest structures (see the discussion by Bernstein and Cashore in Chapter 3). At the federal level, forest issues are now being addressed by the intergovernmental Canadian Council of Forest Ministers (CCFM). Among other activities, CCFM assumes responsibility for coordinating efforts to establish National Forest Sector Strategies, a series of non-binding 'commitments' undertaken by signatory governments and leading organizations relating to 'sustainable development.' Even here, however, CCFM bows to provincial sensibilities by handing off management and reporting of the strategy to a provincially led stakeholders' organization, the National Forest Sector Strategy Coalition.

Labour

The third actor in the Canadian forest policy network is labour, even though labour plays a very minor role in the network compared with industry or government. By 1991 the entire forest products industry, the logging sector, and the capital-intensive pulp and paper industry were highly unionized, although there remains some variation between sectors. The sawmill sector, for example, remains bifurcated with a relatively small number of highly unionized, capital-intensive mills often directly linked to pulp and paper operations and a large number of very small, often family-run, non-unionized mills. As Table 2.4 reveals, while unionization rates remained high, by 1997 total union membership in the forest sector had declined by almost 25 per cent from 1991 levels, as the total number of paid workers dropped by the same proportion. The reasons for this decline are complex, but they are closely linked to technological changes in the sector (as discussed by Hayter and Holmes in Chapter 5 below).

Unionized sectors remain divided by sectoral representation, region, and national affiliation.[30] Moreover, unions in the forest industry have adapted to declining memberships by seeking out new affiliations and mergers throughout the 1990s. In 1985, for example, the individual membership figures for the Canadian Paperworkers Union (CPU) and International Woodworkers of America (IWA) meant that together they would have comprised the seventh largest union and the third largest industrial union in the country, following only the three large public

Table 2.4 Forestry employees covered by collective agreements, by industry sector, 1991 and 1997

	Membership (000s)		Paid workers (000s)		Unionization rate (%)	
Sector	1991	1997	1991	1997	1991	1997
Logging	29.4	12.8	45.0	46.5	65.3	27.5
Sawmills	31.2	37.9	109.3	77.9	28.5	48.6
Pulp and paper	82.4	60.5	109.6	86.3	75.2	70.1
Total	143.0	111.2	263.9	210.7	54.2	52.8

Sources: Statistics Canada, *Annual Report of the Ministry of Industry, Science and Technology under the Corporations and Labour Unions Returns Act – Part II, Labour Unions, 1991* (Ottawa: Ministry of Industry, Science and Technology, 1993) 24 (cat. no. 71–202); and Statistics Canada, *Labour Force Survey, 1997* – special series (unpublished).

service unions – the Canadian Union of Public Employees (CUPE), the National Union of Provincial Government Employees (NUPGE), and the Public Service Alliance (PSA) – and the service-oriented United Food and Commercial Workers International Union, the industrial United Steelworkers of America, and United Auto Workers (UAW) – now Canadian Auto Workers (CAW). By 1996–7 CPU had been merged into the multisectoral Communications, Energy, and Paperworkers Union (CEPU), and the IWA had been transformed into the Industrial Wood and Allied Workers of Canada, ranking as only the twentieth largest union in the country.[31]

The decline in membership is significant, reinforcing the tendency for labour to remain a relatively minor player in forest policy systems. Through the collective bargaining process, organized labour in the forest sector has focused its efforts at the firm level. In most jurisdictions it has not had a significant, long-term, direct impact at the policy level.

The Core Institutions: Land and Resource Ownership and Regulation

The actors in the Canadian forest policy system work within a set of institutional arrangements that have developed over a long period of time. At Confederation, the British North America (BNA) Act followed British colonial practice – itself with a history extending back to the Norman conquest – of according jurisdiction over land and natural resources to the level of government that controlled the territory in which they were located. Hence, Section 109 of the BNA Act (now called the Constitution Act, 1867) awards ownership over land and resources to the provincial governments, while sections 92(5) and 92(13) award provincial governments exclusive rights to legislate the management and sale of public lands and resources and, more generally, 'property' within the province, including privately owned land and resources.[32] The federal government still retains jurisdiction over the land and resources of the remaining Yukon, Nunavut, and Northwest territories, although in recent years it has begun to transfer some responsibilities in these areas to the three territorial governments.

The existence of exclusive federal power in the areas of trade and commerce and of very wide-ranging powers in the area of taxation has limited the thrust of provincial constitutional supremacy in many resource matters.[33] Control over natural resources has often been defined as a question of the rights of provincial ownership versus the federal right to regulate trade and commerce contained in Section 91(2) of the Constitution Act, 1867. This is a direct result of the high percentage of Canadian natural resources destined for interprovincial or international markets. These resources elude provincial property-based jurisdiction and enter into the federal domain as soon as they cross provincial boundaries.[34] This has always been a significant source of federal influence over provincial forest policies, but it has become even more so in the post–Free Trade era, as forest products have fallen under the terms of agreements such as the Canada–U.S. and the North American Free Trade agreements (NAFTA).

In the area of taxation, the provincial governments have also had to defer to the more extensive federal powers in this area. Although provinces are granted the exclusive right under Section 109 to levy royalties on their resources, these relate only to the extraction stage of the natural resource production process. Revenues arising at further stages of the production process can be appropriated by both provincial and federal levels of government. Until 1982 provincial governments were restricted under Section 92(2) to levying 'direct' taxes – that is, taxes paid directly to the government by the taxpayer – while the federal government powers under Section 91(3) are unlimited.[35] After 1982 this situation was altered by the adoption of Section 92(A), the natural resources clause of the Constitution. This section expands some provincial taxation powers to include indirect taxes on natural resources, provided that there is no discrimination in the tax towards different areas of the country.[36]

The result of this institutional situation has been for both levels of government to respect a slowly developed and court-regulated natural resource modus vivendi in which the hallmark of Canadian natural resource policy-making is provincially led intergovernmental collaboration.[37] The federal government has had its largest continuing area of responsibility restricted to the regulation of the forest industry under its trade and commerce powers and to ensuring forest activities do not conflict with federally regulated fisheries or agricultural pursuits. It has also played a significant role in promoting reforestation and other practices within provincial forest lands through the exercise of its spending powers. However, its overall impact and ability to coordinate activities in the sector has been low (see Chapter 13 below). Because of the nature of land and resource ownership and management rights, in the timber management era, Canadian forest policy has been made by provincial governments with coordination among governments achieved first through bilateral dealings between individual provinces and the federal government and, since the Second World War, in multilateral forums such as the Canadian Council of Resource and Environmental Ministers (CCREM) and its offshoots; including the present-day Canadian Council of Forest Ministers (CCFM).[38]

Regime Dynamics: New Problems and Policy Experiments

Over the past two decades, several problems have emerged with the existing regime. These include challenges to the dominant set of ideas present in the sector and the emergence of new actors in the system. Both developments have led to some experimentation with the existing institutional structure in the attempt to reconcile new actors and new ideas with the components of the existing regime.[39]

New Problems

One major set of concerns focuses on the ability of existing institutional arrangements to deal with internal problems generated by the liquidation–conversion project in Canada's old forests. This is essentially a problem of administrative costs. That is, in the first regime of essentially unregulated exploitation, the administrative machinery required of governments was quite limited. From very early in the history of forest exploitation in Canada, the Crown appointed surveyors to map the territorial domain, and licences to utilize certain blocks were sold on payment of ground-rents (sometimes by deposit or promissory note and sometimes accompanied by a licence fee). The only problem with this system involved its enforcement, requiring the appointment of inspectors with the dual task of ensuring that only the licencee utilized leased land and that all cutting occurred on properly leased limits.

Under the second regime of profit and revenue enhancement, however, the range of policy instruments required for effective regulation increased, although it was still limited to those related to licensing, inspection, and collection. Revenue collection schemes were designed to expropriate two types of rents: those associated with forest land and those associated with the trees contained on those lands. The first type of rent was collected through ground-rent charges, usually levied annually for a fixed statutory rate. Although this charge has often included penalty provisions to prevent speculation and monopolization of forest land, its administration was quite straightforward. The second form of rent collection was more problematic and involved the determination of an adequate price to be paid to the Crown for the removal of standing timber from leased lands, or stumpage.[40] One problem involved determining how much wood was actually cut. At first, mensuration was often left to operators and spot-checked by timber inspectors. After numerous scandals and complaints concerning private mensuration, however, most governments moved to appoint public scaling systems and hired additional officials for this task. A second problem, determining how much to charge, still vexes forestry officials and has resulted in a number of different schemes for allocating shares of final prices between governments and corporations.[41] However, once a figure had been determined, collection remained a relatively simple matter.

Once the transition to the forest conservation regime took place, however, the range of required administrative activities was much more extensive. Policy instruments used for conservation purposes ran the gamut from self-regulation[42] to direct government administration.[43] In practice, most Canadian governments chose to operate largely through the use of 'revenue expenditures' (both tax-based and rent-based) and subsidies when dealing with private landowners and holders of long-term leases; and through regulation when dealing with operators utilizing public lands and timber supplies.[44] The result was a significant expansion of government agencies dealing with the forestry sector. Provincial forest protection services designed to protect the forest from natural disaster, especially fire, were created first, and they soon extended their activities to protection against the adverse effects of agricultural settlement and damage from diseases and pests. Protection from fire often involved legislation prohibiting and criminalizing actions that resulted in forest fires. The protection of forest land from agricultural settlement largely involved the creation of forest reserves as areas of land were designated for more or less exclusive forest use. Such designation required compensation for other users already operating in the designated areas and the establishment of land use or zoning legislation. Insect and disease protection involved the creation of sophisticated research establishments capable of lengthy and complex investigations into plant and tree pathology, and other subjects.

A second aspect of the aim of protecting the forest resource base involved increasing efforts to police the utilization of timber by forest companies. Efforts to eliminate waste in harvesting and processing required more effective monitoring of industry operations and, in the case of the actual milling operations, led governments as far as funding joint research efforts with private operators aimed at enhancing yields and finding uses for cast-off by-products.[45]

The transition from a policy of conservation to one of timber management posed a similarly complex set of policy problems.[46] Given its sheer physical size, putting all Canadian forest land under active management has been a monumental undertaking. The scale of forest operations on Crown land in Canada continually threatens to outstrip the capacity of government agencies for hands-on management of even the more significant details. In the conservation era, the cost of provided direct government protection for the resource was, in theory at least, recovered in the form of licence fees and stumpage. Under the management regime, the direction of policy in most jurisdictions was set by the perceived need to offer favourable terms to licensees as part of a wider policy of provincial economic development and as an incentive to undertake management activities. Most jurisdictions began by experimenting with a division of responsibility in which licensees were responsible for cutting timber and government foresters were responsible for regeneration and protection of the new growth, a logical extension of their old protection function. Poor performance, attributed to the inability or unwillingness of provincial governments to reinvest forest revenues in the development of the resource, prompted a general switch to include basic silvicultural activities in the terms of licences. Although this was not clear at the outset, one of the regime's principal effects has been a gradual shift of responsibilities from overworked provincial forestry services to large corporations with their own professional forest staff. Thus, the timber management regime essentially delegates management responsibilities to industry under different forms of forest management agreements or licences.[47]

The general tendency of the timber management regime to attempt to increase the intensity of management over an ever larger area of Crown forest land without either privatizing the forest itself or increasing the scale of direct government involvement in management activity is behind many of the commonly observed problems of the regime. As more tenures have come to include conditions that can only be met by the largest companies, barriers to entry have been created, sometimes deterring new entrants to the market and promoting corporate concentration. Although there have been exceptions, it has also proved difficult to adapt long-term tenures to the needs of potential non-corporate licence holders such as Native bands, municipalities, community forest associations, or individuals. At the same time, as provincial governments have withdrawn from active forest management and assumed a regulatory role, doubts have surfaced about the capacity and even the willingness of provincial forest agencies to monitor licensees effectively and to provide sufficient disincentives for non-compliance with regulations. The extensive grants of public authority that allow licensees to carry out their activities on public land makes the state ever more dependent on licensees themselves for generating much of the information on which everything from forest management planning to compliance and enforcement depends.[48]

New Actors and New Ideas

It was not long before critics emerged claiming that provincial governments had placed themselves in a conflict of interest as both a regulator of forest practices and as the beneficiary of increased revenue from forest industry expansion. Increasingly, small woodlot owners in the east and independent logging contractors in the west, timber-dependent communities and small business associations from these communities, have emerged as interests separate from the large integrated companies and begun to agitate for a voice in policy-making and the articulation of a new policy regime that would address their needs (see Chapter 6).

Other groups shared similar concerns with the timber management regime, although they often did not have the same pecuniary interests in direct resource-related production activities as did small timber-related businesses. These groups varied from province to province but typically included academics, lawyers, recreationists, environmentalists, and Native groups, and sometimes representatives of the fishing and tourism industries. All these groups, together with productive interests, made up the forest policy community, but many were excluded from existing business-government forest policy networks. Three of these groups, however, have in recent years been able to bargain their way into policy networks. The first, very loose, group is made up of other revenue-generating enterprises whose profits are at risk from traditional timber management practices. The major players are commercial fishers in coastal provinces and tourism and recreation organizations, including hunters and sportfishers, everywhere.[49] The second consists of ideologically committed environmentalists concerned with the impact of large-scale timber management on the ecology of forest land and whose fortunes have waxed and waned with the public support and attention that their ideas have commanded.[50] A third group, First Nations, has recently emerged to challenge the state-business network in some provinces where land ownership issues, previously considered settled, have been reopened by court decisions, notably in British Columbia and New Brunswick.[51]

The category of 'environmentalists' houses a very disparate collection of groups and individuals.[52] However, among the three major new actors arriving on the forest policy scene over the past two decades, they are the most significant in terms of bringing a range of new ideas to the forest policy table. There are groups ideologically committed to various versions of environmental creeds, such as Greenpeace, the Sierra Club, or the Western Canada Wilderness Committee; ad hoc bodies seeking protection for specific areas; older naturalist organizations such as the various provincial Wildlife associations; outdoor recreation, hunting, and fishing groups; commercial organizations whose interests were potentially in conflict with industrial forestry, such as the fishing and tourist industries; Aboriginal organizations concerned about traditional-use rights and land claims; and a variety of exponents of smaller-scale, 'local control' resource development.

What these groups have in common, and what justifies combining them under the same head, is a shared hostility to the objectives, instruments, and outcomes of the timber management regime. They do not think that Crown forests should be managed solely or even primarily for the production of industrial fibre; they do not think that provincial governments have proved effective either in planning for the future or in regulating the current activities of their large licensees; and they are concerned that the wealth of forests has been very unequally shared, although here disputes about who has been most disadvantaged and what can be done to remedy this begin to surface fairly quickly. While the commonalities have provided the basis to contest the timber management regime quite effectively, they have not as yet created a new consensus around which a new regime, with new objectives and instruments, new roles for the leading actors, and, above all, new ideas could be created.

Nevertheless, by the mid-1960s in most Canadian jurisdictions, the value of managing forests purely for timber exploitation had begun to be questioned. As a result of this process, a variety of experiments were conducted with various aspects of the timber management policies. Forest policies began to evolve as policy-makers sought to meet objectives other than fibre production.

Policy Experiments 1: Integrated Resource Management in the 1970s and 1980s

At first, the principal impact of environmental ideas was on controversies over land use. The key environmental ideas that human impacts on nature should be limited and that untouched nature is a source of spiritual value fed the demand for protecting wildernesses and pristine areas. Since what an environmentalist means by 'low-impact forestry' and what a forest manager understands by the same phrase are worlds apart, the dispute was generally a raw, redistributive confrontation over successive tracts of forest. The first efforts at accommodating other interests beyond those of government and industry involved spatial segregation of areas designated for forest operations from those designated as parks or recreation areas where forestry was either forbidden or subject to what was considered, at that time, to be stringent constraints.

There were two disabling difficulties with this approach. First, in the larger forest producing provinces, notably British Columbia, Alberta, Ontario, and Quebec, many remote areas that were technically open for logging were operating as de facto wilderness and recreation areas while logging proceeded in more accessible forests. When forest operations began to move into these remote areas, the now-familiar pattern of land use conflict in which environmentalists, often local people, sought to preserve as 'special places' those areas that forest products companies indicated they would log, began to spring up all over Canada. Second, demands for tighter regulation of practices have been provoked by the externalities of industrial forestry even on land uncontested by preservationists: such things as debris choked fish-spawning streams and other kinds of habitat destruction, mutilated viewscapes in tourist corridors, and even localized impacts like reduced air quality from prescribed burning or spray drift from large-scale aerial pesticide applications, as occurred in New Brunswick and Nova Scotia.

The result, in the 1970s and 1980s, was a significant modification of the timber management regime in the direction of integrated resource management (IRM). IRM, which was not a very new idea, seemed like a policy whose moment had arrived. By managing public forests for a variety of goals simultaneously – animal habitat, timber, recreation opportunities, water quality – provincial forest agencies could both capture the whole range of potential values to be found in public forests and satisfy a wide variety of user constituencies. At the same time, and here was the real promise of IRM, by addressing the public perception that throwing open an area to industrial forestry necessarily means the destruction of any other values, IRM might reduce the continuing pressure for preservation and keep the public forests open to forestry.

However, it soon became clear that IRM continued very much within the confines of the old paradigm. Groups complained that new public involvement provisions developed to ensure that all relevant interests received consideration in the establishment of resource plans offered little more than an opportunity to comment on plans already in an advanced stage of completion. Requests for major modifications to plans were routinely dismissed as outside the scope of a process that still appeared to be driven by timber extraction targets set by the same closed network of government and industry. These complaints were echoed by other government agencies who were also encouraged under IRM practices to take part in forest management planning. At the same time, enabling legislation was written as loosely as possible to give forest managers maximum discretion to waive or vary IRM provisions according to their professional judgment. This 'guidelines' approach to logging operations seemed to make little difference on the ground, where the key line managers in provincial forest ministries routinely exercised their powers to suspend or modify the guidelines, and lacked the administrative capacity to enforce them even when guidelines were nominally a condition of the approval and continuation of a logging plan. Far from damping down the preservationist movement, the practice of IRM confirmed preservationists' worst fears, and Canadian forestry found itself in the glare of international scrutiny over high-profile disputes like Clayoquot Sound in British Columbia or Temagami in Ontario.

Policy Experiments 2: Ecosystem Management in the 1980s and 1990s

Whatever its virtues as a tool of forest management, the failure of IRM to solve the political and administrative problems of the timber management regime led directly to new experiments that promise – or threaten – a transformation of the timber management regime itself. One approach (discussed by Jeremy Wilson in Chapter 4), borrowed from the U.S. Pacific Northwest, is 'ecosystem management.' As its name implies, ecosystem management eschews the focus on wood fibre found in the timber management regime in favour of managing for desired ecosystem characteristics, with resources such as fibre, fish, or game becoming residual outputs. In the United States, the adoption of the ecosystem management paradigm on federal lands has been relatively rapid because the paradigm was successfully held up as the solution to a pressing problem that does not exist in Canada: managing public forests to judicially enforced statutory standards that require preservation of native vertebrates and their habitat. U.S. activists were able to use the courts to demand changes in forest management plans that have entailed dramatic reductions in volumes of timber cut to reflect this new understanding.[53]

Lacking many key elements of the U.S. policy framework, such as an endangered species act, the Canadian experience with ecosystem management has been a mixed one. In general, ecosystem management ideas have been adopted as a way of operationalizing the vague and ambiguous rhetoric of 'sustainable development' that dominated the problem definition end of the policy agenda in the early 1990s. Loss of species, habitat, functioning ecosystems, or more controversially, degradation of forest ecosystem 'health' were all taken to be indicators of unsustainable development, and ecosystem management is proposed as the solution. Without courts to make definitive rulings, however, exactly what ecosystem management requires in the Canadian context remains shrouded in uncertainty and locked in continuing disputes between key policy actors and interests. Efforts at implementing ecosystem management principles have varied between jurisdictions, with the most consistent efforts being those carried out on a small-scale basis in the federal-provincial 'model forests' program (as discussed by Beyers in Chapter 7).

The dispute is an intense one largely because the experiment with IRM opened up the forest policy system to many new actors and the ecosystem management paradigm has potentially significant consequences for them all. Under ecosystem management, the overall goal of sustaining healthy forest ecosystems is to be achieved by a two-pronged approach: representative ecosystems will be completely protected from forest operations and the matrix of working forest between the protected areas will be logged by methods that will sustain suitable habitat (not necessarily in the form of continuous linkages or 'corridors') to prevent loss of biodiversity.[54] By reducing the impact of forest operations on the landscape, this approach has the potential to enlist the support of tourism, commercial fishing, and recreation interests. Ecosystem management's intellectual foundation in conservation biology makes it attractive to the older naturalist and conservationist organizations and, because of its experimental character, undermines existing network claims to a monopoly of technical expertise. In both Ontario and British Columbia, the two provinces that have gone furthest with this approach, governments have been able to craft an alliance with moderate environmentalists to promote policies such as a 12 per cent protected area target and stricter regulation of forestry operations.

The Ontario Federation of Naturalists and the Ontario Wildlands League (later joined by the World Wildlife Federation) pressed the case for ecosystem management at Ontario's marathon hearings over the environmental assessment of Crown lands timber management in the 1980s. At length, their efforts were rewarded with the Crown Lands Sustainability Act regulating forestry and the Lands for Life initiative promoting an expansion of protected areas, both supported by these interests as the best that could be achieved in the circumstances (see Chapter 10 below) A similar alliance between the B.C. government and moderate environmentalists, especially tourism and recreation interests, saw the expansion of British Columbia's protected areas towards the 12 per cent target and the implementation of a new Forest Practices Code to regulate harvesting activity (see Chapter 12 below). Although attempts by more radical organizations like Greenpeace to campaign beyond 12 per cent or to expose weaknesses in the new regulations failed to ignite the same domestic public interest as their earlier interventions in the policy debate, pressure has been successfully applied to the corporations themselves in the form of consumer boycott campaigns. The voluntary moratorium on cutting pristine watersheds in British Columbia's central coast – the so-called

Great Bear Rainforest – has been the most striking example of such an international campaign.

However, fully implemented, ecosystem management usually means both further withdrawals from the working forest for reserves and reduced volumes and higher logging costs from what remains. The forest industry has responded with scepticism or outright opposition,[55] and the industry has been supported by many professional foresters and academics concerned about the experimental and untested character of most ecosystem management prescriptions. The more radical environmental organizations, disliking the emphasis that ecosystem management places on science and the technological 'fix,' have not rallied behind it with much enthusiasm, either. They are especially suspicious of the new interest in alternative silvicultural systems to reconcile logging with habitat conservation outside reserves, arguing that ecosystem management is being used as an excuse to log areas that should be preserved. Both the U.S. Forest Service and the government of British Columbia, for example, have made efforts to mitigate the impact of cut reductions by designating some candidate parks or wilderness areas as 'special management areas' instead.[56]

This conflict between competing visions of how to transform the timber management regime is echoed in many of the chapters that follow, and causes us to be sceptical of claims that the timber management regime is already a thing of the past, replaced by 'social forestry,' 'ecosystem management,' or 'sustainable development.' The old policy regime may be moribund, indeed, but the new regime is still struggling to be born and the outcome of the struggle will necessarily be determined in large part by the legacies of the timber management regime itself.[57]

Conclusion: The Politics of Regime Stability and Transition

While there is strong evidence of the continuing 'negotiative' character of the policy network, restricted primarily to state and industry members, environmental interests have nudged the existing bilateral network into an emerging triadic form. This is not to say that environmental groups have the same amount of power and influence as productive and state interests in defining policy options. Rather, an emerging triadic network acknowledges the success of environmental groups in gaining access to the policy table. It is not merely that a much wider range of groups, from those specifically set up to offer sophisticated policy advice, such as the Canadian Environmental Law Association and West Coast Environmental Law Association, to those at the fringes of the environmental movement are now routinely consulted by governments with reference to a range of forest policy issues. More significantly, academics and consultants who are acceptable to environmental interests now find their way onto the technical committees that design forest policy, sometimes as the result of explicit consultation, where such bodies would once have been constituted by government and industry alone.

The significance of this emerging expansion of the policy network is not only that alternative and often conflicting perspectives may be brought forward in formulating policy options. It is also that the state has somewhat greater autonomy in distancing itself from a purely bilateral position with industry. In theory, this may allow the state greater independence not only from productive interests, but from a legacy of past positions accumulated through the historical evolution of policy. Nevertheless, the decision-making stage of the typical Canadian forest policy process continues to reflect the traditional force of productive interests. The institutional structure and material interests of the policy system continue to deter the openness and rationality of the decision-making process, and it is still the case that a great deal of work can be done at the policy formulation stage, including technical policy design, only for behind-the-scenes negotiation between government and interests, particularly industry and electorally significant timber-dependent communities, to result in significant modification or abandonment of these policy initiatives and alternatives.

Policy implementation also continues to feature a very heavy reliance on regulatory instruments. While traditionally there has been some consensus that the financial 'carrot' was a preferable mechanism to encourage compliance, the regulatory 'stick' has been wielded more frequently, with increased fines and stronger enforcement protocols. Continuing reliance on regulatory efforts, rather than planning and other anticipatory and consultative instruments, reinforces the reactive character of administrative actions, and emphasizes the strength of traditional actors in the policy system. This is in large part the result of the constraints under which the state operates. In the forest sector, Canadian governments are faced with a relatively few, powerful actors engaged in a variety of industrial activities. Paradoxically, as the experience of most provinces with renewable licences illustrates, the stricter the regulations and the more extreme the consequences for non-compliance (such as cancellation of the licence), the less likely that these extreme penalties will ever be invoked except as the 'background sanction' against which more extensive negotiation about what the regulations mean in practice takes place.[58]

Policy evaluations in this sector also continue to be largely formal administrative reviews. This means that the policy options considered for possible change tend to be pragmatic considerations about the merits of specific instruments rather than about generalized alternatives to existing policies. The series of royal commissions that were used to prepare the ground for the transition from the conservation regime to the timber management regime in most timber-producing provinces, for example, have not been reproduced in the present era.

In sum, the contemporary Canadian forest policy style has exhibited distinct tendencies to change from a bilateral, 'bargaining,' style to a more complex style that is more open, multilateral, and deliberative – but it has not yet completed the transition. Just as many of the changes to the liquidation-conversion paradigm can be plausibly represented as incremental and experimental modifications, it is clear that the policy style has also failed to completely alter its traditional configuration. That is, most elements of the quasi-corporatist Canadian timber management policy style, especially the restricted pattern of agenda setting, the opaque decision-making process, and the traditional regulatory implementation system, remain in place.

However, as many of the chapters in this book reveal, industry, labour and governments are facing many challenges in the contemporary era. A declining resource base, the needs of a mature industry to heighten productivity through technological change, and the labour displacement that has resulted from changes already implemented all threaten the status quo. In addition, public ownership rights have been challenged by Aboriginal land claims, and provincial governments, generally, are much less dependent on resource rents for their revenues than they were at points in the past. These developments enhance the potential for change in the current regime, a subject to be investigated in the chapters in Parts 2 and 3.

NOTES

1 G.V. La Forest, *Natural Resources and Public Property under the Canadian Constitution* (Toronto: University of Toronto Press, 1969).

2 On the four-regime categorization, see A.J. Herridge, 'The Development of
   Forestry Policy,' in *Forestry Chronicle* 40(4), 1964, 425–8; W.R. Smithies, *The
   Protection and Use of Natural Resources in Ontario* (Toronto: Ontario Economic
   Council, 1974) 5–18.
3 On Quebec's early forest history, see J. Noel Fauteux, 'L'Exploitation de
   Forêts du Canada Sous le Régime Français,' *La Forêt Québécoise* 2(1), 1940, 13;
   Marcel Lortie, 'Les Grands Traits de l'Histoire Forestière,' *Revue Forestière
   Française* 31, 1979, 23–4. On the French naval reserve system of *martelage* sim-
   ilar to the English 'broad arrow' policy, see A.R.M. Lower, 'The Forest in
   New France,' Canadian Historical Association, Report of the Annual Meet-
   ing Held at Winnipeg, 24–5 May 1928, with Historical Papers (Ottawa:
   Department of Public Archives, 1928) 78–89; Jean Bouffard, *Traité du
   Domaine* (Quebec: Les Presses de l'Université Laval, 1977) 27. On the imple-
   mentation of the 'broad arrow' policy itself, see Robert Greenhalgh Albion,
   Forests and Sea Power: The Timber Problems of the Royal Navy, 1652–1862 (Ham-
   den: Archon Books, 1965) 346–69. On Ontario, see Thomas Southworth and
   A. White, 'A History of Crown Timber Regulations from the Date of the
   French Occupation to the Year 1899,' in *Ontario, Clerk of Forestry Annual
   Report* (Toronto: Legislative Assembly, 1899) 154–5; Richard S. Lambert and
   Paul Pross, *Renewing Nature's Wealth: A Centennial History of the Public Manage-
   ment of Lands, Forests, and Wildlife in Ontario, 1763–1967* (Toronto: Depart-
   ment of Lands and Forests, 1967) 17; T.D. Regehr, 'Land Ownership in
   Upper Canada, 1783–1796: A Background to the First Table of Fees,' *Ontario
   History* 55, 1963, 35–48. On the Maritimes, see J. Murray Beck, *Politics of Nova
   Scotia*, vol. 1, *Nicholson-Fielding, 1710–1896* (Tantallon, NS: Four East Publications, 1985).
4 See A.R.M. Lower, 'The Trade in Square Timber,' in W.T. Easterbrook and
   M.H. Watkins, eds., *Approaches to Canadian Economic History* (Toronto: Gage,
   1980) 28–48; A.R.M. Lower, 'The Lumber Trade between Canada and the
   United States,' in A.R.M. Lower, *The North American Assault on the Canadian
   Forest* (New York: Greenwood, 1968) 43–52.
5 See J. Miles Gibson, *The History of Forest Management in New Brunswick* (Vancouver: H.R. Macmillan Lecture, University of British Columbia, 1953);
   J. Howard Richards, 'Lands and Policies: Attitudes and Controls in the Alienation of Lands in Ontario during the First Century of Settlement,' *Ontario
   History* 50(4), 1958, 193–209; George C. Wilkes, 'Ground Rent for Provincial
   Forest Land in Ontario,' *Canadian Journal of Economics and Political Science*
   22(1), 1956, 63–72; Graeme Wynn, *Timber Colony: A Historical Geography of
   Nineteenth-Century New Brunswick* (Toronto: University of Toronto Press,
   1981); Graeme Wynn, 'Administration in Adversity: The Deputy Surveyors

and Control of the New Brunswick Crown Forest before 1844,' *Acadiensis* 7(1), 1977, 51–62; W.S. MacNutt, 'The Politics of the Timber Trade in Colonial New Brunswick, 1825–1840,' *Canadian Historical Review* 30(1), 1949, 61–5; Graeme Wynn, 'The Assault on the New Brunswick Forest, 1780–1850,' doctoral dissertation, University of Toronto, 1974, 122–79. See also E. Minville, ed., *La Forêt* (Montreal: Editions Fides, 1944); Jean Paul Nadeau, 'An Economic Study of Quebec's Sawmill Industry,' doctoral dissertation, Syracuse University, 1969); and Peter Burroughs, 'The Administration of Crown Lands in Nova Scotia, 1827–1848,' in *Collections of the Nova Scotia Historical Society,* vol. 35, 1966, 79–108; Ralph S. Johnson, *The Forests of Nova Scotia: A History* (Halifax: Department of Lands and Forests, 1986) 33–55.

6 Donald MacKay, *Heritage Lost: The Crisis in Canada's Forests* (Toronto: Macmillan, 1985); R. Peter Gillis and Thomas R. Roach, *Lost Initiatives: Canada's Forest Industries, Forest Policy, and Forest Conservation* (New York: Greenwood, 1986).

7 The first mill in Canada to make paper out of wood fibre was opened at Windsor Mills, near Sherbrooke, Quebec, in 1864; the first groundwood pulp mill was built at Valleyfield, Quebec, in 1866. By 1900 there were more than 50 pulp and paper mills in operation in Ontario, Quebec, New Brunswick, and Nova Scotia. On the development of the industry in Canada see Nathan Reich, *The Pulp and Paper Industry in Canada*, McGill University Economic Study no. 7 (Toronto: Macmillan, 1925). In much of Canada, however, the pulp and paper industry is of far more recent vintage. The first mill to manufacture pulp from wood fibre was opened in British Columbia in 1909, Newfoundland in 1910, Manitoba in 1923, Alberta in 1961, and Saskatchewan in 1966. See W.A. Carrothers, 'Forest Industries of British Columbia,' in Lower, *North American Assault*, 251–69. On the Maritime Provinces, see S.A. Saunders, *The Economic History of the Maritime Provinces* (Saint John: Acadiensis Press, 1984). On Newfoundland, see James Hiller, 'The Origins of the Pulp and Paper Industry in Newfoundland,' *Acadiensis* 11(2), 1982, 42–68. On the Prairie Provinces, see John Kennedy Naysmith, *Land Use and Public Policy in Northern Canada,*' (doctoral dissertation, 1975); J.H. White, *Forestry on Dominion Lands* (Ottawa: Commission of Conservation, 1915). On Quebec and Ontario, see Canada, *Report of the Royal Commission on Pulpwood Canada* (Ottawa: King's Printer 1924).

8 See Peter A. Love, 'Renewing Our Renewable Resource: The Legislative Framework,' *Dalhousie Law Journal* 7(3), 1983, 297–314; G.C. Piche, *Forestry Situation in Quebec* (Ottawa: Commission of Conservation, Canada, 1915); James Elliott Defebaugh, *History of the Lumber Industry of America*, vol. 1 (Chicago: American Lumberman, 1906); Lloyd S. Hawboldt, *Forestry in Nova*

Scotia (Halifax: Department of Lands and Forests, 1955); R.B. Miller, 'Forest Resources of the Maritime Provinces,' in Adam Shortt and Arthur G. Doughty, eds., *Canada and Its Provinces*, vol. 14, section VI: The Atlantic Provinces, part II (Toronto: Glasgow, Brook, 1914); Roland D. Craig, *Forests of British Columbia* (Ottawa: Commission of Conservation, 1918); G.W. Payton, *History of Regulations Governing the Disposal of Timber on Dominion Lands in the Provinces of Alberta and Saskatchewan from the 1st September, 1905 to the 1st October, 1930*, 2 vols. (Ottawa: Department of the Interior, 1930).

9 On the development of the profession in Canada, see Andrew Denny Rodgers, *Bernhard Eduard Fernow: A Study of North American Forestry* (Princeton, NJ: Princeton University Press, 1951).

10 For a discussion of the differences between tenure arrangements as they existed in the era of regulation for profits and revenue enhancement and the conservation era, see Judson F. Clark, 'Forest Revenues and Forest Conservation,' *Canadian Forestry Journal* 3(1), 1907, 19–30.

11 The second meeting of the American Forestry Congress was held in Montreal in 1882, sponsored by the Canadian federal government. It elected Henri Joly de Lotbinière, briefly premier of Quebec and later lieutenant-governor of British Columbia, as the first vice-president of the new association. A separate Canadian Forestry Association, with Lotbinière as president, was not formed until 1900. Rodgers, *Fernow*, 62–80.

12 On the Commission of Conservation, see Thomas L. Burton, *Natural Resource Policy in Canada* (Toronto: McClelland and Stewart, 1974).

13 See, e.g., the discussion in British Columbia, Department of Lands, *The Forest Resources of British Columbia, 1937* (Victoria: Forest Service, 1937); and, more recently, Jeremy Wilson, 'Forest Conservation in British Columbia, 1935–85: Reflections on a Barren Political Debate,' *BC Studies* 76, 1987/88, 7–10.

14 Jeremy Wilson. *Talk and Log: Wilderness Politics in British Columbia* (Vancouver: UBC Press, 1998).

15 H.I. Stevenson, *The Forests of Manitoba* (Winnipeg: Economic Survey Board, 1938); Saskatchewan, *Report of the Royal Commission on Forestry Relating to the Forest Resources and Industries of Saskatchewan, Canada* (Regina: King's Printer, 1947); Alberta, *Report of the Post-War Reconstruction Committee* (Edmonton: King's Printer, 1945); British Columbia, *Report of the Commissioner Relating to the Forest Resources of British Columbia 1945*, 2 vols. (Victoria: King's Printer, 1945); Newfoundland, *Report of the Newfoundland Royal Commission on Forestry, 1955* (St John's: Queen's Printer, 1955); Nova Scotia, *Report of the Royal Commission on Provincial Development and Rehabilitation* (Halifax: King's Printer, 1944); W.C. Hazen Grimmer and Fred C. Beatteay, 'Report of the Royal Commission in Respect to Lumber Industry,' in New Brunswick, *Sixty-Sixth*

Annual Report of the Department of Lands and Mines of the Province of New Brunswick for the Year Ended 31st October 1926 (Fredericton: Legislative Assembly, 1927) 16–20; Ontario, *Report of the Royal Commission on Forestry, 1947* (Toronto: King's Printer, 1947).

16 J.F. Gaudet, *Forestry Past and Present on Prince Edward Island* (Charlottetown, PEI: Department of Agriculture and Forests, 1979); J.F. Gaudet, 'Statement on Behalf of the Province of Prince Edward Island,' in Canada, National Forest Conference, *Background Papers and General Information* (Ottawa: Department of Forestry, 1966). See also, Andrew Hill Clark, *Three Centuries and the Island: A Historical Geography of Settlement and Agriculture in Prince Edward Island* (Toronto: University of Toronto Press, 1959).

17 On the varied nature of federal involvement in forest-related issues, see I.C.M. Place, 'Forestry in Canada,' *Journal of Forestry* 76(9), 1978, 557–62; Frances Wetton, 'Evolution of Forest Policies in Canada,' *Journal of Forestry* 76(9), 1978, 563–65, Canadian Forest Service, *The State of Canada's Forests 1996–1997: Learning from History* (Ottawa: Natural Resources Canada, 1997); Monique M. Ross, *A History of Forest Legislation in Canada, 1867–1996* (Calgary: Canadian Institute of Resources Law, 1997), CIRL Occasional Paper no. 2.

18 See J.D.B. Harrison, *Economic Aspects of the Forests and Forest Industries of Canada* (Ottawa: Department of Mines an Resources, 1938); J.D.B. Harrison, *Forests and Forest Industries of the Prairie Provinces* (Ottawa: Department of the Interior, 1936); Michael Howlett, 'The 1987 National Forest Sector Strategy and the Search for a Federal Role in Canadian Forest Policy,' *Canadian Public Administration* 32(4), 1989, 545–63; Kenneth P. Beauchamp, *Land Management in the Canadian North* (Ottawa: Canadian Arctic Resources Committee, 1976).

19 On path dependency and institutional lock-in, see S.J. Liebowitz, and Stephen E. Margolis, 'Path Dependence, Lock-In, and History,' *Journal of Law, Economics and Organization* 11(1), 1995, 205–25; W. Brian Arthur, 'Competing Technologies, Increasing Returns, and Lock-In by Historical Events,' *Economic Journal* 99, 1989, 116–31; David Wilsford, 'Path Dependency, or Why History Makes It Difficult but Not Impossible to Reform Health Care Systems in a Big Way.' *Journal of Public Policy* 14(3), 1994, 251–84.

20 See M. Patricia Marchak, *Logging the Globe* (Kingston: McGill-Queen's University Press, 1995); and Wilson, *Talk and Log.*

21 See Melody Hessing and Michael Howlett, *Canadian Natural Resource and Environmental Policy: Political Economy and Public Policy* (Vancouver: UBC Press, 1997); Ted F. Schrecker, *Political Economy of Environmental Hazards: A Study Paper* (Ottawa: Law Reform Commission, 1984).

22 Ian Radforth, *Bushworkers and Bosses: Logging in Northern Ontario, 1900–1980* (Toronto: University of Toronto Press, 1987); Richard Rejala, *Clearcutting the Pacific Rainforest: Production, Science and Regulation* (Vancouver: UBC Press, 1998).

23 See Marchak, *Logging the Globe.*

24 See Ann Gibbon, 'B.C. Approves MacMillan Bloedel Sale,' *Globe and Mail,* 6 Oct. 1999, B3; Allan Swift, 'Forestry Consolidation Hasn't Turned Up Profits,' in *Vancouver Sun,* 18 Nov. 1999, F8; Ann Gibbon and Tu Thanh Ha, 'Abitibi Snaps Up Rival Donohue,' *Globe and Mail,* 12 Feb. 2000, B1; Ann Gibbon, 'Norwegian Paper Giant Norske Buys Fletcher Challenge Unit,' *Globe and Mail,* 4 April 2000, B1.

25 See, e.g., Canadian Pulp and Paper Association (CPPA), *Response to Challenges and Choices, the Interim Report of the Royal Commission on the Economic Union and Developmental Prospects for Canada* (Montreal: CPPA, 1984) 8. The positions contained in this document parallel earlier positions outlined by industry representatives in an extensive questionnaire survey carried out by the Pulp and Paper Research Institute of Canada (PPRIC) in the early 1970s. See
K.M. Jegr and K.M. Thompson, *The Canadian Pulp and Paper Industry: Threats and Opportunities, 1980–1990* (Montreal: PPRIC, 1975).

26 By 1980 the CPPA represented the interests of 64 companies in the Canadian pulp and paper industry. See William D. Coleman, 'The Emergence of Business Interest Associations in Canada: An Historical Overview,' (paper presented to the Canadian Political Science Association, Montreal, 1985);
W.D. Coleman, *Business and Politics: A Study of Collective Action* (Montreal: McGill-Queen's University Press, 1988) 144–71.

27 The first national association, the Canadian Forest Industries Council (CFIC), was formed in 1983 as a federation of provincial associations joined together to oppose threatened U.S. countervailing tariff action against Canadian softwood lumber imports. By 1986 the provincial associations represented in the CFIC included the New Brunswick Forest Products Association, the Nova Scotia Forest Products Association, the Quebec Forest Industries Association, the Quebec Lumber Manufacturers Association, the Ontario Lumber Manufacturers Association, the Ontario Forest Industries Association, the Alberta Forest Products Association, the Interior (B.C.) Lumber Manufacturers Association, the Cariboo Lumber Manufacturers Association (B.C.), the Council of Forest Industries of British Columbia – Northern Interior Lumber Section, and the Council of Forest Industries of British Columbia. Manufacturers of various wood products have also formed associations in several provinces, as have truck loggers and businesses involved in retail

and wholesale lumber operations. See CFIC, *Canadian Forest Industries 1986 Data Book* (Ottawa: CFIC, 1986) i.

28 Until recently the most important organization representing lumber industry concerns to government and elsewhere has been the Council of Forest Industries of British Columbia (COFI) whose membership was dominated by the large, integrated operators in the coastal region. In recent years, however, major restructuring of the forest industry in British Columbia, and the continuing shift in timber supply from the coast to the interior, has exposed splits in COFI membership, and the organization has become less effective as a general 'umbrella' than it once was.

29 See Natalie Minunzie, 'The Chainsaw Revolution: Environmental Activism in B.C.'s Forest Industry,' Master's Thesis, Simon Fraser University, 1993.

30 In the late 1980s the four largest pulp and paper unions were the Canadian Paperworkers Union (affiliated with the CLC) with 70,000 members in 296 locals; the Federation of Paper and Forest Workers (affiliated with the CNTU) with 169 locals and 14,000 members in Quebec; the Pulp and Paper Workers of Canada (PPWC, affiliated with the CCU) with 17 locals and 7,200 members in British Columbia; and the United Paperworkers International Union (AFL-CIO-CLC) with four locals (three in Ontario and one in Manitoba) and a total of 1,750 members. By 1997 only the United Paperworkers had remained unchanged. The CPU had merged with a larger chemical and energy workers union to become the Communications, Energy, and Paperworkers Union (CEPU) with a total of 167,470 members in 853 locals. The PPWC had lost one local and about 400 members, while the Federation of Paper and Forest Workers had only 132 locals, although its total membership remained at 11,650. Another union, the Independent Paperworkers of Canada, emerged from the takeovers and mergers, with 1,350 members in 13 locals. Canada, *The Directory of Labour Organizations in Canada, 1985* (Ottawa: Ministry of Supply and Services, 1985); Canada, *The Directory of Labour Organizations in Canada, 1992/1993* (Ottawa: Ministry of Supply and Services, 1993. In the woods industry, in the mid-1980s the International Woodworkers of America (IWA, affiliated with the AFL-CIO-CLC) had 65 locals and 51,216 members. The Lumber and Sawmill Workers Union had about 17,000 members, mostly in Ontario and Newfoundland. Woodworkers in Quebec were split into three unions besides those in the Federation of Paper and Forest Workers Union – about 2,500 in the National Federation of Building and Woodworkers Union (CNTU), 3,422 in the Quebec Woodworkers Federation (Independent), and a small number in the one Montreal local of the National Brotherhood of Joiners, Carpenters, Foresters, and Industrial Workers (CLC). Small associations with fewer than 50 members existed in

B.C. – such as the Northern Interior Woodworkers Association and the Cariboo Woodworkers Association – some in company unions and some loosely affiliated with the Christian Labour Association of Canada (Independent) which had 6,513 members. By 1996–7, the IWA had become the Industrial Wood and Allied Workers of Canada with 43,000 members in only 23 locals, the Lumber and Sawmill Workers Union had become merged with the United Brotherhood of Carpenters and Joiners (AFL-CIO-CLC) with 56,000 members in 110 locals, while the Cariboo Woodworkers had shifted allegiance and joined the CCU. In Quebec the Quebec Woodworkers Federation numbered 2,390 members in 21 locals and the National Brotherhood of Foresters and Shopworkers (CNTU) had one local and 3,000 members, while the National Brotherhood of Carpenters, Joiners, Foresters, and Industrial Workers had grown to 2 locals and 9,010 members. Canada, *The Directory of Labour Organizations in Canada 1997* (Ottawa: Human Resources Development Canada, 1998); Canada, *Directory of Labour Organizations in Canada, 1985.*

31 Canada, *The Directory of Labour Organizations in Canada, 1996* (Ottawa: Ministry of Labour, 1996); Canada, *Directory of Labour Organizations in Canada 1997.*

32 La Forest, *Natural Resources*, 3–47 and 164–95. The only significant exception to this rule concerned the fisheries, which under section 91(12) fell into exclusive federal jurisdiction. This 'exception,' of course, befitted the nature of the ocean and anadromous fisheries which transcended provincial boundaries. These terms of Confederation, of course, also gave the federal government the right to control resources on its lands. Although these were minor at the time of Confederation, in 1869 they were greatly expanded by the purchase of the Hudson's Bay Company. British Columbia, Prince Edward Island, and Newfoundland entered Confederation on much the same terms as the original provinces of Nova Scotia, New Brunswick, Quebec, and Ontario and consequently owned and controlled their resources. However, this was not the case with the three provinces carved out of the federally owned Northwest Territories. Manitoba, Saskatchewan, and Alberta did not receive jurisdiction over their land and resources until this power was conveyed to them by the federal government in 1930. This was also true of a small portion of British Columbia originally transferred to the federal government for railway construction purposes in the Terms of Confederation of that province in 1871. Chester Martin, *'Dominion Lands' Policy* (Toronto: Macmillan, 1938).

33 Dale Gibson, 'Constitutional Jurisdiction over Environmental Management in Canada,' *University of Toronto Law Journal* 23, 1973, 54–87.

34 S.I. Bushnell, 'Constitutional Law – Proprietary Rights and the Control of Natural Resources,' *Canadian Bar Review* 58, 1980, 157–69.

35 Gerard V. La Forest, *The Allocation of Taxing Power under the Canadian Constitution* (Toronto: Canadian Tax Foundation, 1981).

36 On Section 92(A), see Michael Howlett, 'The Politics of Constitutional Change in a Federal System: Institutional Arrangements and Political Interests in the Negotiation of Section 92A of the Canadian Constitution Act (1982),' *Publius: The Journal of Federalism* 21(1), 1991, 121–42.

37 Michael Howlett, 'Forest Policy in Canada: Resource Constraints and Political Interests in the Canadian Forest Sector,' doctoral dissertation, Queen's University, 1988. See also, A.R. Thompson and H.R. Eddy, 'Jurisdictional Problems in Natural Resource Management in Canada,' in W.D. Bennett, A.D. Chambers, et al., eds., *Essays on Aspects of Resource Policy* (Ottawa: Science Council of Canada, 1973), 67–96.

38 See Michael Whittington, *CCREM: An Experiment in Interjurisdictional Coordination* (Ottawa: Science Council of Canada, 1978).

39 On the role of ideas and policy change, see Michael Howlett, and M. Ramesh, 'Policy Subsystem Configurations and Policy Change: Operationalizing the Postpositivist Analysis of the Politics of the Policy Process,' *Policy Studies Journal* 26(3), 1998, 466–82.

40 On the general issue of costs involved in timber acquisition, see Arlon R. Tussing, 'An Economic Overview of Resource Disposition Systems,' in Nigel Bankes and J. Owen Saunders, eds., *Public Disposition of Natural Resources* (Calgary: Canadian Institute of Resources Law, 1983) 19–31; Ontario, *Report of the Timber Revenue Task Force to the Treasurer of Ontario and the Minister of Natural Resources* (Toronto: Treasury, Economics and Intergovernmental Relations, 1975) 58–91.

41 On the development of provincial taxation schemes as they affected the forest industry, see A. Milton Moore, *Forestry Tenures and Taxes in Canada: The Economic Effects of Taxation and the Regulating of the Crown Forests by the Provinces* (Toronto: Canadian Tax Foundation, 1957); David Boulter, *Taxation and the Forestry Sector in Canada* (Ottawa: Canadian Forestry Service, 1984). Major taxation revenue schemes included the adoption of specific taxes on logging profits by several provinces in the 1950s. Tax expenditures that affected the sector included preferential tax rates for small businesses and accelerated capital cost allowances on some prominent wood conversion equipment. On the development of these measures, see Alan R. Dickerman and Stanley Butzer, 'The Potential of Timber Management to Affect Regional Growth and Stability,' in Journal of Forestry 73, 1975, 268–9.

42 See David Haley, 'The Forest Tenure System as a Constraint on Efficient

Timber Management: Problems and Solutions,' *Canadian Public Policy* 11 (Supplement), 1985, 315–20.

43 John Cohen and Michael Krashinsky, 'Capturing the Rents on Resource Land for the Public Landowner: The Case for a Crown Corporation,' *Canadian Public Policy* 2(3), 1976, 411–23.

44 Although Newfoundland, New Brunswick, Quebec, Manitoba, Saskatchewan, and British Columbia have all had some experience with public ownership of forest enterprises this has occurred for a variety of reasons, notably large-scale bankruptcy of the enterprise concerned (as was the case in Newfoundland, Manitoba, Saskatchewan, and British Columbia, and later in Quebec) or to provide alternative employment in economically depressed areas of the province (as was the case in New Brunswick, Saskatchewan, and Manitoba). This fits with the observable Canadian pattern concerning public ownership and especially public ownership in the natural resources field. See Economic Council of Canada, *Minding the Public's Business* (Ottawa: Economic Council of Canada, 1986); and Alan Tupper and Bruce Doern, 'Public Corporation and Public Policy in Canada,' in A. Tupper and G.B. Doern, eds., *Public Corporations and Public Policy in Canada* (Montreal: Institute for Research on Public Policy, 1981) 1–50.

45 For a discussion of these mechanisms at the turn-of-the-century, see Judson F. Clark, 'Woodland Taxation,' *Canadian Forestry Journal* 1(4), 1905, 159–72. On present-day forest funding schemes, see Thorne, Stevenson, and Kellogg, *Funding Mechanisms for Forest Management* (Toronto: Canadian Council of Resource and Environment Ministers, 1981); C.M. Johnson, 'Legislative Mechanisms to Balance Public and Private Interests in Forest Management,' paper presented to the International Forest Congress, Quebec City, 1984.

46 Christopher K. Leman, 'A Forest of Institutions: Patterns of Choice on North American Timberlands,' in Elliot Feldman and Michael Goldberg, eds., *Land Rites and Wrongs: The Management, Regulation, and Use of Land in Canada and the United States* Lincoln Institute of Land Policy, (Boston: OGH, 1988), 162.

47 Originally, most provinces offered compensation for all or part of the silvicultural activities carried out by licensees either in the form of tax concessions or reduced stumpage fees. However, from the point of view of governments,' compensating the licensees for management costs places a significant burden on provincial revenues and contributes to a perception that the whole thrust of postwar forest policy is being blunted by insufficient investment in the second-growth forests on which the industry will eventually depend. Many provincial governments have now imposed the full costs of

timber management on licensees, and pressure to recover a greater share is growing in the other jurisdictions. On the basic elements of tenure agreements as they developed, see David H. Jackson, 'Some Structural Components of Contracts as They Relate to Canadian Forest Tenures,' *Forestry Chronicle* 53(1), 1977, 33–6; Jagdish Kumar Rawat, 'Forest Tenure Systems in Canada and Their Role in the Investment Behaviour of Integrated Forestry Firms,' doctoral dissertation, (University of Toronto, 1985); Peter Pearse, 'Property Rights and the Development of Natural Resource Policies in Canada,' *Canadian Public Policy* 14, 1988, 307–20.

48 On the general issues involved in public reliance on private information, see Melody Hessing and Michael Howlett, *Canadian Natural Resource and Environmental Policy: Political Economy and Public Policy* (Vancouver: UBC Press, 1997).

49 See P.W. Williams, 'Tourism and the Environment: No Place to Hide,' *World Leisure and Recreation* 34(2), 1992, 1–9; P.W. Williams, 'ecotourism: An Emerging Tourism Product with Emerging Management Challenges,' *Texas Tourism Trends* 5(3), 1993, 1–5.

50 See, e.g., the environmental position put forward in Michael M'Gonigle and Ben Parfitt, *Forestopia: A Practical Guide to the New Forest Economy* (Madeira Park: Harbour Publishing, 1994); Cheri Burda, Deborah Curran, Fred Gale, and Michael M'Gonigle, *Forests in Trust: Reforming British Columbia's Forest Tenure System for Ecosystem and Community Health* (Victoria: University of Victoria Eco-Research Chair in Environmental Law and Policy, 1997), Report Series R97–2.

51 See National Aboriginal Forestry Association, 'Introduction,' in *Forest Land and Resources for Aboriginal Peoples: An Intervention Submitted to the Royal Commission on Aboriginal Peoples by the National Aboriginal Forestry Association Ottawa, Ontario July, 1993.* Electronic document available at URL: *http://sae.ca/nafa/roycom1.htm#anchor1048476*; Claudia Notzke, *Aboriginal Peoples and Natural Resources in Canada* (Toronto: Centre for Aboriginal Management, Education and Training, 1994).

52 Jeremy Wilson, 'Wilderness Politics in British Columbia: The Business Dominated State and the Containment of Environmentalism, in William Coleman and Grace Skogstad, eds., *Policy Communities and Public Policy in Canada* (Toronto: Copp Clark Pitman, 1990), 141–69.

53 See Robert B. Keiter, 'NEPA and the Emerging Concept of Ecosystem Management on the Public Lands,' *Land and Water Law Review* 25(1), 1990, 45–60; Anna Maria Gillis, 'The New Forestry: An Ecosystem Approach to Land Management,' *BioScience* 40(8), 1990, 558–62.

54 Stan Rowe, 'The Ecosystem Approach to Forestland Management,' *Forestry Chronicle* 68(2), 1992, 222–24; British Columbia, Ministry of Forests, *Draft*

Guidelines to Maintain Biodiversity in Coastal Forests (Victoria: Ministry of Forests, April 1994).

55 Both the Ministry of Natural Resources and the Ontario Forest Industries
. Association opposed proposals for immediate implementation of ecosystem management at the Ontario Environmental Assesment and the board took a 'further study' approach. See Ontario, Environmental Assessment Board, *Decision and Reasons for Decision*, 1994, 392–403.

56 Jim Cooperman, *Keeping the Special in Special Management Zones: A Citizen's Guide* (Gibsons, BC: BC Spaces for Nature, 1998).

57 Ben Cashore, 'Competing for Legitimacy: Globalization, Internationalization, and the Politics of Eco-Forestry Certification (Green Labeling) in the U.S. and Canadian Forest Sectors,' in *Proceedings of the 11th Biennial Conference of the Association for Canadian Studies in the United States* (Pittsburgh: ACSUS 1999); Benjamin Cashore, and Ilan Vertinsky, 'Policy Networks and Firm Behaviours: Governance Systems and Firm Responses to External Demands for Sustainable Forest Management.' *Policy Sciences* 33, 2000, 1–30.

58 Kernaghan Webb, 'Between Rocks and Hard Places: Bureaucrats, Law and Pollution Control,' in Robert Paehlke and Douglas Torgerson, eds., *Managing Leviathan: Environmental Politics and the Administrative State* (Toronto: Broadview, 1990) 201–21.

PART 3
POLICY DYNAMICS

The International–Domestic Nexus: The Effects of International Trade and Environmental Politics on the Canadian Forest Sector

Steven Bernstein and Benjamin Cashore

Canada contains 10 per cent of the world's total forest lands and exports more forest products than any other country.[1] These factors result in two countervailing forces: on the one hand, the world's economic and population growth place heavy demands on Canadian forests as a major source of world fibre; on the other hand, growing international concern about sustainable forestry puts pressure on Canada to maintain its forest ecosystems and old-growth forests. Depending on their fundamental interests, domestic groups identify with one or the other of these pressures. In response, state officials must walk a policy tightrope in their efforts to encourage sustainability and improve Canada's position in the world forest economy.

This chapter highlights the interaction of what Howlett calls the 'domestic forest policy regime,' with a broader set of international institutionalized patterns that also correspond to the regime concept. Canada helps to shape these international forces, but also reacts to them. The 'non-binding' nature and limited regulations of most global forest policies means the case would be overstated to suggest that the domestic regime is fully nested within a global regime. Nonetheless, in a sector vulnerable to the international marketplace and sensitive to increased international scrutiny from a variety of transnational and state actors, these pressures do shape important aspects of Canadian forest policy, and their influence is likely to grow. Understanding Canadian forest policy requires attention to how international policy regime dynamics interact with the domestic regime.

The nature of this international–domestic nexus is most apparent in the international trade and sustainable forestry initiatives since 1990.

We argue that international forest trade and environmental policy have become intertwined, as norms from one permeate the other. The result is the emergence of 'liberal environmentalism' at the global level.[2] Norms of liberal environmentalism predicate environmental protection on the promotion and maintenance of a liberal economic order. These norms reflect the view that environmental protection and the preservation of ecosystems, economic growth, and a liberal international economy are compatible, even necessarily linked. Thus, international environmental and trade agreements are restricted to those that accept economic growth and trade liberalization as ultimate goals. As a result, market-oriented solutions such as the 'polluter pays principle' – which aims to internalize the costs of pollution into the price of a product – dominate, while policies that would restrict trade liberalization or distort markets are rejected. Liberal environmentalism constrains and directs Canadian officials in their attempts to implement their dual and often competing international obligations.

Canadian domestic forest policy has shown signs of both adaptation and resilience to these international pressures. Policy resilience is partly explained by the failure to achieve strong 'binding' international agreements on forestry. Where international trade rules exert more direct pressure, policy resilience also occurs where 'durable' policy legacies make fundamental change difficult to achieve. Adaptation usually occurs in policy areas with high levels of state autonomy from domestic interests opposed to change, or in areas where the state and/or business interests are able to use this international pressure to force their own policy agendas.

This chapter proceeds in five parts. First, we set the context for international pressures by demonstrating the importance of the forest industry to the Canadian economy and its dependence on international trade. Second, we examine how international trade policy directly places pressure on the forest policies of Canada's provinces. Third, we turn to broader international efforts to institutionalize a global set of rules on forest practices and the Canadian response to these initiatives. Fourth, we examine how environmental groups have by-passed international and domestic policy-making processes by using market pressure to target the forest industry directly; these measures range from international boycott campaigns to promoting certification and eco-labelling schemes in processes that sometimes overlap with state–state negotiations. Finally, we assess how the international forces we identify may shape future changes in forest policy in Canada.

The Context

The importance of the forest sector to Canada's economy, and its dependence on foreign markets for its products, makes it unlikely that Canadian forest policy can operate independently of international pressures. Forty-five per cent of Canadian land is forested, 94 per cent of which is publicly owned: 71 per cent by the provinces and 23 per cent by the federal government (most of the federally controlled land is in the Yukon and the Northwest Territories). The forest products sector contributed $20.6 billion to the Canadian economy in 1996, or almost 3 per cent of the gross domestic product. Direct employment in forestry accounted for 2.7 per cent of total Canadian employment. Revenues to provincial governments for rights to harvest publicly owned timber contributed over $2.1 billion to provincial coffers in 1995. Forest products did more than any other sector for Canada's balance of trade surplus, contributing $32.1 billion in 1996[3] and $31.7 billion in 1997.[4] The United States is the most important market for Canadian forest products. In 1997 Canadian forest product sales to the United States were valued at $28.6 billion, to Japan at $3.8 billion, and to the European Union at $3.3 billion (see Figure 3.1).

At the same time, the natural beauty of Canadian forests is a source of tourist dollars, although this revenue is not as important to the balance of payments as is the forest products sector.[5]

Canada's traditional support of multilateral cooperation in international affairs also provides an important context to understanding its role in, and responses to, international forestry negotiations. Since the Second World War, Canadian foreign policy has championed multilateralism as a means to achieve a stable international political and economic environment, a goal reflected in its international forest policies. Canadian governments also view foreign policy as a means to promote Canadian values internationally. In the case of forestry, Canada's position as a forest 'superpower'[6] has afforded the federal government and Canadians acting through non-governmental, business, and international organizations, leadership roles in international activities and negotiations.

Canada and International Trade

Trade Policy Setting

Since the Second World War, tariffs on forest products headed to the

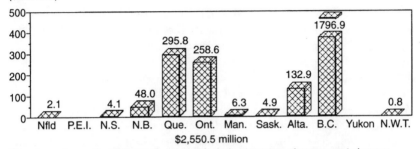

Revenues from the Sale of Timber from Provincial Crown Land, 1997*
($000 000)

$2,550.5 million

*Revenues from sale of Crown timber can include stumpage charges, rent charges, area and holding charges, reforestation levies, protection fees, permit and licence fees, sales and rentals, and other revenues. Revenues collected by the Crown must be considered in the context of the responsibilities and associated costs borne by forest industry.

Source: National Forestry Database

Figure 3.1: Revenues and Economic Profile

United States, Europe, Japan, and other world markets have gradually declined or been eliminated as part of a general pattern of trade liberalization in goods and commodities. International trade agreements, most notably the General Agreement on Tariffs and Trade (GATT) and its successor, the World Trade Organization (WTO), facilitated this process. The Canada–U.S. Free Trade Agreement (FTA) and its successor, the North American Free Trade Agreement (NAFTA) enhance this process on the regional level, pushing towards increased economic integration.

The importance of these agreements extends beyond trade enhancement, since they also provide the rules and mechanisms by which trade and investment is conducted and disputes are channelled.[7] The institutionalization of such rules and mechanisms encourages new practices in conformity with the underlying values and goals of the agreements. Thus, critics note that the agreements aim primarily to promote economic growth and trade liberalization, which tends to encourage resource exploitation over environmental preservation. Recent attempts to promote ecological goals in the context of trade liberalization include the North American Commission on Environmental Cooperation

(NACEC), a side agreement to NAFTA.[8] This agreement fits within the constraints of liberal environmentalism[9] because it predicates a concern with the environment on the promotion of liberal trade. Its power is limited to oversight of existing domestic laws in member countries, and it has no enforcement capability. The creation of NACEC reveals the difficulties of implementing liberal environmentalism in practice, as charges of unfair environmental practices become channelled through mechanisms subordinate to the broader liberal trading regime. Partly as a result, environmental groups have looked to the more developed rules and mechanisms regarding trade subsidies as a way to influence forest policy change.[10]

We use the case of the U.S.–Canada softwood lumber dispute to reveal how trade disputes are channelled and how existing institutions direct patterns of conflict and mobilize producer, consumer, and environmental groups. The dispute offers a good example of how environmental issues and trade are intertwining in the forest sector.

Conflict first arose when Canadian forest exports increased their share of the U.S. market, just when U.S. producers were stung by strict environmental laws governing U.S. national forest lands. Below we examine how the U.S. industry used international trade rules to address this situation, the way trade rules influenced the Canadian response, and the degree of policy resilience that occurred.

The Softwood Lumber Dispute

Since 1982 a coalition of U.S. forest companies has argued that Canadian provincial governments subsidize their forest industries by charging below market prices (stumpage rates) for the rights to harvest publicly owned timber.[11] This coalition argues that the low rates create an unfair competitive advantage, drive down prices, and increase Canadian producers' share of the U.S. lumber market. To neutralize these unfair advantages, U.S. forest companies have launched countervail proceedings under U.S. trade law. Their goal is to have a punitive tax imposed on Canadian lumber to offset perceived subsidies. This case also allows us to see the influence of the FTA/NAFTA bi-national dispute resolution mechanism, implemented six years after the dispute first began.

The dispute has produced both policy convergence and divergence. On the one hand, Canadian stumpage rates increased in response to

U.S. pressures. On the other hand, the policy instrument used in calculating most provincial stumpage fees continues to be driven by the government, rather than by market forces, and the underlying form of
harvesting remains long-term forest licences (tenure agreements).[12]
The softwood lumber dispute also provided environmental groups critical of Canadian forest policy (especially in British Columbia) a controversial tool with which to promote increased environmental protection.
Environmentalists believe that low stumpage rates contribute to an
excessive harvest rate, underplaying the value of the resource to the forest ecosystem and other uses not related to timber.[13] This line of reasoning fits with the 'user pays principle,' a derivative of the 'polluter pays
principle, both of which illustrate the prevalance of liberal environmentalism. This policy norm argues that governments should charge users,
in this case forest companies, the full cost of using resources, so that a
proper social price can be set that would include, or internalize, environmental damage costs or costs of maintaining the resource. In principle, this would promote sustainability in a way that does not distort
markets with government subsidies.[14]

U.S. countervail trade law involves two separate adjudication
processes over whether a subsidy exists (handled by the U.S. International Trade Commission (ITC) of the Department of Commerce) and
whether the imports in dispute injure U.S. producers (which is adjudi-
cated by the department's International Trade Administration or ITA).
Despite changes to U.S. trade law that aided U.S. domestic industry in
launching countervail cases,[15] the U.S. Department of Commerce ruled
in 1983 that no subsidy existed. This was largely because U.S. companies
failed to prove that provincial stumpage programs were tailored to a
'single industry.'[16] Following intense congressional lobbying and legal
precedence regarding definitions of 'subsidy,' U.S. lumber companies
petitioned for countervail relief three years later, and this time the commerce department reversed itself, preliminarily finding that a subsidy
did exist.[17] Amid Canadian charges of political interference, the two
countries agreed to a compromise 'memorandum of understanding'
(MOU) under which Canada would impose an export tariff of 15 per
cent on its softwood lumber exports, with the money going back to provincial coffers.

These pressures by U.S. forest companies sparked a debate in Canada
about the level of stumpage rates that provinces such as British Columbia charged their forest companies to harvest provincially owned forest
land.[18] Those groups and individuals who argued that forest companies

did not pay a fair price for publicly owned timber found a new argument, while cash-strapped provincial governments quickly realized that resolving the problem through higher stumpage fees could also solve their budgetary problems. The B.C. government's support for the MOU was key to its adoption,[19] as was the provision to allow provincial governments to reduce the export tax by increasing stumpage fees. The combination of the countervail action, pressures on stumpage rates, and the B.C. government's wish to increase revenues caused a schism between the provincial government and a forest industry opposed to the MOU. In fact, the B.C. government moved quickly after the MOU was signed to reduce the export tax to zero, through increased stumpage fees. Thus, U.S. law governing international trade resulted in increased stumpage rates, closer to U.S. rates. However, owing to the well-entrenched tenure system in most provinces, which gives large forest companies the right to harvest timber under long-term licensing agreements, large-scale changes to a U.S.-style market-oriented, competitive bidding system did not occur.

The MOU also allowed the Canada–U.S. FTA negotiations to continue. Congress made it known that if the softwood lumber dispute with Canada was not 'fixed,' it would withhold fast-tracking authority for trade discussions with Canada.[20] The subsequent signing of the FTA altered the dynamics of the softwood dispute because of the deal's Chapter 19, which created a bi-national dispute settlement process. Officials of the Canadian federal government championed this new mechanism as a way to de-politicize trade disputes such as the one over softwood lumber. As a result of Chapter 19, and pressure by the Canadian forest industry, the Canadian federal government ended the MOU in 1991, arguing that provincial changes in stumpage rates made it no longer necessary. The federal government believed that because any future challenge would be sent to a bi-national panel, future direct interference by Congress would be less likely to occur.

Upon termination of the MOU, the United States initiated a third countervail proceeding. This move sparked another debate in Canada about sovereignty, stumpage rates, and (this time) environmental protection, which the U.S. lumber lobby raised more explicitly to Congress. Using the argument from environmentalists lobbying in Canada,[21] members of Congress[22] argued that poor forest practices contributed to British Columbia's competitive advantage, even though the formal adjudication process of the ITC and ITA could not officially take environmental issues into account. Following these developments, the U.S.

commerce department's ITA and ITC again ruled that subsidies existed and injuries had occurred to U.S. producers. Yet this time, they ruled that the largest subsidy was British Columbia's raw log export restriction policy, and not provincial stumpage fees.[23] B.C.'s raw log export restrictions were calculated to result in a 3.6 per cent subsidy, while stumpage payments, which earlier had been the key complaint of the U.S. coalition, now amounted to less than a 2.91 per cent subsidy.[24] The finding that export restrictions provided the largest subsidy created a conundrum for environmental groups, who traditionally supported such restrictions because they provided increased fibre supply at home.

Canada appealed the ruling to two FTA bi-national panels, which ruled (eventually along national lines) that the ITA and ITC did not properly follow U.S. trade law and that the United States must remove duties and refund those already collected. Here, the FTA/NAFTA appeared to fend off forces of convergence and to allow Canadian provinces to determine stumpage fees as they saw fit. However, this reading fails to take into account the power of the U.S. coalition to lobby Congress to alter the definition of 'subsidy,' thereby improving the chances for another countervail. Indeed, Congress immediately moved to change U.S. trade law, addressing every single point put forward by the judicial panels to support their ruling in favour of Canada.[25]

The Canadian government became convinced that the recent changes to U.S. trade law made it unlikely it would again prevail at any future bi-national panel process. To avoid a fourth countervail, Canada negotiated a second compromise deal, the Canada–U.S. Softwood Lumber Agreement (SLA), signed in 1996. This time, U.S. negotiators accepted a quota system, offered by the B.C. forest industry, in which exports would enter the United States duty free up to a certain quota, after which an export tax would be imposed.

Owing to a non-derogation clause, U.S. forest companies and North American environmental groups could now use the SLA to limit changes in environmental forestry regulations and stumpage rates. Consequently, when the B.C. government moved to streamline its forest Practices Code and reduce stumpage rates (in order to offset the collapse of the Asian market), it met fierce and sustained opposition from both the U.S. lumber lobby and environmental groups, who argued that the SLA did not permit such changes.[26] In this case, U.S. and NAFTA trade law resulted in an SLA that had the effect of minimizing downward changes to forest practices and stumpage rates.[27] In fact, some industry economists now argue that B.C.'s rates are above market value, much higher than many stumpage rates in the United States and in Eastern Canada.[28] Canada's dependence on the U.S. market and U.S. trade policy thus facilitated higher stumpage rates being imposed in British Columbia, which out-produces all other Canadian provinces in softwood lumber exports to the United States. Indeed, the quota system and the collapse of the Asian market appeared, at first, to give impetus towards the creation of U.S.-style competitive bidding processes in British Columbia. Some hoped that such a move might reduce or eliminate U.S. countervail pressure. For example, MacMillan-Bloedel (before it was purchased by Weyerhaeuser in January of 2000) had produced a white paper in which it proposed a plan to see half of B.C.'s lumber sold through a competitive bidding system.[29]

B.C.'s Fletcher Challenge echoed these views,[30] the B.C. Council of Forest Industries began to publicly raise such ideas,[31] and the opposition Liberal Party followed suit.[32] In this climate, a B.C. government forest policy review called for the establishment of a competitive log market.[33] Despite this increasing interest, the institutionalization of the current tenure system shows no signs of changing. Without changes in this system, a U.S.-style competitive bidding system is not possible.

The softwood dispute has done more to increase stumpage rates than environmental protection per se. Environmental groups have arguably lost some legitimacy by building links with the U.S. timber industry, and whether these links have actually resulted in pressures for increasing or maintaining environmental forestry initiatives remains unclear. This strategy reveals an environmental movement with such limited domestic legal tools that it will cast its net internationally in order to exert pressure to further its goals. At the same time, these groups are split on whether to support or oppose the latest SLA. For example, a coalition of groups in the U.S. Pacific Northwest launched court action in 1998 against the SLA, arguing that it encourages overexploitation of British Columbia's old-growth forests.[34]

As the clock ticked closer to the end of the five year SLA, set to expire at the end of March, 2001, the usual players began to jostle in their attempts to influence any future political or legal solution. The U.S. coalition stepped up its congressional lobbying efforts, including efforts to criticize Canadian environmental forest policies. Likewise Canadian and U.S. environmental groups took the opportunity to argue that Canadian stumpage policy negatively affected the environment.[35] At first, two different industry organizations emerged in Canada, splitting the B.C. industry into one group, and Alberta, Ontario and Quebec forest companies into another. However, by January 2001 these two associations had merged to form the Canadian Lumber Trade Alliance, and immediately called for 'free trade' in Canadian lumber.[36] The new organizations' policy is to oppose extending the SLA, and to help construct a new pact with little or no restrictions on trade.

This manifestation of liberal environmentalism does not guarantee sound ecological practice or environmental protection. The softwood dispute has created odd coalitions, but it has not been the source of increased environmental protection. Changes for greater environmental protection came from domestic pressures and from the international arena through international agreements and environmental groups' use of markets as a tool to further their agenda.

International Institutions and Canadian Forest Policy

The dynamics of liberal environmentalism can be seen most clearly at the international level, where they shape the forest agreements that apply to Canada and militate against the likelihood of a binding international regulatory framework to manage the use and protection of forests. Canada sits uneasily within these dynamics. Since the late 1980s it has stood out as one of the strongest supporters of a global forest convention, which is a major goal of the international plank of Canada's *National Forest Strategy for 1998–2003*.[37] Such a convention would provide Canadian producers and governments with a stable set of rules to guide trade in forest products and ensure access to markets, as well as clarifying commitments for forest management. For similar reasons, Canada has played a major role in the debate over trade and the environment in the WTO and the Organization for Economic Cooperation and Development (OECD).[38] However, while Canadian forest companies benefit immensely from an open international trading system, they have been reluctant to commit to tough environmental standards imposed internationally. Like other northern producer countries, Canada wants a strong reputation as champion of the global environment by pressing for protection of tropical forests, but is as protective of its own sovereignty as are developing countries when it comes to binding commitments at home.

The broader context of liberal environmentalism puts these seemingly contradictory positions in perspective. A fundamental tenet that underlies international liberal environmentalism is that it privileges states as the sole repositories of sovereign authority. International discussions are thus largely directed by this principle, despite policy alternatives that individual countries may offer. Indeed, the foundational norm of international environmental law is that states have a sovereign right to exploit their own resources pursuant to their own environmental and development policies.[39] States remain the privileged actors in negotiating international agreements on forests, and their interests remain paramount. As a consequence, international negotiations tend to reflect North–South conflict over sovereignty issues, rather than hard debate over the proper criteria for sustainable forestry. This section demonstrates how the attempts by the international community to navigate competing pressures of sovereignty, liberal trade, and environmental protection militate against Canada's hopes for a comprehensive forest convention. Indeed, the nature of forests as both a global concern but located within national jurisdictions (unlike commons issues such as ozone depletion) makes these competing pressures particularly difficult to reconcile within the broader liberal environmental framework. The section also shows how the commitments that do exist might influence Canadian domestic policy.

International Forest Negotiations and Agreements

Beginning in the 1980s international efforts began in earnest to achieve a global forestry convention, as a 'second wave' of environmentalism swept over most industrialized countries. At first, northern countries and environmentalists focused their attention on tropical deforestation after public concern mounted over alarming statistics about the rate of deforestation in the Amazon, Asia, and other tropical forest regions. The linkages to threats of climate change and especially to the loss of biodiversity also fuelled demands for action.[40]

This pressure helped to secure the inclusion of a mandate to conserve tropical forests and their genetic resources in the International Tropical Timber Agreement (ITTA) of 1983, and in the organization established by the treaty to promote ITTA goals, the International Tropical Timber Organization (ITTO), even though ITTO's primary mandate remained the facilitation of trade in tropical timber.[41] Then, in 1991, tropical timber producer countries adopted Target 2000 – the date by which tropical timber traded internationally should come from 'sustainable' sources.[42]

ITTO remained committed to norms of free trade and sovereignty, which accounts in large part for the ability of consumer and producer countries to reach consensus on an agreement (as of September 2000, membership consists of thirty producers and twenty-six consumers, including Canada). As Humphreys points out, a primary objective of the ITTA is 'the expansion and diversification of international trade in tropical timber,' and sovereignty over resources is asserted.[43] This combination has led non-governmental organizations (NGOs) such as Friends of the Earth to assert that the incompatibility between environmental and trade goals has resulted in ITTO promoting the former over the latter and not sufficiently encouraging the implementation of sustainable forest management at the national level. For example, ITTO did not respond to requests by NGOs in the late 1980s to seek a waiver from GATT rules to allow discrimination between sustainable and unsustainable timber, which would violate the norm of non-discrimination.

The organization of ITTO along producer–consumer lines has amounted to a North–South split in voting rights and divisions over matters such as aid and the scope of ITTA. Northern and southern countries disagree especially over whether ITTA should be extended to temperate and boreal forests. After prolonged negotiations on a successor agreement (ITTA 1994), consumer countries, including Canada, pledged to manage their own forests sustainably by the year 2000, but outside the context of ITTO. They reasoned that a pledge within ITTO would undermine the prospects for a global forest convention, which they wanted to be much broader than the trade-focused ITTA.

Tropical versus non-tropical divisions also characterized attempts to negotiate a forest convention at the 1992 U.N. Conference on Environment and Development (UNCED) in Rio de Janeiro, popularly known as the Earth Summit or the Rio Conference. In 1990 the Group of Seven industrialized countries, at the Houston Summit, initially gave a strong commitment to negotiating a convention to 'curb deforestation, protect biodiversity, stimulate positive forestry actions, and address threats to the world's forests.'[44] The United States thus proposed a framework convention in Rio, envisaged as requiring no binding commitments to forest conservation. The Bush administration believed such a convention would be easy to achieve and viewed it as the main initiative of the United States at UNCED.[45] While the North originally wanted a focus on tropical forests, it became clear that any global convention would need also to cover temperate and boreal forests if it were to receive support from the South. The group of 77 (G-77), plus China bloc of developing countries, suspicious of northern intentions on a variety of fronts, refused at the second preparatory committee meeting of UNCED

(PrepCom II) to even consider a binding agreement, and U.S. calls for a binding agreement at later PrepComs were to no avail.

The debate on forests during the PrepComs became polarized over the threat to sovereignty, particularly to southern countries, that a binding treaty might entail. In addition, a battle emerged over the level of financial and technological commitments that the North would make in order to aid the South in promoting sustainable forestry.[46] Northern states, such as the United States and Canada, argued for a 'global responsibility' approach, and Malaysia and India, argued for 'sovereign discretion.' The latter view reflected the fears of developing countries that the former approach would lead to forests being viewed as part of the 'common heritage of mankind [sic]' norm. They strongly opposed this norm on the grounds that it would potentially allow northern states to influence how forests within the jurisdictions of southern states should be managed.

What resulted from the Earth Summit was a 'non-legally binding authoritative statement of principles for global consensus on the management, conservation, and sustainable development of all types of forests,' known as the 'forest principles.' As this wording suggests, the statement of forest principles does not capture consensus on how to reconcile the competing visions of forest management, development, and conservation, nor does it bind states to specific commitments. It does, however, contain some support for the principles of biodiversity and the maintenance of ecological processes, while it also recognizes the role of forests as fulfilling economic and social needs.

Despite various attempts by governments and NGOs to reinvigorate movement towards a convention, all have failed to date. Whether a global treaty presents the most appropriate way to protect or manage the world's forests, the lack of movement on a convention, nevertheless, stands in stark contrast to the relative success of international negotiations on climate change and biodiversity. Instead, governments and non-governmental groups have launched various initiatives on specific facets of forestry to get around conflicts that continually arise when discussions turn towards a convention.

Forestry politics after UNCED grew more complex and disjointed for a variety of reasons, including continued distrust between North and South. In place of negotiations focused exclusively on a binding or comprehensive treaty, a variety of narrower international and/or regional initiatives have taken shape since 1992. These initiatives include the Montreal Process on creating criteria and indicators (C&I) for the conservation and sustainable development of temperate and boreal forests (which Canada played a major role in formulating and which have influenced provincial forest policies), the Helsinki Process on protecting forests in Europe (which includes a C&I process), the negotiations already mentioned toward ITTA 1994, initiatives on labelling and certification schemes (largely led by non-governmental groups and/or industry), and a number of expert and governmental forestry workshops.

The only process to focus serious attention on a global convention was the Intergovernmental Panel on Forests (IPF) in 1995, sponsored by the UN Commission on Sustainable Development (CSD). After two years of discussions that failed to reach consensus on a number of key issues, the Intergovernmental Forum on Forests (IFF) succeeded the IPF. Obstacles concerning trade, sovereignty, and aid continued to plague IFF discussions, suggesting progress towards a forest convention will remain slow.[47]

As it became clear that forestry negotiations and activities were likely to continue in an evolutionary process rather than produce a specific outcome, states involved in the IFF process decided to create a permanent UN Forum on Forests (UNFF). Established in October 2000 as a subsidiary body of the UN Economic and Social Council, UNFF is mandated to carry on work to implement existing agreements and initiatives from the IPF/IFF process. In addition, it will 'consider' within five years the possibility of a mandate for negotiating a binding convention.

Effects on Forest Policy in Canada

The lack of binding agreements means that international forestry agreements do not directly affect Canada in the way international trading rules do. Furthermore, Canada's strong economy and global political position buffers Canada from direct pressures that less wealthy countries might face, such as lending conditions the World Bank has imposed designed to influence forest practices in developing countries.[48] Similarly, direct financial incentives from non-governmental groups, such as debt-for-nature swaps, are unlikely to work in wealthy countries such as Canada. However, Canada is susceptible to international pressures that work in less direct ways.

The international realm is the source of important norms and ideas that find their way into the Canadian domestic forest policy agenda. Mere participation in international organizations and negotiations may also alter domestic coalitions or networks since they can develop linkages with transnational or other domestic groups through such forums.[49] Below, we review the effects of norms and ideas, and the way international institutions influence power relations in Canada. We focus especially on the case of British Columbia, where these effects are most evident.

In the case of British Columbia, international influences can be traced back to the U.N.-sponsored 1987 Brundtland Commission report, which set the normative benchmark for forest protection there. The 12 per cent land protection commitment of B.C.'s Protected Area Strategy came from the Brundtland report's call for a tripling of the world's protected areas from the then current 4 per cent.[50]

The formal and informal preparations for the Earth Summit also affected B.C. policy, as did the agreements reached. For example, the biodiversity guidelines in B.C.'s Forest Practice Code reflect values promoted in the Statement of Forest Principles, despite the weakness of the agreement, and the Convention on Biological Diversity. Related concepts such as 'ecosystem management' also influenced B.C. forestry policy. Indeed, international scrutiny over the logging of Clayoquot Sound was largely diffused through the adoption of the Clayoquot Sound Scientific Panel's recommendation that the forest in this region be logged according to the principles of ecosystem management. Panel participants included well-known U.S. proponents of ecosystem management.[51]

At the national level, work under the auspices of the Canadian Council of Forest Ministers (CCFM) led to the establishment of criteria and indicators (C&I) for achieving sustainable forest management in 1995 that fed into the Montreal Process for establishing C&I internationally for temperate and boreal forests. Although debate surrounds the sufficiency of C&I processes for meeting multiple goals of sustainability (ecological, social and economic),[52] international-domestic interactions clearly affected domestic policies since the same CCFM process that fed into international processes also led to C&I being written into legislation governing forests in Ontario and Quebec.

Domestic international interactions are also evident in the CCFM's *National Forest Strategy: 1998–2003*. The report notes that the development of the national forest sector strategy was 'instrumental to Canadian representations at the 1992 Earth Summit and that this allowed Canada to argue in the international sphere that it was a leader in sustainable forest management.[53] The 1998 report focuses Canadian forest policy on the 'forest ecosystem,' something it acknowledges was absent in the CCFM's 1987 *National Forest Sector Strategy* report. The latter focused more on industry timber yield factors and less on environmental concerns. As the 1998 report notes, the Brundtland Commission and the emergence of other international norms caused the council to consider the forest ecosystem and social, cultural forest values alongside economic ones.

A second avenue for influence comes from the ability of international institutions to facilitate the development of transnational coalitions of environmental groups who can share information and force international attention on Canadian forestry practices. Negotiations and international meetings become meeting grounds for various groups to forge links. For example, in addition to scientific linkages, the Earth Summit augmented interaction among world-wide environmental activists. One U.S. activist working on B.C. forest policy explained, 'One thing that came out of the Rio Earth Summit was really a much stronger network of environmental and native people working together on these issues.'[54] New institutions may reinforce these processes. For example, the New North American Commission on Environmental Cooperation also provides incentives for North American environmental groups to coordinate their efforts.[55]

Finally, owing to increased international awareness, transnational environmental groups have used B.C.'s dependence on foreign markets to launch well-publicized boycott campaigns first aimed at Clayoquot Sound, but later expanded to other regions of British Columbia.[56] These pressures influenced B.C. policy change by pressuring, and to a degree aiding, the B.C. government in the early 1990s to continue with its forest practices and land use reforms.[57] They also highlighted the degree to which environmental groups could use the marketplace to force policy change.

The Marketplace

The growing sense of disillusionment that environmental groups felt towards the post-UNCED negotiations, combined with a sense that the prolonged bargaining was draining their time and resources, led these groups to look at directly influencing the private sector as a faster and perhaps more effective way to achieve sustainable forestry. These groups took a dual-track approach. First, they continued the traditional but decidedly negative boycott efforts to force companies to change forest practices and/or purchasing habits by leading consumers away from their products. Second, they launched a proactive certification scheme with the ultimate goal of leading consumers towards purchasing wood products harvested in an environmentally friendly manner.

This proactive process took shape primarily through the Forest Stewardship Council (FSC), formed in Toronto in 1993, and headquartered in Oaxaca, Mexico.[58] Spearheaded by the WWF, FSC accredits organizations (certifiers) who must perform evaluations to see if a company's forestry operation matches ten established principles and criteria. More specific regional standards are then developed based on these broader principles. Regional standards are developed, or are being developed in British Columbia, the Maritimes, Ontario, & the Canadian borel forest.

Forestry industry companies and associations in Canada and the United States began to develop their own sustainable forestry initiatives in the form of systems-based schemes because they were concerned about the influence of environmental groups under the FSC program and its emphasis on environmental performance.[59] The American Forest and Paper Association (AFPA) created its Sustainable Forestry Initiative (SFI) in 1996,[60] while the Canadian Pulp and Paper Association (CPPA) developed Sustainable Forest Management System Standards under the auspices of the Canadian Standards Association (CSA). The Alberta Forest Products Association (AFPA) developed a similar forest certification process entitled Forest Care, which has already certified Weyerhaeuser operations in Grand Prairie. These 'systems'-based approaches are modelled after the International Organization for Standardization (ISO) 14001 Environmental Management System,[61] although only a few companies have explicitly incorporated ISO 14001 guidelines into their operating procedures.[62] Critics argue that these industry processes are less effective because they focus on process rather than performance and because they involve industry associations certifying their own members, rather than third parties under the FSC initiative.[63] Currently only the FSC carries an eco-label.

The future of certification is uncertain, although interest on the part of Canadian forest companies and their competitors is increasing. This interest is in large part owing to FSC efforts to actively target demand-side players such as wood product retailers, home builders, and paper purchasing companies, in its efforts to have these groups require certified forest products. Working in conjunction with its environmental group founders, the FSC first focused on facilitating the creation of buyers groups in the UK, Germany, Holland and elswhere.[64]

These efforts were followed by the creation in the U.S. of the Certified

Hectares

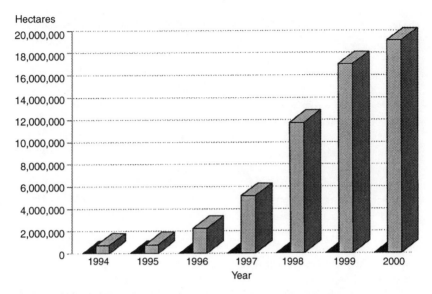

Source: James Sullivan, 'FSC Update,' presentation to the Forest Stewardship Council's Second Annual Conference, Oaxaca, Mexico, 10 November 2000. (For latest updates by country, see FSC's website: www.fscoax.org.)

Figure 3.2: FSC-certified forest land

Forest Products Council (CFPC) in 1997, which provides its members and other businesses with information on purchasing wood from sustainable sources.[65] The CFPC has also been instrumental in supplying information and informing certification choices for such U.S. lumber retailer giants as Home Depot, which, following sustained pressure by the San Francisco based Rainforest Action Network, announced in August 1999 a plan to 'give preference' to certified wood.[66] While the Home Depot announcement does not specify the FSC program, only the FSC would currently comply with the Home Depot guidelines, revealing early success in using a manipulation strategy to achieve legitimacy.

By late winter of 2000, the Rainforest Action Network successfully obtained similar commitments from two of the United States' largest home builders, Centex Corporation and Kaufman & Broad Home Corporation, and Swedish Furniture giant IKEA – all of whom have made commitments similar to Home Depot's.[67] And by the summer of 2000, the WWF had organized the Global Forest and Trade Networks, designed to broaden perceived 'clubs' of buyers groups and retailers so that 'pressures span the industry from forest owner to architect, manufacturer to retailer.'[68]

Still, this issue is far from resolved, and FSC has yet to see its campaigns attempt to alter significantly consumer purchasing habits (largely because they are focusing foremost on creating a supply) from the initial consumer responses noted above. While consumers indicate they will be willing to pay more for certified forest products,[69] the limited research on actual consumer behaviour raises the possibility that consumer behaviour might be different. Currently there are inconsistent price premiums, and often only for niche markets.[70]

Efforts on the part of FSC to facilitate buyers groups have arguably had the largest influence on British Columbia, Canada's largest forest products exporting province.[71] Firms such as MacMillan Bloedel (now Weyerhaeuser) and Canfor have indicated their intention to become FSC certified once regional standards are in place[72] and Western Forest Products is in the midst of attaining FSC certification in this province.[73] Moreover, the B.C. Forest Alliance, an association of mostly forest companies designed to promote the B.C. forest industry locally and abroad, became a member of FSC in 2000, and the Industrial Wood and Allied Workers Union has also applied for membership.

Certification schemes have provoked a reaction from federal and provincial governments who have jointly outlined twelve principles to which certification agreements should adhere.[74] These principles state that any certification system be complementary with government forest policies (which would de facto include the practice of clear-cutting) and, supporting liberal norms, that they be 'consistent with trade law and international principles.' Provincial and federal governments are also concerned that certification might be perceived as a 'non-tariff barrier.' The Dutch government's consideration of only allowing imports of certified wood augmented such fears.

The attraction of certification and labelling schemes is in large part owing to their fit with liberal environmentalism. These schemes aim to internalize environmental costs by including them in the cost of certified products. If educated by the eco-labelling processes, consumers would presumably favour such products, and the market would provide economic incentives to live up to the labelling criteria. The forest products market would then operate with prices that more adequately reflect the costs of environmental protection. Moving from the level of the forest management unit to the national or international level could raise problems for sovereignty, as we discussed earlier.[75] Nonetheless, the appeal of this consumer-driven solution to sustainable forestry stems from its potential to by-pass the sovereignty issue by operating in the marketplace independent of government regulation and authority.

The solution reveals potential contradictions when it comes to sustainability goals. For example, the disjuncture between processes for developing criteria and indicators between governments and certification and labelling schemes by organizations such as the FSC suggests that leaving the latter to forestry companies may not achieve goals of sustainability as dictated by science or even by politically agreed on criteria. Some environmental groups remain sceptical, given past experience with eco-labelling.[76] The Forest Stewardship Council has attempted to sidestep controversies over the term 'sustainably managed' and the C&I process, focusing instead on 'well-managed' forests. In the end, the success of certification may be elusive if it ignores sustainability measures that come out of C&I processes. Whether such market-driven schemes can sufficiently achieve sustainability or other environmental values, including linkages to broader ecosystem concerns such as biodiversity and ecosystem sustainability more generally, remains to be seen.

Conclusion

Canadian forest policy faces increased international scrutiny because of U.S.–Canada forest trade disputes, international sustainable forestry initiatives, and international environmental groups' boycotts and certification campaigns. Because these sources of pressure on Canadian forest policy have themselves become intertwined, trade disputes now include environmental provisions, and international negotiations on forest protection which appear to be limited to solutions that comply with liberal trading norms. Furthermore, environmental groups' strategy of certification and boycotts is dependent on a globalized forest economy where they can pressure consumers in one country to have an impact on industry decisions in another country.

The cumulative impact of these international pressures on Canadian forest management and policy is mixed. The fundamental nature of long-term harvesting rights in return for 'sustained yield management' (the tenure system) and the use of non-competitive methods for setting stumpage rates has not changed. This is despite almost two decades of disputes with U.S. companies who argue that Canada should alter its timber pricing policies along U.S. lines and move towards a competitive bidding system. The explanation for this policy rigidity is the 'policy legacy' of the tenure system, with communities, revenues, and forest jobs all dependent on a fifty-year-old forest management system. However, the softwood dispute has affected policy at the nominal level of timber pricing, which has increased considerably in British Columbia – the central target of U.S. forest companies. Short-term agreements to resolve the U.S.–Canada softwood lumber dispute did serve the purpose of limiting the B.C. government's ability to reduce stumpage rates and even gave the province pause in its efforts to streamline its Forest Practices Code.

Owing to the lack of an international forestry convention, international forestry agreements and processes produce even less direct impact on Canadian forest management practices and policy. The norms and ideas raised in international forums, however, have increased the range of policy ideas considered and implemented by provincial and national governments. Finally, certification and boycotts launched by environmental groups put pressure on individual forest companies to change. Boycott campaigns also contributed a central ingredient in the policy environment that allowed the B.C. government to implement its eco-forest agenda in the early to mid-1990s.

What might we expect in the future? The complexity and fragmentation of international sustainable forestry issues will arguably continue to characterize international discussions as long as a world forestry convention remains elusive. Given Canada's dependence on world forest trade, Canadian forest policy will continue to come under international scrutiny. If Canada wants to shape and direct the type of pressure, it has no choice but to vigorously participate and be proactive in international discussions. Discussions will be carried out within the norms of a liberal trading regime and an increasingly globalized world forest economy. The need for creative solutions to navigate these pressures, and to evaluate whether goals of both sustainability and a healthy forest economy can be easily met within the constraints identified, characterize the challenge ahead if Canadian forest policy is to achieve its competing goals.

NOTES

1 Canadian forest products' share of world forest trade is 20 per cent ('Sustaining Forests, Taking Global Action,' in *1995–1996 State of Canada's Forests* [Ottawa: Minister of Natural Resources, 1998], chapter 2. Forest products constitute 2.9 per cent of the Canadian gross domestic product. Forest prod-

uct exports constituted 14.8 per cent of total Canadian exports in 1997 and contributed $32.1 billion to Canada's balance of trade (Natural Resources Canada, *Natural Resources Fact Sheet* [Ottawa: Natural Resources Canada, 1997]).

2 Steven Bernstein, 'Ideas, Social Structure, and the Compromise of Liberal Environmentalism,' *European Journal of International Relations* 6(4), 2000, 464–512.

3 Natural Resources Canada, *Natural Resources Fact Sheet*.

4 Natural Resources Canada, *The State of Canada's Forests* (Ottawa: Government of Canada, Natural Resources Canada, 1997).

5 The contribution of Canada's forests to its tourism industry is difficult to ascertain. No such data have been compiled.

6 Brian Hocking, 'The Woods and the Trees: Catalytic Diplomacy and Canada's Trials as a "Forestry Superpower,"' *Environmental Politics* 5(3), 1996, 448–75.

7 Paul Stanton Kibel, 'Reconstructing the Marketplace: The International Timber Trade and Forest Protection,' *NYU Environmental Law Journal* 5, 1996, 1–63.

8 Pierre Marc Johnson, and Andre Beaulieu, *The Environment and NAFTA: Understanding and Implementing the New Continental Law* (Washington, DC: Island Press, 1996).

9 One possible exception to liberal environmentalism is the Convention on International Trade in Endangered Species. This convention does provide clear binding rules on the trade of species threatened with extinction. However, the convention is limited in scope and is not part of any agreement on forestry policy. Nevertheless, it may indirectly influence forestry policies, as do similar agreements on climate change and biodiversity. Indeed, part of the debate in international forestry discussions revolves around the relationship of forestry agreements to existing environmental or other related treaties.

10 Kibel argues that 'whether through direct subsidies, low stumpage fees, or lax enforcement of environmental laws, political collusion between government and logging interests adversely impacts native forests. By keeping the production costs of logging low, such collusion has increased the industry's profit margin while simultaneously exerting downward pressure on the market price of timber and wood-based products' ('Reconstructing the Marketplace,' 21).

11 Benjamin Cashore, 'Flights of the Phoenix: Explaining the Durability of the Canada–U.S. Softwood lumber dispute,' *Canadian–American Public Policy* 32.

12 Large forestry companies were given long-term rights to harvest a particular area. In exchange, the companies were required to manage the land on a long-term, 'sustained yield' basis. Companies were also required under these arrangements to operate mills and create employment (Benjamin Cashore, ' *The Role of the Provincial State in Forest Policy: A Comparative Study of British Columbia and New Brunswick,*' Masters thesis, Carleton University, 1988, 57).

13 The argument that higher stumpage rates would lead to a reduced harvest rate is a controversial one. This is because the harvest rate in British Columbia is determined by the government under a 'sustained yield' policy, and stumpage rates do not play a direct role in these calculations. However, the manner in which the government defines 'sustainability' has been highly criticized by environmental groups. See Lois Helen Dellert, 'Sustained Yield Forestry in British Columbia: The Making and Breaking of a Policy (1900–1993),' (York University, Faculty of Environmental Studies, 1994).

14 Charles S. Pearson, 'Testing the System: GATT + PPP = ?' *Cornell International Law Journal* 27, 1994, 353–575. Henri Smets, 'The Polluter Pays Principle in the Early 1990s,' in *The Environment after Rio: International Law and Economics,* ed. Luigi Campiglio et al. (London: Graham & Trotman/Martinus Nijhoff, 1994), 131–47.

15 Judith Goldstein, 1986. 'The Political Economy of Trade: Institutions of Protection,' *American Political Science Review* 80(1), 1986, 161–84; Gary N. Horlick and Geoffrey D. Oliver, 'Antidumping and Countervailing Duty Law Provisions of the Omnibus Trade and Competitiveness Act of 1988,' *Journal of World Trade (Law–Economics–Public Policy)* 23(3), 1989, 5–49.

16 U.S. law dictates that if a government program is available to more than one industry, by definition it cannot be countervailable. See William Lay, 'Redefining Actionable "Subsidies" Under U.S. Countervailing Duty Law,' *Columbia Law Review* 91, 1989, 1495–1518.

17 This time the Department of Commerce argued that although de jure stumpage programs were not available to a single industry, they were de facto. And recent changes in policy loosened up the definition of 'subsidy' to include de facto measures.

18 For a detailed analysis of B.C. stumpage policy over time, see Benjamin Cashore, George Hoberg, Michael Howlett, Jeremy Rayner, and Jeremy Wilson, *In Search of Sustainability: British Columbia Forest Policy in the 1990s* (Vancouver: UBC Press, 2001).

19 James P. Groen, 'British Columbia's International Relations: Consolidating a Coalition-Building Strategy,' *BC Studies*, no. 102, 1994, 25–59; Cashore '*Role of the Provincial State.*'

20 Raymond Vernon, Debora L. Spar, and Glenn Tobin, *Iron Triangles and*

Revolving Doors: Cases in U.S. Foreign Economic Policy Making (New York: Praeger, 1991).

21 Sharon Chow, 'Letter to Congressman Ron Wyden,' Victoria, B.C., Sierra Club of Western Canada, Joe Foy, Letter to Congressman Ron Wyden, Vancouver, B.C., Western Canada Wilderness Committee, 1992.

22 Ron Wyden, Letter to Ambassador Burney, Washington, DC, U.S. Congress, 1992.

23 The final calculation of subsidy was determined to be 6.51 per cent. Unlike 1986, only the top four exporting provinces were subject to the countervail proceedings, with other provinces exempt from any potential tariffs. A subsidy was calculated first for each province and then applied to a national average. British Columbia's subsidy was calculated at 7.95 per cent; Alberta's at 1.25 per cent; Ontario's at 5.95 per cent; and Quebec's at 0.01 per cent. Donald G. Balmer, 'Escalating Politics of the U.S.–Canadian Softwood Lumber Trade, 1982–1992,' *Northwest Environmental Journal* 9(1 and 2), 1993, 85–107.

24 Balmer, 'Escalating Politics.'

25 Charles M. Gastle and Jean-G. Castel, 'Should the North American Free Trade Agreement Dispute Settlement Mechanism in Antidumping and Countervailing Duty Cases Be Reformed in the Light of Softwood Lumber III?' *Law and Policy in International Business* 26(3) 1996, 823–96.

26 Gordon Hamilton, 'Don't Lower Stumpage, U.S. tells B.C., *Vancouver Sun,* 11 April 1997, D1; John Schreiner and Peter Morton, 'Changes to B.C. Forest Code Fail to Please U.S. Environmentalists,' *Financial Post,* 11 June 1997, 7.

27 Canadian Press, 'B.C. May Lower Stumpage,' *Canadian Press Wire Service,* 19 Jan. 1998. Gordon Hamilton, 'Desperate B.C. Boosts Overseas Log Shipments,' *Vancouver Sun,* 5 Feb. 1998, D1, D18. Gordon Hamilton, 'Forestry Assistance Too Late, Report Says' *Vancouver Sun,* 5 March 1998, D1, D14; Justine Hunter, and David Hogben, 'Stumpage Cuts Trigger Rehiring in B.C. Forests: The Premier's Initiative Brings Negative Reaction from U.S. lumber Industry,' *Vancouver Sun,* 29 May 1998, A1–A2.

28 Gordon Hamilton, 'With Cuts, B.C. Stumpage Would Be Double Quebec's,' *Vancouver Sun,* 31 Jan. 1998, H1, H2.

29 MacMillan Bloedel Ltd, 'A White Paper for Discussion: Stumpage and Tenure Reform in B.C.' (Vancouver, MacMillan Bloedel, 1998), 3.

30 See 'It's Time to Cut B.C. Logging Costs Says Outgoing Fletcher Challenge President,' *Financial Post,* 10 Dec. 1998. President Whitehead is quoted as saying, 'Under the present stumpage system, there's no way the U.S. would agree with cuts (to stumpage), so what I'm saying is you've got to cut the

costs to make B.C. competitive ... The only way to do it is a transparent way: We've got to change the system to market bid. What I'm saying is to take some of this TFL and sell it off to be fee simple land.'

31 COFI president Ron MacDonald argued that the Softwood Lumber Agreement should be scrapped only after a new 'free market' solution is in place. His comments were in response to B.C. Premier Glen Clark's charge that, owing to constant scrutiny by U.S. forest companies and difficulty with the current quota system, he might just scrap the deal. MacDonald said that 'unless B.C. was to first adopt a free-market stumpage system (similar to the U.S. in which private landowners sell cutting rights to mills at market-sensitive rates) and address the issue of raw log export restrictions – two issues where the Americans claim B.C. is favouring its forest industry – the U.S. government would likely respond with a countervailing duty on all Canadian lumber exports.

32 See Gerard Young, 'Report Stirs Forest Industry Debate: Push to Tie Stumpage Rates to Market Draws Fire from Both Sides,' *Victoria Times-Colonist,* 6 April 2000, A3; and Gordon Hamilton, 'Campbell's Forestry Solution Ranges Wide: More Access to Timber, Less Regulation, End to FRBC Included as Liberal Leader Unveils Plan for B.C. Industry,' *Vancouver Sun,* 14 Jan. 2000, D1.

33 Gordon Hamilton, 'Industry, Business Condemn Wouters' Forestry Report: Eco-Groups Say the Long-Awaited Review Takes the First Cautious Steps Toward Lower Annual Harvest,' *Vancouver Sun,* 5 April 2000, D1.

34 Northwest Ecosystem Alliance, 'Conservationists Sue Feds over Trade Agreement: Lawsuit Alleges Softwood Lumber Agreement Fuels Deforestation, Undermines Species Recovery' (Seattle: Northwest Ecosystem Alliance, 1998).

35 See Matt Price, 'Submission of the Natural Resources Defense Council to the Trade Policy Staff Committee Regarding Softwood Lumber Practices in Canada and Softwood lumber Trade Between the United States and Canada' (Washington, DC: Natural Resources Defense Council, 2000); and Nigel Sizer, 'Perverse Habits: The G8 and Subsidies That Harm Forests and Economies,' (Washington, DC: World Resources Initiative, 2000).

36 Allan Dowd, 'Canadian Lumber Firms Unite for Trade Battle,' *Reuters,* 16 Jan. 2001. From *www.pacificenvironment.org.*

37 Canadian Council of Forest Ministers, *National Forest Strategy, 1998–2003/Sustainable Forests: A Canadian Commitment* (Ottawa: Canadian Council of Forest Ministers, 1998).

38 Brian Hocking, 'The Woods and the Trees: Catalytic Diplomacy and Canada's Trials as a "Forestry Superpower,"' *Environmental Politics* 5(3), 1996, 448–75.

39 Philippe Sands, *Documents in International Environmental Law* (Manchester: Manchester University Press, 1994).

40 Tropical forests contain an estimated 70 per cent of the world's plant and animal species; see Andrew Hurrell, 'Brazil and the International Politics of Amazonian Deforestation,' in Andrew Hurrell and Benedict Kingsbury, eds., *The International Politics of the Environment* (Oxford: Clarendon Press, 1992), 398–429. Estimates of tropical deforestation are subject to dispute, but recent statistics show it may be increasing despite signs of slowing down in the early 1990s (Ken Conca, 'Environmental Protection, International Norms, and State Sovereignty: The Case of the Brazilian Amazon,' in Gene M. Lyons and Michael Mastanduno, eds., *Beyond Westphalia? State Sovereignty and International Intervention* (Baltimore: Johns Hopkins University Press) 1995; Environmental News Service, 'Amazonas Suspends New Rainforest Logging,' from listserve environnews@envirolink.org 1998; Food and Agricultural Organization, *State of the World's Forest 1997* (Rome: FAO) 1997. A good estimate (by the FAO, 1997) is that deforestation the world over between 1980 and 1995 amounted to 200 million hectares, compensated by only 20 million hectares of forest plantations initiated during that time (primarily in the North).

41 David Humphreys, 'The Global Politics of Forest Conservation since the UNCED,' *Environmental Politics*, no. 5, 1996, 231–56.

42 However, Ross argues that given the low aid budget of the ITTO ($46 million in 1989–1991, for example), it possesses neither the authority nor the resources to significantly affect logging practices in the tropics. Michael Ross, Conditionality and Logging Reform in the Tropics,' in Robert O. Keohane and Mark A. Levy, eds., *Institutions for Environmental Aid* (Boston: MIT Press, 1996, 167–97).

43 David Humphreys, 'Hegemonic Ideology and the International Tropical Timber Organization,' in John Vogler and Mark Imber, eds., *The Environment and International Relations: Theories and Processes* (London: Routledge, 1996) 214–33.

44 Peter Hajanal, *The Seven Power Summit: Documents from the Summits of Industrialized Countries 1975–1989 and Supplement* (New York: Kraus International, 1989).

45 Gareth Porter, and Janet Welsh Brown, *Global Environmental Politics*, 2nd ed. Boulder, CO: Westview Press, 1996).

46 Ibid., Humphreys, 'The Global Politics of Forest Conservation'; Marc Williams, 'Re-articulating the Third World Coalition: The Role of the Environmental Agenda,' *Third World Quarterly*, no. 14, 1993, 7–29.

47 'Report of the First Session of the CSD Interovernment Panel on Forests.' *Earth Negotiations Bulletin* 13(3), 11–15 September 1995; 'Summary of

IPF-2 Geneva.' *Earth Negotiations Bulletin* 13(45), August 24–September 4, 1998.

48 Ross, 'Conditionality and Logging Reform.'

49 Steven Bernstein and Benjamin Cashore, 'Globalization, Four Paths of Internationalization, and Domestic Policy Change: The Case of Ecoforestry in British Columbia, Canada. *Canadian Journal of Political Science* 33(1), 2000, 67–99.

50 World Commission on Environment and Development *Our Common Future* (Oxford: Oxford University Press, 1987), ch. 6.

51 Scientific Panel for Sustainable Forest Practices in Clayoquot Sound, *Progress Report 2: Review of Current Forest Practice Standards in Clayoquot Sound, British Columbia.* The Scientific Panel for Sustainable Forest Practices in Clayoquot Sound, 1994.

52 For a detailed discussion of the conflictual aspects of sustainability criteria and the inadequacy of current C&I processes in Canada to address the diversity of interests and values or the power imbalances between relevant social groups see Sten Nilsson and Michael Gluck, 'Sustainability and the Canadian Forest Sector' (interim report IR-00-250) (Laxenburg, Austria: International Institute for Applied Systems Analysis, 2000).

53 Canadian Council of Forest Ministers, *National Forest Strategy (1998–2003). Sustainable Forests: A Canadian Commitment* (Ottawa: Canadian Council of Forest Ministers, 1998).

54 Personal interview with senior official, National Resources Defense Council, Washington, D.C., June 1994.

55 One of the first environmental challenges using NACEC involved U.S. environmental groups seeking linkages with Canadian and Mexican groups in its efforts to stop a U.S. Congressional decision to allow logging in some forests previously protected for the Northern Spotted Owl. See Patti A. Goldman, 'Submission to Article 14 of the North American Agreement on Environmental Cooperation on the U.S. Logging Rider' (Seattle: Sierra Club Legal Defense Fund, 1995).

56 Canadian Press, 'Greenpeace Steps Up Protests in Europe against B.C. Logging,' *Vancouver Sun*, 28 March 1998, A4. Greenpeace Canada, Greenpeace International, and Greenpeace San Francisco, Broken Promises: *The Truth about What's Happening to British Columbia's Forests* (Vancouver: Greenpeace Canada, Greenpeace International, Greenpeace San Francisco, 1997).

57 Personal interview, Michael Harcourt, former premier, 19 April 1996, Vancouver.

58 Eric Hansen, 'Certified Forest Products Market Place,' in United Nations Timber Committee, ed. *Forest Products Annual Market Review* (Geneva, Switzerland: United Nations Timber Committee, 1998).

59 See Benjamin Cashore, 'Competing for Legitimacy: Globalization, Internationalization, and the Politics of Green Labeling (Eco-Forestry certification) in the U.S. and Canadian Forest Sectors,' paper presented to the 15th Biennial Conference of the Association for Canadian Studies in the United States, Pittsburgh, 1999.

60 American Forest and Paper Association, *Sustainable Forestry Initiative* (Washington, DC: AFPA, 1995).

61 Fred Gale, and Cheri Burda, 'The Pitfalls and Potential of Eco-Certification as a Market Incentive for Sustainable Forest Management, in Chris Tollefson, ed., *The Wealth of Forests: Markets, Regulation, and Sustainable Forestry* (Vancouver: UBC Press, 1997) 414–41.

62 Hansen, 'Certified Forest Products.'

63 The American Forest and Paper Association is currently deciding whether to move to the use of third-party certification.

64 Hansen, 'Certified Forest'; Jean-Pierre Kiekens, 'Certification: International Trends and Forestry and Trade Implications' (Brussels: Environmental Strategies Europe, 1997).

65 Certified Forest Products Council, 'Joining the Certified Forest Products Council' (Certified Forest Products Council, 1998).

66 Home Depot, 'The Home Depot Launches Environmental Wood Purchasing Policy: Company Promises to Reduce Wood Sourced from Endangered Forests during Next Three Years' (Home Depot, 1999).

67 Rainforest Action Network, 'Nation's Top Homebuilders Vow to End Endangered Wood Use: Huge Win for Environmentalists as Pressure Brings Dramatic Turnabout' (San Francisco: Rainforest Action Network, 2000); Gordon Hamilton, 'B.C.'s Green Tag Revolution: Give Our Customers Guilt-free Wood Products, Demanded Home Depot and IKEA,' *Vancouver Sun*, 19 May 2000; Andrew J. Hannigan, 'Centex Ends Use of Endangered Wood,' (2000); Barrie McKenna, 'U.S. Home Builders to Ban Old-growth Wood: Canada's Lumber Exports Would Be Hit Hard by Kaufman & Broad's and Centex's New Policies,' *Globe and Mail*, 31 March 2000; 'Home Builders Give Preference to Certified Wood: Announcements Head Off Nationwide Protests,' *Forestry Source*, May 2000.

68 From World Wide Fund for Nature's 'Forests for Life Campaign' web site at: http://www.panda.org/forests4life/certify ftn.cfm.

69 Keith Forsyth, David Haley, and Robert Zozak, 'Will Consumers Pay More for Certified Wood Products?' *Journal of Forestry*, no. 2, 1999; 18–22; Fred Gale and Cheri Burda, 'The Pitfalls and Potential of Eco-Certification as a Market Incentive for Sustainable Forest Management,' in C. Tollefson, ed., *The Wealth of Forests: Markets, Regulation and Sustainable Forestry* (Vancouver: UBC Press, 1997), 414–41.

70 Hansen, 'Certified Forest Products.'

71 Market-oriented environmental campaigns go beyond forest certification. In the summer of 2000, after ten years of fighting head to head, four key environmental groups operating in the province – the Sierra Club of B.C., Greenpeace, the Rainforest Action Network (RAN), and the Coastal Rainforest Coalition (CRC) – agreed to jointly sponsor with leading B.C. forest companies consultation and scientific research on 'achieving conservation based ecosystem management for temperate rainforests on the North and Central Coast of B.C.' See Coastal Rainforest Coalition, 'Forest Companies and Environmental Groups Pursue Unprecedented Solutions Initiative: Will Jointly Sponsor Consultation and Scientific and Technical Work on Conservation-Based Ecosystem Management for Temperate Rainforests on the North and Central Coast of B.C.' (Vancouver: Coastal Rainforest Coalition, 2000).

72 Benjamin Cashore, Ilan Vertinsky, and Rachana Raizada, 'Firm Responses to External Pressures for Sustainable Forest Management in British Columbia and the U.S. Pacific Northwest,' in *Sustaining the Pacific Coast Forests: Forging Truces in the War in the Woods*, ed. D. Alper and D. Salazar (Vancouver: UBC Press, 2001).

73 Western Forest Products is proceeding with certification by SGC Forestry, one of the FSC's accredited auditors. SGC has developed standards which will be superceded once regional standards are in place. See http://www.westernforest.com/fstew/fcprogressrep.html.

74 Listserve environnews@envirolink.org. Federal-Provincial/Territorial Committee of Assistant Deputy Ministers on International Forest Issues, 'Framework of Guiding Principles for Voluntary Certification System for Sustainable Forest Management: A Federal/Provincial/Territorial Governments of Canada paper, Vancouver, B.C.

75 See Benjamin Cashore, 'Legitimacy and the Privatization of Environmental Governance: Exploring Forest Certification (Eco-labeling) in the U.S. and Canadian Forest Sectors.' Auburn University Forest Policy Center Working Paper No. 14 (June 2000).

76 Gale and Burda, 'The Pitfalls and Potential of Eco-Certification.'

Talking the Talk and Walking the Walk: Reflections on the Early Influence of Ecosystem Management Ideas

Jeremy Wilson

If 20th-century forestry was about simplifying systems, producing wood, and managing at the stand level, 21st-century forestry will be defined by understanding and managing complexity, providing a wide range of ecological goods and services, and managing across broad landscapes.[1]

The proponents of ecosystem management have had a pronounced impact on the discourses surrounding Canadian forest land use and practices issues. Throughout the 1990s, concepts such as biodiversity, natural disturbance-based management, and landscape connectivity figured prominently in both the environmental movement's critiques and the forest industry's defences. As other chapters in this volume show, a number of provincial governments have given ecosystem management perspectives a prominent place in new legislation, policy statements, and planning manuals.[2] Pilot projects implementing these perspectives are under way in various provinces.[3] This chapter considers the difficulties faced by those trying to engineer a shift from discourse change and early experiments to broad-based implementation of ecosystem management ideas. It concludes that if the early history of the 'politics of definition' surrounding these ideas is an indication of what is to come, advocates of this shift are likely to encounter difficult obstacles.

Over the past decade, dozens of resource management theorists and practitioners have tried their hand at defining 'ecosystem management.' After surveying a wide assortment of definitions, Steven Yaffee and his co-authors conclude that 'most authors emphasize a land management approach that incorporates an understanding of ecological systems, considers extended time and spatial scales, and highlights interconnections between landscapes, ecological processes, and humans and other organisms.'[4] Edward Grumbine, who waded bravely into the definitional debate in a 1994 article entitled 'What Is Ecosystem Management?' and a follow-up piece, characterizes ecosystem management as a framework of ideas and principles[5] which 'integrates scientific knowledge of ecological relationships within a complex sociopolitical and values framework towards the general goal of protecting native ecosystem integrity over the long term.'[6] Ken Lertzman and co-authors elaborate on these ideas, suggesting that the set of concepts that has emerged under the ecosystem management banner 'carries with it a gestalt of holism rather than reductionism, a subordination of human desires to ecosystem health, and recognition of a broader range of values in ecosystems than past practices have acknowledged. The goal of ecosystem management is to manage for the long-term integrity of whole ecosystems, not for the production of single resources.'[7]

Steven Kennett warns that no capsule definition can fully capture the content or implications of the term, but ventures that 'in a nutshell, ecosystem management is a set of normative principles and operational guidelines for managing human activities in a way that permits them to coexist, over a specified management area, with ecological processes deemed to be worth protecting over the long term.'[8] Noting the concept's roots in what Aldo Leopold referred to as a 'land ethic,' Kennett goes on to suggest that under ecosystem management, resource use will be constrained by the goal of maintaining ecological integrity: 'Unlike the pure multiple use approach, ecosystem management has a firm normative foundation that imposes an ecological "bottom" line on decision-makers.'[9]

Even this brief sample of definitions indicates that the two words at the centre of our inquiry are carrying a sizeable and diverse load of conceptual freight. Ecosystem management should be viewed not as a concept, but as a cluster of concepts, or perhaps a cluster of clusters of concepts. In his survey of definitions, for example, Grumbine identified no fewer than ten recurring (and interrelated) themes, including some such as ecological integrity and adaptive management that are themselves the centre of ongoing conceptual debate.[10] Kessler and Salwasser enumerate four foundational principles: 'sustain healthy, diverse, and productive ecosystems in the long term; involve people as full partners in land and resources management; strengthen the scientific basis for management by integrating research and management; and integrate all aspects of natural resources conservation through collaboration within the community of interests.'[11]

Lertzman et al. suggest that ecosystem management principles translate into a number of forest management objectives, including modelling management on natural disturbance patterns ('the long-term pattern of the frequency, intensity, spatial extent, and heterogeneity of disturbances'); applying adaptive management and the precautionary principle (an approach that recognizes our uncertainty, acknowledges that all decisions are experiments, and aims to adapt practices in response to learning); maintaining biological diversity (including viable populations of all species making up the indigenous biota of the area, and the integrity of evolutionary and ecological processes); and adequately representing all native ecosystem types within the protected areas system.[12]

The ecosystem management concept, it is clear, is both warm and fuzzy. All or most of the objectives enveloped by definitions of the concept are viewed positively by most people. These definitions overlap to a considerable extent with those offered in elaborations of concepts such as new forestry, holistic forestry, and ecoforestry.[13] Many of the concepts highlighted in definitions of ecosystem management (and in definitions of these related concepts) are themselves the object of rampant definitional pluralism; in a 1998 article, for example, Fred Bunnell noted that he had found at least ninety definitions of 'biodiversity' in circulation.[14]

Not surprisingly, ecosystem management's wide-ranging, multidimensional character has translated into a wide-ranging, multidimensional politics of definition. Debate over how this cluster of concepts should be defined should not be seen as an academic exercise aimed at establishing a neat and tidy scientific consensus. Rather, as Tim Clark puts it, the ecosystem management debate must be seen as a 'complex, competitive, conflictual social process about whose values will dominate.'[15] The politics of definition swirling around ecosystem management are, in a fundamental sense, about which resource management practices (and which resource management actors) will be entitled to bask in whatever symbolic lustre it generates.

The remainder of this chapter presents a detailed reflection on the early impact of ecosystem management ideas. The next section further develops the definitional terrain, exploring the implications of a switch to ecosystem management. The following section elaborates on the general characteristics of the politics of definition surrounding the concept. The next presents a short case study of how these politics have so far played out in one jurisdiction, British Columbia. The concluding section assesses what this experience suggests about the challenges likely to face ecosystem management advocates in the early part of the new century.

The Implications of a Switch to Ecosystem Management

Although the politics of definition surrounding the term 'ecosystem management' are complex and fluid, it is clear that the main cleavage line cuts between biocentric and anthropocentric conceptions.[16] Those on the biocentric side of the continuum argue that where there is conflict, ecological integrity must trump human needs. In the formulation of Noss and Cooperrider, for example, 'biodiversity conservation ultimately requires a rejection of humanism or anthropocentrism ... It requires a biocentric embrace of all life.'[17] Those offering less biocentric conceptualizations keep human needs and uses more squarely in the picture, offering formulations emphasizing the need to find a balance between social priorities and the needs of ecological systems.[18] Furthermore, they argue, the concepts of ecological integrity and health so central to biocentric definitions are, in fact, controversial human constructs that do not translate easily into clear evaluative standards.[19]

Those advancing anthropocentric (or softer, less biocentric) definitions are criticized for offering a naive, 'we can have our cake and eat it too' position that dilutes ecosystem management into something closely resembling discredited concepts such as multiple use and integrated resource management. It is easy, critics say, to 'cherry pick' a few elements from the list of ecosystem management goals and principles. Full and genuine adoption of this list, however, would require and/or entail a comprehensive package of changes, a 'seismic shift'[20] in mindset that would overturn assumptions and practices based on utilitarianism and the 'commodity forest' and replace them with ones based on a Leopoldian land ethic and the 'environmental forest.'[21] Out would go the tacit assumptions underlying traditional resource management practices, including 'earth as a resource for humans, competition over cooperation, control in place of adaptation, viewing all problems as soluble, and viewing nature as stable or balanced.'[22] In would come contextual thinking,[23] management premised on complex conceptions of ecological and organizational systems,[24] and new approaches 'based on the science of surprise, complexity, and nonlinearity.'[25]

These changes in operating assumptions would have to be accompanied by what Grumbine characterizes as a total unravelling and reweaving of the institutional fabric.[26] This transformation, says Errol Meidinger, has to be based on an acknowledgment that neither markets nor hierarchical organizations are up to the task of designing and implementing ecosystem management.[27] Market approaches are inadequate because ecosystems services are unpriced or severely underpriced, and because many of the beneficiaries of those services (for example, future generations) cannot participate in markets. Hierarchical organizations lack the necessary coordination, learning, and reaction capacities. Painful institutional change is required: 'the basic architecture' of existing agencies – including organizational structure, budgetary systems, institutional culture, and traditions – was forged in a distinctly different environment.[28] Ecosystem management requires flatter, less hierarchical organizations, ones able to spread responsibility and authority out among professions at the ground level.[29] It 'calls for more open, participatory practices that emphasize partnerships, shared visions of the land, and decentralized agencies; in this model agencies promote risk-taking, shared initiatives, and adaptive management.'[30]

'Adaptive management,' Kohm and Franklin contend, 'is the only logical approach under the circumstances of uncertainty and the continued accumulation of knowledge. Management must be designed to enhance the learning process and provide for systematic feedback from monitoring and research to practice.'[31] 'Adaptive organizations,' says Grumbine, 'construct networks for information sharing, train and encourage messengers, reward bridge builders, and welcome new learning.'[32] Adaptive managers adopt 'a more humble, tentative, and interpretative approach,'[33] and are 'passionate about interdependent as well as independent thinking.'[34] They have to be 'responsive to the variations, rhythms, and cycles of change' and 'able to react quickly with appropriate management techniques.'[35]

On a more concrete level, it must also be stressed that a genuine commitment to the full ecosystem management package requires strong resource management capacity. In order to make real progress towards the conservation of biodiversity, resource management agencies will need to have the capacity to carry out an extensive array of inventorying, research, planning, and monitoring tasks. Given how little is known about forest ecosystems,[36] the inventorying and research functions alone would require a large expansion in state capacity.

The Politics of Definition

The points made in the previous section could be presented alternatively as a list of the obstacles likely to be faced by biocentric ecosystem management advocates. All facets of the existing forest management paradigm are embedded in political–economic structures that can be counted on to generate resistance to the sort of changes envisaged. Each set of changes would ricochet through the resource management system, creating winners and losers. The resistance of the potential losers could, in most situations, be expected to be intense as well as enthusiastically supported by a diverse assortment of actors with a low tolerance for flux and uncertainty. Lurking always in the background are those who can be depended on to oppose the increases in government capacity and/or regulation that would be required to implement strong biodiversity conservation policy. This section considers the dynamics likely to be generated as ecosystem management advocates confront this array of opponents.

The political experiences of those pushing biocentric versions of the ecosystem management concept represent a test case for consideration of broader questions concerning whether and under what conditions existing practices and power structures can be destabilized by the appearance of challenging new ideas. The role of ideas in policy change processes has been extensively debated for more than a decade.[37] While some would contend that the 'ideational turn' has led to a dead end, there can be no doubt that our understanding of the policy process has benefited from efforts to conceptualize more clearly what goes on at the front end of the policy cycle. It is true though that we have much to learn about the factors that promote or impede attempts to wring lasting policy change victories from gains at the problem-definition and agenda-setting stage of the cycle.

My consideration of the impact of ecosystem management ideas on forest policy discourse and outcomes is guided by a couple of interrelated perspectives. First, packages of concepts and ideas such as those centring on ecosystem management constitute an important element of the 'regime' shaping developments in a particular policy field.[38] The packages associated with established or ascendant ideas define the ideational context or discourse that constrains possibilities within the policy sector. Among other things, the concepts and ideas integral to a given discourse define standards of acceptable practice, thus leaving a mark on the tests that those making and implementing policy must pass in order to retain legitimacy, authority, and derivative advantages. Elsewhere I have offered the following reflection on the factors influencing shifts in the discourses constraining developments in technically complex policy areas such as forestry:

A variety of forces – some rooted in the political arena, others in the scientific community – interact in complex ways to influence how new sets of ideas and knowledge claims appear, take root, gain currency and credibility, and begin to reshape the discourse surrounding a policy area. The strength of the political alliances favouring a set of ideas and claims will obviously make a difference. So too though may factors relating to an idea's merit, such as its ability to account for puzzles, resolve perplexing anomalies, or provide comprehensive and compelling ways of thinking about problems. The accreditation processes may be influenced by the weight of scientific support or evidence, and by whether or not central ideas and claims have gained acceptance in other jurisdictions, particularly admired ones.[39]

It would obviously be naive to believe that 'science' is ever totally insulated from politics. At the same time, however, we need to remain open to the possibility that processes that are not, at least in any manifest sense, political may leave a mark on the discourses surrounding particular policy issues. Discourse-altering ideas may result from shifts in scientific understanding that can, in turn, be linked to new discoveries, new measurement instruments, or new theoretical perspectives. As a result, even actors controlling a preponderance of political resources may not be able to exclude threatening new ideas.

As others have noted, it is difficult to distinguish the effects of ideas from the effects of the political pressures that are the focus of most analyses of policy outcomes.[40] One path towards clarifying the complex dynamics involved centres on the notion of the 'legitimation trap.'[41] The argument here begins with the simple observation that policy choices have to be defended, both to the other intensely involved members of the policy community and to the general public. Policy cannot be legitimated with concepts and ideas that are discredited or outmoded; it must be defended with the concepts and claims at the heart of the currently credible discourse. Shifts in the discourse resulting from the ascendancy of new ideas force recalibration of legitimation arguments. Once the discourse associated with a policy field shifts, all the actors trying to shape outcomes in that field will begin to feel the constraining effects (as well as the creative potential) of the changes. Most importantly, supporters of the status quo will be compelled to defend their positions in terms of the new concepts and understandings. In the process they will expose themselves to possible criticism from those who say that they are not meeting the tests and standards implied. They will run the risk of being caught in the legitimation trap.

The politics of definition swirling around ecosystem management can be conceived in these terms. In most jurisdictions, the main lines of conflict have pitted forest industry actors and their public sector allies (particularly professional foresters) against a coalition of environmental organizations and their professional allies (particularly conservation biologists). Conflict over the definition of ecosystem management and associated concepts has coloured debate over a wide assortment of land use and forest practices issues. These conflicts have also had a pronounced impact on developments at the blurred border between forest science and forest politics, manifesting themselves in debates within professional associations and university departments over curricula, credentials, and related matters. These conflicts have obvious implications for the status of new sub-disciplines such as landscape ecology and conservation biology.

Tensions over ecosystem management are at their starkest in cases where environmentalists and their allies contend that harvesting plans endorsed by the industry and other parts of the development coalition involve a rate of logging too high to allow protection of ecosystem characteristics. Anxious to maintain harvest levels, the industry and its supporters usually adopt as their first line of defence a set of responses based on the sustained yield – multiple use (integrated management) discourse that was employed to legitimate operations throughout the 1970s and 1980s. Industry spokespersons argue that their harvesting practices are designed to sustain the timber supply and protect other important forest values such as wildlife, viewscapes, and riparian zones. Where this response fails to neutralize pressure for ecosystem management, industry interests usually begin to explore what might be referred to as 'old wine in new bottles' strategies.

Typically these combine symbolic manoeuvring with limited substantive concessions. Elements of the ecosystem management discourse are incorporated into rejigged defences of the practices, and if necessary, these practices are adjusted with an eye to convincing at least the undecided portions of the attentive public that these constructions are credible. Throughout this exercise, industry interests try to create and capitalize on the ambiguity surrounding ecosystem management concepts, hoping to maintain a set of meanings loose enough to allow limited modifications of practice to be sold as a genuine response to the new ideas. Ultimately, the development coalition aims to neutralize pressures for policy change by winning support for the claim that it has brought practices into line with the standards embodied in the ascendant discourse.

Ecosystem management advocates, of course, contest each stage of this containment strategy. They counter the first set of industry responses with arguments about the inadequacy of even enriched multiple use measures. Where these arguments force the industry to retreat to its second line of defence, its critics are drawn into iterations of the politics of definition that come to the fore as the focus shifts to the issue of what meaning should be given the subsidiary concepts highlighted in ecosystem management implementation plans. As we will see below, for example, on the British Columbia Coast, attention has now shifted to 'variable retention' and other concepts that have grown in prominence as ecosystem management principles have been fleshed out. In these contests ecosystem management proponents work to achieve favourable reductions in conceptual ambiguity, knowing that clearer and more biocentric definitions will translate into clearer and tougher forest policy standards. Having forced the development coalition to accept at least some elements of the ecosystem management discourse, the environmental coalition seeks ways of forcing the industry to go beyond just talking the talk. It tries to set up and spring the legitimation trap.

Unfortunately for ecosystem management advocates, however, past experience in the forest policy sector suggests that the development coalition will find plentiful escape routes. Those seeking to translate previous shifts in forest policy discourse into improved environmental policy have grown accustomed to the fact that loosely defined tests and standards, and inadequate monitoring and enforcement capacity, usually combine to provide those trying to protect the status quo with plentiful opportunities for avoidance. Most of these opportunities can, in turn, be linked to fundamental characteristics of the forest policy regime. Of particular importance are two characteristics that hinder close public scrutiny of forest policy performance: the technical complexity of the policy field and the vastness and diversity of the forest land base. Using containment strategies that capitalize on these and other 'givens,' the forest industry in different parts of the country has had good success in loosening constraints legislated as part of the policy response to earlier waves of environmental pressures. In various provinces, for example, weak government capacity and obstacles to public scrutiny have combined with the forest industry's structural advantages to shape versions of the story which, in the B.C. context, came during the 1980s to be referred to as 'sympathetic administration.' This story began when a pro-business government under pressure to help a slumping forest industry approved a little noticed set of administrative directives that nullified important components of the sustained yield – integrated management policy supposedly in effect.

It remains to be seen whether Canadian environmentalists and conservation biologists will be able to push the forest industry and its allies towards full and genuine implementation of a biocentric conception of ecosystem management. In order to explore more fully the sort of reform-resistance dynamics likely to play out in the years ahead, we turn now to a case study of the early response to ecosystem management ideas in one jurisdiction, British Columbia.

The Debate over Ecosystem Management in British Columbia

Ecosystem management ideas began to achieve prominence in B.C. forest policy discourse in the late 1980s. Some key dimensions of the discourse shift process can be singled out. First, this process illustrates the critical role of policy entrepreneurs, actors who concentrate on the agenda-setting and problem-definition stage of the policy cycle. According to John Kingdon, 'Policy entrepreneurs, people who are willing to invest their resources in pushing their pet proposals or problems, are responsible not only for prompting important people to pay attention, but also for coupling solutions to problems and for coupling both problems and solutions to politics.'[42] In this case, some leading environmentalists linked up with an emerging cadre of conservation biologists to turn the policy community's focus towards new problem definitions that highlighted the failure of existing policies to address biodiversity conservation concerns. Second, the importation of ideas played a significant role, as Canadian resource managers and interest groups drew on the stories being written as their colleagues in the Pacific Northwest grappled with the spotted owl issue. Third, the processes that brought ecosystem management ideas to the fore were symbiotically connected to those behind the rise of new technologies and academic subdisciplines. The disciplines of forestry and wildlife biology went through complex metamorphoses as conservation biologists and landscape ecologists appeared and expanded their influence. New computer-based technologies such as geographic information system (GIS) mapping facilitated, and to some extent shaped, the shifts. As new subdisciplines and technologies gained a foothold within universities and colleges, curricula and research programs were transformed. Soon, graduates sympathetic to ecosystem management perspectives were knocking on the doors of prospective employers. As these individuals sought projects that would allow them to apply their training, agency perspectives, priorities, and capacities began to change. Both public and private sector bosses were soon persuaded that no self-respecting resource-management bureaucracy of the 1990s could function without tools such as GIS capacity, or maintain credibility unless its officials were capable of deploying the biodiversity discourse.

The interaction of these dimensions is nicely illustrated in the processes that transformed thinking about protected areas planning. B.C. developments were mirrored in other provinces. Prior to 1985, the protected areas policy discourse had been dominated by a problem definition favoured by resource development interests. In essence, these interests said there was no protected areas problem: wildlife, outdoor recreation opportunities, and places with special scenic value were adequately protected by the existing parks system and an ever-expanding collection of integrated resource management measures. By the early 1990s, this perspective was facing a stiff challenge from an alternative problem definition: the protected areas system was neither large enough nor representative enough to play the role it should in the protection of biodiversity.

These shifts were guided by key policy entrepreneurs such as the World Wildlife Fund – Canada (WWF). In its Endangered Spaces Campaign, launched in 1989, the WWF expertly seized on concepts and knowledge claims that had been advanced by international groups such as the International Union for the Conservation of Nature (IUCN). Building on the IUCN-drafted (and U.N.-endorsed) World Charter for Nature's call for preservation of 'representative samples of all the different types of ecosystems,' and on the Brundtland Commission's 'suggestion' that the total world expanse of protected areas should be at least tripled,[43] the WWF brought a cross-section of the country's most respected conservationists together to endorse the Canadian Wilderness Charter.[44] This document called on Canada's federal, provincial, and territorial governments to develop action plans to increase the protected area total to 12 per cent and establish 'at least one representative protected area in each of the natural regions of Canada by the year 2000.'

Although the literature on the functions of policy entrepreneurs has focused mainly on their agenda-setting and problem-definition role, the WWF's ongoing work illustrates the successful policy actor's appreciation of the importance of later stages of the policy cycle. The WWF and its allies in the provinces have had a continued impact on policy development and implementation processes across the country. Their success in this respect is the result of a considerable investment of time and energy in the monitoring and evaluation tasks needed to sustain the pressure for change. The WWF's yearly endangered spaces report cards evaluate the federal government and each of the provinces, providing concise assessments of each in terms of criteria such as 'system planning progress' and 'application of ecological principles.'[45]

The WWF and its allies in the different provinces can take some credit for the fact that, by the mid-1990s, most Canadian jurisdictions had mapped their natural regions and accepted ecological representation as one of the principles that should guide expansion of their protected areas systems.[46] Pressures exerted by these organizations also helped conservation biologists, systems planners, and GIS mappers to entrench themselves in resource management bureaucracies, thereby establishing in-house lobbies for the protected areas goals highlighted in the Endangered Spaces campaign. Clearly, then, environmental groups such as the WWF have been not just importers of ideas, but also diffusers. Recalcitrant governments can expect to be exposed and pressured.

The ascendancy of the eco-representation concept and other elements of the ecosystem management package was obviously not good news for the B.C. forest industry. During the 1970s and early 1980s, it had strongly resisted attempts to implement the environmental agenda. This resistance grew less effective as the 1980s progressed, in considerable part because the environmental coalition exposed a series of cases that seemed to illustrate the failure of both government and industry to deliver on the promises implicit in the province's policies on sustained yield and integrated resource management. These events undercut the legitimacy of the industry and the forest ministry, leaving the traditional policy-making elite in a weakened position as it began to respond to the challenge of how to contain the impact of those pushing ecosystem management ideas.

The forest policy agenda of the New Democratic Party (NDP) government elected in 1991 had been shaped by the discontents and ideational shifts of the previous decade. Most importantly, the NDP was committed to improving forest practices and doubling the size of the protected areas system to 12 per cent of the area of the province. After 1991, ecosystem management ideas had a significant impact on the design and implementation of policy in both areas. As George Hoberg describes in Chapter 12, the new government's Forest Practices Code included components aimed at conserving biodiversity and improving

the protection of riparian zones. Its Protected Areas Strategy highlighted the 12 per cent target as well as the vaguer goal of improving the
park system's ecosystem representation. Between 1991 and 1999, the
NDP governments of Mike Harcourt and Glen Clark added about five
million hectares to the parks system, increasing the proportion of the
province protected from under 6 per cent to nearly 11.5 per cent. These
additions somewhat improved the eco-representativeness of a system
that had long been criticized for its bias towards 'rocks and ice' landscapes, but old-growth ecosystems continued to be under-represented.
Figures from 1999, for example, show that while nearly 21 per cent of
the alpine tundra biogeoclimatic zone is protected, the comparable percentages for the low-lying forest zones range from 2.6 per cent to 9.5 per
cent.[47] A 1998 study showed that about 9 per cent of remaining low ele-
vation old-growth forests are protected, compared with about 16 per
cent of subalpine old-growth.[48]

The regional processes that developed recommendations on additions to the protected areas system also made closely related zoning proposals centring on a new land use category, the Special Management
Zone (SMZ). By 1999 over ten million hectares (about 20 per cent of
the total area covered by approved land use plans) had been assigned to
the SMZ category.[49] Environmentalists initially took some encouragement from talk about practices in these zones being governed by ecosystem management principles. As we will see, however, the process of
fleshing out vague statements of objectives has left environmentalists
increasingly unhappy about what the 'special' in the SMZ designation
actually means.

The most significant ecosystem management experiment to emerge
so far in British Columbia, and perhaps all of Canada, was set in motion
by the controversy over Clayoquot Sound, an area of 263,000 hectares
on the west side of Vancouver Island.[50] The area had been the scene of
conflict between environmentalists and forestry interests throughout
the decade leading up to the NDP takeover. Three consensus-building
processes failed during this period, ensuring that the issue was still front
and centre when the Harcourt government assumed office. After extensive debates in cabinet, Harcourt announced the Clayoquot Sound
Land Use Plan in April 1993. The government added over 48,000 hectares to the 39,000 hectares of existing parkland, increasing the proportion of the area protected to 33 per cent. Introducing a version of the
multizone system that was subsequently applied in other areas, it put
another 17.5 per cent of the area into the newly conceived SMZ cate-

gory. The remainder of the area was placed in a General Integrated Management zone.

Even though the new protected areas included some territory long prized by environmentalists (and even though, according to the government's calculations, the plan would reduce the forest harvest levels in the area by about one-third), many environmentalists reacted very negatively. Their protests led to the arrest of more than 800 people. The resultant world-wide media coverage heightened government and industry worries about consumer boycotts of B.C. wood products. Anxious to defuse the Clayoquot Sound issue, the government made a strong commitment to improving logging practices in the area. In October 1993, Premier Harcourt turned the question of how that might be done over to the newly appointed Scientific Panel for Sustainable Forest Practices in Clayoquot Sound (hereafter, the scientific panel or the panel). The government's goal, said Harcourt, was 'to make forest practices in Clayoquot not only the best in the province, but the best in the world.'[51]

Most of the B.C. government's experiments with forest policy advisory groups over the previous decade had combined government officials and representatives of stakeholder interests. In putting together the scientific panel, the government turned away from this model, leaving government ministries, environmental groups, the Industrial Wood and Allied Workers (IWA), other community interests, and the affected companies on the outside. Instead, it chose to connect representatives from the region's First Nation, the Nuu-chah-nulth, with an interdisciplinary team of scientists and technicians. This second group included specialists on soils, slope stability, roads, yarding systems, worker safety, hydrology, wildlife, biodiversity, fisheries, ethnobotany, and hydrology.[52] Panel members included well-known new forestry advocate Jerry Franklin from the University of Washington, along with several British Columbia academics and consultants with strong conservation biology or alternative silviculture credentials. This group would be joined by four Nuu-chah-nulth representatives.

By 1993 the provincial and federal governments had begun negotiations with the Nuu-chah-nulth over their land claim to the area. While the scientific panel was still in its infancy, the government and the five Clayoquot Sound Native bands negotiated an Interim Measures Agreement establishing joint management under a new entity, the Central Region Board.[53] It was to promote sustainability, reduce unemployment within Aboriginal communities, preserve representative ecological zones, restore fish and wildlife habitat, and provide a sustainable forest industry in the area. As we will see, it also ended up with substantial responsibility for implementing the scientific panel's recommendations.

The panel presented a detailed blueprint for sustainable ecosystem management in Clayoquot Sound, devoting separate chapters of its 200-page final report to silviculture, harvesting, log transportation, planning, and monitoring. Throughout, it applied the precautionary principle and gave primacy to the goal of sustaining the productivity and natural diversity of the region. Its recommendations centred on proposals for long-term, watershed-level planning; a variable-retention silvicultural system; new yarding practices; and full community involvement in intensive, multidimensional monitoring.

In a brief summary, it is difficult to do justice to the intricate linkages the panel developed in elaborating on these elements. The panel recommended an ecosystem approach to planning that would emphasize the maintenance of biological diversity and watershed integrity, along with the protection of cultural, scenic, and recreational values. Conservation of biological diversity, it said, involved 'maintaining ecosystem integrity and connections, and ensuring the survival of all the species and species' variants of plants, animals, and fungi that together form the natural indigenous biota of an area.'[54] Maintaining ecosystem integrity, in turn, meant 'ensuring that ecosystem processes and states do not depart from the range of natural variability exhibited before logging.'[55] The panel's closely related recommendations on ending clear-cutting, discussed below, derived from its observation that in the very wet environment of the region, natural disturbances typically involve small openings produced by 'just a few trees falling over.'[56]

The shift in planning perspectives would be most evident at the watershed level. After dividing the watershed into 'no harvesting reserves' and harvestable areas, planners would specify what portion of the harvestable area could be cut within a defined period.[57] The panel recommended interim standards for these rate-of-cut determinations, arguing that existing evidence about the hydrological (run-off) response to cumulative harvesting showed the need for caution.[58] Emphasizing a theme that had been heavily emphasized by environmentalists, the panel also said that allowable cut levels should be determined by watershed-level resource planning processes, rather than being predetermined and then imposed as constraints governing these processes.[59]

The panel recommended replacing conventional clear-cutting[60] with 'variable-retention,' an alternative silvicultural system that 'emphasizes retaining trees and patches of forest in a managed forest to protect a variety of values and ecosystem components.'[61] Variable retention 'provides for the permanent retention after harvest of various forest "structures" or habitat elements such as large decadent trees or groups of trees, snags, logs, and downed wood from the original stand that provide habitat for forest biota.'[62] As noted, it aims to ensure that ecosystem processes and states remain in the range of natural variability exhibited before logging.[63] The new system, the panel noted, would allow for a variety of options. These ranged from light to heavy retention, and on a second dimension, from dispersed ('retaining trees scattered throughout the cutblock') to aggregated retention ('retaining small areas of undisturbed forest').[64]

Critical decisions on the details of variable-retention prescriptions were to depend on the site's sensitivity and on the presence of non-timber values. Heavy retention would be prescribed for sites with significant non-timber values and ones classified as sensitive because of factors such as visual management objectives or steep slopes. In such areas, said the panel, at least 70 per cent of the forest should be retained in a relatively uniform distribution, opening sizes should be limited to less than one-third of a hectare, and snags, old wood, dying trees, and downed wood should be retained.[65] In less sensitive areas, the aim would be to retain at least 15 per cent of the forest. The panel stopped short of recommending what portion of the land base should be subject to high retention prescriptions. It did, however, note that because of the industry's past focus on low-elevation areas, most of the remaining older forests in Clayoquot Sound are located on slopes greater than 30 degrees.[66] It was clear, then, that if implemented according to the principles laid out, the panel's system would generally mean high retention levels or, that is, harvest levels much lower than those that had prevailed over the previous decade.[67]

The adoption of variable retention would require a transformation of the current harvesting system. After offering a detailed primer on advantages and disadvantages of different yarding, loading, and hauling options, the panel said that the reliance on grapple yarding would have to be reduced. The use of skyline systems and, to a less extent, helicopter logging would correspondingly increase.[68] The new systems would be more complex and labour intensive, and would require additional attention to planning, skills development, and worker safety risks. Falling and yarding efficiency would decrease.[69] The implications in terms of roads were not specified, but it was clear that the switch away from grapple yarding would mean diminished road densities, particularly on mid- and upper slopes.[70]

The scientific panel's report concluded with a chapter on monitoring. 'Effective monitoring,' it said, 'is an essential part of active adaptive management,' yet 'nowhere has sufficient effort been invested in this critical aspect of ecosystem management.'[71] A strong monitoring program should cover diverse indicators of watershed integrity and biological diversity. Implementation of an effective monitoring program would require a considerable commitment from government agencies and the local community. Noting that 'Clayoquot Sound is an excellent place to test the concept of local responsibility for sustainable ecosystem management,' the panel concluded by noting (as it had at a number of other places in its reports) the wealth of knowledge and experience present in Nuu-chah-nulth communities.[72]

The panel characterized its package of recommendations as conservative. It had tried to give 'the benefit of the doubt to the resource rather than to its extraction or development.'[73] All other objectives had to be subordinate to that of maintaining healthy, functioning ecosystems.[74]

It was a foregone conclusion that the scientific panel's recommendations would be accepted. Clayoquot Sound had a very high profile, and Premier Harcourt had committed the B.C. government to making it a showcase for progressive forest practices. In order to hold the green voters who had supported it in 1991, the government needed to erase the blight on its environmental record caused by the 1993 protests. Thanks to the efforts of Greenpeace and the Friends of Clayoquot Sound, the area had truly become a place of 'totemic importance'[75] for environmentalists inside and outside of Canada. These groups had kept the pressure on during 1994 and 1995, leaving little doubt that anything less than full compliance with the panel's recommendations would bring new blockades and a resumption of pressure on U.S. and European consumers to boycott B.C. forest products.[76]

In mid-1995 the forests minister announced that all of the panel's 120 recommendations would be implemented. Conventional clear-cut logging in the area would be replaced by the variable retention system, and harvest levels would be calculated after watershed planning rather than being imposed on the basis of predetermined allowable annual cuts. The Central Region Board was to play a major implementation role. Various measures were promised to help cushion impacts on workers.[77]

In the wake of these decisions, the company with the largest operations in the area,[78] MacMillan Bloedel, suspended operations and then entered into negotiations with the Nuu-chah-nulth and environmentalists, in an attempt to find a mutually acceptable approach to some continued logging. By mid-1999 these negotiations had led to formation of a Nuu-chah-nulth – MacMillan Bloedel joint venture company, and to a pact between this new company and some of the major environmental groups active in the area.[79] Under the terms of this agreement, the company committed itself to logging at a slow, non-industrial pace (to what a MacMillan Bloedel spokesman characterized as 'boutique logging'). Operations would be small scale and governed by variable retention recommendations of the scientific panel.[80] In return, the environmental groups agreed to assist in finding markets for the timber. Among other things, this would mean helping the operation achieve eco-certification under the Forest Stewardship Council standards described in Chapter 2.

Despite these signs of progress, the environmental group most closely involved in the anti-logging protests of the 1990s, the locally based Friends of Clayoquot Sound (FOCS), has now expressed serious reservations about the early efforts to implement the recommendations of the scientific panel. In a 1998 report, FOCS said the process had so far been 'fraught with problems and barriers.'[81] It acknowledged some changes in operational practices, but in a set of criticisms that illustrate the earlier point about the iterated character of the dynamics of the 'politics of definition,' FOCS noted that inspection of recent cutblocks raised questions about whether the aggregate retention version of variable retention actually produced results different from conventional clear-cutting.[82] FOCS was most critical of what it saw as inadequate implementation of the panel's adaptive management recommendations: 'In sum, there have so far been no planning objectives set, no adequate baseline data collection, no monitoring and, therefore, no adaptive management.'[83] These and other problems, said FOCS, had deep roots: 'A lasting implementation of an ecosystem-based forest sector will never happen in Clayoquot Sound until the forest companies themselves abandon volume-based enterprises ... Clayoquot is facing the same pressure as everywhere else in the world, namely the international "race-to-the-bottom" run by logging companies to feed large volumes of timber into commodity markets at the lowest possible costs.'[84] In order for ecosystem management to succeed, companies would have to restructure themselves into operations oriented towards low-volume, high-value opportunities.

The final verdict on the consequences of the scientific panel report will not be delivered for some time. At issue particularly is the question of whether future events will reflect a strong commitment to the 'full package' of panel recommendations, including a conservative adaptive management approach premised on patiently waiting for the results of full inventorying and carefully monitored experiments. Despite the concerns raised in the FOCS report, most ecosystem management supporters remain fairly optimistic about the future of Clayoquot Sound.

Unfortunately for those hoping to see the scientific panel regime applied elsewhere, the Clayoquot Sound recipe involves a rather special combination of elements. The area includes the open ocean beaches of a major national park, Pacific Rim. Since its opening in the early 1970s, the park's coastal scenery and recreation opportunities have drawn millions of visitors. The consequences have included rapid growth in tourist businesses and diversification of the area's economy away from its traditional dependence on resource extraction. Economic diversification has been particularly apparent in Tofino, the village that has been home base for the Friends of Clayoquot Sound. Tofino's political resources have been enhanced by immigration patterns that have brought a continued stream of energetic, committed, and highly qualified environmentalists to settle in the area. The efforts of FOCS to reach national and international audiences have been helped by the fact that a significant portion of the tourists attracted to the area are very sympathetic to the general aims of the environmental movement as well as to the land claims and self-government aspirations of Native peoples. The social bases of environmental protest in the area have also been influenced by the fact that, sitting as it does at the far western (and the mild Pacific) of Canada's transcontinental highway, the area has long been a magnet for restless and idealistic young people trekking across the country or the continent. These elements contribute to Clayoquot Sound's potency as a symbolic focal point for those seeking to find (or give concrete representation to) the sort of pristine nature highlighted in what Candace Slater calls the 'edenic narrative.'[85]

Efforts to diffuse the Clayoquot model to other parts of British Columbia have had limited success. While ecosystem management advocates praise recent increases in protected areas, they are not satisfied with other components of the NDP's land use planning policy. The Special Management Zones are a particular concern. Across the province, the statements explaining decisions to set aside SMZs have been liberally sprinkled with words and phrases from the ecosystem management lexicon, including biodiversity conservation, buffer zones, wildlife corridors, and connectivity. In one instance, reference was made to SMZs being 'vanguard areas for implementation of the principles of Sustainable Eco-system management.'[86] According to environmentalists, the efforts to implement SMZs have so far failed to live up to the promise. After reviewing accounts from environmentalists familiar with early experiences with SMZ planning across British Columbia, the author of one assessment concluded that management in many SMZs 'is too often "business as usual." Problems include continued high rates of logging, continued use of clearcutting, inadequate respect for non-timber values, and the dearth of more detailed, long term planning.'[87] To make the 'special' in SMZ meaningful, he said, the government should commit to the use of ecoforestry practices, in particular the variable-retention silvicultural system recommended by the Clayoquot Sound Scientific Panel.[88]

Outside of Clayoquot Sound, even regional land use disputes involving seemingly promising combinations of political factors have not produced the gains hoped for by ecosystem management advocates. The problems they face are illustrated by the process that was supposed to provide a plan for maintaining B.C.'s population of the northern spotted owl. Officially designated by Canadian authorities as endangered, the owl's range encompasses an estimated 1.1 million hectares in the southwest corner of the province. In 1997, after several years of analysis and debate,[89] the B.C. government acceded to pressure from local timber interests, announcing a plan which, it admitted, would involve a 40 per cent probability of the owl's extirpation.[90] According to an independent ecological assessment by two U.S. researchers, the B.C. plan is far inferior to one adopted to protect the spotted owl in the Pacific Northwest.[91]

Both scientifically and politically, the spotted owl would seem to provide good opportunities for those wanting to try a species-centred approach to making the case for ecosystem management. All of the uncertainties that characterize spotted owl research are compounded in British Columbia by inadequate inventory information, so there are strong grounds to argue that any development should proceed very cautiously. Since this critter rates fairly high on the cute, cuddly, and charismatic scale, considerable public support could be assumed. As well, it lives in old-growth forests that are near and dear to the environmentalists and outdoor recreationists of a large metropolitan area. These advantages were, however, not sufficient to counteract the intense political pressure exerted by a few timber-dependent communities. Their resistance to reductions in harvest levels effectively defeated the chances of an adaptive management approach to spotted owl management.

It should be noted that those pushing to export the Clayoquot Sound model to other parts of the B.C. coast have declared one recent victory. In mid-1998, MacMillan Bloedel announced that it would begin phasing out clear-cut logging in favour of a variable retention system. Despite cause for some doubt about what this move would eventually mean 'on the ground,'[92] the announcement was received positively by even the most hard-line environmentalists. For example, Greenpeace, which had relied heavily on a strategy aimed at foreign audiences after entering the fray over B.C. old growth in 1993, was quick to endorse the company's contention that fears about consumer boycotts of its products had precipitated the shift. Nonetheless, after thirty years of forest industry resistance strategies, including many variants of symbolic barrage tactics, there is a natural tendency to view these events through sceptical lenses. Murray Edelman's writings on the construction of political spectacles provide one inviting interpretative framework.[93]

MacMillan Bloedel (and its successor, Weyerhaeuser) has, however, so far exceeded the targets set in the switch-over schedule laid out in its 1998 announcement, and the initial doubts of company traditionalists appear to have dissipated.[94] Like the Clayoquot Sound case, then, Mac-Millan Bloedel's move may be taken to illustrate a difficult but attainable set of conditions that will allow the legitimation trap to be sprung. It can be argued that the company knew it had to retreat in order to retain legitimacy (and the attendant advantages) in a policy setting increasingly shaped by the discourse on ecosystem management.

Still, cause for scepticism remains. Even if the new approach taken by MacMillan Bloedel (and now Weyerhaeuser) does stand up under scrutiny as a full application of the scientific panel approach, it can be argued that optimism about a wave of industry concessions should be tempered. Some reflection on the analogy between MacMillan Bloedel and Clayoquot Sound suggests that the sound of toppling dominoes may not be heard for some time. In the same way that environmentalists of the 1990s made Clayoquot Sound synonymous with B.C. old growth, they made MacMillan Bloedel synonymous with the forest industry, thus leaving it feeling more vulnerable than most of its competitors to the pressures of boycotts. The obstacles involved in extending the Clayoquot Sound precedent to other areas may be paralleled by those involved in exerting pressure on the industry as a whole. The Clayoquot Sound experience raised the question of whether, by putting so much focus on that one area, environmentalists had left themselves vulnerable to containment strategies premised on area-specific concessions. MacMillan Bloedel's concessions raise analogous concerns.

To round out this account, we should note one other large set of factors that are of considerable concern to B.C.'s ecosystem management proponents. As noted earlier, a genuine government commitment to ecosystem management requires full support for resource management agencies. Forest and environment agencies must be given the financial support needed to carry out the extensive range of inventorying, research, planning, and monitoring tasks involved in a genuine commitment to conservation of forest biodiversity. If anything, these agencies will need larger budgets than those they had during the sustained yield – multiple use era. This point of view has not been embraced by the B.C. government. To the contrary, since 1996 provincial budgetary policies have resulted in a series of major staff cuts at the forest and environment agencies.[95]

Conclusion: Charting the Path Forward

Other chapters in this volume describe the opportunities and obstacles encountered by ecosystem management proponents across the country. By the end of the 1990s, most provincial governments were at least paying lip service to ecosystem management perspectives. As Ian Urquhart's comparison of the Alberta and Saskatchewan experiences indicates,[96] however, efforts to implement these perspectives have moved much further and faster in some provinces than others.

This chapter considered British Columbia's early experiences with ecosystem management. In general, those experiences seem to be mirrored in other jurisdictions that have implanted ecosystem management ideas in new legislation, policy statements, and planning guides. The forces limiting attempts to have the Clayoquot Sound model applied to other parts of the B.C. coast are similar, for example, to those highlighted in Levy, Lawson, and Sandberg's analysis of the factors that have so far constrained and compromised attempts to implement the system laid out in Ontario's new *Forest Management Planning Manual*. As they point out, attempts to realize the potential of the new policy have been undercut by the Ontario government's continued emphasis on satisfying the industry's demand for fibre, as well as by its sharp cuts to resource management staff levels.[97]

The future success of ecosystem management advocacy will be influenced by a complex mix of factors. While the nature of this mix will no doubt vary from jurisdiction to jurisdiction, recent developments in various provinces suggest that prevailing political and ideational contexts will provide proponents of ecosystem management with some opportunities. In attempting to capitalize on these, however, they will face deeply embedded obstacles. The most difficult of these derive from policy legacies; simply put, powerful political resistance will continue to be generated by those who have invested heavily on the assumption that the volume-based industrial forestry paradigm will guide development of remaining accessible old-growth forests. As Howlett and Rayner argue in Chapter 2, the material bases underlying the policy sector will continue to constrain reform possibilities.[98]

Proponents of ecosystem management disagree on how best to achieve implementation of their ideas. Some suggest that the switch to ecosystem management must begin with adoption of strong legislation. In this vein, for example, Steven Kennett cites Scott Hardt's proposal that the mandate of land management agencies be defined by legislation requiring the maintenance of ecosystem viability.[99] Such legislation would designate management indicators that would become the legal standard against which agency performance was assessed: 'Any litigation concerning violation of the ecoystem viability ceiling would focus on the effects that challenged actions would have on the management indicators ... This would allow for meaningful judicial review rather than broad judicial deference to agency expertise.'[100]

A different approach has been emphasized by proponents of eco-system-based community forestry.[101] Here the emphasis is on devolution of management authority. Over the past three decades, communities across Canada have generated an assortment of impressive blueprints for local management. Most are premised on the assumption that, left to their own devices, communities adjacent to forested areas will set and apply principles and objectives that are much more sensitive to ecosystem integrity than those governing centrally managed, volume driven, industrial forest operations. Some proponents of community forestry have suggested that this approach must be combined with the strong legislation model.[102] Local forest authorities would have to operate within an overall legislative framework, such as that envisaged by Kennett.

This chapter suggests that, whatever path they choose, advocates of ecosystem management will continue to face difficult obstacles. Provincial governments, it can safely be predicted, will not be eager to transfer significant authority for forest management to local communities, or adopt legislation reducing discretion and forcing action on the management of ecosystems. The forest interests that have had a large role in shaping present forest policies will certainly not push for changes that would decrease their access to fibre and/or increase their costs of harvesting it.

Under the circumstances, then, those pushing for adoption of strong ecosystem management approaches have little option but to continue with a flexible, multidimensional political approach centring on efforts to identify and capitalize on small opportunities for advancement. Among other things, advocates need to continue working on cultivating allies, on linking plans for ecosystem management to visions of economic health that are attractive to broad cross-sections of people living in resource development regions, and on educating the public about the future costs of ignoring concerns about the conservation of ecosystem integrity.

As they explore political possibilities, supporters of ecosystem management would be advised to consider the conceptualization of the challenge offered in Steven Primm and Tim Clark's reflections on the difficulties encountered in trying to implement an ecosystem management approach for the Greater Yellowstone Ecosystem in the United States. The overall problem, they suggest, might be seen as an onion or as 'a central, on-the-ground problem at the heart of the matter, with successive layers of contextual problems surrounding it.'[103] Peeling away these layers, they encounter 'a lack of: (1) technical experience in "ecosystem management," (2) the bureaucratic will to engage in such management, especially on a cross-jurisdictional basis, and (3) the requisite political support for this sort of research and management.'[104]

Noting that 'any policy alternative that promises to solve the technical problems must also successfully overcome the bureaucratic and political obstacles,'[105] Primm and Clark recommend an approach based on a variety of small-scale, experimental projects. They disagree, then, with those who would argue that ecosystem management pilot projects such as those under way across Canada are (to borrow and adapt a phrase from Chapter 10) Potemkin projects that ultimately retard progress by channelling pressure for change into avenues relatively unthreatening to the supporters of 'business-as-usual' industrial logging. The pilot project tack, according to Primm and Clark, provides the most workable basis for simultaneously solving problems of both technical feasibility and political viability.

Proponents of ecosystem management will continue to debate these and other issues in terms of how best to advance the cause. Those on all sides of these debates will be able to take encouragement from the fact that ecosystem management ideas have gained a foothold in the Canadian forest policy discourse.[106] A systematic cross-time content analysis of rhetorics used to explain and defend forest policy decisions would undoubtedly reveal steady increases in the incidence and centrality of words and phrases such as biodiversity, connectivity, alternative silvicultural systems, and ecosystem integrity. This shift in discourse represents a promising start. So does the increasing incidence of location-specific policy shifts such as those that have transformed the nature of forestry in Clayoquot Sound. History, however, suggests that optimism should be tempered. An examination of how other shifts in forest policy discourse translated into policy change indicates that further gains may be hard won. Those seeking to translate discourse shifts into policies more sensitive to non-timber values have found it difficult to 'spring the legitimation trap.' Talking the talk does not lead easily to walking the walk.

NOTES

1 Kathryn A. Kohm and Jerry F. Franklin, 'Introduction,' in Kathryn A. Kohm and Jerry F. Franklin, eds., *Creating a Forestry for the 21st Century: The Science of Ecosystem Management* (Washington, DC: Island Press, 1997) 1.

2 See, e.g., Lawson, Levy, and Sandberg, this volume, Chapter 10, on Ontario's Crown Forest Sustainability Act (1994); Urquhart, this volume, Chapter 11, on Saskatchewan's Forest Resources Management Act (1996); Hoberg, this volume, Chapter 12, on BC's Forest Practices Code (1994)

3 On some of those conducted under the auspicies of the federal government's Model Forest Programs, see Beyers in this volume, Chapter 7. See also Cheri Burda, 'Ecosystem-Based Community Forestry in British Columbia: An Examination of the Need and Opportunity for Policy Reform, Integrating Lessons from Around the World,' unpublished Masters thesis, University of Victoria, 1999, 82–94.

4 Steven L. Yaffee, Ali F. Phillips, Irene C. Frentz, Paul W. Hardy, Sussanne M. Maleki, and Barbara E. Thorpe, *Ecosystem Management in the United States: An Assessment of Current Experience* (Washington, DC: Island Press, 1996) 3.

5 R. Edward Grumbine, 'Reflections on "What Is Ecosystem Management?"' *Conservation Biology* 11(1), 1997, 41.

6 Grumbine, 'What Is Ecosystem Management?' *Conservation Biology* 8(1), 1994, 31.

7 Ken Lertzman, Tom Spies, and Fred Swanson, 'From Ecosystem Dynamics to Ecosystem Management,' in Peter K. Shoonmaker, Bettina von Hagen, and Edward C. Wolf, eds., *The Rainforests of Home: Profile of a North American Bioregion* (Washington, DC, and Covelo, Calif.: Island Press, 1997) 364.

8 Steven A. Kennett, *New Directions for Public Land Law* (Calgary: Canadian Institute of Resources Law, 1998) 19.

9 Ibid., 20. For surveys of other definitions, see Joyce Berry, Gary D. Brewer, John C. Gordon, and David R. Patton, 'Closing the Gap between Ecosystem Management and Ecosystem Research,' *Policy Sciences* 31, 1998, 56; Brian Czech and Paul R. Krausman, 'Implications of an Ecosystem Management Literature Review,' *Wildlife Society Bulletin* 25, 1997, 668–9; Richard Haeuber, 'Setting the Environmental Policy Agenda: The Case of Ecosystem Management,' *Natural Resources Journal* 36, 1996, 25.

10 Grumbine, 'What Is Ecosystem Management?' 29–31. Grumbine's full list includes: hierarchical context (managers must seek connections between levels of the biodiversity hierarchy); ecological boundaries (managers must work across administrative and political boundaries); ecological integrity (managers must aim to conserve viable populations of native species; maintain ecological processes; protect the evolutionary potential of species; and represent ecosystems in protected areas); data collection (managers require better data and must better use existing data); monitoring (managers must track the results of their actions); adaptive management (managers should assume that scientific knowledge is provisional and treat management as a learning process or continuous experiment); interagency cooperation (managers must learn to work together); organizational change (changes in the structure and operating patterns of land management agencies are required); humans embedded in nature (people must not be separated from nature); and values (human values play a dominant role in ecosystem management goals).

11 Winifred B. Kessler and Hal Salwasser, 'Natural Resource Agencies: Transforming from Within,' in Richard L. Knight and Sarah F. Bates, eds., *A New Century for Natural Resources Management* (Washington, DC: Island Press, 1995) 79–82.

12 Lertzman, et al. 'From Ecosystem Dynamics,' 361–66.

13 David N. Bengston, 'Changing Forest Values and Ecosystem Management,' *Society and Natural Resources* 7, 1994, 516.

14 Fred L. Bunnell, 'Managing Forests to Sustain Biodiversity: Substituting Accomplishment for Motion,' *Forestry Chronicle* 74 (6), 1998, 823.

15 Grumbine, 'What Is Ecosystem Management?' 32, quoting Tim Clark.

16 Czech and Krausman, 'Implications of an Ecosystem Management Litera-

ture Review,' 668; Haeuber, 'Setting the Environmental Policy Agenda,' 3–4, 6.

17 R.F. Noss and A. Cooperrider, *Saving Nature's Legacy: Protecting and Restoring Biodiversity* (Washington, DC: Defenders of Wildlife and Island Press 1994), quoted in Grumbine, 'What Is Ecosystem Management?' 34.

18 See, e.g., Roger A. Sedjo, 'Ecosystem Management: An Uncharted Path for Public Forests,' *Resources* 121, Fall 1995, 10, 20. See also W.L. Adamowicz and T.S. Veeman, 'Forest Policy and the Environment: Changing Paradigms,' *Canadian Public Policy* 24 (Supplement 2), 1998, S51–S61.

19 For a development of this point, see, e.g., D. Wicklum and Ronald W. Davies, 'Ecosystem Health and Integrity?' *Canadian Journal of Botany* 73(3), 1995, 997–9. Wicklum and Davies are agnostic on the subject of ecosystem management, but contend that 'the concepts of ecosytem health and ecosystem integrity are ... ecologically inappropriate. The phrase ecosystem health is based on an invalid analogy with human health requiring acceptance of an optimum condition and homeostatic processes maintaining the ecosystem at a definable optimum state. Similarly, ecosystem integrity is not an objective, quantifiable property of an ecosystem. Health and integrity are not inherent properties of an ecosystem and are not supported by either empirical evidence or ecological theory ... [G]ood or bad ecosystems cannot be defined scientifically and can only be based on the kind of ecosystem desired by society.'

20 Grumbine, 'What Is Ecosystem Management?' 43.

21 Bengston, 'Changing Forest Values and Ecosystem Management,' 528.

22 Grumbine, 'Reflections on "What Is Ecosystem Management?"' 42.

23 Ibid., 43.

24 Kohm and Franklin, 'Introduction,' in *Creating a Forestry for the 21st Century*, 2–3.

25 James W. Crossley, 'Managing Ecosystems for Integrity: Theoretical Considerations for Resource and Environmental Managers,' *Society and Natural Resources* 9, 1996, 465.

26 Grumbine, 'Reflections on "What Is Ecosystem Management?"' 45.

27 Errol E. Meidinger, 'Organizational and Legal Challenges to Ecosystem Management,' in Kohm and Franklin, eds., *Creating a Forestry for the 21st Century*, 361–2.

28 Kessler and Salwasser, 'Natural Resource Agencies,' 183–4.

29 Kohm and Franklin, eds., 'Institutions in Transition,' in *Creating a Forestry for the 21st Century*, 358.

30 Richard L. Knight and Gary K. Meffe, 'Ecosystem Management: Agency Liberation from Command and Control,' *Wildlife Society Bulletin* 25(3), 1997, 678.

31 Kohm and Franklin, 'Introduction,' in *Creating a Forestry for the 21st Century*, 5.
32 Grumbine, 'Reflections on "What is Ecosystem Management?"' 44–6.
33 Margaret A. Shannon and Alexios R. Antypas, 'Open Institutions: Uncertainty and Ambiguity in 21st-Century Forestry,' in *Creating a Forestry for the 21st Century*, 438.
34 Grumbine, 'Reflections on "What Is Ecosystem Management?"' 2, 43.
35 Frances Westley, 'Governing Design: The Management of Social Systems and Ecosystem Management,' in Lance H. Gunderson, C.S. Holling, and Stephen S. Light, eds., *Barriers and Bridges to the Renewal of Ecosystems and Institutions* (New York: Columbia University Press, 1995) 394.
36 On how little is known about forest organisms, their functioning, and the potential impacts of anthropogenic disturbance, see William S. Alverson, Walther Kuhlmann, and Donald M. Waller, *Wild Forests: Conservation Biology and Public Policy* (Washington, DC: Island Press, 1994) 252, 28.
37 See, e.g., John L. Campbell, 'Institutional Analysis and the Role of Ideas in Political Economy,' in *Theory and Society* 27, 1998, 377–409; Peter A. Hall, 'Introduction,' in Hall, ed., *The Political Power of Economic Ideas: Keynesianism across Nations* (Princeton, NJ: Princeton University Press, 1989) 1–11; Judith Goldstein and Robert O. Keohane, 'Ideas and Foreign Policy: An Analytical Framework,' in Goldstein and Keohane, eds., *Ideas and Foreign Policy: Beliefs, Institutions, and Political Change* (Ithaca: Cornell University Press, 1993); and Mark M. Blyth, '"Any More Bright Ideas?" The Ideational Turn of Comparative Political Economy,' *Comparative Politics* 29(2), 1997, 229–50.
38 See George Hoberg, 'Policy Cycles and Policy Regimes: Approaches to Studying Forest Policy Change,' unpublished paper, 1999. In Hoberg's framework, the three components of policy regimes are actors, institutions, and ideas, with institutions defined as 'rules and procedures that allocate authority over policy and structure relations between various actors.'
39 Jeremy Wilson, *Talk and Log: Wilderness Politics in British Columbia, 1965–96* (Vancouver: UBC Press, 1998) 12.
40 See, e.g., sources cited in n37.
41 This paragraph is based on Wilson, *Talk and Log*, 10–16.
42 John W. Kingdon, *Agenda, Alternatives, and Public Policies* (Boston: Little, Brown, 1984) 21. See also Michael Howlett and M. Ramesh, *Studying Public Policy: Policy Cycles and Policy Subsystems* (Toronto: Oxford University Press, 1995) Chap. 5; Leslie A Pal, *Beyond Policy Analysis: Public Issue Management in Turbulent Times* (Scarborough: Nelson, 1997) Chap. 3, 92–4.
43 The Brundtland Commission made only a passing reference to the fact that 'professional opinion' favoured a tripling of the world's protected areas total, which at that point stood at about 4 per cent. For accounts of the

origins of the 12 per cent target, see Larry Pynn, '12 Per Cent Preservation Goal Plucked from Thin Air,' *Vancouver Sun*, 30 Nov., 1994; Harold Eidsvik, 'Canada in a Global Context,' in Monte Hummel, ed., *Endangered Spaces: The Future for Canada's Wilderness* (Toronto: Key Porter Books, 1989) 44; M.A. Sanjayan and M.E. Soule, *Moving Beyond Brundtland: The Conservation Value of British Columbia's 12 Percent Protected Area Strategy* (Vancouver: Greenpeace, 1997) 3–4.

44 Hummel, *Endangered Spaces*, first appendix.

45 World Wildlife Fund (WWF), *Endangered Spaces Progress Report 94–95*; *Endangered Spaces Progress Report 95–96* (Toronto: WWF Canada).

46 See *Endangered Spaces Progress Report 94–95*, 10–11. See Hummel, 'The Upshot,' in *Endangered Spaces* 268–9, indicating that at the start, eight of twelve provincial territorial jurisdictions had system plans.

47 Kaaren Lewis and Susan Westmacott, *Provincial Overview and Status Report* (Victoria: Land Use Coordination Office, 1996), and updated figures from Land Use Coordination Office (LUCO) obtained July 1999. The percentages for forested zones include, 2.6 per cent of the Coastal Douglas Fir Zone, 9.5 per cent of the Coastal Western Hemlock Zone, 8.8 per cent of the Interior Cedar Hemlock Zone, and 4.0 per cent of the Interior Douglas Fir Zone.

48 Andy MacKinnon and Terje Vold, 'Old-Growth Forests Inventory for British Columbia,' *National Areas Journal* 18(4), 309–18. McKinnon and Vold begin with an age class definition of old growth which varies by region and forest type. Old growth consists of coastal forests older than 250 years, and interior forests older than 120 years in the case of lodgepole pine or deciduous species, or older than 140 years in the case of other forest types. They acknowledge that this definition includes areas that would be excluded by an ecological (structural characteristics) definition or by one that excludes 'shorter' old-growth forests.

49 British Columbia, Land Use Coordination Office, 'Special Management Zone Project: Information Report,' (1998), 7–8.

50 Land area; including lakes and ocean inlets the area is about 350,000 hectares.

51 Quoted in British Columbia, The Scientific Panel for Sustainable Forest Practices in Clayoquot Sound, *Sustainable Ecosystem Management in Clayoquot Sound* (Report 5) (Victoria, B.C.: Clayoquot Scientific Panel, 1995) 1.

52 Ibid., Appendix V.

53 British Columbia, The Scientific Panel for Sustainable Forest Practices in Clayoquot Sound, *First Nations Perspectives* (Report 3) 38. For a summary, see Ecotrust Canada, *Seeing the Ocean through the Trees* (Vancouver: Ecotrust Canada, 1997) 25–7.

54 British Columbia, *Sustainable Ecosystem Management*, 201.

55 Ibid., 79.

56 See the quotation from panel member, Laurie Kremsater, in Friends of Clayoquot Sound, 'The Scientific Panel Recommendations,' in *Implementing the Scientific Panel: Three Years and Counting* (1998), 6–7.

57 British Columbia, *Sustainable Ecosystem Management* (Report 5), 80, 166–72.

58 Ibid., 81–83 and 60.

59 Ibid., 72, 154.

60 Ibid., 46–7.

61 Ibid., 78.

62 Ibid., 83; see also 78–89.

63 Ibid., 79.

64 Ibid., 75, 84–5. Although the point has not penetrated the public debate over clear-cutting, the panel did note that depending on what choices were made, the results under variable retention might not differ much from those under conventional clear-cutting. Indeed, its attempt at a figurative comparison of a small clear-cut system and an aggregated retention system showed very little difference. See e.g., Ibid., Fig. 3.3, p. 85.

65 Ibid., 85.

66 Ibid., 12.

67 The volume harvested from Clayoquot Sound had already fallen from 960,000 cubic metres in 1988 to 428,000 cubic metres in 1993. Ibid. 49.

68 Ibid., 109, 114–15.

69 Ibid., 115–16.

70 Ibid., 115.

71 Ibid., 191, 190.

72 Ibid., 218.

73 Ibid., 4, quoting M.R. Kaufman, et al., *An Ecological Basis for Ecosystem Management* (Fort Collins, Col.: U.S. Department of Agriculture Forest Service, 1994) 3.

74 Ibid., 78.

75 A phrase from the 1991 report of the Clayoquot Sound Steering Committee, quoted in Glenn Bohn, 'The Clash over Clayoquot,' *Vancouver Sun*, 13 March 1993.

76 Gordon Hamilton, 'Eco-Group Ready for more War or Peace,' *Vancouver Sun*, 4 July 1995. Gordon Hamilton, 'Time to Make Decision on Clayoquot, MB told,' *Vancouver Sun*, 8 June 1995.

77 British Columbia, Ministry of Forests and Ministry of Environment, Lands and Parks, 'News Release: Government Adopts Clayoquot Scientific Report, Moves to Implementation,' 6 July 1995. See also, Mark Haddock, 'Govern-

ment Adopts Clayoquot Sound Scientific Panel Recommendations,' *British Columbia Environmental Report* (Fall) 1995, 25.

78 The other major company operating in the area, Interfor, has continued its experiments with alternative silviculture.

79 The groups were Greenpeace International, Greenpeace Canada, the Natural Resources Defense Council, the Sierra Club of B.C., and the Western Canada Wilderness Committee. See 'Memorandum of Understanding between Iisaak Forest Resources Ltd. and Environmental Groups,' 16 June 1999.

80 See 'Greenpeace, MB Teaming to Market Clayoquot Timber,' *Vancouver Sun*, 10 Dec. 1998, and 'MB, Environmentalists Agree to Pact on Clayoquot Logging,' *Vancouver Sun*, 16 June 1999.

81 Friends of Clayoquot Sound, 'Collective Summary,' in *Implementing the Scientific Panel: Three Years and Counting*, 1998, 1.

82 Ibid., 'Implementing the Recommendations' 9–11; 'Analysis and Recommendations,' 5–6.

83 Ibid., 'Implementing the Recommendations,' 4.

84 Ibid., 'Analysis and Recommendations' 6–7.

85 Candace Slater, 'Amazonia as Edenic Narrative,' in William Cronon, ed., *Uncommon Ground: Toward Reinventing Nature* (New York: W.W. Norton, 1995) 114–31. See also, in the same volume, Cronon, 'The Trouble with Wilderness; or Getting Back to the Wrong Nature,' 69–90.

86 Low Intensity Area Review Committee, *Low Intensity Areas for the Vancouver Island Region*, 9–10, emphasis in original.

87 Cooperman, *Keeping the Special in Special Management Zones*, 78.

88 Ibid., 78 and executive summary.

89 Results of the analytic exercise are presented in Canadian Spotted Owl Recovery Team, *Management Options for the Northern Spotted Owl in British Columbia*, 1994, n.p.

90 British Columbia, *Spotted Owl Management Plan: Summary Report* (Victoria, B.C.: Spotted Owl Management Inter-Agency Team, 1997) 12. The plan said: 'The probability of spotted owl population stabilization or improvement under this plan is about 60%.' A 60 per cent probability of *stabilization or improvement* in status means a 40 per cent probability of a *worsened* status, which in the case of an endangered species can only mean extirpation.

91 Peter Hodum and Susan Harrison, 'Ecological Assessment of the British Columbia Spotted Owl Management Plan,' Unpublished paper, 1998. According to Hodum and Harrison, the special owl habitat zones provided are too small to support sufficient numbers of breeding pairs, and too far apart to ensure successful dispersal. Harvesting in these zones will be

allowed to continue despite 'considerable scientific uncertainty on whether thinning, salvage operations and other "restoration" oriented silvicultural activities can be used successfully to restore the ecological integrity of an area without significant adverse impacts to ecological elements and processes' 8. By not establishing adequate mechanisms for monitoring these impacts, the plan contravenes fundamental adaptive management principles. In Hodum and Harrison's view, 'It is not realistic to expect that negative effects of various techniques or treatments will be perceived before they have affected owl populations, perhaps severely ... The owl is a long-lived species and there may be substantial time lags in perceived population responses to forest fragmentation' 8. For a comparison of the B.C. and Pacific Northwest spotted owl stories, see George Hoberg, 'Distinguishing Learning from Other Sources of Policy Change: The Case of Forestry in the Pacific Northwest,' paper presented to Annual Meeting of the American Political Science Association, 1998.

92 According to the company, the strongest form of variable retention (based on the assumption that 70 per cent of forest in the zone would never be logged) would apply only in an 'old-growth zone' of about 100,000 hectares, about one-fifth of the total area of old growth controlled by the company. The shift in approaches would be phased in over five years. Over the next ten years, the company anticipated that its allowable annual cut would fall by 8 per cent, a rather small drop considering that the coastal industry is, in any event, in the midst of 'falldown,' a multidecade regression to long-run harvest levels premised on smaller second-growth forests. The company said it would 'increase conservation of old growth on its BC tenures by approximately 20% over what it would have been otherwise,' but gave no indication of what assumptions the 'otherwise' was based upon. See MacMillan Bloedel, 'The Forest Project Backgrounder,' 10 June 1998, at www.mbltd.com/enviro/forest project.

93 Murray Edelman, *Constructing the Political Spectacle* (Chicago: University of Chicago Press, 1988).

94 See 'MB's New Way of Logging Spares Old Growth,' *Vancouver Sun*, 4 Dec. 1998; and 'Foresters Warm to New Methods,' *Vancouver Sun*, 29 May 1999. By mid-1999, however, Weyerhaeuser's takeover of MacMillan Bloedel was raising concerns about the continuation of this initiative and the company's Clayoquot Sound initiatives. See 'U.S. Giant Urged to Honour Environmental Deals,' *Vancouver Sun*, 22 June 1999.

95 See, e.g., 'Clark Government Axes 159 Environment Jobs,' *Vancouver Sun*, 28 May 1999; and Tom Burgess, 'Wildlife Programs in Crisis: An Open Letter to Those Concerned about B.C.'s Wildlife' (1999).

96 Urquhart, this volume, Chapter 11.

97 Lawson, Levy, and Sandberg, this volume, Chapter 10.

98 Howlett and Rayner, this volume, Chapter 2.

99 Steven Kennett, *New Directions for Public Land Law,* 23, quoting Scott W. Hardt, 'Federal Land Management in the Twenty-First Century: From Wise Use to Wise Stewardship,' *Harvard Environmental Law Review* 18, 1994, 393.

100 Hardt, 'Federal Land Management,' 398, quoted by Kennett, *New Directions for Public Land Law,* 23.

101 For a review of proposals and trial runs, see Burda, 'Ecosystem-Based Community Forestry in British Columbia,' 82–94.

102 See, e.g., the argument for a double veto system made by Michael M'Gonigle in 'Developing Sustainability: A Native/Environmentalist Prescription for Third-Level Government,' *BC Studies* 84, 1989–90, 65–99.

103 Steven A. Primm and Tim W. Clark, 'The Greater Yellowstone Policy Debate: What Is the Policy Problem,' *Policy Sciences* 29 (1996) 156.

104 Ibid., 156–8.

105 Ibid., 162.

106 See, e.g., Katja Power, 'Managing the Canadian Forest for Biodiversity,' *Global Biodiversity* 7(4), 1998, 19–23.

Chapter Five

The Canadian Forest Industry: The Impacts of Globalization and Technological Change

Roger Hayter and John Holmes

Over the past two decades or so, Canada's forest industry has experienced profound volatility. All-time record levels of production and profits in the late 1970s and late 1980s separate prolonged periods of downsizing and financial losses. This volatility has been especially pronounced in the long-established, dominant forest regions of the country, none more so than British Columbia. Thus, following the boom of the 1970s, which stimulated a major round of capital investment, by the early 1980s, B.C.'s forest industry was in the throes of the biggest recession since the 1930s. Between 1981 and 1984 the industry lost $1.1 billion, more than 10,000 workers were laid-off, and debt-equity ratios were unusually high.[1] Following the boom of the late 1980s, which more than restored production levels, recaptured many of the jobs lost, and created profits (1987–9) of over $3 billion, fortunes again fluctuated alarmingly. Indeed, in 1994 and 1995 staggering losses of $1.3 billion each year were recorded, and in 1998 the provincial forest industry remained mired in crisis, its costs higher than its revenues. Mills closed and the number of jobs declined again.

These fluctuating fortunes cannot be regarded as the 'normal' ups and downs of the business cycle. Rather, the vulnerability of Canada's industrial forest economy is structural and rests on its evolution as a large volume exporter of a narrow range of low value commodities, specifically, lumber, pulp, and newsprint. During the 'Fordist' long boom of the 1950s and 1960s, the impressive expansion of the forest industry was predicated on access to high-quality, cheap timber and the massive demands of the industrial powers, especially the United States, for lumber, pulp, and newsprint. The 1970s proved to be a turning-point. In particular, Canada's advantage of access to plentiful high-quality, long-fibre softwood has been reduced by continual exploitation, by the increasingly important, much cheaper supplies of wood fibre from plantations in other countries, by technologies that have economically extended the use of hardwoods in wood-processing and pulp- and paper-making, and by increased self-sufficiency in Canada's major market, the United States. In addition, as markets for forest products become more differentiated, demands for standardized lumber, pulp, and newsprint have levelled off or even declined. Moreover, the revolution in micro-electronic technology has thoroughly implicated the forest industry with respect to improvements in efficiency, product development, quality control, skill requirements, and organization. Finally, international environmentalism has become stridently critical of large-scale industrial forestry in Canada, especially in British Columbia.

Within the context of vastly changed competitive conditions, the Canadian forest industry has sought to 'restructure.' In practice, restructuring is closely associated with the idea of 'flexible operating cultures' that are (variously) based on the realization of productivity gains and the achievement of greater product values and diversity. Yet, current problems in the Canadian forest industry, most notably in British Columbia, indicate that the restructuring initiated following the recession of the 1980s is either incomplete and/or in confusion because of the ambiguous meanings of flexibility, especially by whether flexibility means giving priority to cost minimization or to value maximization.

In any event, policy recommendations for restructuring in the late 1990s were remarkably similar to pleas made already in the early 1980s (and before). In the case of British Columbia, for example, a recent report sponsored by the B.C. Science Council argues that the forest industry is still 'locked-in' to a commodity structure and that its future viability depends on a stronger commitment to innovation.[2] Similar sentiments had been expressed in another provincial government report fifteen years previously,[3] as well as by other studies.[4] For Canada as a whole, Smith and Lessard's[5] detailed arguments, made in 1970, for more research and development as the basis for greater innovation in the Canadian forest sector have since been reinforced by several other studies.[6] However, for the Canadian forest industry innovation has proven to be a difficult challenge.

This chapter addresses the 'structural crisis' facing the Canadian forest industry in the current period of globalization. In particular, we seek to understand the scope and limitations of contemporary restructuring. An important focus in our argument is an explanation of why the forest industry has been slow in shifting towards more innovation-based and flexible producers who can provide a diverse range of higher value products – along the lines suggested by a battery of studies over the past thirty years (from Smith and Lessard in 1970 to Binkley in 1995). From this perspective, the Free Trade Agreement (FTA) between Canada and the United States in 1989 and its subsequent extension as the North American Free Trade Agreement (NAFTA) has not been helpful.

Our point of departure is the 'Innisian' observation that the structure of Canada's forest industry has been fundamentally shaped by the trade needs of superpowers. In particular, the large-scale industrialization of Canada's forests in the twentieth century developed for the most part in accordance with the strictures of (North American) continentalism which cast the Canadian forest sector as a staple (commodity) supplier of U.S. industrial and consumer needs. At the beginning of the 1990s, Pacific Rim markets, especially Japan, grew rapidly for Canada, but mainly for coastal B.C. producers, but then they declined precipitously in the mid-1990s. European markets are of less (and generally declining) importance. First and foremost, forest product structures and trade need to be seen as an exercise in continentalism. Moreover, it is important to recognize that, for Canada, the nature and implications of continentalism extend well beyond the issue of free trade.

Continentalism and the Forest Staple: Historical Perspective

In Canada, even before Confederation, the debate about development invariably engages the proponents of continentalism, whose priority is linkages with the United States, against the critics of continentalism – the proponents of nationalism – whose priority is linkages within Canada. The pros and cons of continentalism, or 'reciprocity' as it used to be called, has been a recurring theme in federal elections throughout our history. Indeed, it was the failure of initial attempts at continentalism or 'reciprocity' between the United States and Canada (then comprised of Ontario and Quebec) that encouraged the remaining British colonies to federate, in 1867, to solve their economic problems – for in 1866 the United States abrogated the reciprocity treaty of 1854. Following Confederation, Prime Minister John A. Macdonald's Conservatives failed to obtain a free trade agreement with the United States, but they subsequently (1879) won an election on the promise of the National Policy. This policy, initially on the basis of the establishment of a tariff on manufactured goods, and subsequently through the stimulation of agricultural settlement in the west and the building of transcontinental railroads and related infrastructure, sought to establish the economic and political integrity of Canada. Nevertheless, Canada's relations with the United States remained in the forefront, and in 1911 the federal election was again fought largely on the basis of a proposed free trade treaty with the United States, and again, the Conservative party, representing the forces of nationalism, won. Consequently, this particular free trade proposal was rejected.

It may be argued that the 1911 election represented a watershed for the forces of nationalism. That is, the election result was a victory for the policy of the past rather than of the future. Certainly, the pattern of staple exports differed before and after 1911. Thus, the exploitation of fur from the eighteenth century, the square timber trade from the 1770s to the 1860s, and the export of wheat, the principal engine of growth for the Canadian economy during the 1890s and early decades of the twentieth century, were developed on east–west lines – stimulated by demands in the United Kingdom and other European markets. The fish harvest also served these markets. In addition, these staples were competitive with, or at least alternatives to, ones available from U.S. sources. Thus, Canada's trade in squared timber, which supplied masts for British shipping, developed quickly following the American War of Independence and the Napoleonic Wars which, respectively, restricted British imports of timber from the United States and the Baltic region.[7] In the case of wheat, Canadian and U.S. producers continue to compete for offshore markets.[8]

The extraordinarily rapid industrialization of the U.S. economy inevitably led to demands for Canadian resources, and during the twentieth century, the export of Canadian staples has typically complemented U.S. economic growth. In this regard, soon after the 1911 election, newsprint, pulp, and softwood lumber became the key staple industries on the forefront of north–south continental integration.

Principles of Continentalism

If close integration between the Canadian and U.S. economies was inevitable, the particular geographic, technological, and institutional characteristics associated with continentalism involved choice and questions of policy. Continentalism is not simply a matter of the integration between the Canadian and U.S. economies. Rather, continentalism implies – for Canada – a distinct model of international relations, a distinct set of economic beliefs, and a specific spatial division of labour between the two countries. Continentalism assumes the political hegemony of the United States, and Canada's integration with U.S. defence planning; economically, it means a commitment, to free trade, the free flow of investment, and antagonism towards any kind of political support of economic sovereignty; and in terms of the spatial division of labour, continentalism casts Canada in the role of resource supplier to the U.S. industrial machine.

Defined in these terms, continentalism has long shaped attitudes and policies in both the United States and Canada; it became firmly established during the Fordist long boom of the 1950s and 1960s.[9] From the U.S. side, continentalism was confirmed or at least implied by the Paley report of 1952, which stressed the threat of communism to global security and the need for the United States to import low cost and 'strategic' raw materials to meet its political and economic obligations. Canada was regarded as a particularly desirable source of a wide variety of resources, including newsprint which at that time was considered a 'strategic' commodity. The United States also introduced or retained zero or low tariffs on resource imports while maintaining protection for its secondary manufacturing sector.

For its part, the Canadian federal government had been quietly lobbying for continentalism since at least the 1940s, and both federal and provincial governments were keen to establish Canada as a 'stable and secure' resource supplier. In practice, Canadian economic policy continued its tradition of emphasizing staple exports, principally by subsidizing infrastructure, often on a massive scale, selling or leasing resources to investors on a large scale at a low cost or 'rent,' and by facilitating the entry of foreign capital.[10] Moreover, with few exceptions, such as the log export restrictions first introduced in the late nineteenth century, staple exports are not restricted and are not used to promote domestic manufacturing. Commodities such as oil, coal, natural gas, copper, zinc, gold, uranium, and iron ore have typically been exported with little or no processing.

The failure of Canada to develop a major export-oriented secondary manufacturing sector, which would have been competitive with U.S.-based industrial strengths, is also entirely consistent with continentalism.[11] Canada does have significant automobile exports to the United States. Yet, these exports were created by the 1965 Auto Pact which constituted a rationalization of the industry along continental lines and under the control of the 'Big 3' U.S. auto makers. Other secondary manufacturing industries have typically long been dominated by foreign, especially U.S.-owned branch plants serving Canada's domestic market. Indeed, from the perspective of foreign investment, Canadian economic policies, including the National Policy, have been almost invariably strongly continentalist in both resource and secondary manufacturing sectors.

The Evolution of the Canadian Forest Staple

As Canada's most important staple of the twentieth century, the forest staple offers a quintessential example of what Clark-Jones (1987) terms 'continental resource capitalism.' A few caveats aside, continentalism has been the guiding principle shaping the location, structure, and performance of the Canadian forest staple virtually from its origins. The staple is dominated by commodity production, and these commodities have traditionally enjoyed free access to the United States. The staple has been consistently open to foreign ownership, and U.S. ownership has long been a significant feature. Within the Canadian forest industry attitudes are thoroughly continental: the United States is almost invariably seen as part of the 'domestic' business environment.

Indeed, Canada's pulp and paper industry has been on the leading edge of continentalism. Between 1900 and 1920, this industry expanded its output more than ten-fold from 181,000 to 1,902,000 tonnes.[12] During this period the industry changed from a small domestic industry, with 79 per cent of its output sold locally, to a large-scale export-oriented industry, with 69 per cent of its output exported, largely to the United States. The basic commodity mix of the contemporary pulp and paper industry was essentially established already by 1920: in both 1920 and 1987 about 75 per cent of the industry comprised newsprint and market pulp, most of which was exported.

The basis for the growth of the pulp and paper industry in the critical decades at the beginning of the twentieth century was the escalating U.S. demand at a time when American softwood forests were being rapidly depleted. This demand stimulated the 'northwards migration' of the pulp and paper industry; first, by the introduction of restrictions on raw log exports by Canadian governments between 1900 and 1910, and then by the American decision to remove the tariff, a decision encouraged by newspaper interests within the United States. Since 1911 there has been no U.S. tariff on imports of Canadian newsprint, and by 1913 the tariff on pulp (bleached or unbleached) had been removed, and this, too, has not been reversed. In contrast, tariffs on paper products, such as (cut) printing and writing papers and envelopes remained relatively high; in the case of envelopes, the tariff was reduced during the 1930s and 1940s but it was increased substantially after 1947. Such tariffs, however, have clearly helped constrain the Canadian industry to a commodity orientation on newsprint and pulp.

The situation with respect to wood products is broadly similar. In 1909 the Dingley Tariff reduced the U.S. tariff on imported dimension lumber from $2 to $1.25 per 1,000 board feet, and in 1913 this tariff was eliminated. Until then the markets for lumber had been relatively diverse, as city and railway construction and Prairie settlement generated substantial domestic demands, while a variety of European and Asian markets were served as well, especially from British Columbia.[13] By the 1920s, however, the United States had become the dominant market for Canadian lumber. Although the United States did reimpose tariffs in the early 1930s, during which time Canada entered a Commonwealth Preference Scheme, a 1935 reciprocity treaty between Canada and the United States soon led to the elimination of the tariff on dimension lumber. As with pulp and paper, tariffs on more processed wood products remained, and lumber exports to the United States have typically been of a low value, standardized nature.

Plywood was the only important forestry commodity not granted tariff-free access to the U.S. market. Both the United States and Canada maintained tariff protection around plywood which principally served domestic markets in both countries. Much of Canada's plywood capacity, however, was U.S. owned.

Within the context of an established free trade regime already in place, the structure of the forest industry changed little during the long boom of Fordism. Since 1950, softwood lumber, newsprint, and pulp, especially kraft pulp, all experienced impressive growth (Table 5.1). Kraft pulp was the fastest growing commodity at this time, achieving a per annum growth rate of over 10 per cent between 1950 and 1970 when over 20 new, large-scale mills were built in British Columbia alone. National growth rates for lumber and newsprint were a lot lower, but the absolute increases in production were substantial, and rates of growth in British Columbia were much higher than the national average.[14] Export-sales ratios were consistently high. In 1971, for example, over 85 per cent of Canada's newsprint production was exported, as was almost 67 per cent of Canada's lumber. For these commodities, it is hard to underestimate the importance of the United States as a market in this

Table 5.1 Production levels and growth of selected forest products commodities in Canada, 1950–1970

	Quantity		Average Annual Increase In	
	1950	1970	Quantity[4]	Growth (%)[4]
Newsprint (tonnes)	5,279,000	8,607,000	163,000	2.4
Chemical pulp (tonnes)	3,265,000	9,975,000	338,000	5.9
Kraft pulp (tonnes)[1]	1,054,000	6,707,000	295,000	10.3
Paperboard (tonnes)	771,000	1,838,000	20,000	5.1
Lumber (mfbm)[2]	6,553	11,185	261	3.0
Softwood plywood (M.sq.ft.)[3]	259,000	1,880,000	95,000	9.8

[1]Kraft pulp tonnage also included in chemical pulp output
[2]MFBM: million foot board measure
[3]M.sq.ft.: million square feet, 3/8″ base
[4]Calculated from 'best fit' straight line
Source: Statistics Canada and Canadian Pulp and Paper Association.

period (Table 5.2). Plywood production also grew rapidly in this period but without significant U.S. markets.

The substantial export-oriented growth achieved by the forest industry after 1950 was based on the twin pillars of a Fordist philosophy of production, namely, mass production and Taylorized labour relations.[15] Thus, the three main forest commodity industries were all dominated by large-scale, highly specialized mills producing homogeneous products with few variations. There were hundreds of small sawmills, but by 1970 many of them were closed down, especially in British Columbia. Softwood plywood factories were also committed to producing large volumes of a very limited range of products. The large mills of the time relied on highly specialized (or dedicated) machinery to realize internal economies of scale; the principle of cost minimization was paramount and maximizing 'through-put' (volume) per shift rather than maximizing the value of converted logs underlay production philosophy. Downtime, whether for holidays or repairs, was considered economically wasteful, since it left fixed cost capital and plant idle.

Taylorism, or scientific management, went hand-in-glove with mass production as the dominant form of work organization. Under Taylorism, job tasks were sharply delineated, highly specialized, and preferably simple tasks. 'Blue collar' workers, who performed manual tasks, and

Table 5.2 The Canadian forest sector: Production and exports

Year	Softwood lumber			Newsprint			Wood pulp		
	Production (1,000 t)	Exports (%)	Exports to U.S. (%)	Production (1,000 m³)	Exports (%)	Exports to U.S. (%)	Production (1,000 t)	Exports (%)	Exports to U.S. (%)
1951	5,516	93.3	86.7	14,410	55.3	34.0	2,798	93.0	71.5
1960	6,088	92.2	84.3	17,862	58.8	47.2	6,046	92.4	54.8
1970	7,996	91.8	78.0	25,449	68.0	52.8	8,393	85.8	40.9
1980	8,625	88.6	71.0	43,524	66.7	51.6	9,331	82.4	37.9
1986	9,202	87.9	72.4	51,860	73.3	64.2	10,008	83.4	36.8
1989	9,640	88.1	70.3	57,903	69.2	55.1	9,305	82.6	38.9
1990	9,068	88.2	70.8	53,696	69.1	53.1			

Source: Selected Forestry Statistics Canada 1991 and Council of Forest Industries.

'white collar' managers, who provided the thinking and supervision, were sharply segmented as well. This philosophy of labour relations, along with the principle of seniority, became institutionalized within the unionized collective bargaining of the early 1950s in the Canadian forest industry. Successive collective agreements gave workers continually improving wage and non-wage benefits, as well as a structured labour market in which individual rights and responsibilities were protected and respected. In return, management retained control of a disciplined, specialized workforce that provided the basis for productivity gains in the use of specialized machinery.

The large, export-oriented mills that dominated the Canadian forest industry were often foreign owned, and export patterns have been buttressed by high levels of foreign, especially U.S. investment. The early days of the Canadian pulp and paper industry were fueled by U.S. equity investment involving both forest product firms and newspaper publishers such as the *Chicago Tribune* and the *New York Times*. In 1929, for example, U.S.-owned mills, controlled 38 per cent of Canadian newsprint production and by 1933 this was 51 per cent.[16] U.S. firms and entrepreneurs also participated in the early development of Canada's lumber industry, although without the same implications for foreign control at this time.[17] After 1950, with much encouragement from Canadian governments, foreign investors, led by U.S. multinationals, participated extensively in Canada's forest staple both by investing in new plants and acquiring existing plants (Table 5.3).

By 1977, on the basis of the conventional yardstick, in which control is determined by at least 50 per cent ownership, foreign control varied from 29.9 per cent of capacity (lumber industry) to 44.1 per cent of capacity (pulp and paper) at the national level. If foreign control is calculated on the basis of foreign corporations having at least 25 per cent ownership, then the level of foreign control increases by 5 per cent to 10 per cent in each of the main forest product commodities.[18]

It is also worth noting that, while foreign investment in the Canadian forest staple has long roots, by the late 1960s a few Canadian based forest product companies had established international operations, especially in the United States. If such firms serve as a reminder that the Canadian forest industry cannot be solely characterized as a hinterland, the basic point is that within this sector a central proposition of continentalism has long been met: the free flow of equity investment between Canada and the United States with the dominant locus of control lying in the U.S. metropole. It should also be noted that the trade and international

Table 5.3 Degree (%) of foreign control of selected forest products in Canada, 1977

Commodity	Foreign controlled 50% equity	Foreign controlled 25% equity
Newsprint[a]	39	46
Chemical pulps[a]	50	not calculated
Lumber[b]	28	38
Softwood plywood[b]	46	49
Tissue papers[a]	78	not calculated

[a]Based on corporate and plant capacities as reported in *Lockwoods Pulp and Paper Directory*
[b]Based on corporate and plant production figures as reported in the *Forest Industries Magazine*, July 1979
Source: R. Hayter, 'The Evolution and Structure of the Canadian Forest Products Sector: An Assessment of the Role of Foreign Ownership and Control,' in *Fennia* 163, 1985, 439–50.

investment flows are interdependent; to a significant degree Canadian exports from subsidiary operations are destined for affiliated mills.

Transforming Fordism within a Revised Continentalist Regime

The winds of change began to blow through the Canadian forest industry in the 1970s. Timber supply limits were reached across the country and particularly in British Columbia, where growth had been greatest during Fordism. The 'fall-down effect,' the reduction in timber flow as harvesting shifts from old-growth to managed forests, had been publicly recognized late in the decade. In fact, Canada was losing its cost advantages – which were rooted in natural endowment – to the faster growing forest supply regions of the 'South,' most notably the U.S. South as well as developing countries such as Brazil and Chile.[19] Technological change, which a century previously had favoured northern softwoods, now threatened the economic viability of these same regions. Demand and efficiency changed, too. Indeed, despite its status as a 'mature' sector, technological change in forestry was speeding up rather than slowing down, creating all kinds of possibilities to improve efficiency and quality and enhance product differentiation. Moreover, by the 1970s the Canadian public were demanding a much greater range of values from the forest resource beyond those associated with industrial forestry.[20]

For the forest industry, these wider demands, spearheaded by the rapidly growing environmental movement, have meant a reduction of timber supply and increased costs of logging, trends that have been especially evident in British Columbia.[21]

Since the 1970s, commodity production in the Canadian forest industry has been caught in a growing cost–price squeeze. Costs have increased relentlessly, while prices have fluctuated. To an important degree, commodity production was 'saved' by a declining Canadian dollar which in the late 1990s reached historic lows. Exchange rates are an extremely vulnerable line of defence, however, and in British Columbia the signs are that this defence is already inadequate. Concomitantly, long-run trends towards higher costs, admittedly offset by a declining dollar and more variegated demands, have been complicated by a series of increasingly severe recessions in the industry (1971, 1976, 1981–5, 1993–6), the energy crises of the 1970s, a period of stagflation (early 1980s), the onset of U.S. protectionism towards lumber (since 1983), and selected European boycotts (from the late 1980s), not to mention unusually sharp booms in the late 1970s and late 1980s.

Nevertheless, the central pillars of Fordist production – the mass production of homogeneous commodities and Taylorized labour relations – have been increasingly undermined in the Canadian forest industry, just as they have in other mature industries. The productivity gains associated with Fordism have simply become more difficult, if not impossible to achieve. For the Canadian forest industry, the crisis in Fordism has also been associated with growing vulnerability in U.S. markets. As Fordism has waned, continentalism has been under revision.

Increased Market Vulnerability

During Fordism, the Canadian forest industry was always vulnerable to business cycles in the United States after all, export ratios were consistently very high, and most exports went to the United States. In more recent decades, however, this market vulnerability has worsened because, given continued high export sales ratios and reliance on the U.S. market, Canada's share of U.S. markets has either declined (as in the case of pulp and paper) or it has been put under restrictions (as in the case of lumber).

The United States continues to be the dominant market for Canadian forest products (Table 5.2). In 1990, the output exported still amounted to 88.2 per cent in the case of newsprint, 69.1 per cent in the case of softwood lumber, and 82.6 per cent in the case of pulp. At the same time, by 1990, the *relative* share of exports in all these commodities to the U.S. market had declined. This trend has been especially marked in pulp and paper. With respect to pulp, Canada's share of the U.S. market has always been minor. Even so, since 1951 Canada's share has fallen from 10 per cent to about half that amount. In the case of newsprint, Canada's share of the U.S. market has fallen from a dominant 79 per cent of the total market to just over half – a still important, but consistently declining share. With respect to softwood lumber, Canada's share of the U.S. market traditionally has been in the 20 per cent to 30 per cent range, important without being dominating.

The United States has a substantial lumber industry of its own based in the Pacific Northwest and, increasingly, in the South. To retain their share of the U.S. market Canadian lumber producers have had to maintain high levels of efficiency. In this regard, it has been convincingly argued that the increase in Canada's share of the U.S. lumber market that occurred in the early 1980s, that is, during a recession, primarily occurred because of the superior productivity of Canadian mills in association with the falling value of the Canadian dollar.[22] Nevertheless, these arguments were not successful in preventing the imposition of U.S. protectionist measures on Canada's lumber industry.

Canadian producers have become increasingly vulnerable in U.S. markets with the emergence of the United States as a continental, possibly global, producer of low cost wood fibre. This shift in cost advantage is most marked in the pulp and paper industry. In the case of the newsprint, average costs for a sample of existing mills in selected countries and regions reveals that, in 1990, the U.S. South and West were the lowest cost newsprint producing regions, enjoying significant advantages over Canada and even more so over Sweden and Finland, the traditional optimal locations (Table 5.4). The U.S. South has a huge advantage in wood costs. In 1990, this amounted to Can$40 per finished tonne over Canadian producers, while Scandinavian costs were more than double those of producers in the U.S. South. U.S. regions have substantial advantages in terms of distribution costs.

To some extent, Canada and the Scandinavian countries offset their higher wood and delivery costs with lower chemical costs. Whatever energy cost advantages these regions enjoyed in relation to the United States, however, have been eroded by investment in more energy-intensive pulping methods. In Canada, labour costs accounted for 27 per cent of total mill level costs in 1990, compared with 17 per cent to 20

Table 5.4 Delivered Costs (Can$) of newsprint: principal producing regions

| Costs | 1990 Delivered cost per finished tonne | | | | |
	U.S. South	U.S. West	Canada	Sweden	Finland
Fibre	111	149	149	219	298
Chemicals	29	36	17	7	5
Energy	98	85	92	114	108
Labour	88	71	124	87	72
Other mill costs	109	80	82	104	75
Corp. & selling	20	15	33	14	36
Delivery	32	52	86	83	96
Total	$487	$488	$538	$628	$690

Source: Forest Sector Advisory Council, *Newsprint Cost Study, 1986–1990* (Vancouver: Price Waterhouse, 1991).

per cent in the United States, 15 per cent in Sweden, and less than 13 per cent in Finland. Yet wage rates per hour in Canada are slightly lower than in the United States, and the difference in labour costs per finished tonne is almost entirely the result of differences in labour productivity. A finished tonne of newsprint required 3.6 operating hours to produce in Canada, but only 2.5 hours in the U.S. South and 1.8 hours in the U.S. West. Canada's lower labour productivity, in turn, reflects use of smaller (and older) paper-making machines and traditional labour-intensive pulping technologies.

The situation for market pulp is similar (Table 5.5). The United States has decisive cost advantages over Canadian producers, and in fact, in this industry the B.C. coast was the highest cost producing region in the world. At the same time, developments in recycling technology and emerging environmental concerns, which in many U.S. states have been reinforced by law, have further shifted location advantage to the United States where supplies of waste paper are more economical. Average costs in lumber manufacturing are also higher in British Columbia than in the U.S. South. Moreover, in British Columbia since 1990, higher stumpage charges and new harvesting regulations have pushed up costs considerably, to the point where, in 1998, even the historically low Canadian dollar is not able to sustain viability. For lumber producers, whose exports to the United States have been hit by combinations of export taxes, higher stumpage, and, since 1997, a quota arrangement, these additional costs have been particularly punitive.

Table 5.5 Delivered costs (Can$) of market pulp: principal producing regions

1990 Delivered Cost Per Finished Tonne

Costs	U.S. South	U.S. West	Eastern Canada	Sweden	Finland	B.C. Interior	B.C. Coast
Fibre	138	1204	260	403	460	201	222
Chemicals	79	56	64	54	63	61	61
Energy	24	39	31	14	9	37	59
Labour	70	72	90	102	64	101	148
Other mill costs	62	80	73	58	47	147	138
Corp. & selling	14	17	26	17	16	9	37
Delivery	68	69	64	60	57	97	70
Total	$455	$537	$608	$708	$716	$653	$735

Source: Forest Sector Advisory Council, *Newsprint Cost Study, 1986–1990* (Vancouver: Price Waterhouse, 1991).

What about Free Trade?

The combination of declining market share in the United States and the emergence of U.S. protectionism suggests that as far as the forest staple is concerned the limits to continentalism have been reached. For Canada, the key requirement of the FTA and NAFTA was access to the U.S. market[23] but the forest industry has long had this access, at least as far as commodity production is concerned. Indeed, the Canadian forest industry was among the leading supporters of the Free Trade Agreement with the United States and the North American Free Trade Agreement in order to preserve this access, including support of a trade dispute mechanism, which the forest industry thought vital to its interest. In practice, neither the FTA in general nor the trade dispute mechanism in particular has done little to dissuade protectionism in the United States, and the softwood lumber agreement of 1996 represents the non-tariff barrier considered the antithesis of free trade.

What the Canadian forest industry (and Canadian governments) failed to appreciate was that the FTA (and NAFTA) confirmed continentalism, and that the latter is not the same as free trade. From the U.S. perspective, continentalism implies free trade in association with the role of the United States as hegemonic power, where Canada has the subservient role as resource supplier and subcontractor, as needed. It may be that U.S. protectionism regarding lumber is neither in the U.S. nor Canadian interests. But such an argument misses the point that the United States has hegemony and has decided to exercise its power in relation to Canadian lumber which happens to be largely concentrated in British Columbia. The evolution of the softwood lumber dispute has been messy and complicated.[24] Suffice it to say that the United States has effectively protected its own industry and has gained substantial leverage in shaping forest policy in Canada, especially in British Columbia. The ramifications of this leverage have still to be worked out.

As Canada's forest product exports to the United States have become more vulnerable, some long-standing U.S. corporate ties have been severed, while others have been created. Since the early 1980s at least three U.S. forest product corporations have sold their substantial and long-established Canadian subsidiaries: Canadian International Paper (CIP), Crown Zellerbach Canada (CZ), and British Columbia Forest Products. Both CIP (in the 1920s) and CZ (in 1917) had been established in the early years of the northwards migration of the newsprint industry. In effect, these sales were stimulated by the need to generate cash to modernize capital-intensive facilities within the United States, to partially replace or reduce imports from Canada, and to help fund growth outside of the continent. Other U.S. multinationals, recently exemplified by Weyerhaeuser's acquisition of MacMillan Bloedel (MB), have expanded operations in Canada.

Also revealing of how corporate restructuring is modifying continentalism is the sale, in late 1991, by the *New York Times* (and its American partner, Kimberly-Clark) of its interests in the Spruce Falls newsprint mill, thus ending its sixty-year relationship. A decade earlier, in 1980, the *Times* entered a joint venture with Myllykoski, a Finnish firm, to invest in a paper machine in Maine. This machine came on stream in 1982, one of the first in North America to produce supercalendered uncoated groundwood papers, a high quality paper developed by the Finns and used in magazine publishing. This mill was also the first U.S. source affiliated with the *Times*. As a result of a strike in its Canadian mills, in 1976 the *Times* bought paper from Myllykoski, and because of the superior quality of this paper the *Times* continued to buy it.[25] By 1991, the *Times* had expanded its U.S. supply base to a point where it no longer needed the Spruce Falls mill (which has been downsized and is now owned by employees). In this case, Finnish innovativeness in papermaking (and lack of such innovativeness in Canada), as well as declining cost advantages in Canada, combined to reduce this particular continental link.

Restructuring and the Search for Flexibility

In the context of the new economic environment of the 1970s, the sources of Fordism's former strengths and stability – dedicated production technology and highly structured labour agreements enshrined in law – became the source of its rigidities. A change to more flexible production methods and labour markets became necessary. The transformation from the Fordist model of mass-production to more flexible models of production, however, has been difficult, painful, and remains incomplete. Indeed, in some fundamental respects, flexibility is an ambiguous imperative. In particular, the forest industry had difficulty in clarifying whether it is 'value' or 'cost' that is the prime motivation to restructuring. In the old Fordist model, cost was unequivocally paramount, but in the new flexible regime product differentiation and value claim primacy. Moreover, whether restructuring has been dominated by cost minimization or value maximization the search for labour market flexibility has proven contentious.

Labour Flexibility

In response to problems of competitiveness created by technological change, market uncertainty, and recessions, a consistent theme in forest product restructuring, especially since the mid-1980s, has been the search for employment flexibility. This search has itself been flexible. On the one hand, flexibility implies the direct replacement of the Taylorist system and its strong demarcation of work and management functions, with multiskilled workers who participate in the management as well as the operation of plants. For this core group of 'functionally flexible' employees, adversarial labour relations are replaced with teamwork, quality circles, and skills widening, while wages and other benefits are related to merit as well as to seniority.[26] This kind of employment flexibility is closely associated with the idea of a 'high performance organization' which seeks to fully develop the intellectual as well as manual skills of high paid workforces in continuing efforts to increase productivity and product quality.[27] On the other hand, the search for flexibility is also associated with subcontracting-out functions to lower paid workforces, the use of part-time labour, and in general to the employment of numerically flexible workforces that can be readily adjusted to the swings of the business cycle.

However defined, employment flexibility inevitably implies smaller, 'leaner' operations in which employees are responsible for a much wider range of functions than associated with Taylorist arrangements. Moreover, Canadian forest product firms have found labour flexibility to be much easier to develop in new mills than at existing sites where Taylorism is deeply engrained. A classic example of the new forms of flexible work arrangements is provided by the Whitecourt newsprint mill in Alberta.[28] This new mill started up in 1990 with a non-union workforce of 200 employees who are responsible for operating and maintaining a single newsprint machine and three pulp lines. There is very little job demarcation, and functional flexibility is further promoted by a skills-based pay system. The operation is extremely 'lean' as wood fibre is purchased from outside suppliers and marketing contracted out to an established forest product firm, in stark contrast to the big integrated mills that evolved under Fordism.

Employment flexibility need not imply a non-union workforce. The new sawmill at Chemainus, British Columbia, for example, was completed in 1985 with formal agreement from the union to team work principles. In achieving this flexibility bargain, however, it is important to bear in mind that the firm, MacMillan Bloedel, had 'the hammer.' The previous mill at Chemainus had been closed in 1982, and after two years the firm was no longer obligated to rehire the old workforce according to principles of seniority (the most senior rehired first). Basically, MB built an entirely new mill on the condition that the union accepted flexibility. There are far fewer employees than in the old mill, down from 650 to 155, although several functions, such as planing and kiln drying, are subcontracted out and the suppliers are unionized. In fact, the Chemainus mill has been extremely profitable, and since 1993 union wages have been supplemented by a bonus.

But throughout Canada, the shift to employment flexibility in the major commodity industries has been much more difficult than the examples of Whitecourt or even Chemainus imply. In these established industries, employment flexibility has been primarily sought 'in situ,' that is at existing sites, where Taylorist union agreements have long been in place. In in situ contexts, flexibility is interpreted by workers as a direct attack on the basic union principles of job demarcation and seniority which are there to provide dignity and stability in the workplace. In practice, job flexibility has to be negotiated. In the case of the Powell River mill in British Columbia, these negotiations have been ad hoc, requiring quid pro quo arrangements that have themselves been contentious.[29]

Flexibility bargains have been further compromised because they have typically been sought at a time of considerable employment downsizing. Since 1980, for example, the Powell River mill has reduced its number of employees from 2,400 to about 800, and mills in central and eastern Canada have experienced similar losses with profound consequences for communities and households.[30] To a considerable degree, technological change and rationalization have been the immediate cause of job loss. If job loss might be associated with increased employer bargaining power, it is not a conducive context in which to simultaneously promote flexibility which workers equate with further job loss and the granting of concessions over rights legally won over previous decades. The tendency of firms to increasingly contract out more functions has also been seen as an attempt to reduce costs (wages) and the power of unions.[31]

It is perhaps not surprising that in many cases workers have resisted shifts to flexibility, resistance that has been made effective by the legal rights enshrined in existing collective bargains. The fact is that without considerable job loss a shift to flexibility would not have been entertained. Yet, with job loss it is hard to convince workers about the ideals of the high performance organization which, at root, is based on more cooperative, 'team-oriented' attitudes. Moreover, what might be seen as multiskilling by some can be seen as multitasking or job intensification by others.

Notwithstanding worker resistance, employment flexibility is an inexorable trend across the forest products industry. Among small non-union firms, labour markets have long been extremely diverse. Flexibility is now increasing the diversity of work arrangements among large mills and firms. The attainment of flexibility in situ will likely require retirement of existing workers, but in another ten years or so employment flexibility is likely to be the norm rather than the exception. The extent to which employment flexibility emphasizes core groups of highly paid, stable, multiskilled workers or peripheral groups of low paid, often part-time workers that are readily hired and fired – and variations of these two scenarios – remains to be seen. In part, the answer depends on how product market strategies evolve.

Product Market Flexibility

The same forces encouraging employment flexibility – technological change, market differentiation, and volatile business cycles – have encouraged product market flexibility in the Canadian forest industry. In this context, two main forms can be recognized: flexible mass production and flexible specialization. Flexible mass production, much the stronger of the two shifts, retains the high volumes and economies of scale of Fordism while adopting computerized manufacturing techniques to produce a wider range of product grades in which higher quality is also achieved by more precise specifications and superior performance. Flexible specialization implies the emergence of production systems dominated by transaction among specialized small and medium-sized enterprises (SMEs). While individual SMEs are specialized, the production as a whole can flexibly respond to myriad demands that are themselves small scale and highly differentiated.

The Chemainus sawmill and the Powell River paper mill provide good examples of flexible mass production.[32] At Powell River, for example, in the 1950s and 1960s up to ten paper machines basically all manufactured a few newsprint grades destined for the U.S. market. The restructuring of the plant since the mid-1970s has left three paper machines which produce over fifty grades of paper, as well as newsprint. The plan is for the Powell River mill to become a predominantly specialty paper mill. Similarly, the computerized lumber mill at Chemainus rapidly manufactures a wide range of grades for a wide variety of markets in North America, Europe, and especially Japan.

The trend towards flexible mass production has also required large corporations to rethink their overall investment and products market strategies. Thus, the leading corporations under Fordism were typically highly vertically and horizontally integrated across all major forest products. MacMillan Bloedel for example, Canada's largest forest products corporation manufactured relatively few grades of all the major forest commodities, namely, lumber, plywood, shingle and shakes, market pulp, newsprint, and paperboard, as well as large quantities of paper boxes and folding cartons. Under the imperatives of flexibility, however, it is been too difficult for MB to produce a highly diversified range of products within each of these commodity lines. Thus, for MB restructuring in the 1980s meant divesting shingles and shakes, plywood market pulp, newsprint, and paperboard. Meanwhile, MB diversified within the solid wood and related building materials sectors. This diversification, however, will likely be arrested following Weyerhaeuser's acquisition of MB.

Complementing the shift towards flexible mass production are strategies of flexible specialization, especially in British Columbia and Quebec. In coastal British Columbia, for example, flexible specialization has been primarily represented by the emergence and strengthening of secondary, 'value added' wood-processing activities, notably remanufacturing engineered building components, millwork, and other wood produce industries.[33] The largest of these industries is remanufacturing, which utilizes lumber from the primary wood mill to manufacture a variety of specialty products such as door and window components, interior and exterior paneling, decking, and lumber of various dimensions. Remanufacturers are typically small, specialized firms that produce small batches of products under conditions of timber supply as well as market uncertainty. In contrast to the large forest products corporations the competitive advantages of small remanufacturers are based on 'substantially greater production flexibility, together with a more entrepreneurial approach and a lower overhead/labour cost structure.'[34] This flexibility is fundamentally achieved by specialization and reliance on subcontracting for particular products (of low and high value) and particular services such as sawing, dry kilning, and planing of varying degrees of sophistication. In contrast to flexible mass production, strategies of flexible specialization encourage geographic concentration or clustering of entrepreneurial firms to facilitate personal contact, subcontracting, market access, appropriate labour pools, and access to common services. The main concentration of remanufacturing firms in British Columbia, for example, is in the Vancouver metropolitan area.

In practice, the strategies of flexible mass production and flexible specialization are related, and the distinctions between them can be blurred and even arbitrary. Among the population of SMEs that comprise the remanufacturing industry of metropolitan Vancouver, for example, there are a couple of 'specialty' products branch plants owned and controlled by established large corporations. While to some extent the distinctions between flexible mass production and flexible specialization can be partly explained in terms of factors such as economies of scale, market size, and related uncertainties, firms do have choices concerning whether to 'buy or make'; that is, use the market to obtain a product or service or integrate the activity within their own firm. It is not necessarily clear which alternative is more costly and uncertain to the individual firm, and the implications for local development are also complex. It should also be recognized that making or buying decisions can raise labour issues especially if a union firm wishes to buy ('contract out') from a non-union firm or if the firm has traditionally performed the function in question in-house.

Innovation and the Limits to Product Market Flexibility

There is evidence that the shift to product market flexibility in the Canadian forestry industry has not gone far enough. Indeed, the conclusion of the recent report sponsored by the B.C. Science Council is that the provincial forest economy remains too tied to commodity production. This probably has relevance for the Canadian industry as a whole. Flexible mass production has been an important trend, but it has not developed uniformly across all commodity sectors. Even Powell River, which has pioneered numerous paper grades, still has about half its production in newsprint. Other mills have not been able to change. In kraft pulp production opportunities for differentiation are much more restricted anyway, and most of the new mills in Alberta are large-volume producers of a basic commodity – the Fordist strategy. At the same time, these new highly efficient kraft pulp mills have added to the competitive pressure on the older mills elsewhere in Canada, especially in British Columbia.

Similar observations can be made on the solid wood side. Many large-volume sawmills built in the interior of British Columbia were dedicated to a few construction grade lumber products for the U.S. market, and it has not been easy for them to adjust to a wider product mix. The Asian crisis of recent years further dampened immediate prospects for product market flexibility. Employment increased among flexibly specialized wood producers, but in absolute terms the job gains have not been dramatic.

It needs to be emphasized that strategies of flexible mass production (and flexible specialization) have primarily been based on the adoption of relatively new but still 'proven,' process-oriented technologies.[35] Canadian firms have rarely been the global pioneers of new forest products technology and even more rarely at the forefront of product developments. In this latter regard, MB's research and development of such products as Parallam®, an engineered wood beam with outside and consistent physical characteristics which can be made at any length desired, the variety of new paper grades introduced at Powell River, and Pacifica, a paper grade designed for glossy magazines specifically to be produced at Port Alberni, British Columbia, are exceptions which prove the rule. And, MB's research and development group was closed down in 1998. There are no major in-house research and development groups left in Canada's forest sector, a 'weak link' that helps to explain the sorry record of innovation by Canadian forest products firms, in contrast to Scandinavian or U.S. firms.

By limiting the scope of innovative activity primarily to one of adapting proven process technology to local conditions, the realization of product market flexibilities in Canada has inevitably been curtailed in comparison to major competitors. In the pulp and paper industry, for example, Finland has been particularly innovative in developing higher value papers such as light-weight coated papers and wood-free copy papers.[36] Elsewhere, the United States has maintained technological leadership in tissue papers and is competing with Europe in coated publication grades. In contrast, major Canadian companies have been slow to shift from low and medium value commodities such as kraft pulp and standard newsprint. The story is similar in wood products. Why is IKEA, the firm that designs and markets an enormous range of affordable largely wood-based consumer products and internationalized its operations, from Sweden and not Canada?

The Tradition of Technological Conservatism

In contrast to other advanced forest product nations, technological attitudes and choices within Canada have been conservative. The Canadian forest industry has focused on a narrow range of process technologies consistent with specialization on a limited range of bulk commodities.[37] In practice, the investment choices made by Canadian forest products firms have almost invariably emphasized 'proven' technology. Before choosing equipment Canadian buyers want to see it in operation. Moreover, technological conservatism has had big impacts on Canada's forest equipment supply industry. Relationships between forest products and equipment supply firms in Canada are 'arm's length,' there have been no systematic attempts for the two industries to mutually develop technological strengths, as has occurred in Scandinavia, for example, and Canada does not boast a single world-scale company in this industry. Indeed, Canada's forest firms traditionally have strongly lobbied for free trade in process equipment, and there has been increasing reliance on foreign-made equipment. By the 1980s, for example, imports accounted for about half of Canada's forest staple equipment needs. While the United States remains the dominant source of equipment and research and development patents in Canada, over the past two decades technology imports from Scandinavia and the European Union have increased.

In Canada, the forest industry's technological conservatism directly reflects a lack of commitment to research and development, specifically by industry. By international standards, the research and development investments are relatively underfunded, public sector funding has played an unusually important role, and risky, long-term product research and development is rare. It is well recognized by all indicators of research and development activity – research and development budgets, employment, patent activity – that Canada's efforts are much lower in per capita terms in comparison with its principal forest products competitors, the United States and the Scandinavian countries.[38] The comparisons are especially stark when limited to company or in-house research and development.

Historically, the federal government in Canada sought to compensate for the technological weaknesses of the private sector by investing in a network of public sector research and development laboratories. The government itself recognized the difficulty of transferring technology from public sector research and development to private sector users,[39] and in the early 1980s converted some public sector research and development laboratories to 'cooperative laboratories' funded by forest firms as well as the government. Yet, the purpose of both these forms of research and development is to reduce costs on an industry-wide basis.

In the 1990s there were provincial initiatives, especially in British Columbia and Quebec, to engage in forest products research and development. Unfortunately, neither cooperative nor public sector research and development programs can substitute for in-house research and development in creating firm-specific advantages, especially with respect to product innovation. Product innovation is designed to create firm-specific advantages and needs to be performed by individual firms. Product innovation, however, is critical to product diversification which, in turn, is critical if the vulnerability of the Canadian forest staple is to be reduced.

As a legacy of continentalism, however, the reluctance of forest firms in Canada is deeply rooted and results from the related impacts of the staple's foreign ownership, commodity structure, and boom-and-bust cycles. Virtually all U.S.-owned forest products firms (and equipment suppliers) in Canada have invested in in-house research and development in the United States, but only rarely in Canada. Other foreign-based corporations behave in a similar way. By relying on their parents for research and development, possibilities for similar investments are necessarily undermined. It is also often argued within Canada that concentration on standardized bulk commodities utilizing mature technology simply reduces the need for investment in sophisticated research and development programs. In addition, the susceptibility of bulk commodities for export to the business cycle and to booms and busts has also contributed to attitudes within Canada that have militated against research and development investments. In this context, the conventional argument is that during boom times in-house research and development is not needed and during busts it cannot be afforded; this argument is further reinforced by reference to the inherent uncertainty of research and development which is seen as compounding the inherent uncertainty of commodity trading. Unfortunately, available evidence suggests Canadian forest products firms have become more resistant to the idea of investing in their own research and development as a basis for innovation.

Conclusion: Innovation Is the Policy Priority

All sectors of the economy incorporate attitudes and policies towards technology and innovation. In the case of the Canadian forest sector, these attitudes and policies developed in a highly coherent way that testifies to the legitimacy of the notion of 'policy regime' as developed in this book (see Howlett, Chapter 1). Basically, the forest industry has adopted a conservative approach to technology which emphasizes the adoption of the latest, but proven, equipment in support of large-scale industrial exploitation of the forests for export. Innovation has frequently been required to ensure the effective implementation of the 'latest' technologies to meet the specific needs of site and regional conditions within Canada. Federal and provincial government policies, whatever their other differences, have been fully collaborative in the development of the sector's technological conservatism. The forest labour unions have been silent on the issue.

A combination of the capital intensiveness of the sector and highly distinctive, variable conditions has nurtured a sophisticated level of technological capability in Canada designed to effectively 'adopt' and 'adapt' technology. But Canadian firms have rarely sought to be world leaders in product development, and there has been resistance among Canadian forest products firms to the idea that they should collaborate with local equipment suppliers to ensure that these suppliers become world leaders in equipment design and export. Forest products firms have always insisted on accessing the best technology at the cheapest price regardless of source. In essence, innovation policy in the Canadian forest sector has been fundamentally shaped by a technologically dependent branch plant mentality that is the hallmark of (North American) continentalism.

Established attitudes towards innovation have proven remarkably resistant to change, despite industry-wide restructuring, the entry of significant new forces affecting the forest sector, and consistent advice encouraging more innovatory attitudes. Since 1970, an increasing number of studies, reports, and commissions, some sponsored by industry, have strongly recommended a greater commitment to innovation by the forest industry. Most of these reports suggest investment in research and development as a way of becoming more innovative. As timber costs increase, and timber availability and quality decreases, in Canada, while lower cost supplies are developed elsewhere, innovation is rightly emphasized as the key to productivity improvements. Moreover, these arguments are strongly reinforced by the new forces of environmentalism which would like to see less timber made available to industry, especially from among the remaining supplies of old growth. Similarly, growing Aboriginal land claims and access to forests could stimulate more innovatory behaviour. Admittedly, industry restructuring has revealed a growing commitment to product differentiation in the form of flexible mass production and flexible specialization. But even these trends are limited and conservative; if some provincial governments have increased levels of research and development spending, industry is now spending less on in-house programs than it did in 1970. It would appear that the forces in favour of cost minimization are greater than those of value maximization.

Unfortunately, the parameters set by government policy continue to dissuade more innovative policies. The low Canadian dollar encourages export of low value commodities and makes Canadian forests an attractive proposition for foreign investors, but it does not provide an incentive to firms within Canada to add value. Both federal and provincial governments remain committed to attracting foreign investment, including by acquisition of viable Canadian firms, despite the negative impacts of foreign investment on innovation. Meanwhile, the FTA and NAFTA, so-called free trade agreements, have been associated with growing U.S. protectionism in relation to forest products and have done nothing to inspire innovation.

If there is no shortage of ideas by which research and development and innovation might be stimulated,[40] there seems little hope for change in how the forest industry develops technology in Canada. Yet, the future of the sector, in one way or another, will be shaped by its attitudes towards innovation. Low key policies which provided low key incentives to research and development have not worked. An alternative approach is for federal and provincial governments to collaborate on a new vision for Canada's forests, a vision in which innovation is the central theme. As far as the working forest is concerned, that is, the forest available to industry, the key plank of such a vision is to get timber supplies into the hands of innovators. Rather than provide subsidies to the inefficient who, in more cases than not, also turn out to be the most environmentally damaging performers, all aspects of (industrial) forestry policy should be designed to facilitate and reward innovation. Such a policy would be difficult to construct. But so far, it has never been tried.

NOTES

1 R. Hayter, *Technology and the Canadian Forest Product Industries: A Technological Perspective*, Background Study no. 54, Science Council of Canada (Ottawa: Supply and Services, 1988).

2 Ernst and Young, *Technology and the B.C. Forest Products Sector* (Vancouver: Science Council of British Columbia, 1998).

3 Woodbridge, Reed and Associates, *British Columbia's Forest Products Industry: Constraints to Growth*, prepared for the Ministry of State for Economic and Regional Development in Vancouver, 1984.

4 Hayter *Technology*; C.S. Binkley and S.B. Watts, 'The Status of Forestry Research in British Columbia,' *Forestry Chronicle* 68, 1992, 730–5.

5 J.G. Smith and G. Lessard, *Forest Resources Research in Canada*, Background Study no. 14, Science Council of Canada (Ottawa: Information Canada, 1970).

6 O.M. Solandt, *Forest Research in Canada* (Ottawa: Canadian Forestry Advisory Council, 1979); C.S. Binkley 'Designing an Effective Forest Sector Research Strategy for Canada,' *Forestry Chronicle* 71, 1995, 589–95; Hayter *Technology*.

7 A.R.M. Lower, *Great Britain's Woodyard: British America and the Timber Trade 1763–1867* (Montreal: McGill-Queen's University Press, 1973).

8 T. Cohn, *The International Politics of Agricultural Trade: Canadian-American Relations in a Global Agricultural Context* (Vancouver: UBC Press, 1990).

9 M. Clark-Jones, *A Staple State: Canadian Industrial Resources in Cold War* (Toronto: University of Toronto Press, 1987); D.G. Haglund, ed., *The New Geopolitics of Minerals* (Vancouver: UBC Press, 1989).

10 H.G.H. Aitken, *American Capital and Canadian Resources* (Cambridge: Harvard University Press, 1961).

11 J.N.H. Britton and J. Gilmour, *The Weakest Link: A Technological Perspective on Canadian Underdevelopment* Background Study no. 43 (Ottawa: Science Council of Canada, 1978); G. Williams, *Not for Export: Towards a Political Economy of Canada's Arrested Industrialization* (Toronto: McClelland and Stewart, 1983).

12 R.S. Uhler, G.M. Townsend, and L. Constantino, 'Canada–U.S. Trade and the Product Mix of the Canadian Pulp and Paper Industry,' in R.S. Uhler, ed., *Canada–United States Trade in Forest Products* 106–22. (Vancouver: UBC Press, 1991).

13 R. Hayter and R.M. Galois, 'The Wheel of Fortune: British Columbia Lumber and the Global Economy,' in P.M. Koroscil, ed., *British Columbia: Geographical Essays in Honour of A. MacPherson* (Mission, B.C.: R.S. Graphics, 1991).

14 R. Hayter, 'Corporate Strategies and Industrial Change in the Canadian Forest Product Industries,' *Geographical Review* 66, 1976, 209–28.

15 R. Hayter and T. Barnes, 'Innis' Staple Theory, Exports and Recession: British Columbia, 1981–6,' *Economic Geography* 66, 1990, 156–73.

16 H.A. Marshall, F.A. Southard, and K.W. Taylor, *Canadian-American Industry: A Study in International Investment* (Toronto: Ryerson Press, 1936).

17 R. Hayter, 'The Evolution and Structure of the Canadian Forest Product Sector: An Assessment of the Role of Foreign Ownership and Control,' *Fennia* 163, 1985, 439–50; R. Hayter, 'Corporate Strategies and Industrial Change in the Canadian Forest Product Industries,' *Geographical Review* 66, 1976, 209–28.

18 R. Hayter, 'Patterns of Entry and the Role of Foreign-Controlled Investments in the Forest Product Sector of British Columbia,' *Tijdschrift voor Economische en Sociale Geografie* 72, 1981, 99–113.

19 P. Marchak, 'For Whom the Tree Falls: Restructuring in the Global Forest Industry,' *B.C. Studies*, 90, Summer, 1991, 3–24.

20 A.S. Mather, *Global Forest Resources* (London: Bellhaven, 1990).

21 T. Gunton, 'Forestry Land Use and Public Policy in British Columbia,' in T. Barnes and R. Hayter, eds., *Troubles in the Rainforest: British Columbia's Forest Economy in Transition*, Western Canadian Geographical Series no. 33 (Victoria: University of Victoria, 1997).

22 M.B. Percy and C. Yoder, *The Softwood Lumber Dispute and Canada–U.S. Trade in Natural Resources* (Halifax: Institute for Research on Public Policy, 1987).

23 Canada, *Royal Commission on the Economic Union and Development Prospects for Canada* (Ottawa: Supply and Services Canada, 1985).

24 Percy and Yoder, *Softwood Lumber Dispute*; R. Hayter, 'International Trade Relations and Regional Industrial Adjustment: The Implications of the 1982–86 Canadian–U.S. Softwood Lumber Dispute for British Columbia,' *Environment and Planning A* 24, 1992, 153–70.

25 R. Hohol, 'Why Large U.S. Publishers Own Newsprint Mills,' *Pulp and Paper Journal*, Jan. 1984, 88–92.

26 J. Atkinson, 'Flexibility or Fragmentation? The United Kingdom Labour Market in the Eighties,' *Labour and Society*, 12, 1987, 87–105.

27 R. Hayter, 'High Performance Organizations and Employment Flexibility: A Case Study of In Situ Change at the Powell River Paper Mill 1980–1994,' *The Canadian Geographer* 41, 1997, 26–40.

28 V. Preston, J. Holmes, and A. Williams, 'Working with "Wild Rose": Lean Production in a Greenfield Mill,' *The Canadian Geographer* 41, 1997, 88–104.

29 R. Hayter, 'High Performance Organizations.'

30 G. Norcliffe and J. Bates, 'Implementing Lean Production in an Old Industrial Space: Restructuring at Corner Brook, Newfoundland,' *The Canadian Geographer* 41, 1997, 41–60. D. Rose and M. Villemaire, 'Reshuffling Paperworkers: Technological Change and Experiences of Reorganization at a Quebec Newsprint Mill,' *The Canadian Geographer* 41, 1997, 61–87.

31 J. Holmes, 'In Search of Competitive Efficiency: Labour Process Flexibility in Canadian Newsprint Mills,' *The Canadian Geographer* 41, 1997, 7–25.

156   Roger Hayter and John Holmes

32 T. Barnes, and R. Hayter, eds., *Troubles in the Rainforest: British Columbia's Forest Economy in Transition*, Western Canadian Geographical Series no. 33 (Victoria: University of Victoria, 1997).

33 K.G. Rees and R. Hayter, 'Flexible Specialization, Uncertainty and the Firm: Enterprise Strategies in the Wood Remanufacturing Industry of the Vancouver Metropolitan Area, British Columbia,' *The Canadian Geographer* 40, 1996, 203–19.

34 Woodbridge, Reed, *B.C.'s Forest Products*.

35 Hayter, *Technology*.

36 I. Croon, 'The Scandinavian Approach to the Future of Pulp and Paper,' in G.F. Schreuder, ed., *Global Issues and Outlook in Pulp and Paper* (Seattle: University of Washington Press, 1988) 265–75.

37 Woodbridge, Reed, *B.C.'s Forest Products*; Hayter, *Technology*.

38 Smith and Lessard, *Forest Resources Research*; R. Hayter, 'Research and Development in the Canadian Forest Product Sector: Another Weak Link?' *The Canadian Geographer* 26, 1982, 256–3; Binkley and Watts 'The Status of Forestry Research.'

39 A.J. Cordell and J.M. Gilmour, *The Role and Function of Government Laboratories and the Transfer of Technology in the Manufacturing Sector*, Background Study no. 35 (Ottawa: Science Council of Canada, 1976).

40 Binkley, 'Designing an Effective Forest Sector Research Strategy.'

Chapter Six

Environmentalism and Environmental Actors in the Canadian Forest Sector

Lorna Stefanick

The forest policy regime in Canada has seen dramatic changes in the past two decades. As was noted in the Introduction, this regime is characterized as 'forest management for timber harvest.' Historically, Canada's economic dependence on the extraction of resources meant harvesting the forest, along with other types of primary industrial activities. This was seen as not only an honourable endeavour, but as a critical component of Canada's economic development strategy. In the early years of settlement, felling trees was conceived as an integral component of 'taming' the vast and often hostile Canadian wilderness. As such, little thought was given to the negative externalities associated with resource extraction. In part this was a reflection of the fact that the land mass in Canada was so large (particularly when compared with Canada's small population base) that the ability of the environment to absorb environmental degradation appeared endless.

By the late nineteenth century, however, the limits of many resources became apparent. In particular, the limits of forest resources began to trouble foresters, industrialists and governments concerned with the future of the forest industry. By the latter part of the twentieth century, people other than those directly concerned with the profitability of the industry came to realize the limits and difficulties associated with large-scale resource extraction and the threat it posed to other land values. Although for many years public opinion would fluctuate between support for the industry and for the environment, by the 1990s any ambivalence of the public to environmental issues generally, and forestry practices specifically, had largely disappeared. Forest conservation groups mobilized to prevent the logging of wilderness spaces, challenging the notion that harvesting natural resources is always in the best interest of the public, while other groups objected to the large-scale aerial spraying of herbicides and insecticides on both populated and unpopulated areas.

While many forest-related environmental groups formed on an ad hoc, temporary basis to fight specific battles with industry and regulators (and disappeared as quickly as they arose), others were more permanent and, through various forms of protest and actions, made a much more lasting impact on the forest regime. Anti-logging groups, for example, are particularly prominent in British Columbia; they have been very successful in drawing attention to B.C. logging practices, not only within Canada but also in the international arena. Such groups have been so successful in challenging the hegemony of the forest harvest paradigm that the state is scrambling to find methods to integrate environmentalists into the policy process in order to quell the tide of negative public opinion.

Forest conservation organizations (and more specifically, wilderness conservationists) are now without a doubt among the most visible interest group lobbies in Canada. Groups such as Greenpeace, the Sierra Club of Canada, the Wilderness Committee (WC), the Canadian Parks and Wilderness Society, naturalist clubs, and fish and game societies have utilized methods ranging from direct action to Supreme Court actions, and in so doing have emerged from their position as bystanders on the policy sidelines and have become important forest policy actors. Most wilderness conservation groups, however, still face serious impediments with respect to playing a prominent role in policy formation. This is, in part, caused by the extreme fragmentation of the environmental movement, as well as ongoing problems encountered in funding their organizations and activities.

This chapter analyses the evolving role of environmental groups within the forest policy regime. It begins with a brief overview of the conservation movement in Canada, and in particular the emergence of the wilderness conservation lobby. It then proceeds to analyse wilderness conservation groups as interest groups; it offers an overview of some of the basic characteristics of interest groups and illustrates the particular features of wilderness conservation groups. These features constrain the role of conservation groups in the forest policy regime; however, these features also present them with unique opportunities.

The Conservation Movement in Canada

In contrast to the United States, the impetus to preserve wilderness spaces in Canada came from the government rather than from individual conservation groups. By the 1880s the American frontier was effectively 'closed,' and early conservationists were advocating the preservation of wilderness spaces. Likewise in Canada the realization that resources were indeed exhaustible and might need public management culminated in the decision to create the country's first national park in 1885.

This conservation initiative was spearheaded by the federal government as a method of promoting tourism in the Rocky Mountains. Indeed, Canadian National Parks projects saw the construction of some of Canada's finest hotels by the Canadian Pacific Railway. These were built to entice wealthy patrons to travel across Canada to Banff National Park, spending money on fine dining, sumptuous accommodations, and medicinal hot springs upon arrival at their wilderness destination.

This is not to suggest, however, that the conservation impulse in Canada completely emanated from or was exclusively directed by the state. Mountaineering clubs such as the Alpine Club of Canada and the B.C. Mountaineering Club came into existence in 1906 and 1907 respectively; these groups made wilderness excursions into the backcountry accessible to those who could not afford to hire a Swiss guide. Also in 1906 the Edmonton Natural History Club and the Red Deer River Naturalists were formed. Twenty-five years later the Federation of Ontario Naturalists was born. Fish and game enthusiasts also showed an early interest in conserving wilderness habitat. The first fish and game society in Canada was formed in Prince Edward Island in 1906, and by 1938 Ducks Unlimited had set up shop in virtually every province in Canada.[1] While the primary focus of the mountaineering, naturalist, and game groups was not to preserve the environment, their focus on recreation in natural areas caused them to continually voice conservation concerns over the years.

Canada's most famous conservationist from this period was Grey Owl, the British-born Archie Belaney, who immigrated to Canada from Britain in 1906. Grey Owl strongly identified with Aboriginals, adopting their dress and way of life. By the time his true identity was discovered after his death in 1938, Grey Owl had established an international reputation as a conservationist, publishing such books as *Pilgrims of the Wild*, *Tales of an Empty Cabin*, *The Book of Grey Owl*, and *The Adventures of Sajo and Her Beaver People*. But given the seemingly endless wilderness in Canada, Grey Owl's conservation voice had little impact outside of populated regions where the effects of deforestation were readily apparent.

Most Canadians still thought of the wilderness as a space that needed to be tamed, and the societal consensus was that the harvest of natural resources was desirable because it promoted the economic development of the new nation.[2]

This acquiescence and consensus began to break down in the 1960s and early 1970s. The members of the postwar generation, raised in material affluence without the experience of economic deprivation and tumultuous wartime experiences that shaped the perspective of their parents, began to question whether an unremitting commitment to economic growth had a darker side. Environmental disasters like the Love Canal and the grounding of the oil tanker *Arrow* highlighted this dark side, and publications such as Rachel Carson's famous book *Silent Spring* drove the point home.[3] This period saw the birth of many of Canada's most important environmental groups, including the now internationally renowned Greenpeace. Anti-pollution groups such as Pollution Probe in Toronto, STOP in Montreal, and the Ecological Action Centre in Nova Scotia sprang up across the country. This period also saw the formation of Canadian chapters of prominent American conservation groups such as the Sierra Club, as well as the formation of indigenous conservation organizations. Some of these groups, such as the Canadian Parks and Wilderness Society and the Canadian Nature Federation, had a national perspective on conservation. Groups such as the Alberta Wilderness Association and the Manitoba Environmental Council focused on provincial issues. Others, such as the Bruce Trail Association in Hamilton or the Bow Valley Naturalists in Banff were (and are) primarily concerned with a regional ecosystem or watershed.[4] While these groups began to focus attention on the negative effects of environmental degradation, they also began to question the wisdom of the prevailing resource management paradigm. In doing so, they ultimately began to question how the public's 'best interest' was being defined, and they demanded to have input into the process that was used to make decisions on the public's behalf.[5]

By the 1980s, it was becoming apparent that the world's forests were diminishing at an increasingly rapid rate, and forest industry activity on Canada's Crown lands came under close scrutiny in the international environmental community. This decade saw the veritable explosion of forestry focused environmental groups; over thirty of these were formed in British Columbia in the 1980s alone.[6] This scrutiny was (and is) keenly focused on B.C.'s coastal rainforests, although attention has also been given to clear-cutting practices in B.C.'s interior forests, the northern boreal forest in Alberta and Saskatchewan, and the Temagami region of Ontario and neighbouring Quebec. Concern has been raised over the impact of acid rain on the maple forests of eastern Quebec, and the large-scale insecticide spraying in areas of New Brunswick and Nova Scotia. Across Canada, groups such as the Valhalla Wilderness Society, the Friends of Athabasca, and the Wildlands League emerged as the voice of conservation, while groups such as the B.C. Alternative to Pesticides, the Prairie Acid Rain Coalition, and the Ecological Action Centre (Nova Scotia) focused on the impact of pollution and pesticides on forested areas.[7] Forest conservation activists, particularly those in western Canada, have found allies internationally. Many Europeans, Japanese, and Americans have discovered Canada's comparatively unspoiled wilderness spaces; these outdoor enthusiasts are anxious that the habitat degradation that occurred in their homelands not be replicated in Canada.

Public concern and, in particular, a growing international interest in Canadian forest practices, began to tear down the walls of the fortress that sheltered the decision-making process in the Canadian forest sector. As late as 1985, the idea of soliciting the opinion of an environmental advocate in the making of forest policy was unthinkable. In 1987, the U.N. Commission on Environment and Development (the Brundtland Commission) published its report calling the world to action with respect to environmental sustainability.[8] In response, provinces across Canada began experimenting with various forms of multipartite policy-making processes designed to gain input from conservationists on a host of land-use and resource disposition matters.[9] While the experience of different jurisdictions with such fora has varied, for the most part, consultation with environmentalists has become an essential ingredient of Canadian forest policy-making at the turn of the millennium.

Despite these positive moves forward, forest conservation groups are still faced with some unique organizational challenges that interest organizations in other sectors do not face. These challenges prevent many groups from participating more actively in the forest policy process and will be the focus of the following section.

Forest Conservation Groups as Interest Groups

Canadian interest group scholar A. Paul Pross suggests that interest organizations follow a predictable life cycle. They begin as small, single-issue organizations that form to advocate a particular policy position.

They then gain experience, and if they can expand their resource base, they may 'institutionalize,' gaining the rigid, hierarchical structure characteristics of more established multi-issue pressure groups.[10] This latter organizational form facilitates the penetration of the equally rigid bureaucratic state and increases accountability as the groups' resource bases expand.

Examples of institutional groups within the forest conservation movement abound. Organizations such as Ducks Unlimited or the World Wildlife Fund have grown into multimillion dollar operations with boards of directors, annual reports, and paid staff. These groups have established contacts with not only government personnel but with their industry counterparts. Groups such as the Nature Conservancy avoid confrontation with the forest industry by using market-based tactics. That is, the Conservancy identifies what it considers to be key habitats or unique ecosystems, but rather than lobby for their preservation, it raises money and buys the land with the intention of preserving it in its natural state.

There is a growing body of literature, however, that suggests that some types of interest groups do not follow the developmental pattern of institutionalized groups. European studies indicate that groups belonging to the so-called new social movement phenomenon (used to characterize the peace, women's, and environmental movements in North America and Europe which developed in the late 1960s and early 1970s) have consciously resisted adopting vertically arranged hierarchical structures.[11] These groups have deliberately chosen to continue to use confrontational and media-oriented tactics long after their salience and prestige within the policy community has grown to the point where they could employ more subtle bureaucratic tactics, presumably with some effect. This pattern can be seen among forest conservation groups. For example, the Wilderness Committee has had a budget of over several million dollars for more than a decade, yet it has refused to form coalitions with other conservation groups; it prides itself in being the 'outsider' with respect to government consultation processes.[12] Similarly, Greenpeace Canada has grown into a multinational environmental organization that continues to use media-driven tactics.

Despite the insistence of many of its most powerful members on remaining outside formal policy-making processes, environmentalism has had a major impact on forest policy. At the political level, by 1992 all provinces had committed to creating comprehensive wilderness land management strategies that entailed consultation with conservation organizations. Businesses also began modifying corporate policy in order to avoid criticism from the environmental lobby.[13] Timothy O'Riordan argued as early as 1981 that environmentalists had become one of the most powerful interest group lobbies in Europe.[14] Others argue that environmentalism that is an example of popular reaction to broad social and political changes have affected advanced industrial societies in the post–Second World War era. Moreover, concern for environmental issues has created new bases of political cleavage that challenge long-standing political alignments.[15]

While one could debate the actual strength of the lobby, the critical characteristic of environmental groups is that they do not confine their activities to simply achieving a particular policy outcome but in fact advocate changes in the way we think about our relationship with the natural environment. This pattern is exhibited by wilderness conservation organizations which typically cite 'public education' as a primary goal and lobbying government as a secondary goal.[16] As a policy actor that has really only emerged with any vigour in the past three decades, the non-traditional structure of many Canadian forest conservation groups and their reliance on non-bureaucratic policy activities such as protests and direct action could be attributable to a paucity of resources and inexperience with the policy process. It is also plausible, however, to argue that these organizational differences are primarily attributable to a new ideological perspective that focuses on quality of life rather than on economic issues.[17]

Clearly, challenging the way we think has much greater ramifications for future policy outcomes than does simply achieving a particular goal in a specific policy arena. In the case of the Canadian forestry sector, wilderness conservation groups challenge the notion that trees are simply a resource to be harvested for the economic advancement of humans. These groups articulate the position that trees are part of a larger ecosystem and that felling forests tampers with a finely tuned natural equilibrium, often with devastating consequences for other forms of life. For example, it is argued that massive clear-cutting in the northern boreal forest will have repercussions for the animals and birds that live in that particular habitat and beyond. The survival of other species in other areas is linked to those in the northern boreal forest, particularly if either species is migratory. Most environmentalists would thus question whether an unremitting commitment to economic growth is always justifiable even if the positive spin-offs from this growth were to be evenly distributed among various sectors of society.[18]

This is not to suggest however, that forestry conservationists tend to have similar views. Generally speaking, Canadian forest advocacy groups can be divided into two categories: those that pursue, broadly speaking, 'anthropocentric' or human-centred aims and those that are more 'biocentric' in their aspirations. Anthropocentric forest advocacy groups have a long history in North America. They grew out of the turn-of-the-century conservation movement in the United States led by such individuals as George Perkins Marsh and John Muir. These early conservationists were among the first to question whether wilderness should be viewed simply as a collection of resources to be used and exploited by humans. For these men the very survival of humans was linked to the health of the natural environment, for the latter provided spiritual nourishment and esthetic pleasure. The notion of the environment as a living ecosystem that might have a value to humans quite apart from its economic value was first articulated at this time.

Later social ecologists, such as Murray Bookchin, endorsed a radical ecologism based on this premise. Bookchin, for example, argues that the political and economic systems of the human species are in disequilibrium, and the ability to live in ecological harmony will only be achieved through radical social transformation.[19] Many anti-pollution organizations subscribe to this fundamentally anthropocentric world-view; they are primarily concerned with the human consequences of the negative externalities from industrial processes. These anthropocentric perspectives suggest that ecological equilibrium is a desirable policy end because humans can derive benefits from environmental protection, whether by ensuring clean air or water for human consumption, rejuvenating forests in order to continue harvesting them, or providing natural spaces for human enjoyment at a spiritual or esthetic level.

In contrast, biocentric thinkers in the 1970s advanced the deep ecology perspective that 'all beings have intrinsic worth apart from their usefulness to humans.'[20] This viewpoint questions the notion that even radical social transformation will be of benefit to preserving natural spaces, as the focus remains on improving social relations among people rather than improving the overall relationship established between humans and nature. The more extreme variations of biocentric thought assert that the well-being of humankind is irrelevant and that the central policy issue is habitat preservation for all species.

In Canada, groups active in the forest conservation lobby are generally anthropocentric in focus, and most are not exclusively focused on forest issues. For example, many groups are interested in saving forest habitat in order to preserve the species that live within it for human enjoyment. Some groups focus on bird-watching or natural history (such as the Federation of Naturalists), while others (such as the fish and game federations) promote hunting or fishing. Groups like the Sierra Club are interested in a whole range of environmental issues including forestry issues, while many Aboriginal groups focus on forestry issues because of the ramifications that logging may have for their communities. This is not to suggest that there are no biocentric elements in the Canadian forest conservation lobby. But even groups like the Wilderness Committee, which at times appear to be oblivious to the complex social problems surrounding habitat conservation, have begun to articulate more anthropocentric positions that demonstrate a sensitivity to broader economic and social issues.[21]

The existence of the anthropocentric and biocentric perspectives has led to a split among forest conservationists between those who want conservation for human benefit and those who want it for the benefit of other species with little or no regard for human concerns. Because the ultimate goal is preservation for human enjoyment or enhancing quality of life, the anthropocentric groups are also more likely to entertain concerns about the effects of the cessation of economic activity on those who are employed in the forestry sector. In contrast, the biocentric group focuses on the benefits of conservation for non-human species; issues of unemployment in the forestry sector are not of major concern.

Conservation groups are similar, however, with respect to the constraints they work under. All forest conservation groups, whether anthropocentric or biocentric, can be described as advocating policies that are said to be in the 'public interest.' That is, they argue for a 'good' that is not easily divisible; once it is attained it is available to all. Accordingly, a 'rational' individual allows others to make the necessary sacrifices to attain the good and then 'free-rides' on their efforts by enjoying the benefit without contributing to its acquisition.[22] Because of this free-ridership problem, conservation groups have a more difficult time mobilizing adherents to their cause than do other interest organizations. Added to this problem is the fact that under Canadian tax law environmental groups can have their charitable tax status removed by the government if they engage in lobbying. Because obtaining a tax rebate for contributions is a major incentive for donors, the possibility of the government's punishing troublesome groups for their advocacy activities gives pause for thought in any group tactical session.[23] These problems notwithstanding, conservation groups have managed to mobilize significant latent public support around environmental issues and have emerged as important players in the forest policy community. Groups like Greenpeace and the Wilderness Committee forced their way into the policy arena using confrontational and media-oriented tactics aimed at drawing attention to their marginalized positions. Even after these groups had successfully drawn attention to the environmental perspective, however, neither group dropped its media-driven tactics. Although institutionalized, neither opted for traditional forms of interaction with state actors – given their ideological orientations and organizational constraints.

Conservation Groups within the Environmental Policy Community

As the previous discussion illustrates, Canadian forest conservation groups do not share homogeneous world-views. Conflict among groups is most apparent when conservation is driven by forest uses that are deemed to be incompatible with overall ecological health. In many instances, however, common cause emerges in instances where land is to be designated for forestry use as opposed to a parks and wilderness designation.

All conservation groups devote considerable energy to changing public opinion and raising awareness of environmental issues. These groups have used a range of tactics to raise awareness of forestry issues. These include distributing literature, hosting film and slide shows, building research stations to attract the attention of the scientific community, and constructing 'educational' boardwalk trails in rainforests slated for clear-cut logging to encourage people to 'see for themselves.' More recently, Canadian groups have attempted to raise the profile of Canadian forest issues internationally by conducting protests at foreign legislatures, launching publicity campaigns, and advocating boycotts of Canadian forestry products.

These tactics are particularly effective in the forestry sector because resource-based economies depend on foreign markets to purchase their products. Because of the international nature of the forest industry and the wilderness mystique associated with Canada, forest conservationists have a wide arsenal of tactics available to them that other interest groups in other policy regimes do not have. Groups have capitalized on this advantage, and the international interest in Canadian forest practices (and specifically the threat of product boycott) has forced a degree of change in the forest policy sector that would have been unimaginable as little as ten years ago.[24] Conservation organizations have effectively used visual imagery to juxtapose the beauty of pristine Canadian forests against the ugliness of a clear-cut. This tactic has been especially successful in convincing Europeans that the Canadian wilderness is worth protecting, particularly because this wilderness is the home of many large carnivores not found in Europe. The message to international consumers of Canadian forest products is clear; the most effective method of changing corporate behaviour is to boycott the offending company's products.

To a large extent forest conservationists' emphasis on extranational tactics is a reflection of the organizational structure of the environmental movement. New social movement scholars tell us that one of the defining characteristics of new social movements is that the post-materialist issues they concern themselves with relate to quality of life as opposed to material consumption.[25] As such, the movements that mobilize to promote these values defy political boundaries, as post-materialist issues transcend traditional politics. While the transnational nature of such things as human rights and women's issues can easily be seen, the transnational nature of environmental issues is even more acute. Howlett, Wilson, Bernstein, and Cashore in this volume discuss the ecosystem approach to forest management. This approach clearly reflects and affects the manner in which forest conservationists organize their lobby. Specifically, issues tend to cluster around a particular ecosystem; what happens in one part of the ecosystem will affect the other part because the two sections are interconnected. Thus, groups that focus on a particular ecosystem issue tend to link up with other like-minded groups and individuals regardless of what political unit they belong to and despite the fact that the political jurisdiction for a single ecosystem may reside with more than one government. Indeed, U.S. and Canadian groups residing in the same ecosystem may find they have much more in common with their transnational counterpart than they do with similar national groups on the other end of the continent.[26]

With respect to forest conservation groups, international collaboration is best demonstrated in the western and eastern peripheries of Canada. This is not to suggest that Quebec, Ontario, and the inland Prairies do not have forest concerns that spill into the United States, but simply that the continent's peripheries contain comparatively 'untamed' tracts of intact forest ecosystems that activists on both sides of the border are interested in preserving. The best example of a transboundary focus is the recent Yellowstone to Yukon (Y2Y) conservation initiative. The Y2Y initiative would see the protection of a 2,700 kilometre wilderness corridor through the Canadian and U.S. Rocky Mountains. Conservation biologists argue that large carnivores such as grizzly bears cannot survive in isolated pockets of protected lands because of problems with inbreeding. Environmentalists in the state of Wyoming are increasingly seeing the viability of their species as dependent on the ability of U.S. species to mate occasionally with species in the so-called Serengeti of North America, the Northern Rockies and the Yukon. To get to the 'northern Serengeti,' however, the U.S. animals must pass through the Alberta Rockies. Thus, forestry and mining policy in Alberta has become of great interest to environmental activists in the United States. Groups like the Alliance for the Wild Rockies based in Missoula, Montana, are comprised of leading environmental groups on both sides of the border and have public figures such as singer/song-writer Carole King on their boards of directors.[27]

The structure and activities of forest conservationists impact the policy regime in three important ways. First, policy-relevant ideas are contested, often in a very public forum. This can be seen in recent provincial conservation processes such as Lands for Life in Ontario and Special Places 2000 in Alberta. While the outcomes of these processes were not unequivocal successes, they provided a forum for debate for members of the public who have radically different perspectives. Second, as the political currency of forest conservation rises in the eyes of the public, pressure is exerted to change the constellation of actors within the policy community. It may have been possible to exclude environmental activists from decision-making processes a few years ago, but it is not possible today.[28] And finally, because of their focus on changing public opinion as opposed to influencing policy-makers, the strategies of wilderness conservationists often differ from other interest groups.

Conservation Groups and the Forest Policy Regime

This chapter argues that forest conservation groups are fundamentally different from traditional interest groups in other policy sectors. These differences, related to the ideological nature of environmentalism as a social movement and the nature of environmental protection as a public good, help to explain why conservation groups have not institutionalized as they mature, as do groups in many other sectors. This phenomenon is of interest insomuch as these groups have emerged as important actors within the forest policy regime.

Forest conservationists articulate the position that trees have a value quite apart from the dollar value assigned to them when they are harvested. The emphasis on changing the way Canadians think about forests explains the difficulty governments in Canada have had in integrating conservationists into the forest policy process. The very notion of conservation of wilderness challenges many basic assumptions on which Canada's economic development paradigm has been based. This makes the assimilation of wilderness conservationists into the decision-making process difficult.

The success, however, that environmental groups have enjoyed in reconceptualizing the relationship between humans and the natural environment continues to shift the nature of the policy discourse found in the forest policy regime and causes legitimization problems for traditional actors such as business and labour. While new ideas may have shifted the discourse, the conservation ethic has in no way emerged as the dominant discourse. That is, while it is clear that forest conservation groups have succeeded in drawing national and even international attention to forestry issues, it is debatable that they have succeeded in fundamentally changing the basic values and attitudes of average Canadians or their political decision-makers.

Conservation groups in many provinces have discovered that it is extremely difficult to deal with forestry issues in isolation from larger social and economic issues such a regional development, employment, and community politics. Forest conservation groups are struggling to adapt their agendas to accommodate these concerns, just as policy-makers are struggling to adapt policy in response to the national and international pressure to preserve Canada's forests. As Canada moves into the twenty-first century and the forestry sector adapts to the changing forest products economy, habitat loss, and Aboriginal land claims, the only certainty within the forest policy regime is that change is omnipresent on the horizon.

NOTES

1 Canadian Environmental Network (CEN), *Green List* (Drayton Valley: Pembina Institute for Appropriate Development, 1994).
2 Ibid.
3 Rachel Carson, *Silent Spring* (London: Readers Union, 1964).
4 CEN, *Green List.*

5 Ronald Inglehart, *The Silent Revolution* (Princeton: Princeton University Press, 1977).

6 CEN, *Green List.*

7 Ibid.

8 World Commission on Environment and Development, *Our Common Future* (New York: Oxford University Press, 1987).

9 See Michael Howlett, 'The Round Table Experience: Representation and Legitimacy in Canadian Environmental Policy Making' *Queen's Quarterly* 97, 1990, 580–601. See also, Lorna Stefanick, 'Organization, Administration, and the Environment: Will a Facelift Suffice, or Does the Patient Need Radical Surgery?' *Canadian Public Administration* 41(1) 1998, 99–119.

10 See A. Paul Pross, *Group Politics and Public Policy* (Toronto: Oxford University Press, 1992).

11 Claus Offe, 'New Social Movements: Challenging the Boundaries of Institutional Politics,' *Social Research* 52(4), 1985, 817–68; Stephen Cotgrove and Andrew Duff, 'Environmentalism, Values, and Social Change,' *British Journal of Sociology* 32(1), 1981, 92–110; and Stephen Cotgrove and Andrew Duff, 'Environmentalism, Middle-class Radicalism and Politics,' *Sociological Review* 28(2), 1980, 333–51.

12 In fact, WC passed a resolution at its 1995 annual general meeting stating that it 'does not join coalitions.' Wilderness Committee, <http://www.web.net/wcwild/welcome.html> downloaded Oct. 1996.

13 An example of corporate greening is the 1999 announcement by the world's largest retailer of wood in the world, Home Depot, that it would discontinue sales of redwood, lavan, and cedar from endangered areas by 2002 in favour of purchasing so-called certified wood. Reported in *Victoria Times Colonist*, 27 Aug. 1999, B2.

14 Timothy O'Riordan, *Environmentalism* (London: Pion Publishers, 1981).

15 Kay Lawson and Peter H. Merkl, *When Parties Fail: Emerging Alternative Organizations* (Princeton: Princeton University Press, 1988); Thomas Poguntke, 'New Politics and Party Systems,' *West German Politics* 10, 1987, 76–89; Ferdinand Miller-Rommel, 'New Social Movements and Smaller Parties,' *West German Politics* 8, 1985, 41–54; S. Barnes and M. Kaase, eds., *Political Action* (London: Sage Publications, 1979); Russell Dalton, Scott Flanagan, Paul Allen Beck, James E. Alt, *Electoral Change in Advanced Industrial Democracies* (Princeton: Princeton University Press, 1984); Wilhelm Buerklin, 'The Greens: Ecology and the New Left,' in P. Wallach and G. Romoser, eds., *West German Politics in the Mid-Eighties: Crisis and Continuity* (New York: Praeger, 1985), 187–218.

16 See Lorna Stefanick, 'Structures, Strategies and Strife: The Canadian Envi-

ronmental Movement, unpublished doctoral dissertation, Queen's University, Kingston, 1996.

17 William Chandler and Alan Siaroff, 'Postindustrial Politics in Germany and the Origins of the Greens,' *Comparative Politics* 18, 1985–6, 303–25; Miller-Rommel, 'New Social Movements'; Wolfgang Ridig, 'Peace and Ecology Movements in Western Europe,' *West European Politics* 11(1), 1988, 26–39; Cotgrove, and Duff, 'Environmentalism, Middle-Class Radicalism and Politics'; Cotgrove and Duff, 'Environmentalism, Values, and Social Change.'

18 Robert Paehlke, *Environmentalism and the Future of Progress Politics* (New Haven, Conn.: Yale University Press, 1989).

19 Murray Bookchin, *Defending the Earth* (Boston: South End Press, 1991).

20 Arne Naess, 'The Shallow and the Deep, Long-Range Ecology Movements: A Summary,' *Inquiry*, 16, 1973, 95–100.

21 See Western Canada Wilderness Committee, *Educational Report*, 10(7), 1991, for a discussion of strategies to increase employment opportunities in the forestry sector. This group recently changed its name to Wilderness Committee: a strategic choice reflecting its decision to pursue a national mandate rather than confining itself to Western Canada.

22 See Mancur Olson, *The Logic of Collective Action* (Boston: Harvard University Press, 1971).

23 A. Paul Pross and Ian S. Stewart, 'Lobbying, the Voluntary Sector and the Public Purse,' in *How Ottawa Spends* (Ottawa: Carleton University Press, 1993), 109–33.

24 W.T. Stanbury and I.B. Vertinsky, with Bill Wilson, *The Challenge to Canadian Forest Products in Europe* (Victoria: Pacific Forestry Centre, Canadian Forest Service, 1995).

25 Laurie E. Adkin, 'New Social Movements,' in *Critical Concepts: An Introduction to Politics* (Scarborough, Ont.: Prentice-Hall, 1999), 285–302.

26 The Great Lakes United Coalition (comprising groups based in Ontario, Michigan, and New York State) and the Save Georgia Strait Coalition (comprising of groups based in B.C. and Washington) are two such cases.

27 Alliance for the Wild Rockies, http://www.wildrockies.alliance.org downloaded January 2001.

28 The exclusion of environmental activists was attempted in one local SP2000 process; the ensuing furore had the net effect of nearly derailing the process province-wide. See Lorna Stefanick and Kathleen Wells, 'Conflict, Consultation, and the Castle Crown: Alberta's Special Places 2000,' in Stephen Bocking, ed., *Perspectives on Biodiversity*, (Peterborough: Broadview Press, 2000).

Chapter Seven

Model Forests as Process Reform: Alternative Dispute Resolution and Multistakeholder Planning

Joanna M. Beyers

Multistakeholder decision-making processes as a way of settling the many increasingly urgent and thorny land use disputes have emerged as attractive alternatives to protracted, damaging, and costly fights, whether conducted in the courts or in the bush. These new avenues for decision-making are in the dispute settlement or conflict management tradition.[1] Closely allied with the phenomenon of public participation, multiparty fora provide an opportunity to study the effects, if any, of these innovations in process on policy regimes.

The mediation literature, and the alternative dispute resolution (ADR) literature in general, identifies the structural environment in which policy decisions are made as a determining element in the outcome. There is little hope of success if, for example, there is no procedural equality at the table or if those who are to implement the decisions are missing. This stands to reason but the case examined in this chapter, the Canadian federal government's Model Forest Program (MFP), dating from 1991–2 and now in its second phase, is a strong endorsement of Campbell and Floyd's conclusion that the assessment of ADR projects must be rooted in a 'politically oriented' framework in order to guard against the overly optimistic prognoses that literature is prone to.[2] The existence of an outwardly competent decision-making consensus group easily masks the realities of the structural environment in which ADR must function and with which it is rightly concerned.

Beyers and Sandberg[3] and, in this volume, Rayner and Howlett and Hayter and Holmes have outlined the factors that constrain the Canadian experience in forest policy, among them the lingering effects of colonial times in the form of a staple economy that imposes its own extractive logic on Canada's forest economy. Related and equally important to the Canadian context are federalism and the widespread system of provincial Crown ownership of forest lands, which are nearly all leased out to integrated forest companies enjoying a closed policy network configuration with the provincial government. My contention in this chapter is that this Innisian,[4] historical, and politico-economic view coupled with policy regime analysis will provide the requisite politically oriented theoretical framework for the study of environmental dispute resolution (EDR) in Canada.

The hypothesis guiding this book is that the appearance of new actors and new ideas, together with changes in state capacities, can trigger regime change in the realm of Canadian forest policy. Ottawa's ongoing model forest experiment in multistakeholder decision-making is a good opportunity to test the hypothesis because this novel program installed management units across the country comprised of local parties, some of whom had heretofore never been consulted in the planning and execution of forest management activities. With new ideas and old adversaries at the same table, the hope was that these community-based partnerships would not only innovate forest management practices but also resolve forest management disputes, factors that together had undermined the economic viability of this most important of industries.

My concern here will be with the quality of the attempted process reform and its implications for regime change, hence the potential of an ADR strategy for the long-term resolution of environmental and land use conflict. In a country where forest management is an essentially private matter between a provincial government and large industry, what might be the extent of the influence parties normally excluded from the policy process dispose over in multistakeholder negotiations? Is, as Clement noted of consumer groups, their power that of swaying a decision in a particular direction or do they, in fact, make the decisions and ensure their implementation?[5] I shall argue that, in the Canadian structural environment, the politico-economic situation circumscribes what can be achieved to such a degree that, even where the preferred outcome is joint management (as is the hope in many land use disputes), multistakeholder 'consensus' groups cannot but be, at least on substantial issues, advisory rather than the decision-making instruments they are taken to be. After all, powerful parties are not likely to relinquish their power easily. Concessions will be made in order to gain some advantage otherwise unobtainable; in the case of the forest industry this includes peace in the woods. But shared decision-making turns out to be a route costly in the currency of power and therefore not as desirable as advisory alternatives if the latter can produce similar results.

Following an introductory section to environmental dispute resolution, I turn to the Model Forest Program itself as a specific type of EDR. I then present the principal actors at two of the original model forests and the issues that confront them, paying particular attention to the dynamics among the parties, in order to bring out the structural limitations in their way. The discussion will largely concern policy style; a full treatment of the timber management policy paradigm I have given elsewhere.[6]

Some Background on Dispute Resolution Mechanisms

Mediation as a dispute resolution form is practised widely in many cultures. Typically, in non-industrial societies, one or more well-respected mediators, neutral in the sense of not being a member of either party's kinship group or having some shared interest, shuttle between the aggrieved party and the offender(s) or their families to reach some mutually agreeable settlement appropriate to the status of the plaintiff and the seriousness of the crime. The society itself may exert pressure to settle, especially if the dispute arose between people in close contact with each other; but as relations of dependence weaken and neighbourly relations become less important, the alternatives (the courts or vengeance) are more likely to be resorted to.[7]

Since the model forests place stakeholders in close working relationships, there is indeed pressure on and support for the parties to come to terms. More commonly though, in Western countries, with their highly organized, usually centralized state institutions and communities where family and neighbours are not so closely knit, disputes are brought to the courts or other authorities for a decision. These latter may be fora such as elected or appointed boards and commissions, and public hearings; all are situations in which decisions are deferred to an 'ultimate' decision-maker assisted by expert advisers. Later, decisions are released, and an appeal process may be provided for.[8]

This legalistic approach to decision making, however, has proved difficult to maintain in cases of environmental conflict. Environmental, land use, and natural resources management matters, customarily settled between industry and government organizations, are of vital importance to the people living in the communities where natural resources are extracted or who will be faced with the potential effects of a waste products facility. Such conflicts are frequently about values and set community members against each other: those who make their living from the extractive activity, those whose present living will be jeopardized by it, and those with or without a material interest who oppose the development because of concerns of an aesthetic or larger environmental nature, including cottagers, hunters, and anglers. Inevitably, many different parties become involved in environmental disputes.

Environmental conflict is therefore a fertile field for ADR. Litigation over natural resources management in North America has escalated since the 1950s, when economic pressures and a modernist nature ideology introduced maximum yield policies and intensified resource extraction at the expense of wilderness and of soil and water quality.[9] A second avenue of protest, in the form of blockades and product boycotts often carried out in conjunction with court action, constitutes at least as serious a threat, serious enough for industry and governments to seek alternative solutions. Although the powerful are always free not to implement the terms of resolution, the hope with mediation and participation strategies is that the mutual acceptance of the agreed-upon terms will dissolve the animosity.[10]

Two developments in environmental practice seem to have been of particular import in the evolution of alternative responses to natural resources and environmental issues: ecosystem management, as pioneered in the Great Lakes region, and the 1987 World Commission on Environment and Economy report which introduced the idea of environmentally sustainable development. Both called for public participation because resource decisions concern not only industry and government but also many others, from minor economic interests to the general public. Bocking's observation about the change to ecosystem management of the Great Lakes fisheries in the 1970s applies: regulation has political and economic dimensions besides the usual technical one, requiring negotiation among interests and their comprehensive participation. As a result, the literature in this area of alternative responses to environmental and resource disputes is linked to public participation theory.[11]

Public involvement in decision-making, in an advisory capacity, has been contrasted with more inclusive or shared decision-making. Both are forms of ADR, together with still other possibilities such as arbitration, facilitation, fact-finding, and conciliation, but public consultation has been considered tokenism, and partnerships, citizen control, and delegation of power 'true public participation.' Similarly, Cormick et al.

distinguish between consensus-building processes, which they call mediation, and product-oriented ones. Examples of the former are round tables, joint jurisdictional arrangements, groups that address problems such as facilities siting or water quality and fish and forest management, land use negotiations such as those conducted by British Columbia's Commission of Resources and Environment, and land claims negotiations. In contrast to the position-based bargaining characteristic of product-oriented processes in which the warring parties, unable to find common ground, are committed to their divergent demands, the consensus-building process, known as 'principled' negotiation or 'negotiation on the merits,' is based on a commitment to find common interest.[12] With its partnership structure, the Model Forest Program is of this latter type.

The Model Forest Program

The Model Forest Program is built on the formula of a partnership of the principals. This is in keeping with the character of the problems the program is meant to address, since stakeholder participation is a concept central to environmental management.[13] Canadian precedent for multilateral stakeholder discussions as an environmental policy tool dates back to at least 1984, when the Department of the Environment brought together environmental non-governmental organizations (ENGOs), industry, labour, and government for discussions that came to be known as the Niagara process.[14] Thus, by the time the MFP was launched, in 1991–2, the needed infrastructure (concept and experience) was in place. This included a network of environmentalists, industrialists, and government officials committed to the task of exploring the question of sustainable economic activity.

The MFP, part of the Partners in Sustainable Development of Forests Program outlined in *Canada's Green Plan for a Healthy Environment* of 1990, was proposed by Ottawa, a traditional supporter of the forest industry,[15] in a climate of anti-forestry sentiment stemming from concerns about various environmental issues such as deforestation, climate change, biodiversity losses, and the poor score card of Canadian forestry practices. Environmental, economic, and land use worries at home added their own pressures to the international ones, which also resulted from the globalization of trade and the attendant competition from countries such as Spain and Chile where conditions favour a short growing cycle and costs are low.[16] It became accepted in forestry circles that safeguarding the environment was necessary in order to safeguard the industry's markets and with them the Canadian economy. The MFP, now in its second phase, is an attempt to address the threat coming from the environmental movement by encouraging the industry to 'shift the management of Canada's forests from sustained yield to sustainable development.'[17] It was to create, by national competition, working-scale model management areas where a partnership of stakeholders would put ecological forestry into practice, develop integrated resource management tools to help commercial forestry coexist with other natural resources, conduct research, and apply the most advanced forest management practices.[18]

As already noted, policy decision-making in forest affairs is ordinarily a closed process, taking place between the provincial government and its industrial tenants (sometimes joined by labour), a result of the system of Crown ownership of forest lands that has bred a dependent landlord–tenant relationship.[19] As indicated elsewhere in this volume, this situation, with some variations, is typical of the Canadian forestry sector. It caused Grant to say that British Columbia's 'most appropriate paradigm is that of a "company state".' Speaking of New Brunswick, Colpitts remarked that its Crown forests have gradually been transferred to the large pulp and paper companies such that the government became little more than a 'client spectator,' and Parenteau spoke of the 'limited power of the state to control forest capital.'[20]

That the MFP directed proponents to form partnerships of all key stakeholders and others affected by or interested in forestry activities in the area was therefore a highly innovative way to approach forest land disputes. Industry, whether lease-holding or freehold, was deemed a critical party because of its access to timber, its role in implementing the forest management side, and its technical and managerial expertise. The second critical landholder was the provincial government, having, in contrast to the federal government, complete jurisdiction over Crown forests. The role of both in the partnerships is to provide clear jurisdictional lines to ensure that forest management plans can be implemented.[21] The remaining landholders were, depending on the situation, the federal government (in the case of national parks), First Nations, and small woodlot owners. As initiator and bankroller of the project, Ottawa was at any rate represented by the Canadian Forest Service. Other interested parties, often gaming and angling groups, municipalities, research organizations, and environmentalists, have typically been involved, but depending on the model forest, they either have a seat at the partnership table or are involved in an advisory capacity.

Of the ten original partnerships, here I introduce two. Although the guidelines for the MFP stipulated a broad membership for the partnerships, not all of them complied. As I said, some groups accommodated the less than essential parties through an advisory structure. The first of the model forests I present here is an example of such a restricted partnership, the second of an open or inclusive partnership. However, despite their varying degree of inclusivity, both model forests have encountered similar problems and neither was able to fulfil its mandate.

The Partnerships: Prince Albert and Fundy Model Forests

Prince Albert Model Forest

Prince Albert Model Forest (PAMF) is located in central Saskatchewan, 70 kilometres north of the city of Prince Albert in the southern boreal forest. In 1996, at the time of my interviews there, PAMF comprised nearly 315,000 hectares of which about 160,000 are forested, mostly in softwood and mixedwood (49 per cent and 37 per cent respectively).[22]

At the time, the partnership had seven members: the four landowners (Weyerhaeuser Canada, the Montreal Lake Indian Band, the Canadian Parks Service and the Province through Saskatchewan Environment and Resource Management); two additional levels of aboriginal organization (the Prince Albert Tribal Council and the Federation of Saskatchewan Indian Nations); and the Canadian Institute of Forestry. The Canadian Forest Service appeared ex officio. Some background information on the most important stakeholders follows.

Weyerhaeuser Canada
The Weyerhaeuser Company, the 'aristocrat of the American timber industry,[23] had, in those days prior to its acquisition of MacMillan Bloedel, total assets of more than $13 billion, net sales and revenues of $11.8 billion, and net earnings of $800 million, making it the largest producer of market pulp and softwood lumber in the world. Of the more than 9 million hectares of forest land then owned and/or managed by the company in the United States and Canada, 3.4 million hectares are located in Saskatchewan, north of Prince Albert; 152,200 hectares of these are included in PAMF. Weyerhaeuser's Forest Management Licence Agreement is the largest in the province. Its allowable annual cut stood at 2.4 million cubic metres in 1991, at the time almost one-third of the province's total of 6.645 million cubic metres. With a

pulp mill producing more than 500,000 tonnes per year of bleached kraft pulp and fine paper, and a 225,000 cubic metres per year sawmill, the company is by far the most important regional employer.[24]

Although multivalue forest management and sustainable forestry have recently become operational targets, as they have for the entire industry, and the company pursues minimum-impact manufacturing, Weyerhaeuser has not been able to avoid public resistance to its operations.[25] Roadblocks and other forms of unrest – witness the blockade organized against MacMillan Bloedel by Friends of Clayoquot Sound and Greenpeace in 1993, the stand-off between First Nations protesters and NorSask (partially owned by the Meadow Lake Tribal Council) in the Canoe Lake area of northwestern Saskatchewan in 1992–3, and Weyerhaeuser's own 1996 encounters with the Dore-Smoothstone Lakes Wilderness Protection Association in that same province[26] – put access to timber in jeopardy. Weyerhaeuser's interest in joining on to the Model Forest Program was the opportunity it offered to develop the good relations with its neighbours that are critical to the security of its wood supply (apart from benefiting from the research the model forest would conduct).[27]

Parks Canada

In 1996, nearly 157,000 hectares or 40 per cent of Prince Albert National Park lay within PAMF. The park was established in March of 1927 after Prince Albert's Liberal riding association helped win Prime Minister Mackenzie King a seat there in a by-election, having lost his own in the 1925 general election.[28] The park, which became known as an 'automobile park' (foreshadowing the day when Parks Canada would build access roads into parks as a matter of course), would be developed for its recreational potential.[29] This fitted the thinking of the time; believing that 'the best and highest resource use for these areas lies in recreation,' Parks personnel often placed greater emphasis on the provision of 'artificial' recreational opportunities than on conservation goals.[30]

This emphasis has now largely been abandoned in favour of protection and restoration of the resource using the ecosystem method of land (and water) management. 'Ecological integrity,' 'stewardship,' 'citizen awareness,' and 'diversity' are common terms in recent Parks policy. There is also a clear sense that the ecological integrity of national parks is affected by activities taking place outside of it, and a resolve to address the problem by entering into 'integrated and collaborative management agreements and programs with adjacent land owners and land management agencies.'[31] Hence, from the park's perspective, participation in PAMF is an extension of its mandate. Like other national parks, it is becoming an island within an agricultural and industrial forestry landscape, its ecological integrity threatened. Thus, the park's aspiration in its involvement with PAMF is to contribute to the region's ecological health by broadening the discussion to include, for example, biodiversity, or by raising the possibility of connecting existing protected areas 'either philosophically or geographically.'[32] For similar reasons, park personnel have made Prince Albert National Park available for use in scientific studies. The park has supported hydrological and biodiversity studies of several taxa, among them fungi, birds, and forest plants, and has benefited from some socio-economic investigations into recreational activity and visitor spending patterns in the park.[33]

The Province
Saskatchewan's Department of Environment and Resource Management is the province's representative on PAMF. As the jurisdictional authority and principal landowner, the province is a de facto partner. As at most model forests,[34] it has not been an enthusiastic one, probably because of the federal nature of the model forest project and its potential threat to provincial authority. The relatively small contribution of forestry to the provincial economy may also help account for this reluctance. Saskatchewan's allowable annual cut of 7.6 million cubic metres (up from 7.1 in 1994–5) is not much compared, for example, with Quebec's 57.8 million cubic metres or British Columbia's 71.6 million cubic metres; only Nova Scotia, Prince Edward Island, and Newfoundland/Labrador rank below it.[35] Historically, Saskatchewan's entire manufacturing sector, including forest products, has represented about 5 per cent of a provincial economy dominated by agriculture and mining, reflecting the province's limited forest base.[36] Further, almost all of it lies in the north-central portion of the province, affecting only a small percentage of the population. Direct and indirect employment for 1995 in the sector totalled 9,000 jobs or 1 in 51, with wages and salaries (in 1993) amounting to $123 million.[37]

During PAMF's first three or four years, before a director of the ministry became actively involved, the province's performance was said to be 'disappointing,' a complaint directed only at the board of directors level, since provincial personnel had been highly active on PAMF's technical committee.[38]

Montreal Lake Indian Band
The Montreal Lake Indian Band was the only band in the region to become a partner in the original first-phase PAMF. Montreal Lake Reserve, which is 6,000 hectares large, dates from 1889 when the Montreal Lake Indians signed their adhesion to Treaty 6.[39] With some 2,140 members, it is the smallest of the area's Woodland Cree bands.[40] Joining PAMF was a matter of strategy on the part of the Montreal Lake Cree in their quest for control over resource management and ultimately for the self-government demolished by colonial rule. The PAMF partnership offered an opportunity to build the relationships that will help the Cree move towards meaningful participation in land management and decrease the burden of social ills such as unemployment. This was the motivating force behind Montreal Lake's involvement.[41]

Fundy Model Forest

Fundy Model Forest (FMF) occupies about 420,000 hectares of land in the Acadian mixed conifer and deciduous forest region of southern New Brunswick (29 per cent coniferous, 27 per cent broadleaf, and 23 per cent mixedwood). Unlike Prince Albert Model Forest, Fundy Model Forest has a very large partnership which numbered twenty-eight in 1996. There are four landowners in the partnership. Ownership of forest land in Fundy Model Forest is 63 per cent small woodlots, 17 per cent J.D. Irving freehold, and 15 per cent lease by J.D. Irving from the provincial government; the remainder belongs to Fundy National Park. This pattern is the reverse from that in New Brunswick generally where 70 per cent is held by large pulp and paper companies and the other 30 per cent by small woodlot owners. Apart from these landowners, many others are involved with FMF, among them schools, an angling and hunting club, villages in the area, researchers, and environmentalists.[42] Here I describe only the most important partners.[43]

Greater Fundy Ecosystem Research Group
The Greater Fundy Ecosystem Research Group formed in 1991, spurred on by the work of the Fundy National Park ecologist Stephen Woodley. His work demonstrated the permeability of park ecosystems to outside influences. Fundy National Park's ability to manage biodiversity, Woodley found, was undermined by its isolation in a region fragmented by roads and subjected to intense industrial forestry practices. Created to address this problem, the group's membership includes the province,

the park, researchers at the University of New Brunswick, Dalhousie, and elsewhere, the federal Department of the Environment, and J.D. Irving. It evolved into the independent scientific arm of Fundy Model Forest, its research agenda serving as Fundy's biodiversity agenda.[44]

Fundy National Park

Fundy National Park, located in the traditional sawmilling district of Albert County, was created in 1948 as an alternative strategy in aid of a region subject to chronic economic uncertainty. But the creation of the park, by further diminishing the sawmillers' wood supply in a system where the large pulp and paper companies (in the case of Albert County, the absentee Maine-based Hollingsworth and Whitney) hold the licences to the public woodlands, contributed to the difficulties of the local saw-milling industry; at the same time, the new tourism economy has not yielded the kind of returns hoped for.[45] In 1991, the park had a yearly budget for seventy person-years in employment, $3 million for capital expenditures, and $550,000 for environmental research, and spent another $600,000 annually on goods and services. The value of park tour-ism to the local economy was estimated at $2 million per year.[46]

The problem of the isolation of the national parks as islands in indus-trially developed landscapes is cause for concern at Fundy as well. Never Parks Canada's first choice for the region anyway, industrial for-estry in and around the park has turned it into 'a permeable forest patch,' a fact that puts the survival of reintroduced pine marten in doubt.[47] Thus, although Fundy National Park's participation in the model forest is in large degree the result of its status as landholder, its purpose is to have some means of influence over what happens outside its borders. This ability is its greatest preoccupation and the criterion for its participation.[48]

J.D. Irving

J.D. Irving, Limited is the timber and lumber segment of the Irving fam-ily's holdings, under the direction of its president, J.K. Irving. Including the Fundy licence of which the Fundy Model Forest's Crown lease is a part, J.D. Irving controls through ownership and lease some 1.8 million hectares of timberland in Quebec, Maine, and the Maritime prov-inces.[49] The wealth of the Irving family, estimated at US$3.7 billion in the latest Forbes survey, ranked it 123rd on its list of the world's top bil-lionaires.[50] Its reach includes the country's largest shipyard and largest oil refinery, first deep water port facility, New Brunswick's English-language newspapers and a television station, bus and truck lines, service stations, tugboats and dredgers, hardware stores, a frozen foods company, and a restaurant chain; Irving companies also sell tires, life insurance, heavy equipment, and computers. Its pulp and paper operations include Irving Paper in Saint John (formerly Rothesay Paper). At the beginning of the 1990s, that mill's capacity was 950 tons of newsprint and fine paper daily, employing 700. Forest products at that time brought in $900 million in sales, in part from the ten sawmills the family owns, seven of them located in New Brunswick, which together produced 1.25 million cubic metres of finished lumber per year. About one in every 12 New Brunswickers employed in the province is on the Irving payroll, 25,000 in total around 1990, and one in five New Brunswick private-sector jobs is related to an Irving enterprise.[51]

The company's involvement with Fundy Model Forest is a result of the realization that a softer ecological footprint is necessary if it is to survive in a business whose markets are subject to international boycotts.

Southern New Brunswick Woodlot Owner Organizations

The Southern New Brunswick Woodlot Owner Organizations (SNB) consist of a Wood Cooperative and a Forest Products Marketing Board. Only the first is a partner in Fundy Model Forest. New Brunswick's 41,000 woodlot owners supply 25 per cent of the province's annual forest products sector requirements and contribute $90 million to the economy. SNB, agent for nearly 7,000 woodlot owners, was created by plebiscite in 1979 and operates under provincial statute. There are seven regional marketing boards in New Brunswick, organized into the New Brunswick Federation of Woodlot Owners, formed in 1965, which in turn is a member of the Canadian Federation of Woodlot Owners.[52]

The SNB concerns itself with finding markets for its members, negotiates price, and engages in extension education on growing and cutting wood. While supporting silviculture, SNB's management approach nevertheless differs from the industrial variety in its protection of forest succession and a preference for selection cuts. Plantations, said a spokesperson for SNB, are a sign of management failure. Motivated by its involvement with Fundy Model Forest, SNB has been a key actor in the bid for certification launched by the national woodlot organization through the Canadian Standards Organization.[53]

The key issue for woodlot owners has been and continues to be fair pricing of their products. Marketing boards alone could not guarantee that, because large landowning companies such as J.D. Irving can regulate their rate of cutting, thus setting the price for smaller suppliers. To help remedy the conflict, the provincial government introduced legislation in 1982 that designated woodlots as the primary source of wood fibre and Crown leases as the residual source. To appease the pulp and paper sector, at the same time most Crown lands were consolidated into ten licences to be held by the mill owners. Ten years later, just as the Model Forest Program got under way, amendments to the act revoked 'Primary Source of Supply' status, together with the marketing boards' power to set production and prices. Thus, when SNB joined Fundy Model Forest, there was a feeling that the organization had 'crept into bed with the enemy,' that is, with Irving and the province.[54]

The Province

New Brunswick's Department of Natural Resources and Energy represents the province on the Fundy Model Forest. As at PAMF and elsewhere, it has been a reluctant partner, its participation largely handed over to the regional office in Hampton. Representation by the policy-making level of government has therefore been all but absent, while the provincial staff active on committees have been resource specialists, managers, and scientists.[55] In contrast to Saskatchewan, forestry in New Brunswick is a sizeable component of the provincial economy,[56] so it cannot be provincial indifference towards a natural resource that kept the policy-setting levels from showing more interest. Almost certainly the federal nature of the model forest initiative is to blame. The province, after all, had its own set course to integrated management, its own wildlife habitat management project; the model forest then was a competitor in the eyes of Department of Natural Resources and Energy administrators. Two other factors may contribute to the apparent distancing by Fredericton. One is lack of time in an age when organizations are cutting down on staff; the other the very technical (as opposed to policy-setting) nature of the committees' work.[57]

The province has, all the same, benefited from its involvement in Fundy Model Forest, for example, through the expansion of knowledge. The hope of many participants was that the province would regard the FMF as a valuable partner in advancing the cause of sustainable forest management and hence the well-being of the province's forest industry.[58]

Environmental Groups

A significant difference with PAMF is that, at Fundy, environmental groups are represented on the partnership, five in 1996; only the New

Brunswick Federation of Naturalists and the Conservation Council of New Brunswick are original partners. The interests of these groups cover a wide range of environmental issues, from the local to the regional, from the protection and conservation of nature to ecological forestry and fisheries.

In general, environmentalists at FMF bring a very different, ecological or deep ecology, perspective with which to question the notion held by the majority of its landholders that the area's forests must be working forests. Several saw their role as speaking up for the ecological integrity of the forest and wondered whether they were helping to endorse industrial practices by participating.[59]

Although environmentalists at FMF are partners, here as at Prince Albert Model Forest they face material barriers. Lack of time, and limited financial means and technical expertise are formidable problems that a stipend can only partially meet.[60] Lack of a land base (though several are small woodlot owners) is a further handicap that assigns them to the sidelines of the partnership because land ownership is an indirect factor in the allotment of Fundy Model Forest project funds. Partners without a monetary stake feel they have less credibility.[61]

Yet it is the environmentalists who point out conflicts of interest, press the importance of discussing controversial issues, instil the notion of forests being something more than trees, advance the cause of conservation, and in general raise questions that make pursuing the industrial course a little less comfortable.[62]

Management and Organization at PAMF and FMF

Despite different conceptions of the partnership model, the two model forests are similarly designed along a committee structure. A general manager or administrator looks after the day-to-day affairs of the model forest, assisted by a few essential staff members such as a receptionist/ secretary and a Geographic Information System analyst. Each model forest has a decision-making committee to whom the general manager is answerable; one or more committees made up of volunteers from the partner organizations develop research agendas, educational and outreach programs, and the like.

At PAMF, with its limited (restricted) partnership of landowners and aboriginal organizations, the partners are represented on the partnership management committee or board of directors. Charged with overseeing the commitments of the association, it is PAMF's decision-making body. A new chairman is elected annually, a position that has rotated among native and non-native board members. In 1996, there were three working committees: the technical (or partners) committee, the communications committee, and the consultative committee, a so-called external advisory group necessitated by the exclusion of other interests from the limited partnership base. Said to be a bit 'lost' and easy-going, its capacity to speak from an alternative viewpoint has never been great; the committee preferred to avoid controversy and, on the whole, was supportive of PAMF. Prior to 1996 there was also a volunteer research committee, composed of university researchers from diverse disciplines, whose role it was to advise PAMF's board of directors on how to best integrate research results into its management plan.[62] During 1997–8, as the model forest adjusted to the transition from first to second phase and after the present study had ended, the position of communications officer was suspended and the communications committee appeared no longer to be functioning. In addition, the existence of the consultative committee too was in doubt. Together these developments suggested a worrisome concentration of powers by the board. Since then, however, the advisory structure has been reorganized. Currently there are three working groups arranged by theme: ecosystem health and local-level indicators, integrated resource management, and communications and knowledge exchange. Each is open to all interested parties, but the third attracts less outside interest than the others, as communication is mostly an internal concern. Meetings take place regularly, and communication among the groups has improved, especially with the institution of a large meeting a year, which, in addition to the annual general meeting, brings the working groups together. Previously, participation in PAMF was made difficult for partner and non-partner organizations alike by a lack of communication between the committees and the board of directors, and among committees. For example, one representative on the communications committee noted that the board of directors seldom informed committee members of decisions it made and that minutes of board of directors meetings were not circulated, nor were they informed about the activities of the other committees except rarely. But an old obstacle faces those who still wish to participate: funding for the program's second phase has been cut in half, depriving interested organizations of their travel subsidy. One consequence has been to minimize environmentalist representation, a constituency already in 1997 much disenchanted with the entire experience.[63]

The most important distinction between management at Fundy and at PAMF is that the former has an inclusive or open partnership. There are at least two advantages to an inclusive partnership — each member of a committee belongs to an organization that is a partner, thus increasing accountability, at least in theory, and the open structure gives the otherwise marginal members of the policy community, those with little more than knowledge to their names, a forum more equitable than where partnerships are restricted. But it is very difficult to make a large consensus-based group function well; FMF has tried to accommodate its needs through two leading committees.

The first of these is the management committee, at the time chaired by Louis LaPierre, a professor in the department of biology at the Université de Moncton and member of the New Brunswick Premier's Round Table on the Environment and Economy. In 1996, it consisted of the four land tenure groups (permanent seats), a representative of the education, research, and environment sectors of FMF (annually elected seats), and three ex officio members (Canadian Forest Service, Fundy Model Forest's General Manager, and a lawyer). It met monthly to approve work plans and to administer funds and schedules, and took responsibility for the staff. Parallel to this was the partnership committee through which the twenty-eight partners had another, more direct voice; it met less frequently to review the strategies and recommendations of the management committee, the various technical committees (e.g., biodiversity, wood supply), and the information and education committee. At the time some believed that, in fact, it was this partnership committee where the real decisions were made and where the important management concepts arose that the model forest discussed. They thought of it as a board of directors, except that it met less often than the management committee and was hampered by its unwieldy number, irregular attendance, and incomplete information base (which remained with the management committee since technical committees and staff are accountable to it). In this view, the partnership committee's decisions ideally would instruct the management committee which, as executive, would implement the partnership's wishes. Most of the partners, however, have not seen themselves as providing strategic direction or as the decision-makers. But as far as FMF's management plan is concerned, the partnership committee does seem to have become the 'executive's' principal adviser.[64]

Partnership Dynamics

At both model forests the partnerships have succeeded in developing working relationships that demonstrated good will and have inspired trust. At Fundy, for example, SNB and J.D. Irving have cooperated on projects and, when the park brought to Irving's attention that a particular planned cut would damage a popular view, the company changed its plans. It has also begun to implement results from FMF's research program.[65] Likewise, at PAMF, Weyerhaeuser showed flexibility and willingness to accommodate others when it invited its partners and others in the area to design the cut blocks in the Bull Moose harvesting area. The company also decided not to cut the Thunder Hills, an area just north of Prince Albert National Park and sacred to native people, although it had been slated for cutting.[66] Another accomplishment at PAMF has been that the park has let up on its veneration of Grey Owl, a British conservationist who adopted native ways and lived in the park from 1931 to 1938.[67] This had been a sore spot with the Montreal Lake Cree since they, the people whom Grey Owl imitated, had been 'booted out' of Prince Albert National Park at the time of the park's creation in accordance with early Parks Canada policies.[68]

These and other achievements demonstrate that at least on some fronts ADR instruments such as the Model Forest Program partnerships can be effective in resolving specific, sometimes long-standing disputes, and certainly help establish trust and understanding. But there are limitations on what they can do. These result from the structural factors identified above and elsewhere in this volume, and are therefore significant: in a general way, they can prepare practitioners of and participants in ADR more realistically for what they may expect; in terms of a mechanism for process reform, however, it is important to recognize structural factors because they affect the distribution of power at the negotiating table. This can be illustrated by looking at how the two partnerships have tackled the problem of developing their management plans.

The information brochure soliciting proposals for the MFP did not specifically say that the model forest partnerships would have to produce a management plan — there was not to be actual joint management of the model forest area. However, they did have to identify management goals and the values the management regime was to include, identify the activities to be undertaken that would support reaching the goals, and experiment with new and innovative management techniques. They were to demonstrate the relevance of their particular program to sustainable forestry, and propose how 'trade-offs among conflicting objectives' (or values) might be dealt with and managed.[69] For all intents and purposes, these requirements translate into a management plan. At the least, as Gardner Pinfold consultants noted in their evaluation of the MFP, the partnerships should develop the management planning process that would fulfil the MFP's objectives.[70] The fact that trade-offs are involved between competing values means that at both Fundy and PAMF producing the integrated resource management plan has been a struggle. That deeply held values or principles make mediation more difficult than when just facts are at stake (the more common situation) is well known in ADR.[71]

At Fundy, the principal points to be accommodated by the management plan were obtained by consulting the public in the area. Issues include road building and maintenance, riparian buffer zones, and biodiversity conservation. Conflict within the Fundy partnership arose when these abstract concerns had to be translated into concrete objectives, specifically into the numbers that would lend themselves to the generation, by decision support system, of alternative what-if scenarios. As one partner put it, it seemed that the technocrats had taken over; to him and others the problem is that the ecological integrity of the forest may not be quantifiable. The technocratic preoccupation with quantification is associated for some of these partners with 'male super-rational language.'[72]

Quantification is about seeking the minimum one can get away with or a compromise – the trade-offs. Alternative scenarios, in fact, come into play only because of economic concerns. Economic impacts might have been discussed by referring to an ecological bottom line (and the Greater Fundy Ecosystem Group did produce a guiding document for that purpose), but the FMF membership was forced to debate scenarios that were driven by the economic logic of a timber-based industry with its quantifying methodology.[73] Thus, if environmentalists were to put a clear-cut ban on the table, the company would respond that they cannot manage forests without making some.[74] And the park's strongly felt position that adjacent landowners (J.D. Irving in this case) have a responsibility towards the ecological integrity of Fundy National Park and ought to curtail their activities along its border, fell on deaf company ears.

At PAMF, writing a management plan has also met with difficulties because of the economic logic and force of industrial forestry. Early attempts to produce the plan almost ran aground on Weyerhaeuser's resistance because of the priority of the Environmental Impact Assessment that the company was performing on its own provincial management plan. In the process, Weyerhaeuser came to be seen as a selfish company, unwilling to share its database while gaining access to information PAMF had generated. Of course, PAMF's share is just 4.5 per cent of the Forest Management Licence Agreement, making it necessary for Weyerhaeuser to conduct additional studies of its own.[75] This is one reason why PAMF may not be important enough to Weyerhaeuser, but the marked differences among the partners about the meaning and implementation of sustainable forest management have not helped. Industrial forestry means a focus on young forests, with attendant problems such as the use of pesticides and fertilizers, cut-block logging, loss of genetic and species diversity, soil impoverishment and impairment, damage to waterways, and loss of habitat. 'Managing for other values' in this case is seen to be a problem additional to the first task of producing timber, to be approached incrementally.[76] The Cree, on the other hand, believe that forestry should take a patchwork approach in order to maintain harmonious relations with nature, leaving some areas untouched and varying uses in others.[77] To the national park, protection of forest integrity is the most important. 'We will never agree on common objectives,' said one PAMF partner.[78]

An ongoing but muted conflict at PAMF highlights another reason why producing the management plan has been so difficult. Responsibility for forest management lies with only two players: the company and the province. Although the partnerships are involved with devising strategies and carrying out activities that would accelerate sustainable forestry by the lease-holding company, none is expected to make actual management decisions.[79] That would be an interference with the closed and unique legal relationship between the province and the company. True co- or joint management of a model forest's lands, in which power-sharing between the parties occurs,[80] is therefore not envisioned. At PAMF, it was clear right from the start that this could not be: when the Cree, during the early stages of PAMF, spoke in terms of co-management (the 'C-word'), Weyerhaeuser reportedly threatened to pull out. The underlying condition for PAMF's formation was to accept existing power relations. The company believes that the existing contractual relationship with 'the landlord' (Saskatchewan Environment and Resource Management) is the key, in conjunction with stakeholder consultation, to its security of wood supply.[81] In its own dealings with advisory or guidance groups on its leasehold lands outside of PAMF, Weyerhaeuser's position is that these so-called co-management boards not have the last word on forestry decisions, because these ultimately rest with Saskatchewan Environment and Resource Management.[82] For its part, the province, intent on keeping its jurisdictional powers unimpaired, agrees, seeing co-management only as an advisory function to improve the way resources are managed.[83] Although some boards think of themselves as co-jurisdiction boards, the province has informed them that they have no such authority.[84] This situation is not at all unique. Thomas Beckley concluded that, at the few co-management projects in existence in Canada today, decision-making is unequal and the boards function as advisory bodies.[85]

Discussion and Conclusions

Of all the principles or conditions that experience in environmental dispute resolution has identified as necessary for a successful outcome, the one calling for a relatively equal distribution of power may be the least straightforward to assess.[86] This observation applies to the general alternative dispute resolution literature where the presence of a consensus structure tends to be equated with the equitable distribution of power and resources.[87] It is appropriate also in the case study before us. There the partnership structure gives, in theory, equal power to each partner; the fact that decisions were made by consensus caused even the participants themselves sometimes to believe it was so. On this count Nixon makes what may be a useful distinction: true consensus is a community-building process, misuse of the term presumes the need for full agreement among the parties.[88] However, the Model Forest Program suggests that the outcome of the process is a more reliable gauge of actual equality than the method whereby decisions are reached. For example, in the wrangling about alternative scenarios for the FMF management plan, the decisions about the scenarios may well have been made by consensus (in either sense of the word), but the fact that the scenarios were necessary at all reflects the powerful logic of the timber imperative as well as the strength of the province–company alliance to force the hand of all involved, leaving many participants to wonder whether they were helping to green-stamp a program of industrial forestry.

It is also important to distinguish between the kinds of issues the partnership must decide. The partnerships were able to resolve some lesser grievances to the satisfaction of all those concerned, but they were not able to resolve the more fundamental disputes: those to do with actual land use and those involving regime change. At PAMF, for example, the focus on timber by those most powerful generated the feeling that agreement on the content of the management plan would not be possible, and Weyerhaeuser's discomfort over power sharing was behind its resistance to the notion of true co-management. We may speculate also that the determination on the part of the company and the province not to compromise the existing power arrangement helped institute a structure that marginalized non-material interests, when the whole MFP had been called into existence with the express hope of bringing them to the table. This underscores the importance of ideas and principles (or values) in the outcome of an ADR project, but also the crucial role played by institutional structures. Thus Cormick et al. may well write that the protective stances of governments (towards their legal authority to make the final decisions) and of certain societal agents (towards their exclusive rights to manage leasehold forest lands) are problematic only 'on the surface.' But the practical MFP experience suggests, on the contrary, that these structural impediments are critical to the ability of ordinary citizens, 'stakeholders' without much material interest, to participate as equals in consensus-building groups, and indeed to loosen the grip of the timber production paradigm (and the staple economy) on the forest industry.[89] Clearly, as these authors point out, the provinces should not be excluded from the table because they are, after all, part of the process and possess valuable technical information; similarly, the forestry corporations should participate since they hold the legal rights to management and have the needed resources to implement management decisions. But, just as clearly, the alternative decision-making process is impeded by what Clogg called 'corporate intransigence' and the tendency of government representatives to set the rules. In her examination of British Columbia's Commission of Resources and Environment and its subregional processes, Clogg found that the negotiated land use outcomes ratified the forest industry's priorities. She concluded that the existing policy and legal framework favours certain resource-based business sectors over others and that the procedural equality of round-table mediation is not enough to overcome structural barriers.[90] In the case of the Clayoquot Sound Steering Committee, important issues never came up for discussion because agreement could not be reached on their relevance. Government and industry officials continued to make decisions outside the process, seemingly unwilling to compromise their existing powers and privileges.[91] In short, the appearance of equality does not undo the reality of structural inequality.

Looking again at the MFP, there is a certain kind of equality in that any party could threaten to walk out, and some did, such as Fundy's SNB in a dispute over the allocation of project funds, which led to many late-night meetings to convince it to stay.[92] But it is J.D. Irving which has the final say about how much it will pay local woodlot owners for their wood, and it is J.D. Irving which decides whether it will oblige Fundy National Park by tempering its logging activities outside the park; likewise, Weyerhaeuser is the partner who will decide how much of a say the others may have in the management decisions that concern its licence. By the same token, everyone in the model forests is free to fight industry at the table, but to play that kind of game, one FMF activist thought, is 'a terrible ordeal.' Finally, decisions whether to alter the existing policy regime by delegating power to the model forests or similar bodies will be made by the provincial governments (in consultation with industry), not by the lesser folk at the table: the interested public.

In light of this structural inequality, the question arises whether the partnerships in the MFP might not better be seen as privileged, well-endowed advisory groups rather than alternative decision-making fora. The appearance given by procedural equality suggests that the partners are 'far more than advisors';[93] this is enhanced by the fact that they have had to hammer out a modus vivendi sufficient to allow them to submit a successful proposal and carry out their contractual obligations to each other and the Canadian Forest Service. They are also well funded and engage in research. In these respects the MFP is superior to any advisory board. Against that, however, must be put the fact that the MFP does not actually threaten the existing privileged relationship between the companies and their home province because whatever agreements a partnership reaches, even by consensus, they are not legally binding. A model forest may yet succeed in creating a management plan but its subordinate position is evident in that the company need not implement it,[94] and the content of the plan is likely to reflect the overwhelming influence of industrial forestry. In sum, the experience of the Model Forest Program gives little reason to believe that such partnerships, just because they are based in the consensus process, are much more than advisory.

Finally, what can the experiment of the model forests tell us about the potential of process reform for regime change? The evidence of the MFP agrees with Rayner and Howlett's observations presented earlier (in Chapter 2). The MFP instituted unprecedented decentralization of resource planning and management by introducing new actors with new ideas, yet the traditional policy style has been only contested, not seriously challenged, let alone replaced by a new network coalition. Similarly, although the involvement of the new actors did lead to modifications in operational practices, it was not able to alter the timber extraction paradigm itself. The model forests also successfully resolved problems in neighbourly relations, showing the validity of the partnership concept as an ADR tool. This alone is a truly important achievement for which the MFP must be commended. However, when it comes to the issue of forest policy paradigm and policy style, the burden of structural and politico-economic realities means the partnerships function rather as an unusual advisory group to their large industrial partners, not as their equals. Indeed, in view of the concerns about model forests not taking on a responsibility they are not entitled to, Gardner Pinfold consultants suggested their role might be to 'advis[e] local land managers, and demonstrat[e] what could be done.'[95] As in the larger world of forestry policy, the MFP reflects (and was created because of) the increasing contestation of the existing policy regime, but the role of the new actors is firmly checked by the same macro-conditions that helped create the regime in the first place. Full regime change therefore seems unlikely, although we may witness institutionalized process reform in the form of widespread use of advisory boards, established in order to enlist the public's views and so counter the threat of environmental unrest.

At best then, the Model Forest Program will have injected incremental change into the existing regime and generated some much needed practical experience with alternative management models. As Beckley remarked, 'New experiments build upon the experiences of previous ones,' and they may yet mature into new workable models.[96] Incremental change is not necessarily a bad thing. Beckley argues that it gives hope for increased public accountability, greater and more meaningful public participation, and may even lead to healthier forests. Incremental change also empowers policy activists, but may only demonstrate the resilience of the dominant policy regime and the ability of the dominant actors to usurp the new ideas. If long-term solutions are wanted, and if the Model Forest Program is any indication, then process reform will need to be embedded in structural reform. Whether gradual adjustments will ever result in such a comprehensive regime overhaul remains, it seems to me, an open question.

NOTES

1 Environmental mediation is a subset of this. See Jessica Clogg, 'Tenure Reform for Ecologically and Socially Responsible Forest Use in British Columbia,' unpublished MES Major Paper, York University, Toronto 1997);

Marcia C. Campbell and Donald W. Floyd, 'Thinking Critically about Environmental Mediation,' *Journal of Planning Literature* 10, 1996, 235–47.

2 Campbell and Floyd, 'Thinking Critically.'

3 See Joanna M. Beyers and L. Anders Sandberg, 'Canadian Federal Forest Policy: Present Initiatives and Historical Constraints,' in L. Anders Sandberg and Sverker Sörlin, eds., *Sustainability – The Challenge: People, Power and the Environment* (Montreal: Black Rose Books, 1998) 99–107.

4 For a succinct statement of 'Innisian' theory, see Roger Hayter and John Holmes, this volume: 'the structure of Canada's forest industries has been fundamentally shaped by the trade needs of superpowers.'

5 Wallace Clement, *The Canadian Corporate Elite: An Analysis of Economic Power* (Toronto: McClelland and Stewart, 1975).

6 Joanna M. Beyers, 'The Forest Unbundled: Canada's National Forest Strategy and Model Forest Program 1992–1997,' unpublished doctoral dissertation, York University, Toronto, 1998.

7 Sally E. Merry, 'Mediation in Non-Industrial Societies,' in Kenneth Kressel and Dean G. Pruitt and Associates, eds., *Mediation Research: The Process and Effectiveness of Third-Party Intervention* (San Francisco and London: Jossey-Bass, 1989) 68–90.

8 See Gerald Cormick, Norman Dale, Paul Emond, S. Glenn Sigurdson, and Barry D. Stuart, *Building Consensus for a Sustainable Future: Putting Principles into Practice* (Ottawa: National Round Table on the Environment and the Economy, 1996), 19.

9 On forestry conflicts, see Paul W. Hirt, *A Conspiracy of Optimism: Management of the National Forests since World War Two* (Lincoln: University of Nebraska Press, 1994); on modernist nature ideologies, see Beyers, 'The Forest Unbundled'; Anders Öckerman, 'Culture versus Nature in the History of Swedish Forestry: A Case for Pluralism,' in Sandberg and Sörlin, eds., *Sustainability – The Challenge*, 72–9.

10 See Merry, 'Mediation in Non-Industrial Societies.'

11 See Stephen Bocking, *Ecologists and Environmental Politics: A History of Contemporary Ecology* (New Haven: Yale University Press, 1997) 177; Kim Brenneis and Michael M'Gonigle, 'Public Participation: Components of the Process,' *Environments* 21(3), 1992, 5–11; Charles F. Cortese and Linda Firth, 'Systematically Integrating Public Participation into Planning Controversial Projects: A Case Study,' *Interact / The Journal of Public Participation* 3, 1997, 6–23.

12 See Cormick et al., *Building Consensus*, 10–12; Brenneis and M'Gonigle, '*Public Participation*,' 6; Roger Fisher, William Ury, and Bruce Patton, *Getting to Yes: Negotiating Agreement without Giving In* (New York: Penguin, 1991), 10.

13 See S.M. Born and W.C. Sonzogni, 'Integrated Environmental Management:

Strengthening the Conceptualization,' *Environmental Management* 19, 1995, 167–81; R.J. McLain and R.G. Lee, 'Adaptive Management: Promises and Pitfalls,' *Environmental Management* 20, 1996, 437–48.

14 See G. Bruce Doern and T. Conway, *The Greening of Canada: Federal Institutions and Decisions* (Toronto: University of Toronto Press, 1994).

15 See Michael Howlett, 'The 1987 National Forest Sector Strategy and the Search for a Federal Role in Canadian Forest Policy,' *Canadian Public Administration* 32, 1989, 545–63; Michael Howlett and Jeremy Rayner, this volume.

16 See C. Godbout and L. Bouthillier, *Forestry Issues in Canada*, paper for the Canadian Council of Forest Ministers: Hull, 1991; M. Patricia Marchak, *Logging the Globe* (Montreal and Kingston: McGill-Queen's University Press, 1995); Lorna Stefanick, this volume.

17 See Beyers and Sandberg, 'Canadian Federal Forest Policy'; Beyers, 'The Forest Unbundled.'

18 See Forestry Canada, *Partners in Sustainable Development of Forests Program* (Hull, no date), 1; Forestry Canada, *Model Forests: Background Information and Guidelines for Applicants* (Hull, 1991); Graham Savage, Fredericton, telephone interview, 23 April 1996.

19 See Michael Howlett and M. Ramesh, *Studying Public Policy: Policy Cycles and Policy Subsystems* (Toronto: Oxford University Press, 1995); H. Vivian Nelles, *The Politics of Development: Forests, Mines and Hydro-Electric Power in Ontario, 1849–1941* (Toronto: Macmillan, 1974).

20 See W.P. Grant, 'Forestry and Forest Products,' in W.D. Coleman and Grace Skogstad, eds. *Policy Communities and Public Policy in Canada: A Structural Approach* (Toronto: Copp Clark Pitman, 1990), 120; Nancy Colpitts, 'Sawmills to National Park: Alma, New Brunswick, 1921–1947,' in L. Anders Sandberg, ed., *Trouble in the Woods: Forest Policy and Social Conflict in Nova Scotia and New Brunswick* (Fredericton: Acadiensis Press, 1992), 96; Bill Parenteau, ' "In Good Faith": The Development of Pulpwood Marketing for Independent Producers in New Brunswick, 1960–1975,' in *Trouble in the Woods*, 138.

21 Interviews with Jeff Patch, Fredericton, 2 May 1996, and Lois Dellert, Toronto, 9 Aug. 1996.

22 See S.N. Kulshreshtha and H.V. Walker, *Strategic Planning for the Prince Albert Model Forest* (Prince Albert: Prince Albert Model Forest Association, 1994); Prince Albert Model Forest Planning Committee (PAMFPC), *Prince Albert Model Forest: Proposal Submitted to National Advisory Committee, Model Forest Program, Ottawa* (Prince Albert: Prince Albert Model Forest Association, 1992).

23 See G. Herndon, *Cut and Run: Saying Goodbye to the Last Great Forests in the West* (Telluride: Western Eye Press, 1991), 170.

24 Since MacMillan Bloedel held a timber licence in Saskatchewan as well, Weyerhaeuser's holdings in that province will probably greatly increase there. For the numbers quoted here, see Weyerhaeuser, *Canada Overview* (Folder) (Kamloops, no date); PAMFC, *Prince Albert Model Forest*; Canadian Council of Forest Ministers, *Compendium of Canadian Forestry Statistics 1992* (Ottawa: Forestry Canada, 1993).

25 See Weyerhaeuser Canada, 'Eco-Labeling the Forest: Will New Certification End the War in the Woods?' *BC Life* 8(5), 1996, 4–5; R.C. Gozon, 'Minimum Impact, Ecological Balance and Public Expectations,' paper presented to the Third Global Conference on Paper and the Environment, 28 March 1995, London.

26 For the events at Clayoquot Sound, B.C., see Jeremy Wilson, this volume; for the Canoe Lake protest, see Elizabeth May, *At the Cutting Edge: The Crisis in Canada's Forests* (Toronto: Key Porter Books, 1998) 165–8; on Dore-Smoothstone, see Canadian Press, 'Co-Management Upsets Northwest,' in *Prince Albert Daily Herald*, 25 May 1995, 1.

27 See J.W. Creighton, 'Facing the Future: Sustainability through Continuous Improvement,' paper presented to Papercast, 1994, Frankfurt; J. Spencer, 'Partnership Building for Sustainable Development: An Industry Perspective from Saskatchewan,' in O. Thomas Bouman and David G. Brand, eds., *Sustainable Forests: Global Challenges and Local Solutions* (New York: Food Products Press, 1995) 163–9.

28 See B. Waiser, 'The Political Art of Park Making: Mackenzie King and the Creation of Prince Albert National Park,' paper presented at the Themes and Issues in North American Environmental History Conference, 25 April 1998, Toronto.

29 See P. Goode, J. Champ, and L. Amundson *The Montreal Lake Region: Its History and Geography* (Saskatoon: Sentar Consultants, 1996).

30 See Canada, *National Parks Policy* (Ottawa: Indian Affairs and Northern Development, National and Historic Parks Branch, 1969). The terms 'conservation' and 'preservation' are often used interchangeably. Here I refer to ecological goals of the kind associated with the field of conservation biology.

31 See Canada, *Parks Canada Guiding Principles and Operational Guidelines* (Ottawa: Natural Resources Canada, Parks Service, 1994), 35:3.2.9.

32 Interview with Paul Tarleton, Waskesiu, 10 June 1996.

33 See O. Thomas Bouman, *Third Annual Report of the Prince Albert Model Forest Association Inc.* (Prince Albert: Prince Albert Model Forest Association, 1995).

34 See Gardner Pinfold Consulting Economists, *Evaluation of the Canadian Model Forest Program* (Ottawa: Audit and Evaluation Branch, Natural Resources Canada, PE 223/1996, 1996).

35 See Natural Resources Canada, *The State of Canada's Forests, 1996–97: Learning from History* (Ottawa: Canadian Forest Service, 1997).

36 See T.W. Steele, D.M. Boylen, and A. Baumgartner, *Saskatchewan's Forest Industry, 1985* (Ottawa: Canadian Forestry Service, Information Report Nor-X-295, 1988); Michael Howlett, 'The Forest Industry on the Prairies: Opportunities and Constraints to Future Development,' *Prairie Forum* 14, 1989, 233–57.

37 See Natural Resources Canada, *The State of Canada's Forests, 1995–1996: Sustaining Forests at Home and Abroad* (Ottawa: Canadian Forest Service, 1996).

38 Interviews with Tony Richmond, Ian Monteith, Michael Newman, and others, Prince Albert, June 1996; this situation has improved since 1996.

39 See Goode et al., *Montreal Lake Region.*

40 See Saskatchewan Health, *Covered Population, 1996* (Regina: Health Registration File, 1996).

41 Interviews with Gene Kimbley and Ed Henderson, Prince Albert, 11 and 13 June 1996.

42 See Fundy Model Forest (FMF), 'The Fundy Model Forest: A Model Forest Proposal,' submitted under the 'Partners in Sustainable Development of Forests' Program of Canada's Green Plan for a Healthy Environment (Saint John, 1992).

43 For a complete discussion, also of PAMF, see Beyers, *The Forest Unbundled.*

44 See Stephen Woodley, 'The Greater Fundy Ecosystem,' *Greater Fundy Ecosystem* 1(1), 1993, 1; and telephone interview with Stephen Woodley, Ottawa, 1 Aug. 1997.

45 See Nancy Colpitts, 'Sawmills to National Park: Alma, New Brunswick, 1921–1947,' in *Trouble in the Woods,* 90–109.

46 See FMF, 'The Fundy Model Forest.'

47 See Colpitts, 'Sawmills to National Park'; L. Cooper and Douglas Clay, *An Historical Review of Logging and River Driving in Fundy National Park* (Alma: unpublished manuscript of Parks Canada, Research Notes of Fundy National Park no. 94–05, revised, 1994), 2; interview with Stephen Flemming, Alma 3 May 1996.

48 Interview with Dan Mullaly, Alma, 3 May 1996.

49 See J. DeMont, *Citizens Irving: K.C. Irving and His Legacy – The Story of Canada's Wealthiest Family* (Toronto: Doubleday Canada Limited, 1991); D. How and R. Costello, *K.C.: The Biography of K.C. Irving* (Toronto: Key Porter Books, 1993).

50 See B. Milner, 'Bill Gates Leaves Pack Behind at $90-billion,' *Globe and Mail,* 21 June 1999; the Irving family placed 84th with $3.5 billion in 1996, see Associated Press, 'Gates Leaves other Top Tycoons in the Dust,' *Globe and Mail,* 14 July, 1997, A9.

51 See DeMont, *Citizens Irving*; J.D. Irving (www.ifdn.com, 9 June 1998). As well as in New Brunswick, the family operates in Japan, Maine, and South America.

52 See New Brunswick Federation of Woodlot Owners (NBFWO), *New Brunswick Woodlot Owners' Code of Practice* (no place, no date).

53 See Brian Belyea, 'Developing a Sustainable Forest Management Planning System for Private Woodlots Using the Canadian Standards Association Protocol,' *Forestry Chronicle* 72, 1996, 605–7; Canadian Federation of Woodlot Owners, 'Woodlot Owners Getting Ready for Certification,' press release, Fredericton, 15 April 1996; Gardner Pinfold, *Evaluation of the Canadian Model*.

54 See Anonymous, 'Woodlot Owner Survey,' *SNB Woodlot Advance* 6(1), 1996, 7; NBFWO, *Code of Practice*; Parenteau, "In Good Faith,' 110–41; May, *At the Cutting Edge*; plus an anonymous interview, FMF, May 1996.

55 Interviews with Tom Pettigrew, Hampton, 30 April 1996; Blake Brunsdon, Dan Mullaly, and Doug Clay, Alma, 3 May 1996. More recently there has been some movement in this position: the Department of Natural Resources and Energy's Director of Sustainable Development, Policy and Planning Branch has accepted a position on the national Model Forest Network's board of directors, signaling a new attitude towards FMF (Peter Etheridge, written communication, 1997).

56 See Natural Resources Canada, *The State of Canada's Forests, 1996–97*. New Brunswick's annual allowable cut was 11.2 m^3 in 1995, greater than that in previous years. Provincial exports of forest products were valued at more than $2 billion in 1996, three-quarters coming from the wood pulp and paper products sector, with a trade balance of $1.9 billion. Forest industries provided 26,000 direct and indirect jobs, or 1 in 12.

57 Interview with Doug Clay.

58 Interview with Peter Etheridge, Sussex, 29 April 1996.

59 See Karen Townsend, 'Comments to the FMF Partnership Workshop,' mimeograph, 18 Jan. 1996; interviews with David Coon, Fredericton, and Karen Townsend, Alma, 3 May 1996.

60 Interview with Peter Pearce, Fredericton, 2 May 1996.

61 Interview with Anna Holdaway, Alma, 3 May 1996.

62 Interviews with Marilyn Powell, Cambridge Narrows, 3 May 1996, Karen Townsend and Peter Pearce.

63 Anonymous interview, PAMF, June 1996; Allyson Brady, written communication, 1998; Keith Chaytor, personal communication, 2000.

64 See FMF, 'The Fundy Model Forest'; interviews with Dan Mullaly, Peter Pearce, Graham Forbes, and David Coon.

65 Interview with Dan Mulally; Peter Etheridge, written communication 1997.
66 Interviews with Gene Kimbley and Michael Newman, Prince Albert, 11 and 13 June 1996.
67 Canada, *National Parks System Plan* (Ottawa: Environment Canada, Parks Service, 1990).
68 Interviews with Paul Tarleton, Gene Kimbley and Michael Newman. Considering the changed attitude the park has brought to this issue, it is difficult to believe that the world premiere of the Hollywood film *Grey Owl* was held, in September 1999, in Waskesiu, the site of Prince Albert National Park's headquarters. See Canadian Press, '*Grey Owl* to Premiere in Canada,' *Globe and Mail*, 8 May 1999.
69 See Forestry Canada, *Model Forests: Background Information and Guidelines for Applicants* (Hull, 1991), 8–9.
70 See Gardner Pinfold, *Evaluation of the Canadian Model Forest Program*, 29, also 8: the outcome of the weighing of alternative strategies and trade-offs is 'an explicit management plan' to implement the strategy.
71 See Kenneth Kressel and Dean G. Pruitt, 'Conclusion: A Research Perspective on the Mediation of Social Conflict,' in Kenneth Kressel, Dean G. Pruitt and Associates, eds., *Mediation Research: The Process and Effectiveness of Third-Party Intervention* (San Francisco and London: Jossey-Bass, 1989), 404; Brenneis and M'Gonigle, 'Public Participation,' 5–11; Chris Maser, *Resolving Environmental Conflict: Towards Sustainable Community Development* (Delray Beach: St Lucie Press, 1995).
72 See Townsend, 'Comments.'
73 Interview with Mullaly, telephone follow-up, Alma, 24 May 1996; the ecological 'bottom line' was prepared by the Greater Fundy Ecosystem Group in the form of guidelines – see Greater Fundy Ecosystem Research Group, *Forest Management Guidelines to Protect Native Biodiversity in the Fundy Model Forest*, Stephen Woodley and Graham Forbes (Fredericton: New Brunswick Cooperative Fish and Wildlife Research Unit, University of New Brunswick, 1997).
74 Interview with Etheridge.
75 Telephone interview with Jack Spencer, 19 June 1996.
76 See Creighton, 'Facing the Future.'
77 Interview with Henderson; anonymous interview, PAMF, June 1996.
78 As reported by Thomas Bouman, personal communication, 1997.
79 See Gardner Pinfold, *Evaluation of the Canadian Model Forest Program*, 6.
80 See E.W. Pinkerton, 'Overcoming Barriers to the Exercise of Co-Management Rights,' in Monique Ross and J.O. Saunders, eds., *Growing Demands on a Shrinking Heritage: Managing Resource-Use Conflicts – Essays from the Fifth Institute*

Conference on Natural Resources Law (Calgary: Canadian Institute of Resources Law, 1992), 277.

81 Telephone interview with Spencer.

82 See D. Oleksyn, 'Timber Harvest Battle Brewing,' *Prince Albert Daily Herald*, 6 June 1996, 1.

83 See G. Urbanoski, 'Province Rejected Co-Management Plan from Ottawa Year before It Became Public,' *Prince Albert Daily Herald*, 18 Aug. 1995, 1, and 'Self-Government Sticking Point in Co-Management,' *Prince Albert Daily Herald*, 19 Aug. 1995, 1; R. Gosse, *Searching for Common Ground: First Nations and the Management of Natural Resources in Saskatchewan – A Background Paper to Assist Discussions on 'Co-management' Issues* (prepared for DIAND, Victoria, 1995).

84 Anonymous interview, PAMF, June 1996.

85 See Thomas M. Beckley, 'Moving Toward Consensus-Based Forest Management: A Comparison of Industrial, Co-Managed, Community, and Small Private Forests in Canada,' *Forestry Chronicle* 74, 1998, 738.

86 Under 'equality' I include related concerns such as the availability of resources to all equally. Other conditions include: the parties must want to settle or feel that there is good reason, such as the need for a good relationship with the adversaries, to participate; all parties must be at the table (the principle of inclusivity), including the departmental public servants who will be responsible for implementation; and the negotiations must be open and accompanied by extensive community outreach; decision-makers must show their commitment to the process, for example by making sufficient resources available to all participants, involving them in the final decision-making, giving adequate notification and making information available, and the like; the focus should be on interests, not position, a situation that will favour the discovery of common ground and will inspire faith in the possibility of a settlement; the process must be flexible, designed with care and respect, and agreed upon by all interests in order to build up trust and counter adversarial attitudes and strategies, and it should be supervised by the major users. See Kressel and Pruitt, 'Conclusion: A Research Perspective on the Mediation of Social Conflict,' 404. Also Brenneis and M'Gonigle, 'Public Participation,' 5, 7; Maser, *Resolving Environmental Conflict*, 7; Cormick et al., *Building Consensus*, 20; Fisher, Ury, and Patton, *Getting to Yes*; Campbell, and Floyd, 'Thinking Critically about Environment Mediation,' 237; Jonathan Brock and Gerald W. Cormick, 'Can Negotiation be Institutionalized or Mandated? Lessons from Public Policy and Regulatory Conflicts,' in *Mediation Research*, 138–65; Barry Stuart, 'The Potential of Land Claims Negotiations for Resolving Resource-Use Conflicts,' in *Growing Demands*, 129–54.

87 See Cormick et al., *Building Consensus*; interview with Newman; telephone interview with Doug Mazur, 19 June 1996.

88 Bob Nixon, 'Public Participation: Changing the Way We Make Decisions,' in Ken Drushka, Bob Nixon, and Ray Travers, eds., *Touch Wood: BC Forests at the Crossroads* (Madeira Park: Harbour Publishing, 1993) 23–66.

89 Cormick et al. *Building Consensus*, 109.

90 See Clogg, 'Tenure Reform,' 69–71, 82.

91 See Nixon, 'Public Participation,' 32–5.

92 Telephone interview with Woodley.

93 Telephone interview with Mazur.

94 The second phase of the MFP may be somewhat more demanding. Among other things, its guidelines stipulate that the new five-year 'action plan' must show how each model forest will implement sustainable forestry practices and to what degree those responsible for forest management will be participating in the model forest's activities. See Natural Resources Canada, Canada's Model Forest Program: Proposal Guidelines for Phase II (Ottawa: Canadian Forest Service, 1996) 14.

95 Gardner Pinfold, *Evaluation of the Canadian Model Forest Program*, 29.

96 See Thomas M. Beckley, 'Moving Toward Consensus-Based Forest Management: A Comparison of Industrial, Co-Managed, Community and Small Private Forests in Canada,' *The Forestry Chronicle* 74, 1998, 743.

PART 4
CASE STUDIES IN INSTITUTIONAL ADAPTATION
AND POLICY CHANGE

Chapter Eight

Atlantic Canada: The Politics of Private and Public Forestry

Peter Clancy

An Overview

The forest politics of the Atlantic provinces is a study in contrasts, although not without several strong common themes. Of the four, only New Brunswick figures among the leading provincial jurisdictions by size. Ranked by timber harvest volume or value, it rounds out the top five, following British Columbia, Quebec, Ontario, and Alberta. It was even more prominent in earlier times, when New Brunswick served as Britain's 'timber colony' in North America. When the profession of forestry was launched, at the beginning of the twentieth century, the University of New Brunswick founded Canada's second degree program in 1908. If there is a regional leader in terms of provincial forest policy and administration, New Brunswick has the best claim to the title. The remaining Atlantic provinces sit in the bottom half of the national forest tables.[1] With an industry less than half the size of its western neighbour, Nova Scotia ranks sixth in Canada by most standard measures. Half reduced again, Newfoundland stands eighth (or ninth), while tiny Prince Edward Island rivals the northern territories for last spot (see Table 8.1).

However, these factors only begin to capture the rich and surprising contrasts of forestry in the Atlantic region. The nature of the resource is an important variable. Here Newfoundland stands apart from the others. The three Maritime provinces share the distinct Acadian forest region, which combines significant proportions of softwood conifers (such as spruce and balsam fir) and hardwood broad-leaf species (such as maple and birch).[2] The Acadian forest varies between predominantly softwood or hardwood areas and mixed-wood areas, and this complex composition makes possible a diverse range of industrial applications.

Table 8.1 Comparison of Atlantic provinces forestry sectors (provincial ranking in parentheses)

Province	Forest land, 1997 (million ha)	Annual harvest, 1996 million m³	Shipment value, 1995 (billions of $)	Employment, 1997
Newfoundland	22.5 (7)	2.1 (8)	N/A	8,000 (8)
P.E.I.	0.29 (10)	0.4 (10)	$0.034 (10)	N/A
Nova Scotia	3.9 (9)	5.6 (6)	$1.4 (6)	18,000 (6)
New Brunswick	6.1 (8)	10.8 (5)	$3.9 (5)	29,000 (5)

Source: *State of Canada's Forests, 1997–98* (Ottawa: Natural Resources Canada, 1998).

Whether the forest has been effectively managed towards this end is a question taken up below. The Province of Newfoundland and Labrador, by contrast, forms part of the boreal forest region, which stretches across Canada's mid-north from east to west. Here the species composition is over 90 per cent softwood, particularly black spruce and balsam fir. In terms of natural endowment, then, Newfoundland's forest shares more with Ontario and Quebec than with her Maritime neighbours. This has implications for both forest management policies and for industrial utilization.

A different perspective emerges from a consideration of forest tenure (i.e., ownership) relationships. Canada's forests are predominantly a 'Crown' resource, with 70 per cent of inventoried forests in provincial ownership, 24 per cent in national (federal) ownership, and only 6 per cent in private hands.[3] As a result, provincial authorities play a central role in defining the terms of access, management, and use of the resource. The Maritime provinces, however, register a strong exception to the national pattern. Owing largely to eighteenth- and nineteenth-century land grant policies that encouraged settlement, a uniquely high proportion of forested rural land rests in private hands to this day. Expressed in terms of total inventoried forest land, the privately owned share is 90 per cent for Prince Edward Island, 70 per cent for Nova Scotia, and 49 per cent for New Brunswick. In no other province does the private forest share exceed 14 per cent (Ontario) and in Newfoundland it is less than 3 per cent.

The prominence of private tenure is a defining social relationship of Maritime forestry. First, it creates a major rural small producer segment in a sector where neither Canadian government authorities nor industry are accustomed to yeoman ownership. The prevalence of private tenure also makes possible a market in forest land (as well as forest products), whereby corporations have accumulated significant holdings by purchase. Thus, the private forest segment includes two potentially antagonistic forces: small woodlot owners and industrial corporate owners. Politically, this transforms the producer alignment from a business–government polarity into a woodlot–corporate–Crown triangularity. Finally, the scale of private forest holdings complicates the application of provincial government policy in the Maritimes. These authorities lack some of the policy levers enjoyed elsewhere in the country. Both legal and political considerations have discouraged provincial governments from aggressively regulating private forest lands. For landowners, this has been a mixed blessing. While it has brought freedom from cutting rules and export controls, it has also posed a barrier to forest tax reform and organized commodity marketing. Given the diffusion of ideas and practices in forest training, professional practice, and policy-making, it is interesting to gauge the impact of this Maritime particularity. Provincial government officials regularly lament the burdens they face from private forest tenure, and the absence of creative policy for this segment is striking. Indeed a Freudian psychologist might be tempted to diagnose a regional syndrome of 'Crown land envy.'

On this issue, too, Newfoundland stands apart. As colonial settlement was confined largely to coastal fishing ports, the island's interior remained in Crown hands. Thus, when commercial interest first turned to the forest resource, in the late nineteenth century, it was available for lease to British business on highly concessionary terms. One significant exception, however, ensured a small producer presence of a unique sort. In 1906 a coastal forest belt three miles deep was reserved for the use of fishing communities requiring sawlogs and fuel. Although these lands have been heavily used over the course of the twentieth century, they went essentially unregulated until the 1970s and as such constituted an open access (albeit Crown-owned) resource. For Newfoundland, then, Crown tenure was not a sufficient condition for progressive forest management. Nor was this simply a colonial (i.e., pre-1949) condition. In fact, Newfoundland lagged well behind the norms of both British and Canadian forest policy until the 1970s.[4]

In exploring forest policy regimes in Atlantic Canada, we face a dual challenge. It is clear that there are few simply observed generalizations across the four jurisdictions. Fundamental differences of forest ecology, political economy, party politics, and administrative development account for significant variations in the timing, the sequences, and the substance of policy. At the same time, however, there are certain common forces (shared with other provinces as well) that exert some continuity. The provinces form part of a shared national and international marketplace for forest products, which dictates comparative product values, business cycles, and investment opportunities. Provinces are also linked through national government initiatives in forestry, which have been mounted in several waves since the Second World War. Ottawa has concentrated on forest science, the joint financing of silvicultural programs, and forest product export development. More specifically, the Government of Canada underwrote a national program of forest inventories in the 1950s, land improvement programs in the 1960s, intensive silvicultural treatments in the 1970s and 1980s, and third-party certification for sustainable management systems in the 1990s. Indeed, it was the 1995 termination of the joint forest resource development schemes, after more than twenty years of continuous federal support, that triggered the current forest management crisis which has been particularly severe in Atlantic Canada.

Clearly, it is not possible to offer in this chapter an exhaustive treatment of the four jurisdictions. Yet in seeking to capture the broad trends of regime change through time and space, examples will be drawn from all provinces. Our goal is to chart the parameters of forest policy regimes throughout Atlantic Canada. In so doing, the discussion must be sensitive to the range of variation within the set, and to the grounds for generalization and difference. While the policy literature on Atlantic forestry is not burgeoning, neither is it minimal. It does remain uneven, however, which means that there is much to learn from a cross-provincial comparison. Several propositions will be explored in the sections that follow: (1) all Atlantic forest regimes underwent structural transformations in the generation immediately following the Second World War; (2) here the defining features include the decline of a partisan and clientelist forest regime and the rise of a professional and administrative forest regime (although the shift is relative rather than absolute); (3) the driving forces for this change included escalating industrial demand for wood fibre, and unprecedented federal transfers to underwrite intensive management; (4) by virtue of its structure, the modern Atlantic forest regime services a core set of industrial producer interests; (5) its failures to accommodate alternative claims from woodlot, environmental, and Aboriginal interests have weakened the regime's political legitimacy in the 1990s.

Regime Formation: Colonial Foundations

Forest policy occupies a vast field, and some preliminary distinctions will help to organize the territory. *Primary* forest policy involves measures directed at the timber resource itself, and the activities of growing, harvesting, and marketing wood fibre. Here the prime aim of forest management is to maximize the growth of standing timber and the yield of logs. *Industrial* forest policy involves measures directed at the forward processing activities whereby raw logs are manufactured into higher value commodities such as lumber, pulp and paper, furniture, and other wood products. Of course, the two can never be strictly separated. As will be clear below, the terms and allocation of timber-cutting rights (through measures such as granting and leasing policies, stumpage, and tax rates, manufacturing conditions, log export rules, private wood-marketing arrangements, and timber-cutting regulations) will directly affect the prospects for industrial processing, and determine which agents acquire logging rights. At the same time, measures directed at secondary processing (such as special timber concessions, forest tax and stumpage reductions and exemptions, fresh water and electricity supply deals, special terms on effluent discharge, railroad and highway transport support, and capital cost relief through grants and tax breaks) will shape the demand structure for primary products.

It was almost three centuries ago that the imperial Crown began to assert proprietorial claims to timber. Between 1690 and 1765, British colonial governors and their agents negotiated a series of treaties with the Aboriginal peoples of the Mi'kmaq and Maliseet tribes. While their precise terms have been subject to continuing legal dispute, the colonial treaties recognized Indian sovereignty and rights to traditional land while securing neutrality or alliance in the English–French wars.[5] In addition, the English Crown reserved woodlands by species and by territory. The Broad Arrow Policy was proclaimed in colonial Nova Scotia in 1729, reserving all white pine trees on Crown lands (whose diameter exceeded twenty-four inches) for the masting requirements of the British navy.[6] Later, in 1774, vast tracts of many major watersheds were designated as timber reserves and thereby exempted from land grants.[7]

By the early nineteenth century, Atlantic Canada had assumed its modern political boundaries. Ile St Jean (renamed Prince Edward Island) and Ile Royale (now Cape Breton) passed from France to England in 1763. Six years later, Prince Edward Island became a separate colony, whose lands were allotted to English aristocrats. New

Brunswick was carved out of the old colony of Nova Scotia in 1784, in response to the pressures of Loyalist immigration. And throughout this time, Newfoundland remained an English colonial outpost in the western Atlantic, dedicated chiefly to the fishery.

Throughout the nineteenth century, the foundations of *forest tenure* were the central question in dispute. This revolved around the politics of settler societies. One axis involved the struggle between appointed colonial officers and elected representatives for control of Crown lands. In New Brunswick the historic transition came in 1837, when the Lords of Treasury surrendered timber, land, wildlife, and mineral powers to the House of Assembly.[8] Another axis set the merchant compact class, eager to control large land blocks for settlement or timbering, against the immigrant underclass which aspired to smallholdings. On the one hand, the demand for farmland, secured by either grant or sale, placed continuing pressure for the transfer of Crown holdings. On the other hand, the revenue needs of colonial governments made Crown forest holdings strategic assets. Colonies responded in different ways to the challenge of the lumber trade. New Brunswick opted for Crown reserves and timber licensing by the 1830s.[9] Nova Scotia continued to grant sizeable tracts of land up to 1900. In Prince Edward Island, the political challenge of tenant farmers to absentee landowners took the form of the Escheat Movement, which eventually forced the surrender and sale of these properties after 1878.

Regime Change: The Impact of Conservation and Industrial Expansion

With crown tenure secured for the residual forest, attention shifted in the early twentieth century from the 'disposition' of timber to its 'management.' In earlier times, forest owners and leaseholders were largely unregulated in their approach to the resource. There were several threads to the new thinking. The North American resource conservation movement had demonstrated the abuses of unregulated capitalist exploitation, and made the case for controlled public management of renewable resources such as forests.[10] While this movement was well launched by the 1890s among national authorities and big resource businesses, it was slower to penetrate subnational governments and hinterland enterprises. Second, the shift of focus from the alienation of Crown land (for settlement) to the conservation of Crown land (in forest) involved a complex transition of values, administrative techniques, and political alliances, which could only be accomplished with time. As an administrative instrument, the early twentieth century provincial Department of Lands and Forests was often a forced amalgamation of distinct and opposed cultures, particularly as the lands component declined and the forests component rose to prominence. Even here, while forest 'management' might have been given new statutory expression in the years following the First World War, it was another matter to translate these impulses into administrative programs, much less implement them on the ground.[11]

Third, the partisan and clientist dimensions of forest policy remained decidedly traditionalist during the first half of the twentieth century. This was a time when ministers and elected legislative members remained key political brokers between rural interests and forest policy outputs such as Crown cutting licences and leases, roads and railroads, and seasonal jobs. Not only did the allocative channels run between the political and rural economic elites, but also between elite and subordinate personnel within the state. At a time before professional forest accreditation had won widespread acceptance in resource management, field positions remained important patronage plums. Forest ranger positions, where the duties centred on fire protection and enforcement of game laws, were allocated to politically connected sawmillers or outdoorsmen, as were the sub-ranger positions beneath them. Fourth, the values of scientific research, professional training, and administrative expertise were considered central to the new conservation management. This held vast implications for financing, recruitment and decision-making in state agencies for lands and forests. However the pace and extent of the transition between old and new regimes hinged on the political alliances, representative vehicles, and resource.

Well into the twentieth century, the old regime remained strong. In New Brunswick, the organized lumber interest was virtually hegemonic, while in Nova Scotia it held a leading if less absolute role in most rural regions. In Prince Edward Island the forest interest was relegated to a minor theme within farmer politics, while in Newfoundland British capital carved vast concessions out of a colonial government desperate for commercial growth. The continuing symbiosis between politician and timberman fuelled regular electoral controversies, large and small.[12] Still reeling from the recession that followed the Great War, New Brunswick lumbermen demanded that the Liberal Veniot government cut stumpage and workers' compensation charges. Unhappy with the response, the industry shifted its support to the Conservative party which was elected in 1925.[13] A Nova Scotia election in the same year saw a similar shift of partisan fortunes. The election of the Conservative Rhodes government brought the dismissal of the entire ranger field staff and its replacement with Tory friendlies. The Liberal return in 1933, under Angus L. MacDonald, reversed this process while more than doubling the number of positions.[14] Four years later, Nova Scotia voters were treated to the 'woodpecker election.' This centred on allegations of the illegal cutting of 20,000 cords of pulpwood upon Crown land in Guysborough County, by a company whose president served as minister without portfolio in MacDonald's cabinet.[15]

Such incidents attest to the continuing parochialism and the patronage-based allocations of forest politics in New Brunswick and Nova Scotia through the first half of the twentieth century. It would be wrong, however, to ignore the slowly building counter-tendency towards nonpartisan administrative management based on professional standards and technical expertise. This had been central to the U.S. and Canadian Conservation movements from the outset. It was in Montreal that the first Conservation Congress convened in 1882. President Teddy Roosevelt's close adviser was Gifford Pinchot, a European-trained forester who pioneered professional education in the United States in the 1890s and was appointed the founding head of the U.S. Forest Service in 1905. In Ottawa, the Laurier government revived the momentum by hosting the National Forestry Convention of 1906. It also sponsored the Commission of Conservation (1909–20), a federally funded agency to promote studies and cooperation with its provincial and industry counterparts. This entire movement placed great faith in technical support for resource planning. Optimal use depended on surveys and measurement, regulated harvest, and planned renewal. Significantly, the University of New Brunswick followed Toronto's lead and inaugurated Canada's second degree program in forestry in 1908. Early graduates found federal and provincial forestry agencies (rather than industrial firms) to be their most likely sites of employment. It was in the decade after the First World War, when the pulp and paper industry boomed, that trained foresters began to find work in industrial woodlands. Given the far greater capital costs and amortization periods associated with pulp and paper mills, guaranteed access to woodlands and an orderly supply of logs was essential to secure finance, and foresters played an integral role in this.

In Atlantic Canada, the rise of pulp and paper and the decline in lumbering signalled a structural change of historic proportions. It altered the power structures of the respective forest industries, the administrative mandates of state forestry departments, and the underlying assumptions of forest policy regimes. This transformation occurred first in Newfoundland and New Brunswick, where the balance had tilted before the Great Depression. Not until the 1960s did it register in Nova Scotia, while Prince Edward Island remained virtually untouched until the 1980s.

The colony of Newfoundland experienced a brief lumber boom after 1890, when a small number of large mills exported significant volumes to Britain.[16] As the white pine resource declined, attention turned to the pulp potential of lesser diameter spruce and fir, and many sawmill leases were acquired by groundwood pulp operators. However, the giant 1905 lease of forest, mineral, and water rights to the Anglo-Newfoundland Development Company (AND), for a term of ninety-nine years, began the rise of the pulp industry.[17] A subsidiary of the Harmondsworth publishing empire in England, AND augmented its initial lease for a total of 3,670 square miles of timber during its first decade. Although no fewer than six pulp plants were built in the colony of Newfoundland before 1920, AND's Grand Fall's mill was the only long-term survivor of the initial generation. The second pillar arrived in 1925, when another British firm established a large integrated complex at Corner Brook in western Newfoundland. This time a major lease was conferred upon Newfoundland Power and Paper Company, which also acquired freehold and licensed Crown forests.[18] In turn, it was purchased in 1938 by Bowaters, the British newsprint giant. For half a century these two enterprises dominated Newfoundland's forest industry, controlling between them a full two-thirds of all forested land with minimal state oversight.

In New Brunswick and Nova Scotia, small groundwood pulp mills began to appear at river mouths as early as the 1890s. Limited by their low capacities (twenty tons per day was common), and the U.S. tariff on newsprint (not removed until 1913), the groundwood mills nonetheless brought new, chiefly U.S., capital to the industry. They also bid up the competition for Crown and private timber stands, as much for speculative as for harvesting purposes. With the postwar recession, and the rash of bankruptcies that it triggered among sawmills, many timber limits changed hands. This opened the way for a new wave of larger enterprises, based on chemical pulping processes and often linked to the manufacture of paper. For New Brunswick, the 1920s 'pulp triumvirate' included the Fraser, Bathurst, and International Paper companies, each of which aggressively accumulated both freehold forest and Crown leases.[19] It was almost a generation before the second wave of New Brunswick pulp and paper firms arrived in the postwar period. While K.C. Irving inherited a sawmill and woodlands in 1933, it was not until the 1950s that he incorporated Irving Pulp and Paper. By this time, Irving had secured timber rights to much of the lower St John river valley, and a new regional complex was born.[20]

The pattern in Nova Scotia differed again. Here no indigenous lumber giants like Fraser or Bathurst led the way into pulp and paper. Instead, the 1919 sawmill slump saw the timber resource locked into a series of speculative holdings. The prototype was the 'Oxford Lease' of Cape Breton lands, concluded in 1899. While great expectations accompanied this 620,000 acre deal, Nova Scotia lacked the leverage to force a major manufacturing investment.[21] With such a political climate well established by 1914, the land dealers and exporters went to work with a vengeance This prompted debates not only on speculative trading but on primary wood export controls.[22] One leading project that came to fruition, just prior to the crash of 1929, was the Mersey Paper Company on the province's south shore. Here the driving force was Isaac Walton Killam, a Royal Securities associate of Roy Aitken (later Lord Beaverbrook) in Montreal.[23] While Mersey survived the lean times of the depression, it was more than thirty years before another major mill appeared in the province. Thus, Nova Scotia's transition from lumber to pulp remained incomplete. A split developed in the sawmill sector between a progressive lead element aiming at technical improvement, both in the woods and before the saw, and a more tenuous high-grading segment of small portable ('woodpecker') mills.[24] The former established the Nova Scotia Forest Products Association (1934), which was recognized by the Department of Lands and Forests as the voice of the lumber interest until the pulp and paper sector won the lead in the 1960s.

Regime Change in the Era of Pulp and Paper

Despite the evident differences, all three provinces underwent a forest industry transition during the first half of the twentieth century. This, in turn, forced complicated changes in primary forest policy regimes. They are seen most clearly in debates over policy ideas, institutions, and programs. New Brunswick was the first Atlantic province to respond, through a series of measures beginning in 1906. The Public Domain Act authorized a province-wide timber survey and regulations to preserve forested areas. Yet, as was often the case, a lack of funding and administrative capacity meant that no actions followed. By this time the political rivalry between sawmill and pulp licensees, small operators and large, meant that any talk of cutting limits, increased stumpage, or licence reallocations would be hotly contested. At the same time, a shared interest in the need for fire protection, and control of wasteful cutting offered some common ground for reform. After a scandal involving the swap of campaign contributions for licence renewals, New Brunswick hired its first professional forester in 1915 and began the long-expected inventory. Three years later the first consolidated Forest Act was passed, creating a distinct Forest Service, a permanent staff, and a tax-supported fire protection fund.[25]

However, the postwar recession shook the lumbermens' commitment to forest management, as they pressed for stumpage and tax cuts in the battle to survive. The young Forest Service found itself under challenge for its use of 'undersize permits' in supervising logging. The chief conservation measure of the day was a diameter limit (12 inches for spruce and 9 inches for fir, measured at the stump) to protect undersized trees from premature felling. While this was effective in sawlog stands, special permits were designed to allow pulp loggers to take smaller stock under certain conditions. Desperate sawmillers pressed, with success, to win undersize permits for their own operations. Gillis and Roach capture the situation aptly, noting that 'after a reasonably good and practical start in 1918, events had conspired to give the province the form but not the substance of a forestry programme. Strapped for funds and encumbered by a rapidly declining sawmill sector, the province's one attempt at sophisticated forest management [before the Second World War] could not be counted a success.'[26] The only measure to attract consensual support was fire protection, and it was here that all Atlantic forestry departments focused their interwar efforts.

Nova Scotia entered the twentieth century in a similar fashion. A long-standing Liberal government nurtured close ties with the sawmill segment. Here, however, the preponderance of forest land lay in private hands. Consequently, there was less pressure on Crown forests, but also considerable doubt about the extent of provincial jurisdiction over freehold forest. This opened the way for virtually unregulated logging and extensive forest degradation. As elsewhere, concern over declining supply brought growing support for conservation. The Western Nova Scotia Lumbermen's Association supported the Fernow forest inventory of 1908, the first of its kind in the province.[27] The departments of lands and forests were consolidated in 1926, when Chief Forester Otto Schierbeck, the first trained professional, was hired. Despite ambitious plans, Schierbeck foundered on the twin shoals of indifferent political masters and resentful county rangers.[28] After his dismissal in 1933, the job was reclassified as Provincial Forester without any formal terms of reference. Despite a comprehensive policy brief from the Nova Scotia professional foresters in 1944, it was not until the 1950s that the next steps towards professional management were taken.[29]

In sum, the provincial forest programs of the interwar years showed an awareness of technical management possibilities but lacked the social and political foundations to deliver. Instead, they fell back on activities that drew more consensual support: fire protection, fish and wildlife regulations, and the disposition of Crown cutting rights. This has sometimes been labelled 'extensive management,' since it relies on apportioning the naturally grown forest to supply cheap fibre under conditions of natural regeneration. Whether this merits the term management at all is open to question. However, it certainly contrasts with the 'intensive management' paradigm that followed. And as the foresters of the day freely acknowledged, key management tools such as the inventory, growth, and harvest data necessary for sustained yield regulation were lacking.

The Postwar Policy Regime: 1949–1995

Significantly, the modern forest policy regime begins and ends with federal government initiatives, even though its institutional base rests in the Atlantic provinces themselves. It begins in 1949 with the Canada Forestry Act, which made possible new levels of federal financial and research support for provincial agencies. It ends with Ottawa's decision to terminate the series of federal–provincial forest management agreements which had fuelled intensive forestry in the Atlantic region for more than twenty years. As will be seen below, the federal presence accelerated and facilitated programs as diverse as forest insect control, forest inventory work, marginal land improvement, forest service modernization, and intensive silviculture on both private and public lands.

In addition to the federal initiative, there were other postwar changes. The supply of trained professional foresters increased by several orders of magnitude. The four university forestry schools found their intake of students swelled by returning veterans in search of career possibilities. The depression years of shrinking classes and unemployed graduates seemed to be gone forever, as the Canadian forest industry experienced another investment boom and provincial forest agencies reorganized in response. At the University of New Brunswick, for example, the average number of graduates in the years 1938–47 was nine, while in the period 1948–57 the average number jumped to fifty-two.[30] As this professional cadre filled out the forest management ranks of business and state, their capacities to plan and deliver more sophisticated growth and harvesting programs increased accordingly.

A third driving force for change was the transformation in woods production. Part of this involved mechanical innovations which accelerated the potential rate of felling and removal, while another part involved the social reorganization of woods work. As late as the 1950s, most pulp and paper firms directly employed a woods labour force numbering thousands at peak season. Winter cutting was by axe or saw, with short length logs hauled by horse and sled to river brows. During the spring run-off the logs were driven downstream to mills or trans-shipment points.[31] However, by the mid-1960s, logging systems had changed beyond recognition. Fellers used chainsaws at the stump, and articulated skidders gathered short or long lengths for transport overland to roadsides. Here they could be loaded onto trucks or railcars for delivery to the mill site. By the late 1960s, more complex harvesting machinery began to appear in Atlantic woods. 'Wood processors' offered various combinations of felling, delimbing, junking, and hauling functions, at considerable gains in physical productivity. In less than a decade, extensive clear-cutting became the harvesting system of choice for large operators.[32]

Dramatic social changes accompanied the new systems. Not only was the size of cutting crews reduced, but the work shifted from manual labour to machine operation, and woods work became a year-round activity. Another trend saw corporate woodlands divisions cease to employ bush crews directly and contract, instead, with independent logging and hauling operators. Although the modern logging operation is capital intensive and highly leveraged financially, corporate support in the form of assured or preferred contracts and surety guarantees made possible the formation of an independent logging segment whose class politics was closely aligned with the manufacturing firms it serviced. In the process, much of the risk shifted to the contracting segment, caught between the pressures of debt servicing and competitive tendering.

While these broad conditioning factors brought sustained pressure on interwar policy regimes, they cannot account for the particular responses to be found in the Atlantic provinces. For this purpose it is necessary to look for the key issues and conflicts around which coalitions were built and perpetuated, and these varied considerably by jurisdiction.

In New Brunswick, as already explained, the pulp and paper industry bid for business hegemony before the Second War. A number of firms had emerged with the timber limits and productive assets to dominate the forest sector for generations. As anchors for regional sub-economies in the northwest, northeast, and central areas of the province, they far overshadowed the sawmill operators with whom they competed for fibre. Yet, as wartime memories faded, the political alignments of the transitional client state could not yet guarantee this pre-eminence. More durable commitments were necessary for the alliance to be sealed. In New Brunswick, these emerged through a convergence of interests on one particular issue, which welded together a formidable power bloc including paper firms and provincial and federal forestry agencies. Rooted in the forest protection focus of interwar policy, it was deepened and extended in the late 1940s as concern for threat of fire was joined by the threat from defoliating insects. In effect, the spruce budworm epidemic fused these institutions together in a shared science-based strategy, harnessing chemistry and engineering in a long-term battle to preserve the resource base.

The Dominion Forestry Service brought entomological expertise, a generous budget, and senior political support. Liberal ministers such as C.D. Howe, who represented forest constituencies, well appreciated the economic scale of the budworm threat. As forest owners and operators, the province and the industry were willing collaborators. New Brunswick led the nation in linking long-term Crown licences to silvicultural obligations as early as 1937, and neither 'partner' was willing to accept massive losses from insect or disease. Under the terms of the first Canada – New Brunswick agreement, the largest aerial spray program in North American history was carried out. A special tripartite enterprise known as Forest Protection Ltd (FPL) handled the contract work for more than a generation. A fleet of surplus aircraft was assembled at a staging facility known as 'Budworm City' for the annual campaigns.[33] In the process, the Canadian Forestry Service became a leading institutional advocate and authority on the chemical protection of forests. This produced somewhat different results when the issue surfaced twenty-five years later in eastern Nova Scotia.[34]

If industrial forestry congealed in New Brunswick around the budworm issue, it reached Nova Scotia in a different manner entirely. Here the DLF faced a far more fractured forest industry, a legacy of the unfinished transition from lumbering to pulp and paper. Significant tracts of Crown land remained uncommitted, and others languished under obsolete leases. But no management strategy was possible without reliable data. Thus, the central project of the 1950s was a province-wide forest inventory, financed by Ottawa.[35] On the strength of its results, and the Crown regaining control of the Oxford lands, Nova Scotia mounted an aggressive drive for new manufacturing facilities. With the help of extensive Crown leases at low stumpage rates, Stora Kopparberg agreed to build a sulphite pulp mill in eastern Nova Scotia (1959), while Scott Paper agreed to a sulphate pulp mill in the central region (1965). By committing the balance of the Crown lands to these projects, the province shifted abruptly to a pulp and paper supply model. This also marked a decisive political defeat for Nova Scotia sawmillers, particularly those operating in the Cumberland-Colchester-Hants counties 'horseshoe' where the lumber industry had been strongest. Without independent access to Crown lands, they were left to buy private stumpage, ally with the pulp lessees, or scale back their businesses altogether.[36]

The new leasing arrangements also prompted a review of logging policies. The chief conservation measure at the time was the Small Tree Act, a diameter limit rule designed to protect potential sawlog stock from premature cutting. It was replaced by the Forest Improvement Act (FIA), modelled upon Swedish forest policy and delegating the formulation of logging regulations to a series of district boards bringing together private and public foresters and representatives of woodlot owners. It quickly became the target of a hostile industry lobby, which postponed its proclamation, blunted its application, and ultimately led to its repeal in 1986.[37] In the meantime, the policy vacuum created by the FIA was filled incrementally, as the Department of Lands and Forests struck separate arrangements for corporate leaseholders, corporate forest owners, and small woodlot owners. These are discussed in the following sections.

In Newfoundland, the postwar decades are best described as an era of corporate prerogative. Management responsibility rested completely with the licence-holders. The terms of the original concessions obliged the companies to protect the forests from fire and to harvest and utilize all timber fit for use. Given the length of the agreements (and the absence of periodic review clauses), the absence of stumpage payments on pulpwood, and the lack of a state forest service before 1960, the delegation of woodland management was virtually absolute. One compelling measure of this comprador position can be found in the Small-wood government's role in the 1959 loggers' strike.[38] Under the leadership of Landon Ladd, the International Wood Workers of America (IWA) came to the province from British Columbia in 1956. The IWA sought to organize some 12,000 loggers, whose wages and working conditions were heavily exploitative even by hinterland standards. After winning legal recognition, entering contract negotiations, and accepting a conciliation report (which the companies rejected), the IWA launched a legal strike early in 1959. As the loggers gained the upper hand, the mills threatened closure. Having already denounced the IWA as outsiders who brought only hate and fear to Newfoundland, and having sponsored a new pro-government union, Smallwood passed special legislation to decertify the union. He also linked its leadership (without evidence) to Jimmy Hoffa's Teamsters, who were under criminal investigation in the United States. Violent exchanges escalated on the picket lines, culminating in the 'Badger Riot' in which a policeman was killed. Although the IWA had been shattered by the spring of 1959, Smallwood's union did not survive either. In ten years' time the base wage had doubled, under the International Brotherhood of Carpenters, although the labour force had dropped below 5,000 in the face of mechanization.

While modern forest management may have been impossible in Newfoundland, New Brunswick was setting the pace in the postwar generation. It pioneered an incentive-based tenure system in which long-term licences were granted in return for sustainable management plans approved by state foresters. Even then, it required periodic adjustments to curb corporate discretion. To prevent licensees from extracting excessive stumpage fees from third party operators, regulations were passed. To prevent a misallocation of sawlogs to pulping and to encourage 'integrated logging' (the exchange of sawlogs and pulpwood between operators), special stumpage discounts were given on combined operations. By 1965 the Crown timber resource was fully committed (with the addition of several new pulp mills), and attention shifted sharply towards improving yields from existing forests. As Fellows observed, 'one cannot date its beginnings exactly, but it is fair to say that the period from the mid-sixties to mid-seventies represented the height of the transitional stage from the controlled exploitation of renewable resources to their planned and cultivated exploitation.'[39] Some implications of this new stage in Crown forest management will now be discussed.

Forestry Policy and the Woodlot Owners Movement

In both New Brunswick and Nova Scotia, the depth of the industry–government alliance is evident in the battles over the organized marketing of privately owned pulpwood. With 40 per cent of the New Brunswick forest controlled by small woodlot owners, it was hardly surprising that a commodity marketing movement emerged to challenge the industry's reliance on Crown and corporate forests. Beginning with the low prices accompanying the forest sector recession of the early 1960s, the organizing drive continued for more than a decade.[40] At issue here was the need and the means for an increased share of small private pulpwood sales and improved returns for the product. After one regional supply board was established in Madawaska, a royal commission was struck in 1963. Headed by UNB forestry professor Louis Seheult, it recommended a minimum price for private pulpwood but advised against compulsory boards across the province. When the Robichaud government refused to act, a federation was formed by seven regional woodlot groups. During the next recession, in the early 1970s, concerns were raised about the competitiveness of provincial mills and the prospects of lay-offs. This time the Conservative Hatfield government identified increased woodlot supply as part of its reform package, and a 1973 amendment to the Forest Products Act stipulated that corporate access to Crown leases would be blocked if firms refused to enter meaningful negotiations with woodlot supply groups. Although this prevented firms from ignoring private suppliers, as Parenteau points out, talk and agreed contracts are quite different outcomes. Despite a campaign extending for more than a decade, during which their solidarity was continually tested, woodlot organizations were unable to achieve mandatory bargaining. Furthermore the New Brunswick government proved extremely reluctant to use the Crown lease threat as a lever. However, the relative success of the New Brunswick movement in establishing new civil structures does need to be noted. As deMarsh points out, the provincial policy of the 1980s accepted the legitimacy of collective bargaining and the right of individual owners to make management choices.[41] This was new, and it is still not universally the case.

In Nova Scotia, where woodlot producers faced even lower 'market' prices in the 1960s, a simultaneous campaign took a somewhat different turn. Here the pulp and paper segment was less solidly entrenched at the outset. In 1963, the Cape Breton–based woodlot movement won recognition of 'forest products' as a commodity under the farm marketing regime. It was only after the forest lobby (department and firms) inter-vened to block the issuance of the authorizing regulation that the entire matter was turned over to a commission of inquiry. After being advised that collective marketing should be delayed pending the province-wide organization of woodlot owners, the government sat back to await the outcome. With financial support from the federal Agricultural Rehabili-tation and Development Act (ARDA) program, the extension depart-ment of St Francis Xavier University mounted a three-year organizing campaign which led to the founding of the Nova Scotia Woodlot Own-ers Association (NSWOA) in 1969. When a strong majority of woodlot owners voted in favour of an organized scheme in 1971, Halifax announced that a separate statute would establish a separate pulpwood marketing board to supervise certification and oversee bargaining. The balance of the decade was consumed by litigation, as the mills mounted continuing challenges to the statute and procedures of the new board.[42] It was telling that the provincial government never used moral suasion with the forest industry to defend the legitimacy of its marketing initia-tive. As a result, corporate interests were able to delay group marketing for more than fifteen years, during which alternative supply channels were confirmed, and the woodlot movement was fragmented and de-mobilized. This syndrome was repeated after 1986, when the minister of lands and forests announced the reform of the marketing board to secure improved prices and market share.[43] An intense industry lobby was renewed against the proposed marketing procedure, while a sus-tained attack on the board chairman led to his dismissal, and the aban-donment of the reform package, in 1990.[44]

In contrast to the ready consensus on the need to protect vast tracts of Crown and industrial freehold, no such urgency accompanied the questions of mobilizing and managing small private lands. While the woodlot segment could not be ignored, neither could it be easily accom-modated. Both governments' weak and belated compromises on private pulp marketing contrast sharply with their readiness to commit resources, virtually in perpetuity, for massive chemical spray campaigns (in New Brunswick) and extraordinarily cheap Crown stumpage (in Nova Scotia). At the same time, New Brunswick's accommodation of the woodlot movement compares favourably with the Nova Scotia response. More generally, the campaign for higher returns through collective marketing challenged the concession of cheap Crown stumpage and ran counter to the dictates of conventional forest economics. Finally, it was mounted by interests at the fringe rather than the core of the forest policy network. As such this was more easily deflected, by a policy discourse that dismissed woodlot owners as part-timers interested in a fast buck, with little potential for long-term management.

The Federal Power and Regime Change

In some respects, the expansionary phase of postwar forestry had run its course by the 1970s. Most provincial resource departments had modernized their timber administrations. Field staffs led by professional foresters pursued sustained yield (limiting annual cut to the level of annual growth) as required by statute. In the process, Crown limits had been fully committed (some would argue overcommitted) to industrial production. It was at this stage that the federal government launched a program that would transform Atlantic forestry. Certainly, Ottawa was not new to resource policy, having promoted the conservation movement, the postwar forestry act, and the ARDA program for rural development. However, the most recent initiative ranks as a pivotal influence on modern forest policy regimes.

In the years following 1973, federal and provincial governments negotiated a series of forest resource development agreements. These continued through several five-year periods until 1995. They held a triple significance for policy. Through its shared-cost participation, Ottawa injected significant new funds to enhanced management programs. In Atlantic Canada, this ranged from 55 per cent to 90 per cent of designated costs. Second, the qualifying conditions for these programs forced provincial authorities to launch policy reviews, to engage in strategic planning, and to reconfigure previous activities in light of the results. Across the region, the early 1970s witnessed a cascade of royal commission, task force, and professional consultant investigations. No provincial policy regime escaped examination, although this led to differing degrees of change. Third, the resulting agreements pushed provincial departments towards comprehensive and intensive silviculture programs, which went well beyond the 'extensive' (fire control and natural regeneration) management practices of earlier decades.

The origins of these programs had little to do with forestry. The federal Department of Regional Economic Expansion (DREE) was searching for a successor to its 'designated areas' approach. In this, business investment in low-growth areas qualified for significant locational incentives. This program was, however, firm driven. The new approach was based on the negotiation of strategic economic plans between federal and provincial authorities, to determine sectoral and project priorities. Embodied in general development agreements (GDAs), they would be implemented by sub-agreements that committed funds to agreed programs. New Brunswick was among the first provinces to conclude a GDA, in 1973.[45] Even before this, project talks were under way and a forestry development sub-agreement was virtually inevitable (given its foundational role in the provincial economy). As Table 8.2 reveals, the other Atlantic provinces were not far behind, and substantial sums became available in the forestry field.

In each province, the sub-agreement reflected the burdens and opportunities of past forest policy. In Newfoundland, it facilitated virtually the first management program ever sponsored by the provincial forest service. Ottawa covered 90 per cent of the costs as the service took on staff, designed a field structure, expanded its nursery capacity, and prepared for a full set of silvicultural treatments for understocked areas. Two decades of royal commissions, reporting in 1955, 1966, and 1970, had failed to take hold of forest issues. In sharp contrast, the 1973 federal–provincial task force tackled the anachronistic concessionary regime head on.[46] One year later, the Forest Land (Taxation and Management) Act provided the authority, and the 1974 Forest Subsidiary Agreement provided the fiscal muscle.

In Prince Edward Island, the entire DREE initiative was channeled, in 1968, into one comprehensive economic plan of fifteen years' duration. Not surprisingly, it was built on the agricultural and secondary manufacturing sectors. However, the development plan noted that 43 per cent of the land area was wooded. The provincial forest development agency was charged with cutting and planting the productive forest area on a fifty-year rotation.[47] It is important to place this forestry program in perspective. A forestry division was established in 1951 (following the Forestry Act of that year), and the province hired only its second extension forester in the 1960s. One policy review at that time identified management on freehold lands as the core issue, declaring that fragmented ownership and small-scale harvesting operations 'are not conducive to good forest management.'[48] Another report stressed the 'badly neglected condition' of Island forests as a result of 'repeated high grading and by abandonment of agricultural land.'[49] Nevertheless, the forestry component of the P.E.I. plan remained modest.

There was one moment in the mid-1970s when the province faced a clear political choice about the shape of its future forest. The newly hired chief of the forestry branch outlined a plan to restore the forest

Table 8.2 Federal–provincial forestry agreements, 1975–1995

Agreement	Dates	F:P%	Total $000	Federal	Pro-vincial
Canada–New Brunswick					
Forest Subsidiary Agreement	1975–80	80:20	58,000	46,400	11,600
Forest Subsidiary Agreement II	1980–4	80:20			
Forest Renewal Agreement	1984–9	55:45	77,400	42,300	35,100
Cooperation Agreement					
for Forest Development	1989–94	55:45	91,000	55,600	35,400
Canada–Nova Scotia					
Forest Subsidiary Agreement	1977–82	60:40	57,800	36,100	21,700
Forest Subsidiary Agreement II	1982–9	53:47	92,600	49,800	42,800
Forest Renewal Agreement	1984–7	67:33	25,500	17,000	8,500
Cooperation Agreement					
for Forest Development	1989–91	55:45	45,000	24,750	20,250
Cooperation Agreement					
for Forest Development	1991–5	50:50	98,000	49,000	49,000
Canada–Prince Edward Island					
PEI Plan	1968–83	Small Forest Sub-Component			
Forest Resource Development					
Agreement	1983–8	68:32	20,144	13,688	6,456
Forest Resource Development					
Agreement	1988–93	60:40	24,083	14,200	9,883
Canada–Newfoundland					
Forest Subsidiary Agreement	1974–9		N/A		
Forest Subsidiary Agreement II	1980–5		63,400		
Forest Resource Development					
Agreement	1986–90	70:30	48,000	33,600	14,400
Cooperation Agreement					
for Forest Development	1990–5	70:30	64,300	45,000	19,300
Canada–Labrador Development					
Agreement	1990–95		N/A		

Note: This table is constituted from several sources that are not in complete agreement about dates and allotments. Consequently, it should be considered as illustrative but not definitive.
Sources: Forestry Canada, *Annual Report, 1989–1990* (Ottawa: Supply and Services, 1991); J.L. Bourdages and J.P. Amyot, *Canada's Forests: No Future without Good Management* (Ottawa: Library of Parliament, 1992); texts of Forest Agreements for New Brunswick and Nova Scotia.

estate to its Acadian roots by a program of diverse planting of native species, featuring white pine, red oak, eastern hemlock, white ash, yellow birch, butternut, and beech. However, by 1979 the government opted for a softwood development strategy for pulp production, and the forester in question, Steven Manley, left the service.[50] The softwood strategy, funded by the federal agreements, built a substantial nursery capacity, which provided more than two million seedlings per year, 96 per cent of which were pine, spruce, and larch softwoods.

The federal–provincial forest agreements of 1983–93 dealt with the industrial management issue more comprehensively, and in a fashion similar to Nova Scotia. Within five years, some 2,000 woodlot owners (of a potential 16,000) had agreed to management plans. This was driven in part by a soaring hardwood harvest as fuelwood replaced more expensive energy sources. While these agreements injected more than $40 million into Island forest improvement, they also illustrated how the federal presence instils a formal planning impulse as a cost of compliance. In return for the new inventory and the landowner assistance measures, the P.E.I. government was obliged to prepare a twenty-year plan and a forest policy framework. It also revised the Forest Management Act prior to the 1988 renewal negotiations, and adopted the discourse of sustainability (with its public 'reporting' format) in recent documents.[51]

The two largest agreements covered New Brunswick and Nova Scotia. Here the experience of New Brunswick will be used to illustrate the design and negotiation process for forest 'agreements' in general, while Nova Scotia will be used to illustrate the transformations set loose during these years. Of the four Atlantic provinces, New Brunswick enjoyed the longest and closest association with federal forest agencies. The Maritime regional office of the Canadian Forest Service is based in Fredericton, and ties among technical officials were forged during decades of spruce budworm aerial spray collaboration beginning in 1951. Yet these long-standing relationships among forestry professionals did not guarantee an easy fit when DREE proposed the GDAs, since they were framed at higher political and bureaucratic levels. Nonetheless, the forestry agencies were well positioned to develop a sub-agreement. Ottawa was already funding a provincial forest resources study, focused on improved methods of resource allocation which would maximize economic potential.[52] This was, in effect, the sort of strategic review on which DREE was insisting. Even before the release of its final report, in 1974, the study findings were reflected in the federal–provincial negotiations. In fact, the New Brunswick forest 'sub' was concluded before the

Canada–New Brunswick GDA was formally signed in 1974. It was the first of four New Brunswick forest deals, extending to 1994.

The process of fashioning forest sub-agreements was one of intergovernmental negotiation. The initiating role lay primarily with the provincial forest services, while Ottawa stipulated some basic parameters. For example, strategic focus was necessary, to draw together the specific initiatives in support of overarching goals. Thus, the 1977 Canada–Nova Scotia agreement identified employment opportunities, enhanced forest productivity, and improved wood allocation and utilization as prime goals.[53] Neither was Ottawa willing to fund normal programming, with the result that the negotiations led sometimes to new delivery mechanisms and eligibility criteria. Accordingly, the 1977 agreement sponsored a new concept of group management ventures to achieve economies of scale and cost in bringing small woodlots into management. In the federal team, departmental priorities also surfaced. The delegates from DREE were particularly sensitive to the urgency of restructuring marginal enterprises. Consequently, they pushed for 'rationalization' measures to modernize the lead element of the sawmill sector while squeezing the small seasonal operators out of production. In other cases, federal officials resisted provincial plans whose rationale could be questioned. Ottawa refused to finance Nova Scotia's ambitious plan to purchase one million acres of small private woodlands, and insisted that the funds allotted to forest management be allocated among industrial, Crown, and woodlot lands in rough proportion to their total forest areas. In the end, 92 per cent of the $25 million was devoted to management planning and treatment, with the balance allotted between industry development, research and training, and public information.

Forest Regime Change in the 1990s

Regime change is generally measured in slow rather than fast time, as the process of crisis and recomposition is seldom sudden. In this sense, the decade of the 1990s was transitional: the pillars of an earlier structure had eroded but the shape of its successor was far from firm. This section outlines the constituent elements from which a new regime may spring, together with the contradictory pressures standing in the way. This portrait of recomposition should not imply that the management policies of past decades have ceased to exist, although their application and impact may well be compromised by the obstacles sketched below.

There is no question that for Atlantic Canada, the 1990s was a turbulent period in forest politics. The decade opened with the most severe recession since the Depression, leaving long-established processing plants in doubt for their future. In New Brunswick, Fraser's Atholville mill was shuttered, the Bathurst mill changed hands, and the Repap complex on the Mirimichi staggered at the verge of bankruptcy. In Nova Scotia, the Stora mill faced closure for years before a major reinvestment was announced in 1996, while the Scott Maritimes mill passed to Kimberley-Clark, which then put it up for sale. As in earlier slumps, provincial governments mounted relief efforts. Frank McKenna announced a 'renewal' program in New Brunswick, centring upon tax relief, pulpwood price cuts, and lower stumpage charges.[54] The Liberal Savage government in Nova Scotia mounted more modest efforts in this regard.

Yet for Atlantic forestry, perhaps the greatest victim of the slump came at its close. In April 1993, Ottawa signalled that all federal–provincial forest development agreements would be terminated at the end of the existing round. Announced in the waning months of the Mulroney government and confirmed later by the Chrétien Liberals, this was a casualty of Ottawa's deficit reduction campaign.[55] For small provinces struggling with their own fiscal problems, the prospect of life after the agreements was chilling. It left the future of comprehensive silviculture very much in doubt. The intensive forest management and harvesting regime was by now deeply entrenched, and the loss of silvicultural inputs on the familiar scale left all four provinces facing serious overcut situations.

There were differing responses to this sword of Damocles. The government of Nova Scotia sponsored the creation of a new advocacy body known as the Coalition of Nova Scotia Forest Interests (CNSFI). This grouping of industry interests, ranging from woodlot owners to processing firms, first lobbied for the renewal of the agreement and then spent two years exploring options for a post-agreement approach to silviculture. In Newfoundland, the Department of Forest Resources prepared a new Forest Development Plan to cover a twenty-year period.[56] Released in draft form in 1997 and finalized one year later, it was described as 'a dramatic shift in forest management in this province from a timber management approach to an ecosystem management approach.' This suggested a much closer attention to both harvesting and utilization, decentralized to the district level, to squeeze the maximum impact from increasingly scarce program funds.

The factors above demonstrate the ability of wider economic forces to buffet the forest policies of small provinces. There was, however, a more positive and deliberate planning process at work, in the Atlantic region as elsewhere. This was the encounter between intensive forest management and the sustainable development imperatives. It was unleashed by the Brundtland Commission report of 1987, and later embraced by the Canadian Council of Forest Ministers. As illustrated elsewhere in this volume, 1992 was a pivotal year which saw the Rio Conference, Agenda 21, the Canadian Forest Strategy, and the Canada Forest Accord. Having sponsored and endorsed many of these measures, provincial authorities faced the challenge of adapting their own programs accordingly. The most significant responses have involved biodiversity measures (particularly in relation to protected areas), and third-party certification schemes for sustainable forest management (as an alternative to state-sponsored or state-regulated systems).

The unfolding of the sustainability debate in Atlantic forestry has seen some fascinating collisions between the organized forest estate and elements of the civic public, as they advance alternative visions of a new forest regime. The state and corporate institutions at the clientelistic core of these policy networks have sought the shortest line connecting the unsustainable present and the sustainable future. Recognizing the mounting market value of sustainable management practice (to both customers and public), they have embraced the notion of third party certification of primary forest care. This forms part of a wider trend to enhance commodity value by injecting standardized attributes (such as 'sustainably managed timber'). The first such certification system, ratified by the Canadian Standards Association (CSA) in 1997, has generated a growing web of 'stewardship agreements' linking forest manufacturers, landowners, and logging contractors.[57]

Provincial authorities face a number of highly charged issues as they bring such practices into public policy: Who will certify the certifiers? How many certification schemes will be recognized? How will the schemes reallocate the costs and benefits of management in the forest estate? How does 'sustainable management' relate to the demise of the joint forestry agreements? When its advisory coalition suggested such a scheme in 1996, the Province of Nova Scotia discovered an unexpected level of public scepticism with the new discourse of sustainable forestry.[58]

To the extent that third-party certification shifts the focus from legislation and public expenditure to voluntary standard setting and compliance, it redefines the power relations of forestry.[59] Consequently it should not be surprising that some prominent social interests have mounted new challenges of their own.

After an initial acquaintance with the CSA consultative process, a coalition of environmental organizations repudiated it as a corporate 'greenwash' of sustainable values. They then threw their support behind an alternative certification scheme sponsored by the non-governmental Forest Stewardship Council (FSC). In Canada, the FSC developed its first set of sustainable forest standards for the Acadian forest region of the Maritimes.[60] The environmental critique sees the certification process as a means to rationalize the forest-holding status quo. Adopting the logic of quality management appraisal, the CSA process centres on the applicant's forest management system – the inventory records and cutting plans – as distinct from the impact of harvesting on the ground. As such, it sidesteps most of the difficult issues of environmental forestry, including clear-cutting, mechanized harvesting, and chemical spraying. The critics are left with serious doubts on whether the practice of 'sustainable forest management' will be any different from the earlier 'maximum sustained yield.'

Aboriginal peoples have launched a different political challenge to the Crown forest regime, through the assertion of treaty and Aboriginal rights of ownership. This began with the Innu of Labrador, whose land claim to their traditional territory of Nitassinan (in Labrador) has been asserted for more than a decade.[61] It has been advanced against state encroachments ranging from military overflights to nickel mining to hydro-electricity and logging. Against the Newfoundland government's forest leasing system, the Innu have advanced an alternative system of selection logging which they defend as more appropriate to the ecological conditions of their territory.[62]

The Mi'kmaq and Maliseet Peoples have mounted separate challenges to Crown forest tenure in the Maritimes. Basing their claim on the terms of eighteenth-century treaties, a number of Mi'kmaq led by Thomas Peter Paul commenced logging without licence on New Brunswick Crown lands in 1996. After the charges against Paul were dismissed in Provincial Court, his acquittal was upheld on appeal to Court of Queen's Bench.[63] This prompted hundreds of Indian people to begin logging late in the autumn of 1997, while the province took the case to the New Brunswick Court of Appeal. When the senior court overturned Paul's acquittal, the Department of Natural Resources faced an explosive situation as Mi'kmaq loggers refused to withdraw from the woods. Only after extended negotiations with band authorities, and an offer to include Mi'kmaq interests as sub-licensees under the Crown Lands and Forest Act, was the stand-off defused in June 1998. By this time, Nova

Scotia Mi'kmaq were also moving into the Crown forests in several parts of the province. Again charges were laid, and by the summer of 1999 there were three separate cases before Maritime trial courts. While the final determination of these legal issues will occur at the Supreme Court of Canada, they have already transformed the course of Mi'kmaq politics, and shaken both provincial governments' assurance of the character of Crown title.

Conclusion

It is clear that Atlantic forestry involves not one story but four. In each province, state authorities have struggled over the disposition of this formidable resource. Political decisions in the nineteenth century shaped the patterns of forest tenure, forest use, and forestry income. As the older and more diversified colony, Nova Scotia continued to grant and sell land until 1900, with the result that three-quarters of the provincial forest passed into private hands. This same pattern applied to Prince Edward Island, once the absentee English landlords were dispossessed after 1878. In New Brunswick, by contrast, the colonial Crown reserved vast tracts at an earlier date, and timber revenues were a mainstay of public finance. This left state authorities in control of more than half of the resource. With settlement confined to the coastal belt, Newfoundland forests remained overwhelmingly in Crown hands, in closer likeness to the Canadian norm.

The forest processing industry has evolved through several distinct stages, from masting timber and square timber to lumbering and pulp and paper. Once again, each province reveals a distinct mix. After a brief lumber boom, Newfoundland became a pulp and paper enclave by the 1920s. New Brunswick shared this interwar transition, although without entirely displacing the sawmill segment; their political and economic rivalry was channeled, in time, as integrated logging operations and a layered leasing system of prime and sub-licensees encouraged symbiotic relationships. In Nova Scotia the transition was frozen for nearly half a century, before the arrival of several large pulp processors in the 1960s; in the interim, Nova Scotia lumbering was far more fragmented than its New Brunswick counterpart and it was only since the 1970s that a cluster of high volume mills have achieved dominance. In Prince Edward Island, a small sawmill sector utilized logs from farm woodlots, historically, although mainland competition brought its decline in the postwar years.

In each province, such developments translated into complicated political alignments and equally elaborate state policies. Not surprisingly, New Brunswick was the first to establish a forest service charged with the orderly development of the publicly and privately owned resource. Nova Scotia followed shortly after, although in both cases the acquisition of political legitimacy and technical capability took decades rather than years. Because of the colonial-style pulp concessions in Newfoundland, the formation of a provincial forest service was delayed until the 1960s. Before that the concessionaires were virtually unregulated in their woods activities.

By 1970 the industrial hegemony of pulp and paper interests had been secured in three provinces (and reflected in P.E.I.), although the processes differed significantly in each. Common to all was the willingness of state forest agencies to commit Crown forests for long periods in return for silvicultural and management plans geared to increased yields. The federal–provincial agreements of the 1970s provided a new funding quantum, and technical forestry doctrines provided an operational blueprint, for their implementation. Reacting to this, the woodlot owner movements in New Brunswick and Nova Scotia asserted alternative claims in the management and marketing realms. The contrasting outcomes suggest greater autonomy on the part of the New Brunswick state in accommodating forest interests outside of the industrial core. This is being tested again at the time of writing, in the treaty rights challenge by New Brunswick's Aboriginal loggers. In any event, the demise of the federal–provincial agreements hastened the emergence of new political challenges in the 1990s. The decade ended once again in transition, as the Atlantic governments, industries, and publics explore the prospects for reconstituting their forest policy regimes.

NOTES

1 See, e.g., Canadian Council of Forest Ministers (CCFM), *Compendium of National Forestry Statistics, 1995* (Ottawa: Natural Resources Canada, 1996).
2 Strictly speaking, the northwest corner of New Brunswick falls within the Great Lakes–St Lawrence forest region, which is distinguished by red and white pine, hemlock and oak, as well as birch and maple.
3 CCFM, *Canada's Forest Heritage* (Ottawa: Forestry Canada, n.d.) 16–17.
4 For one survey, see J.M. Butler, A.B. Case, J. Richardson, and A.G. Raske, 'Forest Management Practices in Newfoundland,' in J. Hudak and A.G.

Raske, eds., *Review of the Spruce Budworm Outbreak in Newfoundland* (St John's: Newfoundland Forest Research Centre, 1981) 180–213.

5 Of particular importance are the treaties of 1725, 1726, 1728, and 1752. For an overview of the colonial treaty process, see P. Cumming and N.H. Mickenberg, eds., *Native Rights in Canada* (Toronto: Indian-Eskimo Association, 1972).

6 Ralph S. Johnson, *Forests of Nova Scotia* (Halifax: Four East Publications, 1986) 39–40. The Broad Arrow Policy was extended to freehold land in 1785.

7 Barbara R. Robertson, 'Trees, Treaties and the Timing of Settlement: A Comparison of the Lumber Industry in Nova Scotia and New Brunswick, 1784–1867,' *Nova Scotia Historical Review,* 4(1), 1984, 37–55.

8 This period is explored in detail in W.S. MacNutt, 'The Politics of the Timber Trade in Colonial New Brunswick, 1825–40,' in G.A. Rawlyk, ed., *Historical Essays on the Atlantic Provinces* (Toronto: McClelland and Stewart, 1967) 122–40.

9 Graeme Wynn, *Timber Colony* (Toronto: University of Toronto Press, 1981).

10 R. Peter Gillis and Thomas R. Roach, *Lost Initiatives* (Westport: Greenwood Press, 1986) Chaps. 2 and 3.

11 The most detailed history of a forestry administration in Atlantic Canada is E.S. Fellows, *New Brunswick's Natural Resources: 150 Years of Stewardship* (Fredericton: Natural Resources and Energy, 1989).

12 These relations have been explored through the medium of political cartoons in L. Anders Sandberg and Bill Parenteau, 'From Weapons to Symbols of Privilege: Political Cartoons and the Rise and Fall of the Pulpwood Embargo Debate in Nova Scotia, 1923–1933' *Acadiensis* 26(2), 1997, 31–58.

13 Gillis and Roach, *Lost Initiatives*, 185.

14 Wilfrid Creighton, *Forestkeeping* (Halifax: Department of Lands and Forests, 1988), 40.

15 J. Murray Beck, *Politics of Nova Scotia*, vol. 2 (Halifax: Four East Publications, 1988) 172.

16 Graham Page, W.C. Wilton, and Tony Thomas, *Forestry in Newfoundland* (Ottawa: Environment Canada, 1974) 41–3.

17 James Hiller, 'Origins of the Pulp and Paper Industry in Newfoundland,' *Acadiensis* 11(2), 42–69.

18 J.K. Hiller, 'The Politics of Newsprint: The Newfoundland Pulp and Paper Industry, 1915–1939,' *Acadiensis* 19(2) 1990, 3–39.

19 Bill Parenteau, 'The Woods Transformed: The Emergence of the Pulp and Paper Industry in New Brunswick, 1918–1931,' *Acadiensis* 22(1), 1992, 5–43.

20 For the early Irving sawmill period, see Russell Hunt and Robert Campbell, *K.C. Irving: The Art of the Industrialist* (Toronto: McClelland and Stewart,

1973). For Irving's skirmishes with rival Rothesay Paper, see Douglas Howe and Ralph Costello, *K.C.: The Biography of K.C. Irving* (Toronto: Key Porter Books, 1993). For Irving's relationship with Premier Louis Robichaud in the 1960s, see Della Stanley, *Louis Robichaud: A Decade of Power* (Halifax: Nimbus Publishing, 1984).

21 Sandberg, 'Forest Policy in Nova Scotia: The Big Lease, Cape Breton Island, 1899–1960,' in L.A. Sandberg, ed., *Trouble in the Woods* (Fredericton: Acadiensis Press, 1992).

22 Bill Parenteau and L. Anders Sandberg, 'Conservation and the Gospel of Economic Nationalism: The Canadian Pulpwood Question in Nova Scotia and New Brunswick, 1918–1925,' *Environmental History Review* 19(2), 1995, 57–83.

23 Thomas Raddall, *The Mersey Story* (Liverpool: Bowater Mersey Company, 1979); Douglas How, *Canada's Mystery Man of High Finance* (Hantsport, NS: Lancelot Press, 1986).

24 L. Anders Sandberg, and Peter Clancy, 'Property Rights, Small Woodlot Owners and Forest Management in Nova Scotia,' *Journal of Canadian Studies* 31(1), 1996, 28–36.

25 Gillis and Roach, *Lost Initiatives*, 180–7.

26 Ibid., 187.

27 B.E. Fernow, *Forest Conditions in Nova Scotia* (Ottawa: Commission on Conservation, 1912).

28 L. Anders Sandberg, and Peter Clancy, 'Forestry in a Staples Economy: The Checkered Career of Otto Schierbeck, Chief Forester, Nova Scotia Canada, 1926–1933,' *Environmental History* 2(1), 1997.

29 Nova Scotia Members of the Canadian Society for Forest Engineers, 'Forestry, Economy and Post-War Reconstruction in Nova Scotia,' *Annual Report* (Halifax: Nova Scotia Department of Lands and Forests, 1944).

30 Calculations were derived from U.N.B. Forestry Association, *The Fiftieth Anniversary of the Faculty of Forestry at the University of New Brunswick, 1980–1958* (Fredericton: UNB Forestry Association, 1958).

31 Eric Muller, *In the Mersey Woods* (Liverpool: Bowater Mersey Paper Company, 1989).

32 This transition is captured in Atlantic Development Board, *Forestry in the Atlantic Provinces* (Ottawa: Queen's Printer, 1968), passim.

33 Sandberg, and Clancy, 'A Study in Contrasts: Politics, Science and the Spruce Budworm in New Brunswick and Nova Scotia, Canada,' unpublished manuscript, 1998.

34 Elizabeth May, *Budworm Battles* (Halifax: Four East Publications, 1982).

35 The results are reported in R.M. Bulmer and L.S. Hawboldt, *The Forest*

Resources of Nova Scotia (Halifax: Department of Lands and Forests, 1958). For a wider perspective on Nova Scotia's forest politics, see L. Anders Sandberg and Peter Clancy, *Against the Grain* (Vancouver: UBC Press, 2000).

36 For a profile of one such sawmiller, see Harry Thurston, 'Prest's Last Stand,' *Harrowsmith* 30, Aug.–Sept., 1983.

37 L. Anders Sandberg, 'Swedish Forestry Legislation in Nova Scotia: The Rise and Fall of the Forest Improvement Act, 1965–1986,' in D. Day, ed., *Geographical Perspectives on the Maritime Provinces* (Halifax: Saint Mary's University, 1988); and Glyn Bissix and L. Anders Sandberg, 'The Political Economy of Nova Scotia's Forest Improvement Act, 1962–1986,' in L.A. Sandberg, ed., *Trouble in the Woods*, 168–97.

38 For details see Richard Gwyn, *Smallwood, the Unlikely Revolutionary* (Toronto: McClelland and Stewart, 1968), chap. 18; and H. Landon Ladd, 'The Newfoundland Loggers' Strike of 1959,' in W.J.C. Cherwinski and Gregory S. Kealey, eds., *Lectures in Canadian Labour and Working Class History* (Toronto: New Hogtown Press, 1985).

39 E.S. Fellows, *New Brunswick's Natural Resources*, 141.

40 Bill Parenteau, 'In Good Faith': The Development of Pulpwood Marketing for Independent Producers in New Brunswick, 1960–1975,' in L.A. Sandberg, ed., *Trouble in the Woods* (Fredericton: Acadiensis Press, 1992).

41 Peter deMarsh, 'Pulpwood Producer Marketing Organizations in New Brunswick' in Bryant Fairley, Colin Leys, and James Sacouman, eds., *Restructuring and Resistance* (Toronto: Garamond, 1990) 231.

42 P. Clancy, 'The Politics of Pulpwood Marketing in Nova Scotia, 1960–1985,' in L.A. Sandberg, ed., *Trouble in the Woods*.

43 Nova Scotia, *Forestry: A New Policy for Nova Scotia, 1986* (Halifax: Department of Lands and Forests, 1986).

44 P. Clancy, 'Crossroad in the Forest,' *New Maritimes* 9(5), 1991; and P. Clancy, 'On the Axe's Edge: The Graham Langley Saga,' *New Maritimes* 11(5), 1993.

45 Donald J. Savoie, *Federal-Provincial Collaboration* (Montreal: McGill-Queen's University Press, 1981), chap. 4.

46 F.C. Pollett, J.A. Munro, and J. Hudak, 'Forest Policy and Implementation,' in Hudak, and Raske, eds., *Review of the Spruce Budworm Outbreak.*

47 Canada, Department of Regional Economic Expansion, *Development Plan for Prince Edward Island* (Ottawa: Queen's Printer, 1970) 43.

48 A.W. Blyth et al., *Forestry in the Atlantic Provinces* (Ottawa: Atlantic Development Board, 1968) 5–15.

49 Prince Edward Island, *A Forest Policy for Prince Edward Island* (Charlottetown: Department of Energy and Forestry, 1987) 1–2.

50 Elizabeth May, *At the Cutting Edge* (Toronto: Key Porter Books, 1998) 111–14.

51 See Prince Edward Island, *P.E.I. State of the Forest Report, 1988–1990* (Char-
    lottetown: Department of Agriculture, Fisheries and Forestry, 1993); Prince
    Edward Island, *A Report on Forest Resource Issues* (Charlottetown: DAFF, 1995).
52 New Brunswick, *Report of the Forest Industries Resources Study* (Fredericton:
    Department of Natural Resources, 1974).
53 *Canada–Nova Scotia Subsidiary Agreement – Forestry*, 28 June 1977, 19.
54 P. Clancy, and L.A. Sandberg, 'Maritime Forest Sector Development: A Ques-
    tion of Hard Choices,' in Sandberg, ed., *Trouble in the Woods* ,212–15.
55 The initial announcement came from Natural Resources Minister Bobby
    Sparrow on 27 April 1993. It was confirmed by Finance Minister Paul Martin
    in his Feb. 1995 budget.
56 Newfoundland and Labrador, *20 Year Forestry Development Plan: 1996–2015*
    (St. John's: Department of Forest Resources and Agrifoods, 1998).
57 P. Clancy, 'The Politics of Stewardship: Certification for Sustainable Forest
    Management in Canada,' in L.A. Sandberg and Sverker Sorlin, eds., *Sustain-
    ability: The Challenge* (Montreal: Black Rose Books, 1998) 108–20.
58 For the original proposal, see Coalition of Nova Scotia Forest Interests, *A
    New Forest Strategy for Nova Scotia: Discussion Paper* (Halifax: Department of
    Nat. Resources, July 1996). The results from an extensive series of public
    hearings are reported by the Forest Sector Committee of Voluntary Plan-
    ning, *Public Response to Coalition of Nova Scotia Forest Interests' Discussion Paper*
    (Halifax: Voluntary Planning Nov. 1996). The Department of Natural
    Resources revived most of the Coalition proposals one year later, in *Toward
    Sustainable Forestry: A Position Paper* (Halifax: Department of Natural
    Resources Nov. 1997). Draft legislation had been introduced at the time of
    writing.
59 P. Clancy, and L.A. Sandberg, 'Formulating Standards for Sustainable Forest
    Management,' *Business Strategy and the Environment* 6, Oct. 1997.
60 Materials related to the Acadian Forest Regional Standards process can be
    found at the following internet website: www.canadian-forests.com/fsc.html
61 Marie Wadden, *Nitassinan* (Vancouver: Douglas and MacIntyre, 1991).
62 For details on the Innu approach to forest management, see the internet
    website: www.innu.ca/
63 *R. v Peter Paul*, New Brunswick Provincial Court (Arsenault, P.C.J.), 27 Aug.
    1996. *R. v Thomas Peter Paul*, New Brunswick Court of Queen's Bench, Trial
    Division (Turnbull, J.), 28 Oct. 1997; *R. v Paul*, New Brunswick Court of
    Appeal, 22 April 1998, *LawPost N.B.C.* no. 4453.

Chapter Nine

Quebec: Consolidation and the Movement towards Sustainability

Luc Bouthillier

Contemporary Quebec forest policy is the result of a process that started at the beginning of European colonization. Today, it is a political–administrative edifice of such forbidding complexity that its very legitimacy can be called into question. The purpose of this chapter is to describe how the edifice was constructed, and more specifically the origins of Quebec's forest domain – the forest owned and controlled by the government, or, put more generally, by the public – and how it has been managed. Various 'diagnostic' elements are identified in this chapter, and facilitate the evaluation that follows of the management of Quebec's forests. The perspective is one of continuity of the forest and its usage: if there is one recurrent theme throughout the history of Quebec's forest policy, it is very much that of sustainability. The idea of 'sustained yield' thus provides coherence in describing the long-term dynamics of Quebec's forest policy.

The Recent Recognition of an Idea with Deep Roots

Today, forestry policy in Quebec, as in other Canadian provinces, rests on the concept of 'sustained yield.'[1] However, Quebec forest legislation has but few explicit references to it. Indeed, until 1984, in Quebec, 'sustained yield' remained a term used only by forestry policy managers, or other forestry professionals. Nevertheless, the principal characteristic of the Quebec forest regime is that the public (government) exercises its jurisdiction over forests through the activities of private (industrial) interests and the philosophical underpinning of this joint management of the public-private forest domain is the principle of sustained yield.

Close to 90 per cent of Quebec's forest is under direct state control.

This fact alone goes a long way towards explaining why the concept of sustained yield has so long been part of the Quebec policy landscape. Sustained yield expresses a management philosophy that defends the notion of the public interest in a manner that is both concise and adaptable to the changing context of forest practices.[2] The government of Quebec has long been accustomed to delegating forest management to the forest industry, in the expectation of industry implementation of the government's general policies. It took until June, 1985, however, for the government of Quebec to establish sustained yield as a primary management directive with the force of law. In fact, the first mention of the concept of sustained yield in an official document is found in the Quebec Ministry of Forests' 1985 policy statement entitled *Bâtir une forêt pour l'avenir* (*To Build a Forest for the Future*),[3] where the ministry announced that the future management of public forests is to be 'predicated on aiming for sustained yield.'

That policy statement took legislative form in December 1986, when with a lot of fanfare, the government proclaimed that the principle of sustained yield was to be the key structural element of the new Forest Act.[4] This was quickly recognized as a new departure in official Quebec forest legislation.[5] It is important to emphasize, however, that the government wished to employ the concept primarily in order to legitimize the re-allocation of forest area among private industrial interests.

From 1986 onward, each pulp or saw mill was associated with a 'management unit,' and mill operators have to sign a forest supply and management contract (CAAF) covering management practices in the unit.[6] The law stipulates that the volume of cuts stated in the contract cannot be greater than the potential annual sustainable cut determined for the management unit. By sustained yield, the legislature means the maximum annual volume of wood that can be harvested in perpetuity without diminishing the capacity of wood production in that unit. This policy marked a rupture with the management style in place since the beginning of the twentieth century under which North American legislatures generally considered the forests to be inexhaustible and scientific management or Taylorist principles provided the rationale for how it was to be harvested.[7] Insofar as the 1985 document signalled a regime change in Quebec, it is in the legislation's altering this philosophical basis of the relationship between Quebec society and the its forest domain. Let us consider some details of this alteration.

Prior to December 1986, the forestry regime did not consider forest growth in the harvest plans of industry. Although the government did oblige entrepreneurs to harvest only a certain volume of wood within a given area, the government worried little about incremental natural growth of exploitable fiber when fixing harvest volumes. The concern, above all, was the stock already at hand: the state of the forest at the time the allocation was completed constituted the sole basis of planning.

The 1986 Forestry Act called for an assesment of biological productivity, as a reference point in determining the state of the forest and its potential productivity. This use of a biological indicator to demonstrate and measure the impact of production targets has been met with general approval.[8]

It must be pointed out, however, that the concept of sustainable yield, as the element underlying regulation, made its way into the Forestry Act in a particular context. The concept was invoked by the government in 1985 as a way to dampen the outcry and concern about the overexploitation of provincial forests. At that time, government experts estimated that by the year 2005 there would not be enough softwood available to meet industrial demand. The preservation even of an 'extensive' management regime would involve a diminution of the possible harvest over time. Without energetic intervention it was estimated that the harvest would fall some 56 per cent, from 31 to 14.2 million cubic metres in forty years.[9]

Many stakeholders have described pre-1987 operations as overexploitative,[10] and have encouraged rapid movement towards a management policy dictated by sustainable yield. However, this fear of shortages of raw wood is not new. Already in 1927, a study of the Canadian forest, by P. Fontanel, concluded that the forest did not grow fast enough to replace what was taken out.[11] This observation has, of course, been reaffirmed afterwards on many occasions.[12] However, each time, the geographic size of Quebec, the importance of the demand for wood, or yet another definition of the productive capacity of the forest permitted the argument to be advanced that 'there was no threat in sight.'[13]

Is it possible that the recent interpretation of the concept of sustained yield over time has allowed Quebec governments to once again rationalize destructive forest policy to favour 'responsible' development? The concept (implied or explicit) of sustained yield provides a very loose definition of reality that allows the setting of policy goals and allocations to cope with the problems of the day. However, one must recognize that political advocacy of sustained yield does not necessarily imply that the forests will get healthier in the long run. This is because the concept of sustained yield has two aspects. It is a decision to manage public lands in a defensive manner, keeping an eye open for surprises that the future can bring. Indeed, since the beginning of the twentieth century, managers of the public forest domain have had a tendency to manage the forest as a natural system which must be protected from unforeseen dangers.[14] Concretely, they seek to conserve the forest lands. However, the same managers also consider the forest as a source of wealth to be enhanced in order to prepare for future harvesting. Once in place, these two goals can be contradictory.

Managing for sustained yield is intended to permit a reconciliation of these two tendencies. Rationalizing harvest levels by allowing for natural increments is intended to permit the simultaneous satisfaction of socioeconomic demand for timber and the biological permanence of the forest.[15] Technically, sustained yield imposes a measured and controlled harvest of the forest which speaks to a rational context for managing natural resources; presaging the sustainable development project that the promoters of ecodevelopment presented to the world. But there are still links between Taylorism and ecodevelopment and these links are revealed by an examination of how the concept of sustainability has been interpreted over the history of forest policy in Quebec.

The Making of the Public Forest Domain and the First Attempts at Forest Management

The French Regime

Quebec has long been thought to be part of the virgin territories of America, distinguished by the abundance of resources it sustains. This image still fascinates Europeans today.[16] One should not be surprised, therefore, that during the colonial period the authorities did little for the economic management of wood stocks. Champlain's tales of the forest as hostile and impenetrable depict a situation in which the tree was considered to be a nuisance. Three centuries later, Dupuis would still speak of 'Maisonneuve's syndrome' to depict the situation of a forester who is quicker to cut than to tend the forest.[17]

Quebec forest policy begins in 1669, when Colbert ordered the planting of oak trees on the royal domains of the King of France.[18] Echoes of this ruling were felt, as well, on both sides of the Atlantic. In 1672 the Intendant Talon reserved the wood of oak trees from the land titles of seigneurs,[19] with the object that these reserves would establish a large supply of wood for naval construction. Interestingly, Talon's promulgation of reserves began the first conflict over the use of forests in Quebec. While enhancing potential production, the reserves limited the possibility of immediate exploitation: should the colonists be deprived of a large quantity of usable wood today in order to permit ship-building tomorrow?

The question could only be answered by public authority and at the beginning of the eighteenth century, the Intendant Dupuys was clear: 'We must think of the wood as a Canadian fruit that will succeed the fur trade.'[20] But in a 1722 judgment, Intendant Bégon authorized subjects to cut wood reserved for the Crown. The colony was interested in land improvement, and there was no other way to do this than by clearing the trees. Bégon exempted the colonists from the reserve clause in exchange for the assurance that the harvested wood be 'usefully employed.'[21] In doing so, he reaffirmed a ruling made nine years earlier, in 1713, that allowed the taking of wood on lands nearby for the construction of bridges over rivers. In the choice between the usefulness of the forests now or their anticipated use later, the Crown's representative almost invariably chose the former. The impact of this choice on the domestic economy was immediately evident. As Bouffard remarks, Bégon's decision presents an early lesson in development theory and practice. It contained the embryo of a Quebec forest policy which addressed the question of different production functions competing for the same raw material but at different points in time.

A fourth significant colonial-era forest ruling appeared in 1742. At the request of Intendant Hocquart, the reserve clause imposed by Talon was extended to include red pine.[22] With this clause, the governing authorities returned to the idea of preparing for the future. However, let us not be fooled. The notion of forest reserves was imported from the metropolis. In Europe, government authorities anticipated drastic shortages of wood that were of great concern because wood was feeding the technological and industrial progress of the day. This was not a worry for the local population in North America. Despite some fears that surfaced in 1757 over the physical limits of colonial forests,[23] most Canadians thought that they would never have to use the forests to the point that they would have to wonder about their availability. They let the royal representatives resolve their metropolitan worries with wood ordinances which were only poorly and infrequently observed. In short, a preoccupation with the measured exploitation of the forest meant very little to the 65,000 habitants scattered on the shores of the Saint Lawrence in the middle of the eighteenth century.

The British Regime

The British Conquest, in 1763, did not change the forest regime put in place by the French. Governor Murray also had to set aside pine reserves – for the Royal Navy. Above all, the imperial administration asked him to reserve woodlands to cultivate trees for masts for the imperial fleet.[24] Although the pine woods of the Ottawa basin were then in fact reserved, the instruction to cultivate the forest became a dead letter.

In laying out their township tenure system, the British colonial authorities also made provisions for woodlands reserves. But they included the standing wood as a autonomous source of revenue for the clergyman and the schoolteacher that moved into each district. The order to cultivate the forest was even more incongruous in the regions of Quebec that were uninhabited as this area was already covered with forest. Since the market for wood at this time was dormant,[25] nature's generosity coupled with the weak demand for wood nullified the early prescription for enhanced silviculture.

The trade in timber from British North America only started to flourish during Napoleon Bonaparte's 1808–12 continental blockade of the United Kingdom.[26] The large-scale harvesting of white and red pine for the British market preoccupied forest companies and their workers throughout the nineteenth century. In 1805, 170 large ships left Quebec City with their holds full of pine. Five years later, 661 ships, fully loaded with pine, left Quebec for England.[27] Pine exports multiplied thirteen-fold, from 19,000 to 230,000 loads,[28] between 1808 and 1812.[29]

Following the passing of the Corn Laws in 1841, British tariff barriers protecting colonial forest products were lowered, beginning in 1842. By 1846, wood leaving Quebec was no longer competitive with that shipped from the Baltic.[30] But this depression in the forest sector was temporary. Commerce in wood began to pick up again in 1849, and the new imperial policy allowed the forest industry to profit from U.S. demand for lumber. Broadly speaking, the exchange of sawn products continued to be a lively commerce until the end of the nineteenth century. It peaked in the 1850s, when a reciprocity treaty between Canada and the United States was put in place, and slowed down with the combined effects of the treaty's end in 1866 and world recession in the 1870s.

Although the exploitation of the provincial forest was carried out by private organizations, the Crown did not for a moment give up its property rights as government decision-makers wanted to preserve their control over the land. Forest lands possessed a strategic character. The abundance of nature was, however, so obvious that forest resource management amounted to the refusal to alienate property rights for the production of wood. From the beginning of industrial logging, the forest was considered to be a public good that the private sector would enhance. This perception was transmitted from generation to generation and had a considerable impact on the forestry policies of the government of Quebec. For their part, the commercial sector involved in forest utilization kept its own future interests and ideas in mind. Throughout the nineteenth century the wood trade gave the colony a measure of purchasing power which resulted in the formation of a new hierarchy of Quebec society.[31] The new commerce, taking into account its path of exchange, favoured the English-speaking merchants and entrepreneurs.

The exploitation of the forest left the Francophone population with a status equivalent to that of a permanent woodland proletariat.[32] Consequently, this population became uninterested in forest resources management. Sometimes, they even saw management activities as obstacles preventing them from attaining their collective goals. The competition between the colonists and the forest exploiters for control over land in Quebec hence took the form of an ideological struggle that persisted for a very long period.

As Canada gradually acquired more autonomy from London, the strategic value of the forest ceded its place to that of the value of exchange. The cash value of wood products seduced the elites of the nineteenth century and the forests became an important generator of funds to pay for infrastructure costs. A.R.M. Lower believes that entrepreneurs, at this time, viewed the forest as a temporary source of wealth, permitting individuals to become established on the land, so that they could then try their luck at other types of activities.[33] The life stories of a few wood merchants, like the Booths or Wrights, are the folkloric representations of this scenario. But, to sustain his case, Lower singles out the development of agriculture which followed the forest operations. From the government's perspective, the forest was also perceived as a short-term, almost ephemeral opportunity for economic development. The internal diversification of an economy by means of external trade in raw materials or 'Staples' is the most common explanation for the emergence of the Canadian economy. The thesis was developed by Innis and popularized by other authors under the term 'staples economics.'[34]

In the middle of the nineteenth century, however, the government had not yet reached the stage where it could consciously elaborate a theory of economic development. Businessmen were content just to invest in the land, stopping in front of the beautiful stands of pine, logging at the lowest cost possible, and starting again a little further on. By 1835, some lumber camps were already situated more than 650 kilometres from the confluence of the Saint Lawrence and Ottawa Rivers.[35]

The public power, therefore, seemed to consider the forests as an economic springboard to be discarded once the initial propulsion had taken place. This vision lasted a long time. Bernard Fernow, a German forester who immigrated to Canada in 1907 and participated in the founding of the faculty of forestry at the University of Toronto, denounced this attitude. For him, the public well-being and posterity were sacrificed when the forest was reduced to a temporary source of revenue.[36] Fernow thought that the forest should be used on a more permanent basis and suggested that the government ought to adopt a more interventionist attitude or, at least, that it should use its fiscal power to direct the action of industry towards sustainability.

Mackay also reports that in 1850 certain individuals judged that the attitude of the public authorities towards the sustainability of the forest was reprehensible. In particular, there are two people known for their writings on the subject. The first, Charles R. Weld, asked how long would the Canadian forest last under the huge pressure that the U.S. market was putting on its wood. The second, James Dawson, concluded that many of the wood-producing forests were in imminent danger of vanishing. In 1863, Alexander Campbell, superintendent of Crown lands, delivered a plea for the cause of sustained yield before a parliamentary committee on forest depletion. Campbell wanted the harvesting of wood to be systematic, and he believed it was necessary to take measures to prevent the squandering of the forest. However, the deliberations of the committee were lost during the turmoil of Confederation. A bit later, Henri Joly de Lotbinière raised the question again. He exhorted silviculture by example, while practising a forestry inspired by the European tradition on his own seigniorial land. The idea of balancing the harvest of wood with the periodic regrowth of the forest was beginning to come to life on the Canadian scene.[37]

Scientific Forestry

The Legislature of the United Canadas passed the Administration of Woods and Forests on Crown Lands Act in 1849.[38] It sought to clarify the powers of government to award cutting licences on public lands. The rights of the licensee, like his obligations *vis-à-vis* the government, comprised the central elements of this first forestry legislation. In return for stumpage and other forms of rents given to representatives of the Crown, entrepreneurs obtained a free hand on the ground. They took advantage of these circumstances to try to place their industry on a larger and more solid base. Thus, they were among the leaders of the first wave of conservationists when they went up Parliament Hill in 1866. They relied on a factory metaphor to describe a forest which could run forever under their 'care.' They tried to guarantee the production of wood by gaining control over the largest possible amount of land for exclusive forestry purposes. The 'wood barons' became promoters of forest resources management centred on the stability of their industry. Moreover, they thought that they were best placed to ensure that such management took place and 'to serve the needs of humanity.'

The possibility of extending their fiscal base at the low price of delegating power to industry pleased the politicians of the day. They consented, therefore, to give the administration of Crown forests to the beneficiaries of the forest licences. At this point, notions of forest 'concession' or timber limits came on the scene. These arrangements gave exclusive rights to all the wood in a specified area to those who held forest permits, thus, confirming the delegation of management powers. It was up to the industry to manage the harvest of the forest within the limits of their concession and thereby to maximize societal well-being.[39] However, the government never ceded propriety rights to these lands as the forests were still considered a national good which could not be privatized.[40] An act passed in 1851 had confirmed this position by making it impossible to sell Crown lands other than for the purposes of colonization.

The expansion of the state apparatus following Confederation led to adjustments to the Woods and Forests Act, whose jurisdiction was transferred to the provinces in 1868. In Quebec, legislation had three objectives: first, to increase state revenues; second, to give a fair chance for entrepreneurs to have access to the public forest; and, third, to prevent overexploitation of forest wealth.[41]

The Quebec legislation specified the length of time that a licence could be held. It could be renewed annually, but had to be held by the same entrepreneur for an obligatory period of twenty-one years. In addition, the timber limit had to be used. The annual exploitation of 500 feet of square wood and twenty logs per square mile, or the making of permanent buildings such as logging camps and horse stables, was required if a doubling of the rent was to be avoided or the licence given to someone else.[42] In exchange for these undertakings on the part of the licensee, the government promised not to increase stumpages more than once during the twenty-one years.[43] Also the licence-holders were authorized to use their licence as a guarantee of security to obtain money from the banks as necessary for their operations.[44] This gesture reinforced the feeling of security for the licence-holders, who were already motivated by their exclusive twenty-one-year contracts. In certain respects this was the first step that made the sustainability of the forest politically desirable. However, as Bouffard reminds us, forest tenure was still not characterized by absolute permanent ownership. It was precarious, and it could be revoked according to the exigencies of the public interest. Agreements between forest concessionaires and financial institutions only held that, in case of revocation, the government would do its best to expedite the recovery of the bank's capital.

In this period, despite the opposition from the colonization movement, it was generally understood that Quebec land was divided into two types, forest and agricultural.[45] On 24 December 1875, the government gave a legislative basis to the idea that some forest land must remain forested. The Forest Lands Act now turned to the creation of forest reserves. It became legal for the lieutenant governor in council to put vacant Crown woodlands aside to ensure the perpetual production and cultivation of wood.[46] The government aimed to reserve lands for forest exploitation for at least 150 years. In this manner, the government hoped to ensure constant supplies of commercially available wood as well as to regulate water flows. The recognition of the forest character of the province even went so far as to oblige settlers to maintain forest cover on 15 per cent of the land they were given.[47]

The preoccupation of the government with the forest translated into new regulations for Crown lands. The cabinet tried to preserve forests for future harvests by preventing the cut of small-sized trees. A ruling on diameter limitation was modified thirteen times between 1868 and 1943 and was a great source of controversy throughout this period. As early as 1882, Fernow maintained that ignorance of the physiology of trees made the famous 'silviculture clause' ineffectual: 'The small ones are not necessarily the youngest, they can also be the less vigorous,' he said at a congress held in Montreal. The question involved emotional and technical debates that lasted until 1922, when the government tried to ensure the renewability of the forest by giving substance to the idea that the correct scheduling of harvests could guarantee a regular supply of wood material.

The scarcity of large trees, combined with the rising rate of literacy (and ensuing proliferation of newspapers), as well as technological progress in the making of pulp, allowed the pulp and paper industry to supersede the lumber industry in the early twentieth century.[48] The amount of land ceded to contractors grew considerably under the influence of this new industrial actor; between 1910 and 1920, the forest area controlled by pulp mills doubled.[49] As the dynamism of the pulp sector was maintained until 1931, so was its need for raw wood. Between 1925 and 1935, the productive capacity of mills jumped from 1.6 million to 3.9 million metric tonnes of pulp and paper.[50] The pulp and paper industry was dependent on vast areas of white and black spruce forests in the Quebec hinterland. It is estimated that in order to be sustainable each cubic metre of wood harvested in Canada during the Second World War required 9.4 hectares of forest under concession.[51] In Quebec this ratio was estimated to be only 2.43 hectares per cubic metre in 1940.[52] At this time the makers of paper held 80 per cent of the forest lands under concession.

Industry's voracious appetite for Quebec forest lands worried both supporters of provincial political autonomy and agricultural messianism. In 1911, the Gouin government succeeded in appeasing nationalist fears by establishing district forests.[53] The idea was to keep a proportion of the forest public to ensure that settlers moving into rural Quebec would have a supply of wood for heat and construction.[54] Each settler was authorized to take only a maximum of 15 cords (approximately 55 cubic metres) of wood per year. Otherwise the idea of permanent reserves, put forward in 1875, although interesting on paper, seemed to do no more than give business opportunities to insolvent contractors. The government put an end to the experiment with permanent reserves in 1915, but it did not repeal the sections of the forest act that permitted their existence.

Nevertheless, the government did become more demanding of industry. The Forest Inventory Act came into effect in 1922. It made the creation of timber inventories and intervention plans the key to obtaining a cutting permit,[55] and required that all logging operations be carried out according to a 'rational framework.' The Lands and Forests Act was later amended to stipulate that no clear-cutting could be undertaken on Crown lands without special authorization. To obtain such authorization, a licence-holder had to produce a management plan based on a proper inventory undertaken in accordance with instructions set out by the Lands and Forests Department.

For the chief forester Gustave C. Piché, the aim of the Forest Inventories Act was to 'sustain the exploitation of the forests.'[56] Piché summarized that, first, one had to determine the volume of the annual cuts with reference to the growth of the forest so as not to hurt its 'capital.' Then, one had to gradually regularize the forest cover. With a good knowledge of the inventories, the cuts could be oriented towards obtaining an even distribution of age classes, thus, working towards the creation of a 'normal' forest. However, the spirit of the Forest Inventories Act took some time to be implemented on the ground. In 1929, only five management plans were deposited with the government. In the end, the lands and forests department issued Directive B-44, aimed at all timber limit-holders. The note, dated 28 October 1929, outlined what the contents of the development plan should be in twelve steps:[57]

1 Description of the place where harvests will take place
2 The area of each cutting block
3 Local topography
4 Identification of forest types for stands that are the object of logging
5 Distribution by species
6 Volume by class of breast height diameter (BHD) and by species
7 Average height and BHD per species
8 Average age of the stands
9 State of forest regeneration (average height and number of stems per acre)
10 Foreseen difficulties of exploitation
11 Proposed logging method
12 Justifications for proposed logging method

In the middle of the 1930s, few companies took the initiative to complete this list with a calculation of the allowable annual cut on their limit. They used the celebrated 'area-volume regulation' formula:[58]

$$(A/R) * V = \text{Allowable cut (m}^3/\text{year)}$$

where A is the productive area (in hectares), R is the rotation age (in years), and V is the volume at maturity (m^3/ha). The government generalized the formula's application from 1939 onward. After that, the content of the forest management plan was firmly established, only subject to marginal changes until 1974.

The government demands appeared acceptable to industry. Indeed, the act only required a management plan that was a mere sketch indicating where the wood was to be removed, and how the exploited volume related to forest productivity.[59] Public managers expected that, once overmature stands were accounted for, loggers would harvest a quantity of wood equal to the net annual increment.[60] After the Second World War, it was suggested a rotation period of eighty years be adopted for planning the cut. The idea was to maximize the average annual increment. In this way, government experts thought that it would be feasible to harvest the Crown lands at a 2 per cent annual rate without impairing the sustainability of the forest.[61]

In this system limit-holders were in a position of strength as they were responsibile for collecting and analysing inventory data. Therefore, the limit-holders held the necessary information to estimate the physical productivity of the forest. In addition, government regulators were advised to tolerate a certain flexibility to accommodate the volatility of the market for forest products.[62] Some critics quickly rebuked companies for taking control of the environment away from the people in order to carry out their operations without any spirit of conservation.[63] Minville, for example, believed that land had to be redistributed in such a way that it reinforced the peasantry, not industry. According to him, farmers could spend time cutting wood and tending the forests during the their off season. Minville also thought the regulations framing the supervision of the harvest, defined largely with industry participation, had compromised the forest stock in the long run.

Some professional foresters, like Ellwood Wilson, chief forester at the 'Laurentide' company responded. Wilson challenged his industrial colleagues to seek profits while, at the same time, maintaining a commitment to the sustainability of towns based on paper mills. He went so far as to say that the survival of these communities depended on the ability of the industry to get a sustained yield from the forest it controlled. For the Canadian Association of Pulp and Paper Producers, the industry's responsibility for public wealth was to administer the forest so as to obtain the maximum quantity of wood products in perpetuity.[64] The concept of sustained yield, well assimilated by industry, was used to counter Minville's followers' arguments in favour of a less industrial approach to forest management.

From the Industrial Golden Age to the Interventionist State

At the beginning of the 1950s, the consumption of wood from industrial forestry in Quebec totalled close to 15 million cubic metres per year.[65]

This had an enormous impact on the 19,425,000 hectares of public land placed under the timber limit system by 1949.[66] The situation troubled forest managers within the government who raised fears of an impending wood shortage in order to justify the reorganization of the administration of the state forests.[67] The apprehension of most observers came, above all, from the fact that growing trees was not a profit-making activity for large corporations. The forest appeared to be a source of spending, as opposed to profitable manufacturing.

In theory, on an area of almost 20 million hectares, the annual removal of 15 million cubic metres might be compensated for by the natural growth of the forest.[68] However, since most forests were in an advanced state of maturity, the system brought wood losses and underutilization of the productive capacity of the land. The postwar boom reaffirmed the continuing strong U.S. demand for construction material and accelerated questioning of the capacity of provincial forests. The pulp and paper industry's domination of the forest sector was soon seen as an impediment to the intensification of management activities.

The general public began to contest the established management system.[69] Many of the new parishes that emerged in rural areas after the '1929 crisis' showed signs of decline and government officials started to realize that forest tending could revitalize these settlements.[70] In 1956, the Agricultural Products Marketing Act gave woodlot owners negotiation powers over the price of pulp wood harvested on their lots. This action permitted them to overcome the monopsony tactics of the pulp and paper industry that were revealed by a federal commission of inquiry in 1958. In 1971, the closure of a dozen villages in the Gaspé peninsula strengthened popular will to cultivate the forest in order to justify the continual occupation of the land.

The importance of forest concessions was weakened at this time for several reasons. Foremost, the underutilization of the resources *vis-à-vis* market opportunities, and the desire to stimulate 'indigenous Quebec entrepreneurship' from development opportunities justified calling the timber limits into question.[71] The public managers' desire to play a more important role in the economy and the ambition to transform the forest into a profit centre also added to the arguments in favour of redefining the existing forestry regime.

The perception of the forestry environment, which stems from this period of political realignment, is still strongly tainted by technological positivism. As the demand for wood continued to increase, the managers saw the possible scarcity of wood as a justification to begin industrial diversification under state coordination. This context made another future feasible for the public forest. However, as much as one had now to convince oneself of the natural ability of Quebec land to support a forest cover as it had a century before, the permanence of the forest was still a given even at the beginning of the 1960s.[72]

By this time, large paper companies ruled over the Quebec forest domain. In 1969, eight pulp and paper companies held 16.5 million hectares in their hands, totalling over 72 per cent of the conceded territory.[73] The barriers limiting access to the public forests under the concession system were abundantly used as a symbol to ferment a 'feeling of humiliation' in the population.[74] The government was practising generous industrial intervention strategy in order to modernize the Quebec economy, and the idea of taking back silviculture and harvest planning activities from large companies became very popular. However, the government did not want to exclude the private sector, but wanted, instead, to develop a partnership between the state and industry.

In 1971 a white paper advanced two new ways of carrying out forest management work on the ground.[75] On the one hand, the government would create a large state forest company. On the other, it would regionalize the structure of the Department of Lands and Forests and give it a more operational mandate. In both cases, the government wanted to give back to its agents the responsibility for management units which would be reorganized to meet the real needs of existing mills. The regionalization option was put in place at the end of 1973.

In choosing this path the government revoked timber limits, radically changing the rules of the forestry game. It wanted to disassociate the granting of raw wood concession from the disposition of the ground on which the trees stood. The government wanted to be linked to industry by means of supply agreements which were not directly tied to territory. Accordingly, it proposed to replace concessions by planning units which would reflect a distinct biophysical character. The formation of these units would facilitate the task of making the forest able to satisfy global demand for raw wood as well as optimizing the use of small-diameter stems.

The government indicated that state intervention would consist of making ten-year development plans for each planning unit. The objective would be to ensure the permanent harvest of raw wood at competitive prices.[76] To realize these plans, the state recognized the importance of industry, and it endeavoured to give all the implementation work to industry through guarantees of supply. This was an enormous change.

Accordingly, the government anticipated an eight-year transition period to phase out timber limits on public lands. This process started in December 1974 and barring insurmountable difficulties, all public lands producing forest materials were to be part of the public forest domain by 1982. From that point on, no private companies would hold exclusive property rights over trees on public lands.

Officially, the regulation that controlled the forest harvest maintained the simple norms in use by industry for the previous forty years. The forest managers, who worked for the state, set the allowable cuts from one year to the next and the volume of the annual harvest had to be within the limits defined by the net growth of the forest for the year in question.[77] In focusing the calculation of annual allowable cut on the forest growth and on the transition to a 'normal' forest, however, they perpetuated the mechanical application of the concept of sustained yield held since the 1930s.

Nevertheless, debate over the relevance of this mechanical application of sustained-yield concepts in forest management was high in Canada at the end of the 1960s.[78] Without taking a direct part in the talks, Quebec sided with those who contested such approaches. The government wanted a forestry administration sensitive to socio-economic change.[79] Quebec policy developers were about to reformulate the idea of sustained yield to attain this objective.

Public managers had already put forward the idea of 'periodic' sustained yield for some time.[80] This implied that the volume of wood cut over ten years was to be balanced with the yields resulting from forest growth for the same period. Some annual gaps, therefore, were permitted. It is important to emphasize that since 1968 the expression 'allowable cut' did not include the regularization or normalization of the forest. Managers simply focused on the determination of an annual volume of raw wood that could be taken continually during the whole rotation period.

Periodic sustained yield was slightly more flexible than that determined by an annual base. As the authors of a forestry policy brief outlined,[81] the maintenance of an even flow during the rotation would come at the cost of the stagnation of forest growth and the slowdown of industrial expansion. This situation was caused by the structural imbalance of timber age classes within Quebec forests. More than 65 per cent of the province's forest lands was occupied by forests that were mature or senescent. To overcome this, the government wanted to alter the way the inventories of standing wood were allocated.

This type of management was to be aimed to guarantee the supply for mills during a given period and, at the same time, to restore the integrity of the productive capacity of the provincial forest. A break with the continuity of supply was acceptable if it met these criteria.[82] The concept of sustained yield contained in this model was, therefore, only an indicative one. The concept was used to discern the impact of a supply shortage according to three criteria: the time it would occur, as well as the duration and size of the shortage. The further the period of rupture was from the time of its calculation, the more the forest manager could hope a qualitative change in the demand for raw wood could meet the situation. Sustaining annual harvests became a way of using a model to simulate the future, to imagine possible scenarios. The calculation of allowable cut levels informed decision-making, but was not a substitute for them.

In implementing this model, government planners explicitly tried to incorporate the effects of market forces of supply and demand for forest products. However, this interpretation of the concept of sustained yield only included consideration of the production of wood for commercial use. The understanding of the different functions of the forest was hardly mentioned in the forestry policy documents of the day. Multiple use concepts did not enter the analytical framework established to develop forest policy-making.

To be sure, the authors of those policy documents mentioned the importance of the forest's multifunctional character to define measures of its productive capacity.[83] However, a high industrial priority remained.[84] During the 1970s, the preservation of the forest capital meant preservation of industrial potential. The government formulated management regulations by taking account of the needs of mills, assuming the extreme limits of the natural possibilities of forest renewal. The overabundance of old stands suggested accelerated harvesting whose rhythm would depend more on economic opportunities than on the forests' recuperative ability.

The Withdrawal of the State

The early 1980s brought an economic slowdown to Quebec as a whole. Petroleum shocks, rising inflation, and monetarism dampened the global economy. Supply-side economics focused on economic growth through less or no state intervention in production processes.[85] The promoters of this 'new' medicine hoped to increase productivity through the elimination of the artificial barriers constraining the supply of goods and services. According to them, privatization held the seeds of a strong economy and the state should withdraw from most production activities.

The Quebec government hid behind its responsibility for prudent forest management to abandon its entrepreneurial role. It wanted to mitigate its budget deficits and therefore the government claimed it had to correct some structural problems with the provincial economy such as reducing its supports to labour and to investors.[86] In this context, the forest policy implemented in 1972, which included forty-four management plans covering the entire public forest domain, appeared to be out of date. The will to ensure that forest management be carried out directly by the state or through mixed private-public arrangements fell out of step with the prevailing economic view.

The 'dirigiste' forest policy developed during the 1970s was worsened by problems of administrative inertia and underfunding. Moreover, the power the government had exercised over forest planning put the industry on the defensive. To assure that its raw material needs be fulfilled, the industry consolidated its wood reserves by accumulating supply guarantees. By 1984, the authorized consumption of round softwood for the whole industry totalled 52 million cubic metres per year,[87] an absurd figure given that the annual allowable cut was estimated to be approximately 30 million cubic metres.[88]

In operational terms, government analysts identified three factors of change. First, despite the discourse in place since 1922, forest managers had not really oriented their harvest operations to the more mature stocks. A report on the situation by the minister responsible for the forests[90] indicated, rather, that loggers continuously privileged volume over age without considering the 'normalization issue.' Also, since 1976, a spruce budworm epidemic had altered the state of the forest, causing a loss of 6 per cent of the total forest stock, or 235 million cubic metres. This was equivalent to ten years of harvest.[91] Thirdly, the impact of the mechanization of the cuts was felt. Experts agreed that only 40 per cent of the forest area exploited by mechanized harvest of coniferous stands[92] since 1965 had regenerated in a satisfactory manner.[93]

Public expectations about forests had also changed. Since 1979, for instance, wildlife management operations[94] had opened the forest to 300,000 outdoor recreationists. The expansion of activities in these natural settings was so great that analysts estimated that, by 1987, 1.5 million Quéebecois had enjoyed a recreational activity on some part of the forest located in seventeen parks, thirty wildlife reserves, sixty controlled development zones, and the 150 outfitter inns of the province.[95]

As a result, for the first time the environmental agenda gained ground in Quebec forestry.[96] Forest managers started to realize that they should pay much more attention to the interdependence between elements in an organized dynamic system in order to maintain that dynamism.[97] Quebec foresters, it was argued, had been mistaken in assuming that the forest would regenerate after cutting to its previous state.[98]

Nevertheless, wood shortages dominated discussion of the reorientation of Quebec forest policy when reforms were proposed in 1984. The so-called danger of the shortage of wood was the dominating factor in policy review discussions. State managers were obsessed by a possible shortage: and the possibility of a scenario in which 'Quebec will no longer have sufficient forestry resources to ensure the development of the forestry industry or even to simply maintain production at its present levels.'[99] The 1984 Ministry of Lands and Forests analysis was clear: the available stock would meet global demand in 1983 and for the next thirty years. After that period, industrial decline was anticipated if corrective measures were not started immediately.

To rectify the situation, the ministry suggested replacing the harvest priority by a silvicultural one. They argued that accomplishing this regeneration went well beyond the capacity of the state, and therefore recommended that the government announce loudly and clearly that it was no longer able to substitute itself for the private sector in managing logging. The ministry suggested that the government should take the following three steps. First, it had to define the territorial areas of the harvest. Second, it had to guarantee the continuity of the production function for raw wood. Finally, it had to push a dynamic conservation framework that must be used for forest renewal.

The first two steps of the proposed strategy to compensate for the possible wood shortage simply constitute the repetition of history. Government planners argued that the users of the forest must experience a feeling of belonging to the land if large-scale regeneration was to occur. The ministry thought that such a result could be had through a definitive allocation of a portion of Quebec lands to the production of wood. In tying the users of wood to a duly identified area, they wanted industry to abandon its role as exploiter of the forest in favour of a new role as producer of wood. That is where the last step in the strategy became important.

But this third step suffered from as much confusion in 1984 as it had in the 1972 project. The forest review did not concretely define the dynamic conservation framework which it was recommending. It seemed that the government wanted to set the allocation of cuts according to the productive capacity of the land. The basic postulate underlining the reorientation of Quebec forestry policy was therefore that of underproduction; the idea that the annual volume of wood produced in Quebec was less than the biophysical capacity of the forest. In the long term it was argued, the annual production of commercial softwood on a sustained basis had to be greater than 28.6 million cubic metres.[100] However, two centuries of harvesting had modelled the composition of standing stock in such a way that it impeded the realization of the full potential of the forest.[101] The Quebec government wanted to create a new forest reality through an enormous replanting program. In the meantime, it admitted that it would be difficult to bridge the gulf between the need for and the availability of wood. In a few parts of the province the volumes that would sustain an annual harvest equal to the given industrial demand were limited to only a few years' reserve. Therefore, the government bet on the presumption that the supply of wood constrained by natural causes would result in higher prices and release the necessary economic forces to resolve the shortage.[102] Those economic forces would be the prelude to a spatial redistribution of industrial demand and to the adaptation of industry to the new context of substantial fibre reduction.

To adapt, in this sense, meant to make better use of available resources while making them last longer. To aid this process they wanted to enlarge, one last time, the boundaries of productive territory. They expected to complete the opening of forests in the middle north of Quebec, a movement started during the latter part of the 1960s. Quebec still had 7 million hectares of quite productive forest in this area, but it was judged to be too far away to contribute to provincial inventories of commercial wood.[103] Those areas would support reserves of 500 million cubic metres, of which more than 87 per cent would be made up of 'decadent' stands. According to government planners,[104] the exploitation of the pulp zone situated north of the 50th parallel would leave time for the forest to regenerate in the more southern sites. Harvesting the forests of the middle north represented a way of ensuring the supply of wood during the thirty years needed to remodel the Quebec forest landscape. Also, despite the quite high operating costs, the exploitation of this zone appeared to offer the possibilities of industrial expansion.

The government's forest policy proposal was released in June 1985 in a document entitled *To Build a Forest for the Future*. The hypothesis underlying the ministry's study was an idea dear to professional foresters in Quebec. They took for granted that maintaining a tree cover sufficient to meet the needs of the wood industry would preserve all of the functions of the forest. This hypothesis brings us back to the classic interpretation of the concept of sustained yield. Focusing on the trees, this concept reduced the function of the forest to wood. This reasoning sacrifices the complexity of the forest to bolster a reductionist and technical approach. The merit of the report, however, was that it simplified the aims of the emerging forest policy and consequently enhanced its short-term chances of success.

The government proposition comprised two mutually complementary objectives. First, the government wanted to maintain a forest cover of quality. Second, it was committed to satisfying the present and future needs of the forest industry. In the minds of the government's forest managers, an increase in the quality forest cover would simultaneously allow for the sustainability of industrial activities while meeting other needs and expectations. The production of wood and the role of the industry remained, therefore, at the centre of the policy project.

These aims were to be achieved by two means. It was, first, about giving the government a land use plan for the entire forest territory, where the multifunctional character of the forest was expressed in the degree of priority given to wood production. The second objective was to guarantee the application of basic silviculture to all parts of the territory used for the production of wood, through the elaboration of specific contracts geared towards that end.

On the whole, the 1985 propositions marked a return to the pre-1972 situation. The framers confined government intervention to two traditional roles: the allocation of the forest territory between diverse users of wood and the administrative control of the harvest. The authors of *To Build a Forest for the Future* insisted on a precise legal orientation. They retained the idea of calculating allowable cut through the sustained yield model. On the one hand, they wanted to reallocate the available resources according to the fibre productivity of the territory. On the other hand, they thought that they could stimulate harvest operations compatible with the silvicultural principles. Sustained yield was presumed to play the role of a catalyst that would change stakeholders' behaviour. However, the rhetoric did not accomplish much: 'The management of wood resources on the basis of sustained yield is a necessity to ensure the sustainability of the resource and the economic activities that follow it.'[105] One could see the same expectations put forward seventy years earlier.

The Present-Day Quebec Forest Regime

After three years of discussion, the idea of renewing the Quebec forest regime came to an end in December in 1986 when the National Assembly approved the new Forest Act on Christmas Eve. The Land and Forests Act was completely repealed. The timber limits, Crown forest lands administered by the state, and forest reserves were abolished. At the same time, the rights and privileges attributed to them were revoked. All the forest areas administered by the state were designated as public domainal forests.

The legislature's intention was to find a solution to the underutilization of Quebec forests that resulted from inappropriate management techniques.[106] The act was presented as a framework to control all the activities affecting the productivity of forest areas on the public domain. In fact, above all, it addressed the role of the stakeholders who cut the wood. The legislation was particularly directed to industry which wanted to have a guaranteed long-term fibre supply.

An official handbook on forest management was published in 1987. It explained the contractual relations between the government and the tenure-holders in accomplishing the task of restoring and preserving the forest cover of the management units located on public lands. In 1988, the handbook became a technical annex to the forest supply and management contracts. It has since had numerous additions, particularly concerning stands of mixed wood. Its application allowed the state to subtly refine its governance of the forest. But the calculation of wood yields posed the problem of the dichotomy between the government that acts as a landlord and the government that defines social standards. Over ten years later, the importance of having an agency that would bring together industry and government representatives to set productivity goals and means to reach it is apparent.[107]

The protection of all forest resources was the second objective of the act approved in 1986. The legislature wanted to allow expression of the multifunctional character of the forest. The contract-holders were indeed saddled with a set of regulations aimed at standards on forest intervention.[108] The main objective of these regulations was to preserve the diversity of the forest environment during harvesting activities.[109]

They were the fruit of collaboration between departments and they spelled out authorized forestry practices regarding the interdependence of forest components. They identified, as well, the protective measures enforced by means of cutting licences.

In a melee over a revised forest protection strategy adopted in 1994, these regulations were profoundly modified. The regulations focused, for the most part, on riparian areas and wildlife habitats, so that control over the size of cutting blocks and the use of pesticides represented their most visible manifestation. The goal of some academics, of having a more adaptive process, one that would be specific to each ecosystem, remained, however, unmet. In its assessment of the implementation of the forest regime over the previous ten years, the Ministry of Natural Resources (1998) continued to list development of such an adaptive process among its intentions.[110]

The 1986 regulations confirmed, as well, the use of land use plans for public lands. In fact, the government took advantage of the public interest in the forest as an ecosystem to lay down a plan that classified public lands according to the possibility of exploiting their wood. The zone where the extraction of raw wood was excluded comprised only 1 per cent of public forests. The zone where the production of wood was classified as secondary occupied 16 per cent of the public forest domain, whereas priority was accorded to wood crops that could serve industrial ends on the remaining 83 per cent.[111] The law foresaw the convergence of this plan with the development schemes that had been elaborated by each of the regional governments[112] which had public domain forests on their territory. This was an opening to get the public more involved in the decision-making process about forest management.

The 1986 act was above all, however, a response to the industrial imperative. Through it, the legislature acceded to a wish that the users of raw wood had held for more than twenty years: the allocation of volumes of timber by the government would be tied to specific lands. However, as announced in 1985, the government had agreed only on a very conditional basis to identify forest areas with private enterprise. First of all, the government defined the public forests as a residual source of wood. This position was meant to encourage wood production by the growing number of small woodlot owners as well as owners of private timber lands. The government wanted to optimize the yield by type of product, forcing the pulp and paper giants to use sawdust, wood chips, and recycled fibres before giving them a production area on the state domain.

The second condition was more ambitious. In exchange for access to an inventory of fibre on a designated public territory, the government wanted to force the large forest exploiters to transform themselves from loggers into forest attendants. Ten years of assessment showed that a rapid decline in yield per hectare had resulted from the lack of silviculture in harvesting operations. To be allowed to harvest wood in the public forest, a potential contract-holder would have to commit to a forest regeneration program that would result in improved yields at maturity. Respect for this condition was fundamental to the awarding of contracts.

Unlike the forest regime on the public forest domain that prevailed between 1974 and 1986, the entrepreneurs who took advantage of the public forest now represented the main motor of the new management plan. They had to actively participate in the silviculture effort. Accordingly, the legislature announced that stumpage would be calculated on volume allocated by the government representatives rather than on the wood harvested by forest entrepreneurs. The forest industry lobbied hard against this position and would obtain its repeal in 1990, and the re-establishment of the calculation of stumpages following the volume harvested.

Only the stems of those species that satisfied the needs of a specific mill were considered in the definition of a management area. Because of forest diversity, these areas were often shared by different firms. A new generic term appeared to designate these areas: common area.[113] The supply and forest management contract (CAAF) may be applied to numerous common areas. It confers to private parties the right to get annual licences to harvest the volume of wood required to meet the needs of a mill in excess of what can be obtained from woodlot owners, residual sources, and recycling facilities. In return, the contract-holder undertakes to attain a level of wood yield set by government officials. The contract has a twenty-five-year term, but its possible renewal every five years effectively makes it permanent as long as the user adequately lives up to the contract commitments. There were 124 common areas on the public forest domain to accommodate 262 CAAF-holders in 1997.[114] Only the volume attributed to the specific species used by that enterprise is included in the franchise it is awarded by the state. In addition, companies are not allowed to sell unused portions of their allocated standing timber. The proliferation of common areas posed the problem of how to elaborate a coordinated position in face of the exigencies of the forest regime. A mechanism to ensure collegial decision-making was absent in the act.

The dynamic of the present Quebec forest present regime rests on the five-year review of the general management plan. This review is done under the initiative of government representatives who evaluate the work of the contract recipient. Their main task is to adjust the yield of wood fixed in the contract. Despite its importance, the promoters of the new regime did not elaborate further on the review process. Above all, they concentrated their energy on setting up the regime. They agreed to a period of three years, starting in April 1987, to make the transition from the mixed tenure system comprising forests in the public domain and timber limits to that of the new forest supply and management contracts. Some 300 contracts had to be negotiated.[115]

When allocating the contracts, the determining emphasis has been placed on opening up forests in Quebec's middle north. The strategy was presented, at first, like a well-known traditional song about pushing back the frontier. But, from the perspective of industrial sustainability, pushing back the frontier in order to expand the cutting zone was no longer an alternative to forest cultivation. The exploitation of the middle north forest appeared as a complement to silviculture efforts undertaken in the south. It was interpreted as a concrete way to satisfy present demands, while at the same time, preparing for the future. This is where the use of the concept of sustained yield came into play. The legislature took upon itself the task of making entrepreneurs shed their short-term harvester mentality. The aim of the imposition of sustained yield management was to force forest exploiters to be preoccupied with the future as they intervened in the forest. This constraint on stocks was seen as a reinforcement of market signals, thus, adding another mechanism of adaptation. The new regime legally obliged industry to become aware of the limits to the supply of raw wood. Simultaneously, it intended to promote new development opportunities by freeing volumes of species that did not contribute to the actual supply of mills.

At the same time, the middle north reserves met the need for wood during the period when industry learned how to cultivate the forest. Interpretation of the concept of sustained yield led government authorities to consider controlled access to the middle north forest as a means of establishing a transition period. Such an interpretation made it possible to take wood from the last virgin forests of Quebec in order to maintain a steady supply of timber. It authorized the identification of allowable cut effects that would result from an increase of silviculture work in the south. Geoffroy's analysis of the strategic value of the northern reserves substantiates these relationships.[116] Therefore, the size of forest operations north of the 50th parallel had to be in proportion to the gains in volume resulting from the silviculture work carried out in the south but not yet available for harvest. The situation was not without worry for those who live in the middle north. For them, this strategy was incomplete because it provided no clear vision concerning the sustainability of the middle north forest.[117]

The system adopted in 1986 was the expression of a will to better control the cut in the public forests. The government wanted to show that this time it had really taken matters into its own hands. In these circumstances, the idea of sustained yield became attractive. As underlined by Minville-Deschênes, it represented the ideal objective for forestry policy.[118] The sustained yield idea promoted by the government since the 1985 release of *To Build a Forest for the Future* has also gained support from most stakeholders within the industrial forest sector.[119] The consensus around this concept seemed also to be the state's best argument to direct the use of forests. The accuracy of that policy was reaffirmed in an assessment of the new regime made by the Quebec government in 1998.[120]

Sustained Yield: A Five-Part Model

As the term is used in Quebec, sustained yield characterizes a dynamic relationship between the forest and the communities inhabiting it. Five main interpretations of the idea of sustained yield have been at play over time and in particular socioeconomic contexts in Quebec and the United States (Figure 9.1).[121] These five interpretations bring to light political projects that have been distinct in terms of means and objectives.

Physiological Interpretation of Sustained Yield

This is the classic vision of sustained yield. It consists of adjusting the annual forest harvest, which is determined by the state, to the annual growth of the trees growing on the territory harvested. The forest is analogous to a bank account where one might play with the interest without reducing the capital. But forest capital is a heritage, a gift from nature. Harvesting the forest is not only about timber. Socially, the objective is to motivate wood harvesters to establish themselves on a given territory and ensure the regrowth of their trees; this is the only way of guaranteeing them a renewal of supply. Industrial policy should

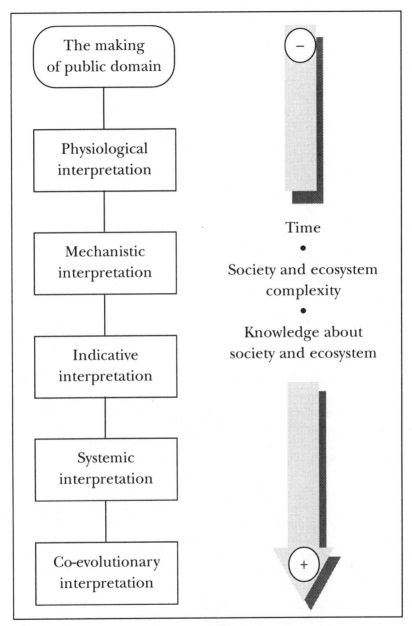

Figure 9.1. Interpretation scale of sustained yield forestry – a model

bend to the forces of nature and limiting the yield is intended simply to ensure the sustainability of the forest.

The physiological interpretation may guide the forest management policy as long as stocks are abundant. However, it contains an important flaw. Industry focuses solely on the available quantity of raw wood. Therefore, limiting harvesting to levels of sustainable yields constitutes a constraint that tells industry nothing about the available volumes, and it takes no account of the (variable) demand for wood products. Market conditions for wood products have no influence on cut allowances. Thus, one should not be surprised if this interpretation has a short shelf-life. It corresponds, in fact, to the initial phase of rational forest management and society and forests are seen as operating in a steady state. The physiological interpretation permits one only to rationalize forestry and to set the stage for a forest policy.

Mechanical Interpretation of Sustained Yield

The growing demand for forest products led the government to quickly take measures to manipulate the forest cover to obtain more wood or to justify larger harvests. To attain increased productivity, forest policy tried to change to make industry more responsible in exploiting the forest in a manner that redistributes the stock of trees on its areas. Under the mechanical interpretation, harvesting the forest is to be structured in such a way that after a transition period, average annual growth is maximized. This is what is meant by 'normalizing the forest.' The policy has two objectives. One is always to try to promote industry. The second, however, is to ensure that the commercial forest has the maximum quantity of available wood for harvesting. The forest becomes a variable factor of production. The 'normal' forest, where each age class of tree occupies the same space over time, is the desired goal because it represents a condition of social stability and maximizes all the functions of the forest.

This model of a normal forest raises a number of questions. The idea that an even flow of wood could stabilize human communities betrays, once more, a lack of understanding of economics. Normalization does not take into account the profit motive in the mills, where the wood is transformed, although the pursuit of profit is a basic rule of business. We find rhetorical and mysterious the assertion that the normal forest would eventually lead to a situation in which all the functions of the ecosystem are optimized. It does have the trappings of an ecosystem approach. Nevertheless, in our view, the objective of the normal forest, or the normalization of the forest, is merely an elegant way to justify an increase in allowable cuts without increasing the responsibilities of industry.

Sustainable Yield as an Indicator

An examination of the history of forestry in Quebec reveals that the demand for wood has not only continually increased, it has also diversified. Above all, forest managers are starting to expressly consider other forest functions as a justification for public sector intervention, such as the regularization of water supplies, the management of wildlife habitat for particular species such as deer, and developing recreational sites. In addition, the explosion of scientific knowledge in recent decades and its applications also modify the relationship between nature and society. Technological progress now provides an ethical challenge. It is no longer a given that we can do better than nature and that our works are always socially progressive. The volume and the variety of the needs to be satisfied, as well as the increased possibilities of manipulating the forest environment, thus, bring about a third interpretation of sustained yield.

By now, the influence of the economic approach on industry and government is obvious. Governments realize that the stability of human settlements depends on strong markets for wood products and a continuous supply of raw material. Technological progress reallocates the factors of production. Economists emphasize that available wood must be used to the maximum when in demand. The public forest domain occasionally faces development opportunities that have to be seized as they come.

The integration of economic considerations into the concept of sustained yield defines the forest in response to the needs of the market. It becomes important to locate, in time and space, ruptures in the continuity of the supply of wood. The duration, magnitude, and above all, the time when these ruptures are likely to appear are the important and necessary parameters of indicative planning. Governments count on market forces to send messages to active economic agents and, by doing so, to prompt them to improve their productivity. All the government has to do is to provide information, to build scenarios of the future states of the forest.

With this interpretation the government moves away from the goal of normalizing the forest. It wants, above all, to stimulate the adaptive capacity of the forest ecosystem as well as the industrial structure. This

point of view contains a very simple social project: if the forestry industry grows, then the human settlements dependent on it will also develop
satisfactorily.

Systemic Interpretation of Sustained Yield

The philosophy of production contained within the indicative planning
interpretation of sustained yield clashes with the multifunctional character of the forest domain that is now beginning to be recognized by
government. The simplicity of the social project animated by indicative
planning does not reflect the more complex reality well. It does not take
into account our ignorance about ecosystems and human communities.
Furthermore, it makes worse the existing unsolvable conflicts between
the two. The parties involved in the formation of a forest policy want to
reclaim a truly diverse production from the public forests.[122] The government has to, therefore, conceive of a forest policy regime composed
of an ecosystem offering multiple production possibilities, excluding
those below or above certain thresholds.[123] At the same time, the government must respond to public anxiety concerning the consequences
of manipulating the forest cover[124] and become committed to a continual process of improving forestry knowledge and practices.[125]

Knowledge of the interdependence among forest functions leads to
caution and diversity rather than the defiant attitude underlying the
indicative planning interpretation. On the biophysical level, Brown and
Carter emphasize that the complexity of the interactions between the
plants and their physical environment as well as the speed with which
these interactions change, make it hazardous to predict the state of the
stocks of raw wood based solely on the rate of growth of a forest stand.[126]
On the economic front, Worrel and Zinn remind us that the objective
of forest policy consists of maintaining the continuity of the flow of a
variety of benefits stemming from the public forest.[127] This portfolio
approach offers a lot of room for change in forest policy.

With this perspective, the concept of sustained yield can supply conceptual support to modelling efforts to project the state of the forest
and to select a development scheme that could integrate various functions of the forest. This is the systemic interpretation of sustainable
yield. In other words, when development projects allow the realization
of a continuous flow of benefits the result will be a compromise between
stakeholders participating in the same management regime. This will be
a systematic application of sustainable yield. The forest will then be per-

ceived as a system. Sustainable yield will then act as a catalyst to bring systematic thinking into the heart of civic dialogue. It will induce a redeployment and diversification of the 'forest industry' with regard to the multiplicity of expectations of the forest.

Co-evolutionary Interpretation of Sustained Yield

Human intervention modifies the forest in a way that, in its turn, forces society to adapt. Both the ecosystem and society are part of a mutually interactive system.[128] It is possible to see interactions between the two that can lead them to change in a way that is favourable to human collectivities without slowing down the dynamics of the ecosystem. This is what Norgaard called co-evolution.[129] The co-evolutionary approach also rests on the observation that society, in becoming more complex, assumes a growing proportion of the regulatory functions that used to be endogenous to ecosystems.[130] For instance, those functions in the boreal forests would arise through natural disasters rather than the senescence of dominant trees.[131] 'Good' logging practices would mimic natural disturbances.

A co-evolutionary interpretation of sustained yield brings us new ways of viewing forest policy. This interpretation allows human institutions to substitute themselves for certain ecological processes that are powerful forces in the forest. Sustained yield, thus, remains a normative concept that compels, this time, human intervention to maintain the integrity of the forest. For Perry the question of the integrity of the forest is tackled with parameters defined by the regime of natural disturbances individual to each ecosystem.[132] It becomes important to define the social acceptance of the consequences of a management program where natural disturbances such a fires or insect epidemics play a major role. Technically, the application of the co-evolutionary interpretations of sustained yield can help devise management options across time and space to ease a decision process inherently plagued by the uncertainties of ecosystem processes.

Such an interpretation forces us to take account of the complexity that characterizes forest ecosystems and to integrate this complexity within the policy process. Concretely, it invites us to understand how natural disturbances have modified the forest's capacity to adapt and to visualize that human manipulation has the same power. The objective of this interpretation is to adapt the behaviour of individuals and institutions to the dynamics of the forest. Despite its productivist origins, the idea of co-evolutionary sustained yield offers a very simplified approach to deal with the complexity of the forest. This model aims to answer some questions concerning the flow of goods and services that the forest can provide and to integrate an understanding of the dynamics of the forest with a political process that facilitates responsible and attainable human behaviour.

The Application of the Model to Quebec Forest Policy

The promoters of the existing Quebec forest regime insist on using 'sustained yield' to differentiate it from what came before.[133] They are right, insofar as they use productivity measures to weigh the potential productivity of the public forest domain to determine the area of development for industry. Nevertheless, the idea of using sustained yield as an operational standard to calculate possible harvest is not a new one (Figure 9.2). In its modern form it has been around Quebec since the middle of the 1920s. Its earlier antecedents can be traced back to the regime in New France.

The 1986 rehabilitation of sustained yield constitutes, all the same, a positive step towards better management of the forest in the public domain. The concept permits us, in effect, to shed the harvester mentality. The desire to obtain more raw wood than nature can furnish without human assistance appears compatible with the accomplishment of social progress. However, the concept of sustained yield as currently practised in Quebec does not yet integrate the multiple functions of the forest ecosystem very well. It has reductionist characteristics stemming from its limited focus on the supply of wood as the main parameter of management policy.

Sustained yield has, nevertheless, furnished the logic necessary to constitute and preserve a large public domain. Intendant Dupuys, in 1757, and Commissioner Campbell, in 1866, wanted simply to systematize the harvesting of wood and to prevent the ruin of the forest in order to protect the public good. But, just as they focused on the maximum volume of wood per hectare, today's forest managers are insensitive to the socioeconomic evolution that has led to awareness of all of the many values of the forest. They have strayed from their task which is to meet society's and industry's demand for goods and services while respecting our forest heritage. Distinguishing sustained yield from its current technical objective would give a new lift to the dynamics of provincial forestry policy.

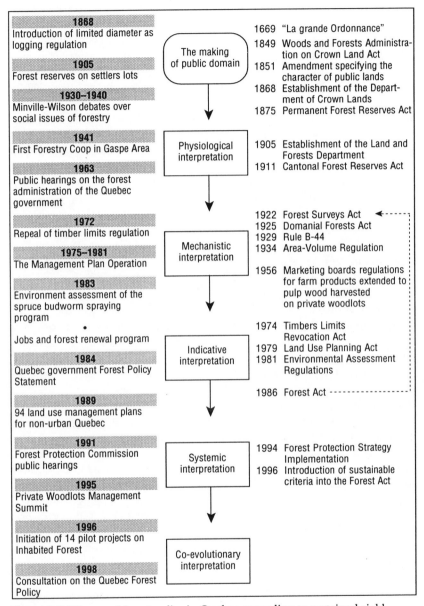

1868
Introduction of limited diameter as logging regulation

1905
Forest reserves on settlers lots

1930–1940
Minville-Wilson debates over social issues of forestry

1941
First Forestry Coop in Gaspe Area

1963
Public hearings on the forest administration of the Quebec government

1972
Repeal of timber limits regulation

1975–1981
The Management Plan Operation

1983
Environment assessment of the spruce budworm spraying program

Jobs and forest renewal program

1984
Quebec government Forest Policy Statement

1989
94 land use management plans for non-urban Quebec

1991
Forest Protection Commission public hearings

1995
Private Woodlots Management Summit

1996
Initiation of 14 pilot projects on Inhabited Forest

1998
Consultation on the Quebec Forest Policy

The making of public domain

Physiological interpretation

Mechanistic interpretation

Indicative interpretation

Systemic interpretation

Co-evolutionary interpretation

1669 "La grande Ordonnance"
1849 Woods and Forests Administration on Crown Land Act
1851 Amendment specifying the character of public lands
1868 Establishment of the Department of Crown Lands
1875 Permanent Forest Reserves Act

1905 Establishment of the Land and Forests Department
1911 Cantonal Forest Reserves Act

1922 Forest Surveys Act
1925 Domanial Forests Act
1929 Rule B-44
1934 Area-Volume Regulation
1956 Marketing boards regulations for farm products extended to pulp wood harvested on private woodlots

1974 Timbers Limits Revocation Act
1979 Land Use Planning Act
1981 Environmental Assessment Regulations

1986 Forest Act

1994 Forest Protection Strategy Implementation
1996 Introduction of sustainable criteria into the Forest Act

Figure 9.2 History of forest policy in Quebec according to sustained yield principles

The 'physical' yield to be maintained is only a technical means of controlling the harvest of wood in a specific area and assuring regularity of that harvest. One should not confuse this 'physical' yield with 'sustainable' yield, where the result is to maintain forest cover over a management unit permitting a diverse flow of goods and services. Conservation of the forest cover means that the forest is utilized while preserving its essential characteristics.[134] Therefore, to reduce forest management to a question of cubic metres of wood is a dangerous simplification of the ongoing debate that surrounds the general organization of space affected by the support of forest cover. This was evidenced by the public excesses and outbursts that were typical of the period when indicative interpretation of sustained yield was in place in Quebec during the 1970s. With the regime adapted in 1986, the government returned first to the classical interpretation of sustained yield, stating that, from now on, the inventories of raw wood would be managed in such a way that harvest equilibrium would be effected that would continue over time.[135] The explanation for the 1986 changes can be found in the government's desire to show that it would keep a close eye on the forest industry. The government's attitude also coincided with the growth of an ethic of caution within some segments of Quebec society.[136] Let us recall that along the path leading to the new forest regime a number of people denounced the latitude given to industry with respect to cutting blocks. As far as the informed public was concerned, industry had excessive room to manoeuvre.[137]

The 1986 Forest Act stipulated the tangible form that sustained yield would take. As planned, it conformed to the classical interpretation of the concept. The act (sec. 45) specified that the aim was to reach a situation where the volume of raw wood attributed annually to a management unit could be taken forever. But the act's proponents inferred that this conjuncture was imminent, so that the day after the contract was signed, a company would sustain a perpetual yield. They glossed over the conditions necessary for a regular balanced harvest. They forgot that in the classical case the physiological and mechanical interpretations of the concept of sustained yield are closely intertwined for a period at least equal to a rotation before there can be a constant harvest across time and space. Above all, they forgot that this period is sufficiently long that demands on the forest area could meanwhile change.

Lortie et al. maintain that the Forest Act did not present a means to permit diverse groups within Quebec society to express their wants and needs.[138] We draw the same conclusion regarding Quebec forest policy.

The obligation to make available information concerning management plans, contained in the law since 1994, is not sufficient to activate local or regional debates on forest development. A systemic interpretation of sustained yield is still in the making, considering the government's lack of commitment to respond to society's expectations: commercial, cultural, ethical.[139] The notion of taking into account natural disturbances and other various needs of the ecosystem in order to realize a co-evolutionary interpretation of sustained yield is nowhere echoed in Quebec politics. Despite the 1994 Forest Protection Strategy and the integration, in 1996, of criteria defining sustainable development as the primary objective of the Forest Act, the forest regime remains, as ever, primarily oriented towards industry.[140]

Conclusion

A constraint freely accepted will be better integrated into the practices of a group of stakeholders sharing the same field of activities than a directive imposed from above.[141] A new forest agreement generalized around the ideas of sustainable yield, even if suspect with respect to the dominant entrepreneurial culture, would be a political triumph. It could be exploited to favour the development of an ethic of responsibility with respect to the productive capacities of the forest. Such a consensus is always fragile, however. In Quebec, the current one is founded on an incomplete understanding of the concept of sustained yield. The government relies a great deal on the mirage of a harvest in equilibrium. To it, the equilibrium of forest harvest and annual growth represents a sort of final destination. Without denying idealism its power to mobilize, we worry about the relevance of decisions that do not address the difficulties of attaining the ideal. Equilibrium cannot exist other than in the minds of those who want it to sanction the use of the forest. What must be remembered is that the reality of the forest and its social institutions is dynamic.

We conclude this overview of the history of Quebec forestry by reiterating that it acquires coherence through use of the concept of sustained yield as a tool permitting both a viable formulation of the problems of the forest regime and reflection of its dynamics. Quebec forest policy could well jump to another stage of social and economic progress – the co-evolutionary stage of sustained yield – if it could successfully nourish continuing debate at the community level on the needs to be satisfied, the functioning of the forest, and the possible modes of intervention. For the moment, however, the will of the Quebec government is to concretely translate sustained yield on the ground into a continual flow of raw wood, and so stimulate a technocratic approach which is incompatible with a management regime that is sensitive to a diversity of forest values and processes.

NOTES

1 Michael Howlett and Jeremy Rayner. 'The Framework of Forest Management in Canada,' in M. Ross, ed., *Forest Management in Canada* (Calgary: Canadian Institute for Resources Law, 1995) 43–118.

2 L. Bouthillier, 'Le concept de rendement soutenu en foresterie dans un contexte nord-américain,' doctoral dissertation, Université Laval, 1991.

3 Ministère des forêts (MFO), *Bâtir une forêt pour l'avenir: la politique forestière* (Quebec: Gouvernement du Québec, 1985).

4 MFO, *Modalités d'intervention en milieu forestier* (Quebec: Gouvernement du Québec, 1986) 75.

5 M. Lortie, L. Bélanger, F. Fortier, J. Pfalzgraf, and M. Pineau, 'Vers l'utilisation durable des ressources forestières du Québec,' *L'Aubelle*, no. 70, 1989, 6–8.

6 Contrat d'approvisionnement et d'aménagement forestier (CAAF).

7 G.R. Smith, 'Making Decisions in a Complex Environment,' in K.A. Kohm and J.F. Franklin, eds., *Creating of Forestry for the 21ˢᵗ Century* (Washington DC: Island Press, 1997) 419–36.

8 Ordre des ingénieurs forestiers du Québec, 1983. 'Faire le point,' *L'Aubelle*, no. 32, 1983, 4–7.

9 G. Paillé, and R. Desffrasnes, 'Le nouveau régime forestier du Québec,' *Forestry Chronicle* 64(1), 1988, 3–8.

10 Association des industries forestières du Québec, *La politique forestière du Québec*, mémoire déposé au Ministre de l'Énergie et des Ressources, 1984. Fédération des travailleurs forestiers du Québec, *Mémoire déposé au Ministre de l'Énergie et des Ressources au sujet de l'énoncé de politique forestière de 1984* (1985). Ordre des ingénieurs forestiers du Québec, 'Faire le point,' *L'Aubelle*, 1983.

11 P. Fontanel, *La forêt canadienne* (Montreal: L'école sociale populaire, 1927) 64.

12 T. Maher, *Pays de Cocagne ou terre de Caïn?* (Quebec: Les presses universitaires Laval, 1952) 252. E. Minville, 'La forêt,' *L'actualité économique* 1(3), 1941, 241–74. Ministère au terres et Forêts (MTF), *Livre blanc sur l'administration du territoire public et la gestion des forêts au Québec* (Quebec: Gouvernement du Québec, 1968).

13 Tachereau in Fontanel, *Le forêt canadienne.*

14 G.H. Manning, 'Evaluating Public Forestry Investments in British Columbia: The Choice of Discount Rate,' *Forestry Chronicle* 53(3), 1977, 155–8.

15 A.C. Worrell, *Principles of Forest Policy* (New York: McGraw-Hill, 1970).

16 M. Becker and F. Le Tacon, 'Santé de la forêt: importance d'une sylviculture adaptée aux conditions de milieu,' *Revue Forestière française,* vol. 37, 1985, 7–28.

17 H. Dupuis, *Le syndrome de Maisonneuve* (Sainte-Foy: Ordre des ingénieurs forestiers du Québec, 1988) 41.

18 A. Lafond, *Forest and Forestry in Québec* (Vancouver: University of British Columbia, 1974).

19 C. Beaudoin, *Historique de la forêt privée au Québec* (Laval: Laboratoire de recherche en forêt privée, Université Laval, 1986.

20 A. Bédard, *Le milieu forestier* (Laval: École d'arpentage et de génie forestier, Université Laval, 1941).

21 J. Bouffard, *Traité du domaine, reproduction de l'édition originale réalisée en 1977* (Laval: Les Presses de l'Université Laval, 1921).

22 Ibid.

23 Beaudoin, 'Historique de la forêt privée.'

24 Bouffard, *Traité du domaine.*

25 F. Ouellet, *Histoire économique et sociale du Québec 1760–1850,* 2 vols. (Montreal: Fides, 1971).

26 M. Lortie, 'Les grands traits de l'histoire forestière,' *La revue forestière française,* vol. 31, special issue: *La forêt au Québec,* 1979, 22–7.

27 J. Lacoursière, J. Provencher, and D. Vaugeois, *Canada-Québec: Synthèse historique* (Montreal: Éditions du renouveau pédagogique, 1977) 631.

28 One load equals 1.42 cubic metres.

29 Ouellet, *Histoire économique.*

30 A.R.M. Lower, *North American Assault on the Canadian Forest* (New Haven: Yale University Press, 1938).

31 Ouellet, *Histoire économique.*

32 Maher, *Pays de Cocagne.*

33 Lower, *North American Assault.*

34 H.J. Innis, 'The Importance of Staple Products,' in W.T. Easterbrook and M.H. Watkins, *Approaches to Canadian Economic History* (Toronto: McClelland and Stewart, 1956) 16–19; M.H. Watkins, 'A Staple Theory of Economic Growth,' *Canadian Journal of Economics and Political Science* 34(2), 1963, 141–58; M.H. Watkins, 'The Staple Theory Revisited,' *Journal of Canadian Studies* 12(5), 1977, 83–95; G.W. Bertram, 'Economic Growth in Canadian industry, 1870–1915: The Staple Model and the Take-Off Hypothesis,' *Canadian Jour-*

nal of Economics and Political Sciences 29(2), 1963, 159–84; D.J. Savoie, 'Some Theoritical Considerations,' in D.J. Savoie, ed., *The Canadian Economy: A Regional Perspective* (Toronto: Methuen, 1986) 9–24.

35 J. Swift, *Cut and Run: The Assault on Canada's Forests* (Toronto: Between the Lines, 1983) 28–90.

36 Ibid.

37 Donald Mackay, *Heritage Lost: The Crisis in Canada's Forests* (Toronto: Macmillan, 1985).

38 M. Lortie, 'Les grands traits de l'histoire forestière,' *La revue forestière française* vol. 31, special issue: *La forêt au Québec*, 1979, 22–7.

39 MTF, *Exposé sur l'administration et la gestion des terres et forêts du Québec* (Quebec: Gouvernement du Québec, 1965).

40 Fontanel, *La forêt canadienne.*

41 N.P. Patry, *Historique de la foresterie au Québec de 1849 à 1938*, 2 vols. (Quebec: MTF, 1940).

42 Ibid.

43 Bouffard, *Traité du domaine.*

44 Association des ingénieurs forestiers du Québec (AIFQ), *Le problème forestier du Québec* (Montreal: Fides, 1949).

45 Fontanel, *La forêt canadienne.*

46 MTF, *Exposé sur l'administration.*

47 AIFQ, *Le problème forestier.*

48 Swift, *Cut and Run.*

49 P.-A. Linteau, R. Durocher, J.-C. Robert, and F. Ricard, *Histoire du Québec contemporain: le Québec depuis 1930* (Montreal: Éditions du Boréal, 1986) 20–50, 207–55, 416–92, 625–34.

50 Ibid.

51 Swift, *Cut and Run.*

52 Bouthillier, *Le concept de rendement soutenu en foresterie.*

53 Forêt cantonale.

54 AIFQ, *Le problème forestier.*

55 Lafond, *Forest and Forestry.*

56 Patry, *Historique de la foresterie au Québec.*

57 Quebec Forest Industries Association, *The Québec Limit-holders' Manual*, 1932, 53–5.

58 Ibid.

59 Ibid.

60 Piché (1936) in Patry, *Historique de la foresterie au Québec.*

61 N. Lafleur, *La drave en Mauricie* (Quebec: Édition du bien public, 1970). 30–41, 101–19.

62 Piché in Patry.
63 E. Minville, E., *Histoire économique du Québec* (Montreal: Librairie Beauchemin Limitée, 1934).
64 Association canadienne des producteurs de pâte et papier, *La récolte du bois* (Montreal: Canadian Pulp and Paper Association, 1954) 67.
65 Ibid.
66 Association des ingénieurs forestiers du Québec, *Le problème forestier.* Montreal: Fides, 1949.
67 Maher, *Pays de Cocagne.*
68 Lachance (1952) in R. Bellefeuille, *Notes d'aménagement forestier,* Teaching material (Quebec: Université Laval, 1963).
69 Lortie, 'Les grands traits de l'histoire forestière.'
70 A. Careless, *Initiative and Response: The Adaptation of Canadian Federalism to Regional Economic Development* (Montreal: McGill-Queen's University Press, 1977).
71 Bouthillier, 'Le concept de rendement soutenu en foresterie.'
72 MTF, *Exposé sur l'administration.*
73 Careless, *Initiative and Response.*
73 Bouthillier, 'Le concept de rendement soutenu en foresterie.'
74 Lévesque, L.-P., 'Atelier: exploitation forestière,' in *Pour une politique québécoise, collection Les idées du jour* (Montreal: Édition du Jour, 1967) 79–86.
75 MTF, *Exposé sur la politique forestière,* vol. 1, *Prospective et problématique* (Quebec: Gouvernement du Québec 1971).
76 MTF, *Exposé sur la politique forestière,* vol. 2, *Réforme et programme d'action* (Quebec: Gouvernement du Québec, 1972).
77 MTF, *Exposé sur l'administration.*
78 K.V. Smith and J.V. Krutilla, 'The Economics of Natural Resource Scarcity: An Interpretative Introduction,' in K.V. Smith, ed., *Scarcity and Growth Reconsidered: Resources for the Future* (Baltimore: Johns Hopkins University Press, 1979) 1–35.
79 MTF, 1972, *Exposé sur la politique.*
80 Bellefeuille, *Notes d'aménagement forestier.*
81 MTF, *Exposé sur la politique.*
82 L.J. Lussier, M. Boudoux, C. Godbout, and N. Laquerre, *Quelques notes en marge du calcul de possibilité forestière* (Quebec: Gouvernement du Québec, 1976).
83 MTF, 1971. *Exposé sur la politique forestière.*
84 G. Bouliane and D. Guibert, 'Libres propos au sujet de l'aménagement des forêts publiques,' in *La revue forestière,* vol. 31, special issue: *La forêt du Québec,* 1979, 150–2.

85 M. Beaud and G. Dostaler, *La pensée économique depuis Keynes* (Montreal: Éditions du Seuil, 1993) 157–9.

86 G.D. Lévesque, *Les finances publiques du Québec, l'urgence d'un redressement* (Quebec: Ministrère des Finances, Gouvernement du Québec, 1986).

87 MER, *La politique forestière du Québec: problématique d'ensemble* (Quebec: Gouvernement de Québec, 1984.

88 Ibid.

89 MFO, *Ressource et industrie forestières: Portrait statistique 1987–1988* (Quebec: Gouvernement du Québec, 1989).

90 MER, *Le secteur forestier Recherche et développement, préparé par un groupe de travail comme rapport de conjoncture sur la recherche et le développement dans le secteur forestier au Québec* (Quebec: Gouvernement du Québec, 1983).

91 Ministère de l'environnement du Québec (ME), *Politique d'utilisation des pesticides en milieu forestier* (Quebec: Document de support à la Commission parlementaire, 1988).

92 L. Holt, A. Linteau, P.H. Tremblay, and W.L. Johnson, 1965. 'Some Aspects of Balsam Fir Management,' in *Pulp and Paper Canada*, p. 322–38.

93 MFO, *The New Forest System* (Quebec: Gouvernement du Québec, 1986).

94 *Opération gestion faune* puts an end to private fishing and hunting clubs located on Crown lands.

95 ME, *Politique d'utilisation des pesticides.*

96 Bouthillier, *Le concept de rendement soutenu.*

97 J. de Rosney, *L'avenir en direct* (Paris: Fayard, 1989).

98 M. Jurdant, *Le défi écologique* (Quebec: Boréal compact, 1986).

99 MER, *La politique forestière.*

100 Ibid.

101 MER, *Le secteur forestier.*

102 Bouthillier, *Le concept de rendement soutenu.*

103 MFO, *Ressource et industrie forestières: Portrait statistique 1986–1987* (Quebec: Gouvernement du Québec, 1987).

104 MER, *La politique forestière.*

105 MFO, *Bâtir une forêt pour l'avenir.*

106 MFO, *The New Forest System.*

107 MRN, *La mise à jour du régime forestier* (Quebec: Document de consultation, Gouvernement du Québec, 1998).

108 Standards on forest intervention are called *règlement sur les normes d'intervention en milieu forestier.*

109 Y. Barrette, '*De nouvelles modalités d'intervention,*' in *Forêt Conservation* 53(8), 1987, 21–2.

110 MRN, *La mise à jour du régime forestier.*

111 MER, *La politique forestière.*
112 Sixty-five regional governments (municipalités régionales de comté) are impacted by forest development on public lands.
113 Common area, literal translation for *aire commune.*
114 MRN, *Les droits consentis dans les forêts du domaine public du Québec, Bilan du régime forestier,* vol. 1 (Quebec: Gouvernement du Québec, 1997).
115 MFO, *Ressource et industrie forestières: Portrait statistique 1987–1988.*
116 G. Geoffroy, *Effet de possibilité, Service des plans d'aménagement* (Quebec: Ministère de l'Énergie et des Ressources, Gouvernement du Québec, 1986).
117 Bureau d'audiences publiques sur l'environnement (BAPE), *Des forêt en santé, rapport de la Commission sur la protection des forêts* (Quebec: Rapport spécial no. 2, Gouvernement du Québec, 1991, 43–62.
118 R. Miville-Deschênes, *Analyse d'objectifs de production de matière ligneuse pour la région administrative du Bas-Saint-Laurent Gaspésie* (Quebec: Ministère des Terres et Forêts, Service de la recherche, Mémoire no. 46, 1978).
119 Bouthillier, 'Le concept de rendement soutenu.'
120 MRN, *La mise à jour du régime forestier.*
121 Bouthillier, 'Le concept de rendement soutenu.'
122 BAPE, *Des forêts en santé.*
123 K.P. Davis, *Land Use* (Toronto: McGraw-Hill, 1976) 259–83.
124 S.K. Fairfax and G.L. Achterman, '*The Monongahela Controversy and the Political Process*' in *Journal of Forestry* 75(8), 1977, 485–87.
125 C.S. Holling, 'The Resilience of Terrestrial Ecosystems: Local Surprise and Global Change,' in W.C. Clark, and R.E. Munn, eds., *Sustainable Development of the Biosphere* (Cambridge: Cambridge University Press, 1986) 292–317.
126 T.C. Brown and D.R. Carder, 'Sustained Yield of What?' *Journal of Forestry* 75(11), 1977, 722–3.
127 G.W. Zinn, 'Regional Development and Forest Resources Management,' *Journal of Forestry* 73(5), 1975, 287–305.
128 Holling, *The Resilience of Terrestrial Ecosystems.*
129 R.B. Norgaad, 'Sociosystem and Ecosystem Co-evolution in the Amazon,' *Journal of Environmental Economics and Management* 8(3), 1981, 238–54.
130 R.B. Norgaard, 'Sustainable Development: A Co-Evolutionary View,' *Futures* 15(6), 1988, 606–20.
131 Becker and Le Tacon, 'Santé de la forêt.'
132 Perry, *Forest Ecosystems.*
133 MRN, *La mise à jour du régime forestier.*
134 J.S. Maini and A. Carlisle, *La conservation au Canada: aperçu général, ministère de l'Environnement* (Ottawa: Service canadien des forêts, publication no. 1340-F, 1974, 3–30, 63–101.

135 MFO, *The New Forest System.*
136 F. Dumont, *Raisons communes* (Montreal: Boréal, 1995).
137 Jurdant, *Le défi écologique.*
138 Lortie, 'Le développement de la politique forestière'; Lortie et al. 'Vers l'utilisation durable.'
139 MRN, *La mise à jour du régime forestier.*
140 J. Robitaille, 'Les défis partagés du gouvernement du Québec et de son industrie forestière,' *Forestry Chronicle* 73(1), 1997, 121–5.
141 H. Simon, 'Decision-Making and Administrative Organisation,' in *Administrative Behaviour* (New York: Free Press, 1965).

Chapter Ten

'Perpetual Revenues and the Delights of the Primitive': Change, Continuity, and Forest Policy Regimes in Ontario

Jamie Lawson, Marcelo Levy, and L. Anders Sandberg[1]

Managed prudently as a public estate, [a vast wilderness at the back door of its settlements] would ensure to the province perpetual revenue and the delights of the primitive. But regarded as a hoard of buried treasure, it naturally is ransacked and looted by all to whom the opportunity presents itself.[2]

Communities of living things are always characterized by ceaseless mutual interactions and adjustments. In Ontario, human beings have been part of that process for thousands of years, but it is during the past two centuries that the province's vast forests have come under unprecedented pressure from human intervention. In southern Ontario, forests have been cleared to provide land for farming and cities, and in the western and northern parts of the province trees have fuelled industrial development. The suppression of fires and the establishment of parks have also done their parts in changing forest ecosystems.

In this chapter, we employ the concept of policy regime to explain the changing pattern of forest use and sectoral institutional structure in Ontario. Beyond this general approach, which we share with the other contributors to this volume, we emphasize the influence of ascendant interests for the different periods of the Ontario forest regime's history. By contrast, Howlett and Rayner (in Chapter 2) emphasize the equally important question of ascendant policy philosophies or approaches, and show that the same developments emerge within the policy network in virtually every province. Our approach results in minor deviations, which are complementary rather than incompatible, with the general historical patterns identified by Howlett and Rayner. The concept of a forest policy regime not only deals with policy issues per se, but also with how policy is shaped by the history, politics, economics and – indeed – forests of a particular jurisdiction. The major influences on a regime's evolution are markets, politics, workplace arrangements, and environmental change. All of these influences have been shaped by the increasing globalization of the economic activities as the latter affect local communities and environments.[3]

In Ontario forest policy, we identify two elements of change and continuity worthy of special exploration. The first is the pattern of benefit from the forest resource. For much of Ontario's history, we argue, provincial officials with a mandate to allocate forest resources have pursued a strategy of limiting non-fibre uses of the forest, in order to guarantee the industry a more secure and competitively priced wood fibre supply. In this matter, state agencies themselves have had varying degrees of interest in the revenues that royalties or increased economic activity provided. Over the years, this has meant fighting or containing First Nation rights to forest lands, reserving lands in prime forests for the industry's use, scaling down conservationist measures, and containing the preservationist ambitions of some environmentalists.[4] With respect to environmentalist interests, the establishment of protected areas that specifically exclude the industry has accordingly been limited and highly selective. However important these environmentalist achievements may be in comparison with other jurisdictions, they have tended to be more cosmetic than real in ensuring the undeniable benefits that healthy ecosystems offer to society as a whole. They have also been more narrowly beneficial to well-to-do southern urban interests rather than job-related rural or northern ones.

In recent decades, the industry's accelerating pace of logging and job-shedding in the province has caused woods workers to view with alarm pressures to preserve forests. Over time, the pace of these changes has also left individual firms with few competitive choices besides unsustainable harvest levels. Real change, involving a more systematic rethinking of the human relationship with nature, would include a review of every substantial aspect of the human use of trees. In reducing the destructiveness of major forest related activities, and hence the 'ecological footprint' of every forest-related job, it could accordingly reduce the current overemphasis on the zoning or quarantine of 'untouched nature' from the destructive human uses. This challenge still has not been thoroughly integrated into the policy agenda.

If the first element of change and continuity in Ontario's forest policy regimes was the general question of benefit, the second element derives from the political debate about how those benefits (as they are variously conceived) are to be extended. While historical treatments of the forest industry and policy, such as the writings of A.R.M. Lower, have tended to emphasize tensions between the industry and farming interests, we emphasize the growing tension between industrial–governmental forest interests ('perpetual revenues') and preservationist ones ('the delights of the primitive').[5]

The industrial–governmental interests constitute the principal promoters and users of Crown lands, and their dual goal is to extract as much fibre from the forest as possible while viewing other forest uses as mere constraints on extraction. These actors are of overwhelming political importance in determining policy over the large majority of the province's forest lands, Crown lands making up 88 per cent of the total provincial forest area. Initially, these actors harvested the wood supply with little concern for regeneration.[6] Between the beginning of the twentieth century and the Great Depression, the mounting scale of timber extraction, most notable in the pulp and paper industry of the northwest, was forcing many observers to question the ongoing viability of this difference. After the Second World War, however, the provincial government built up a professional bureaucracy, which used the new tools and theories of forest science and more interventionist means to intensify the process. In paying more attention to extending the benefits of the forest as a resource into the future, this constituency understood its purpose as the continuance of a complex renewable resource. At its most visionary, it foresaw forest conservation; at its most narrow, it foresaw sustained yields of timber alone.

As Ontario emerged from a period of sheer indifference to the future of the forests, it became more important to distinguish among various policy approaches to forest reproduction. In these distinctions, U.S. models have been especially influential. In this chapter, by conservation, we follow the meaning of U.S. Forest Service Director Gifford Pinchot. In the first half of the twentieth century, Pinchot advocated maximum use of the forest under the dictum 'the greatest use for the greatest number.' At the time, this meant a lot more than maximizing the wood fibre yield. It also included the use of forests as protection of water supplies, as windbreaks to prevent soil erosion, and as keepers of wild game.[7] In Ontario, as we shall see, conservationist concerns are applied selectively, both socially and spatially. They tend to be expressed and administered separately from, and not in unison with, the primary concern over fibre. In the end, it is the interest of fibre and other forest benefits that conservation seeks to serve in Ontario, and it is in the language of conservation that both industry and government can speak most readily of the forest's future.

With preservation we mean the movement inspired by the U.S. naturalist John Muir. On the one hand, Muir advocated the preservation of forest lands in their 'wild state,' feeling that nature ought to be protected for its intrinsic value. While this 'pure' view of preservationism is shared by many today, the so-called utilitarian preservationist position is more common. This position stresses that vital human needs can be satisfied by preserved areas. These may include parks as a source of recreation and a home of various 'useless' species of flora and fauna, principally on the grounds that some may one day prove beneficial to humans.

While the stylized conflict between industrial ('log it all') and preservationist ('leave it all') interests seems present everywhere today, it is especially well illustrated in the history of Ontario. At the beginning of the twentieth century, the central focus was clearly on producing wood fibre for industry be it for lumber or pulpwood for export or other use. But already then an incipient preservationist movement existed to challenge the dominant forest industry. By the end of the twentieth century, this conflict had increasingly resolved itself into a stand-off over marginal amounts of land: we see an intensive rate of industrial forest use in intimate coexistence with a mounting number of preserved forest areas.

Having laid out two particularly important elements in forest policy regime development in Ontario, we turn to a discussion of five successive policy regimes that have guided the Ontario forestry sector. The first two are (1) a political–military regime aimed at settling Loyalist refugees, ensuring the colony's loyalty and viability, and providing timber for the blockaded British navy (1800–28), and (2) a period of intergovernmental struggle over jurisdiction and the control of revenue (1829–47). Under these regimes, exploitative and profoundly wasteful measures towards the forest were dominant under the pretext that cleared lands were ideal for agricultural settlement. Preservation and conservation concerns were non-existent, as Howlett and Rayner's characterization suggests – it was a single period of unregulated exploitation. At the same time, the two periods may be distinguished by the distinct interests and purposes that were ascendant.

At mid-century, a critical turning-point was reached, in both policy approach and ascendant interests. A progressive spatial separation of industrialists, conservationists, and preservationists is characteristic of the subsequent forest policy regimes. Typical, too, is a social convergence for these interests, as the voices of all three positions were overwhelmingly the voices of elites rather than the voices of distinct classes.[8] The mid-century turning-point led to (3) a regime of active stimulation and conservation, guided for the first time by the growing hegemony of the forest industry (although still subservient to the promotion of settlement and agriculture), and supported by an emerging government bureaucracy and forester profession (1848–1941). Under this regime, conservation and preservation concerns were raised, but were subordinated to industrial needs and geared towards the mores and aspirations of well-to-do urban constituents. At the timber frontier, conservation and preservation issues continued to be considered irrelevant. In important instances where the consequences of resource exhaustion seemed poised to force a more conservationist position on core regional branches of the industry, the industry reinvented itself under provincial stimulus, centred on a new product mix and a richer, more distant frontier. The associated periods of innovation in the policy community itself (notably the conservationist period of the 1880s) were cut off from effective, sustained implementation. Competitively driven overcapacity at this new centre then met the global depression, drawing the provincial forestry industry into a condition of profound vulnerability. Thus, (4) out of the Second World War's empowerment of a now-Keynesian state, a regulatory regime accordingly emerged, characterized by a growing expert community, the rise of forest science, and increased government capacity. This was a regime intended to promote sustained yield practices, horizontal integration of forest exploitation, and multiple forest use (1941–1992). Finally, (5) a more recent forest management regime has focused on preserving and sustaining forest ecosystems through government regulation that encourages the use of voluntary measures to guide forest uses.

In the following section, these periods will be discussed in greater depth. It should be noted that the names given to them are nearly all oriented to the stated intentions of leading interests of the period, and do not often correspond with actual achievements in the bush.

The Political–Military Regime, 1800–1828[9]

Three massive transformations within fifty years ensured that the earliest forestry concerns in Ontario would be political and military. The first event, the conquest of New France, could only be secured militarily by providing to First Nations guarantees that colonial territorial expansion would be controlled and negotiated with them.[10] This policy was consolidated most decisively in the Royal Proclamation of 1763. The second event, the American Revolution, created a government-supported influx of refugees. By 1791, one eddy of this Loyalist tide had made southern Ontario a separate common-law jurisdiction within a reconstituted empire. The third event was the spread of the Napoleonic blockade to Britain's Baltic timber suppliers. U.S. trade policy during the blockade intensified Britain's supply dependency on its colonies, and this dependency struck at its famous navy, not just at its commerce.[11] Baltic timber suppliers were cut off from Britain by 1809, and U.S. trade policy during the blockade enhanced its impact.

This third event launched the first full-scale timber industry in Ontario, but on terms inconceivable without the other two. The Royal Proclamation of 1763 ensured that in an expanding exploitation and settlement area, the state would have an entrenched position between the First Nations and a number of industries. From this position, the state would have a new interest in discouraging high payments to the first, and encouraging a lucrative gap between those payments and the revenues from the second. The American Revolution had ensured that colonial officials would reserve navy timber in the remaining colonies with a greater sensitivity to settlers' need for wood, and the blockade would open naval suppliers' minds to many competing varieties of timber from around the globe. Ontario's first forest policy was merely implied by these larger policy goals and no separate written treatment was deemed necessary. Initial instructions, for instance, that the governor establish Crown reserves in all local townships went largely unheeded, and the liquidation of the forests within an expanding range of settlement became so central to the regime as to be taken for granted. The real interest lay in allocating the benefits: pine and oak for the navy; land for colonial institutions and a colonial aristocracy; and the remainder – by fire or by felling – for local farms. As a practical set of arrangements, these approaches to the forest entirely marginalized forest conservation during the reactionary peace that followed Napoleon. Forest preservation was a non-issue; the forest constituted either a source of quick profit for colonial businessmen-cum-politicians or an obstacle to the settlement process.

The Struggle over Revenue, 1828–1848[12]

In a sense, forest regimes are always about allocating benefits from the bounty of nature. In Ontario, any alternative allocation that integrated the costs of reproducing the forest have been marginalized or contained. After 1828, however, a naked allocative struggle became the core of the regime. Colonial officials recognized the final market's rapid commercialization in peacetime and allowed commercial interests to trade directly with the British metropole. Offices were established at Bytown, present-day Ottawa, to exact a rudimentary stumpage fee from these interests along the Ottawa Valley.

Almost immediately, these fees became controversial in the larger struggles for responsible government at home and for a liberal trade policy in Britain. The revenues from resources on Crown land flowed from protected metropolitan trade in timber, directly to Crown officials and the interwoven colonial elites. Substantial monopoly rents went to British shipping interests in the process. The fees were not under control of the local assemblies. On the other hand, the transition to a fully liberalized commercial policy was never fully accepted, as this implied allowing the colonies both American and European direct trade, the associated security risks, and the adoption of core elements of American republican ideology. The task of those seeking a more rational economic alternative was to overcome these concerns. Local responsible government, colonial autonomy and control over customs, and British free trade were laid out as interlocked alternatives in this period; and in the 1840s, step by step, all of these policies were implemented. As during the previous regime, conservation and preservation measures were minimal, and merely confined to 'protect' the resource from the trepidations of the favoured few.

The Stimulation/Conservation Forest Policy Regime, 1848–1941[13]

Liberal by intent, this forest policy regime was presented as a *laissez-faire* regime, particularly in its early stages. It served to place the market and specifically market-driven actors at the centre of policy concerns. It addressed, however incompletely, many inefficiencies of the previous system, inefficiencies associated notably with overtly privileged non-market access to land and resources, to final markets, and to political power. Overtly, it eliminated the privileges that Britain accorded entrenched political favourites in the lumber trade and facilitated in part by protective Imperial tariffs. But in substantive terms, many of these privileges persisted. In fact, with the new regime the liquidation of the forest resource could proceed on an accelerated basis with state encouragement and attention. It was this organized assault on the Canadian forest that led to the first call for forest conservation and preservation in the latter parts of the nineteenth century and beginning years of the twentieth. Howlett and Rayner rightly point to the conceptual complexity of this period by subdividing it. In the subsections that follow, we first comment on the growing industrial focus of the period and then explore emergent conservationist and preservationist issues. We conclude with comments on social bias.

Industrial Use, and Emerging Conservation and Preservation Issues

With Imperial free trade, the potential for profits (and new abuses) turned on the link between the market and a Crown-owned cabinet-regulated resource. This linkage proved liable, as in previous regimes, to nakedly political land allocations. This was so both before and after Confederation, notwithstanding the jurisdictional transfer of natural resources to the province of Ontario. Assigning Crown leases and cutting rights to lumbermen was aimed at generating local political support, short-term gains in provincial revenue, and jobs in strategic constituencies.[14]

The politics of timber quickly acquired an intergovernmental character after Confederation. The only way to gain access to more of this strategic resource over time was by treating with First Nations for increasingly remote forest lands, an exclusively federal responsibility. The governing parties in Ottawa and in Toronto vied during the 1880s for the right to allocate timber on such Crown land.[15] Some First Nations' reserved lands were largely cut over by the lumbermen to enrich the latter and to form federally controlled trust funds. Other First Nations, overlooked in treaties, often lost their homelands' forests without even this consideration.

As Crown-administered lands passed into the control of lumbermen and pulp companies, a major, if also highly transient labour supply was needed to cut the wood and operate the mills. Being highly labour-intensive at the time, the forest industry thus provided seasonal employment for a huge number of itinerant workers and local farmers. First Nations also formed an integral part of this workforce.[16]

In spite of retaining Crown forest ownership with provincehood, the provincial government did not develop a forest management system.[17] Instead, it used its powers to systematize support for industry on concessionary terms. While sometimes taking an interventionist role, such as imposing a manufacturing condition on the export of wood products beginning in the 1890s, the provincial government always saw the long-term interest of business and its own fiscal needs as its priorities.[18] That these interests did not include provisions for regeneration reflected an institutional assumption that the industry was, as with previous regimes, drawing on an infinite supply as well as preparing lands for agricultural settlement.[19]

Organized expressions of concern for the wood supply were confined to specific geographic regions. Peter Gillis has argued that the Ottawa Valley's forest barons were not unaffected by the conservation movement and the messages espoused by American forest reformers such as Gifford Pinchot and Theodore Roosevelt, as well as by Bernhard Fernow.[20] But their merchantable timber, and hence their political clout, were mostly exhausted in the late nineteenth century. At the timber frontier of Ontario's northwest, few lumbermen expressed similar views. Conservationist sentiments were more often expressed by farmers in some areas of southern Ontario, such as the Oak Ridges Moraine north of Lake Ontario. Many such farmers had suffered from being settled on sandy infertile soil patches which had been hastily stripped of trees. In this geographic area, Mark Kuhlberg has argued that Ontario foresters implemented some of the more innovative forest management schemes in Canada in the earlier parts of the twentieth century.[21]

During this regime, Patricia Jasen has also documented the rise of the tourism industry in Ontario. This resulted for the first time in an incipient preservationist concern for the forests, albeit expressed at first primarily in the wild things that inhabit them.[22] Gerald Killan has documented the early origins of the Ontario parks system in an industry–conservationist alliance forged in the creation of Algonquin Park.[23] It was in some of Ontario's earliest parks that the Canadian Group of Seven found the inspiration to create a unique Canadian tradition of landscape painting. This tradition was rooted in the mythically rugged and unpeopled landscape of the north.[24] Hodgins and Benedickson have documented the preservation of old-growth forests along the shores of Lake Temagami at the behest of the local recreational cottagers, tourism operators, and canoe outfitters at the beginning of the twentieth century.[25] Temagami would become distinctive politically decades later, in no small part because these constituencies experienced the surrounding landscape through the canoe and portage routes that tourist workers in the local First Nation knew intimately.[26]

The Social Convergence and Spatial Divergence of Forest Issues

The growing disparate notions of the Ontario forest landscape – the forest as source of a limitless supply of industrial fibre versus the forest as an element to be conserved (used wisely) or protected – formed the basis of future Ontario forest policy regimes. They also reflected a complementarity in forest policy, both forces serving a very similar constituency. The forest as an industrial source of fibre clearly served a wealthy segment of lumber- and pulp-men. Conservationist thinking clearly favoured the same class. For instance, local forest management theorists blamed forest fires and forest devastation on farmers, and advocated stepped-up fire prevention and dedicated forest reserves off-limits to settlers in order to promote forest growth. This ignored the farmers' legitimate claims to the forest resource, the central role played by the lumbermen themselves in degrading the forest, the important place of fires in regenerating pine, and the potential of silviculture in improving the forest situation.[27] Except in allowing private, unprocessed roundwood to flow to the United States after the manufacturing condition blocked such flows from public land, it ignored the dire position of farmers in the less fertile parts of eastern and central Ontario, earning meagre supplementary cash in monopolistic pulpwood markets.[28] Finally, having enticed settlers into the remote clay belt, it then failed to recognize the extent of their needs, if they were to establish combined farming and forest operations at the northern forest frontier.[29]

Conservationist policy at the time also served a wealthy constituency. Recreationists, sports hunters, and fishermen were overwhelmingly from this very small portion of the population. Few poor or middle-class people had ready access to the 'cottage country' of central Ontario – or the vacation time in which to enjoy it. Parks policy clearly favoured a utilitarian conservationist cause that supported elite interests. On the positive side, this included milestone commitments to watershed protection, and the conservation of game animals, as well as less enviable practices such as the aggressive extirpation of animals of prey, alongside the provision of wood fibre.[30] But consistent with the business interests of many of these recreationists when they returned to the city, wood fibre acquisition was, at most, physically separated in preservationist fashion from the other activities in order to accommodate them. The manner of fibre acquisition was for the most part not subjected to an alternative basis for accommodating other activities. Towards the end of this period in Algonquin Park, for example, Frank MacDougall kept tourist and log-

ging interests increasingly separate through a rudimentary land allocation programme.[31] He also conducted forest surveillance with the use of
airplanes, and maintained wildlife protection through the 'poaching'
boom of the 1930s.[32]

This is not to say that such pioneering efforts were counterproductive
or undesirable. But through such zoning practices, a more thorough
going reform, both in how industry operated in the bush and in how
resource-users fit into the forest economy, became less visible issues to
the vacationing public. Nor do we say that the more exacting preservationist position typical of contemporary environmentalism was already
present. The true preservationist cause, as advocated by John Muir – the
protection of nature and natural processes for their own sake – had still
not gained substantially in popularity at the time, unless one considers a
statement articulated by the Federation of Ontario Naturalists in the
early 1930s.

The complementarity of industrial and conservationist goals is well
expressed in the works and the backgrounds of the Group of Seven.
Rather than depicting pristine wilderness landscapes, many of the
group's motifs were the result of the resource exploitation, such as
second-growth forests, and the group also embraced and benefited from
the conveniences and sponsorship of the resource economy in their
quest for a uniquely Canadian art.[33] Yet their images have provided
Ontarians – indeed, Canadians more generally – with foundational
images of a striking, largely empty north. First Nations and other peoples were conspicuously absent from most of these depictions.

The stimulation–conservation period therefore reflected a paradox:
the complementarity of three seemingly contrasted Ontario forest interests, the industrial, conservationist, and preservationist stands. The
extent of conservation and preservation should not, however, be overstated. Most lumbermen characterized even minimal preoccupation
with conservation and preservation as impractical. The opening of the
Upper Great Lakes to commercial exploitation in the early twentieth
century meant that Algonquin Park and a series of significant forest
reserves across central Ontario were never to live up to their planned
role as zones for conservation and forest management. Similarly, during
the Great Depression of the 1930s most of the forest management and
conservationist initiatives crumbled entirely, and Ontario fell from its
leadership position in Canadian forest policy.[34] The populist Liberal
premier Mitch Hepburn portrayed conservation as a mere outgrowth
of an unaffordable overpaid bureaucracy during a fiscal crisis. These

events left conservation in Ontario's forest policy (and its most accessible forests) at a relatively low point by the beginning of the Second World War.[35]

The Sustained Yield Forest Policy Regime, 1941–1994

Beginning during the Second World War, the Ontario forest policy regime changed substantially. It was characterized primarily by the relative decline of sawmilling and the growth of the pulp and paper industry in the northern and northwestern parts of the province. The promotion of the pulp and paper industry had long called for a different forest policy regime, and the fact that it suffered from profound overcapacity during the 1930s depression drove the message home. This branch of the industry was in need of long-term and extensive Crown leases as securities for large-scale investments and as fibre supply for their mills. The factory methods that allowed Henry Ford to perfect the mass production of automobiles required the application of capital-intensive, fossil-fuel driven methods when applied to timber extraction, and they also required the maximum return in fibre for the deployment of such equipment. 'Waste' and unstable tenure were no longer compatible with profitable production. Clear-cutting for horizontally integrated firms or for contractually allied firms replaced separate species- and size-specific licensing for pulp and wood products.

Factory methods were relatively well suited to the narrow species range and fire-induced single-aged patches of trees that the boreal forest offered. Better than the sawlog industry, the pulp and paper industry could use the northern forest's smaller logs. Ian Radforth argues that the bogs and rugged terrain of the Canadian Shield held such machinery back until the 1960s, with the exception of truck loading and chainsaws. But in other respects, including unionization and well-paid, year-round jobs, this forest regime allowed for the development of 'Fordist' work relations in forest operations in northern Ontario. As increasingly capital-intensive practices developed in the bush, an accelerating process of labour-shedding and improved labour conditions also occurred.[36]

Such an ambitious regime had little time for the petty allocation process of earlier regimes. The system of short-term wood allocation based on patronage gave way to a system of centralized control and the assignment of long-term leases by the provincial government and its bureaucracy in Toronto. These leases were typically let on concessionary terms in a climate of close corporate–government cooperation and fierce competition among the provinces for pulp and paper industry investment.

The Rise of Sustained Yield

In 1941, Frank MacDougall was appointed deputy minister of the provincial Department of Lands and Forests. It signified the beginning of the growing ascendancy of professional foresters in the bureaucracy.[37] A reorganization of the department ensued aimed at putting into place a 'planned conservation programme' based on sustained yield, the principle of maintaining the harvest within the rate of growth. One central measure was the replacement of the old woods and forest branch, whose function was to collect timber dues, with a new division of timber management, which was to administer twenty-one-year Crown leases and ensure their management on a sustained yield basis. Other tasks expanded by the department were new forest inventories and the expansion of the provision of fire protection.

After the Second World War, the Kennedy Royal Commission proposed a revised program of reform.[38] Kennedy, a high-ranking veteran of the war and a man familiar with the industry, toured the province to complete his investigations with the Department of Lands and Forests. He attacked the waste in the bush and issued a ringing endorsement for scientific management and professional control of the resource on a sustained-yield basis. But he also challenged the business hegemony in the forest sector by proposing a system of government ownership and operation. Kennedy, thus, called on the expertise of Ontario's government to underwrite both growth and employment by the stable full utilization of the province's forests – a guarantee of resource supply.

These recommendations need to be placed in a wider context. Kennedy's urgings corresponded with Lord Keynes's call for the expertise of all national governments to ensure stable full employment of people by a guarantee of aggregate demand. It also fitted with Keynes's refocusing of state revenues to the national taxation of incomes, a condition that took the pressure off the provincial taxation of public lands and resources. The revenue question had hitherto complicated such a stabilizing forestry role for the province.

Keynes's ideas were linked in principle to workers' survival needs, at least through high and stable wages and a welfare state. The pressures implied by full utilization of the forest resource, however, conflicted with Kennedy's insistence that the government operate forestry activities.

Thus, Kennedy's enthusiasm for government ownership among Ontario decision-makers quickly waned, and scotched one dimension of his plan.

A combination of a centuries' old analytical tradition with a postwar tendency towards standardized production, the forest management practices based on sustained yield focused on the production of only one commodity: forest fibre for the mills. The multiplicity of human forest concerns other than about forest fibre were classified as 'non-timber values.'[39] For the first time, a series of guidelines prescribed so-called areas of concern (i.e., zones where forest operations were restricted) to protect such non-timber values. Under these guidelines, however, non-timber values only entered timber decisions as constraints.[40] Such an approach created buffer zones around water bodies, eagles and hawks' nests, and moose calving sites and wintering areas, but only within a framework of a forest managed for timber production. The factorylike approach the industry was adopting towards the producing forest meant that firms typically would ignore such areas entirely rather than adapt their cutting methods to them.

As constraints on timber production, non-timber values were thus incorporated into a larger system of 'multiple-use by adjacency,' that is, 'timber was harvested in one place, recreation services provided somewhere else and multiple-use was claimed overall.'[41] This replaced the earlier view of the forest in which various non-industry interests (and various branches of the industry) were supposed to coexist, and only those strictly incompatible with the industry, such as farming, were separated out. Stranger than a single-variable management program, in this era of supposed government control and expertise, was the continuation of industry harvests well in excess of tree growth levels. Since this is precisely in conflict with the temperament of the reforms during the immediate postwar period (whereas a focus on timber was precisely what was intended), this continuity requires an explanation.

The Role of Science in Rationalizing Increased Fibre Use

The emerging coniferous wood supply crisis during the sustained yield forest policy regime was principally the result of two factors: overharvesting and poor regeneration. Paradoxically, the new science of forestry was instrumental in contributing to the wood supply crisis. At the time, the science of forestry determined annual rates of extraction for each species or group of species mainly (although not only) by their rate of growth. But these so-called annual allowable yields were thoroughly manipulable and heavily influenced by the industry's objective to maximize an economic return on investment. The forest industry, thus, consistently overharvested the forest. This overharvesting showed up most clearly in the mounting costs incurred by the pulp and paper companies in transporting wood to their mills from increasingly distant locations.[42]

The science of forestry contributed to the overharvesting in other ways. The age distribution of Ontario's boreal forest was considered skewed, that is, overrepresented by mature and overmature stands, a condition to which prior fire suppression may have contributed. In order to correct this situation, forest managers used the so-called acceleration factor to cut above the rate of growth. The intent was to 'normalize' the age distribution in the forest. In principle, this practice was intended to soften the future inevitable reduction in available timber after all original timber stands had been cut over. In fact, this practice encouraged companies to continue their preference for cutting previously uncut forest lands instead of tending and cutting well-managed secondary growth closer to home: it was mostly the rationale that had changed. By the 1980s, various authorities had become highly critical of this procedure. In 1981, the Lakehead Report to the Royal Commission on the Northern Environment concluded that the acceleration factor had resulted in short-term overharvesting, contributing to the decline in the supply of wood.[43] And in 1986, Gordon Baskerville identified the use of the acceleration factor as a 'principal cause of the decline in harvest volume over time.'[44]

The poor regeneration of certain species of commercially valuable conifers during the postwar period was also responsible for the crisis in forest supply. In 1992, an audit on the regeneration of cutovers in the boreal forest found that 'the spruce cover type ha[d] been reduced substantially,' from 18 per cent in the original forest harvested to 4 per cent in the regenerating second forest. The rate of re-establishment of conifers was only 9 per cent on planted spruce sites cut in the 1970–5 period and 18 per cent in spruce sites cut in the 1980–5 period.[45] In addition, Baskerville determined that the amount of silvicultural (regeneration) investment was unwisely based on regional or district budgetary targets and not on biological and site-specific considerations.[46]

The forestry practised in Ontario also had various negative ecological consequences that went beyond the poor regeneration of trees. Many wildlife species were threatened or endangered as their habitats shrunk dramatically. For instance, woodland caribou, which once ranged as far south as Lake Nipissing (near North Bay), receded to northwestern

Ontario.[47] Its southern range coincided with the northern limit of forest operations.

The wood supply crisis and the negative environmental consequences of sustained yield forest practices, as documented by both forest experts and environmental critics, resulted in several forces calling for change. Wilderness advocates, dissenting foresters, and ecologists began to call for changes in the sustained yield forest policy regime. In 1987, Forest for Tomorrow, a coalition of environmental groups, submitted to the Ontario Environmental Assessment Board (EAB) that a more integrated approach to timber management was needed. The coalition argued that timber and non-timber users and uses needed to be considered equally. Otherwise, Ontario's forests would continue to be managed mainly for their timber, with even more disastrous consequences. The coalition argued successfully that under the Environmental Assessment Act, the Ontario Ministry of Natural Resources (OMNR) was compelled to seek approval for its timber management planning process by undertaking a class environmental assessment (CEA). Starting in 1987, five years of hearings scrutinized MNR's proposed planning process.

In the end, the Environmental Assessment Board approved the minister's timber management planning process, but imposed a number of terms and conditions. These included limits to clear-cut size, the development of environmental guidelines, and the design of a more transparent process of involving the public. The board also ruled that the OMNR must adopt a more integrated approach to forest management.[48] Interestingly enough, and despite having resisted such an approach during the hearings, the OMNR, now under a New Democratic Party cabinet, moved towards just such an ecosystem-based approach.

In response to the class environmental assessment, the OMNR launched a series of initiatives in search of a different form of forest management. Perhaps the most important step was the appointment of the Ontario Forest Policy Panel, a multistakeholder group, which was commissioned to write a report guiding Ontario forest policy development into the twenty-first century. The report, putting forest ecosystems ahead of forest fibre, had a major impact on subsequent forest legislation.[49]

The Sociospatial Bias of Conservation and Preservation

Beyond the issues directly attached to the supply of wood fibre for industry, a prominent part of the Ontario forest policy regime continued to be forest conservation and preservation. But, as during the previous regime, in many respects these programs were applied selectively, and their proponents' concerns were centred in the southern parts of the province, or in those areas that could be readily reached by an increasing number of automobile-driving vacationers. Some important elements of forest management, notably in the area of silviculture, were ignored, or were oriented primarily to southern Ontario. After the reorganization of the Department of Lands and Forests in 1941, 'Ontario's first forester,' E.J. Zavitz, who had been instrumental in the province's reforestation efforts earlier in the century, remained head of the existing reforestation division. This division retained its independence from the new timber management division until Zavitz's retirement in 1957. The reforestation division concentrated its efforts on reforesting the 'waste lands' of southern Ontario and operating the provincial forest nurseries.[50] It was in urban and less fertile, sandier parts of the south that deforestation had given rise during the Depression and in the postwar period to flooding and erosion, and the expansion of a network of conservation authorities. These were designed to mobilize municipal support for reforestation along flood-prone southern Ontario watersheds.[51] It was also in the south that most other reforestation efforts continued to be located.

The Ontario parks system expanded and took a prominent place in the Department of Lands and Forests. A growing urban vacation boom followed the postwar transformation of demographic patterns and working conditions. This boom made a wider portion of the public conscious of the value of wilderness areas and parks (and through its own excesses, made the public conscious of their fragility). Algonquin Park emerged as a contested terrain in the 1960s, and the southern-based Algonquin Wildlands League was formed. The latter lobbied for the preservation of the park, and the scaling down of logging within its boundaries. Similar contested terrains emerged at Quetico Provincial Park and in Temagami, and by the 1980s over the preservation of 'old growth' forests generally. As the vacation boom crested in the 1970s, ever-nationalist Ontarians emulated the wilderness pursuits of Pierre Trudeau, their canoe-paddling prime minister, more and more. Even those who remained at home drew increasingly on the mythic connections, fixed a half-century before, between their nationhood and the mixed forests of central Ontario's Canadian Shield.[52] For many who experienced a sense of timeless beauty while in central Ontario, the preservation of forests with long histories of low-disturbance development became a significant political goal. For the members of First Nations whose homelands were at stake, the 1960s and 1970s were a period of political recovery and organization, and the wider public began to hear Aboriginal arguments about the destructive and exclusionary implications of both 'multiple-use by adjacency' and preservation.

In 1978, Ontario published a new provincial parks policy, which outlined the types of parks, the zoning within parks, and the activities to take place within the provincial parks system.[53] In 1982, the Ministry of Natural Resources began to integrate the formation of the parks system into a larger strategic land use planning process, allowing prospective parks to compete with other land uses. Tensions ensued with respect to the function of these parks, one faction arguing in favour of utilitarian preservation and the other total protection. Utility and ecology, thus, emerged as important competing ingredients in park planning.[54] In the early 1990s, the debate continued. An Old Growth Forests Policy Advisory Committee was formed in 1992, to develop recommendations for conserving old-growth ecosystems in Ontario, and in 1993 it presented its report.[55] Environmental groups became more vocal, too, with organizations such as the Federation of Ontario Naturalists calling for more preserved and roadless areas, and the World Wildlife Fund launching its endangered spaces campaign.

Towards a New Initiative?

By the early 1990s, the wood supply crisis, the ecological problems associated with wood harvesting, the concern over old growth in provincial parks and elsewhere, and the increasing demand for recreation and commercial remote tourism provided calls for a more environmentally sensitive forestry. This resulted in the commitment, at least in policy, to a new ecosystem-based approach to forest management. It faced immense obstacles. The division between industrial values, conservationist policies (now including sustained yield policies) and preservationist measures remained. Conservation efforts were centred in the south, and preservation policies were aimed at the disproportionately wealthy, urban-based, and non-Aboriginal constituencies' demand for recreation and retirement areas in relatively easily accessible northern forests and protected areas. Furthermore, the landmark 1993 forest panel's policy document, *Diversity: Forests, People, Communities,* was matched by two other policy documents endorsing the old sustained yield forest policy regime.[56] The industry itself had clearly come to see existing 'multiple-use' arrangements, with different activities divided into separated spatial areas, as perfectly satisfactory to industry competitiveness. And as the economic turmoil of the 1980s and 1990s eroded the vacation time, real incomes, and job security of lower- and middle-income families, the tensions distinguishing the forest as a place of work, as a homeland, and as a 'protected' place of timeless renewal broke into open confrontations.

The Forest Ecosystem Policy Regime, 1994 to the Present

The introduction of the Crown Forest Sustainability Act (CFSA) in December 1994 signified the official endorsement of a forest ecosystem policy regime. This new regime incorporated environmental and recreationist organizations and advocates in determining policy, alongside the still-dominant industry. The act, with its corresponding implementation manuals and regulations, was a first attempt at promoting tree harvesting while maintaining healthy forest ecosystems. The ecosystem approach is based on two general principles: the conservation of biological diversity and the mimicking of natural disturbance patterns. The approach places special emphasis on the residual forest, that is, the forest structure that is left after harvesting. Clear-cuts should be conducted in a range of sizes. Snags, dead trees, and debris should be left on site, and a certain percentage of live trees, including individuals from commercial species should be left standing. Prescribed burning combined with shelterwood cutting is proposed as a means of regenerating white pine. This approach is based on the idea that by leaving enough of the current forest structure, the forest ecosystem would be able to renew itself. While much knowledge still needs to be gained on how ecosystems work, it is still felt that an ecosystem approach can sustain, in the long run, both the forest and the forest industry.

The act incorporated the principles of forest management developed in the Ontario forest policy panel's *Diversity* document of 1993. Its purpose was to 'provide for the sustainability of Crown forests and, in accordance with that objective, to manage Crown forests to meet social, economic and environmental needs of present and future generations.' It further required that the determination of forest sustainability should be carried out in accordance with a new *Forest Management Planning Manual* (*FMPM*).[57] The act, thus, represented an important shift from the old Crown Timber Act, which made all other values secondary to timber extraction.

The new planning system required that management strategies and forest operations not jeopardize the long-term health of the forest ecosystem. The starting point was the so-called current forest condition (CFC), which was to be described and quantified in detail before planning began. A thorough knowledge of the CFC was considered essential to establish objectives and strategies, and to monitor and determine whether proposed management strategies created a sustainable future forest condition (FFC). The OMNR has so far developed a series of measurable 'indicators of sustainability' covering biodiversity, wildlife habitat, forest productivity, soil and water conservation, and benefits to society against which management strategies are to be measured.[58]

The development of objectives and strategies was also bounded by legislation, regulations, and policies beyond the Crown Forest Sustainability Act, including regional objectives. This framework was referred to in the planning process as 'direction from other sources.' Within it was clear policy direction with respect to biodiversity, with a mandate in the policy framework for sustainable forests for conservation or, where possible, enhancement. This meant that forest management plans could not significantly change the level of biodiversity at the forest management unit level. Another important consideration was provision for specific local issues. This meant that the plan must incorporate the protection of significant habitats, the operations of remote tourist outfitters, the treatment of spruce budworm outbreaks, or any other local circumstance that needed special consideration. In short, the development of objectives and strategies had to take into consideration provincial, regional, and local interests at multiple levels.[59]

A critical aspect of the use of indicators of sustainability, particularly those related to ecosystem measurements, was that it provided a framework for forest managers to stay within the limits of natural variation. One example of such disturbances is fire, which is the main natural disturbance in the boreal and, to a lesser extent, the Great Lakes–St Lawrence forest. This meant that forest operations could not change fundamental characteristics of the ecosystem beyond what occurs naturally. To do this, forest managers were to be assisted by various computerized models developed by OMNR. The modelling of potential scenarios resulting from different management alternatives was to be compared with the no-management option which reflects the natural development of the forest. In sum, the new management approach emphasized that harvesters should strive to mimic natural disturbance patterns, and pay special attention to the residual forest.

The Limitations of Science

As elsewhere, the drive towards ecosystem management has been directed by the environmentalist critique of Canadian forest practices. It has also been driven by the negative effects of the old sustained-yield paradigm, and by the undoubtedly sincere efforts of foresters and industry to do things differently. But these efforts are in many ways constrained and compromised by various ecological, political, and economic factors.

There are first of all problems associated with some of the ecological assumptions underpinning the ecosystem management approach. While clear-cuts are often assumed to resemble fire disturbances, they are typically more different than similar. A forest fire typically leaves trees, debris, and ashes which protect the soil from erosion and provide nutrients for the regeneration of the stand.[60] Clear-cuts, by contrast, remove all the trees in a stand, and in whole- tree cutting operations a large part of the nutrients as well. Similarly, wild fires do not discriminate between commercial and non-commercial species, while industry removes only merchantable trees, by-passing those stands containing non-commercial species, thus, skewing the composition of future species in the forest.

More specifically, the system of clear-cutting ignores the fact that many boreal forest species in northern Ontario, such as jack and red pine, trembling aspen, white birch, and white and black spruce, are adapted to fire disturbances for reasons only partly related to intolerance of shade.[61] Fires provide the conditions for the rapid growth of jack pine, whose cones only open with the heat. The seeds germinate rapidly taking advantage of the bright sun and soil conditions. White and black spruce can grow in open or lightly shaded conditions, often under jack pine and other rapidly growing species such as trembling aspen and white birch. But being longer lived, spruce may eventually replace them. In the Great Lakes–St Lawrence forest, white pine is also a less shade-intolerant species of fire origin. Its bark is fire resistant and usually large mature trees survive the fires. They shed cones which open and release their seeds that germinate in an appropriate seedbed prepared by the fire. There are, thus, limits to the extent to which humans can understand and mimic forest ecosystem dynamics. The approach remains instrumentalist and technocratic rather than accommodating to the dynamics of ecosystems.

There are also political and economic constraints in implementing the forest ecosystem policy regime. For instance, there are difficulties in gaining acceptance for controlled fire in northern communities where wildfires have marked many lives. But more generally, the present Conservative government's approach to forest management indicates that the fundamental innovations of the Crown Forest Sustainability Act process may be very difficult to realize. The government is currently scaling down the regulatory framework, and it clearly continues to emphasize the need to satisfy the forest industry's demand for fibre. This trend is reinforced by the emergence of a new set of policy instruments based on industry-driven initiatives, such as voluntary compliance and certification schemes ensuring that industrial goods are produced on an environmentally sustainable basis. One critical impediment to the implementation of the CFSA is the resulting reduction in enforcement capacity. The Ministry of Natural Resources staff and forest management budget was cut by 50 per cent between 1995 and 1998, and tenure holders are now themselves responsible for the enforcement of the CFSA.[62] Other public programs have suffered. Ontario's conservation authorities have clearly fallen victim to the government's financial cutbacks, apparently on the ground that the authorities strayed from their original mandate of watershed protection to providing recreation.[63]

One recent development in the implementation of the CFSA is instructive with respect to the government of Ontario's commitment to the act. In February 1998, a three-judge panel of the Ontario divisional court ruled that the Ontario Ministry of Natural Resources violated the act by not having a comprehensive plan in place to regulate logging in six major areas, including Algonquin Park, Temagami, and the Algoma Highlands.[64] Meanwhile, the industry is conducting its own campaign to put its house in order, which includes measures to certify its management systems and/or wood products at the national level, and the formulation of a new code of forestry practices provincially.[65]

Conservation and Preservation Issues

Those preservationist and conservationist policies that remain have continued to be kept separate from the all-important fibre objectives. In some cases, positive initiatives have even tended to provide a screen for the continued pursuit of industrial forestry. Typically, such policies still provide only marginally and selectively for forest ecosystem management. In the southern part of the province, a tax rebate for managed forest areas is now provided for private woodlot owners. It is relatively easy to qualify for, but its provisions may have more to do with political than forest management motives.[66] The provincial and federal governments have also established model or community forests based on multi-stakeholder negotiations and planning. Their operations are, however, compromised by the lack of tenure reform, with the majority of stakeholder groups holding little if any control over the affected forest lands; the larger leaseholders, therefore, tend to hold a dominant position.[67] Various federal and provincial programs to assist First Nations' forest management ventures are also double-edged. While they may go some distance towards promoting a more integrated and ecosystem-sensitive forest management, they may also lessen the chances for more radical changes by drawing attention away from land rights (or land claims) settlements.[68] One should also note the recently formed Canadian Ecology Centre in Mattawa, which is both a training facility for the forest industry, and an education centre for local school boards, Nippising University, and Canadore College, as well as a centre of ecotourism. It is perhaps not coincidental that the centre, and the institutions it serves, are located in premier Harris's constituency of North Bay.

Some initiatives in urban forestry have also been advanced. The city of Toronto, for example, has pioneered a by-law protecting trees above a certain size growing on private lands. While these initiatives may provide some opportunities for less well-to-do urban residents to experience nature, perhaps not surprisingly, the public protests that led to the by-law emanated from wealthy inner-city neighbourhoods, where trees not only serve an environmental and amenity function, but also enhance property values. Meanwhile, more and more private policy initiatives are taken in support of '[p]reserved areas,' especially in the southern part of the province.[69]

The Emerging Provincial Picture: Multiple Use by Adjacency?

The larger stakes for Ontario's ecosystems still lie in the north. The next moves of the current government depend on the outcome of yet another new consultation process. In the northern districts of the province, the Lands for Life process has taken the principle of 'multiple use by adjacency' to a province-wide level, based on the ecological and social divisions evident in the Great Lakes–St Lawrence, Boreal East, and Boreal West regions of the provincial Crown forest.[70] Ostensibly, the approach speaks also to local alienation from the centralized postwar forest management process, in creating separate planning processes for each large region under the official control of appointees from local communities. While the full implications of this rapidly concluded process are not fully clear at the time of writing (December 2000), it appears likely that on the whole, industrial interests will predominate overall. But they will likely be complemented with tourism in the northwest and northeast; and tourism and preservationism in the Great Lakes–St Lawrence region.

The latter arrangement is possible only because relatively limited commercial industry is viable in these extensively cutover forest lands, and its cottage-country mixed forest landscape is already firmly linked with wilderness in the minds and practices of southern and urban Ontarians. In the end, the Lands for Life process yielded a 12 per cent target for reserved lands in Ontario, a figure derived through negotiations among the government, industry, and the so-called Partnership for Life, composed of three major environmental groups (the World Wildlife Fund, the Federation of Ontario Naturalists, and the Wildlands League).[71] The Partnership for Life and even the radical environmentalist group Earthroots have praised the deal. Although the endorsement has been cautious, the hope is that the so-called Ontario Forest Accord, a multistakeholder forum (which includes the partnership), will facilitate the expansion of future preserved areas.[72] But the process has also been criticized for its secret negotiations, the sell-out or greenwash by the Partnership for Life and Earthroots, the exclusion of First Nations and other groups, and the possibility of 'floating park designations' to accommodate the forest and mining industries.[73] Recent meetings between the Partnership For Life and Nishnawbe Aski Nation to develop a memorandum of understanding may point in a new and constructive direction. The memorandum would include the concerns, goals, and aspirations of each group as well as a broad set of principles to guide future interactions.[74]

The case for real local control in forest policy, particularly for those at the short end of labour-shedding 'efficiencies' and monopoly control, has always been strong, but these groups have seldom been able to win the day.[75] All too often, local input can be skewed towards those interests with the most political clout. Large corporate interests hold unparalleled real political power, but vacationers who come and go with the season, and who are considered the very opposite of 'local,' also have considerable political voice. Often, repeat visitors and cottage-owners in particular develop deep affection for a wooded place – and the determination to safeguard it.[76] Local people who live permanently in the region often feel constrained to side with either one of these two power-ful constituents, and their position in such situations is a powerful and understandable source of resentment. Some people have insisted more and more emphatically on support for local issues and local control. Coming out of the turbulent forest debates of the 1980s, many environ-mental groups have also begun to incorporate the concerns of local forest workers and First Nations in order to be taken more seriously. But such dialogues on the ground over programs like the Wildlands League's 'Forest Diversity – Community Survival,' which may point in a new and constructive direction for these sometimes conflicting inter-ests, are few and far between.[77]

The real concerns – for local control, jobs, and the environment – may now be successfully harnessed instead to a policy of 'Potemkin wil-derness,' spearheaded by a new breed of forest professionals, in the Great Lakes–St Lawrence and Boreal East areas.[78] This includes the cre-ation of smaller tourist sites and waterways in places such as Algonquin Park. In Temagami, we may see the development of something even more spectacular. For there, the preservationist lobby is strong, and where thorough scientific investigations suggest that the old-growth pine forests possess unique multiple values, are increasingly rare, and contain a greater amount of ancient northern temperate forest than in most other parts of Ontario. Together with the Lower Spanish Forest and the Algoma Highlands, Temagami is held out as a unique ecosystem belt which can be held together by one wilderness corridor (and per-haps not coincidentally, a continuous canoe route as well).[79] But so far, these wilderness areas are far from being recognized as a means to get to the very nub of the issue: to achieve a sustainable relation between all human activities – properly ordered – in all their surroundings. Instead, ecological insights and the best of scientific analyses may promote a mere spatial constraint on industry, one that contents itself with the minimum of protected areas for road-, trail-, and canoe-based tourism.

Overall, while preservation policies and preserved areas are becom-ing more numerous, they are also becoming more and more the reserves of the better-off. In the past fifteen years the preserved area to be managed in Ontario has increased by 50 per cent, visits to these areas have increased by 60 per cent, but the budget for management has decreased by 62 per cent. The 'business-like' management response to such budget cutbacks has led to increased user fees for those able to pay and restricted access for those who cannot.[80] As an indication of what may come, in Frontenac County, the Ministry of Natural Resources has issued a land use permit to the municipality which is charging user fees for road access and camping in exchange for basic maintenance.[81] Alongside trends that favour industrial interests, the seeds are also there for more preservationist areas, primarily in the south and in the Great Lakes–St Lawrence regions, with a few enclaves in the Boreal Northeast and Northwest regions as well. The question of how much area should be preserved in this way dominates discussions. This is not likely to change, regardless of which political party is in power.

New Initiatives?

Are there no examples in Ontario where a combined ethic of human use and ecosystem preservation coexist? As in most other jurisdictions, there are isolated cases of less destructive harvesting operations based on a deliberate revival of horse teams, the combination of forest cuts with other forest uses, or integrated forest use.[82] One example that is often referred to in this category is the Haliburton Forest and Wildlife Reserve Limited.[83]

The Haliburton Reserve deserves considerable attention among those who seek to go beyond the current dynamic of separately zoned industrial forestry and preservation. Founded on heavily degraded land in the 1930s, Haliburton's forests are managed under a deliberate policy of 'low-grading' (leaving the best, taking the rest) in response to past 'high-grading' (taking the best, leaving the rest). Reserve lands are not formally zoned for 'multiple use by adjacency': distinctive forest management is applied to the whole reserve to be compatible with sustainability and other human activities. The Forest Stewardship Council, an international organization certifying wood products harvested on a sustainable basis, has endorsed the operations of the Haliburton Forest, one of only two operations to have earned such a label in Ontario. The Haliburton operation is conducted by Tembec, a large integrated forest corporation, which is also the certified manager for a group of small woodlots in the Huntsville area of Ontario. Both operations supply wood to Tembec's specialty products division of hardwood flooring in Huntsville.

Such operations are, however, far and few between, and generally not viable on a larger scale, given the competitive edge enjoyed by the firms operating less sustainable forest operations.[84] Not even the Haliburton Forest Reserve's practices can be seen as an example that is easily integrated on a wider basis, for its current generation of forest operations are 'subsidized' by the presence of recreational business activities, one being 'the only wholly privately owned snowmobiling operation in North America.'[85]

In such crucial areas where forest lands have been historically degraded, no model is readily evident that can sustain recovery operations on a profitable basis, at least in the short term. The front-loading of reinvestment in Ontario's most damaged forest lands is economically and ecologically essential. But such efforts can be filled only by sustained intersectoral transfers (on the Haliburton model), by government action, or – most promisingly – by properly supported First Nation, civil-societal, and community initiatives. The next era of Ontario forestry will have to be one in which such 'interests' have a prominent role.

Conclusion

Traditional harvesting methods used in Ontario have been based on meeting fibre demands rather than on considerations for the after-harvest condition of the forest. Natural regeneration under these conditions resulted in widespread conversion from a conifer- to a hardwood-dominated forest. The planting programs for key commercial species have for the most part been unsuccessful. In the case of white pine, the planting program was scrapped in the 1980s, and in many areas remaining stands have been slated for depletion cut (i.e., harvesting with no intention of regenerating the stands in white pine).[86] These practices have been unsustainable whether we look at them from an ecological or industrial perspective.

The new approach, based on maintaining the long-term health of the ecosystem, appears to be more sustainable. As long as the forest is sustained, all its values can be sustained, including commercial timber operations and the northern communities dependent on it. The difficulties in this approach are considerable. From a strictly scientific perspective, the knowledge needed to make accurate projections is incomplete. Indices for diversity have been used in scientific studies for a long time. However, they are currently on track to be used in long-term and large-scale management decisions. The issue of whether they are sensitive enough has been raised during the development of the models. Wildlife habitat requirements are being studied and incorporated. However, only long-term studies along with ongoing monitoring and evaluation of the models would provide reliable information.

More fundamentally, however, the Ontario forest continues to be overcut and the fibre supply continues to decline. The previous decline of the pine, the present decline of the spruce, and the growing cut of various hardwood species, suggest a continued degradation and decline of the wood supply.[87]

From a political perspective, the Progressive Conservative government has made deregulation and cutting government spending its priorities. Staff cuts at the OMNR have shut down many opportunities for public scrutiny and input, and thrown legally required regional and provincial committees for broader land use planning issues into limbo. The ability of the OMNR to research, monitor, evaluate, and enforce the new approach has also been seriously hampered. Environmental groups have even had to go to court to force the government to comply with its own regulations. The forest management units that OMNR have managed for the wood supply of smaller independent sawmills have been quietly transferred to large companies. Whatever their fiscal effects, these consequences of recent policy have effectively stalled progress towards more sustainable forest management in Ontario.

Whatever the commitment of future governments to conservation and preservation may be, it will have consequences which are played out in space. Here, the risk is that existing functional divisions and social inequalities will simply be 'spatialized,' in other words, expressed in and intensified through separate social and physical spaces. In the southern part of the province, conservationist and preservationist measures, such as the protection of urban trees, the restoration of damaged or profoundly altered ecosystems, or the creation of protected places is now taking on a more private than public character. Ecology is tied to wealthy neighbourhoods or the demand of the wealthy for nature experiences.

The Lands for Life process is putting a further spatial dimension to this process in the northern regions of the province, carving out three discrete spatial management units where industrial use is prioritized, and conservationist or preservationist goals are variably stressed. The 12 per cent designation of Crown forest lands as preserved areas and parks, however, appears highly suspect because of several loopholes. The debate of forest-related issues in this context tends to be confined to how much preserved lands should be maintained, not how the human relationship with nature should be reorganized overall.[88] The problem with this is that there is no debate over how forest management can be improved in space, and how industrial, conservationist, and preservationist values could coexist.[89]

NOTES

1 This chapter is a collaborative effort and our names appear in alphabetical order. Sandberg acknowledges the financial support of the Social Sciences and Humanities Research Council of Canada, Grant No. 410-91-0460.

2 A.R.M. Lower, 'Review: Report of the Ontario Royal Commission on Forestry,' *Canadian Journal of Economics and Political Science* 14, 1948, 508.

3 MW Analysts, Contemporary Information Analysis, *Ontario's Forests: The Driving Forces* (Report prepared for the Ontario Forest Policy Panel, 1993).

4 Donald Mackay, *Heritage Lost: The Crisis in Canada's Forests* (Toronto: Macmillan, 1985) 45; Bruce W. Hodgins and Jamie Benedickson, *The Temagami Experience* (Toronto: University of Toronto Press, 1989) 31–2. Compare also Jeremy Wilson, 'Wilderness Politics in British Columbia: The Business Dominated State and the Containment of Environmentalism,' in William Coleman and Grace Skogstad, eds., *Policy Communities and Public Policy in Canada: A Structural Approach* (Toronto: Copp Clark Pitman, 1990) 141–69.

5 Peter Gillis and Thomas Roach, *Lost Initiatives: Canada's Forest Industries, Forest Policy and Forest Conservation* (New York: Greenwood Press, 1986); A.R.M. Lower, *The North American Assault on the Canadian Forest* (Toronto: Ryerson, 1938).

6 Mark Kuhlberg notes an exception which in the end proved unsuccessful, 'We have "sold" Forestry to the Management of the Company: Abitibi Power and Paper Company's Forestry Initiatives in Ontario, 1919–1929,' *Journal of Canadian Studies* 34(3) 1999, 187–209.

7 For a closer examination of the distinction between conservation and preservation, see Curt Meine, 'The Oldest Task in Human History,' in Richard Knight and Sarah Bates, eds., *A Century of Natural Resources Management* (Washington, DC: Island Press, 1995).

8 On this use of 'spatialization' to mean a particular structuring of social space into mutually exclusive functions, see Jamie Lawson, 'Nastawgan or Not? First Nations Land Management in Temagami and Algonquin Park.' In L. Anders Sandberg and Sverker Sörlin, eds., *Sustainability – The Challenge: People, Power, and the Environment* (Montreal: Black Rose Books, 1998) 189–201.

9 The following section draws on Douglas McCalla, *Planting the Province: The Economic History of Upper Canada, 1784–1870* (Toronto: University of Toronto Press, 1993) 13–42; Ontario, Department of Lands and Forests, *A History of Crown Timber Regulations from the Date of the French Occupation to the Year 1899*. Reprinted from the Annual Report of the Clerk of Forestry for the Province of Ontario, 1899 (Toronto: Queen's Printer, 1957) 154–77.

10 Peter Kulchyski, *Unjust Relations: Aboriginal Rights in Canadian Courts* (Toronto: Oxford University Press, 1994) 7–8.

11 Robert G. Albion, *Forests and Seapower: The Timber Problem of the Royal Navy, 1652–1862* (Hamden, Conn.: Archon Books, 1965 [1926]).

12 The following is based on McCalla, *Planting the Province*, 45–66; Ontario, *A History of Crown Timber Regulations*, 177–201.

13 For sources, see McCalla, Planting the Province, 225–31; Ontario, *A History of Crown Timber Regulations*, 201–84; MacKay, *Heritage Lost*, 22–7; Gerald Killan, *Protected Places: A History of Ontario's Provincial Parks System* (Toronto: Dundurn Press, 1994) 1–73.

14 For more details, see A. Paul Pross, 'The Development of a Forest Policy: A Study of the Ontario Department of Lands and Forests,' doctoral dissertation, University of Toronto, 1967; Jamie Swift, *Cut and Run: The Assault on Canada's Forests* (Toronto: Between the Lines, 1983); H.V. Nelles, 'Timber Regulation, 1900–1960' unpublished manuscript. RG-1, BB-1, Box 14, file 2-15-1, Archives of Ontario, Toronto.

15 Christopher Armstrong, *The Politics of Federalism* (Toronto: Queen's Printer, 1981) 22–30; Bruce W. Hodgins, 'The Temagami Indians and Canadian Federalism, 1867–1943,' *Laurentian University Review* 11(2), 1979, 71–100.

16 On their role as wage labour, see Sheila M. Van Wyck, 'The Fruits of their Labour – Native Indian Involvement in the Canadian Wage Economy: A Regional Case Study of the Upper Ottawa Valley, 1850–1930,' master's thesis, University of Toronto, 1979. For an equivalent account in British Columbia, see Rolf Knight, *Indians at Work: An Informal History of Native Labour in British Columbia, 1858–1930* (Vancouver: New Star Books, 1978). For an interesting case of the wealth accumulated by a First Nation able to resist the predations of the lumbermen, see J.T. Angus, *A Deo Victoria: The Story of the Georgian Bay Lumber Company, 1871–1942* (Thunder Bay: Severn, 1990) chapter 14.

17 H.V. Nelles, *The Politics of Development: Forests, Mines and Hydro-Electric Power in Ontario, 1849–1941* (Toronto: Macmillan, 1974).

18 Peter Sinclair, 'The North and the North-West: Forestry and Agriculture,' in Ian M. Drummond, ed., *Progress without Planning: The Economic History of Ontario from Confederation to the Second World War* (Toronto: University of Toronto Press, 1987) 77–83.

19 Richard S. Lambert and Paul Pross, *Renewing Nature's Wealth: A Centennial History of the Public Management of Lands, Forests, and Wildlife in Ontario, 1763–1967* (Ontario: Department of Lands and Forests, 1967) 300–12.

20 R. Peter Gillis, 'The Ottawa Lumber Barons and the Conservation Movement, 1880–1914,' *Journal of Canadian Studies* 9(1), 1974, 14–30.

21 Mark Kuhlberg, 'Ontario's Nascent Environmentalists: Seeing the Foresters

for the Trees in Southern Ontario,' *Ontario History* 88 (June) 1996, 119–43. See also Helen E. Parson, 'Reforestation of Agricultural Land in Southern Ontario before 1931,' *Ontario History* 86(3), 1994, 237–48.

22 Patricia Jasen, *Wild Things: Nature, Culture, and Tourism in Ontario, 1790–1914* (Toronto: University of Toronto Press, 1995).

23 Killan, *Protected Places.*

24 Paul Walton, 'The Group of Seven and Northern Development,' *Canadian Art Review* 17(2), 1990, 171–9; W.J. Keith, *Literary Images of Ontario* (Toronto: Queen's Printer, 1992) 7–12; Jonathan Bordo, 'Jack Pine–Wilderness Sublime or the Erasure of the Aboriginal Presence from the Landscape,' *Journal of Canadian Studies* 27(4), 1992–3, 98–128.

25 Hodgins and Benedickson, *The Temagami Experience.* See also Bruce Littlejohn and Lori Labatt, eds., *Islands of Hope: Ontario's Parks and Wilderness* (Toronto: Firefly Press with the Wildlands League, 1992).

26 On the peculiar political importance of this shared experience, see James Lawson, 'First Nations, Environmental Interests and the Forest Products Industry in Temagami and Algonquin Park,' doctoral dissertation, York University, 2000.

27 Peter Gillis and Thomas Roach, 'Early European and North American Forestry in Canada: The Ontario Example,' in H.K. Steen, ed., *History of Sustained Yield Forestry* (Santa Cruz, CA: Forest Society, 1984) 211–19.

28 Thomas Roach, 'Farm Woodlots and Pulpwood Exports from Eastern Canada, 1900–1930,' in H.K. Steen, ed., *History of Sustained Yield Forestry,* 202–10.

29 George McDermott, 'Frontiers of Settlement in the Great Clay Belt, Ontario and Quebec,' *Annals of the American Association of Geographers* Sept. 1961, 261–73.

30 Gerald Killan, 'Ontario's Provincial Parks and Changing Conceptions of "Protected Places,"' in John S. Marsh and Bruce Hodgins, eds., *Changing Parks: The History, Future, and Cultural Context of Parks and Heritage Landscapes* (Toronto: Natural Heritage/Natural History, 1998) 14–49. Alan MacEachern, 'Rationality and Rationalization in Canadian National Parks Predator Policy,' in C. Gaffield and P. Gaffield, eds., *Consuming Canada: Readings in Environmental History* (Toronto: Copp Clark, 1995) 197–212; Janet Foster, *Working for Wildlife: The Beginning of Preservation in Canada* (Toronto: University of Toronto Press, 1978).

31 Killan, *Protected Places,* 1–16.

32 Ibid., 59–73. We place 'poaching' in inverted commas to stress that local people, but especially First Nations people, have historically considered the taking of game in such circumstances entirely normal and justifiable, based as it

is on practices that far predate contemporary game problems, and to which First Nations assert an Aboriginal right.

33 See, e.g., Robert Stacey, 'The Myth – and Truth – of the True North,' in Michael Tooley, ed., *The True North: Canadian Landscape Painting, 1896–1939* (London: Lund Humphries, 1991) 37–63; Walton, 'The Group of Seven.'

34 Gillis and Roach, *Lost Initiatives*; Lambert and Pross, *Reviewing Nature's Wealth*, 335–53.

35 Lambert and Pross, *Renewing Nature's Wealth*, 335–53; Killan, *Protected Places*, 13–35.

36 Ian Radforth, *Bushworkers and Bosses: Logging in Northern Ontario, 1900–1980* (Toronto: University of Toronto Press, 1987) 3–8, 155–220.

37 Lambert and Pross, *Renewing Nature's Wealth*, 354–89.

38 Swift, *Cut and Run*, 110–13.

39 Ontario Ministry of Natural Resources (OMNR), *Timber Management Planning Manual for Crown Lands in Ontario* (Toronto: Queen's Printer, 1986).

40 Gordon Baskerville, *An Audit of the Crown Forests of Ontario* (Toronto: ONMR, 1986).

41 Richard Behan, 'Multi-resource Forest Management: A Paradigmatic Challenge to Professional Forestry,' *Journal of Forestry* 88(4), 1990 12–18.

42 OMNR, *Ontario Forests Products and Timber Resource Analysis,* Vols. 1 and 2 (Toronto: Queen's Printer, 1992).

43 F. Anderson and N. Bonsor, *The Economic Future of the Forest Products Industry in Northern Ontario* (Report Prepared for the Royal Commission on the Northern Environment by Lakehead University, Thunder Bay, Ontario, 1981).

44 Ibid.

45 Ontario Independent Forest Audit Committee, *A Report on the Status of Forest Regeneration* (Sault Ste Marie: OMNR, Forest Audit Secretariat, 1992).

46 Ibid.

47 W. Darby, H. Timmerman, J. Snider, K. Abraham, R. Stefanski, and C. Johnson. *Woodland Caribou in Ontario: Background to a Policy* (Toronto: Queen's Printer, 1989).

48 Ontario Environmental Assessment Board, *Reasons for Decision and Decision: Class Environmental Assessment for Timber Management* (Toronto: Queen's Printer, 1994).

49 Ontario Forest Policy Panel, *Diversity, Forests, People, Communities: A Comprehensive Forest Policy for Ontario* (Toronto: OMNR, 1993).

50 Lambert and Pross, *Renewing Nature's Wealth*, 365.

51 Arthur Herbert Richardson, *Conservation by the People: The History of the Conser-*

vation Movement in Ontario to 1970 (Toronto: University of Toronto Press, 1970); Arthur Herbert Richardson, *A Report on the Ganaraska Watershed* (Toronto: Department of Planning and Development, 1946); John R. Fisher and Donald H.M. Alexander, 'The Symbolic Landscape of the Oak Ridges Moraine: Its Influence on Conservation in Canada,' *Environments* 22(1), 1993, 100–4.

52 Killan, *Protected Places*, 120–204.

53 *Ontario's Provincial Parks: Planning and Management Policies* (Toronto: OMNR, 1978).

54 Killan, 'Ontario's Provincial Parks and Changing Conceptions of "Protected Places,"' 14–49.

55 Old Growth Policy Advisory Committee, *Old Growth Forests: 1993 Public Consultation Report* (Sudbury: n.p., 1993).

56 These included Forest Industry Action Group, *Ontario's Forest Products Industry: Hard Choices – Bright Prospects: A Report and Recommendations from Labour, Industry, and Government to the Ontario Minister of Natural Resources* (Ontario: OMNR, 1993); OMNR, Policy Development and Transfer Section, *Developing a New Timber Production Policy* (Sault Ste Marie: OMNR, 1993). For a detailed analysis of the diverging goals of these documents and *diversity*, see Marcelo Levy, 'The Policies and Politics of Ontario Forestry,' master's Major Paper, York University, 1995.

57 Ontario, *Crown Forest Sustainability Act* (Toronto: Legislative Assembly of Ontario, 1994).

58 The process involves four steps: (1) An assessment of the value of the indicator at the beginning of the planning period; (2) a projection of the value of the indicator at the end of the planning period as a result of management actions; (3) an assessment of whether the projected value of the indicator is acceptable (e.g., an assessment of whether it compromised sustainability under the plan); and (4) ongoing monitoring and evaluation of the accuracy of the projection at the end of the planning period. David Euler, J. McNicol, D. Parker, M. Levy, A. Bisschop, and R. Tomchick, 'Indicators of Sustainability Used in Forestry in Ontario,' in *Training Module II, Forest Management Planning Manual* (Toronto: OMNR, 1995).

59 OMNR, *Forest Management Planning Manual for Ontario's Crown Forests (Final Draft)* (Sault Ste Marie: OMNR, 1995).

60 For instance, a summer fire in Quetico Provincial Park in 1995, covering about 25,000 hectares, left a great number of trees standing (either dead or alive), and some pockets of trees completely unaffected. R. Suffling, 'The Red Hot Summer of '95,' in *Quetico Foundation Newsletter* (Toronto: Quetico Foundation, 1995).

61 Terence Carleton and Patricia MacLellan, 'Woody Vegetation Responses to
    Fire versus Clear-Cutting Logging: A Comparative Survey in the Central
    Canadian Boreal Forest,' *Ecoscience* 1(2), 1994, 141–52. See also Terence
    Carleton, 'More than A Change of Heart is Needed to Preserve the Forest,'
    Globe and Mail, 1 Aug. 1995, A14.

62 Environmental Commissioner of Ontario *Annual Report 1997* (Toronto:
    ECO, 1998) 37. For a critical account of recent events, see Elizabeth May, *At
    the Cutting Edge: The Crisis in Canada's Forests* (Toronto: Key Porter Books,
    1998).

63 On the cutbacks, see Scott Piatkowski, 'Tories Undermine Conservation in
    Ontario,' *Alternatives* 22(3), 1996, 8. On the last point, see Jennifer Anne
    Cardwell, 'The Origin and Changing Role of Recreation in Ontario's
    Conservation Authorities,' master's thesis, York University, 1996.

64 Ontario Court of Justice (General Division), Divisional Court Judgement of
    O'Leary, Campbell and Cosgrove, JJ, 6 Feb. 1998, Court File No. 539/96;
    'Province breaking own logging laws,' *Toronto Star*, 7 Feb. 1998, A23; Sierra
    Legal Defence Fund and Wildlands League, *Cutting around the Rules: The
    Algoma Highlands Pay the Price for Lax Enforcement of Logging Rules* (Toronto:
    SLDF, WL, 1998). This decision was upheld by the Ontario Court of Appeal.

65 There are two major nationally based forest certification schemes in Canada.
    The pulp and paper industry supports an initiative by the Canadian
    Standards Association to certify forest management systems. The Forest
    Stewardship Council, an international environmental non-governmental
    organization, approves auditors who inspect and certify sustainable forest
    management operations. For the development of an ethical code among
    Ontario forest producers, see 'Ontario Inks New Forestry Code: Ontario For-
    est Industry Association Members Hope New Operating Guidelines Will
    Help Restore Public Confidence,' *Logging and Sawmill Journal* 24(4) (June
    1993) 5–6.

66 James Fieldhouse, 'Politics versus the Environment: The Ontario Managed
    Forest Tax Rebate Program,' honours thesis, York University, 1998.

67 Sara Costa, 'Community Involvement in Community Forestry,' major project
    report, York University, 1993.

68 P.S. Smith, 'A Survey and Evaluation of Natural Resource Agreements
    Signed with Aboriginal People in Canada: Do They Result in Autonomy or
    Dependence?' BS paper, Lakehead University, 1991.

69 Norm Richards and Tom Beechey, 'Planning and Managing for Protected
    Heritage Areas in Ontario: Accomplishments, Challenges, Directions,' *Envi-
    ronments* 24(1), 1996, 42–56.

70 For selective documents from various perspectives, see OMNR, *Boreal East*

Planning Area, Boreal East Land Use Strategy: Workbook for Commenting on Draft Planning Objectives and Preliminary Planning Options, 26 March, 1998; Enzo Di Matteo, 'Timber! There Go Half the Trees of Ontario,' *Now,* 5–11 March 1998, 19, 25; 'There is no wall around Ontario's Lands for Life,' *Globe and Mail,* 20 April 1998, A13; 'Fight for Northern Ontario Escalating,' 5 August, 1998, A5; 'Lands for Life or Logs for Jobs?' *Toronto Star,* 28 June 1998, F4.

71 For the final deal, see OMN. *Ontario Living Legacy – Land Use Strategy* (Toronto: Ministry of Natural Resources, 1999).

72 For a statement of Monte Hummel of the World Wildlife Fund, see 'Not Perfect, but a Historic Deal,' *Toronto Star,* 16 Aug. 1999, A12. For Earthroots, see Lea Ann Mallett, 'Lands Deal Won by Working Together,' *Toronto Star,* 5 Oct. 1999, A21.

73 For a selection of different critical comments, see Tony Weis and Anita Krajnc, 'Greenwashing Ontario's Lands for Life,' *Canadian Dimension* 33(6), 1999; Anita Krajnc, Andrew Pask, and Anna Maria Valastro, *Ontario's 'Living' Legacy: One Year Later, the Harris Government Gets a Failing Grade* (Boulter, Ont.: Pronature Network, 2000); John Ibbitson, 'Environmentalists Swap Backpacks for Back Rooms,' *National Post,* 8 Feb. 1999, A16; L. Anders Sandberg, Raymond A. Rogers, and Catriona A.H. Sandilands, 'Lands for Life Fails to Serve the Environment,' *York University Gazette* 29(33) 1999, 12; Insider, 'Hard Work Ahead Says Conference Speakers,' *Seasons* 39(3) 1999, 37; and Canadian Environmental Law Association, 'Mining "Side Deal" Undermines Lands for Life Proposal, Says Environmental Law Group,' *Media Release,* 21 May 1999.

74 Lorne Johnson, Consultant for the World Wildlife Fund, personal communication, 30 May 2000.

75 Gillis and Roach, *Lost Initiatives.* Bruce Hodgins, 'Nationalism, Decentralism and the Left,' in Viv Nelles and Abraham Rotstein, eds., *Nationalism or Local Control: Responses to George Woodcock* (Toronto: New Press, 1973) 39–46; Herb Hammond, 'Community Forest Boards: Gaining Control of Our Forests,' in *Putting Power in Its Place: Create Community Control!* (Gabriola Island: New Society Publications, 1992) 100–3.

76 Ron Prefasi, 'Temagami,' in *At the End of the Shift: Mines and Single Industry Towns in Northern Ontario* (Toronto: Dundurn Press, 1992) 156–60.

77 Wildlands League, *Forest Diversity – Community Survival,* Fact Sheets 1–10, n.d.

78 G.A. Potemkin (1739–1791) was a chief adviser to Catherine the Great of Russia. He is alleged to have arranged elaborate facades depicting whole villages and hired peasants to walk beside them along the tour routes of Holy Emperor Joseph II during Joseph's state visit to Russia. The ruse was intended to convince Joseph that Russia was more advanced than it actually

was, and so spare Catherine the embarrassment over her achievements, given the Enlightenment values the monarchs shared. In a similar fashion, separate recreational and intensive logging zones are not only safety or waterway-conservation measures. They reduce social conflict over forests merely by keeping logging out of the sight of most vacationers. The fundamental ecological impacts of existing logging techniques, of course, need not change, and need not be challenged. *Encyclopedia Americana* (international ed.), vol. 22 (Danbury, Conn.: Grolier, 1997), 468.

79 Peter A. Quinby, ed., *Ancient Forest Ecology and Conservation in the Lake Temagami Site Region: Selected Studies*, vol. 1, 1993–1997 (Toronto: Ancient Forest Exploration and Research, 1997).

80 Paul F.J. Eagles, 'Ecotourism and Parks: Do or Die,' in Marsh and B. Hodgins, eds., *Changing Parks* 276–7.

81 Canadian Broadcasting Corporation, FM Radio 99.1, 16 Feb. 2000.

82 See, e.g., Peter Hendry, 'The Working Woodlot: Ever Heard of a Chestnut Farmer?' *Earthkeeper* 4(4), 1994, 18–21. For a First Nation's perspective, see Lawson, 'Nastawgan or Not?' See also, Wildlands League, 'Ecological Forestry ... A Cut Above,' 'Crafting More Jobs with Less Wood,' 'Nurturing Diversity Through Ecotourism,' and 'Planting the Seeds of a New Economy,' *Forest Diversity – Community Survival*, Fact Sheets Nos. 6–9, n.d.

83 'Haliburton: A Multi-Use Model,' *Logging and Sawmill Journal*, 27(9), 1997, 41–2. L. Anders Sandberg and Christopher Midgley, 'Recreation, Forestry and Environmental Management: The Haliburton Forest and Wildlife Reserve, Ontario, Canada,' in Xavier Font and John Tribe, eds., *Forest Tourism and Recreation: Case Studies in Environmental Management* (Wallingford, England: CAB International, 2000) 201–15.

84 These companies would clearly dispute the claim that their operations are unsustainable. Indeed, the forestry industry is now promoting its own certification scheme for 'sustainably produced' wood products. These efforts are organized by the Canadian Standards Association, which is promoting a certification scheme based on sustainable management systems rather than third-party inspections of forest practices on the ground. Such industry-driven efforts have alienated most environmental groups. Elizabeth May refers to them as a forestry industry 'scam' to market its products more efficiently.

85 The point here is that there are limits to the expansion of businesses providing forested areas for snowmobile use. Recreational snowmobile use is also a highly polluting activity. Sandberg and Midgley, 'Recreation, Forestry, and Environmental Management.'

86 OMNR, *Timber Management Plan for the Superior Forest* (Chapleau: Ontario

Ministry of Natural Resources, 1992); OMNR, *Algoma Crown Management Unit* (Sault Ste Marie: OMNR, 1994).

87 For a clear statement on this, see Environmental Commissioner of Ontario, *Annual Report 1997* (Toronto: ECO, 1997) 42.

88 For an excellent treatment of this point, see James D. Proctor, 'Whose Nature? The Contested Moral Terrain of Ancient Forests,' in William Cronon, ed., *Uncommon Ground: Rethinking the Human Place in Nature* (New York: W.W. Norton, 1995) 269–97.

89 For such alternative ways of seeing the forest, from the perspective of labour and First Nations, see Thomas Dunk, *It's a Working Man's Town: Male Working Class Culture* (Montreal and Kingston: McGill-Queen's University Press, 1991); 'Talking about Trees: Environment and Society in Forest Workers' Culture,' *Canadian Review of Sociology and Anthropology* 31(1), 1994, 14–34; '"Is It Only Forest Fires that Are Natural?": Boundaries of Nature and Culture in White Working Class Culture,' in Sandberg and Sörlin, eds., *Sustainability – The Challenge*; Jamie Lawson, 'Nastawgan or Not? First Nations Land Management in Temagami and Algonquin Park,' in Sandberg and Sörlin, eds., *Sustainability – The Challenge*, 189–201.

Chapter Eleven

New Players, Same Game? – Managing the Boreal Forest on Canada's Prairies

Ian Urquhart

The phrase 'Prairie forestry policy' may strike more than a few readers as either overly optimistic or an oxymoron. After all, trees are a rare sight when you are driving on the asphalt ribbon of highway joining Calgary to Winnipeg. The view from the TransCanada Highway, however, camouflages the ecosystem reality of the three Prairie provinces – more than half of their territory is forested, mostly by the species making up the boreal forest, Canada's largest. In terms of forest industry development in Canada, the boreal is a late bloomer, a forest which has become commercially attractive only with the shrinking of fibre supplies located closer to the markets traditionally served by Canadian pulp, paper, and lumber industries.

This chapter addresses in several ways this volume's interest in policy regimes. It opens with a discussion of forest industry development. This is used to draw attention to two significant features of the policy regimes that one finds on the Canadian Prairies. The first feature is that, through a very powerful state–corporate policy network, Alberta has grown a forest products industry that is much more economically and politically significant than what may be found in its Prairie neighbours to the east. Second, recent events in Saskatchewan offer some promise to introduce new players to forestry policy-making; the increased presence that Aboriginal-owned businesses seem likely to assume in the Saskatchewan forest products sector over the next several years may change the relative importance of the actors in the policy subsystem in potentially significant ways. The chapter then looks at forestry legislation and management practices. Here we discover what Bernstein and Cashore refer to in a different context as 'adaptation and resilience.' Elsewhere in this volume Wilson reflects on the influence that 'ecosystem management' has had on the way we talk about forestry issues today and the political obstacles policy-makers face in 'walking the walk.' In the context of adjusting government policy to incorporate the idea of ecosystem management, Saskatchewan wears the face of adaptation, Alberta and Manitoba that of resilience. As Lindquist and Wellstead also have noted, Saskatchewan has made significant changes to the province's forest management legislation.[1] On 1 April 1999, Saskatchewan proclaimed the 'most comprehensive, forward looking forest management legislation in North America.'[2] While there is undoubtedly some inflation in the government's self-congratulatory assessment of this initiative, there is potential in Saskatchewan's new legislative and regulatory framework to modify significantly the policy expectations associated with the timber management regime. The resilience worn in Alberta and Manitoba refers to the stubbornness of policy-makers to go beyond the symbolic recognition of ecosystem management and its associated principles and practices in provincial legislation. There are few signs from the latter two provinces that environmental interests have accomplished what Howlett and Rayner detect elsewhere, namely, an emerging triadic policy network.

A third objective of this chapter is to suggest that the evolving structure of the international economy is one of the more important factors responsible for the resilience shown by Alberta. This segment of the essay highlights the importance of internationalization, 'a process by which various aspects of policy or policy-making are influenced by factors outside national territorial boundaries.'[3] The approach taken here differs in important ways from other works in this collection that highlight the importance of international factors to domestic behaviour. While it shares Bernstein and Cashore's interest in using international factors to account for domestic policy patterns, it does not give pride of place to international trading rules, international forest negotiations, or international forest agreements in explaining domestic policy. Rather it stresses the pressures that episodic and structural features of the international economy and pulp and paper industry are putting on those who are charged with governing Canada's forests. In looking for a causal linkage between the international political economy and government policy, the chapter differs from the work of Hayter and Holmes, concerned as they are with the relationship between globalization and the behaviour of firms.

The face of internationalization appearing in this chapter is sketched by detailing the long-term challenges that a second group of new players – Indonesian forest products companies – pose for public policy-makers in the northern hemisphere. These companies are euphemistically called the Dragons of Pulp because, like the Komodo Dragons native to Indonesia's Komodo and Sundra Islands, they are large, aggressive, and opportunistic. They are proving to be dangerous competitors for the Alberta pulp and paper industry. In the hands of Canadian pulp and paper producers, the Dragons' competitive threat becomes an important political obstacle to regime change. The threat, with all that it implies for the workers and communities who rely upon pulp and paper operations for their livelihoods, may be used as a brake on policy change that would take forest policy in a more sustainable direction.

Forestry Industry Development in the Prairie Boreal Forest

To the preservationist voices in the environmentalist choir, Canada's boreal forest, the predominant Prairie forest, is under ferocious assault.[4] Writing from a landscape protection and biodiversity conservation perspective, the Alberta ecologist Richard Thomas writes that 'today the Boreal Forest is undergoing anthropogenic changes of unprecedented magnitude and rapidity, many of whose effects are potentially irreversible.'[5] In Alberta, the Peace River lowland is one locale where human impacts have been especially damaging to the forested landscape. Between 1961 and 1986, 20 per cent of the northern dry mixed-wood boreal forest was cleared for agriculture – a rate of deforestation (0.81 per cent annually) comparable to that reported in Amazonia between 1975 and 1988 (0.87 per cent annually).[6] Thomas estimated that in the southern dry mixed wood zone in Alberta the annual rate of deforestation over a forty-five-year period was higher than the annual Amazonian rate of deforestation noted above – a situation he suspected has been aggravated recently by the clearing of private lands in the Athabasca–Lac La Biche area of aspen to feed new pulp mills.[7] By comparison, the annual rate by which productive forest area was lost in the boreal forest of central Saskatchewan between 1984 and 1994 was 0.35 per cent, which is considerably slower than the rates Thomas calculated for the dry mixed-wood portions of Alberta's boreal forest.

In Thomas's account of the challenges human activities pose to sustaining biodiversity in the boreal forest, the forestry industry plays a major role.[8] If the balance and the structure of the boreal forest is still changing faster in Alberta than in Saskatchewan, much of the explanation rests with the fact that, in the late 1980s and early 1990s, the pace of forest industry expansion in Alberta was much quicker and its geographic reach much wider. In Alberta, the pulp and paper industry grew explosively, fueled by significant amounts of unallocated timber in the boreal forest and a provincial government (under Premier Don Getty, 1986–93) prepared to offer generous financial assistance to the companies it selected to develop the boreal. Between 1986 and 1995 nearly $4 billion was invested in the forest products sector.[9] Alberta's taxpayers subsidized and financed, to a very considerable degree, these investments; environmental groups were excluded from participating in the decisions regarding how the boreal forest should be used.[10] The provincial government extended just over $1.2 billion in loans, loan guarantees, and infrastructure expenditures to the companies it chose to establish or expand pulp and paper facilities in Alberta.

These investments reaped impressive gains in pulp and paper production. From the early 1970s until the late 1980s Alberta's pulp production was stable at just under 500,000 tonnes per year (tpy). By 1995, pulp production had quadrupled to 2.2 million tpy.[11] This increased level of pulp production (as well as newsprint) made a major contribution to boosting the value of Alberta's forest products exports to $2.333 billion in 1997 (from $658 million in 1990).[12] Such increases raised the economic and political importance of the industry. The forest products industry now is described variously as the third or fourth largest industrial sector in Alberta (behind energy, agriculture, and, perhaps, tourism). In 1995, the dollar value of forest products exports stood above the value of exports from either the grains and oilseeds or the livestock and red meat sectors.[13]

As Table 11.1 shows, in the late 1990s the Alberta forest products sector dwarfed the forest products sectors of Manitoba and Saskatchewan. Neither of Alberta's sister provinces followed its lead and searched the globe aggressively in the late 1980s for investment capital. Little in the way of new large-scale forest project development has occurred in Manitoba recently. The grand promises Repap made in 1990 to invest $1 billion in its paper mill at The Pas (now owned by Tolko Industries) disintegrated with the firm's profitability and stock price. The one major new facility added in Manitoba – an $80 million Oriented Strandboard (OSB) mill built by Louisiana–Pacific in Swan River – only went ahead after Repap forfeited its timber harvest rights after failing to proceed with its promised investments.

Until very recently Saskatchewan's story was very similar to Mani-

Table 11.1 Selected forestry industry statistics, Alberta, Saskatchewan, Manitoba (various years)

	Alberta	Saskatchewan	Manitoba
Harvest volume (1997)	22.2 million m^3	4.1 million m^3	2.1 million m^3
Harvest area (1997)	50,697 ha	17,500 ha	15,544 ha
Value of exports (1998)	$2.6 billion	$673 million	$480 million
Value of shipments (1996)	$4.2 billion	$867 million	$873 million
Direct employment (1998)	26,000	6,000	9,000
Wages & salaries (1996)	$622 million	$149 million	$172 million

Source: Natural Resources Canada, Canadian Forest Service, *The State of Canada's Forests, 1998–99.*

toba's. Only one significant addition was made to the Saskatchewan forest sector during the heyday of forest industry expansion in Alberta. Saskatchewan's Crown Investments Corporation formed a partnership with Millar Western Industries and brought a 280,000 tpy zero-effluent bleached chemi-thermo-mechanical pulp (BCTMP) mill to Meadow Lake. The pace of industrialization began to accelerate in May 1998 with Weyerhaeuser's announcement that it would invest $315 million in its twenty-year-old Prince Albert pulp mill in order to improve the facility's environmental performance and economic efficiency.

However, the catalyst for the most significant changes to Saskatchewan's forest products industry arose somewhat ironically out of Weyerhaeuser's submission to the provincial government of a twenty-year forest management plan. The plan would guide the firm's forestry operations and investments from 1999 to 2019. As part of Saskatchewan's environmental assessment of the Weyerhaeuser plan, the company's proposals were examined by a forestry consulting firm, and the consultants' views were submitted for further evaluation to four forestry professors from Canadian universities. These reviews concluded that the sustainable harvest level from Weyerhaeuser's forest management licence agreement (FMLA) area was considerably higher that the company first estimated (4.19 million cubic metres per year vs 2.77 million cubic metres per year). The area contained 'a surplus sustainable harvest.'[14] These conclusions led Saskatchewan to withdraw 1.5 million hectares from Weyerhaeuser's FMLA area (30 per cent of its cutting area) and, in view of the expert consensus, gave the company conditional approval to triple the production of softwood lumber from the area it retained. The plans to triple lumber production required a business plan that proposed the doubling of the capacity of Weyerhaeuser's Big River sawmill and the possible expansion of the Wapawekka sawmill – a joint venture between Weyerhaeuser and three northern Saskatchewan First Nations.[15]

The press release announcing provincial approval of Weyerhaeuser's business plan stated that the company, by relinquishing a significant percentage of its cutting area, made new developments possible. Less than a week later a wave of new projects was announced, projects that would primarily draw on timber in the Weyerhaeuser forest management area. The firm's previously announced upgrades and partnerships plus these new developments amounted to more than $850 million in private sector investment. Politicians predicted that these projects would create nearly 10,000 jobs (3,300 direct; 6,600 indirect) and double the size of the province's forest industry. It was, Premier Romanow said, 'the single biggest announcement of private-sector job creation in the history of the province.'[16]

For the policy regime, the current direction of forest industry development in Saskatchewan is interesting because government is trying to incorporate some of the interests that usually have been excluded from the forestry sector – Aboriginal peoples and local communities. Any allocations of timber from the Weyerhaeuser FMLA area must involve Aboriginal peoples and/or northern communities. Aboriginal peoples and/or local communities were involved in all of the seven new projects announced. The government's insistence that northern forest use follow this direction was confirmed later when a forest company applied for a land allocation but was refused because it did not have a 'community partnership.'[17] Saskatchewan stands as an important exception to the point made earlier by Howlett and Rayner regarding the difficulty in adapting long-term forest tenures to the interests of groups which usually are excluded from the policy network.[18]

Will this addition of new actors transform forestry practices in Saskatchewan's boreal forest? It's far too soon to know. To listen to some of northern Saskatchewan's Aboriginal and northern community leaders it might seem that, under their management philosophy, the boreal forest will be something more than a source of lumber and pulp. For example, Chief Michel of the Peter Ballantyne Cree Nation said that his people's partnership with Ainsworth Lumber 'will follow the patterns of sustainable forest use traditional to the Woodland Cree.'[19] Similarly, Chief Head of the James Smith Cree Nation welcomed forestry partnerships because his people 'have always been concerned with the forest and wanted to be directly involved in the activities within the forest itself.'[20] Others, however, articulated the economic and employment concerns that Weyerhaeuser found to be the most striking sentiment among northerners when it consulted the public about its twenty-year forest management plan. 'We are pleased,' Chief Cook of the Lac La Ronge Indian Band said, 'that the province has recognized that the people who live in the local communities should gain some of the benefits from the development of the forestry resources.'[21] Of course, intentions aside, the extent to which new directions will be taken also will be shaped by the laws and regulations governing the operations of forest companies. It is to that framework that we now turn.

Forestry Legislation and Management

It has become customary to open discussions of forestry practices by noting that since the release of the Brundtland Report in 1987 the phrase 'sustainable development' has been added to the vocabulary of forest managers. The phrase was the centrepiece of *Sustainable Forests: A Canadian Commitment*, the report published by the National Forest Strategy Committee in 1992. For forestry this general principle demands moving beyond the long-held view that the essence of good forest management was maintaining a 'sustained yield' (of wood products) from the forests. Instead, good management will see the value of forests as also resting in uses other than timber production. The implications of this more holistic view include a more participatory decision-making environment. In the words of a Saskatchewan environment and resource management report: 'Forests must be viewed and understood as ecosystems performing a variety of interrelated functions that can only be sustained if the integrity of the ecosystem is protected. The process for making forest land use decisions must be expanded to seek a balance among the interests of all parties with a stake in the outcome.'[22] Here we consider the extent to which the legislative–managerial frameworks for forest use have endorsed the more holistic view called for by sustainable development. In this sort of discussion we would be prudent to recall what Wilson said earlier about the stages of the policy cycle and the difficulties that those who favour change face in seeing the gains made at the problem-definition and agenda-setting stage sustained in the policy formulation and implementation stages.

Elsewhere in this volume, Howlett and Rayner call our attention to changes to the Timber Management Paradigm. They argue that this paradigm is no longer hegemonic, that ideas such as integrated resource management and ecosystem management have helped to push the Timber Management Paradigm to the stages of fragmentation of authority and contestation. Such changes did not previously have nor are they now having a great impact on the government's approach to forest use planning in Alberta. Integrated resource management did not guide the province as it assigned the vast majority of the province's boreal forest to pulp and paper producers in the late 1980s – integrated resource plans had not been prepared for most of that area.[23]

Today, references to integrated resource management have been joined or have given way to ecosystem management and public participation. Alberta's legislative and regulatory commitments to increased public participation and incorporating non-timber values into its decision-making processes are found in the Natural Resources Conservation Board (NRCB) Act (1990), the Environmental Protection and Enhancement Act (1992), and some forest management agreements made pursuant to the Forests Act.

Through the NRCB Act, the NRCB was established to review natural resource projects (excluding oil and gas projects) to determine whether the projects serve the public interest. This determination should consider the socioeconomic effects of the proposals, as well as the effects the projects would have on the environment. All forestry projects which are ordered to prepare an environmental impact assessment (EIA) report according to the terms of the Environmental Protection and Enhancement Act are subject to NRCB review. The environmental impact assessment report should describe the proposal's possible positive and negative environmental, social, economic, and cultural impacts; it also should consider the cumulative, regional, temporal, and spatial impacts of the proposals and offer plans to mitigate adverse effects. Not all forest industry projects, however, are necessarily subject to an NRCB review. Pulp, paper, newsprint, and recycled mills producing more than 100 tonnes per day are subject to NRCB review because the province's environmental assessment regulations require them to produce EIA reports.

Oriented strandboard (OSB) mills and sawmills, on the other hand, escape NRCB review if they are not asked to prepare an EIA report. Whether these latter projects must prepare EIA reports is left to the discretion of the director or the minister of environmental protection. In the event that neither the director nor the minister call for an EIA on these latter projects, the cabinet still has the authority to order that the NRCB review them. An NRCB review does not necessarily mean that public hearings into a project will be held. The convening of public hearings is left to the board's discretion. From the public participation perspective then, the only legislative guarantees of public participation in evaluating the suitability of forest projects comes first, from the right to express concern about a proposed activity; second, from the right to make suggestions regarding the EIA terms of reference; and third, from the right to comment on any application made to the NRCB.

One piece of legislation that is silent on the issue of public participation is the Forests Act. The act is silent on the issue of public consultation, either by government or by companies, in respect to the most fundamental forestry decisions – creating FMAs, granting other timber allocations such as quotas, or in issuing timber licences. Once an FMA is signed and a forestry project receives its necessary approvals, the FMA may call for public involvement in forest management planning. In some cases, such as Alpac Forest Products, the FMA requires a company to 'conduct public presentations and reviews of its forest management plans' and respond in the plan it submits to the minister 'to the concerns raised by the public.' In the case of Alpac, holder of the largest FMA in Alberta, the consultative exercise is not required to be ongoing, and it need not take place until the eve of the deadline for the company's submission of a revised detailed forest management plan – November 2007.

Another indication of the weakness of the Alberta government's commitment to ecosystem management and public participation may be found in its response to the Alberta Forest Conservation Strategy. The Forest Conservation Strategy emerged in the aftermath of the conflicts sparked by the province's pulp and paper strategy. Those conflicts led the government in 1993 to invite industry, environmental groups, and academics to help it formulate a Forest Conservation Strategy for Alberta, a strategy that would reflect 'the diversity of forest values and uses.'[24] In May 1997, a report entitled *The Alberta Forest Conservation Strategy: A New Perspective on Sustaining Alberta's Forests* was presented to the minister of environmental protection; in February 1998 the minister responded to this report with the pamphlet *The Alberta Forest Legacy: Implementation Framework for Sustainable Forest Management.*

For a document claiming to offer an implementation framework for sustainable forest management *The Alberta Forest Legacy* is vague and disappointing. Nowhere does the pamphlet, or its accompanying news release, offer a signal that the government intends to follow the first recommendation found in the conservation strategy – to revise statutes, regulations, rules, policies, and practices to reflect the essential features of the strategy. In fact, *The Alberta Forest Legacy* really provides little guidance to how the vision of sustainable development found in the strategy will be implemented, a characteristic which may mean that the minister of environmental protection believes that government should step aside and let the users of the resource decide how to proceed.

From the standpoint of sustainability one of the most worrisome features of *The Alberta Forest Legacy* is its outline of the management approaches which should be taken towards Alberta's forests. There, the minister discarded the 'protection' designation found in the strategy. This designation clearly intended that protected areas 'must exclude industrial development and other activities that disturb the land surface.'[25] The minister replaced the 'protection' designation with 'heritage' and refused to endorse the strategy's suggestion that there are places in Alberta where industrial development should be prohibited. Suspicions that this shift tacitly endorses the importance of industrial development are confirmed, ironically, by the *Legacy*'s statement that, where they are necessary, heritage areas will be maintained through the Special Places 2000 Program – the provincial government's response to the Endangered Spaces program launched by World Wildlife Fund Canada in 1989. In 1998, World Wildlife Fund Canada gave Alberta an 'F' on its annual 'protecting endangered spaces' report card, and two of the province's most moderate environmental organizations – the Canadian Parks and Wilderness Society and the Federation of Alberta Naturalists – resigned from the special places coordinating committee. All of these actions were sparked by the province's refusal to concede that industrial activity should not be allowed to occur in areas which were recommended for 'protection' by the special places program. What, they wondered, was the point of a protected areas strategy if not to protect some areas of the province from industrial activity?[26]

In Manitoba, the legislative commitment to environmental assessment is found in the Environment Act (1987). The act created the Clean Environment Commission (CEC) and gave it the responsibility to develop and maintain public participation in environmental matters. The minister of the environment has the power to direct the commission to hold public hearings, lend advice, and make recommendations concerning proposed developments requiring an environmental licence. The minister's discretion – in calling for a hearing and in acting upon the CEC's recommendations – is wide. For example, despite requests for public hearings from nineteen of twenty public submissions regarding a proposal by Pine Falls Paper Company (now Tembec) to modernize its Pine Falls mill, neither the department nor the minister felt a public hearing was required.[27]

Some suggest that the Minister has used this discretion to try to defuse opposition to projects favoured by government and industry. When Repap proposed to expand and convert the mill it had just purchased from the provincial government (Manfor) the minister of the environment split the public hearings into two phases. The first phase considered the expansion and conversion of the mill; the second phase considered forest practices. 'Thus,' Novek writes, 'public scrutiny of the controversial forest management agreement would be delayed until after the mill expansion was well under way.'[28] While the minister is under no legal obligation to accept and implement recommendations coming from the CEC's investigation, if the minister rejects the commission's findings written reasons for the minister's disagreement must be provided and made public.

Unlike the NRCB in Alberta, the CEC, if requested by the minister, may conduct environmental assessments of forestry management plans. When the commission has been asked to consider these plans its mandate has been broad. For example, the commission, when asked to hold public hearings into Louisiana–Pacific's ten-year forest management plan in 1995, was invited to offer recommendations on subjects such as the potential impact of the plan upon the sustainability of all forest values including ecosystems and biological diversity; socioeconomic, social, cultural, and health aspects flowing from the plan's environmental impacts; and monitoring and research activities which may be needed in light of the forest management activities proposed in the plan. When the CEC examined the Tolko Manitoba (formerly Repap) 1997–2009 forest management plan, a variety of concerns were raised during the public hearings. Protection of wildlife populations, endangered spaces, impacts on Native communities and the treaty land entitlement negotiations, and departmental resources for monitoring increased harvest levels were among the concerns raised. When the commission recommended that Tolko receive the environment licence it sought it attached twelve conditions. All of them, except for one establishing annual allowable cut ceilings, were incorporated into Tolko's 1997–2009 forest management plan licence.[29]

Environmentalists remain critical, however, of the effectiveness of the

CEC as an independent environmental assessment agency. The minister's wide discretionary powers is one focal point for those criticisms. Also, environmentalists are critical of the fact that, as in Alberta, there is no environmental assessment of the initial decision to assign a forest management licence (FML). Fundamental issues such as the amount of timber that may be cut annually are settled in the FMLs and are thus not subject to an environmental assessment. Furthermore, the commission lacks the institutional capacity a strong environmental assessment agency requires; its members have tended to be laypeople who lack the sorts of expertise that would strengthen their ability to evaluate projects and management plans; the commission's staff capacity to conduct investigations is too limited. Consequently, the CEC is viewed as an example of political symbolism, an agency that has strengthened, not challenged, the industrial forestry model in Manitoba.[30]

Saskatchewan stands out as the Prairie administration that has gone the farthest to incorporate formally the values of ecosystem management and public participation into its forestry decision-making process. Through the Canada–Saskatchewan Partnership Agreement in Forestry, an integrated forest resource management plan was developed, a plan distinguished by extensive public consultations and the preparation of the *State of the Resource Report.*[31] This report, an attempt to detail the then-current state of the province's forests, was described as 'an indispensable foundation for developing an integrated forest resource management strategy.'[32] The legislative foundation for this more holistic and participatory approach to forest management was provided by the Forest Resources Management Act of 1996 (FRMA) which replaced the Forest Act.

Although the Saskatchewan legislature passed the FRMA in 1996, the act did not come into effect until 1 April 1999. During that nearly three-year period, Saskatchewan Environment and Resource Management developed the regulations that would bring the act into effect. The public was consulted extensively during this period: mailouts, discussion papers, questionnaires, workshops, and public meetings were among the mechanisms used to gauge public support for sustainable forest management. One of the key features of this new forest management framework is the commitment to planning at three levels: provincial, regional, and local. At least once every ten years a forest accord will be drafted. This provincial framework will outline the broad principles and goals that will guide regional and local plans. Regionally, the government will prepare integrated forest land use plans for the various management units. These land use plans provide the context for twenty-year forest management plans that companies must prepare for the regions where they hope to operate. Locally, companies will prepare annual operating plans detailing what they will be doing and when they will be doing it.

A second key feature is the requirement that public consultation occur in each of these planning exercises. A third notable feature is the requirement that industry monitor, on an ongoing basis, the impact of their activities on other users of the forest and on the ecosystem itself. This monitoring program will be supported by a science advisory board, established to advise the minister on the development and effectiveness of the program.[33] Firms will also be required to produce independent audits of their operations every five years to gauge the extent to which forest management goals are being realized. Ecosystem management and participatory values also have been strengthened by the fact that the twenty-year forest management plans prepared by companies are subject to mandatory environmental assessments.

The first plan subject to this process, with its attendant public review, was that of NorSask Forest Products, a company jointly owned by the Meadow Lake Tribal Council, Millar Western Pulp, and Techfor. Nor-Sask described its forest management plan as 'an adaptive management approach based on the principles of integrated resource management, ecosystem sustainability, and maintenance of biodiversity.'[34] Ministerial approval was contingent upon the company taking concrete steps to realize these principles and to involve the public, as well as co-management and advisory boards in its forest management responsibilities.[35] In 1998, two more twenty-year forest management plans – one by Saskfor MacMillan,[36] the other by Weyerhaeuser – were laid before this new environmental impact assessment process.

Unlike the NorSask plan, these plans were reviewed by a private sector forestry consulting firm. The consultants' reports were then critiqued by a panel of forestry professors from various Canadian universities. In the case of the Saskfor MacMillan environmental assessment, all of the reviews and reports were open to public review for sixty days. Few objections were raised to the environmental impact statement (EIS) Saskfor MacMillan prepared for its twenty-year plan. Only seven letters were received commenting on the EIS. They were described as a 'mixed bag' by an environmental assessment branch official – some general criticisms, some criticisms of clear-cutting, and some specific criticisms of the plan.[37]

Saskatchewan's new legislative and regulatory framework certainly suggests that ecosystem management values have made important gains in the agenda-setting and policy-formulating stages of the policy cycle.[38] Will these values prevail in the later stages of the policy cycle – such as policy implementation? Given the novelty of Saskatchewan's initiative, it is clearly too early to answer this question. In his discussion of the strength of ecosystem management ideas in British Columbia, Wilson noted that the technical complexity of forest policy issues was one important political obstacle to realizing significant forest policy change.[39] This comment may prove to be just as applicable to the future of Saskatchewan's efforts to embrace ecosystem management.

Environmental groups such as Nature Saskatchewan, the Canadian Parks and Wilderness Society, and the Dore–Smoothstone Lakes Wilderness Protection Association, skilled and dedicated as their members may be, likely lack the organizational capacity needed to offer the sophisticated analyses that effective participation in Saskatchewan's new decision-making arrangements will require. This likelihood may well be compounded by other factors. First, there is the question of organizational energy – will environmental groups, given their often meagre resources and frequent reliance upon volunteers, have the energy to participate in the myriad of processes that now seem open to them in Saskatchewan? Second, there is the state of public knowledge and concern about Saskatchewan's forests. Public knowledge has been described as low[40] while Weyerhaeuser reported that the general public had few concerns about its twenty-year forest management plan: 'Only twenty-four out of 140,500 clip-out coupons in newspapers and brochures, asking about people's concerns, were returned. No phone calls were received from well over a thousand newspaper or magazine advertisements which invited participation.'[41]

The push to expand forestry operations in the north may also complicate efforts to implement ecosystem management. Already environmental groups have claimed that public participation and the environmental impact assessments of proposed projects have suffered because of the government's enthusiasm for increasing the production of timber and the number of forestry jobs. Nature Saskatchewan criticized the government for approving Weyerhaeuser's revised business plan before the environmental assessment of the company's forest management plan was completed. 'We can only conclude,' the group said, 'that the government has sacrificed the environmental review process in its haste to announce expansion of (Weyerhaeuser's) Big River mill.'[42] Seven of the ten member Dore–Smoothstone co-management board resigned in protest over government behaviour that 'has grown increasingly favourable to industry.' One disgruntled board member felt that Weyerhaeuser effectively vetoed the majority view on the board and that the economic interests of the industry were given priority over all the other interests in the area. For Weyerhaeuser, the majority on the board misinterpreted what the objectives of public participation should be: 'Their view is not where and when we should cut but if we should cut, and that was really outside of the terms of reference of the advisory committee. The purpose of the committee is to help us carry on our business in a way that is least disruptive to others and other resource users.'[43] Such disputes over what key concepts like public participation really mean, occurring as they do in settings where a power imbalance exists, signal another of the difficulties faced by those who would like to take advantage of Saskatchewan's legislative and regulatory changes.

Internationalization: Another Obstacle to Regime Change

When we consider the prospects of regime change we sometimes assume that, on balance, international factors are, at the very least, nudging governments to move their forestry practices away from the timber management paradigm, towards a new, somewhat ill-defined sustainable paradigm where the commitment to ecosystem management is more than symbolic. Boycotts, certification, and international forestry convention negotiations all push in this direction. In the final section of this look at management of the boreal forest on the Prairies, I want to play devil's advocate. Here, I will argue that, at least one major international development – the structural evolution of the international forest products economy – actually serves to prop up the established paradigm. In fact, because the changing international structure presents an important competitive threat to Canadian firms, particularly in the pulp and paper sector, governments are under significant pressure to lower the costs of producing pulp and paper in Canada. As the Canadian Pulp and Paper Association (CPPA) told the Senate subcommittee examining the future of the boreal forest, the forest industry needs 'secure access to competitive sources of fibre' and 'a more efficient regulatory structure to achieve environmental and other policy objectives at lower cost to the industry.'[44] These are not needs that are well served by moving to non-traditional, more expensive, forest management practices such as ecosystem management. These needs may question traditional policy instruments but not in a way that leads to a more sustainable paradigm of exploitation. At present, the structural changes in the international economy are posing the largest threat to Alberta's pulp and paper sector, and the obstacles to regime change that this form of internationalization poses are explored in the context of Alberta.

Earlier, we noted that Alberta saw explosive growth in the size of its pulp and paper sector between 1986 and 1995. To explain the explosive growth in this industry we should look in two directions. The first factor to consider is the globalization of the forest industry – the internationalization of manufacturing and services and the efforts of transnational firms to improve their competitiveness by spreading and shifting their production around the globe. In the pulp and paper sector, forest products companies have tried to lower their costs of production by shifting their operations offshore, often to jurisdictions offering them unexploited forests. Japanese transnationals epitomized this face of globalization throughout the 1980s. Their search for fibre was clearly global, taking them to the tropical forests of the southern hemisphere as well as to the boreal forest that blankets the northern half of Alberta.

In Alberta, the interest of transnationals in securing timber resources and in shifting overseas the lower value-added dimensions of the paper business – like pulp production – complemented a second factor, the interest of successive provincial governments in diversifying the economy. Those familiar with modern Alberta history will recognize the claim that diversification has been a Holy Grail for every Progressive Conservative government this province has had since 1971. Premier Lougheed argued that Alberta's dependence on revenues from depleting oil and gas reserves made the province too vulnerable.[45] Lougheed's government played an active, interventionist role in Alberta's economic life in pursuit of a 'more balanced economy.'[46] In July 1984, his government released the *White Paper on an Industrial and Science Policy for Alberta*, a document that made it very clear that it was the government's job, not the market's, to select winning industries and use financial assistance to ensure that firms would come to Alberta, rather than locate elsewhere.[47]

This fundamental plank of the Lougheed government – that the state should play an active role in diversifying the provincial economy – was central to the industrial policy-making of the Getty government. What Mansell and Percy refer to as a 'forced-growth' or a 'hothouse' approach to diversification was followed by Lougheed's successor.

According to this approach, 'one or a few industries (or firms) are targeted for special assistance in the form of capital grants, wage subsidies, loan guarantees, tax expenditures, etc.'[48]

It has been more than a decade now since Alberta took the forestry diversification path. For some, the significance of the pulp and paper industry we noted earlier signals the success of this diversification initiative. To be sure, the arrival of companies like Daishowa, Mitsubishi, and Oji Paper brought badly needed jobs to northern Alberta. A closer look, however, reveals some nagging concerns about the industry's health and profitability. The new mills have lost more money than they have earned. In the 1990s, 1995 was the only year when the industry generated a positive return on its pulp investments. As the province's pulp and paper producers told the Standing Policy Committee on Natural Resources and Sustainable Development in August 1995: 'Investment returns have been awful for five of last six years [sic].'

Nowhere have the problems besetting the Alberta industry been more serious than in respect to Alpac Forest Products (formerly known as Alberta–Pacific) – a joint venture controlled by Mitsubishi Corporation and Oji Paper, and the largest beneficiary of the province's willingness to subsidize pulp and paper development. The province spent $75 million on transportation infrastructure required by Alberta–Pacific and supplied the company with a $250 million loan from the Heritage Savings Trust Fund. With a price tag of $1.3 billion the Alberta–Pacific pulp mill, northeast of Athabasca, was the largest pulp mill built during the post-1986 wave of investment. When the mill neared completion in 1993 the business press congratulated Alberta–Pacific's then principal owner, Crestbrook Forest Industries,[49] on its business acumen. Pulp prices were on the rise, and Alberta–Pacific's output would boost Crestbrook's profits.[50]

The worlds of Crestbrook and Alberta–Pacific did not unfold as the experts in the business press expected. The upswing in pulp prices was short-lived and Alberta–Pacific has seldom been profitable. Citing poor pulp prices, Alberta–Pacific took advantage of the province's generous loan agreement and postponed paying any of the interest owed to the provincial government arising from its $250 million loan. Consequently, Alberta–Pacific's debt to Alberta taxpayers grew monthly to nearly $400 million. Alberta–Pacific's miserable financial performance helped plunge its parent, Crestbrook, into a deep financial crisis. This crisis led Crestbrook, in March 1999, to arrange the sale of its 40 per cent share of Alberta–Pacific to Mitsubishi and Oji Paper.[51]

**The International Economy and the Tribulations of
Alberta Pulp and Paper Producers**

The roots of the difficulties facing Alberta pulp producers rest in a changing international political economy. Two features of this political economy – one episodic, the other long term and structural – pose serious threats to Alberta's industry. The episodic feature is the financial crisis that swept through Asia in 1997–8. The importance of the Asian collapse to the Canadian pulp and paper industry arises first, from the region's growing importance as an export market for Canadian pulp and paper. Between 1965 and 1974, Japan and other Asian countries accounted for 9.7 per cent of Canadian wood pulp exports (by volume); between 1985 and 1994, these markets took 23.6 per cent of these commodities.[52] According to the Canadian Pulp and Paper Association, by 1997 Asia had passed the domestic Canadian market to become the second largest market for Canadian pulp.[53] Second, the Asian appetite for paper was important fuel for the recovery of pulp prices that all pulp and paper producers benefited from between 1993 and 1995. The price support that Asian demand gave to pulp prices is suggested by the following: from 1990 to 1995, paper and board consumption in the Asia Pacific region rose by 39 per cent; per capita growth rates in countries such as Korea (64 per cent), Malaysia (73 per cent), Indonesia (75 per cent), and Thailand (81 per cent) were 'phenomenal.'[54] While U.S. paper and board consumption was basically stagnant in 1995, Asia Pacific consumption rose by 8.6 per cent. Consequently, most predictions of a return to healthier pulp prices assumed that the Asian growth rates of the early 1990s would be sustained. Without strong Asian demand, it is likely that international pulp prices will stagnate or deteriorate in the short term.

In light of the Asian crisis, demand from Korea, Japan, and Southeast Asia for Canadian pulp and paper weakened. The currency and stock market crises that erupted in East Asia in the summer of 1997 were expected to slash the region's 1998 growth rate in half. Instead of growing by 7.2 per cent in 1998, the region grew by only 3.6 per cent in 1999. This modest regional economic growth figure masked the severity of the crisis in several East Asian nations. South Korea, Indonesia, and Thailand all slipped into recession in 1998. Real gross domestic product in Indonesia, Thailand, and South Korea was predicted to fall respectively by 5 per cent, 3 per cent, and 1 per cent.[55] The consensus view among independent analysts, as well as Canadian pulp and paper producers, was that the Canadian industry had been, and would continue to be, damaged by serious economic weakness in Asia.[56]

This drop in demand was exacerbated by the sharp currency devaluations that accompanied Asia's economic slowdown. Since pulp and paper products usually are traded in U. S. dollars, the steep currency devaluations in Indonesia, South Korea, and Thailand increased the local costs of paper products and depressed demand further. While the Asian crisis damaged the prospects of the Alberta industry, a preoccupation with Asia's current problems ignores the fact that Alberta producers struggled during much of the period when Asian markets had a growing appetite for Canadian pulp.[57] This situation suggests that there are other, possibly more long-lasting or structural, characteristics of international pulp markets that Alberta's producers have to wrestle with. The structural hurdle they must overcome, somewhat ironically, is a product of the same globalization and state-led diversification imperatives that contributed to the rapid growth of the Alberta industry in the 1980s – the state-supported development of inexpensive sources of timber. The structural threat that the Alberta pulp and paper industry faces now is the emergence of very low-cost pulp producers in Indonesia, Brazil, and Chile. Although this chapter focuses only on the challenges posed by the Indonesians, the logic of the argument may be applied to South American pulp producers as well.

The emergence of low-cost producers in countries like Indonesia has helped sustain a perennial feature of the international pulp industry – overcapacity. Overcapacity – too many mills producing more pulp than the market demands – has been a chronic feature of recent pulp market cycles, a feature that generally has had a depressing effect on pulp prices. In the 1990s, Indonesian pulp and paper producers hatched aggressive expansion schemes to capture market share. Currently, the Indonesian industry, the fourteenth largest in the world, is dwarfed by the Canadian industry. Indonesia's 1995 production of two million tonnes of pulp – as much as Alberta produced – was less than 10 per cent of Canada's output. Nonetheless, the Indonesian industry is in the midst of what one review of the international trade in wood products calls 'explosive growth.'[58] Between 1986 and 1997, the capacity of the Indonesian pulp industry rose by more than 1,200 per cent, from 317,000 million tonnes in 1986 to 3,905,600 million tonnes in 1997.[59] The Indonesian Pulp and Paper Association predicted, as the Asian crisis deepened, that by 2010 Indonesia will produce 10 million tonnes of pulp annually and will be planted firmly among the world's ten largest producers.[60] Much of the additional capacity that the Indonesians have added to their industry is aimed at export markets. In 1996, 1,127,390 million tonnes of pulp were exported, more than ten times the amount exported in 1992.[61]

It is important to note that these observations and predictions have been tempered but not dashed by the Asian crisis. For example, the ambitious expansion plans of Indonesia's most significant pulp and paper producer – Asia Pulp and Paper (APP) – remain intact despite the crisis gripping the country. Asia Pulp and Paper, characterized before the crisis as 'clearly the most aggressive pulp and paper company on earth in the late 1990s,'[62] remains committed to its ambitions to become the world's largest pulp and paper producer within the next decade. Indonesia's financial meltdown, which led to the downgrading of corporate as well government debt, did not force APP to abandon expansion plans in Malaysia and Indonesia. Through projects in those two countries APP's pulp capacity should rise by 50 per cent (from two to three million tonnes) by the end of 1999.[63]

The Indonesian crisis has led a second significant player – Asia Pacific Resources International Ltd (APRIL) to postpone some of the expansions it had scheduled for 1998. In a press release intended to calm its investors, APRIL announced that there would be a delay in its plans to expand the output of the largest pulp mill in the world – the Riaupulp mill (in Borneo).[64] Meanwhile, plans to add paper capacity proceeded. One of its subsidiaries started up its first paper machine in Sumatra and a partnership with UPM-Kymmene, the Finnish forest products giant, ensured that the company's fine paper mill in China would be completed in early 1999.[65]

APRIL, like APP, has tried to protect and improve its position in the global economy by forming a number of strategic alliances with Japanese, European, and North American pulp and paper producers, alliances that should strengthen the firm's medium- and long-term prospects. The most noteworthy of these alliances is with Finland's UPM-Kymmene. According to the terms of a March 1998 agreement, the Finns' investment of $235 million in APRIL's Chinese fine paper mill project gives them the option of converting that investment into a 30 per cent interest in the Riaupulp mill – the largest and arguably the lowest cost mill in the world. The arrangement promised the Finns access to low cost production while offering the Indonesians access to the paper-making expertise of Europe's largest paper producer. This is not the only alliance struck by APRIL. Agreements with Champion and Canfor of North America, DaiEi of Japan, and CYPAP Pulp and Paper Limited (BOMO Paper Ltd) of the Middle East, are part of APRIL's efforts to increase its share of the Japanese, European, and North American paper markets.[66]

The seriousness of the Indonesian challenge to hardwood pulp producers in Alberta stems from several underlying strengths of the Indonesian industry. First and foremost, Indonesia is one of the world's lowest cost pulp producers. According to a draft report prepared in June 1997 for the Alberta government by KPMG Consulting, Alberta bleached hardwood kraft pulp producers are much less competitive than Indonesian producers.[67] The Indonesians enjoyed a 30 per cent cost advantage over Alberta producers – an advantage which grew because of the 70 to 80 per cent devaluation of the Indonesian currency (the rupiah). The average cost of pulp production for APRIL in 1997 was just US$188 per tonne – a figure comparing very favourably to the costs per tonne of pulp produced at the Daishowa-Marubeni, Weldwood, and Weyerhaeuser mills in Alberta.[68] This envious position has many contributors. Indonesia's wood and labour costs are arguably the world's lowest. KPMG concluded that, for hardwood pulp producers, wood costs in Indonesia are between 20 and 29 per cent lower than in Alberta. Indonesian labour costs are at least 30 per cent below Alberta's. Geography also makes Indonesian transportation costs to Asian buyers cheaper than Alberta's. Unlike the technologically backward stereotype some have of low-wage competitors, the Indonesians are technologically sophisticated competitors. Their state-of-the art facilities enhance their economic performance and enable them to meet or exceed the environmental performance of their North American competitors.

Finally, through strategic alliances with the European, North American, and Japanese firms mentioned earlier, the Indonesians have developed important marketing networks for their products. For example, APP's alliance with Itochu, combined with APP's cost advantages, has helped the Indonesian company grab nearly a 10 per cent share of the Japanese copy paper market.[69]

Several of the cost advantages enjoyed by Indonesia's modern mills were strengthened by the currency crisis that gripped the country. From August 1997 to the summer of 1998 the value of the Indonesian rupiah evaporated. By July 1998 the rupiah was worth approximately 80 per cent less against the U.S. dollar than it had been a year earlier.[70] This dramatic devaluation, while sparking the food riots and political unrest that led to Suharto's resignation, benefits Indonesian exporters such as the country's pulp and paper producers who sell their products in U.S. dollars. The president and chief executive officer of the American Forest and Paper Association warned the U.S. Congress in late February 1998 that the devaluations in East Asia had made the region's forest products firms 'hyper competitive,'[71] an observation borne out by the fact that Indonesian paper exports jumped by 50 per cent in 1997.[72] The Brazilian pulp and paper sector, another very low cost producer, feared that the rupiah's devaluation – more colourfully referred to as 'exchange rate dumping' – would cost Brazilian producers some of their export markets.[73]

The devaluation will be especially rewarding for those Indonesian producers who are paying a high percentage of their local costs in the devalued rupiah. At APRIL's massive Riaupulp mill, for example, approximately 53 per cent of the mill's production costs are denominated in rupiah.[74] APP's operations paint a similar picture. There, approximately 65 per cent of the firm's consolidated cash operating costs are paid for with rupiah.[75] The rupiah's devaluation, when contrasted with the much, much smaller devaluation of the Canadian dollar since the autumn of 1997, has probably further strengthened the competitiveness of Indonesia's already very formidable pulp and paper industry.

Improving Competitiveness: Alberta's Response to Internationalization

The troubles facing Alberta's pulp and paper industry are no strangers to the rest of the Canadian pulp and paper industry. Overcapacity, tough global competition, volatile pricing, and abysmal financial returns have led the industry to appeal to government for assistance. Lise Lachapelle, the president and CEO of the Canadian Pulp and Paper Association, served notice that her industry is looking for 'public policy initiatives to create a more competitive environment for pulp and paper in Canada.'[76]

The problems the Alberta industry faces plus the sentiments that government should address these problems, pose something of a dilemma for the provincial government. On the one hand, the government has committed itself to avoiding the offer of direct financial assistance as a means of economic diversification. The Klein government's vision of Alberta's economic future argues that 'government has an essential role to play in encouraging economic growth, but its role must change from that of direct intervenor to partner and facilitator ... In place of direct financial assistance, we will look to new methods of stimulating economic development – methods like removing taxes and regulations that impair business competitiveness; and improving small business access to financing.'[77] On the other hand, direct financial aid has proven to be exactly what some of the children of the Getty government's forestry diversification strategy need as they strive to compete in global markets. Consequently, the government's forestry policies may speak the rhetoric of 'getting out of the business of business,' while extending direct financial assistance to Alberta pulp and paper producers to help them restructure their debt in order to improve their competitiveness.

Two examples illustrate the government's willingness to offer direct financial assistance to struggling forest products companies. On 1 April 1997 Alberta's Treasurer announced that the government had agreed to sell its investment in a Whitecourt pulp mill owned by Millar Western Industries. Millar Western's Whitecourt pulp mill was the first project to benefit from the Getty government's enthusiasm for subsidizing forest industry diversification. The province, through a $120 million loan, financed the majority of the cost of the pulp mill.[78] In its first ten years of operation, the mill only made a profit once, in 1995.[79] Consequently, the company had never made any payment on its provincial loan. When the government announced that it had sold its loan to the Canadian Imperial Bank of Commerce for $27.8 million, Millar Western owed the provincial treasury $272 million. In other words, the province's loss on this loan was $244.2 million. By forgiving nearly a quarter of a billion dollars in debt, the province reduced Millar Western's long-term debt by 60 per cent.[80] This direct financial assistance to the company helped position Millar Western to try to raise capital in the equity markets.[81]

In March 1998 the province once again bailed out a struggling pulp and paper company. This beneficiary was Alberta–Pacific. The provincial government supported the Alberta–Pacific project by spending $75 million on infrastructure and by extending a $250 million loan from the Heritage Savings Trust Fund. When the government announced that Mitsubishi and Oji Paper had agreed to buy back the province's loan for $260 million, the total owing the province stood at approximately $400 million.[82] As in the case of Millar Western, the province's loss on this loan, estimated at $145 million by the Liberal party's treasury critic, was a direct provincial financial contribution to the efforts of the company to restructure its debt and become more competitive.[83]

This type of direct financial assistance to struggling pulp and paper companies did not exhaust the range of policy options which the government was under pressure to adopt in order to strengthen the competitiveness of Alberta's pulp and paper industry. The Alberta pulp industry seized the opportunity presented by the emergence of its East Asian and South American competitors to pressure the province for policy concessions that will reduce the 20 to 30 per cent cost disadvantages they face *vis-à-vis* the Indonesians and Brazilians. On the subject of stumpage – the money paid to government for the right to harvest timber from provincial lands – these companies have argued that provincial stumpage rates must be sensitive to the fact that most of the costs of producing pulp in Alberta are higher than the production costs competitors pay in the southern United States, Brazil, Indonesia, and Chile. In other words, the provincial government should modify its stumpage regime to improve the competitiveness of Alberta producers against firms who enjoy lower wood, transportation, and labour costs.[84]

The pulp and paper companies use a simple and politically compelling lever – jobs – to lobby government to excuse them from paying virtually any timber royalties for the foreseeable future (a situation Alberta oil sands producers now enjoy in their royalty arrangement with the province). AlPac is a major employer in the Athabasca–Lac La Biche area – providing more than 400 jobs in its mill and 660 jobs in the woods. The same may be said for the importance of Weyerhaeuser in the Grande Prairie area, Weldwood in the Hinton area, or Daishowa-Marubeni in the Peace River area. The government moved to meet the producers' requests in February 1999. Little-noticed regulatory changes to the province's timber management regulation had the effect of reducing dramatically the stumpage most of the province's pulp and paper producers will pay for deciduous timber during periods when the price of hardwood pulp is less than C\$750. In the case of Alpac, the company's deciduous timber dues were reduced by more than 50 per cent (to \$.20 per cubic metre).

It will be interesting to watch if a political debate emerges in Alberta regarding these measures to strengthen the international competitiveness of the forest products sector. By modifying the stumpage system in the direction preferred by the pulp and paper industry, the province has taken another step to strengthen a forest management model where employment is the overwhelming consideration. For some members of the public, a worrisome environmental dimension may accompany any further movement in an 'employment-centred' policy direction. Spokespersons for the pulp and paper industry do not hesitate in attributing some of their current financial difficulties to excessive, scientifically suspect environmental regulations.[85] At the same time, there is a recognition that the price competition the Canadian industry faces is so severe that firms must redouble their efforts to reduce operating costs.[86] If Canadian companies must focus on cutting their operating costs, what will be the future of potentially more environmentally friendly forest management practices, such as ecosystem management, which will be more expensive to put in place?

Conclusion

In this chapter, I have argued, through examining patterns of forest industry development, provincial legislative and regulatory frameworks, and a changing international economy, that new players have joined the forestry policy game. In Saskatchewan, government policy has recognized Aboriginal peoples, local communities, and the general public as legitimate players in forestry policy-making. There, it is possible, but not certain, that we may see the contestation of the timber management regime mentioned by Howlett and Rayner. However, not all of the new players identified in this chapter reside on the Prairies, and the influence of the new foreign competitors described here on provincial forest policy-making runs counter to regime change. As the case of Alberta shows, the challenges that internationalization poses may lead governments to adopt whatever policy mix is needed to improve the competitiveness of the forest products sector. It would be naive to believe that this mix will necessarily be favourable to those who wish to strengthen ecological considerations in the management of the boreal forest on the Canadian Prairies.

NOTES

1 Evert Lindquist and Adam Wellstead, chapter 14 in this volume.
2 Saskatchewan Environment and Resource Management, 'Saskatchewan Leads North America with New Forest Legislation,' news release no. 99–244, 31 March 1999.
3 G. Bruce Doern, Leslie A. Pal, and Brian W. Tomlin, ed., *Border Crossings: The Internationalization of Canadian Public Policy* (Toronto: Oxford University Press, 1996) 3.
4 See, e.g., 'Canada's Future Forest Alliance,' in *Brazil of the North: The National and Global Crisis in Canada's Forests* (New Denver, BC: Canada's Future Forest Alliance, 1993); Elizabeth May, *At the Cutting Edge: The Crisis in Canada's*

Forests (Toronto: Key Porter Books, 1998); or the material found on the webpage of the Taiga Rescue Network, an International Alliance of Non-Governmental Organizations. The network's webpage is http://www.snf.se/TRN/

5 Alberta Environmental Protection, 'The Final Frontier: Protecting Landscape and Biological Diversity within Alberta's Boreal Forest Natural Region,' *Protected Areas Report* 13, March 1998, 9.

6 Ibid., 150–2.

7 Ibid., 159. See also the testimony of Richard Thomas in Senate, Standing Senate Committee on Agriculture and Forestry, *Proceedings of the Subcommittee on the Boreal Forest, First Session, 36th Parliament, 1997–98*, issue no. 13 (16 Nov. 1998), 4–9.

8 But, Thomas points out that significant risks to the biodiversity of the boreal forest arise from a wide range of industrial, settlement, and recreational activities. See *The Final Frontier* 63–172.

9 Alberta, Economic Development and Tourism, *Alberta International Export Strategy, 1995–96: Marketing the Alberta Advantage* (Edmonton: Alberta Economic Development and Tourism, 1995) 124.

10 On Alberta's forest development strategies during this period see Larry Pratt and Ian Urquhart, *The Last Great Forest: Japanese Multinationals and Alberta's Northern Forests* (Edmonton: NeWest Press, 1994).

11 Alberta Newsprint Company et al., 'Presentation to Standing Policy Committee on Natural Resources and Sustainable Development,' brief, mimeo, 21 Aug. 1995.

12 Canadian Council of Forest Ministers, National Forestry DataBase Program, Table 8.1.

13 $2.6 billion versus $1.792 and $1.342 billion respectively. Petroleum products dominate the provincial export picture. Crude petroleum exports in 1995 amounted to $6.9 billion; natural gas exports totaled $5.135 billion. See Alberta, Economic Development and Tourism, *The Alberta Advantage in Action: Highlights of the Alberta Economy* (Edmonton: Alberta Economic Development and Tourism, 1997) 4.

14 Saskatchewan, 'Government Gives Approval to Weyerhaeuser Business Plan,' news release, 22 April 1999.

15 *Ibid.*; 'Weyerhaeuser Takes Cut,' *Saskatoon Star-Phoenix*, 23 April 1999; 'Weyerhaeuser "Disappointed" with Reduction in Forest Area,' *Saskatoon Star-Phoenix*, 24 April 1999. In light of the revised sustainable harvest levels Weyerhaeuser sought to triple its softwood lumber production and offered to relinquish timber harvesting privileges on approximately one million hectares of Crown land.

16 Saskatchewan, 'Major Forest Industry Expansion Announced: Industry's Plans Could Create Up to 10,000 New Jobs,' news release, 26 April 1999; 'Forest Industry Spurs Job Growth,' *Saskatoon Star-Phoenix*, 27 April 1999.

17 'Dwindling tree supply threatens salvage mill,' *Saskatoon Star-Phoenix*, 20 July 1999.

18 The National Aboriginal Forestry Association has made similar observations about the incompatibility of Aboriginal involvement and long term tenure arrangements. See Peggy Smith in Senate, Standing Senate Committee on Agriculture and Forestry, *Proceedings of the Subcommittee on the Boreal Forest, First Session, 36th Parliament, 1997–98*, Issue no. 4 (10 April 1997).

19 'Forest Deal Lauded,' *Saskatoon Star-Phoenix*, 27 April 1999.

20 Saskatchewan, 'New Forestry Partnership in Zenon Park,' news release, 30 April 1999.

21 Saskatchewan, 'New Forestry Partnership in La Ronge,' news release, 10 May 1999.

22 Rod Thompson, *Sustainable Forest Development: Perspectives on a New Forestry* (Saskatchewan: Forestry Branch, Saskatchewan Parks and Renewable Resources, 1992). Quoted in 'Canada-Saskatchewan Partnership Agreement in Forestry,' *Saskatchewan Long-Term Integrated Forest Resource Management Plan*, March 1995, 1–2.

23 Andrea Moen, *Demystifying Forestry Law: An Alberta Analysis* (Edmonton: Environmental Law Centre, 1990), see esp. Appendices 6 and 11.

24 Alberta, Environmental Protection, *The Alberta Forest Conservation Strategy: Report of the Initiating Workshop March 10, 11, 1993* (1993), 22.

25 Alberta, Alberta Forest Conservation Steering Committee, *Alberta Forest Conservation Strategy* (1997), 17–18.

26 Interestingly, the government's insistence that industrial activity is compatible with protecting an area has been rejected by the leading organization in the province's petroleum sector – the Canadian Association of Petroleum Producers.

27 Manitoba, Department of the Environment, 'Summary Report,' 20 Sept. 1999. http://www.gov.mb.ca/environ/pages/archive/summaries/173–3.html

28 Joel Novek, 'Environmental Impact Assessment and Sustainable Development: Case Studies of Environmental Conflict,' *Society and Natural Resources* vol. 8, 1995, 153.

29 Manitoba , 'Environment Act Licence Issued to Tolko Manitoba Inc.,' news release, 15 Jan. 1998.

30 Telephone interview, Don Sullivan, Taiga Rescue Network, 3 Sept. 1999; see also Don Sullivan, 'A cut too far ... Logging the Manitoba/Saskatchewan bor-

der,' in *Taiga News* 24, April 1998; and Don Sullivan in Senate, Standing Senate Committee on Agriculture and Forestry, *Proceedings of the Subcommittee on the Boreal Forest, First Session, 36th Parliament, 1997–98*, no. 13, 16 Nov. 1998. Dissatisfaction with the CEC and the provincial environmental assessment process has led environmentalists to use the courts to try, so far unsuccessfully, to force the federal government to conduct environmental assessments of forestry operations such as road and bridge construction.

31 Canada-Saskatchewan Partnership Agreement in Forestry, *Saskatchewan Long-Term Integrated Forest Resource Management Plan*, March 1995.

32 Monique M. Ross, *Forest Management in Canada* (Calgary: Canadian Institute of Resources Law, 1995) 174.

33 Saskatchewan, 'Scott Announces Unique Forest Science Advisory Board,' news release, 20 May 1999.

34 Saskatchewan, 'Minister Announces Decision on NorSask's 20 Year Forest Management Plan,' M2 presswire, 15 May 1997.

35 For an account of the development of co-management in the NorSask FMA, see T. M. Beckley and D. Korber, *Clear Cuts, Conflict, and Co-Management: Experiments in Consensus Forest Management in Northwest Saskatchewan*, Northern Forestry Centre, Information Report, NOR-X-349 (Edmonton: Canadian Forestry Service, 1996).

36 Saskfor MacMillan is now part of Weyerhaeuser's Saskatchewan operations. This resulted from the sale of the Saskatchewan government's 49 per cent share of Saskfor MacMillan to MacMillan Bloedel in May 1999 and Weyerhaeuser's takeover of MacMillan Bloedel one month later.

37 Confidential correspondence with author, 30 Aug. 1999; 'Tree Plan Takes Root,' *Saskatoon Star-Phoenix*, 20 April 1999. The environmental assessment of Weyerhaeuser's twenty-year plan was delayed because of the revisions it made to its business plan and its loss of a significant portion of its cutting area. The assessment of Weyerhaeuser's EIS still was not completed in September 1999.

38 On policy cycles see Howlett and Rayner.

39 Wilson, this volume.

40 Michael Finley, 'The Future of Saskatchewan's Forests,' http://www3.sk.sympatico.ca/mfinley/future.html 20 September

41 http://www.link.ca/20 year plan/

42 'Forestry Expansion Draws Fire,' in *Saskatoon Star-Phoenix*, 27 April 1999.

43 'Co-Management Board Members Fed Up with Government,' in *Saskatchewan Star-Phoenix*, 8 May 1999.

44 See the testimony of Steve Stinson of the CPPA in Senate, Standing Senate Committee on Agriculture and Forestry, *Proceedings of the Subcommittee on the Boreal Forest, First Session, 36th Parliament, 1997–98*, no. 6 (17 April 1997), 9.

The CPPA also felt that three other key issues needed to be addressed: capital tax levies that harmed investment in capital-intensive industries; the cost implications of regulatory changes to the energy and transportation sectors; access to international markets.

45 Larry Pratt and John Richards, *Prairie Capitalism: Power and Influence in the New West* (Toronto: McClelland and Stewart, 1979) 168.
46 Ibid., 215.
47 Pratt and Urquhart, *The Last Great Forest*, 50.
48 Robert L. Mansell and Michael B. Percy, *Strength in Adversity: A Study of the Alberta Economy* (Edmonton: University of Alberta Press, 1990) 118.
49 At the time, Crestbrook also was controlled by Mitsubishi and Oji Paper. In January 1999 Tembec Inc. made a takeover bid for all of Crestbrook's common shares. Mitsubishi and Oji sold their shares to Tembec and the Quebec-based forest products company now is the sole owner of Crestbrook.
50 'Crestbrook Wagers on a Brighter Pulp Future,' *Financial Times (of Canada)*, 81(39), 24 April 1993.
51 Crestbrook Forest Industries, 'Crestbrook Announces Sale of Al-Pac Mill and Results for the Year Ended December 31, 1997,' news release, 3 March 1998.
52 See Natural Resources Canada, Canadian Forestry Service, *The State of Canada's Forests, 1995–1996*, Figure 3.9, Trends in the destination of Canada's wood pulp exports (volume), 1996, 54.
53 See http://www.cppa.org/english/info/graph3g.htm
54 D.A. Neilson and Robert Flynn, *The 1997 Edition: The International Woodchip and Pulplog Trade*, 6. (Petoria: D.A. Neilson and Associates, 1997)
55 Bank of Montreal, *Global Monitor*, 5 Feb. 1998. http://www.bmo.com/economic/ econ.htm The specific predictions are from Craig Alexander, Toronto-Dominion Bank, 'The Aftermath of the Asian Crisis,' http:// www.tdbank.ca/tdbank/Research/Economic_Reports/issues/May7/asian.htm
56 Carolyn Leitch, 'Asian Crisis Blow to Forestry, Noranda Says,' *Globe and Mail*, 14 Nov. 1997, B5; Alberta Forest Products Association, 'Forest Product Markets Uncertain as Asian Crisis Continues,' news release , 28 Jan. 1998; Crestbrook Forest Industries, 'Press Release,' 23 Oct. 1997; Canadian Pulp and Paper Association, 'Press Release,' 30 Jan. 1998; Bank of Montreal, 'Asian Flu: Minor Flu or Major Malady?,' 9 Dec. 1997, http://www.bmo.com/economic/econ.htm
57 Much of the damage in the pulp sector may be attributed to Alberta's importance as an exporter of hardwood market pulp to several Asian countries. For example, in 1996 Alberta supplied 59 per cent of Canada's hardwood pulp exports to South Korea. On the general impact of the Asian crisis see

Alberta Forest Products Association, 'Forest Product Markets Uncertain as Asian Crisis Continues,' (news release), 28 Jan. 1998 and Alberta Forest Products Association, 'Lumber and Pulp Still the Drivers for Solid Market Recovery,' (news release), 23 July 1998.

58 Neilson and Flynn, *The 1997 Edition: The International Woodchip and Pulplog Trade*, 54.

59 The 1986 figures are taken from AAP Newsfeed, 'Profile – Indonesia's Pulp & Paper Industry,' 18 Feb. 1998. The 1997 figures are taken from J.H. Manarung and Anton Santoso, 'Profile – Indonesia's Pulp and Paper Industry,' *Asia Pulse*, 15 July 1998.

60 'Nearly a Tiger,' *Asian Business* 33(9), 1997.

61 AAP Newsfeed, 'Profile – Indonesia's Pulp & Paper Industry,' 18 Feb. 1998.

62 Neilson and Flynn, *The 1997 Edition: The International Woodchip and Pulplog Trade*, 54.

63 PR Newswire, 'Asia Pulp And Paper Reports Financial Results For The Third Quarter And Nine Months Ended 30 September 1997,' 17 Dec. 1997; PR Newswire, 'S&P Takes Action on 18 Indonesian Corporate Entities,' 9 Jan. 1998.

64 PR Newswire, 'APRIL Reviews Current Financial Position, Operations and Expansion Plan,' 3 Feb. 1998. The current 500,000 tpy expansion program is delayed due to the failure of European equipment suppliers' banks to accept Indonesian banks' letters of credit that have been established by company.

65 See PR Newswire, 'APRIL Fine Paper Announces Start-Up of First Paper Machine,' 6 April 1998; 'Finnish Firm to Fund April's China Mill,' *Business Times (Singapore)*, 7 March 1998.

66 For a North American transnational such as Champion, this alliance promises to deliver earnings greater than the firm's cost of capital, give the company access to products which fit well with Champion's Brazilian and North American products, and improve the company's knowledge of Asian markets. Source: Business Wire, 'Champion International Corporation and The APRIL Group Sign Marketing and Sales Agreement,' 11 January 1998. APP has formed a similar marketing alliance with Itochu in Japan. See 'Itochu, APP Alliance Will Aid Sourcing,' *Pulp and Paper Week*, 17 March 1997.

67 The Minister of Environmental Protection refused to release the final report to the author, citing commercial confidentiality.

68 APRIL's costs are taken from PR Newswire, 'APRIL Announces Full Year 1997 Results,' 6 April 1998. The costs per ton (year unspecified) for the three Canadian mills were $300, $342, and $368 respectively. These figures are taken from Fred Wilson, 'The Unanswered Questions for Alberta's Pulp and Paper Industry,' unpublished paper, Sept. 1997.

69 'Analysis – Japan's Paper & Pulp Makers Face Competition,' *Asia Pulse*, 19 Dec. 1997.
70 'Forex Losses a "Time Bomb" for Listed Firms,' *Jakarta Post*, 15 July 1998.
71 Federal News Service, 'Prepared Testimony of W. Henson Moore, President and CEO, American Forest and Paper Association (AF&PA) Before the House Ways and Means Committee, Subcommittee on Trade,' 24 Feb. 1998. See also his testimony before the Senate Finance Committee in July 1998. Federal News Service, 'Prepared Testimony of Henson Moore, President and CEO, American Forest and Paper Association (AF&PA) Before the Senate Finance Committee,' 14 July 1998.
72 'Profile – Indonesia's Pulp and Paper Industry,' *Asia Pulse*, 15 July 1998. The attractiveness of Indonesian pulp also may be seen in reports of increasing imports to the United States and news that an Australian paper mill will close its pulping operations and replace the locally produced pulp with Indonesian pulp. See 'Forest Product Rates nose-dive,' *Journal of Commerce*, 17 Aug. 1998 and Don Woolford, 'AMCOR says Burnie Pulp Mill to Close,' AAP Newsfeed, 3 June 1998.
73 Gazeta Mercantil Online, 'Paper Industry Will Adjust to Prices,' 10 Dec. 1997.
74 PR Newswire, 'APRIL Announces Third Quarter 1997 Results and Updates Progress on Expansion Projects,' 1 Dec. 1997.
75 PR Newswire, 'Asia Pulp And Paper Reports Financial Results For The Third Quarter And Nine Months Ended 30 September 1997,' 17 Dec. 1997.
76 Canadian Pulp and Paper Association, 'Canada's Pulp & Paper Industry Posts Record Shipments; 1998 Focus on Restructuring and Cost Competitiveness,' press release, 30 Jan. 1998. See also the CPPA's.
77 Alberta, *Seizing Opportunity: Alberta's New Economic Development Strategy* (Edmonton: Government of Alberta, 1993) 4.
78 Millar Western Industries only injected $6.5 million into the $204.5 million mill. The other sources of financing for the mill were a $70 million bank term loan and an $8 million bank operating loan. See Millar Western Industries, 'Millar Western Industries Ltd. Responds to Alberta Government's Announcement,' (news release), 3 April 1998.
79 'Province Put Loan at Risk When It Wouldn't give $20 M More,' Larry Johnsrude, *Edmonton Journal*, 4 April 1997, A1.
80 59.8%. As of 30 Sept. 1997 the company's long-term debt was $163.7 million. See Millar Western Forest Products Ltd., *Preliminary Prospectus Dated October 21, 1997*, 34.

81 Millar Western's timing could not have been worse when it came to its initial public offering. The Asian financial crisis devastated the market values of Canadian forest products firms and led Millar Western, Harmac Pacific, and E. B. Eddy to withdraw their initial public offerings.

82 According to the terms of the loan, interest on the loan accrued and was capitalized until 28 Feb. 1997. Beginning in March 1997 the loan called for Alberta–Pacific to make monthly payments on the additional accrued interest to the extent of available project cash flow. No payments were ever made.

83 The Liberals' estimate of the provincial loss is reported in 'Government lets Al-Pac off the hook,' Allan Chambers, *Edmonton Journal*, 4 March 1998, A1. Critics of the sale argued that the Klein government, like the Getty government before it, did not bargain hard enough with the Japanese. This argument would seem to be supported by the announcement that Mitsubishi and Oji Paper would be putting approximately $US 175 million of new capital into the business. See 'Japan/Far East economic/corporate news summary,' *AFX News*, 30 April 1998.

84 The position of the Pulp and Paper Producers is summarized in Paul McLoughlin, *Alberta Political Scan*, no. 209, 5 Dec. 1997, 7–8.

85 See, e.g., 'Speaking Notes for a Speech by K. Linn Macdonald, President and C.E.O., Noranda Forest Products Inc., to the Empire Club, Toronto,' 13 Nov. 1997. The speech is available from the Canadian Pulp and Paper Association's website. See http://www.cppa.org/english/news/speech81.htm

86 Jim Shepherd, the C.E.O. of Alberta–Pacific before its sale in 1998, said in Crestbrook's 1996 Annual Report that his focus would be to 'reduce costs vigorously.' See http://www.crestbrook.com/finance/ar4.html

Chapter Twelve

The British Columbia Forest Practices Code: Formalization and Its Effects

George Hoberg

Overview[1]

Throughout the 1990s, the forests of British Columbia have been the flashpoint for some of the most dramatic environmental controversies in Canada. Conflicts have raged between forest companies and workers, on the one hand, and environmental groups, both domestic and international, on the other hand. The provincial government has struggled to manage the controversy, and introduced a number of significant policy reforms, including a strategy to resolve land use conflicts, a review of timber supply, and a 'forest renewal' program to invest in ecological restoration and improving the productivity of the land base. The centrepiece of policy reform efforts was the B.C. Forest Practices Code (FPC), a comprehensive new legislative framework to guide forest planning and regulate forest practices.

Forest practices regulations address the issue of how to design policies to mitigate the undesirable consequences of timber harvesting. For example, there are significant controversies over the practice of clear-cutting – harvesting all the trees in one area at a time – and policies have been designed to limit the size of clear-cuts, and how much the new forest has to grow before adjacent areas can be harvested. Logging also affects fish and wildlife habitat, and policies have been designed to limit those impacts. The construction and maintenance of roads to provide access to harvestable stands is another major concern of forest practices regulations.

In designing regulations, policy-makers strive to strike an appropriate balance between the economic benefits of logging and the consequences of logging for other values of concern in the forest, including ecological, esthetic, and recreational values. One of the great dilemmas in forestry is tailoring policy design to the exceptionally varied and complex nature of the problem. Historically, this has been done by granting large amounts of discretion to professional foresters (public and private) to manage the forests according to their best professional judgment. As public values changed, forestry became a far more contested policy arena. As the public demanded more environmental values from the forest, trust in professional foresters declined significantly. One of the resulting trends has been an effort to *formalize* policy into binding rules and regulations. While this serves the objective of making forest management more transparent and accountable to the public, it creates problems if overly rigid and uniform rules prevent foresters from implementing the most appropriate practices. The B.C. Forest Practices Code, enacted in 1994, is a dramatic example of formalization and the dilemmas it poses.

This chapter examines the B.C. government's attempts to formalize forest policy through the code. The first section provides an overview of the concept of formalization. The second section analyses the historical background of the code. The focus then shifts to an analysis of the content and structure of the code through the lens of formalization, including the significant changes that were introduced in 1998. The final section addresses the impacts of these changes on the dynamics within the policy regime.

Formalization: A Conceptual Introduction

Formalization is an issue of both policy and institutional design. This chapter focuses on two aspects of formalization. The first, which I will call *regulatory formalization*, involves elevating the legal status of the policy instruments designed to influence forest practices, for example, moving from a voluntary guideline to a mandatory regulation. In addition to the legal formality of the instrument, policy-makers face a number of other complex issues of regulatory design. The second aspect of formalization, which I will call *procedural formalization*, involves opening up the regulatory procedures and processes to foster more public input and awareness. In both cases, the government is usually sacrificing discretion and flexibility for some other value.

In terms of regulatory design, the first issue is the level of legal formality. Policy-makers can rely on guidelines, which are meant to inform the judgment of those implementing the policy but are not supported by any kind of administrative or legal sanctions. In contrast, formal rules and regulations are legally required and are backed up with sanctions, either administrative penalties such as stop-work orders or fines, or criminal penalties pursued through the judicial process.

In addition to the legal formality of the instrument, regulatory design involves complex questions about how to configure the rule to match the problem. One of the few efforts to articulate criteria for policy design is put forth by Colin Diver in his framework for thinking about 'optimal regulatory precision.'[2] Diver distinguishes between three criteria: simplicity, transparency, and congruence. Simplicity refers to the number of steps involved in the decision rule. Transparency refers to the clarity of the rule: in the same situation, different people will interpret the rule in the same manner. Congruence is the most difficult of the criteria to articulate. It refers to the match between the design of the rule and the problem it is intended to address. A congruent rule will not 'overinclude' by being applied in situations where it is inappropriate, nor will it 'underinclude' by failing to be applied in situations where it should be applied.

Diver uses the example of a speed limit to illustrate the differences in the criteria and the dilemmas confronting efficient rule design. A uniform speed limit, such as 80 kilometres per hour, has the virtue of simplicity and transparency. It rests on a single variable that is relatively easily measured, whether by a speedometer or a radar gun. The problem is that the rule is not congruent – there may be some situations (e.g., a clear dry day with little traffic) in which higher speeds are safe, and others (snow or ice) in which only substantially lower speeds are safe. A speed limit that would attempt to address this problem of congruence, for example, one that says 'drive safely depending on the conditions,' would increase problems of transparency.

Clearly, policy-makers face a much more complex task in establishing forest policy. Not only do they face difficult trade-offs between economic and environmental values, but they also confront a wide variety of conditions across different landscapes and across different biogeoclimatic zones. Different animal species have different habitat requirements. Appropriate requirements for stream protection will differ, depending on whether fish are present, the species in question, and the size of the stream, among other things. British Columbia has fourteen major biogeoclimatic zones – forest practices that may be perfectly appropriate in some places may be quite inappropriate in others. The ecological impacts of large clear-cuts may be substantially different in a forest ecosystem, such as boreal forests in the northern interior, where large fires are a frequent occurrence in nature, than they would be in the coastal zone where such natural disturbances are less frequent and less dramatic.

Given this dramatic situational and geographic variation, uniform, one-size-fits-all rules are likely to be inappropriate. A uniform rule designed to protect the most sensitive site will overregulate a less sensitive one. One designed to protect the least sensitive will underregulate more sensitive ones. A rule designed to address the mean will overregulate in some areas and underregulate in others.

In such a situation, there are two quite different approaches to improving congruence. One is based on dramatically increasing the complexity of the rules so that they vary to take into account all possible permutations. While improving congruence, this approach departs from simplicity, and may be administratively impractical to develop, and very cumbersome to implement. The alternative approach is to rely on professional discretion by delegating significant authority to working foresters to adopt the practice they deem to be appropriate in the circumstance. This approach has the advantage of simplicity, but it sacrifices transparency.

The challenging task of policy-makers is to strike an optimal balance between simplicity, transparency, and congruence, given the particular problem confronting regulators. In trying to strike this balance, policy-makers consider economic criteria of costs (administrative and compliance) and benefits of different combinations of the three variables. But they also need to consider political criteria, such as legitimacy and accountability. In some cases there may be significant tensions between economic and political criteria. For example, policy design that relies on professional discretion may be economically desirable, but the lack of transparency may create significant problems with accountability.

Regarding procedural formalization, the key issue is the design of the process for making, implementing, and evaluating policies, in particular who participates in the process and who has access to what information. Processes may be relatively closed, for example, a clientelist relationship between the government and a regulated industry, where other interests lack effective input and little information is revealed about policies and their effects. When the policy environment becomes more pluralistic, such a closed system is typically hard to sustain. Competing interests demand a greater say in policy, and they pressure the government to open up the process and provide them with easily accessible information so they can monitor policy implementation.

In designing procedures, policy-makers have two main concerns. First, they need to maintain sufficient legitimacy of the policy process, so they have to accommodate the procedural demands of powerful interest groups. Second, they need to monitor bureaucratic implementation to ensure that it is meeting government objectives and, thus, confront the problem of obtaining adequate information to do so. In a clientelist, bipartite system in which the government is only concerned about serving one interest (in this case, the forest sector), the government can be relatively certain that bureaucrats will not depart too far from the interests of their clients, or if they did so, the industry would be sure to inform the government.

In a more pluralistic environment, in which the government is concerned about placating diverse interests, the monitoring problems increase. The government may be willing to increase the freedom of information so that it can receive a more balanced assessment of its policies. There are costs to the government, however. It needs to be careful not to hamstring bureaucracy so much that it becomes incapable of effectively delivering policy benefits. And it runs the risk that greater openness will expose bureaucratic activities that are a political liability to the government.

These concepts help illuminate the significance of the transformation of forest policy embodied in the B.C. Forest Practices Code. The history of the code is the history of the government responding to increasingly powerful environmental interests by dramatically increasing both regulatory and procedural formality. That move was made to address the threat to the legitimacy of forest sector policies posed by escalating environmental demands. As we will see, formalization has come with considerable costs.

Historical Background

Prior to the 1990s, forest policy in British Columbia was strongly oriented towards promoting the forest industry and did not provide much protection for environmental values. As the environmental movement gained power in the late 1960s, the government responded in largely symbolic ways.[3] Environmental values did not find their way into governing statutes until 1978.[4] The Forest Act referred to environmental values only by implication, proclaiming that among the factors to be considered in the determination of the allowable annual cut were 'the constraints on the amount of timber produced from the area that reasonably can be expected by use for purposes other than timber production' (sec. 7(3)(a)(v)). In laying out the 'purposes and functions' of the Ministry of Forests, the act outlined five objectives, only one of which directly mentioned environmental values, and even then it did so in the context of balancing them with industrial values. Section 4(c) directs the ministry to 'plan the use of the forest and range resources of the Crown, so that the production of timber and forage, the harvesting of timber, the grazing of livestock and the realization of fisheries, wildlife, water, outdoor recreation and other natural resource values are coordinated and integrated.'

Prior to the enactment of the code, in the mid-1990s, forest practices were regulated in British Columbia largely through the licence agreements between forest companies and the government. While there have been no systematic studies of forest practices in this earlier period, enforcement of these standards was very spotty, especially during the notorious period of 'sympathetic administration' that characterized provincial forest policy during the first part of the 1980s. In some areas and for some specific resources, there were regional guidelines that were used as the basis for provisions in licences. In the case of clear-cutting, there were no limits in statute or regulation on clear-cut size. As a result, limitations on clear-cutting varied significantly from area to area, both in the average and maximum size of clear-cut allowed, and the regulatory force of the limits. For instance, the Okanagan timber supply area plan contained a limit on the maximum average cutblock size of less than 30 hectares, but allowed clear-cuts up to 50 hectares.[5] On the coast, the initial 1972 *Coast Planning Guidelines* established a maximum cutblock size of 80 hectares, but, as a result of 'sympathetic administration,' this limit was not enforced after 1980.[6] The 1992 *Coast Harvest Planning Guidelines* stated that new-cut blocks 'should average 40 hectares.' Prior to 1992, there were also no limits on adjacency, or how soon an area next to an existing clear-cut could be logged. The 1972 coast guidelines required 'leave areas' between cutblocks, but that guideline was not enforced after 1980. The 1992 coast guidelines for the Vancouver region required that clear-cut blocks need to reach 'free growing stage' before adjacent blocks could be logged. [7] In 1990, 92.3 per cent of the area harvested province-wide was clear-cut.[8]

In the case of riparian area protection, forest practices were also governed by non-binding guidelines with substantial regional variation.

Coastal areas were governed by the *British Columbia Coastal Fisheries Forestry Guidelines,* initially established in 1988 and updated in 1993. These guidelines were established in a classic bargaining process between the federal Department of Fisheries and Oceans,[9] the B.C. Ministry of Forests, the B.C. Ministry of Environment, and the industry trade group, the Council on Forest Industries.[10] The guidelines defined four classes of streams, each class being associated with specific fisheries values and forest management objectives. The guidelines set out 'Streamside management zones' that were 10 to 30 metres wide, depending on the stream width. Within the first 10 metres adjacent to the stream, harvesting was not permitted, although exceptions to prevent destructive windthrow were allowed. Partial cutting was permitted in the rest of the zone, subject to the relatively restrictive requirement of maintaining 'original stand characteristics.' There were no region-wide guidelines for the B.C. interior, but some specific areas had them. For example, the Okanagan timber supply area had its own guidelines. The minimum width of a streamside management zone was greater (20 metres) but the limits on harvesting within the zone were far less stringent – there was no 'no harvest strip' and harvesting within the zone could remove up to 50 per cent of the preharvest closure.[11] While these guidelines were non-binding, they did attain greater legal force if they were included in stand-specific cutting plans.

In addition to this relatively informal set of policies on forest practices, there was a somewhat more formal procedural framework for planning and appeals. Since the implementation of the Forest Act of 1978, a complex planning process emerged, in which timber companies and the government engaged in a multilevel process of developing plans and getting approvals before road-building and logging was to commence. These procedures provided for public notice and comment at various stages, the significantly increasing the access of the public to information about planning process. The effect of the framework was limited somewhat by the uncertain legal nature of the planning framework, revealed through several lawsuits initiated by environmental groups in the early 1990s.

In one case, the Western Canada Wilderness Committee attempted to halt old-growth logging in the Nahmint Valley on MacMillan Bloedel's tree farm licence 44, arguing that the chief forester violated the Forest Act by (1) extending MB's management and working plan (MWP) for the tree farm licence past its expiration date while MacMillan Bloedel completed a new MWP, (2) approving preharvest silviculture plans and cutting permits and allowing logging road construction in the absence of a new management and working plan. In May 1991, the B.C. Supreme Court held that the chief forester is entitled to extend the term of the MWP. In justifying the decision, the judge cited Section 152 of the Forest Act: 'Except with respect to the Crown, the minister may extend a time required for doing anything under this Act.' The court also upheld the silviculture plan and cutting permit. The lone environmental victory was the ruling that MacMillan Bloedel could not build roads beyond those areas where logging has been approved unless it had a valid road permit.[12]

Logging companies quickly adapted to this court ruling. In a similar case in the Tsikita Valley, another area highly valued by environmentalists, MacMillan Bloedel temporarily suspended road building and applied for a road permit, which was quickly approved by the district manager of the Ministry of Forests. The Western Canada Wilderness Committee returned to the courts arguing that the district manager cannot issue a road permit until the company has the 'right to harvest' timber which, in turn, is not granted until a preharvest silviculture plan is filed under the Forest Act. The B.C. Supreme Court disagreed in this case and one other case,[13] and in a similar case involving the approval of logging in the absence of an approved five-year development plan.[14] The effect of these rulings was to insulate the ministry's approval of timber-harvesting activities from environmental challenges through the courts, and reduce the effect of more comprehensive planning requirements on particular harvesting activities.

These cases show the limited opportunities available for environmental groups to use the courts to influence forest policy. Environmental groups also lacked the right to launch administrative appeals. Under the Forest Act, licence holders could appeal government decisions about plans or allowable cut determinations in a quasi-judicial process, but members of the public or their representatives could not.

Historically, timber-oriented objectives dominated forest policy. The dominant mode of policy instruments was a complex and confusing mix of non-binding guidelines and site-specific provisions contained in permits or licences. In terms of Diver's concepts, they were complex, relatively opaque, and congruent. As a result of this mode of regulation, forest practices regulations were characterized by a limited or uncertain legal basis, substantial regional variation, and weak enforcement. Regarding procedures, a planning framework was in place, but the lack of procedural formality limited its effectiveness, at least in the eyes of environmentalists.

Pressures for Reform

There were four essential sources of pressure for change in B.C. forest practices regulation.[15] The first was public opinion. When the environmental issue exploded onto the public agenda in the late 1980s, B.C. forestry came under intensive scrutiny. These pressures were strong enough to lead even a recalcitrant Social Credit government to initiate code development. In the summer of 1991, Socred Minister of Forests Claude Richmond issued a 'discussion paper' requesting input into what kind of approach should be pursued. In the overview to the six-page brochure, Richmond stated, 'I believe the question is not whether we need a code ... but how we can put a code into place.' The letter concludes, 'Based on your response, the Ministry of Forests will develop a forest practices code.'[16]

The second pressure for change was the election of the Harcourt government. The momentum for change in B.C. forestry accelerated dramatically after the election of the NDP government in late 1991 brought to power a government far greener in orientation than its predecessor. Indeed, the NDP platform explicitly called for the enactment of a Forest Practices Act as part of its environmental agenda.[17] The existence of a new party in power lessened the chances that the government would reverse its plans to develop a code.

The third source of pressure for change was a series of reports suggesting the existing approach to forest practices was failing. In particular, the publication of two reports (the so-called Tripp reports) investigating the impacts of forest practices on salmon habitat embarrassed forest companies and the government, and prompted calls for reform. An investigation of compliance with the fisheries guidelines on Vancouver Island exposed practices that led even the minister of forests to claim that he was 'absolutely appalled' and that the practices were 'completely unacceptable.'[18] The report found that when the guidelines were followed, they were reasonably effective, but in general compliance with the guidelines was poor, including those for streamside management zones. The report concluded: 'There was, on average, one major or moderate impact on one stream for every cut block inspected.'[19] A follow-up report examining the entire coastal region found similar levels of non-compliance.[20]

These fisheries reports were important not only because they contributed to the view that there were significant problems with the existing policy framework, but they promoted a particular definition of the policy problem that promoted formalization as a solution. The reports found that when the guidelines were implemented, they worked. The problem was that the guidelines were not being followed in enough situations. The recommended solution was two-fold: strengthen the legal force behind the standards, and step up enforcement.

The fourth, and ultimately most influential, source of pressure for change was the international campaign orchestrated by the environmental movement. Environmentalists began laying the groundwork for the campaign in the late 1980s and early 1990s. One of the tactics was to frame B.C. forestry as the 'Brazil of the North' to take advantage of the strong public sentiment against deforestation of tropical rainforests.[21] The campaign intensified dramatically in the wake of the Clayoquot Sound controversy during the summer of 1993, attracting considerable attention from prominent environmental groups and celebrities. Visits by the Australian rock band Midnight Oil and Robert Kennedy, Jr, a representative of the U.S. group the Natural Resources Defense Council attracted a great deal of attention to the cause. Environmentalists began pressuring consumers, especially in Europe, to boycott B.C. forest products. While few contracts were actually cancelled, the campaign was influential enough that it convinced the industry that regulatory reform was necessary in order to maintain market share.[22]

As a result of this distinctive combination of pressures for change, the major solution that emerged was the consolidation of the existing patchwork of guidelines and regulations into one over-arching piece of legislation. The official genesis of the proposal seems to be the 1991 *Report of the Forest Resource Commission*. The report recommended 'a single, all-encompassing code of forest practices through the introduction of a Forest Practices Act.'[23] The Ministry of Forests' July 1991 discussion paper explicitly mentions the report as the genesis for the idea. The NDP picked up on this idea and included it in its platform for the 1991 election.

The proposal for a comprehensive legislative code emerged from a particular definition of the policy problem in the early 1990s. In a 1993 public document, the government defined the problems as follows:[24]

- 'Insufficient legal powers – lack of a single, consistently applied forest practices act':[25] At the time, forest and range management activities were said to be governed by twenty-six statutes, 700 regulations, and 3,000 guidelines, and this bewildering patchwork needed to be consolidated and rationalized.

- 'Lack of strong, up-to-date rules governing all areas of forest and range practices': Standards have been applied inconsistently across regions and in some cases do not exist at all.
- 'Occurrences of poor and inconsistent industry performance' in ensuring 'basic stewardship requirements.'
- 'Inadequate monitoring and enforcement': Staff cutbacks in the 1980s reduced monitoring and placed greater responsibilities on companies for monitoring and reporting.
- 'Weak penalties': In some areas the government lacked authority to fine non-compliance; in areas where fines were authorized, the maximum penalty of $2,000 was considered inadequate to deter violations.
- 'Insufficient auditing' by government of company forest practices.

In the context of heightened domestic and international political scrutiny of B.C. forest practices, the pre-code framework created two specific problems. First, to the extent that the government did have standards in place, the exceptionally complex nature of the regulatory framework made it difficult to present and explain them to the public, both domestically and internationally. Second, as the Tripp reports revealed, the non-binding nature of the standards was undermining their effectiveness. The solution that emerged was a formalization of the regulatory framework into a comprehensive, statutory code of practice.

In November 1993, the NDP government released a discussion paper on the code along with proposed rules. The basic process was one of assembling and improving existing standards, and the paper proposed to codify many of them in law. No great break from the past was envisioned, such as a move to an incentives or a 'result-based' approach.[26]

Adopting the Forest Practices Code

Promising a 'new regime of accountability,' the government introduced the Forest Practices Code Act of British Columbia to the legislature in mid-May 1994.[27] In doing so, it emphasized the enactment of 'world class forest practices' and stiff enforcement penalties of up to $1 million a day. The government estimated the code would cost between $250 and $300 million per year.[28] Draft regulations were issued later that month. In releasing the proposed standards, Minister of Forests Andrew Petter stated: 'Unlike many current standards, the proposed new standards are mandatory and enforceable. They limit the size of cutblocks, protect community watersheds and will ban clear-cuts where alternative harvesting systems are more appropriate. Ecological requirements will drive decisions on appropriate harvesting methods.'[29] The code act was enacted by the legislature on 7 July 1994. On 12 April 1995, eighteen regulations and sixteen high-priority guidebooks were released, followed by others over the next month. The code provided for a transitional period of implementation that began in June 1995 and was completed in June 1997.

Structurally, the FPC has three layers: the code act enacted by the B.C. Legislature, a series of binding regulations issued through order-in-council, and a set of non-binding guidebooks meant to guide implementation of specific provisions. Functionally, the code has three components: forest practices, planning, and enforcement.

Regulatory Formalization in the FPC

It is difficult to assess precisely how the code changed policies in specific areas of forest practices. Following through on the two specific types of forest practices we examined earlier, we can see that there has been substantial change both in the formality of the instrument, the setting of the instrument, and to some extent the design of the instrument. In the case of clear-cutting, as described above, there were no clearly defined rules prior to the code. In the code's operational planning regulation, specific legal limits were placed on clear-cut size: 40 hectares in the coastal and southern interior regions, and 60 hectares in the northern interior regions. In coastal regions, this changed a guideline average of 40 hectares to a legal maximum of 40 hectares. In the interior, legal limits were imposed where none had existed before. Note that there is still some regional variation here in an effort to make the regulations congruent – to a certain extent they are designed to capture the different 'natural disturbance types' in the divergent ecological regions of the province.

The case of stream protection follows a similar pattern. On the coast, non-binding guidelines on required buffer strips and other features were transformed into binding regulations. In addition to formalizing the instrument, the settings on the instrument were also changed to be more protective of the resource. The *Coastal Fisheries / Forestry Guidelines* (*CF/FG*) required 'streamside management zones' for fish-bearing streams to be as long as channel widths on both sides of the stream. The guidelines stated that 'Generally, all trees within 10 m of the stream-banks should be retained,' but allowed for exemptions with the

Table 12.1 B.C. Forest Practices Code stream protection rules

Riparian class*	Average channel width (m)	Reserve zone width (m)	Management zone width (m)	Total RMA width (m)
S1 large rivers	≥100	0	100	100
S1 (except large rivers)	>20	50	20	70
S2	>5≤20	30	20	50
S3	1.5≤5	20	20	40
S4	<1.5	0	30	30
S5	>3	0	30	30
S6	≤3	0	20	20

S1–S4: Fish stream or community watershed
S5–S6: Not fish stream and not in community watershed
Source: *Riparian Management Guidebook.*

approval of fisheries departments. As shown in Table 12.1, the code increased the buffer strips significantly for streams greater than 1.5 metres in width. (Fish streams less than 1.5 metres in width (S4 under the code), often important co-habitat, get less protection under the code than under the *CF/FG.*) In addition to the no-harvest buffer strip, the code provides for 'management zones' beyond the 'reserve zone' where limited logging was intended. Thus, the code significantly increased stream protection on the coast. In the interior, the province-wide standards in the code meant even more dramatic change, because there were no regional guidelines in place.

While the stream protection rules apply province-wide, the *Riparian Management Area Guidebook* developed to supplement the regulations does contain recommendations that vary regionally. For instance, the 'best management practice' suggested for small fish streams on the coast (S4) is to retain 50 per cent of trees within 10 metres of the bank. In the interior it is recommended that all the trees within 10 metres of the bank be retained.[30]

Thus, for the two examples of forest practices, the biggest change was in the degree of legal formality of the instrument. There were also changes in the setting. The level of congruence also changed, but not as dramatically. For clear-cuts, a patchwork of different regional guidelines was simplified into two categories. In the case of stream protection, the general level of congruence seems to be relatively constant – both policies were quite complex. The code combines a formal rule with variation by stream type with non-binding guidelines that enhance regional variation.

Procedural Formalization in the FPC

Planning

Arguably, the Forest Practices Code is more of a framework for planning than it is a 'forest practices code' per se. 'Higher level plans' are essentially zoning decisions about what sorts of emphasis are given to what values – they include resource management zones, landscape unit objectives, and sensitive area designations. These higher level plans guide the development of 'operational plans' oriented towards more specific aspects of forestry. Originally the FPC provided for six operational plans: forest development plans, logging plans, silviculture prescriptions, stand management prescriptions, five-year silviculture plans, and access management plans. The central planning document was the Forest development plan (FDP), a five-year plan laying out all the proposed management activities for the area. The most important site-specific plan is the silviculture prescription (SP). One of the most important features of the act was that once higher level plans were in place, operational plans had to be consistent with them. The FPC significant increased the formality of the planning procedures and provided environmentalists with new legal resources. Under the new rules, if the ministry behaved the same way it behaved in the court case described above, it would clearly be in contravention to the law.

Although it does significantly increase formality, the planning framework (and the regulatory framework) still rests on a significant amount of discretion. The code invests an enormous amount of discretionary authority in the district manager of the Ministry of Forests (there are forty-three in the province) who are responsible for approving operational plans. As a result, there is built-in flexibility to adjust requirement to local conditions. The added potential for congruence comes with the risk of abuse of discretion.

Enforcement

In addition to practices and, the FPC also introduced a new system for enforcement and compliance, including a dramatic increase in the maximum fine, from $2,000 to $1 million. In its public relations on the code, the government gave considerable emphasis to the stringent fines available as an indicator of their tough new enforcement approach. A compliance and enforcement branch was created in the Ministry of Forests, and extensive requirements for public reporting of enforcement and compliance statistics were created. The code act also provided for a Forest Appeals Commission to hear the complaints of licencees about enforcement actions.[31] The FPC did not give other members of the public, such as environmentalists, the right to appeal regulatory or enforcement decisions (or non-decisions).

Rather than freezing environmental interests out of the appeal process entirely, however, the government followed the innovative path of creating a new administrative entity, the Forest Practices Board, to act as a public watchdog. The board does not have any legal or regulatory power, but it has the authority to conduct investigations into the Ministry of Forests' implementation of the code and audit corporate forest practices. It is also established as the organization to hear complaints from the public, including environmentalists, about ministry decisions under the FPC or corporate forest practices. The board does not have authority to take action on a complaint, but it can investigate a complaint and make recommendations to the ministry. It can also launch an appeal to the Forest Appeal Commission on behalf of the public.

Thus, the Forest Practices Board acts as a buffer between public complaints and the ministry – a bureaucratic floodgate holding back the rush of complaints demanding ministry attention that would likely occur if a U.S.-style process was adopted. While ministry decisions are still insulated from direct public challenge, the Forest Practices Board – through its investigatory and auditing roles – grants the public much more access to information about ministry decisions. Much of the impact of this reform clearly depends on the role that the board chooses to play. The process has become more open and more formal, but the procedural rights of environmentalists still pale in comparison to their U.S. counterparts. Environmentalists south of the border can directly appeal administrative decisions, and when they go to court, they have far more formidable tools to bring to bear than B.C. environmentalists do.[32]

The Effects of Regulatory Formalization

The Forest Practices Code took effect in June of 1995, with a transition period for full implementation ending in June 1997. Clearly, it is too early to provide an appropriate evaluation of its implementation, but we can point to certain patterns and pressures. From a political perspective, the FPC seems to have solved some of the government's problems but not others. The good news is that polls of provincial public opinion show the government has received credit for introducing the code (although the public remains sceptical about its enforcement). The bad news comes on several fronts. The FPC has done nothing to chill the criticisms of the environmental community, and international market pressures still loom large. At the same time, the costs of implementing the code have been burdensome and have contributed to an economic crisis in the industry. In that the code's primary objective is 'balancing productive, spiritual, ecological and recreational values of forests,' it must be deemed a failure. The FPC has not provided adequate ecological benefits, and at the same time it has been a major cost burden.

Impact on Forest Practices

The government has invested little effort in tracking implementation of forest practices, at least in a manner that has been communicated to the public. Statistics on clear-cut size do exist. In 1988 and 1998 average clear-cut size across the province dropped from 43 to 26 hectares, a decline of 40 per cent, but virtually all of this decline occurred before 1995 when the code came into effect.[33] Greater attention to environmental concerns and clear-cutting, particularly in the late 1980s and early 1990s, seems to have had more direct impact on clear-cut size than the code.

On stream protection, the government has been harshly criticized for its implementation of the new regulations by the Sierra Legal Defence Fund (SLDF). In an apparent attempt to replicate the methods and influence of the Tripp reports of the first half of the decade, the SLDF issued a report blasting government and industry performance. They argued that some streams were not identified at all in plans and some streams were misclassified (e.g., as non-fish bearing when in fact fish were present). Their most striking finding was that 83 per cent of the streams they surveyed were clear-cut to their banks. For small fish-bearing streams (e.g, S4 streams which can serve as important co-habitat), 79 per cent were clear-cut to the bank. The report did note that these impacts were legal under the FPC. While no-harvest reserve zones exist for larger fish streams, the smaller streams are protected only by 'riparian management zones,' where the harvesting prescription is at the discretion of the company recommending the plan and the district manager of the Ministry of Forests approving the plan.[34]

What the SLDF report did strongly suggest is that the best practices recommended in the *Riparian Management Area Guidebook* were not being followed. Recall that on the coast, the guidebook suggests that for small fish streams on the coast (S4), 50 per cent of trees within 10 metres of the bank should be retained. The SLDF report says that 79 per cent of the streams are clear-cut to their banks. While this aspect of the report has received little attention, it does undermine one of the strongest industry criticisms of the FPC: that the non-binding guidebooks become de facto regulations because company foresters fear that the government officials will approve nothing less. If the SLDF figures are correct, they suggest that company foresters routinely recommend, and government officials routinely approve, riparian protection far less stringent than recommended in the guidebook.

The SLDF report received considerable attention from the press and sent off alarm bells in the government. The government ordered its own review, which although not nearly as critical as the one by the SLDF, did raise some significant concerns, particularly about the proper identification and classification of streams. Unlike some of the industry critics of the SLDF report, the government review emphasized the importance of small streams for fish habitat. At this point, the government took the extraordinary step of requesting that the Forest Practices Board conduct its own independent investigation.

After considerable delay, the Forest Practices Board issued its report in June 1998. The board was far more positive about riparian area protection than Sierra Legal Defence Fund, but it did note some significant problems with policy implementation. It found relatively high compliance with planning and practice requirements, and it found that the amount of alteration to streams has decreased significantly since the FPC was introduced. The biggest problem that the board found was with the classification of streams, particularly smaller streams. Nearly half the two classes of small fish streams (S3 and S4 under the code) audited were 'underclassified,' leading to 'inappropriate practices in a number of cases.'[35] The board also noted that the recommendations in the guidebooks for retention in riparian areas were frequently not followed. Among other things, the board recommended increased training to improve classification and the enactment of more specific requirements for retention

Logging Costs

Environmentalists have denounced the FPC as ineffective, and industry has complained bitterly about the costs of complying with it. In response to industry concerns, the government commissioned a study performed by the reputable accounting firm KPMG. Published in April 1997, the study suggested that the costs of the code were indeed significant. The study compared 'delivered wood costs' in 1992 and 1996, and divided the increase according to a highly refined set of categories.[36]

The results state that delivered wood costs increased from $50 per cubic metre in 1992 to $87 per cubic metre in 1996, an increase of 75 per cent. Increases in stumpage accounted for 45 per cent of the increased costs, the FPC accounted for 33 per cent of the increase, and a miscellaneous category of 'non-code-related cost drivers' accounted for the remaining 22 per cent. The fall-out from this study was confirmation of the industry's claims of dramatically increased costs. Despite the fact that stumpage hikes were shown to be a more important driver behind the cost increases than the code, the additional $12 per cubic metre of FPC-related costs – 14 per cent of total delivered wood costs – was still considered unquestionably significant in an industry with small (or negative) profit margins.[37]

The Effects of Procedural Formalization

Higher Level Plans

One of the principal objectives of the FPC was to develop a more comprehensive and integrated system of planning. Planning at the operational level appears to be working relatively well, but very significant delays have been experienced in the establishment of higher level plans. As of the end of mid-1999 only three higher level plans have been put in place for the entire province, one based on the regional land use plan for the Cariboo-Chilcotin area, and the other two based on land and resource management plans established in Kispiox and Kamloops. This leaves the overwhelming majority of the provincial forest land base without the guidance of higher level plans. The absence of higher level plans does not vitiate the code's planning framework, because district managers have a great deal of guidance in planning regulations and guidebooks.

The absence of higher level plans does create particular problems for the province's approach to protecting biodiversity. Landscape units, a type of higher level plan, are the main instrument for the implementation of biodiversity objectives. Despite the code being law for over five years, only three landscape units have been designated. The government has also yet to designate any of the other two types of higher level plans designed to protect biodiversity, namely, old-growth management areas or sensitive areas. In the absence of these plans, biodiversity is not going without protection, but the 'default' provisions to be used in the absence of landscape units is the lowest form of biodiversity emphasis provided in the *Biodiversity Guidebook*.[38]

Enforcement and Compliance

Another major thrust of the FPC was to strengthen enforcement and compliance. The code appears to be relatively successful in this regard; the compliance record is quite good. For the period June 1995 to June 1998, provincial officials conducted 113,000 inspections, about 94 per cent of which were found to be in compliance. [39] On those instances where compliance was not found, many were resolved in the field. The remainder resulted in some type of contravention decision.

The rate of compliance is quite impressive. However, the pattern of enforcement actions applied to contravention reflects overwhelming reliance on the 'softer' end of the remedy spectrum. Of a total of 1,283 contravention decisions over the three years, there have been only nine prosecutions under the tougher criminal provisions of the statute. Despite the much ballyhooed $1 million fines emphasized by the government when it introduced the FPC, no fine has come anywhere close to that maximum. The highest fine issued has been $265,000, and that to the federal government for unauthorized harvesting of Crown timber in the construction on the Alaska Highway. No other penalty has been greater than $100,000: 40 per cent of all monetary penalties have been less than $500, 60 per cent less than $1,000, and 89 per cent less than $5,000.

The dramatically expanded access to information about forest policy in the province is reflected by the fact that all of these statistics, including information revealing which particular companies have had fines levied against them, are publicly available, on the Ministry of Forests website.

Expanding Public Access to Information

One of the most important effects of the FPC was to dramatically increase the access to information by the public, including critics of forestry in the environmental movement. Perhaps the most important institutional innovation has been the Forest Practices Board, set up as an independent entity by the code to serve as a public watchdog. Because of the combination of start-up problems, limited resources, and, apparently, timid leadership, the board started very cautiously. By late 1998 and early 1999, however, the board had begun to play a far more active and confident role.

By early July 1999, the board had published eighteen audits, sixteen complaint investigations, and two special investigations. In public presentations, the board has developed a four-part assessment of the FPC. First, the board believes 'there have been changes and a significant improvement in forest practices since the code came into effect.' Through its activities, the board has observed improvements in stream protection and road building and that there is a generally high level of compliance. Second, the board notes, 'There is a need for better compliance with code requirements and a need for more effective opportunities for public involvement.' The board is less sanguine about compliance than the Ministry of Forests enforcement reports. The board observes that 'although compliance is generally high, we have identified some significant non-compliance with code requirements in more than half of the operations we have audited.' Third, 'there are important pieces of the code that have not yet been implemented,' particularly with regard to the higher level plans necessary to protect wildlife and biodiversity. Finally, the board believes that improvements are needed in the quality of plans developed under the code.[40]

The Forest Practices Board has taken a relatively low-key approach, while environmental groups have taken a very aggressive approach to policy evaluation. Led by the Sierra Legal Defence Fund, environmentalists have submitted numerous reports harshly critical of the FPC and its administration. In terms of the effects of formalization, it is important to note that much of the information revealed in these reports would not previously have been available to environmental activists.

The major reports include the following statements:

- Clear-cutting: Despite the rhetoric of the FPC, clear-cuts are still overwhelmingly the harvesting method of choice across the province – they were used in 92 per cent of approved cutblocks surveyed by SLDF.[41]
- Stream protection: An audit of coastal streams showed a surprising

number of incorrectly classified streams and that 79 per cent of small fish-bearing streams were clear-cut to the banks.[42]

- Biodiversity: The government has yet to introduce any of the major elements of the biodiversity components of the FPC, including landscape units, old-growth management areas, identified wildlife species, wildlife habitat areas, and sensitive areas.[43]
- Steep terrain logging: The government has not adequately implemented the FPC provisions designed to regulate logging on steep slopes to prevent landslides and soil erosion.[44]
- General forestry performance: Based on grades for twelve individual aspects of forestry policy, the government's forestry report card contains 8 F's and 4 D's, for a final grade of F.[45]

These reports contain a great deal of polemical, evocative, pro-environment rhetoric. However, what is distinctive about the SLDF effort (funded largely by U.S. foundations) is the detailed, careful documentation underlying the analysis. While they may not meet the standards of a professional audit, they do reflect a level of analytical sophistication that is unusual in the B.C. environmental community. The SLDF reports have helped focus environmental pressures on the government and industry and hammered home the message, lest anyone forget, that members of the public are watching. In its international campaign, Greenpeace has picked up on these reports in an effort to show the world it, too, is watching.[46]

Revising the FPC: The Surprising Persistence of Formalism

In the first half of the decade when the code was in the development stage, the B.C. economy generally was doing very well and the forest industry in particular was booming. By 1996, however, the latest cyclical downturn was well under way and the industry found itself reeling from a combination of pressures. Although lumber prices remained strong, pulp prices plummeted. Logging costs increased dramatically, as a result of the introduction of the code and the significant stumpage increases of 1994 as part of the forest renewal plan. As product substitutes emerged and low-cost southern hemisphere suppliers increased their output, British Columbia risked pricing itself out of the global market.[47]

Meanwhile, the 1996 Softwood Lumber Agreement with the United States placed constraints on how much the Canadian industry could export south of the border. The implementation of that agreement required the allocation of company-specific quotas. Interior firms that historically relied on the U.S. market acquired the necessary quotas; coastal firms that sold most of their products to the Asian markets did not. When the Asian economic crisis developed in 1997, coastal firms were left without any markets. Production declined dramatically with the accompanying job losses at pulp and saw mills.

The crisis in the industry left the government scrambling for ways to reduce costs, and revisions to the FPC were a fundamental part of the agenda. Thus, despite the strident environmental criticisms of the code's implementation, the economic context ensured that when revisions to the code emerged on the government agenda, the focus was to be on reducing costs, not expanding environmental protection. In fact, much of the rhetoric from industry and the forestry profession about the code targeted what has been referred to here as formalization. Critics of the code attacked the procedural formalization of the complex planning framework which made it difficult to get timely approvals for logging. Critics also attacked the regulatory formalization of the code. In particular, they complained about excessive reliance on 'process-oriented standards' that were unduly complex and rigid and insufficiently responsive to professional judgment. They advocated process-oriented standards be replaced with 'results-oriented' ones which would specify a clear result required and leave the means to do so up to professional judgment. Such results-oriented standards would have the advantage of simplicity, and, if well implemented, improve congruence. But they have the disadvantage of not being transparent, and thus, they create potential problems for accountability.

In June 1997, the Clark government introduced Bill 47, the Forest Statutes Amendment Act. In announcing the changes, Minister of Forests David Zirnhelt stated: 'We introduced the code over two years ago to ensure our forests were managed to meet present needs without compromising the needs of future generations. We made it clear there would be ongoing adjustments, based on experience in the field, to ensure we maintain a balance of world-class sustainable forest practices. We have consulted widely and these initial changes *will make regulations simpler and less costly for government and industry, while preserving our high environmental standards*'[48] (B.C. Ministry of Environment Lands and Parks and Ministry of Forests 1997, emphasis added). Despite the emphasis on cost-savings, the government had seen enough polls showing continued domestic support for strong environmental measures,[49] and were sufficiently fearful of provoking a renewed international boycott campaign, that it took pains to emphasize that the streamlining would not compromise environmental standards.

For the better part of a year, the government developed the regulations to implement the new legislation, which were finally announced in April 1998. The principle focus of the changes was a simplification, or streamlining, of the planning process. The number of operational plans was reduced from six to three.[50] Companies were given greater stability and certainty by changes in the process for approving plans. Given the instability in the context of higher level plans, plans would have to meet the requirements in place four months before they are submitted, rather than at the time of submission. A process of 'gating' was established, so that once a cutblock was approved, it need not be re-evaluated in the forest development plan unless dramatic new information emerged. These changes allow companies to maintain a larger inventory of timber approved for harvest, thus, increasing the operational certainty and flexibility. Important paperwork requirements were reduced. Assessments of various resources required to develop plans, such as streams, no longer have to be submitted with plans. They do, however, need to be made available to the government (or members of the public) upon request.

There were modest moves in the direction of more results-based standards, particularly in the silviculture prescription. But many important areas, such as stream protection, were explicitly exempted from the move away from process standards. While no regulatory changes were involved, the government also promised procedural changes to increase average cutblock size closer to the legal limits. According to the government, 'Smaller cutblocks significantly increase administrative workload, road requirements, the cost of logging and environmental risk, such as fragmentation of wildlife habitat' (ibid.).

Industry groups offered lukewarm support of the changes.[51] Environmentalists denounced the changes, claiming they gut environmental standards.[52] In their press releases, however, environmental groups struggled to demonstrate how environmental standards were being gutted. They referred to two changes: the commitment to increasing clear-cut size, and a procedural change permitting firms to exceed the maximum amount of soil disturbance for road construction if the company commits to remedying afterwards.[53] Neither claim supports the accusation that FPC standards have been gutted. The issue of clear-cut size has emerged because de facto clear-cut sizes are substantially smaller than regulatory limits (and there are significant ecological concerns that environmental groups are hesitant to discuss with small clear-cuts). The soil disturbance change does reflect a modest relaxation of standards but nothing fundamental.

Although the case is much harder to make, environmentalists are far more concerned about the changes in process designed to reduce paperwork and simplify the planning process. Procedures that industry views as bewildering, unjustified red tape are considered by environmentalists to be fundamental to their ability to act as a watchdog on the industry and government for environmental values. For example, they are very concerned about the increased difficulty in acquiring the assessments performed by companies in support of planning and reductions in some of the avenues for public review. These concerns have been echoed by the independent Forest Practices Board, which criticized some of the proposed changes in a formal letter to the government that was eventually made public.[54]

In enacting the original code, the government significantly increased both the regulatory and procedural formalism of forest practices regulations, as well as expanding environmental protection measures and giving them force of law. The Bill 47 amendments provide a modest retrenchment in some of the procedural elements, but leave the bulk of the new policy framework intact, including the most important environmental standards. Given the magnitude of the economic crisis in the forest industry, it is actually somewhat surprising that they were unable to attain greater regulatory relief. The modest nature of the changes is testimony both to the power of the status quo, but also to the enduring public commitment to environmental values and the continuing pressures of the international marketplace fostered by international environmentalists.

Conclusion

When faced with mounting public criticism of its framework for regulating forest practices, the government of British Columbia responded with the Forest Practices Code, a dramatic formalization of the regulatory system. Many standards were moved from non-binding guidelines to legal rules backed up with sanctions in the event of non-compliance. In many cases, the settings of the instruments have been changed to be more protective of the environment. Background documents supporting the code developed stress in the inordinate complexity of the pre-code framework. While the code may have reduced complexity somewhat, it is still sufficiently complex to frustrate public, and at times even professional understanding.

It is certainly more *transparent* than the previous framework. Prior to the FPC, there was even misunderstanding about the legal status of certain standards. Despite its complexity, the code has significantly increased the clarity of the standards. In addition, various mechanisms, ranging from requiring annual reports on enforcement and compliance to the watchdog role of the Forest Practices Code, have significantly increased public access to information about forest practices.

Regarding congruence, it is not possible to say whether the FPC has increased or decreased congruence. In some cases, it does seem to have decreased regional variation. The most significant shift in variation is the increasing uniformity of the legal status of rules. Prior to the code, standards existed in some places but not others, creating problems of a level playing field for the industry. By increasing regulatory formality across the province, the code has reduced variation on that variable. In terms of regulatory design, the code still permits significant regional variation, and it is difficult to make any kind of blanket statement as to whether or not the code has increased or decreased variation overall. The FPC promotes congruence through several mechanisms. Some regulations vary by situation (buffer strips on streams differ by stream type) or region (clear-cut size limits vary by region). In many cases, exemptions are granted to local implementing officials, district managers, to vary rules to fit the circumstances. There is also a great deal of variation built in to the guidebooks that provide non-binding suggestions to foresters. Despite this significant degree of variation, the code is still far more formalistic than the preceding framework which addressed the dilemma of variation largely through reliance on professional discretion. In terms of the effects of formalization, it has certainly achieved one of its objectives of increasing public information about forest practices. This has helped improve the legitimacy of B.C. forestry with the domestic public, but apparently not with the environmental movement, especially its international wing. In fact, one of the ironies of the change to formalization is that it has helped develop the information that has in turn been used to attack the B.C. forest sector.

Generally, we know very little about how the FPC has improved forest practices or environmental quality. But there is some evidence that the formalization in the code has also improved forest practices. The Forest Practices Board has documented significant improvements in forest practices around streams since the introduction of the FPC. While there is no similar report on this, one of the greatest environmental benefits of the code has apparently been to significantly improve the quality of forest roads. The main question is whether these improvements have been achieved in a cost-efficient manner. The industry has been harshly critical of the code for being far too expensive. Industry critics also continually state that they do not favour backing off the environmental standards in the code, so they are attacking the structural elements of the code that decrease its cost-effectiveness.

Their proposed solution focuses on simplification – of the complex planning framework, and of the overly complicated and rigid 'process-oriented' approach to regulation. The critics prefer 'results-oriented' regulations, combined with much greater delegation to professional foresters. Bill 47 and its accompanying regulations move the FPC marginally in that direction, but the changes were not fundamental. The government has thus far been reluctant to go farther. Environmentalists are quite fond of formalization because it gives them access to information that they can use to pressure industry and government, and they have had enough clout to thwart more dramatic significant changes. Whether that clout can endure in the face of the escalating economic crisis in the forest industry remains to be seen.

NOTES

1 Research for this paper was funded by the Social Sciences and Humanities Research Council and the Hampton Fund of the University of British Columbia. It relies heavily for empirical matter presented earlier in 'The Formalization Dilemma: The Forest Practices Code of British Columbia,' presented at the annual meeting of the Canadian Political Science Association, June 1998.

2 Colin Diver, 'Regulatory Precision,' in Keith Hawkins and John Thomas, eds., *Making Regulatory Policy* (Pittsburgh: University of Pittsburgh Press, 1989), 199–232.

3 Jeremy Wilson, *Talk and Log: Wilderness Politics in British Columbia* (Vancouver: UBC Press, 1998).

4 Jeremy Wilson, 'Wilderness Politics in B.C.,' in William Coleman and Grace Skogstad, eds., *Policy Networks and Policy Communities* (Toronto: Copp Clark Pitman, 1990), 155.

5 B.C. Ministry of Forests, *Okanagan Timber Supply Area: Integrated Resource Management Harvesting Guideline* (Victoria: Ministry of Forests, 1992), 10.

6 British Columbia, The Scientific Panel for Sustainable Forest Practices in Clayoquot Sound, *Sustainable Ecosystem Management in Clayoquot Sound, Report 5,* 57.

7 Ibid., 59.

8 B.C. Ministry of Forests, 'Forest Service Disagrees with Federal Report on Ancient Forest in B.C.,' *News Release,* 14 April 1992.

9 In contrast to virtually all other areas of environmental regulation of forestry in British Columbia, the federal government plays a significant role in fisheries protection. This results from the federal government's constitutional authority over inland fisheries and anadromous fish. The Fisheries Act, first enacted in 1868, is perhaps the strongest federal tool for environmental protection. Section 32 requires that 'no person shall destroy fish by any means other than fishing except as authorized by the minister or under regulations made by the minister.' Section 35 states that 'no person shall carry on any work or undertaking that results in the harmful alteration, disruption, or destruction of fish habitat' and Section 36 says that 'no person shall deposit or permit the deposition of a deleterious substance of any type in water frequented by fish or in any place under any conditions where such deleterious substance or any other deleterious substance that results from the deposit of such deleterious substance may enter any such water.'

10 B.C. Ministry of Forests, *British Columbia Coastal Fisheries-Forestry Guidelines* (Victoria: B.C. Ministry of Forests, 1993).

11 B.C. Ministry of Forests, *Okanagan Timber Supply Area,* 18–20.

12 *Western Canada Wilderness Committee et al. vs. the Attorney General for British Columbia et al.,* Action no. A911359, Supreme Court of B.C., 24 May 1991.

13 *Western Canada Wilderness Committee vs. The Attorney General for British Columbia et al.,* Action no. A912174, Supreme Court of British Columbia, 24 June 1991, 4–5. *Sierra Club of Western Canada vs. British Columbia (Attorney General)* [1992] B.C.J. no. 1293 (QL). B.C. Court of Appeal, Judgment, 3 June 1992.

14 *Fountain vs. British Columbia (Minister of Forests, District Manager, Golden Forest District)* [1992] B.C.J. no. 1556 (QL). B.C. Supreme Court, Judgment, 7 July 1992.

15 George Hoberg, 'The Politics of Sustainability: Forest Policy in British Columbia,' in R. Kenneth Carty, ed., *Policy, Politics, and Government in British Columbia* (Vancouver: UBC Press, 1996); Wilson, *Talk and Log,* Chapt. 11. 272–89.

16 B.C. Ministry of Forests, 'A Forest Practices Code: A Public Discussion Paper' (Victoria: BCMOF, 1991).

17 New Democratic Party, *A Better Way For British Columbia: New Democratic Election Platform,* 1991.

18 B.C. Ministry of Forests, *News Release*, 30 July 1992.

19 Derek Tripp, et al., *The Application and Effectiveness of the Coastal Fisheries Forestry Guidelines in Selected Cut Blocks on Vancouver Island* (Victoria: Ministry of Environment, Lands, and Parks, 1992) iii.

20 Derek Tripp, *The Use and Effectiveness of the Coastal Fisheries Forestry Guidelines in Selected Forest Districts of Coastal British Columbia* (Victoria: Ministry of Environment, Lands, and Parks, 1994).

21 Aaron Doyle, Brian Elliott, and David Tindall, 'Framing the Forests: Corporations, The B.C. Forest Alliance, and the Media,' in William Carroll, ed., *Organizing Dissent: Contemporary Social Movements in Theory and Practice*, 2nd ed. (Toronto: Garamond Press, 1997) 250.

22 W.T. Stanbury and Ilan Vertinsky, 'Boycotts in Conflicts over Forestry Issues: The Case of Clayoquot Sound,' *Commonwealth Forestry Review* 76(1) 1997, 18–24; Steven Bernstein and Benjamin Cashore, 'Globalization and Fourth Paths of Internationalization: The Case of Eco-forestry Policy Change in British Columbia,' *Canadian Journal of Political Science*, 33(1), 2000, 67–99.

23 Forest Resources Commission, *The Future of Our Forests* (Victoria: Queen's Printer, 1991), 88.

24 B.C. Government. 1993. *British Columbia Forest Practices Code – Discussion Paper* (Victoria: Government of British Columbia, 1993).

25 This element of the problem is poorly defined and confuses two aspects: the clarity of legal powers and the complexity of the regulatory framework. The clarity issue is dealt more directly with the second element below.

26 W.T. Stanbury and Ilan Vertinsky, 'Governing Instruments for Forest Policy in British Columbia: A Positive and Normative Analysis,' in Chris Tollefson, ed., *The Wealth of Forests: Markets, Regulation, and Sustainable Forestry* (Vancouver: UBC Press, 1998).

27 For an overview of policy instruments used in the Code, see previous note.

28 Gordon Hamilton and Keith Baldrey, 'Forest Critics Seek Meat in NDP's Plan,' *Vancouver Sun*, 17 May 1994, A1.

29 B.C. Ministry of Forests and Ministry of Environment, Lands, and Parks, 'New Mandatory Standards to Improve B.C.'s Forest Practices' (Victoria: Ministry of Forests, 1994); 'New Mandatory Standards to Improve B.C.'s Forest Practices.' *New Release*, 30 May 1994.

30 B.C. Ministry of Forests and Ministry of Environment, Lands, and Parks, *Forest Practices Code of British Columbia – Riparian Management Area Guidebook* (Victoria: Ministry of Forests, 1995).

31 Under the Forest Act, licencees had the right to appeal but specially constituted boards had to be established for each appeal.

32 Hoberg, *Regulating Forestry: A Comparison of British Columbia and the U.S.*

Pacific Northwest, UBC Forest Economics and Policy Analysis Unit Working Paper 185, 1993.

33 Government of Canada, B.C. Ministry of Forests, *Just the Facts – A Review of Silviculture and Other Forestry Statistics,* 1997. Available at http://www.for.gov.bc.ca/hfp/forsite/jtfacts/cutblock.htm

34 Sierra Legal Defence Fund, *Stream Protection Under the Code: The Destruction Continues* (Vancouver: Sierra Legal Defence Fund, Feb. 1997).

35 B.C. Forest Practices Board, *Forest Planning and Practices in Coastal Areas with Streams – Summary Report* (Victoria: Forest Practices Board, 1998), 4.

36 KPMG, *Financial State of the Forest Industry and Delivered Wood Cost Drivers* (prepared for the B.C. Ministry of Forests, April, 1997).

37 Of the $12.22 per cubic metre code costs, $4.52 was credited to planning and administration and $7.70 was credited to forest practices. The significance of forest practices, in order, were cutblock size, road and landing requirements, soil conservation requirements, riparian management requirements, greenup and adjacency, and visual quality objectives. KPMG, *Financial State.*

38 B.C. Ministry of Forests, *Forest Practices Code of British Columbia – Biodiversity Guidebook* (Victoria: Ministry of Forests, Sept. 1995), 8.

39 B.C. Ministry of Forests, Compliance and Enforcement Branch, *The Annual Report of Compliance and Enforcement Statistics for the Forest Practices Code,* for the years 1996, 1997, 1998, available at http://www.for.gov.bc.ca/tasb/legsregs/fpc/fpc.htm.

40 Keith Moore, Chair, Forest Practices Board, 'Presentation to House of Commons Standing Committee on Natural Resources and Government Operations,' 14 May 1999. At www.fpd.gov.bc.ca/background/MPs.htm.

41 Sierra Legal Defence Fund (SLDF). *British Columbia's Clear Cut Code* (Vancouver: SLDF) Nov. 1996.

42 SLDF, *Stream Protection* (Vancouver: SLDF, Feb. 1997).

43 SLDF, *Wildlife at Risk* (Vancouver: SLDF, April 1997).

44 SLDF, *Going Downhill Fast: Landslides and the Forest Practices Code* (Vancouver: SLDF, June 1997).

45 SLDF, *British Columbia's Forestry Report Card, 1997–98* (Vancouver: SLDF, 1998).

46 Greenpeace, *Broken Promises: The Truth About What's Happening to British Columbia's Forests* (Vancouver: Greenpeace, April 1997).

47 Clark Binkley, 'Preserving Nature through Intensive Plantation Forestry: The Case for Forestland Allocation with Illustrations from British Columbia' in *Forestry Chronicle* 73(5), 1997, 553–9; M. Patricia Marchak, *Logging the Globe* (Montreal: McGill-Queen's University Press, 1995).

48 B.C. Ministry of Environment, Lands, and Parks and Ministry of Forests,

'Revisions Make Forest Practices Code More Efficient, Effective,' *Government Press Release*, 9 June 1997.

49 For a revealing look at the government's assessment of the opinion climate at the time, see Ministry of Forests Public Affairs Branch 1997.

50 The Five-Year Silviculture Plan was eliminated and replaced by policy requirements; relevant provisions of the Access Management Plan, were incorporated into the Forest Development Plan; and the Logging Plan was incorporated into the Silviculture Prescription.

51 Forest Alliance of B.C., 'Code Changes a Progressive Step,' *News Release*, 2 April 1998.

52 Gordon Hamilton, 'B.C. Chops Red Tape to Save Forestry Firms $300 Million,' *Vancouver Sun*, 3 April 1998, A1.

53 SLDF, 'Forest Practices Code Rollbacks Confirmed,' *Media Release*, 2 April 1998.

54 The letter was eventually published on the board website at http://www.fpb.gov.bc.ca/reports/brd.htm

Chapter Thirteen

The Federal Role in Canadian Forest Policy: From Territorial Landowner to International and Intergovernmental Co-ordinating Agent

Michael Howlett

Introduction: The Federal Role in Canadian Forest Policy-Making

Understanding the development of the federal role in the formation of Canadian forest policy is somewhat more problematic than is the case with the development of forest policy in the provinces. This is because of the constitutional division of powers which awards control over forests to the landowner and the fact that, at present, the federal government owns or controls forest resources only in minor patches on Native reserves, in national parks, on such federal installations as armed forces bases and airports, and in the generally poor forest lands of the Northwest and Yukon territories. Unlike in the provinces, then, where the development of forest policy can be seen to have occurred in the interplay of governments, capital, and labour over the creation and distribution of resource revenues, in the case of federal forest policy formation, the fundamental interest of the federal government is much less certain. Although it has considerable powers over the forest industry, without a direct interest in forest rents the federal government has had a less conflictual orientation towards the industry than have provincial governments. Federal forest policy has tended to be more sympathetic to industry concerns for continued profitability than have provincial governments forced to compete with industry in order to maximize their own returns from the forest resource.

Historically, however, this was not always the case. Although the British North America (BNA) Act continued the precolonial practice of awarding control and jurisdiction over forest resources to the provinces, not all land in the country was under provincial control and not all of the provinces that entered Confederation did so on the same terms as the original four: Nova Scotia, New Brunswick, Ontario, and Quebec. Between 1867 and 1905 the federal government also attempted to use its powers over trade and commerce, fisheries, and through other means, to extend its control over provincial resources. By 1900, however, it had lost three major constitutional battles with the provinces over the delineation of the Ontario–Manitoba border, concerning the validity of the Ontario Rivers and Streams Act, and in a judicial interpretation of the validity of Ontario's forest 'manufacturing condition.' These losses restricted its role to co-equal status with the provinces, controlling only forest resources on federal lands.[1] By 1905 a process of full-scale devolution of federal forestry powers had begun with the creation of the new provinces of Alberta and Saskatchewan. By 1930 this transfer was complete and the federal role shifted to attempting to coordinate provincial policy to benefit a national industry, and more recently to coordinating provincial efforts in the name of international environmental initiatives and trade imperatives.

Federal Resource Ownership and Control

The manner in which sparsely settled areas of the country were incorporated into Canada allowed the federal government, until 1930,[2] a role similar to that of a provincial government when dealing with forest resources in territorial areas. Manitoba, Saskatchewan, and Alberta share a common history of federal control of provincial forest lands and resources from 1869 to 1930, while the Northwest Territories and the Yukon, despite significant devolution of powers in the 1980s and 1990s, technically remain under federal control to the present day.

Forest Policy in the Northwest Territories and Manitoba before 1905

At first merely an extension of the area granted to the Hudson's Bay Company (HBC), the North-Western Territory was distinguished from the area of Rupert's Land under the company charter of 1821. At that time the HBC was granted an exclusive monopoly to trade in the area. Renewed on several occasions, this licence expired in the late 1850s, and after a protracted debate in British and colonial circles, it was included in the territory purchased from the HBC in 1869–70 by the recently confederated Dominion of Canada.[3]

Canadian authority in the area was first exercised through the provisions of the 1869 'Act for the Temporary Government of Rupert's Land and the North-Western Territory When United With Canada.'[4] The act specified government by Parliament through the device of an appointed local lieutenant governor and council for the entire territory. Although the act was overridden in the case of the small area in the southeastern corner of the territory, which became the Province of Manitoba in 1870, it was reenacted at that time, and again upon its second expiration in 1871.[5]

The federal government quickly extended to the newly acquired area of the country a forest resource policy regime inherited from the United Provinces of Canada after 1867. This policy, incorporated in the Dominion Lands Act of 1872, was based on the Crown Timber Act adopted by the union government in 1849. Administered in the territories by the Department of the Interior, the policy institutionalized the notion of extracting government revenues from resource exploitation by private sector interests through the use of area-based licences and volume-based stumpage fees.

Exploitation of the forest resources of the area, however, was at this point well in the future. The 200-year domination of the North-West Territory and Rupert's Land by the HBC and rival fur traders had prevented the early exploitation of the area's timber resources for domestic consumption. Local settlement being discouraged,[6] the only other market for territorial timber would have been either the United Kingdom or the United States. Transportation barriers and a lack of valued species such as oak or white pine prevented the former from exercising any influence on local trade, while the plentiful resources and ease of access to competitive stands of timber in Michigan and the Minnesota Territory served as effective barriers to entry of territorial timber into the neighbouring United States. Although population growth continued, it was nowhere near the size required to establish a local market, and the lack of adequate transportation facilities continued to prevent the exploitation of domestic resources for external markets.[7]

In 1870, following the Riel rebellion, legislation was introduced to create the province of Manitoba.[8] The new province entered Confederation on different terms from those of the other provinces, in that Section 30 of the Manitoba Act specifically removed the control over lands vested in other provincial governments by Section 109 of the BNA Act. The section reserved all ungranted lands to the Crown in the name of the Dominion government. This, of course, prohibited the province from obtaining revenues from the lands or the minerals or timber they contained, although this was the largest source of revenue for most provincial governments at the time.[9]

The desire of the Dominion government to promote settlement of the area led it to regulate timber removal from Crown lands required to build houses, farms, telegraph lines, rail beds, and other needed services and infrastructure. In order to further this end, in 1872 the first Dominion Lands Act was passed. Although amended on many occasions, the act would govern agricultural settlement and timber exploitation on Crown lands in the prairie provinces until 1930.[10] The act was concerned primarily with agricultural settlement and, concerning timber, provided that small stands of prairie timber would be shared equally among quarter-section holders 'to prevent petty monopoly.' It also established a system of licences for timber removal contingent on the licence-holder establishing a sawmill of set size within a specified period of time to process the timber. No limits were placed on size and the leases were set for a twenty-one-year period.[11]

The main timber resources of the present-day Province of Manitoba, however, lay to the north and east of the original provincial boundaries.[12] The timber potential in these areas had been recognized by the Dominion surveys of 1869–70, and by the late 1870s so had the limits of continued cultivation.[13] Given the limits of the resources located within provincial borders and in settled territorial lands in the northwest, the system of twenty-one-year licences proved unworkable, and major amendments to the system of timber allocation were made in 1883.[14]

In the area covered by what is now the province of Saskatchewan, the exploitation of provincial forests awaited the arrival of settlers and the establishment of railway links both to the rest of Canada and the world, and to the areas of the territory which contained the largest timber resources. The lumber industry in Saskatchewan only began in earnest in 1878–80 with the construction of a major stationary sawmill at Prince Albert.[15] The prospects of the fledgling forest industry, however, received a blow when the route of the Canadian Pacific Railway (CPR) was altered in a southerly direction in 1881. While the southern districts traversed by the railway were to grow quickly, the exploitation of the territory's forest resources awaited the construction of the Canadian National Railway and branchlines into the north.[16]

In Alberta, unlike in the other two prairie provinces, however, the mainline of the CPR did extend into forested lands in the eastern slope

Rockies section. As such, the development of the provincial forest industry could begin immediately upon commencement of construction of the CPR in the 1880s.[17]

The first sawmill development in what was to become the province of Alberta occurred in the extreme southwesterly corner of the unorganized NWT in 1880 – the area that became the provisional District of Alberta in 1882 – in conjunction with railway construction. The first Crown timber agent was appointed in 1881 and was stationed at Edmonton, which became part of the provisional District of Athabaska in 1882.[18] The CPR both owned and leased timber berths in Alberta to fulfil its own needs for ties, mining lumber, cordwood, and posts.

Lumbering in the province began in the Padmore area in 1883 and in the Kananaskis area in 1884. The two companies involved, the Bow River Lumber Company and the Eau Claire Lumber Company, operated sawmills in Calgary to serve the rapidly expanding local market. Other companies quickly became involved in the exploitation of the coal and timber resources of the Canmore area, such as the Canadian North-West Coal and Lumber Syndicate in 1890.[19]

By the late 1890s the extent of lumbering on the eastern slope was such that the Dominion government began the process of land reservation which eventually culminated in the creation of Banff and Jasper national parks. In 1887 the government established a small nature reserve at Banff, and in 1892 enlarged it to include the area around Lake Louise.[20]

Federal Forest Policy in Manitoba, Saskatchewan, and Alberta, 1905–1930

The first decade of the twentieth century was an active one for the federal government and its system of forest administration, with the first introduction of conservation measures into its system of forest regulation.[21] In 1906 the federal government sponsored the first National Forestry Congress. Held in Ottawa, the conference brought together foresters from across the country and represented the first major inroad into Canada of ideas popularized by the conservation movement in the United States.[22] Partly in response to the sentiments expressed at the Congress, the same year the government passed the Dominion Forest Reserves Act, establishing twenty-one permanent forest reserves in the country.[23] This period also saw demands for provincial autonomy come to fruition in Alberta and Saskatchewan.

In 1882 by Dominion order-in-council, the Northwest Territories had been divided into four 'provisional districts' of Assiniboia, Saskatchewan, Alberta, and Athabaska – the northern area remaining unorganized. Although not as swiftly as in the case of Manitoba, action on the grievances of local residents was taken by Parliament soon after the end · of the second Riel rebellion. In 1886–7 representation of the Northwest Territories in Parliament was established[24] and in 1888 an elected Territorial Assembly replaced the Legislative Council.[25]

In 1895, following the Klondike gold rush, the Yukon Territory was created. In 1897, after a decade of struggle in the Territorial Assembly, a new Northwest Territories Act granted responsible government to the territories.[26] With the rapid increase in settlement in the post railway era, the agitation for separate provincial status grew as residents sought democratic government and the authority to finance educational and economic infrastructural development. [27]Full control over Crown lands, however, was not achieved when the new provinces of Alberta and Saskatchewan were created in 1905.[28]

By the terms of the Saskatchewan Act,[29] the districts of Assiniboia and Saskatchewan were merged into the new province of Saskatchewan. Under Section 21 of the act, control over provincial lands, including minerals and timber, remained with the Dominion government.[30] Successive provincial Liberal governments from 1905–29 remained in power largely by catering to the demands made by farmers,[31] and they did little to support other sectors of the economy, including a forest industry located for the most part in the sparsely settled northern regions of the province.[32]

The Alberta Act of 1905,[33] like its Saskatchewan counterpart, reserved timber for the Dominion government, allowing the jurisdiction of the Dominion Lands Act and the Dominion Department of the Interior to continue unimpeded in the province until 1930.[34] Both the first Liberal administrations and then the United Farmers of Alberta (UFA) government of Herbert Greenfield had little to do with forest administration, concentrating their efforts on improving the agricultural situation. The UFA government, during its second term under J.E. Brownlee, however, had a significant impact on the forest sector when it negotiated the transfer of control over natural resources to the provincial government in 1930, ending sixty years of federal control over the lands, forests, and minerals of the territory and province.

In 1924 the federal Royal Commission on Pulpwood noted that many of the large tracts of timberland suitable for lumbering operations in the three Western provinces had already been cutover and allowed to deteriorate. It also noted that provincial cuts of spruce for lumbering purposes had declined rapidly after the First World War and were by 1922 at only

10.9 per cent of their 1917 level. The two largest mills in Saskatchewan, for example, at Prince Albert and Big River, had closed, and the prospects of a pulp mill at Prince Albert mooted in 1912 had been cancelled because an associated power project did not come to fruition. The commission prophesied a very limited role for the forest industry in the future of the province.[35] Nevertheless in Manitoba in 1920 pulpwood berths had been authorized, and in 1921 the first pulpwood berth was awarded covering 2,864 square kilometres of land north of the Winnipeg River. This eventually resulted in the opening of the first prairie pulp and paper mill at Pine Falls in 1927, the only such mill ever developed under federal administration anywhere in the country.[36]

Federal Forest Policy in the Northwest Territories and the Yukon after 1930

In 1930 the natural resource transfer agreements ended the role of the federal government as a significant owner of forest resources. By the late 1930s the federal presence was restricted to the remaining lands under federal control in the Yukon and NWT.[37]

The potential for forest exploitation in the NWT was largely ignored throughout the early period of federal government forest policy, as the Dominion government concentrated on developments in the prairie lands under its control.[38] Although explorations of the area had determined the existence of some timberlands in the Mackenzie and Keewatin districts, and these facts were well known by 1914,[39] the difficulty of access and the existence of large stands of higher quality timber in more accessible southern areas of the country prohibited their exploitation.[40] Nevertheless, by 1921 Dominion timber regulations had been extended to the northern areas of the NWT. A Crown timber agent was established at Fort Smith, and annual permits were issued to mill operators on payment of a rental charge per square mile.[41]

The situation in the Yukon was a little different. Early sawmilling efforts associated with the Klondike Gold Rush and the building of the territorial capital at Dawson resulted in the removal of most of the timber in the northern section of the territory. Extensive use of wood fuel both for residential purposes and in the steamboat traffic on the Yukon River and its tributaries resulted in the depletion of most other easily accessible forests by 1930. Until the construction of the Alaska Highway opened up previously inaccessible areas along the Liard watershed in 1942, the lumber requirements of the Yukon were met by shipments of materials from British Columbia.[42]

In the two territories a gradual transfer of administrative responsibility for forests to the territorial governments was accomplished throughout this period.[43] In the natural resource area the most important step involved the promulgation of the territorial land use regulations under the Territorial Lands Act of 1950.[44]

Under the terms of the act, in each territory timber removal was governed by territorial timber regulations under the supervision of a superintendent of forestry. The regulations authorized free removal of timber by trappers, settlers, or federal, territorial, educational, or religious agencies. For commercial purposes, a charge for timber permits was levied and land leased on a required volume basis. The regulations also provided for ten-year renewable timber harvesting agreements, although only one – that of the Yukon Forest Products Company – was ever issued. The federal Department of Indian and Northern Affairs (DIAND) operated lands and forest services in both territories, and these were responsible for inspection, fire protection, conservation activities, and other duties, although many of them have been taken over by territorial agencies in recent years.[45]

Under DIAND control, forest exploitation in the north was not undertaken on a sustained yield basis. Only the single timber harvesting agreement called for the submission of cutting plans. Rather than close utilization or reforestation, federal policy explicitly called for utilization of the forest for employment purposes.[46] Following the transfer of jurisdiction to the territorial government in 1987 this policy was continued, although the situation has been complicated by the conclusion of Aboriginal land claims agreements in both the Yukon and the NWT which contain First Nations' rights to timber harvests for a variety of commercial and non-commercial purposes.[47]

While legislation passed in 1988 and 1990 allows for the issuance of forest management agreements in the NWT which would involve additional management activities, none has yet been issued.[48] The most recent Yukon government forestry statement, *A Vision for Yukon Forests*, called for the implementation of an ecosystem management approach after the transfer of management responsibilities to the territory on 1 April 2000. The plan attempts to incorporate community level planning with traditional Aboriginal knowledge and practices into the territory's forest management regime.[49]

Federal Efforts to Coordinate Provincial Forest Policies, 1930–1987

Despite the gradual reduction of its territorial land base after 1930, the federal government has never given up its attempts to influence Canadian forest policy. However, it has been reduced to attempting to use its various powers over regional development, international trade, and the environment to indirectly affect the development of provincial forest policies. It has, for example, always been concerned with the effect on product prices and national economic development of high levels of concentration of ownership in the forest products sector. This concern has manifested itself from time to time in federal inquiries and anti-combines investigations which transcended provincial and territorial boundaries. These included a special inquiry in 1885, a legislative inquiry in 1907, royal commissions in 1901 and 1916, a session of the parliamentary standing committee on banking and commerce in 1934, a series of anti-combines investigations between 1939 and 1966, and inquiries conducted by the Royal Commission on Corporate Concentration in the late 1970s.[50]

It is also the case that Ottawa assumed control over production and pricing of forest products during the Second World War, and after the war's end continued to attempt to direct the development of provincial forest policies.[51] In 1949 the government of Mackenzie King attempted to use the federal spending power to exert influence on provincial policy development. The government passed the Canada Forestry Act[52] which was the basis for a series of federal–provincial shared-cost programs in areas such as forest protection, inventories, reforestation, education, and road construction. The funding was established under the Minister of Resources and Development and allocated at a federal–provincial meeting in 1951.[53] Most of the money was spent on access road construction and forest inventories.[54] However, forest research also received a large boost. The federal government sponsored a reorganization of the Pulp and Paper Research Institute, funded the Canadian Institute of Forestry, and established its own forest research centres – located in the Canadian Forest Service of the Department of Resources and Development and the Forest Biology Division of the Department of Agriculture.[55]

The Diefenbaker government (1957–62) increased the profile of federal forestry activities as part of a general thrust towards increased natural resource development endorsed by the Gordon commission. Increased federal activity in the natural resource field was evident in the establishment of a federal Department of Forests in 1960 and an attempt made to secure a national consensus on federal reserve policy through the holding of the Resources for Tomorrow Conference in

Montreal in 1961.[56] This process culminated in the establishment of the first National Forest Congress since 1906, held at Montebello, Quebec, in 1966 under the auspices of the Department of Forests. The congress failed to secure provincial approval of federal leadership in the formulation of national forest policy, however, and by the end of the year the Pearson government had to acknowledge the limited direct role of the federal government in regulating an industry dependent on the exploitation of provincially owned resources. Pearson dissolved the Department of Forests and began the process of terminating the shared-cost forestry programs put into place since 1951.

Nevertheless, after 1966 the federal government continued to include forest projects as part of its regional development efforts, providing assistance to industries to construct roads, establish plants, and the like.[57] By 1974, when the federal government's regional assistance programs were rationalized under the general development agreement (GDA) program, forestry had become the subject of specific sub-agreements signed with several provinces.[58] These regional development expenditures reflected both a concern for the forest resource itself and the renewed concern for the viability of the forest industry. As federal regional development efforts decreased in the late 1970s and early 1980s, however, the role of the federal government in Canadian forest policy again became uncertain.

Throughout the 1970s, the need for a new federal forest policy was repeatedly urged by the Science Council of Canada and the Canadian Council of Resource and Environment Ministers (CCREM), among others. The Science Council in particular stressed the need to ensure that Canadian forests were managed in such a manner that environmental damage was limited and long-term supplies of timber were assured. Towards these ends it urged the federal government to moderate its historical emphasis on industrial development and renew its commitment to forest-related research – both biological and industrial.[59]

Inheriting the mantle of the 1960s natural resources conferences, the Canadian Council of Resource and Environment Ministers continued to promote intergovernmental cooperation in the natural resource fields. Like the Science Council, the CCREM promoted the adoption of sustained yield forest management efforts by Canadian governments and undertook a systematic inventory of forest policies then in place in Canadian jurisdictions. Like the Science Council, its aim was to ensure the availability of long-term supplies of timber to meet the needs of industrial users.[60]

By 1972 these concerns had received an institutional voice in the form of the establishment of a Canadian Forestry Advisory Committee (CFAC) to the minister of the environment – to whom jurisdiction over the Canadian Forestry Service had been transferred in 1970–1.[61] CFAC lobbied hard for the establishment of a national forestry policy. After 1973 the Economic Council of Canada also began to champion the need for a federal policy regarding the forest sector. The council included forestry in its general review of the needs of the national economy and established a forest products committee as one of sixteen industry committees reporting to its 1973 National Economic Conference.[62]

Within the government itself, the problems faced by an aging pulp and paper industry had by this time also begun to receive additional attention. In August 1973 the Canadian pulp and paper industry's needs to secure raw materials and to update manufacturing technology were addressed by the forest products group in the Department of Industry, Trade, and Commerce.[63] By 1974 the federal government had moved to establish a joint working group with the provinces, the Federal–Provincial Forest Industries Development Committee (FIDC), to study the merits of proposals to 'rationalize' the industry. FIDC examined possibilities for matching supply and demand for paper products and forest resources through restructuring the industry by modernization, mergers, integration, and diversification, and established the province of New Brunswick as a pilot study area.[64] Partially on the basis of the study results, and partially because of moves made by the Quebec government to establish its own programs, the federal government provided funding to older mills in eastern and central Canada to upgrade and modernize their plants and manufacturing process. To this end several pulp and paper modernization agreements were signed with several provinces under the general GDA process.[65]

Between 1973 and 1978 the federal government worked on the establishment of a sector-by-sector industrial strategy. The forest sector was included in the process of policy review which led up to the 1978 first ministers conferences on the economy.[66] Four major areas of concern were identified, all of which reflected the renewed federal concern for the future viability of the forest industry. These were: (1) the cost disadvantages of Canadian producers *vis-à-vis* competitors, especially in the United States; (2) a poor investment climate in Canada for major new investment especially *vis-à-vis* the United States; (3) difficulties in generating adequate capital to improve productivity and reduce costs; and (4) forest resource problems, especially 'the concern that unless a more intensive level of forestry was practised, the resource would not for many more years be able to play its traditional role as the foundation of so much of the nation's economic growth.[67]

To resolve these problems, a total of thirty-nine recommendations were made in the areas of investment, modernization and taxation, forest resources and management, environmental control and pollution abatement, energy, transportation, research, market development, and labour-management relations, including unemployment insurance and manpower.

By 1978–9 both the forestry community and the forest industry were demanding the enunciation of a clear federal policy on the forest sector.[68] The forestry community, bolstered by new studies indicating the approach of supply limitations in various regions of the country,[69] demanded that the government renew its financial efforts in research and take some steps to regulate forest resource use. The forest industry also demanded that the government halt its ad hoc subsidy of producers located in specific regions of the country or operating obsolete mills and provide a package of more generally available tax concessions and subsidies. These demands were made directly to the government at a third National Forest Congress held in Toronto in 1980.[70]

The federal government published a short outline of existing forestry policy in 1979,[71] but did little else until after the brief Clark interregnum in 1979. The re-elected Liberal government met at Lake Louise in September 1980 and decided to undertake major policy reviews in the areas of fisheries, forestry, agriculture, and minerals. An interdepartmental federal forest sector strategy committee was established and instructed to examine measures to strengthen the resource base, improve research and development, and aid new market development.[72]

The various federal proposals were discussed at the 1980 National Forest Congress, and in 1981 this process resulted in the issuance of *A Forest Sector Strategy for Canada*, a discussion paper released by the Ministry of the Environment.[73] After a review of the current status of the resource base and forest industry, the discussion paper proposed that the federal government follow a strategy aimed at maximizing economic and social development. Forest policy was to be explicitly recognized as part of federal economic development priorities, which included a renewed emphasis on natural resource exploitation.[74]

Although the preamble to the strategy document appeared to lay the foundation for a major federal role in Canadian forest policy, the strategy itself identified only a relatively few areas for active federal government involvement. The federal role was restricted to 'lessening trade barriers in international markets and promoting Canadian exports; ensuring a positive economic and regulatory climate for new investment; improving the resource data base; maintaining forestry research and development at a level consistent with ... international competition; ensuring the gap in scientific and professional manpower is closed; supporting provincial forest renewal programs where regional and transitional considerations may warrant, in order to ensure permanent viability of the resource, [and] provision of national and international statistics.'[75]

These areas all lay within well-established federal jurisdiction. The larger issue of directing the content of existing and future forest policies remained within provincial jurisdiction and outside the 1981 strategy.[76]

Following publication of the *Forest Sector Strategy*, the federal government adopted several short-term programs aimed at alleviating unemployment in the sector and especially in regions hard-hit by declines in lumber prices. Among the measures the government adopted were a renewed policy of funding 'mission-oriented forest research; a new series of federal provincial agreements aimed at forest renewal;[77] and the placement of market access for forest products high among its trade policy objectives.[78] Although the Trudeau government had failed to secure a major role for the federal government in the forest sector in 1981, the Mulroney government was determined to raise the profile of the central government in the forest sector after assuming office in 1984.[79]

The government quickly unveiled several major forest policy initiatives. Funding for forestry activities was increased under a series of subsidiary forestry agreements under the Economic and Regional Development Agreement (ERDA) process – although many of these spending plans had been developed and negotiated by the Liberals in 1983–4. The Conservatives formed a new Ministry of State for Forests and quadrupled planned federal expenditures in the forest sector from about $225 million to over $1 billion for the period 1985–90. The Conservatives also moved to rationalize an array of over 90 ad hoc interdepartmental committees and task forces working on forest sector problems within the federal administration and combined two major private sector advisory groups to the minister of the environment and the minister of regional industrial expansion into a single forest sector advisory committee to the minister of state for forests.[80] On the intergovernmental level, the government also supported the withdrawal of forest ministers from the more or less moribund Canadian Council of Resource and Environment Ministers (CCREM) and the formation of a separate Canadian Council of Forest Ministers.[81]

In addition, the government began a major policy development process aimed at enunciating a new Conservative national forest policy to replace the *Forest Sector Strategy* for Canada adopted by the Liberals in September 1981.[82] The government provided funding for a series of 'forestry fora' held in various cities around the country in 1985–6 leading up to the establishment of another National Forest Congress in Ottawa in April 1986. The fora were intended to bring together company officials, government personnel, labour representatives, academics, and other interested parties to discuss the future direction of forest policy in Canada. The recommendations of the fora[83] were brought to the National Forest Congress for ratification,[84] and a committee of federal and provincial officials struck to set down the guidelines for a new national strategy. These were referred to the Canadian Council of Forest Ministers at a final forestry forum in St John, New Brunswick, in July 1987. In due course a document, *A National Forest Sector Strategy for Canada*[85] appeared, and this was accepted by the government as representing federal forest policy.

The 1987 strategy paper addressed five major areas of concern: trade and investment, forest management, employment, research and development, and public awareness; making a total of thirty-four recommendations for action. Specific mention of the role of the federal government, however, was made in only six recommendations; two in each of the areas pertaining to trade and investment, forest management, and employment. It was suggested that the federal government take the concerns of the forest sector into account in negotiating liberalized trading arrangements with the United States, that the federal role in funding forest management be confirmed, and that the federal government take action on the question of acid rain damage to forests. In addition, it was recommended that the federal government participate in programs to compensate labour for employment losses suffered through technological change and aid the development of university forestry programs.

The 1987 strategy was a failure in the sense that the major role originally envisioned for the federal government in coordinating provincial governments failed to come to fruition, largely because of the continued insistence of provincial governments upon their sole jurisdiction in this sector.[86]

Federal Efforts at Coordinating National and International Forest Policies after 1987

The failure of the 1987 strategy marked the end of federal efforts to influence provincial forest policy through financial means, and after 1987 the federal government shifted tactics and concentrated its efforts on two areas in which it has sole jurisdictional authority: international trade and international relations, especially towards the global environment.

The Trade Agenda

The federal government of Canada has had, and continues to have a major role affecting national industries through its powers over international trade. In the forest sector, its efforts have focused on eliminating both tariff and non-tariff barriers to increased trade in Canadian forest products. While in the case of the former it has had great success and successive rounds of international trade negotiations have eliminated virtually all tariff barriers in natural resource products, the same is not true of non-tariff barriers.[87]

Non-tariff barriers to trade in Canadian forest products have been and continue to be significant, both in the softwood lumber and the newsprint industries. The Japanese market for Canadian softwood lumber, for instance, has been limited by the lack of acceptance in the Japanese building code of platform frame construction of apartment buildings of three or more stories and by the need to regrade lumber to Japanese standards.[88] Ex quota duties against Canadian newsprint were also imposed by the European Union,[89] on imports of Canadian newsprint exceeding a 650,000 tonne quota established when Britain entered the common market.[90]

Successive Canadian federal governments have made efforts to eliminate these barriers. However, the effects of these barriers remain marginal as long as Canadian forest products trade is oriented primarily towards the U.S. market. Much more serious have been U.S. antidumping and countervailing duty actions[91] over shakes and shingles[92] and softwood lumber[93] exports which have resulted in the establishment of temporary punitive duties and quotas on Canadian products in this key marketplace.

The softwood lumber dispute concerns claims made by U.S. producers that Canadian lumber is being sold at artificially low prices on the

U.S. market because of low Canadian government stumpage rates charged on Crown timberlands. Such claims have arisen on many occasions, notably in 1962, 1982, 1985, and 1991 when formal proceedings in the U.S. into the imposition of countervailing tariffs were undertaken.[94] Although the complaints of U.S. producers were dismissed in the 1962 and 1982 cases, in October 1986 the U.S. International Trade Commission ruled in a preliminary determination that Canadian exports were unfairly subsidized and that they damaged U.S. industry.[95] In order to avoid a negative final determination, on 30 December 1986 the Canadian and U.S. governments signed an eleventh-hour memorandum of understanding instituting a 15 per cent Canadian federal government export tax on a variety of Canadian softwood lumber products.[96]

The dispute prompted a major re-examination and restructuring of Canadian timber pricing systems, established a precedent for extensive countervailing action in other trade areas, and was one of the reasons cited for the need to negotiate a comprehensive Canada–U.S. Free Trade Agreement (FTA) that would exempt Canadian programs from U.S. trade remedy law.[97] Nevertheless, when the actual free trade package was sent to the U.S. Congress for its approval, in October 1987, the softwood lumber export duty was specifically exempted from the general tariff reduction.[98]

In 1991 the federal government cancelled the 1986 agreement. This immediately prompted another countervailing action on the part of U.S. lumber producers.[99] When the U.S. International Trade Administration again ruled that the U.S. industry had been harmed, the dispute made its way to the dispute resolution process established by the terms of the Canada–U.S. FTA. Although the FTA panels upheld the Canadian case and Canadian producers received a windfall when punitive U.S. duties were rebated to them, in 1994 under new World Trade Organization rules the United States changed its trade laws, making it clear to Canadian officials that a new countervailing action would succeed. As a result, in 1996 a second Canada–U.S. softwood lumber agreement was signed, this time establishing a quota on Canadian exports to the United States and an escalating export tax on amounts exceeding the quota.[100]

In all aspects of these negotiations, the federal government coordinated and guided provincial governments and the forest industry, primarily in order to provide a single and united voice resisting U.S. trade pressure. This role continued in 2001 when the 1996 agreement expired and led to a new round of U.S.–Canada softwood lumber talks.

The Sustainability Agenda

This coordinating role was also a central feature of the two national forest strategies developed in Canada in 1992 and 1998. These two efforts were linked together, as the 1998 initiative arose out of a five-year review of the 1992 effort. Both of these strategies differ from those that preceded them, however, since they reflect not so much the desire of the federal government to directly influence the content of provincial forestry policies so much as the aim of coordinating Canadian activities with those at the international level, especially with respect to the role played by forestry in sustainable development and other environmental initiatives.[101]

The 1992 document *Sustainable Forests: A Canadian Commitment* contained nine strategic priorities intended to help implement the government's international commitments in this sector.[102] In the 1992 process, the federal government attempted to avoid some of the mistakes made with previous strategies. Significantly, the main responsibility for its implementation rested with the intergovernmental Canadian Council of Forest Ministers. An effort was made to cement intergovernmental agreement through the signing of a formal Canada Forest Accord, and a process was established to review progress towards implementation of the accord over the next five years. Signatories to the accord formed the National Forest Strategy Coalition which was charged with developing a successor document in 1998 based on the results of the 1992 process.

The 1998 document[103] contained the same basic structure as the 1992 document. Its strategic directions were related to the areas of forest ecosystems, forest management, public participation, the forest industry, forest science, communities and the workforce, Aboriginal peoples, private woodlots, and the global forests. Thirty-one specific objectives and 121 commitments were contained in the document.

The principle initiative for the 1992 and 1998 strategies arose in the international arena. Tropical timber issues had been discussed since the 1970s in international fora and issues more generally related to forestry had been raised by the 1987 report of the U.N.-sponsored Brundtland Commission on Environment and Development.[104] In preparation for the 1992 U.N. Conference on Environment, and Development (UNCED), also known as the Rio conference, proposals had been mooted for the negotiation of an international convention on forests. Canada supported this convention, along with the European Union, although it was opposed by the United States. What resulted from the Rio conference was not binding international law, but rather a voluntary action program on forests set out as part of the conference's *Agenda 21* document. The document enunciated several principles of sustainability as they related to forests and called on governments, like Canada, to establish 'national forest policies' to ensure their implementation.[105]

Following the conference, in 1994 the Canadian and Malaysian governments co-sponsored an Intergovernmental Working Group on Forests (IWGF) which met twice. In June 1994 a World Commission on Forest and Sustainability was created, and in April 1995 the U.N. Commission on Sustainable Development (CSD) created an Intergovernmental Panel on Forests (IPF) to take over from the IWGF in actively promoting these policies. The IPF panel met several times but was unable to reach an agreement on whether a binding international law could be attained. As a result the U.N. agreed to create an intergovernmental forum on forests that would attempt to develop a recommendation by the year 2000.[106]

Canada has been intimately involved in all aspects of this recent set of international developments. The entire process has been termed 'the Montreal process' stemming from the original meeting in Montreal in 1993 which led to the formation of the IWGF,[107] although technically the Montreal process involved only the development of criteria and indicators for the conservation and sustainable management of temperate and boreal forests. These were adopted by the governments involved in the Santiago Declaration of 1995.

The overall impact of the 1992 and 1998 federal documents on the ground, however, have been minor.[108] A review undertaken by a panel of experts found that only local improvements had been made and urged greater involvement and commitment on the part of senior governments.[109] Nevertheless, faced with difficulties encountered due to consumer boycotts of Canadian old growth forest products, the federal government has found a new niche from which to influence, or attempt to influence provincial forest policies. Along with initiatives such as certification and promotion of sustainable practices worldwide, they have helped ensure continued access for Canadian forest products in international markets.[110]

Summary and Conclusion: The Politics of Constitutional Constraints

This historical overview has revealed a continually changing and shifting federal role in Canadian forest policy. Despite the fact that the BNA Act perpetuated provincial ownership of unalienated forest land, granted exclusive legislative authority over these lands to the provincial governments, and accorded the exclusive right to levy royalties to these governments, the federal government maintained a position equal to that of the provinces through its control over the Crown lands of the Northwest Territory and Hudson's Bay Company purchases. I retained this control despite the creation of the three prairie provinces in 1870 and 1905.

Losing several important jurisdictional battles with the provinces over lands and resources, however, after 1905 the federal government had to be content to administer its own forest lands through the Department of the Interior, and to attempt to influence provincial policy through reason and persuasion. This was accomplished, for instance, in Prime Minister Wilfrid Laurier's convening of the first National Forest Congress in 1906, and by the efforts made by both the Laurier and Borden governments to promote forest conservation through federal participation in the long-standing Commission of Conservation, as well as through the provision of assistance for the formation of various professional associations of foresters and forest engineers.

This particular modus vivendi with the provinces ended in 1930 with the natural resource transfer agreements which conveyed control over Crown lands in the three prairie provinces to the governments of Manitoba, Saskatchewan, and Alberta. Following this development, the federal role in the forest sector was thrown into a quandary from which it has never entirely emerged. Left with only the poor forest lands of the Yukon and Northwest territories to administer, the Department of the Interior was disbanded by the Mackenzie King government in 1936 and federal forest administration reduced to a small lands, parks, and forest branch in a new Department of Mines and Resources.[111] Only the imposition of federal wartime controls on timber production and prices between 1939 and 1945 rescued federal forest policy from oblivion.

After the Second World War, the forest sector figured prominently in federal reconstruction efforts and in efforts to expand the national economy through resource development. Although the federal role remained limited by the constitutional division of powers and provincial resource ownership, the Mackenzie King government attempted to influence the direction of provincial forest policies through the federal spending power. This initiative was embodied in the enactment of the Canada Forestry Act in 1949 which authorized the federal government to enter into shared-cost, conditional grant programs with the provincial governments.

Following the resource development orientation of the Gordon Commission on Canada's Economic Prospects, the Diefenbaker government attempted in 1960 to establish a direct federal presence in the forest sector through the creation of a specific federal Department of Forests. The Pearson government continued the resource development policy begun under Diefenbaker, but was forced to acknowledge the need for provincial participation in the development of forest policy. In 1966 the government, through the Department of Forests, convened only the second National Forest Congress in Canadian history in an effort to secure provincial support for new federal initiatives.[112]

What should have been the culmination of a process leading up to a new federal presence in the Canadian forest sector, however, turned out to be its nadir. Faced with provincial opposition to federal conditional grant programs and an inability to overcome constitutional barriers to an increased direct federal role in forest regulation, Pearson dissolved the Department of Forestry and began the process of ending the shared-cost programs.[113]

Federal expenditures in the forest sector continued to be made, however, but now took on the form of regional development incentives. The decline of forest issues in federal priorities during this period was reflected in the fact that the primary responsibility for the administration of remaining federal forest programs was transferred from the Department of Forestry to several different agencies, including new departments of Forestry and Rural Development, and of Fisheries and Forestry, before ending up in 1970 divided between a small branch of the Ministry of the Environment and a division of the Department of Regional Economic Expansion (DREE).[114]

Nevertheless, by the early 1970s the federal government was once again prompted to intervene in the forestry sector by its perception that the forest industry was in a crisis situation. Attempts were made to alleviate mill closures stemming from overcapacity in several declining industry sectors like the dissolving pulp industry in Quebec in 1970, and a concern for the need to modernize outdated plants and equipment surfaced. As a result, DREE began a process of ad hoc modernization subsidies to producers that culminated in the federal–provincial pulp and paper modernization programs signed with most eastern provinces between 1978 and 1982.

Concerns for the future of the national industry continued to be elaborated by several federal government agencies and advisory committees during this period, including the Economic Council of Canada and the

Science Council of Canada. Attempts to define the nature of the industry's problems and the appropriate policy response included the inclusion of the forest sector in the twenty-three sectoral task forces established by the Trudeau government to develop a basis for a national industrial strategy in the days leading up to the 1978 first ministers conferences on the economy.

The lack of an effective federal government policy in the forest area generated a federal response in the re-elected Trudeau government's 1980 decision to undertake major policy reviews in several key natural resource sectors, including the forest sector. Part of the staples-led economic development strategy unveiled in the 1981 federal budget, the national energy program, and other major federal resource initiatives of the early 1980s, the Liberals envisioned a major role for the federal government in promoting backward and forward linkages for the forest sector industries through government procurement associated with resource development mega-projects. The Liberals undertook to call a third major National Forest Congress in Toronto in 1980 to aid in the development of a new policy for the sector which would have room for a major federal role in directing future forest sector development. As the Parliamentary secretary to the minister of the environment stated at the time, the federal government was very concerned with establishing a federal presence in the development of the forest sector and in ensuring provincial policies favoured national goals and not 'parochial provincial interests.'[115]

Nevertheless, when the government finally announced its new strategy in 1981, although its preamble and background sections accurately reflected the federal concern for economic and industrial development, the proposals for actual government action were very restricted. Indeed, the proposals were limited to those that had been recommended by the provincially dominated Canadian Council of Resource and Environment Ministers (CCREM) in a separate policy exercise carried on outside the formal federal policy process.

Both the 1981 Liberal strategy and the 1987 Conservative strategy began with a process of policy development oriented towards increasing the federal role in forest policy. Both processes, however, ended with documents limiting the federal role to forest research, export enhancement, and, most importantly, providing continued funding for provincial forest management efforts – without any input into the establishment of those programs themselves.

The record of federal efforts to influence national forest policy shows that, between 1930 and 1987, successive federal governments of differing political persuasions had all been motivated by a concern for the health, vigour, and continued profitability of the forest industry. That is, each effort – in 1949, 1966, 1978, 1981, and 1987 – was motivated by the perception of an impending production or financial crisis in the industry or by the desire to promote additional industrial investment in resource exploitation. Each effort had involved the federal government in the provision of financial assistance to the industry either in the form of infrastructural development or subsidies for industry rationalization and modernization.

On each occasion, the federal government responded first by the imposition of temporary, ad hoc measures and then attempted to move towards the implementation of a policy framework that would allow room for a continued, ongoing, federal presence in the regulation of forest sector activities. On each occasion, however, while the government may have been successful in establishing a short-term presence in the sector, provincial opposition resulted in the limitation of the federal role to providing funding for provincial programs and direct involvement in only a relatively minor range of areas like research and development, trade promotion, and public awareness.

After 1987 the federal government changed tactics and concentrated its efforts on aspects of the forest sector that fall within its own jurisdiction. With the exception of the model forest program discussed in previous chapters, its efforts in the 1990s have focused on international trade issues, specifically managing the Canadian response to the U.S. softwood lumber countervail actions, and in integrating Canadian policy with that of the United Nations through its representation at UNCED, through the Montreal Process and more generally in a number of international initiatives in the forestry, biodiversity, and climate change areas. This latter activity has involved it in the establishment of two recent national forest strategy processes in 1992 and 1998. Although important, like their predecessors in the post-1930 period, these initiatives have had a limited impact on actual forestry practices in Canada.

While significant, the new role of the federal government as an agent of international and intergovernmental coordinator represents a significant decline from earlier eras. No longer a major landowner or a significant provider of funds for forest sector development, the federal government has lost its ability to affect most aspects of Canadian forest policy and practices.

NOTES

1 Christopher Armstrong, *The Politics of Federalism* (Toronto: University of Toronto Press, 1981); F.C. Morrison, 'Oliver Mowat and the Development of Provincial Rights in Ontario: A Study in Dominion-Provincial Relations 1867–96' in Ontario, Department of Public Records and Archives, *Three History Theses* (Toronto: Department of Public Records and Archives, 1961); H.V. Nelles, *The Politics of Development* (Toronto: Macmillan, 1974); and Gerard V. La Forest, *Reservation and Disallowance of Provincial Legislation* (Ottawa: Department of Justice, 1955). The most significant case was *Smylie v Queen*, O.A.R. vol. 27, 1900, which upheld Ontario's manufacturing condition on pulpwood exports against the federal trade and commerce power.
2 At the turn-of-the-century, the federal and provincial governments were treated identically in contemporary prescriptions for 'national' forest policy. See, for example, B.E. Fernow, 'A Forest Policy for Canada' in *Industrial Canada* 8(3), 1907, 175–9; B.E. Fernow, 'What We Want,' in Canadian Forestry Association, *Tenth Annual Report of the Canadian Forestry Association* (Toronto: Warwick Brothers, 1909) 75–83; and Judson F. Clark, 'A Canadian Forest Policy' *Canadian Forestry Journal* 2(1), 1906, 41–8.
3 For a discussion of events in this protracted period see Norman Fergus Black, *History of Saskatchewan and the Old North West* (Regina: North West Historical Publishers, 1913) 5–142
4 Act 32 and 33 Victoria Chapter 3, 1869. This act, among other things, formally changed the name of the area to the 'North-West Territories.'
5 'An Act to Amend and Combine the Act 32 and 33 Victoria Chapter 3; and to Establish and Provide for the Government of the Province of Manitoba' 33 Victoria Chapter 3, 1870, and 'An Act to Make Further Provision for the Government of the Northwest Territories ' 34 Victoria Chapter 16, 1871.
6 At this time the entire area of what is now Alberta, Manitoba, and Saskatchewan had a European population of 6,691 persons and an estimated 50,000 persons of Aboriginal descent. Less than 3,650 hectares of land were under cultivation. W.A. Mackintosh, *Prairie Settlement: The Geographical Setting* (Toronto: Macmillan, 1934) 1; and Chester Martin, 'Confederation and the West,' in Canadian Historical Association, *Report of the Annual Meeting Held in the City of Toronto May 27–28 1927 with Historical Papers* (Ottawa: Department of Public Archives, 1927) 20–8.
7 The area did continue to develop and change, however, as successive Dominion governments continued the process of establishing rudimentary political institutions and encouraging immigration to the area. Concerns over the proper administration of the territory to the east of Manitoba led to its

exclusion from the Northwest Territories and its creation as a separate territory by the terms of the 1876 Keewatin Act. 'An Act Respecting the Northwest Territories and to Create a Separate Territory Out of Parts Thereof,' 39 Victoria Chapter 21, 1876. Although the original Northwest Territories Act (1875) had an enumerated list of powers of the Territorial Government (Section 7) which included territorial control over forest protection – subject to federal paramountcy – it was replaced in a major revision of the act passed in 1877. The new act specified that the powers of the Territorial Government would be set by Federal Order-in-Council. See the Northwest Territories Act, 40 Victoria Chapter 7, 1877.

8 'An Act to Amend and Continue the Act 32 and 33 Victoria Chapter 3; and to Establish and Provide for the Government of the Province of Manitoba' 32-3. Victoria Chapter 3, 1870.

9 Unlike Prince Edward Island, which received a grant from the federal government in lieu of land revenues when it joined Confederation in 1873, Manitoba received no compensation until 1882. See Chester Martin, *The Natural Resources Question: The Historical Basis of Provincial Claims* (Winnipeg: King's Printer, 1920) 43-53, 81.

10 'An Act Respecting the Public Lands of the Dominion' 35 Victoria Chapter 23, 1872. On the early period of federal control see J.D.B. Harrison, *Forests and Forest Industries of the Prairie Provinces* (Ottawa: Department of the Interior, 1936) 47-51.

11 The 1872 Dominion Lands Act was also amended to provide that the Hudson's Bay Company would receive one twentieth of the revenue derived from any timber limits established in 'unsurveyed territory within the fertile belt.' Payment was to continue until a township had been surveyed and established. 'An Act to Amend the Dominion Lands Act' 37 Victoria Chapter 19, 1874.

12 In 1876, by the terms of the Keewatin Act, the large forested areas immediately adjacent to the province – from Fort William to the western border of the province at Lake Manitoba and north to the Arctic Ocean (a total area of over 1,022,000 square kilometres) – were incorporated into the District of Keewatin. Most of the area south of latitude 60 was eventually transferred to Manitoba by 1912. The eastern area beyond Lake of the Woods was subject to a long dispute between the Federal government and the Province of Ontario and was eventually granted to Ontario. See Norman L. Nicholson, *The Boundaries of Canada: Its Provinces and Territories* (Ottawa: Queen's Printer, 1964) 71-6.

13 Mackintosh, *Prairie Settlement*; Martin, *'Dominion Lands' Policy* (Toronto: Macmillan, 1938) 443-4.

14 The best sources on the early system of timber administration and the early

forest industry in the province of Manitoba are C.B. Gill, 'Forest History' in E.S. Fellows, ed., *Potential Development of the Primary Forest Industries* (Winnipeg: Report Prepared for the Committee on Manitoba's Economic Future, 1961) 28–49; H.I. Stevenson, *The Forests of Manitoba* (Winnipeg: Economic Survey Board, 1938) 159–79.

15 See, e.g., Saskatchewan, *The Natural Resources of Saskatchewan* (Regina: Department of Natural Resources and Industrial Development, 1945) 111–12.

16 The first railway branch line into the north was built in 1890 from Regina to Prince Albert but was largely unsuccessful in opening the area up to either settlement or exploitation. By 1902 settlement had proceeded by only about 48 kilometres north of Regina. See T.D. Regehr, *The Canadian Northern Railway: Pioneer Road of the Northern Prairies 1985–1918* (Toronto: Macmillan, 1976) 179–86; Arthur S. Morton, *History of Prairie Settlement* (Toronto: Macmillan, 1938) 65–95.

17 The last area of the Eastern Slope to be exploited for timber was the area surrounding Jasper which awaited the arrival of the Canadian Northern Railway in 1903 and the Grand Trunk Pacific Railway between 1909 and 1910. James C. MacGregor, *A History of Alberta* (Edmonton: Hurtig Publishers, 1981) 201. The lumber industry was especially aided by the arrival of the Grand Trunk Pacific Railway – which opened up rich timber country surrounding Edson and received another boost from the extension of the Canadian Northern to Lake Athabaska between 1906 and 1912. Ibid. 201–2, and Leo Thwaite, *Alberta: An Account of Its Wealth and Progress* (Toronto: Musson Book, 1912) 142–3. The more heavily timbered northwestern area of the province was opened to logging between 1914 and 1916 by the construction of the Edmonton, Dunvegan, and British Columbia Railway which reached into the Peace River country. MacGregor, *A History,* 205–6. By 1918 numerous mills were in operation in the Peace River area, notably at Fort Vermillon and Peace River itself. See F.H. Kitto, *The Peace River District, Canada: Its Resources and Opportunities* (Ottawa: Department of the Interior, 1918) 14.

18 See David H. Breen, '"Timber Tom" and the North-West Rebellion,' in *Alberta Historical Review* 19(3), 1971, 1–7.

19 On the early industry see Phil Lewis, 'Resource Development in the Canmore Area,' in *Alberta History* 32(2) 1984, 9–18; Christopher Youe, 'Eau Claire: The Company and the Community,' *Alberta History* 27(3), 1979, 1–6.

20 J.H. White, *Forestry on Dominion Lands* (Ottawa: Commission of Conservation, 1915) 13–14.

21 This is not to say that the revenue-generating potential of the nation's forests

was forgotten. See, for example, the statement on revenue potential made by the federal government's first Superintendent of Forestry, Elihu Stewart, contained in Defebaugh's early history. James Elliot Defebaugh, *History of the Lumber Industry of America* (Chicago: American Lumberman, 1906) 83–4.

22 See Canada, *Report of the Canadian Forestry Convention Held at Ottawa, January 10, 11 and 12, 1906* (Ottawa: Government Printing Bureau, 1906); Nelles, *The Politics of Development* (Toronto: Macmillan, 1974); Thomas L. Burton, *Natural Resource Policy in Canada* (Toronto: McClelland and Stewart, 1974) 23–46; Peter Gillis and Thomas Roach, *Lost Initiatives* (New York: Greenwood, 1986); Donald MacKay, *Heritage Lost* (Toronto: Macmillan, 1985).

23 'An Act Respecting Forest Reserves,' 6 Edward 7 Chapter 14, 1906; see H.N. Whitford and Roland D. Craig, *Forests of British Columbia* (Ottawa: Commission of Conservation, 1918) 145–6. The best source on this era of federal forest policy is an unpublished Department of the Interior manuscript in the Public Archives of Canada in Ottawa; G.W. Payton, *History of Regulations Governing the Disposal of Timber on Dominion Lands in the Provinces of Alberta and Saskatchewan from the 1st September, 1905 to the 1st October, 1930 Two Volumes* (Ottawa: Department of the Interior, 1930).

24 In the House of Commons via 'An Act Respecting the Representation of the Northwest Territories in the Parliament of Canada,' 49 Victoria Chapter 24, 1886 and in the Senate via 'An Act Respecting the Representation of the Northwest Territories in the Senate of Canada,' 50–1 Victoria Chapter 3, 1887.

25 'An Act to Amend the Revised Statutes of Canada, Chapter Fifty, Respecting the Northwest Territories,' 51 Victoria Chapter 19, 1888.

26 'An Act Further to Amend the Acts Respecting the Northwest Territories,' 60–61 Victoria Chapter 28, 1897. The difficulties over appropriations and the gradual emergence of party government in the Territorial Assembly is discussed at length in Lewis Herbert Thomas, *The Struggle for Responsible Government in the North-West Territories 1870–97* (Toronto: University of Toronto Press, 1978) 161–263. Relevant documents and legislative records are contained in E.H. Oliver, *The Canadian North-West: Its Early Development and Legislative Records* (Ottawa: Government Printing Bureau, 1914); Publications of the Canadian Archives No 9 – 2 vols. A more popular account is contained in Grant MacEwan, *Frederick Haultain: Frontier Statesman of the Canadian Northwest* (Saskatoon: Western Producer Prairie Books, 1985).

27 See C. Cecil Lingard, *Territorial Government in Canada: The Autonomy Question in the Old North-West Territories* (Toronto: University of Toronto Press, 1946); Lingard, 'Economic Forces Behind the Demand for Provincial Status in the Old North West Territories,' *Canadian Historical Review* 21(3), 1940, 254–67.

28 Although both governments received some financial compensation for the Dominion Government's retention of control over Crown lands and natural resources, both issues were to remain contentious until they were transferred to provincial jurisdiction in 1930. See Black, 453–80; Oliver, 'Saskatchewan and Alberta: General History' in Adam Shortt and Arthur G. Doughty, eds., *Canada and Its Provinces: A History of the Canadian People and Their Institutions by One Hundred Associates* (Toronto: Glasgow, Brook, 1914) 19(10) – The Prairie Provinces Part I, 147–280; Lingard, 'Territorial Government in Canada,' 207–31.

29 'An Act to Establish and Provide for the Province of Saskatchewan,' *The Saskatchewan Act*, 4–5 Edward 7 Chapter 3.

30 In return the provincial government received a Dominion per capita subsidy which escalated upwards according to each census return along a fixed formula. Until the provincial population reached 400,000 persons the subsidy amounted to $375,000 per year. In addition, the province was granted an initial five year subsidy of $93,750 annually to cover the costs of establishing public buildings.

31 On the origins of the farmer protest movements in the Territorial Grain Growers Association and the Saskatchewan Grain Growers Association prior to the First World War, see S.M. Lipset, *Agrarian Socialism: The Co-operative Commonwealth Federation in Saskatchewan – A Study in Political Sociology* (Berkeley: University of California Press, 1959) 37–72; and John Archer, *Saskatchewan: A History* (Saskatoon: Western Producer Prairie Books, 1980) 133–65. On the impact of the National Policy tariff on the farmer see V.C. Fowke, 'Political Economy and the Canadian Wheat Grower' in Norman Ward and Duff Spafford, eds., *Politics in Saskatchewan* (Toronto: Longmans, 1968) 207–20.

32 On the Liberal era in Saskatchewan see David E. Smith, *Prairie Liberalism: The Liberal Party in Saskatchewan, 1905–71* (Toronto: University of Toronto Press, 1975); Escott Reid, 'The Saskatchewan Liberal Machine Before 1929,' *Canadian Journal of Economics and Political Science* 2(1), 1936, 27–40.

33 'An Act to Establish and Provide for the Government of Alberta' 4–5 Edward 7 Chapter 3, 1905.

34 See N.D. Bankes, *Crown Timber Rights in Alberta* (Calgary: Canadian Institute of Resources Law, 1986) 14–24.

35 Canada, *Report of the Royal Commission on Pulpwood* (Ottawa: King's Printer, 1924) 68–72. A survey of the natural resources of the prairie provinces by the Department of the Interior in 1925 shared the same bleak conclusion, noting only that the province contained large stands of under-utilized pulp-wood in inaccessible areas and in stands of low volume per hectare. Canada,

Natural Resources of the Prairie Provinces (Ottawa: Department of the Interior, 1925) 35–6.

36 Gill, 'Forest History' in Fellows, *Potential Development of the Primary Forest Industries* (Winnipeg: Report Prepared for the Committee on Manitoba's Economic Future, 1961) 32; Canada, 'Royal Commission on Pulpwood,' 64.

37 The boundaries of the two northern territories remaining under federal government control were established between 1895 and 1905. Following the large influx of people to the previously sparsely populated area following the 1896 Klondike Gold Rush, the provisional district of the Yukon was constituted as a separate territory in 1898 by 'An Act to Provide for the Government of the Yukon District' 61 Victoria Chapter 6, 1898. In 1905, when new provinces were created in Alberta and Saskatchewan, the northern boundaries of the two prairie provinces were extended and the area above 60 degrees of latitude, including the District of Keewatin, defined as the North-west Territories. See 'An Act to Amend the Act Regarding the North-West Territories' 4–5 Edward 7 Chapter 27, 1905.

38 The best source on this early period is John Kennedy Naysmith, 'Land Use and Public Policy in Northern Canada,' doctoral dissertation, University of British Columbia, 1975, 57–87.

39 See Ernest J. Chambers, *The Unexploited West: A Compilation of All the Authentic Information Available at the Present Time as to the Natural Resources of the Unexploited Regions of Northern Canada* (Ottawa: King's Printer 1914) 64–80, 261–80, 317–23.

40 No mention of Dominion government forestry activities in either territory are contained in contemporary government accounts. See, for example, W.N. Millar, 'Organization Work of the Dominion Forestry Service Branch in Western Canada' in Canadian Forestry Association, *Report of the Fourteenth Convention of the Canadian Forestry Association* (Quebec: Dussault and Proulx, 1913) 80–4; J.H. White, *Forestry on Dominion Lands*; and E. Stewart, 'Forestry on Dominion Lands,' *Report of the Second Annual Meeting of the Canadian Forestry Association* (Ottawa: Government Printing Bureau, 1901) 19–22.

41 See F.C.C. Lynch, *The Lower Athabaska and Slave River District* (Ottawa: Department of the Interior, 1921). For descriptions of the early establishment of small sawmills by the federal government and various church groups see F.H. Kitto, *The North West Territories 1930* (Ottawa: Department of the Interior, 1930) 72–3; Canada, Department of Mines and Resources, *The Northwest Territories: Administration – Resource – Development* (Ottawa: Department of Mines and Resources, 1943) 24, 44–6.

42 See W.F. Lothian, *Yukon Territory: A Brief Description of Its History, Administra-*

tion, Resources and Development (Ottawa: Department of Mines and Resources, 1947).

43 Changes to the system of territorial administration arising from the recommendations of the Carrothers Commission were contained in 'An Act to Amend the Northwest Territories Act' 14–15 Elizabeth 2 Chapter 22, 1966. See also C.M. Drury, *Constitutional Development in the Northwest Territories: Report of the Special Representative* (Ottawa: Ministry of Supply and Services, 1980).

44 'An Act Respecting Crown Lands in the Yukon Territory and the Northwest Territory' 14 George 6 Chapter 22, 1950, replaced the Dominion Lands Act of 1872. See Peter Pearse, *Forest Policy in Canada* (UBC: Forest Economics and Policy Analysis Project, 1985) T4–T5; Naysmith, 120–36. The Act was amended in 1970 to include environmental considerations. On the 1970 Act and regulations see Kenneth P. Beauchamp, *Land Management in the Canadian North* (Ottawa: Canadian Arctic Resources Committee, 1976). On the 1977 amendments see Gurston Dacks, *A Choice of Futures: Politics in the Canadian North* (Toronto: Methuen, 1981) 168–95.

45 See Beauchamp, *Land Management* 16–17, 32–3; and Pearse, op.cit. T5–T9.

46 See Naysmith, 'The Future Value of Canada's Northern Forests,' in *Forestry Chronicle* 46(4), 1970, 277–80. Although timber inventories in the north are poor, it was known that existing operations are removing timber at a rate greater than any allowable cut system would permit. This was allowed simply to permit these logging firms to survive. Correspondence with C.R. Carlisle, Regional Manager, Forest Resources, Department of Indian and Northern Affairs, 30 April 1986.

47 Forest Management Act, *SNWT* 1986(2), Chapter 3.

48 See Forest Management Act *RSNWT* 1988, Chapter F9 and Forest Management Regulations, 1990, *RRNWT* Chapter F14.

49 See Canadian Forest Service, *The State of Canada's Forests 1998–1999* (Ottawa: Natural Resources Canada, 1999).

50 See Canada, 'Report, Relative to the Manufacturing Industries in Existence in Canada,' in House of Commons, *Sessional Papers* vol. 18(10), 1885, paper no 37; Canada, 'Report of Commissioner and Other Documents in Connection with The Royal Commission in re: The Alleged Combination of Paper Manufacturers and Dealers,' in House of Commons, *Sessional Papers* vol. 36, 1902 and vol. 13, sessional paper no 53; Canada, 'Proceedings of the Select Committee Appointed for the Purpose of Inquiring into the Prices Charges for Lumber in the Provinces of Manitoba, Alberta and Saskatchewan,' in the appendix to the *Forty-Second Volume of the Journals of the House of Commons, Dominion of Canada Session 1906–7 Part II* (Ottawa: King's Printer, 1908);

Canada, *Inquiry into the Manufacture, Sale, Price and Supply of Newsprint in Canada: Interim Report* (Ottawa: Ministry of Finance, 1918); Canada, *Proceedings of the Select Standing Committee of the House of Commons on Banking and Commerce: March 6, 1934 – June 14, 1934* (Ottawa: King's Printer, 1934) 762–926. The anti-combines investigations began with Department of Labour Canada, *Investigation into an Alleged Combine in the Manufacture and Sale of Paperboard Shipping Containers and Related Products* (Ottawa: King's Printer, 1939), while the Royal Commission on Corporate Concentration included many large forest companies in its investigations. See, for example, H.T. Seymour, *Royal Commission on Corporate Concentration Study No. 1: Argus Corporation Ltd. – A Corporate Background Report* (Ottawa: Ministry of Supply and Services, 1977); and Murray Savage, *Royal Commission on Corporate Concentration Study No. 6: Domtar Ltd – A Corporate Background Report* (Ottawa: Ministry of Supply and Services, 1976). However, the Commission determined that Canadian firms required large-scales – necessitating high levels of concentration in a small domestic market – in order to compete on international markets. See Canada, *Report of the Royal Commission on Corporate Concentration* (Ottawa: Ministry of Supply and Services, 1978).

51 As early as 1944 Opposition leader John Bracken had proposed the establishment of a national forest policy, arguing that the federal government had to take a more active role in regulating the forest resource if the forest industry was to prosper. The Conservatives proposed establishing a federal-provincial advisory board to draft a new National Forestry Policy to help 'conserve and manage our forest resources in a manner which would give the widest and most lucrative employment to as many Canadians as possible' while remaining competitive in world markets. See John Bracken, *A National Forestry Policy* (address by the Honourable John Bracken delivered in Campbellton N.B. 15 May 1944), election pamphlet, 2.

52 'An Act Respecting Forest Conservation' 13 George 6 Chapter 8, 1949 replaced the Dominion Forest Reserves Act of 1911.

53 Canada, *Canada's Forests 1946–1950: Report to Sixth British Commonwealth Forestry Conference* (Ottawa: Department of Resources and Development, 1952) 25–6.

54 Under the terms of the Canada Forestry Act, between 1951 and 1967, the federal government spent $63.8 million (about $180 in 1980 dollars) on forestry activities. While the majority of this money was spent aiding forest inventory and fire protection efforts in the provinces, $23.5 million was spent on the construction of access roads to aid industry's ability to exploit previously inaccessible resources. See Canada, *Forest Inventory and Reforestation Under the Canada Forestry Act: 1952 to 1956* (Ottawa: Department of

Northern Affairs and National Resources, 1957); and Thorne, Stevenson, and Kellogg, *Funding Mechanisms for Forest Management* (Toronto: Canadian Council of Resource and Environment Ministers, 1981) p. 16. On the process leading up to the 1949 Act see Gillis and Roach, 237–50.

55 K.G. Fensom, *Expanding Forestry Horizons: A History of the Canadian Institute of Forestry – Institut Forestier du Canada, 1908–1969* (Ste Anne de Bellevue: Canadian Institute of Forestry, 1972).

56 The inter-provincial Steering Committee of the Conference became the Canadian Council of Resource Ministers in 1964 and undertook several major studies of the forest sector and forest policy. The council became the Canadian Council of Resource and Environment Ministers (CCREM) in 1971. On CCREM see M.S. Whittington, *CCREM: An Experiment in Interjurisdictional Co-ordination* (Ottawa: Science Council of Canada, 1978).

57 Between 1965 and 1971 forestry related activities of $83.1 million accounted for 17.4 per cent of total expenditures under these programs. Forestry expenditures were included in the Regional Development Incentives Act (RDIA) programs, the Agricultural and Regional Development Act (ARDA) programs, the Fund for Rural Economic Development (FRED) programs, the Industrial Research and Development Act (IRDIA) programs, the Programme for the Advent of Industrial Technology (PAITC), and the Industrial Research Assistance Program (IRAP) among others. See Price Waterhouse Associates, *A Study of Taxation Practices Related to the Pulp and Paper Industry: Part II, Phase II – Other Fiscal Measures Volume II* (Ottawa: 1973) 1–27.

58 Between 1974 and 1980 the federal government spent $205 million on forestry projects. Of this total, the largest single item continued to be access road construction; which accounted for $65.1 million or about one third of all funding. See Thorne, Stevenson, and Kellogg, *Funding Mechanisms* 21 and relevant provincial sections above. On the overall development of regional economic development policies in Canada see Donald J. Savoie, *Regional Economic Development: Canada's Search for Solutions* (Toronto: University of Toronto Press, 1986); James Bickerton and Alain G. Gagnon, 'Regional Policy in Historical Perspective: The Federal Role in Economic Development in the Atlantic Provinces and Eastern Quebec,' paper presented to the Annual Meeting of the Canadian Political Science Association, Vancouver 1983.

59 See Science Council of Canada, *Seeing the Forest and the Trees* (Ottawa: Science Council of Canada, 1970) Report no 8.

60 See Canadian Council of Resource and Environment Ministers, *Forestry Seminar Background Papers – Winnipeg 1970* (Manitoba: Canadian Council of

Resource and Environment Ministers, 1970); and Canadian Council of Resource and Environment Ministers, *Forest Policies in Canada* (Manitoba: Canadian Council of Resource and Environment Ministers, 1976).

61 In 1971 an Inter-Departmental Committee for the Review of the Forest Products Industry had been formed to follow-up on the proceedings of the Forest Industry Consultative Committee (FICC) established in 1970. For a list of members of the FICC see Canada, *Review of the Canadian Forest Products Industry* (Ottawa: Department of Industry, Trade, and Commerce, 1978) Appendix III, 263–7.

62 The analysis and recommendations of the 1973 *Outlook Paper* were endorsed by the Canadian Forest Advisory Council in its third report of September 1975. Canadian Forest Advisory Council, *The Forestry Situation in Canada – Major Concerns and Proposed Remedies* (Ottawa: Canadian Forest Advisory Council, 1975) 4.

63 Canada, Department of Industry, Trade and Commerce, 'A Working Paper Concerning the Canadian Pulp and Paper Industry' (Ottawa: Department of Industry, Trade, and Commerce, 1973). Prior to this, the need for a new overall strategy for the industry had been recognized in the problems associated with disjointed federal and provincial government efforts to aid the dissolving pulp industry in Quebec. In this instance, federal and provincial subsidies had given rise to new capacity coming onstream at an ITT-Rayonier mill at Port Cartier at a time when markets were glutted; resulting in layoffs in other Quebec mills. An excellent study of the arrangements, results, and lessons from the situation is Nitin Tarachand Mehta, *Policy Formation in a Declining Industry: The Case of the Canadian Dissolving Pulp Industry*, doctoral dissertation, Harvard University, 1978. See also, Walter Johnson, 'Striking in a Quebec Paper Town: East Angus and the Pulp and Paper Industry,' *Our Generation* 12(3), 1978, 32–44.

64 See Darveau, Grenier, Lussier and Associates, *Forest Industry Rationalization: A General Approach and Pilot Study* (Ottawa: Federal-Provincial Forest Industries Development Committee, 1978).

65 See Wood Gundy Ltd., *Historical and Future Sources and Uses of Capital for the Pulp and Paper Sector of the Canadian Forest Products Industry* (Ottawa: Department of Regional Industrial Expansion, 1977).

66 On the first and second tier process of policy reviews of 23 sectors of the economy carried out by the Ministry of Industry, Trade, and Commerce, and the outcome of the 1978 conferences see Richard French, *How Ottawa Decides: Planning and Industrial Policy-Making, 1968–1980* (Toronto: Lorimer, 1980); and Douglas Brown, Julia Eastman, and Ian Robinson, *The Limits of Consultation: A Debate among Ottawa, the Provinces and the Private Sector on an*

Industrial Strategy (Ottawa: Science Council of Canada, 1981). This process included the first sectoral overview prepared by the federal government. Significantly it did not discuss policy towards forest resources, but only the status of the forest industry. See Canada, *Review of the Canadian Forest Products Industry.*

67 First Ministers Conference on the Economy, *Report of the Consultative Task Force on the Forest Products Industry* (Ottawa: First Ministers' Conference on the Economy, 1978) 2.

68 A good summary of the policy process followed between 1979 and 1984 by the federal government, including synopses of the major policy statements produced over the period is Stephen McBride, 'Canadian Forestry Policy 1979–84,' paper presented to the Annual Meeting of the Canadian Political Science Association, Guelph, 1984).

69 F.L.C. Reed and Associates, *Forest Management in Canada* (Ottawa: Canadian Forestry Service, 1978).

70 The unity of foresters and industry on the need for a new federal policy is apparent in the discussions which took place at the 1980 Congress. See Canadian Pulp and Paper Association, *The Forest Imperative: Proceedings of the Canadian Forest Congress September 22–23, 1980* (Montreal: Canadian Pulp and Paper Association, 1980) .

71 Canada, *Federal Policy on the Canadian Forestry Sector* (Ottawa: Canadian Forestry Service, 1979).

72 Roger Simmons, *Federal Forestry Commitments in the 1980s*, Lecture Series No. 7 (Edmonton: University of Alberta Forest Faculty, 1980).

73 Canada, *A Forest Sector Strategy for Canada* (Ottawa: Ministry of the Environment, 1981).

74 See Doern, 'Spending Priorities: The Liberal View,' in Doern, ed., *How Ottawa Spends Your Tax Dollars: Federal Priorities 1981* (Toronto: Lorimer, 1981) 1–55; Canada, *Economic Development for the 1980s* (Ottawa: Ministry of Finance, 1981); and Canada, *Major Canadian Projects, Major Canadian Opportunities: A Report of the Major Projects Task Force on Major Capital Projects in Canada to the Year 2000* (Ottawa: Department of Industry, Trade and Commerce, 1981).

75 Canada, 'A Forest Sector Strategy for Canada,' 5.

76 The limited federal role specified by the 1981 strategy was in keeping with the role envisioned for the central government by the provinces. The Canadian Council of Resource and Environment Ministers, had undertaken at its June 1977 meeting to develop a framework for a national forest policy which would reconcile forest and industrial interests and take into account federal and provincial jurisdictional limitations. By 1979 the CCREM had developed

an 11 point proposal for a national forest policy. The proposal recognized provincial jurisdiction over most issues; endorsed multiple use management of the forest resource; employment creation; producing additional industrial wood; regional stability; maintaining export earnings and a positive contribution to the Canadian balance of payments; and the maintenance of 'social capital' – that is, the contribution of the forest sector to provincial and federal treasuries. See Canadian Council of Resource and Environment Ministers, *Forestry in Canada: Background Paper for the Federal-Provincial Consultation on the Economy, Ottawa January 25, 1978* (Manitoba: Canadian Council of Resource and Environment Ministers, 1978); G.S. Nagle, 'What Is National Forest Policy in Canada?' *Forestry Chronicle* 54(6), 1978, 291–5; and Canadian Council of Resource and Environment Ministers, *Forestry Imperatives for Canada: A Proposal for Forest Policy in Canada* (Manitoba: Canadian Council of Resource and Environment Ministers, 1979).

77 See Canada, *Policy Statement: A Framework for Forest Renewal* (Ottawa: Ministry of the Environment, 1982). The intention of the government was to enter into these agreements with the provinces subject to certain conditions – such as the adoption by the provinces of a long-term 20-year plan for forest management. See Anonymous, 'Millions Needed to Save Woods Industry' *Globe and Mail*, 30 December 1982, 4.

78 See Canada, *A Review of Canadian Trade Policy: A Background Document to Canadian Trade Policy in the 1980s* (Ottawa: Department of External Affairs, 1983); Canada, *Trade Policy for the 1980s: A Discussion Paper* (Ottawa: Department of External Affairs, 1983).

79 The Progressive Conservatives while in opposition from 1979–1984 had criticized Liberal 'inactivity' in the forest sector and promised action in the area. See Frank Oberle and Warren Everson, *The Green Ghetto: Can We Save Canadian Forestry?* (Ottawa: Mimeo, 1983). Existing federal programs in the forest sector survived virtually unscathed from the program review undertaken by the Neilson Task Force, with only minor programs such as biomass research recommended for cancellation. See Canada, *Natural Resources Program: From Crisis to Opportunity* (Ottawa: Task Force on Program Review, 1985).

80 Interview with Warren Everson, Executive Assistant to Minister of State for Forestry, March 1985. See also Roman Hohol, 'Interview: Gerald Merrithew – Federal Forestry Minister Reviews His First Year in Spotlight,' *Pulp and Paper Magazine* 39(1), 1986, 78–80; and Chris Wood, 'Q and A With Forestry Minister Gerald Merrithew: Preventing the Decline and Fall of One of Our Key Industries' *Financial Post*, 22 December 1984, 40. Two useful overviews of developments in federal forest policy at this time are Canadian Forestry Service, *Progress Report 1980–84 on Canada by the Canadian Forestry Service,*

Prepared for the Twelfth Commonwealth Forestry Conference 1985 (Ottawa: Canadian Forestry Service, 1985); United Nations, *State of Forestry in Canada* (Rome: Food and Agriculture Organization, 1986) Presented at the North American Forestry Commission – thirteenth session Chetumel, Mexico 3–7 February 1986.

81 Brian Mulroney, 'Opening Statement' in Canadian Forestry Association, *National Forest Congress 1986* (Ottawa: CFA, 1986), 303–5.

82 Canadian Forestry Service, *A Forest Sector Strategy for Canada* (Ottawa: Ministry of the Environment, 1981).

83 See Canadian Council of Forest Ministers, *Canadian Forestry Forum, 1985–1986* (Ottawa: Agriculture Canada, 1986).

84 Gilbert Paille, 'The Major Elements of a Forest Sector Strategy for Canada,' in Canadian Forestry Association, *National Forest Congress 1986* (Ottawa: Canadian Forestry Association 1986) 392–6.

85 Canadian Council of Forest Ministers, *A National Forest Sector Strategy for Canada* (Ottawa: Ministry of Supply and Services, 1987).

86 Michael Howlett, 'The National Forest Sector Strategy and the Search for a Federal Role in Canadian Forest Policy,' *Canadian Public Administration*, 32(40), 1987, 545–63.

87 One sector which continued to operate under tariff protection was the Canadian fine paper industry. The industry was also kept out of foreign markets by foreign tariffs on fine paper products. Until 1977, Canadian fine papers faced a U.S. tariff of 2.8 per cent, which, under the Multilateral Trade Negotiations agreement of that year, was to be reduced to 0.8 per cent by 1987. Tariffs in the EEC remained at 12 per cent until 1980 when it was agreed to reduce the tariff to nine per cent by 1987. J.D. Johnson, *The Effect of Tariff Reductions on the Canadian Fine Paper Industry* (Thunder Bay: Canadian Forestry Service Great Lakes Research Centre, 1984), 7–8. Tariffs in the fine paper sector were much higher earlier in the century, however, falling from a high of 33 per cent in 1900 to 23 per cent by 1968, before dropping sharply in that year to 15 per cent. The 1979 GATT round agreed to reduce tariffs on fine paper from 15 to 6.5 per cent between 1980 and 1987.

88 A longstanding issue in Canadian–Japanese relations, these were the subjects of Canadian complaints to GATT. See Brian Milner, 'Canada Seeks GATT Ruling on Japan's Lumber Duties,' *Globe and Mail*, 9 March 1988, B1.

89 The EEC has also charged Canadian producers with price-fixing in the European market. See Myra MacDonald, 'Pulp Producers Appeal EC Fine for Price-Fixing' *Globe and Mail*, 13 January 1988, B15.

90 DRIE, 'Sectoral Competitiveness Profiles.' See also GATT Secretariat, *Problems of International Trade in Forestry Products: Background Study by the Secre-*

tariat (Geneva: General Agreement on Tariffs and Trade Secretariat, 1984); Ministry of Industry, Trade and Commerce, *The Pulp and Paper Sector: A Background Study for GATT Negotiations* (Ottawa: Industry, Trade and Commerce, 1972).

91 For a general discussion of U.S. trade remedy laws see J.M. Finger, H. Keith Hall, and Douglas R. Nelson, 'The Political Economy of Administered Protection,' *American Economic Review* 72(3), 1982, 452–66 and Rodney de C. Grey, *United States Trade Policy Legislation: A Canadian View* (Montreal: Institute for Research on Public Policy, 1982).

92 On the 35 per cent duty imposed on Canadian redwood shakes and shingles in the mid-1980s see Anonymous, 'Shakes and Shingles Operating Full Steam,' *Globe and Mail*, 14 October 1986, B1–B2; K. Noble, 'No Let Up In Sight for Revitalized Forest Industry,' *Globe and Mail*, 4 September 1987, B1.

93 General reviews of the on going softwood lumber dispute are contained in David Leyton Brown, 'Hewers of Wood: The Forest Products Sector,' *International Journal* 42(1), 1986–1987, 59–77; Michael B. Percy and Christian Yoder, *The Softwood Lumber Dispute and Canada-U.S. Trade in Natural Resources* (Montreal: Institute for Research on Public Policy, 1987); Benjamin Cashore, 'Flights of the Phoenix: Explaining the Durability of the Canada-U.S. Softwood Lumber Dispute,' *Canadian-American Public Policy* 32, 1997.

94 On the 1962 episode see Sperry Lea, *The U.S. Softwood Lumber Situation in a Canadian-American Perspective* (Toronto: National Planning Association and the Private Planning Association of Canada, 1962). On the 1982–1983 countervailing case, which resulted in a negative determination, see U.S. International Trade Administration, *Final Negative Countervailing Duty Determinations: Certain Softwood Products from Canada* (Washington DC: U.S. Department of Commerce, 1983); Gordon W.V. Jansen, 'Canada-United States Trade Relations: The Lessons of the Softwood Lumber Countervail Case,' in Conference Board of Canada, *Executive Bulletin* 27, 1984. On the 1985 action see Michael B. Percy and Christian Yoder, *The Softwood Lumber Dispute*. On the 1991 action see Cashore, 'Flights of the Phoenix.'

95 See U.S. International Trade Administration, *Preliminary Affirmative Countervailing Duty Determination: Certain Softwood Lumber Products from Canada* (Washington DC: U.S. Department of Commerce, 1986); On the situation between 1982 and 1986 see Kenneth F. Englade, 'Stumped by the Lumber Issue,' *Across the Board* 23(2), 1986, 25–32. A detailed discussion of the preliminary determination is contained in Michael Howlett, 'Softwood Lumber and Extra-Territoriality,' *Policy Options* 8(2), 1987, 27–30.

96 Canada, *Memorandum of Understanding to Resolve Differences with Respect to the Conditions Affecting Trade in Softwood Lumber Products* (Ottawa: Ministry of

International Trade, December 30, 1986); U.S., International Trade Administration, *Termination of Countervailing Duty Investigation.*

97 On the rationale for the free trade talks see Ministry of International Trade, *Canadian Trade Negotiations: Introduction, Selected Documents, Further Reading* (Ottawa: Department of External Affairs, 1985).

98 See Canada, *Trade: Securing Canada's Future – Overview of The Canada-United States Trade Agreement* (Ottawa: Ministry of International Trade, 1987). On the specific effects of the deal on the softwood lumber trade see Kimberly Noble, 'Softwood Lumber Agreement Remains Unaffected by Comprehensive Treaty,' *Globe and Mail,* 6 October 1987, B5.

99 Mary Pierson, 'Recent Developments in the U.S./Canada Softwood Lumber Dispute,' *Law and Policy in International Business,* 25, 1994, 1187–1203.

100 See Benjamin Cashore, 'Flights of the Phoenix.' See also Ken Drushka, 'It's the Same Old Softwood Lumber War,' *Vancouver Sun,* 7 March 2001, D2.

101 See Brian Hocking, 'The Woods and the Trees: Catalytic Diplomacy and Canada's Trials as a "Forestry Superpower,"' *Environmental Politics* 5(3), 1996, 448–75.

102 Canadian Council of Forest Ministers, *Sustainable Forests: A Canadian Commitment* (Ottawa: Canadian Forest Service, 1992).

103 Canadian Council of Forest Ministers, *Sustainable Forests, A Canadian Commitment: National Forest Strategy 1998–2003 – National Forest Congress Version* (Ottawa: Canadian Council of Forest Ministers, 1998).

104 See World Commission on Environment and Development, *Our Common Future* (New York: Oxford University Press, 1987).

105 See David Humphreys, *National Forest Programmes in a Global Context* (paper prepared for the International Seminar on the Formulation and Implementation of National Forest Programmes, Freiburg, Germany, 1998).

106 See Peter Gluck, "National Forest Programs – Significance of a Forest Policy Framework." In P. Gluck, G. Oesten, S.H. and, K.-R. Volz, eds., *Formulation and Implementation of National Forest Programmes: vol. 1 – Theoretical Aspects* (Joensuu: European Forest Institute, 1999). 39–52; Derek Humphreys, 'National Forest Programmes in a Global Context,' in Gluck et al., eds., *Formulation and Implementation of National Forest Programmes,* 53–72. See also Tage et al., 'Hot Spot in the Field: National Forest Programmes – a New Instrument within Old Conflicts of the Forestry Sector,' *Forest Policy and Economics.* 1(1), 2000, 95–106; Monique M. Ross, *A History of Forest Legislation in Canada 1867–1996* (Calgary: Canadian Institute of Resources Law, 1997) CIRL Occasional Paper no. 2.

107 See Canadian Forest Service, *The State of Canada's Forests 1995–1996: Sus-*

taining Forests at Home and Abroad (Ottawa: Natural Resources Canada, 1996).

108 See Joanna M. Beyers and L. Anders Sandberg, 'Canadian Federal Forest Policy: Present Initiatives and Historical Constraints,' in L. Anders Sandberg and Sverker Sörlin, eds., *Sustainability – the Challenge: People Power and the Environment* (Montreal: Black Rose Books, 1998) 99–107.

109 See Canadian Council of Forest Ministers, *National Forest Strategy Final Evaluation Report – Blue Ribbon Panel, 1997* (Ottawa: CCFM, 1997).

110 See Steven Bernstein and Ben Cashore, *The Internationalization of Domestic Policy-Making: The Case of Eco-Forestry in British Columbia* (Paper Presented to the Annual Meeting of the Canadian Political Science Association, St. Catharines, Ontario, 1997); Chris Elliott and Arlin Hackman, 'The Forest Stewardship Council and Forest Certification in Canada,' *Policy Options* 17(9), 1996, 18–20; and Peter Clancy, 'The Politics of Stewardship: Certification for Sustainable Forest Management in Canada' in Sandberg and Sörlin, *Sustainability – the Challenge*, 108–20.

111 On these administrative changes see J.E. Hodgetts, *The Canadian Public Services: A Physiology of Government, 1867–1970* (Toronto: University of Toronto Press, 1973).

112 See National Forestry Conference, *Background Papers and Proceedings* (Ottawa: Department of Forests, 1966) .

113 Pearson told the Canadian Institute of Forestry that the decision to abolish the Department of Forestry originated in the constitutional limits placed on federal powers in the area and in provincial opposition. See Fellows, 'Forestry's Future Frustrated or a Condensed History of a Canadian Forester's Concern for Forest Renewal,' *Forestry Chronicle* 62(1), 1986, 35–50; F.L.C. Reed, *The Role of the Federal Government in Forestry*, Lecture Series no. 5 (Edmonton: University of Alberta Forest Industry, 1980).

114 See Ken Johnstone, *Timber and Trauma* (Hull: Forestry Canada, 1991).

115 Roger Simmons, *Federal Forestry Commitments in the 1980s*, Lecture Series no. 7 (Edmonton: University of Alberta Forest Faculty, 1980).

PART 5
CONCLUSION

Chapter Fourteen

Making Sense of Complexity: Advances and Gaps in Comprehending the Canadian Forest Policy Process

Evert Lindquist and Adam Wellstead

This book demonstrates that the Canadian forest policy regime is an increasingly complex policy area to analyse. There is now an impressive web of policy actors, institutions, ideas, bureaucratic capacities and processes, and governing arrangements that affect policy outcomes and attempt to grapple with many overlapping issues that do not respect jurisdictional divides. Our goal is to remind readers, however briefly, of the complexity that analysts confront and then examine how some scholars have attempted to make sense and impart coherence on contemporary policy-making in Canada. We also seek to evaluate the progress made to date in applying these models and frameworks to forestry policy-making and identify gaps in scholarship.

We begin by reviewing how complexity in the Canadian forest policy sector derives from an expanding number of policy actors, evolving federal arrangements, and a variety of international forces. We review some models and frameworks that describe and evaluate complex policy-making processes, and then consider how forest policy scholars have attempted, over time, to impart coherence on what has always been a complicated policy area to monitor and comprehend. We identify several gaps in the literature to date, such as closer analysis of organizational capacities and commitments, the roles of field staff as well as experts and scientists working on behalf of provincial and federal departments, the increasingly critical dynamics of forestry policy management at the community level across Canada, the systematic investigation of values and policy-making rhythms at play in the sector, and the development of an overarching framework or taxonomy for understanding the progress of research in this field. We outline a research agenda that could fill many of these gaps.

While there is much to be done, we argue that scholars working on forestry policy and management have made important theoretical and empirical strides over the past few years. By doing so, these scholars have not only advanced the boundaries of the fields of political science, public administration, and public policy, but they have also illuminated how policy-making occurs in traditionally closed networks. We are confident that this productive group of scholars will take up the research agenda we outline in this chapter and continue with the tradition of using the forestry policy sector as a basis for developing new theoretical and empirical contributions, and for more inclusive, healthier and, we hope, wiser policy communities.

Sources of Complexity: Interests, Federalism, Globalization

This volume shows that the Canadian forest sector is entering an era of rapid change. In this section, we review the sources of complexity through three lenses: the expanding range of actors involved in forestry policy and management, the evolving domestic governance arrangements, and the shifting nature of international influences on domestic policy-making. However, the real source of complexity derives from how these forces and actors *intersect* across these artificial categories, and how they express themselves differently at the regional and local levels.

The Proliferation of Policy Actors

All of the chapters in this volume acknowledge, in varying degrees, the multiple, intersecting levels of government. Moreover, there is a host of actors and institutions *outside* government that seek to influence forest policy-making. We could talk about these actors in a generic sense (e.g., business, labour), but it is important to recognize that they exercise influence at different levels of jurisdiction as well as across different sectors, and include the following:

There are hundreds of environmental, conservation, and recreation-related organizations. Some are large and national or international organizations such as the Sierra Club or the Canadian Wilderness Association. Other groups are small, sometimes very ideologically committed, and often pursue local level issues (e.g., the Friends of the Athabasca in Alberta were opposed to the construction of the Alberta and Pacific pulp mill in northern Alberta). Others groups may focus on a single issue or approach. An important feature is their access to media and information – their members are increasingly knowledgeable (and often critical) about the scientific issues related to the management of forested areas.

Industrial forestry firms are usually better organized and have access to more resources than environmental groups. These firms can exercise influence at the local, provincial, and national levels as independent entities or through associations that reflect the different functional areas of the industry and various levels of jurisdictions.[1] Although complex, these associations are not as fragmented as environmental groups. Increasingly, some associations take on regulatory functions as a response to environmental protests and emerging regulatory sustainable forestry regimes, and as an alternative to government intervention. The largest industry group, the Canadian Pulp and Paper Association, is promoting the International Standard Organization's (ISO) 1400 certification standards for member companies. Some firms collaborate with provincial associations in voluntary audits of forest management practices. For example, the Alberta Forest Products Association has undertaken audits of its member's forest management practices through the Forest Care Program.

Labour organizations have also had to change their traditional role in the forest sector. They are faced with a difficult contradiction. On the one hand, unions are faced with protecting a declining membership as labour-saving technology has been introduced at a rapid rate. On the other hand, business and labour groups are often allied with each other in opposition to the environmental movement. Again, the labour movement itself is complex, with unions exerting influence at the local, provincial, and national levels, and often in association with other union organizations. Some of the most militant labour action against the environmental protests has come at the community level, often in concert with business interests.

An increasingly important set of policy actors are organizations and researchers involved in research and development. In addition to the Canadian Forest Service (CFS) Science and Technology Networks, other research institutions such as universities and private research institutes have expanded beyond traditional forest issues such as silviculture and now must consider new lines of research such as biodiversity, ecological classification, and socioeconomics. The largest forest research project is the $20 million Network of Centres of Excellence in Sustainable Forest Management (NCE) program at the University of Alberta. Universities, the training grounds of forestry professionals, have developed new curricula that address new forest management issues. Moreover, forest-related research has emerged from disciplines such as economics, sociology, geography, psychology, and political science.

In contrast to ten or twenty years ago, although government and industry remain the principal actors, they must contend with many more actors, issues, and forces that cut across jurisdictions. There has been growing public support for groups arguing against traditional timber management practices. More importantly, these groups serve to increase the policy discourse space and in many cases have brought different values to bear on forest management.

Forest policy decisions and international developments have their greatest impact on local communities and individuals, particularly in areas that are remote and resource dependent. Local governments are usually the most affected by policy decisions, but they have little or no impact on policy-making. In some cases, communities will be negatively affected by these changes, while others will enjoy alternative sources of employment and tax revenue (retraining, accommodation between labour and business, which in some cases will be Aboriginally owned). Other alternatives such as tenure reform and community forestry have also been touted as alternatives for forest-dependent communities. It is often the case that local concerns and initiatives such as community forests, participation, and tenure are channelled through provincial governments, while local or regional governments host or participate in symbolic consultative processes. However, the devolution of provincial powers may lead to a greater role for municipal governments in forest management decisions. For example, Harvey and Hillier describe examples in northern Ontario where local governments are bridging the gap between community development and resource management.[2] Wilson (this volume) suggests that community-based forestry may be an alternative route towards achieving ecosystem management, which has not been achieved on a larger provincial scale.

Perhaps the most significant change in community-level dynamics has been the recent efforts to address Aboriginal treaty rights and land claims. The 1996 Royal Commission on Aboriginal Peoples made specific recommendations for interim measures to improve Aboriginal access to forest resources on Crown lands and to increase participation in managing and developing forest lands and resources.[3] The results of these negotiations, usually between First Nations and provincial and federal governments, are beginning to have a significant impact on resource management at the community level, creating new patterns of ownership and stakeholders in policy-making, and these will vary significantly from community to community.

Domestic Governance Regime: Evolutionary Federalism

Provincial governments are the dominant governmental jurisdiction in the forest sector because they control 71 per cent of Canada's forests. Provincial governments are responsible for all legislation related to forest management such as reforestation, fire and pest control, and collecting land rents. In most provinces, issues related to forest management are typically the responsibility of large omnibus ministries that have authority over other resources such as mining and agriculture.[4] However, these brute facts mask the complexity inherent in a large and geographically diverse country with a federal system of governance, which results in diverse responses to international and domestic challenges associated with forest management.

The five case study chapters in Part 4 of this volume illustrate how the provinces have responded differently to the emerging environmental and market demands. Clancy's chapter shows how historical factors, mainly settlement patterns, combined with current dilemmas such as the elimination of the federal–provincial forestry development agreements have led to different forest policy regimes in the Atlantic provinces. Bouthillier describes how Quebec's forestry policy regime is a 'political–administrative edifice of such forbidding complexity,' shaped by 300 years of history and a state that has oscillated in the degree of its intervention. Some authors point to rapid policy change as a contributing factor to the complexities faced by provincial regimes, but different pressures often lead to different outcomes. Both British Columbia and Ontario overhauled forest management legislation in the early 1990s. However, Hoberg (this volume) attributes change in British Columbia to the force of public opinion, the election of the NDP government, a number of expert reports critical of current forest practices, and most importantly, international environmentalist pressures; whereas Levy et al. argue that in Ontario the Crown Forest Sustainability Act stemmed from the class environmental assessment recommendations supported by a NDP minister of natural resources who favoured ecosystem-based forest management. Generally, though, provincial governments have resisted adopting such ambitious forest practices. One exception is Saskatchewan, where the forest regime has undergone substantial policy changes in response to rapid development, with the impetus for change coming from the forest industry itself (Urquhart, this volume).

All provincial governments have, since the early 1990s, undergone fiscal restructuring. Many ministries and departments responsible for forest management experienced major budgetary reductions. Whole programs have been eliminated, ministries have been reorganized, and staff reduced. In 1993, for example, the Alberta Department of Forests, Lands, and Wildlife was consolidated into the new and larger Department of Environmental Protection. The total budget allocation of the Alberta Land and Forest Service declined by 27 per cent between 1993 and 1995, and 30 per cent of its services were eliminated.[5] Such cutbacks and reorganization were experienced, in varying degrees, across the country. It has been argued, particularly by environmentalists, that these reductions have led to decreased bureaucratic capacity which will hinder the enforcement of sustainable forest management practices on forest companies that might not otherwise comply with new regulations.

The federal nature of the Canadian political system means that intergovernmental relations also affect the forestry sector. Two types of intergovernmental relations matter most: federal–provincial relations, and now, federal–provincial–Aboriginal relations. Most recently, federal and provincial governments have responded to global and national pressures for sustainable forest management in a collaborative manner. The federal government makes important policy contributions to the sector, although, as Howlett (this volume) points out its influence in this area has been less expansive than that of the provinces. The federal government has steadily declined in this area after losing struggles with the provinces over control and jurisdiction in the early part of the twentieth century. However, after the 1930 national transfer agreements, Howlett points out, the federal government, which had been sympathetic towards the forest industry, began to develop a new role: bolstering the industry through regional development programs and scientific research. This was accomplished by negotiating, on a bilateral basis with provincial governments, general development agreements during the 1970s, and later, economic regional development agreements during the 1980s. The federal government tried, albeit unsuccessfully, to influence provincial policy on a national basis (as illustrated by the failure of the 1987 forest strategy).

Strategies aimed at reducing budget deficits decreased funding available for bilateral agreements for forest management and research, and this has affected federal–provincial arrangements. Most noticeable was the non-renewal of the $1 billion forest resource and development assistance (FRDA) programs in the early 1990s. Nevertheless, cooperation persists, most notably in the creation of the Model Forest Program. Unlike the FRDA agreements, each of the eleven model forests are more complex alternative program delivery arrangements with many stakeholders. In all of the model forests there is involvement and financial contribution by industrial and community-based partners (see Beyer, this volume). While the Model Forest Program has not led to fundamental regime change, it does underwrite innovative experiments which, however incremental in impact, may provide examples of how to govern future forest management.

The federal government continues to exert influence in the areas of international relations, international trade, and forest research. It has taken a leadership role in negotiating international environmental and forestry agreements (e.g., the 1992 UNCED Earth Summit in Rio de Janeiro or the 1998 Kyoto agreement on climate change and global warming). These international concerns and the need for a coordinated sustainable forest management regime led the federal government to initiate the 1992 forest accord and to create the Canadian Council of Forest Ministers (CCFM), and later, an extensive 'criteria and indicator' program. The federal government has also been actively involved in trade agreements such as the development of the Canada–U.S. softwood lumber agreement. Despite a major organizational restructuring and downsizing in 1993, the Canadian Forest Service remained the leading forest research organization, with ten National Science and Technology Networks located across Canada, each dedicated to a component of forestry.[6]

It should also be noted that, in this context, federal and provincial forest departments increasingly intersect with other federal and provincial departments responsible for agriculture, the environment, recreation, fisheries, labour, industry, and tourism. Such interactions have been driven not only by budgetary imperatives but also by increasing recognition of the horizontal nature of forest-related policy issues. And, as we noted earlier, we must acknowledge the rapid emergence of Aboriginal communities as a distinct level of government. Recent treaties and negotiations with Aboriginal communities have often centred on a significant and genuine shift in access and control of natural resources. This injects a new set of players into the policy-making mix, further complicating the field of intergovernmental relations.

The International Dimensions: Protest, Competition, Constraints

All Canadian governments and communities are contending with the effects of initiatives and decisions at the international level. Indeed, to focus on national and provincial crises and policies would be to lose sight of the impetus for such developments. However, as many chapters in this volume indicate, the international dimension has always been an important and defining feature of the Canadian forest policy regime because of its colonial past and export orientation. In short, we are now witnessing not only how international forces express themselves in different ways, but also how increasingly sophisticated domestic actors utilize international pressures and forums to further their respective objectives.

Perhaps the single most important international event influencing forestry management was the United Nations Conference on Environment and Development (UNCED) held in Rio de Janeiro in June 1992. The conference not only provided a forum that amplified the concerns of environmental groups, but it also led to several international forest-specific commitments and policy initiatives by national governments, and precipitated subsequent debate, discussion, and negotiation. There have been concerted efforts to improve coordination among producing nations in developing sustainable forestry practices. The most prominent includes the Intergovernmental Working Group on Forests (IWGF) and the FAO's Commission on Sustainable Development's Intergovernmental Panel on Forests (IPF).[7] It was through IWGF that the groundwork for a global level criteria and indicators for SFM was initiated, and the Canadian government agreed to develop national level indicators. The IPF has made proposals for action on national forest programs in such areas as monitoring and evaluation of SFM and involving First Nations peoples and local communities in decision-making. Bernstein and Cashore (this volume) refer to this as the rise of 'liberal environmentalism' whereby the ecological preservation has been directly tied to the 'promotion and maintenance of a liberal economic order.' As a result, forestry policy decisions can no longer be made in isolation and now contain an international context.

An interesting international 'cross-pressure' concerns a rapidly changing, more competitive, and volatile forest export market (Hayter and Holmes, this volume). Despite market volatility, forest products (pulp and paper, lumber, and newsprint) remain Canada's leading net export and are key contributors to the economy's of British Columbia and northern Ontario.[8] Although the total world market continues to grow, Canada's overall share of the world forest products exports has experienced a long-term decline.[9] Part of the decline can be explained by emerging competition from countries such as Russia, Spain, Chile, Malaysia, and Indonesia. Urquhart's study of Prairie forest policy illuminates the impact of the Asian financial crisis, coupled with low-cost producing countries, such as Indonesia, on Alberta's forestry policy regime. Often these countries have large untapped natural forested areas or large productive plantations and lower labour costs.

At the same time, other traditional forest exporters – such as the Nordic countries – also experienced a decline in their export market share. They, as well as American producers, have responded by introducing technological advances such as more efficient pulp and paper production, and enhanced competitiveness in international markets. In addition to taking advantage of technological changes in machinery and biotechnology, the forest industry has responded to the information revolution by utilizing geographical information systems (GIS) and improving the transfer of market information. The industry has had to respond to this competitive market by re-skilling its workforce, and the value of per worker output has increased over the past twenty years from 3.5 jobs/tonne of pulp and paper produced to just under 2 jobs/tonne.[10] All of this is further complicated by North American and international multilateral trade agreements, which can liberate and constrain trade.

All of this has created opportunities for the myriad of international, national, provincial, and local groups who form the Canadian forest policy community. Until recently, those who have for the most part been excluded from the tight-knit business–government nexus are questioning and scrutinizing the traditional practices associated with the timber management regime (Howlett and Rayner, this volume). At the national level, the Canadian environmental movement has been faced with challenges that have prevented their active participation in the forestry policy-making process, which according to Stefanick (this volume) is a result of its resistance to adopting vertically arranged hierarchical structure. However, conservation groups have been able to change public opinion and raise awareness of environmental issues through the media by highlighting Canadian forest practices in international forums. This has been particularly effective given Canada's dependence on exports of forest products. Provincial governments and industry have been forced to consider new forest management issues and values such as biodiversity, landscape scale management, wildlife, recreation, subsistence, aesthetic and watershed management, recycling, and climate change. On the other hand, Bernstein and Cashore (this volume) note that non-binding agreements have only had a minimal impact on changing Canadian forest policy and practices; 'the state/and or business have been able to use this international pressure to force their own policy agendas.'

Providing accounts of forestry policy-making is bound to be a complex enterprise with so many issues, jurisdictions, and actors to take into account. Here we illustrate this point with two examples. First, local-level or grassroots environmental protests can have profound influences on provincial and national governments and industry to change policies. The 1993 blockades in Clayoquot Sound on Vancouver Island or in Temagami in northern Ontario were militant efforts to either change existing forest management policy, and in the case of British Columbia has precipitated a new forest policy regime. In contrast, groups located in other countries, particularly in Europe, have taken up the cause of local communities and also had a profound effect on forest policy. In the early 1990s, Greenpeace and the Sierra Club targeted the harvesting of old-growth forest on North America's Pacific northwest coast. In Canada, Greenpeace's campaign against logging in British Columbia's temperate rain forest, and a resulting call to British consumers to boycott MacMillan Bloedel's products, came in response to a failed 1993 blockade. The B.C. government took numerous steps to respond to local and foreign environmental groups, which included measures such as the Scientific Advisory Panel, Commission on Resources and Environment (CORE), reducing the average annual cut, announcing protected areas, adopting the forest practices code, negotiating with the Nuu-Chah Nulth band, and implementing the Forest Renewal Plan. In short, global, environmental, and economic concerns from above have led to changes in the sector but at the same time change has been induced by pressures from below.

Making Sense of Complexity in the Forest Sector

This section reviews several different analytic frameworks that have been utilized to comprehend the complexities of forest policy-making. We begin with the traditional approaches used to understand forestry policy-making, which focused on the policy cycle and the use of different policy instruments by government authorities. We then review the application of more recently developed frameworks, such as policy community or network analysis, and a complementary approach that emphasizes the role of beliefs and expertise in policy learning. Finally, we consider the related literature on agenda-setting in policy domains. We outline key elements of each tradition, and review the applications of each to understanding forestry policy-making.

Traditional Frameworks for Forestry Policy-Making

Until recently, the mainstream approach for understanding policy-making in the forest sector drew on two important frameworks from the public policy and political science literature, which focused on the state's policy cycle and the selection and rationale for policy instruments. The policy-cycle approach attempted to make sense of complexity by dividing the policy-making process into several discrete stages. Howlett and Ramesh provide a useful account of the evolution and variants on this approach that first emerged several decades ago, but they argue that the most parsimonious framework included the following stages: agenda setting, policy formation, decision-making, implementation, and policy evaluation.[11] When applied to understanding forest policy-making in Canada, most attention was directed to the stages of policy implementation and evaluation – that is, the results and outcomes of policy regimes, rather than on other parts of the process. This reflected the fact that forestry policy was a state-based enterprise undertaken in collaboration with industry in a relatively stable environment, with little contest over policy goals or the nature of the policy process itself.

Likewise, analysis of forest policy – dominated by economists – which focused more attention on implementation and evaluation, also evinced interests in the choice and effectiveness of alternative policy instruments. The policy-instruments framework was developed during the 1970s and endeavoured to catalogue the means by which governments sought to achieve its objectives. At the broadest level, these instruments included self-regulation, exhortation, expenditure, regulation, and public ownership. Doern and Phidd argued that policy instruments differ with respect to the amount of 'legitimate coercion' the state employs in persuading citizens, firms, or other governments to follow its objectives, while others suggested choice had more to do with protecting various types of capital.[12]

These instruments, and more subtle variants, are often used in combination. Traditionally, forest policy involves an extensive state involvement because most of Canada's forested land is publicly owned. Most forested lands fall under provincial ownership and a forest management agreement (FMA) defines tenure arrangements (the annual allowable cut and management responsibility) the government has with a company. A typical FMA comprises an extensive number of regulations and guidelines regarding harvesting, regeneration, and protection. Also, there are fines and penalties for non-compliance with guidelines. Moreover, in some provinces, such as Alberta, grants and subsidies are paid to tenure holders who build mills. In short, several instruments have traditionally been employed simultaneously to secure government objectives.

More recently, Adamowicz and Veeman argue that a new set of policy instruments is required in the shift from focusing solely on timber and fibre production, based on the principles of sustainable forest management, in order to balance social and economic concerns while maintaining ecological integrity.[13] They include self-regulatory measures such as joint tenure rights to reflect landscape-scale management and links to market-based mechanisms (certification) that are based on consumer preference for environmental performance. Other tools include shifting prescriptive regulations to incentive-based schemes, enhanced management, non-timber valuation, and increased public participation. This reflects a desire by those who favour a shift towards more self-regulatory market-based policy instruments. On the other hand, many environmental groups are calling for greater regulation and control by the state as the more appropriate or effective policy instrument that will ensure a forest's ecological well-being.

For many years frameworks that focused primarily on the features and choice of policy instruments – old and new – held considerable appeal for analysing policy-making in the forest sector. The expanding menu of instruments reveals the increasing complexity in forest policy-making; the traditional instruments, as well as the merits of underpinning values and processes by which they are designed, have been called into question. This reveals that adopting policy instruments is not just about the exercise of legitimate coercion by governments, nor should it be limited to assessing their effectiveness and efficiency; it also involves struggles over who gets to choose, and monitor the use of, instruments. As the forestry policy arena became more contested, and therefore more complex, it was not surprising that academic observers turned to other frameworks to guide their analysis.

Taking a Wider View: Embracing Forest Policy Networks and Communities

An important development in political science in recent years has involved developing sectoral perspectives on policy-making. This approach can be traced back to the work of Pross, who sought to account for the full range of actors involved in designing, monitoring, and challenging public policy in a given policy domain.[14] He referred to the entire cluster of actors as a policy community, but he made an important distinction between the 'subgovernment' comprising government and industry actors, whose vested interests were in maintaining the status quo, and the 'attentive public' comprising observers and other interested parties who, although without access to power, nevertheless provided critical perspectives and developed alternatives. This work was taken an important step forward by Atkinson and Coleman, and later Coleman and Skogstad, who essentially argued that subgovernments (which they referred to as policy networks) could vary significantly due to different balances in authorities, capacity and autonomy among state actors and key societal (usually business) groups.[15] Atkinson, Coleman, and Skogstad as well as many other scholars have produced many typologies of policy networks. They have sought to be comparative, not only to account for different patterns in different sectors, but also to explore how the patterns of interests in similar policy domains may vary across jurisdictions.

The policy community framework has been applied to forestry policy-making in several studies. In a study of the development of the National Forestry Sector Strategy, Grant found that the Canadian pulp and paper industry had a close collaborative relationship with provincial governments.[16] This collaboration led to the major forestry issues networks resembling concertation networks or 'company states' – provincial governments provided favourable environments for the operations of large companies. Wilson's case study of British Columbia's forest environmental movement also examined a closed forest-management network.[17] During the 1980s, the industry and the Ministry of Forests were openly hostile to the emerging environmental movement. The industry feared that any changes to forest-management practices would undermine their market strength. Wilson showed that although the fragmented environmental movement was often denied contact with key ministry officials and lacked financial resources, it was able to win support by direct appeals to the public by appearing at regulatory hearings, protesting, law suits, and so on. In a study of forest management across Canadian provinces, Howlett and Rayner argue that despite mounting pressure on forest policy networks from environmental groups and international forces, only incremental change in policies has occurred because of well-entrenched subgovernments; new ideas about forest management were generally shunted aside by networks, or dealt with in largely symbolic ways, even if the relative strength of governments with respect to firms varies somewhat across provinces.[18] More generally, the federal government has found it difficult, or been reluctant, to assert a strong role in an area that falls more or less squarely in provincial jurisdiction.[19]

Academics studying forestry policy-making turned to policy community and network perspectives because they captured the wider circle of actors challenging the policy regime. It should also be noted that the clashes of forestry, environmental, and Aboriginal interests have provided an excellent set of cases through which to explore the utility of the analytical framework. A large proportion of the policy network cases in Canada have focused on forestry and environment issues. Interestingly, the scholars who studied these issues became part of the attentive public, serving to broaden perspectives on the practices and dynamics of forest policy communities, as well as developing views on how well those communities are coping with, and adapting to, a variety of mounting pressures. This points to yet another element of complexity in forestry policy-making, which has to do with the capacity of policy communities to adapt and learn in conflictual and value-laden environments. To take up these issues, scholars have turned to a complementary set of frameworks.

Policy-Making as Contending Beliefs and Policy Learning

In reviewing the literature on forestry policy-making, one encounters a palpable sense of unease. Some observers (Lindquist 1992; Wellstead 1996) worry about the ability of policy networks and communities to respond to building pressures, to rise above strongly held beliefs or powerful interests, and to find ways to accommodate them in new policy regimes.[20] As a result, there has also been an abiding interest in tapping into and elaborating frameworks that deal with belief systems and policy-oriented learning. In part, this interest has emerged because policy-makers and their critiques have increasingly better access to the practices of counterparts in other jurisdictions, and sometimes these constitute exemplars or competitive threats.

The literature on policy learning itself is difficult to wade through; Bennett and Howlett have pointed out that many contributors have different notions of learning and focus on different levels of analysis.[21] For example, Rose explores how policy-makers learn selectively from other jurisdictions, while Hall focuses more on how governments as a whole learn and embrace policy paradigms.[22] Perhaps the most systematic approach, and one that embraces the complexity of policy communities, is the advocacy coalition framework introduced by Sabatier and Jenkins-Smith.[23] They see policy communities (or, in their words, policy subsystems) as arenas where struggles over policy proceed among networks of actors with shared belief systems. They presume that conflict is endemic in policy communities, and also argue that it is necessary for policy learning to occur. Their emphasis on beliefs, rather than economic and organizational interests and capacities, makes their approach distinct. Since belief systems are difficult to change, Sabatier predicts that significant policy change is unlikely to occur as result of skirmishes between advocacy coalitions. Rather, if significant policy change does occur, it is presumed to be a result of exogenous events outside a policy community, such as rapidly changing socioeconomic conditions, the election of new governments, and the impact of decisions from other policy domains.

The advocacy coalition approach has been applied in several studies on forestry policy-making in Canada. Wellstead reviewed forest policy change in Alberta and Ontario, and his findings were consistent with the hypothesis that policy change tends to occur at the secondary aspect of belief systems rather than at the core.[24] In their survey of forestry policy change in British Columbia, Lertzman, Rayner, and Wilson employ the framework to outline the values and belief systems of the 'development' and 'environmental' advocacy coalitions, and demonstrate how the environmental coalition developed strategies that forced changes on the part of the development coalition.[25] They also demonstrated that the environmental coalition was considerably more loosely coupled than the development coalition, not simply because it had fewer resources, but also because of a further and increasingly important complexity: the diverging interests of environmental groups and Aboriginal communities. Lertzman et al. also challenged a central Advocacy Coalition Framework (ACF) hypothesis by arguing that dominant advocacy coalitions can learn and adapt policy by means of a 'non-crisis' path, which is consistent with the cross-national study of Coleman, Skogstad, and Atkinson that outlines different trajectories for policy change in agriculture policy sectors.[26]

The advocacy coalition approach is a relatively recent addition to the analytic tool kit of academics in Canada, one which has been embraced uneasily,[27] or indirectly. Several contributors to this volume, for example, have explored belief systems without invoking the framework. In part this stems from the overlap between interests, institutions, and ideas – and the slipperiness of concepts related to policy learning. More-over, it is difficult to discern where, say, the structuralist policy network approach ends, and learning models begin; indeed, Lindquist has argued that a good analysis of policy sectors should proceed by simulta-neously investigating belief systems and institutional capacities.[28] Mat-ters are further complicated by the fact that it is difficult to determine the effectiveness of recent policy changes, and therefore the amount of learning; this, of course, is a frustrating reality that confronts scholars and practitioners alike. These issues aside, it has been the case that, as with the policy community approach, Canadian scholars interested in forestry and environmental issues have evinced considerable interest in the advocacy framework: Sabatier and Jenkins-Smith report that, since 1988, there have been over twenty-five applications from scholars work-ing in a diversity of fields and countries, and, of the four Canadian applications, three involved to the forest sector.[29]

Policy Change through Chance and Convergence

Another complementary, but fairly distinct, line of research is now focusing on agenda-setting and the forces underpinning policy change. As noted earlier, agenda-setting is the first stage of the policy cycle, and in the early days of analysis of the forest policy sector was not an interest-ing area for analysis. A growing policy community and diverging inter-ests have made this a subject worthy of exploration. It is true that the other conceptual frameworks reviewed above broach the matter of policy change, particularly the learning and advocacy coalition perspec-tives, but only as one component of a larger set of issues. In recent years, considerably more scholars have sought to understand agenda-setting processes per se and model the seemingly rare circumstances under which significant policy decisions take place.

One avenue of work builds on Kingdon, and more recently Baum-gartner and Jones, who have elaborated a model based on garbage can models of decision-making from organization theory and on biological concepts of punctuated equilibria developed to explain periods of speci-ation.[30] Essentially, the challenge is to explain why some policy ideas or alternatives become public policies but also to explain why others *do not* move high up on the policy agenda, or if they do, fail to get adopted as decisions. Kingdon specifies three relatively independent streams of influence – the problem stream, the political stream, and the policy stream – that have the potential to affect policy-making priorities. Policy decisions occur when policy windows open (budgets, elections, international agreements, etc.) and policy entrepreneurs find ways to join ideas, problems, and people as windows quickly open and close. The emphasis here is on timing and chance, but also that when decisions do occur, they can have a defining influence on a policy domain. Another avenue focuses more on the extent to which different policy subsystems overlap, and whether decisions in one policy domain have a significant impact on another. One example of such work is Zafonte and Sabatier's study of overlapping subsystems in San Francisco Bay–Delta Water policy.[30]

To date, these models have not been systematically applied to the forest policy sector, although key contributors to the literature are certainly aware of their existence.[32] Some scholars have explored, however, whether or not policy innovation in the forestry policy sector is a function of external as opposed to internal forces, and it is abundantly clear that many contributors to this volume see international forces as constituting an important impetus for change. Keeping this in mind, we would like to draw attention to the work of Hoberg and Morawski, who argue convincingly that some of the most interesting features of change in forestry policy in British Columbia can be traced to the collision of previously distinct policy networks, the forestry network (which also included environmental groups) and the Aboriginal network.[33] The intersection of these networks brought different players to the table in the respective networks, and thus generated new tensions but also provided new possibilities for policy.

Forest Policy and Complexity: The Trajectory of Analysis

Our cursory review should indicate the analysis of forestry policymaking has made great strides during the last decade. The apparent shortcomings of the policy cycles and instruments approaches, combined with an increasingly complex policy field, led many analysts to seek out more realistic models of state–society relationships. One result is that more nuanced and contextualized accounts of policy making have been developed. Economists no longer hold a monopoly in forest policy analysis. In addition, there now exists a critical mass of forest policy researchers in Canada who can comprehend and analyse the growing complexities of the sector. Indeed, our review has emphasized the fact that the forest policy sector has been very well served by a dedicated cohort of scholars at the cutting edge of the discipline, who have used case studies in the sector to explore a succession of analytic approaches;

it would be difficult to find a substantive domain that has been better served by this literature.

It must be emphasized, however, that the relatively new approaches are attempting to understand many of the same issues: why are certain policy instruments adopted in different jurisdictions, and on what occasions do interests and policy-makers seek to exert influence and make decisions? We have provided a quick review of key approaches that can be used to understand the complexity of forestry policy. Although we have emphasized the differences in the approaches, they can and should be used in combination. Indeed, although the policy network, advocacy coalition, and agenda-setting frameworks operate at different levels of analysis and embrace more variables, they ultimately seek to explain why certain instruments are chosen, the manner in which they are used, and why governments move to new instruments over time. This leads to the obvious point that a multitude of competing or complementary frameworks can produce their own complexities, perhaps obfuscating central trends and essential points in the name of analytical nuance and completeness. To the extent that this observation is true, it is incumbent on researchers to consolidate frameworks and to specify more clearly precisely how they vary from each other.

Modelling Complexity: What Are the Gaps?

The four general models of policy-making introduced above reveal the progress made by analysts in understanding the process of forest policy-making in light of the complex interaction of different issues and actors. However, in this section we question whether these approaches capture the entire range of issues and the policy-making dynamics in the Canadian forest sector. Below we outline some of the theoretical and empirical dimensions that appear to be overlooked in the literature to date.

Organizational Capacities and Commitments

A critical shortcoming in each of the approaches and applications to date is the inadequate attention devoted to investigating and assessing organizational capacities. Whether policy actors – individually, in groups or associations, or as a sector – can respond to challenges is a function of organizational capacity. By capacity we mean the number of staff, the knowledge of relevant issues, and the requisite skills to achieve objectives. It is well understood in the organization theory literature that asking organizations to take on certain tasks without them addressing their capacity is a recipe for ineffectiveness. Likewise, the biggest gap to date in the ACF and other normative approaches has been the tendency of analysts to presume that all members of advocacy coalitions have similar beliefs; however, we know that differing values and degrees of commitment can be found within coalitions. We think more attention should be directed to understanding the emergence and the distinctiveness of Aboriginal advocacy coalitions, which are evincing very distinctive positions on forest management issues from either the timber management or environmental coalitions. While some progress has been made by Lertzman et al., Hoberg and Morawski, and Wilson (this volume), more nuance and detailed data-gathering are required.[34]

Perspectives and Role of Field-Workers

To date, the theoretical literature has done a good job of identifying the range of government interests and recognized that the policy regime and style are products of negotiated agreements or imposed solutions. What is less understood are the day-to-day interactions taking place among professional and political staff that serve to share information and develop common understanding of policy issues – even though the public posturing of political leaders may indicate otherwise. Are front-line staff and agencies with similar responsibilities, such as environment and forestry bureaus, more likely to share similar views than other agencies with other functional responsibilities such as economic development? How do front-line staff from different agencies balance the conflicting demands of ministers and other stakeholders? Although the more general literature examines the challenges for front-line staff, forest-based researchers have not developed an understanding of how the views and actions of field staff in federal or provincial forestry agencies may diverge from those of political and bureaucratic leaders working from the centre, nor has there been an analysis of field staff as 'street-level bureaucrats' handling complex tasks and over-determined policy fields.[35] This is a particularly important area of concern because of the highly technical nature of forest management issues, and the increased reliance on decentralized and community-based management regimes. Sabatier et al. found that there were different factions of professionals in the U.S. Forest Service, but similar research has yet to be undertaken in Canada.[36]

Role of Science and Experts

One way to envision forest management and planning is as a technical and scientific endeavour. However, even with the move from sustained yield management to sustainable forestry management principles, technical and scientific issues will continue to be at the heart of change in forest policy. Forestry policy development will involve a wide and diverse circle of experts and professionals (see Wilson, this volume). As has been the case in other policy domains, the organization, disposition, and influence of forestry-related experts and professionals has not been systematically studied in Canada. This is surprising because forestry professionals have been closely aligned with the dominant advocacy coalition,[37] and, over the past ten years, there has been an infusion of new types of expertise with different core beliefs who have challenged the dominant coalition in various forums. This shortcoming is not specific to the analysis of forest policy-making,[38] but there is increasing interest in the management of science and technology.[39] Sabatier has argued that debates between experts and professionals can play a key role in the policy process and in facilitating policy learning because they have 'a desire for professional credibility and the norms of scientific debate will lead to a serious analysis of methodological assumptions, to the gradual elimination of the more improbable causal asserting and invalid data, and thus probability to a greater convergence of view of time concerning the nature of the problem and the consequences of various alternatives.'[40] Examples of professional forums might include the Ontario Timber Environmental Assessment hearings (Levy, Lawson, and Sandberg, this volume) or the Scientific Panel for Sustainable Forest Practices in Clayoquot Sound (Wilson, this volume). In some cases professionals may moderate conflict and enhanced learning between competing coalitions, but on the other hand, they may tend to exacerbate conflict and reflect (and, indeed, harden) the positions and values associated with each advocacy coalition.

Community Adaptation and Governance

Surprisingly little attention has been paid to community-level policy-making, even though many protests are initiated at this level, and it is where the consequences of policy shifts are experienced most acutely. The models outlined above examine complexity at the sectoral or meso level by examining vertical patterns of policy interactions; that is, the analysis of actors at several different levels (international, national, provincial). Beyer's chapter on Model Forests (this volume), and Wilson's chapter on Clayoquot Sound (this volume), provide good starts, but more effort must be devoted to understanding horizontal patterns of interaction at the local level. We need to understand how local patterns of ownership and politics affect the implementation of public policies, the process of adapting to new realities, and the nature of vertical linkages with higher orders of government and associational systems. This will be particularly important to study since many provinces have attempted to decentralize the responsibility for decision-making and monitoring of performance, and many local decision-makers have demanded greater participation in forest management and policy development. Particularly important to monitor will be the resolution of Aboriginal land claims and the establishing of unique self-government models which will unfold fundamentally as a local phenomenon, even if preceded by 'nation-to-nation' negotiations with provincial and federal governments. We will need to employ models that do better jobs at capturing the diversity of arrangement at the local level across a large land mass (either provincially or federally) as well as providing a basis for comparing those arrangements and their performance.[41]

Measuring Values and Beliefs

Political scientists know that ideas, values, beliefs, and interests influence public policy and administration. We have indicated that several of the newer analytical approaches take these variables very seriously and link them to the matter of policy learning. Many of the chapters in this volume directly or indirectly adopt this approach. However, no one has undertaken a systematic analysis of belief systems. Beyond a superficial description of the environmental and timber management advocacy coalitions, neither Lertzman and his colleagues, nor Wellstead, provide empirically based operationalization and measurement of competing belief systems. Thus, while plausible, the existence of advocacy coalitions is empirical assertion. Zafonte and Sabatier have employed quantitative scaling techniques to measure the intensity of competing core and secondary beliefs.[42] In addition, qualitative in-depth interviews can provide valuable insight into the belief systems of policy elites, such as the extent of organizational commitment to the broader values ascribed to advocacy coalitions, and the extent to which those beliefs remain stable and the circumstances under which they change. We already noted that particular attention should be focused on how Aboriginal communities take up responsibility for forestry management, and how different communities balance the demands for employment, environment, resource management, and recreation. However, full application of the ACF approach requires systematic and longer term surveys of public and elite opinion using quantitative and qualitative instruments, not unlike those employed in the Canadian Election Survey. Such work needs to be repeated at regular intervals, and should compare the beliefs of groups in several communities, as well as those of federal and provincial policymakers and representatives of various interest groups. This represents an interesting opportunity because not even the ACF progenitors have employed time series analysis to test their propositions.

Policy-Making Rhythms

Canadian academics are beginning to turn attention to subject of agenda-setting and policy windows.[43] Drawing on the work of U.S. scholars such as Kingdon and Baumgartner and Jones, this research is quite sophisticated in terms of modeling and statistical techniques. In these studies the tendency has been to study very different policy areas and to identify and compare the opening and shutting of windows, the extent to which alternatives move up the agenda, and the circumstances under which significant decisions occur. However, we would like to suggest that more mundane, yet productive research could be carried on the forest policy sector. We believe that contributors to the literature have done an excellent job of conveying the range of complexities, but not provided systematic accounts of the rhythm of policy-making. By this we mean that further efforts should be made to identify the various policy windows in the forest sector – government budgets, throne speeches, key court decisions, the meetings of pertinent intergovernmental ministerial meetings (sectoral and the annual premiers' conference) and the many working committees they spawn, legislative hearings, international conferences, task forces and commissions, and meetings of various associations and groups. The objective would be to closely monitor the progress of ideas and proposals, and to consider more carefully the connection among different windows and the policy problem and political streams. Such research would produce information that would also illuminate the work-a-day world of ministers, public servants, and outside interests alike.

Aggregating Specific Approaches

In reviewing the contributions to this volume, we were struck by how contributors draw upon different traditions, and yet deal with many common levels of analysis, notwithstanding different points of departure and areas of focus. We believe there is a need for an integrating framework that encompasses all of the variables associated with each of the approaches, whether they involve historical, geographical, technological, economic, social, normative, institutional, international, federal, provincial, local, and Aboriginal levels of analysis. We are not suggesting a 'systems' approach that would have to be adopted by all scholars, but rather, a way to show how different types of theoretical and empirical inquiries relate to each other, and to identify opportunities for further research. The Sabatier framework may provide a point of departure, but it would have to be greatly elaborated to embrace the federal, provincial, local, and Aboriginal levels of governance, and to deal with the distinctiveness wrought by the geographical and historical realities of Canada. In other words, it would be prudent to develop a framework that marries Sabatier with Innis, and links both to how federalism and its supporting structures have evolved in Canada. Such a framework would discipline and liberate: it would allow scholars to bracket their own specific theoretical and empirical inquiries, and yet provide more systematic linkages to pertinent forces and variables, allowing for influences to be traced more easily, whether they emanate from community, international, or federal contexts.

Concluding Remarks

Forestry policy-making in Canada continues to be dominated by closed networks of government and industry actors, even though the processes by which decisions are made have come under increasing scrutiny and challenge from environmental interests working at the local, provincial, federal, and international levels, and from First Nations land claim, treaty and self-government initiatives. Although inter-governmental mechanisms are in place to negotiate and exchange information on a variety of issues between federal and provincial governments, the responsibility for adopting new forest management practices, investing in new technologies and value-added processes, and negotiating with First Nations are clearly provincial responsibilities. International pressures remain important and fluid conditioning factors: environmental groups can threaten regional forestry markets from the other side of the globe, international markets can send commodity prices spiraling in one direction or another, new technologies and scientific techniques regularly emerge and thus create new competitive threats and demand alternative skill requirements from employees, and the U.S. Congress continues to effect protectionist measures that can cripple the industry. A major challenge confronting all Canadian governments, then, is to ensure that firms and communities alike adapt to these pressures.

The challenge confronting analysts of forestry policy-making in Canada has been to find ways to capture these trends and to embrace the inherent complexities of the forestry policy sector. In many regards, these complexities resemble those of other policy areas in Canada, such as the federal fact, with relatively autonomous provinces exercising powers and the federal government seeking influence and having impact at the margins; such as a more open, less deferential society, which has led interests in broader policy communities to challenge the arrangements governed by relatively closed networks; and geographical and historical diversity, which caused the mix of factors at play to vary considerably across the country. Forest policy, politics, and business have contributed, of course, different sets of complexities to the mix. We have argued that scholars analysing forestry policy-making moved from the policy cycle and policy instrument frameworks in order to capture these complexities and increasing contestation by utilizing frameworks that focused on the entire policy community and sought to comprehend the underpinnings of existing regimes and the forces for change, which ultimately reveal more clearly the workings of power and influence. We believe that this policy domain has been well served by a new generation of scholars who have taken great interest in the policy domain while using the cases to explore issues on the boundaries of their discipline. By doing so, these scholars have not only broadened the intellectual perspectives brought to bear on analysis of forestry policy, but they have also become part of the broader discourse on policy-making.

Notwithstanding the encompassing qualities of the policy frameworks that have been employed by these scholars, we have identified some gaps in scholarship, although this comment must be termed a 'quibble,' given the small numbers and productivity of this group. We have suggested that more attention should be devoted to assessing the actual capacities of various policy actors and the role of professionals and experts, rather than simply analysing beliefs, interests, and authorities. We have also suggested that far more attention needs to be devoted to

understanding how local communities are adapting to a rapidly changing environment, and to develop a more explicit and systematic picture
of the belief systems at work as well as the policy-making rhythms in the
forestry sector. Should our colleagues working on forest policy issues
take up these matters, we have no doubt that they will continue their tradition of also advancing analytic practice that can be applied to other
sectors.

NOTES

1 See Michael Howlett and Jeremy Rayner, Chapter 2 in this volume, and Wyn
   P. Grant, 'Forestry and Forest Products,' in William Coleman and Grace
   Skogstad, eds., *Policy Communities and Public Policy in Canada* (Toronto: Copp
   Clark Pitman, 1990), 118–40.
2 Stephen Harvey and Hillier Brian, 'Community Forestry in Ontario,' *Forestry
   Chronicle* 70(6), 1994, 725–30.
3 National Forestry Strategy Coalition, 'National Forestry Strategy,' *Sustainable
   Forests: A Canadian Commitment* (Ottawa: National Forestry Coalition, 1997).
4 Monique M. Ross, *Forest Management in Canada* (Calgary: Canadian Institute
   of Resources Law, 1995).
5 Adam M. Wellstead, 'The Role of the Advocacy Coalitional Framework in
   Understanding Forest Policy Changes: Two Case Studies of Alberta and
   Ontario,' Master's thesis. University of Toronto, 1996.
6 As of 1 November 2000, there are now five National Science and Technology
   Networks.
7 W.T. Stanbury, Ilan B. Vertinsky, and Bill Wilson. *The Challenge to Canadian
   Forest Products in Europe: Managing a Complex Environmental Issue* (Vancouver:
   Canada–British Columbia Partnership Agreement on Forest Resource
   Development: FRDA II), 1995.
8 Canada. Canadian Forest Service, *The State of Canada's Forests: The People's
   Forests, 1997–1998* (Ottawa: Natural Resources Canada, 1998).
9 Canadian Forest Service, *The State of Canada's Forests: Sustaining Forests at
   Home and Abroad, 1995–1996* (Ottawa: Natural Resources Canada, 1996).
10 Canadian Forest Service, *The State of Canada's Forests: Learning from History,
   1996–1997* (Ottawa: Natural Resources Canada, 1997).
11 Michael Howlett and M. Ramesh, *Studying Public Policy: Policy Cycles and Policy
   Subsystems* (Toronto: Oxford University Press, 1995).
12 G. Bruce Doern, and Richard W. Phidd, *Canadian Public Policy, Ideas Structure, Process*, 2nd ed. (Scarborough: Nelson Canada, 1992); Nicolas Baxter-

Moore, 'Policy Implementation and the Role of the State: A Revised Approach to the Study of Policy Instruments,' in R.J. Jackson, D. Jackson, and Baxter-Moore, eds., *Contemporary Canadian Politics: Readings and Notes* (Scarborough: Nelson Canada, 1987).

13 W.L. Adamowicz and T.S. Veeman, 'Forest Policy and the Environment: Changing Paradigms,' *Canadian Public Policy* 24 (supplement 2), 1998, 51–61.

14 A. Paul Pross, *Group Politics and Public Policy* (Toronto: Oxford University Press, 1986).

15 Michael Atkinson and William D. Coleman, 'Policy Networks, Policy Communities and the Problems of Governance, *Governance* 5(2) 1992, 154–80; William D. Coleman and Grace Skogstad, eds., *Policy Communities and Public Policy in Canada: A Structuralist Approach* (Toronto: Copp Clark Pitman, 1990).

16 Grant, 'Forestry and Forest Products.'

17 Jeremy Wilson, 'Wilderness Politics in BC: The Business Dominated State and the Containment of Environmentalism,' in Coleman and Skogstad, *Policy Communities*, 141–69.

18 Michael Howlett and Jeremy Rayner, 'Do Ideas Matter? Policy Network Configurations and Resistance to Policy Change in the Canadian Forest Sector,' *Canadian Public Administration* 38(3), 1995; 382–410. Michael Howlett and Jeremy Rayner, 'Opening Up the Woods?: The Origins and Future of Contemporary Canadian Forest Policy Conflicts,' *National History: A Canadian Journal of Enquiry and Opinion* 1(1), 1997, 35–48.

19 Michael Howlett, 'The 1987 National Forest Sector Strategy and the Search for a Federal Role in Canadian Forest Policy,' *Canadian Public Administration* 32(4), 1989, 545–63.

20 Evert A. Lindquist, 'Public Managers and Policy Communities: Learning to Meet New Challenges,' *Canadian Public Administration* 35(2), 1992, 127–59; Wellstead, *The Role of the Advocacy Coalitional Framework.*

21 Colin J. Bennett and Michael Howlett, 'The Lessons of Learning: Reconciling Theories of Policy Learning and Policy Change,' *Policy Sciences* 25, 1992, 275–94.

22 Richard Rose, *Lesson-Drawing in Public Policy: A Guide to Learning Across Time and Space* (Chatham, NJ: Chatam House, 1993); Peter A. Hall, 'Policy Paradigms, Social Learning and the State: The Case of Economic Policy-Making in Britain,' *Comparative Politics* 25(3), 1993, 275–96.

23 Paul Sabatier, 'An Advocacy Coalition Framework of Policy Change and the Role of Policy-oriented Learning Therein,' *Policy Sciences* 21, 1988, 128–68; Paul Sabatier and Hank C. Jenkins-Smith, 'The Advocacy Coalition Frame-

work: An Assessment,' in Sabatier, ed., *Theories of the Policy Process* (Boulder: Westview Press, 1999) 117–66.

24 Wellstead, 'The Role of the Advocacy Coalitional Framework.'

25 Ken Lertzman, Jeremy Rayner, and Jeremy Wilson, 'Learning and Change in the British Columbia Forest Policy Sector: A Consideration of Sabatier's Advocacy Coalition Framework,' *Canadian Journal of Political Science* 29, March 1996, 111–33.

26 William D. Coleman, Grace D. Skogstad, and Michael M. Atkinson, 'Paradigm Shifts and Policy Networks: Cumulative Change in Agriculture,' *Journal of Public Policy* 16(3) (1997) 273–301.

27 George Hoberg, 'Putting Ideas in Their Place: A Response to "Learning and Change in the British Columbia Forest Policy Sector,"' *Canadian Journal of Political Science* 29(1), 1996, 135–44.

28 Lindquist, 'Public Managers and Policy Communities.'

29 Sabatier and Jenkins-Smith, 'The Advocacy Coalition Framework.'

30 John W. Kingdon, *Agendas, Alternatives, and Public Policies* (New York: Harper Collins, 1984); Frank R. Baumgartner, and Bryan D. Jones, *Agendas and Instability in American Politics* (Chicago: University of Chicago Press 1993).

31 Matthew Zafonte, and Paul Sabatier, 'Shared Beliefs and Functional Interdependence as Determinants of Ally Networks in Overlapping Subsystems: An Analysis of San Francisco Bay–Delta Water Policy,' unpublished manuscript, 1997. University of California.

32 Michael Howlett, 'Issue-Attention and Punctuated Equilibria Models Reconsidered: An Empirical Examination of Agenda-Setting in Canada,' *Canadian Journal of Political Science* 30(1), 1997, 3–29; Michael Howlett, 'Predictable and Unpredictable Policy Windows: Institutional and Exogenous Correlates of Canadian Federal Agenda-Setting,' *Canadian Journal of Political Science* 31(3), 1998, 3–29.

33 George Hoberg and Edward Morawski, 'Policy Change Through Sector Intersection: Forest and Aboriginal Policy in Clayoquot Sound,' *Canadian Public Administration* 40(3), 1997, 387–414.

34 Lertzman et al., 'Learning and Change in the British Columbia Forest Policy Sector.' Hoberg and Morawski, 'Policy Change through Sector Intersection.'

35 B.W. Carroll and D. Siegal, *Service in the Field: The World of Front-Line Public Servants* (Montreal: McGill-Queen's University Press, 1999).

36 Paul Sabatier, John Loomis, and Catherine McCarthy, 'Hierarchical Controls, Professional Norms, Local Constituencies, and Budget Maximization: An Analysis of U.S. Forest Service Planning Decisions,' *American Journal of Political Science* 39(1), 1995, 204–42.

37 Wellstead, 'The Role of the Advocacy Coalitional Framework.'

38 Lindquist, 'Public Managers and Policy Communities.'
39 G.B. Doern, *Science and Scientists in Federal Policy and Decision Making* (Ottawa: Policy Research Secretariat, Government of Canada, 1999). Web site: http://policyresearch.schoolnet.ca/keydocs/Doern/index-e.htm. G.B. Doern and T. Reed, *Risky Business: Canada's Changing Science-Based Policy and Regulatory Regime* (Toronto: University of Toronto Press, 2000).
40 Paul A. Sabatier, 'Knowledge, Policy-Oriented Learning, and Policy Change: An Advocacy Coalition Framework,' *Knowledge: Creation, Diffusion, Utilization* 8(4), 1987, 680.
41 See R. Warren, 'The Interorganizational Field as a Focus for Investigation,' *Administrative Science Quarterly* 12 March, 1968, 590–613; W.R. Scott, 'The Organization of Societal Sectors: Propositions and Early Evidence,' in P.J. DiMaggio and W.W. Pavell, eds., *The New Institutionaism in Organizational Analysis* (Chicago: University of Chicago Press, 1991) 108–40.
42 Paul Sabatier and Matthew Zafonte, 'Who Do Policy Elites Look to for Advice and Information? Policy Networks in San Francisco Bay/Delta Water Policy,' unpublished manuscript, University of California, Aug. 1997.
43 Howlett, 'Issue-Attention and Punctuated Equilibria Models'; Howlett, 'Predictable and Unpredictable Policy Windows.'

Contributors

Steven Bernstein, University of Toronto
Joanna M. Beyers, York University
Luc Bouthillier, Laval University
Benjamin Cashore, Auburn University
Peter Clancy, St Francis Xavier University
Roger Hayter, Simon Fraser University
George Hoberg, University of British Columbia
John Holmes, Queen's University
Michael Howlett, Simon Fraser University
Jamie Lawson, York University
Marcelo Levy, York University
Evert Lindquist, University of Victoria
Jeremy Rayner, Malaspina University-College
L. Anders Sandberg, York University
Lorna Stefanick, University of Alberta
Ian Urquhart, University of Alberta
Adam Wellstead, University of Alberta
Jeremy Wilson, University of Victoria

Studies in Comparative Political Economy and Public Policy